Introducing Philosophy

A TEXT WITH INTEGRATED READINGS

Tenth Edition

Robert C. Solomon
University of Texas at Austin

Kathleen M. Higgins
University of Texas at Austin

Clancy Martin
University of Missouri-Kansas City

New York   Oxford
OXFORD UNIVERSITY PRESS

Oxford University Press, Inc., publishes works that further Oxford University's
objective of excellence in research, scholarship, and education.

Oxford New York
Auckland   Cape Town   Dar es Salaam   Hong Kong   Karachi
Kuala Lumpur   Madrid   Melbourne   Mexico City   Nairobi
New Delhi   Shanghai   Taipei   Toronto

With offices in
Argentina   Austria   Brazil   Chile   Czech Republic   France   Greece
Guatemala   Hungary   Italy   Japan   Poland   Portugal   Singapore
South Korea   Switzerland   Thailand   Turkey   Ukraine   Vietnam

For titles covered by Section 112 of the US Higher Education Opportunity Act,
please visit www.oup.com/us/he for the latest information about
pricing and alternate formats.

Published by Oxford University Press, Inc.
198 Madison Avenue, New York, New York 10016
http://www.oup.com

Oxford is a registered trademark of Oxford University Press

Library of Congress Cataloging-in-Publication Data

Solomon, Robert C.
Introducing philosophy : a text with integrated readings / Robert C. Solomon, Kathleen M. Higgins,
    Clancy Martin. — 10th ed.
        p. cm.
    ISBN 978-0-19-976486-0 (alk. paper)
    1. Philosophy—Introductions.   I. Higgins, Kathleen Marie. II. Martin, Clancy W. III. Title.
    BD21.S629 2012
    100—dc23   2011031839

ISBN 978-0-19-976486-0

9 8 7 6 5 4

Printed in the United States of America
on acid-free paper

For our parents
Vita P. Solomon (1916–2005) and Charles M. Solomon (1914–1986)
Kathryn A. Higgins (1925–2003) and Eugene A. Higgins
Anna Victoria Moody and John William Martin (1941–1997)

Contents in Brief

Contents

Part Two | Know Thyself 283

CHAPTER 4 | SELF 285

CHAPTER 5 | MIND AND BODY 332

Philosopher Biographies

Preface

Introducing Philosophy: A Text with Integrated Readings, Tenth Edition, is a thorough introduction to the core problems of philosophy. Organized topically, the chapters present alternative perspectives—including analytic, continental, feminist, and non-Western viewpoints—alongside the historical works of major philosophers. The text provides the course materials that allow instructors and students to focus on a variety of philosophical problems and perspectives. The goal is to present students with alternative views on philosophical issues and let them arrive at their own conclusions, which should be based on arguments in class and with classmates, as well as on the discussions in this book. The book presupposes no background in the subject and no special abilities. The purpose of philosophy is to encourage each person to think for himself or herself; no single source of arguments or information can take the place of personal dialogues and discussions. A textbook is ultimately a sourcebook—everything in it is to be taken as a cause for further argument, not as a final statement of results.

New to the Tenth Edition

- Chapters 1 and 2 have changed positions, making Chapter 1 on Religion and Chapter 2 on Reality.
- The following readings have been added to the new edition:
  - William Paley, "The Watch and the Watchmaker" (Chapter 1)
  - John Locke, from *An Essay Concerning Human Understanding* (Chapter 2)
  - Bertrand Russell, from *The Problems of Philosophy* (Chapter 3)
  - W. V. O. Quine, from "Epistemology Naturalized" (Chapter 3)
  - St. Thomas Aquinas, from *Summa Theologica* (Chapter 7)
  - John Dewey, from *The Quest for Certainty* (Chapter 7)
  - Dr. Martin Luther King, Jr., "Letter from Birmingham Jail" (Chapter 8)
- The following readings have been omitted from the new edition:
  - Charles Hartshorne, on the Ontological Argument (Chapter 1)
  - Paul Davies, from *The Mind of God* (Chapter 1)
  - Cory Juhl, on the "Fine-Tuning" Argument (Chapter 1)
  - Jean-Paul Sartre, from "The Desire to Be God" (Chapter 1)
  - Philip Bricker, on David K. Lewis, *On the Plurality of Worlds* (Chapter 2)
  - David Reisman, on Individualism (Chapter 4)
  - Friedrich Nietzsche, on Consciousness as Communication (Chapter 4)
  - G. W. F. Hegel, on "Spirit" and the Individual (Chapter 4)
  - G. W. F. Hegel, from *Reason in History* (Chapter 4)

- Søren Kierkegaard, "A Retort" from *Concluding Unscientific Postscript* (Chapter 4)
- Karl Marx, on the Social Self (Chapter 4)
- Harry Frankfurt, from "Coercion and Moral Responsibility" (Chapter 6)
- Tara Smith, on the Necessity of Egoism (Ayn Rand) (Chapter 7)
- Emma Goldman, from "Anarchism: What It Really Stands For" (Chapter 8)

Key Features

- A second color to visually enhance the text and further engage students and instructors (NEW)
- More than 230 images that illustrate key concepts and encapsulate famous philosophical figures (NEW)
- More than 100 brief profiles of philosophers interspersed throughout the text (NEW)
- Substantial readings from significant works in the history of philosophy, with helpful commentary from the authors
- Key terms bolded in the text and collected at the end of each chapter
- Marginal quotations from famous philosophers that keep the student engaged and focused
- Questions for further consideration at the end of every subsection and additional chapter review questions at the ends of chapters
- Bibliographies and Further Reading at the end of each chapter
- A Glossary of the most important and widely used philosophical terms at the end of the book

Ancillaries

The Instructor's Manual on CD and a Companion Website for students and instructors (www.oup.com/us/solomon10e) that accompany this text have been fully revised according to the new edition. The Instructor's Manual includes

- Chapter Summaries and Goals
- Section Summaries
- A Test Bank that includes multiple-choice, essay, true/false, and fill-in-the-blank questions
- Lecture outlines
- Downloadable PowerPoint presentations

The Companion Website includes all the material from the Instructor's Manual, along with the following resources for students:

- Interactive flash cards with key terms and definitions
- Self-quizzes that give students the opportunity to test what they have learned
- Glossary

Acknowledgments

From Kathleen M. Higgins and Clancy Martin

For this edition, we want to thank especially our editor, Robert Miller, and his assistant Christina Mancuso. We also want to thank Megan Rickel, who helped tremendously with permissions, and the readers who advised us in the preparation of this edition: Daniel Campana at the University of La Verne, Teresa Cantrell at the University of Louisville, Michael Clifford at Mississippi State University, Christian Coseru at the College of Charleston, Miguel Endara at Los Angeles Pierce College, Robert S. Gall at West Liberty University, Michael Gendre at Middlesex Community College, William S. Jamison at the University of Alaska Anchorage, Andrew Jones-Cathcart at College of the Canyons, Jonathan Scott Lee at Colorado College, Nancy Matchett at the University of Northern Colorado, Matthew McGrath at the University of Missouri, Gregory Oakes at Winthrop University, David Scott at Coppin State University, David Sherman at the University of Montana at Missoula, and Jiyuan Yu at the State University of New York at Buffalo.

From Robert C. Solomon

This book and its previous editions have been made possible through the encouragement and help of many people, most important of whom are the several thousand introductory students I have had the pleasure of meeting and teaching. For the ninth edition, I want to give special thanks to my friend and colleague Clancy Martin. For the original edition, I thank Susan Zaleski for her very special insights and criticism of the manuscript in its early stages. I also thank Robert Fogelin, John McDermott, Janet McCracken, Stephen Phillips, Paul Woodruff, Stephanie Lewis, Michael Tye, George Cronk, Roland D. Zimany, Terry Boswell, Lisa Erlich, David Blumenfeld, Harry O'Hara, Barbara Barratt, Billy Joe Lucas, Cheshire Calhoun, Peter Hutcheson, Richard Palmer, Norman Thomas, Greta Reed, Edward Johnson, Don Branson, Hoke Robinson, Meredith Michaels, Bruce Paternoster, Maxine Morphis, Bruce Ballard, Jeffery Coombs, Timothy Owen Davis, Conrad Gromada, Gregory Landini, Dan Bonevac, Kathleen Higgins, Kristy Bartlett, Marilyn Frye, Jonathan Westphal, David J. Paul, Edward Johnson, Fred Tabor, Brian Kutin, Karen Mottola, John Rowell, Christopher Melley, John Carvalho, Michael Clifford, Timothy Davis, Ronald Glass, Isabel Luengo, Thomas Ryckman, William Smith, and Clancy Martin. At Harcourt College Publishers, my editors—Bill Pullin, Bill McLane, and David Tatom—were helpful and encouraging for many years and through many editions. Finally, I would like once again to thank my first philosophy teachers—Robert Hanson, Doris Yokum, Elizabeth Flower, James Ross, and C. G. Hempel—who provided me with the models and the materials for an ideal introductory philosophy course—and the many students who still continue to make the teaching of philosophy one of the more satisfying professions in a not easily satisfying world.

For the Student: Doing Philosophy

Your attempt to develop your own thoughts—to "do" philosophy, as well as to read what others have done—is central to any study of philosophy. Philosophy, more than any other field, is not so much a subject as it is a way of thinking, one that can be appreciated fully only by joining in. While reading each section, therefore, do not hesitate to put down the book at any time and do your own thinking and writing. When reading about metaphysics, for example, think about how you would develop your own view of reality and how you would answer the questions raised by the first philosophers of ancient Greece or the Orient. When confronted by an argument, consider how you might argue for or against a given position. When facing an idea that seems foreign, try to put it in your own terms and understand the vision that lies behind it. And when facing a problem, always offer your own answer as well as the answers offered by earlier thinkers. In philosophy, unlike physics or biology, your own answer may be just as legitimate as those given by the philosophers of the past, and there may be equally interesting answers from different traditions. This is what makes philosophy so difficult to learn at first, but it is also what make it so personally valuable and enjoyable.

Most of the sections and all the chapters are followed immediately by questions for you to answer, either out loud with other students or in class or in writing, perhaps by way of a class journal or as an addition to your class notes. Most of the questions are intended simply to encourage you to articulate the point of what you have just read, putting what you have just read in (more or less) your own words. All too often when we are reading new or difficult material, we just allow it to "pass through" on the way to the next reading. We all have had the experience of reading a long passage, even spending a considerable amount of time on it, and then afterward finding that we are unable to say anything about it. The aim of the questions, therefore, is to force you to say or write something. Some of the questions are thought provoking, but most are aimed simply at providing immediate feedback for you. We ask, therefore, that you take the questions seriously and consider them an integral part of your reading assignment.

Writing Philosophy

With the foregoing ideas in mind, it should be obvious why talking about philosophy with friends and classmates, raising important questions and objections in class, and writing down ideas are so important. Articulation reinforces comprehension, and arguing against objections broadens understanding. Writing papers in philosophy is a particularly important part of any philosophy course, and there are certain general guidelines to keep in mind:

1. Begin your essay with a leading question. "Thinking about" some philosophical issue can be fun, but too easily loses direction and purpose. For instance, thinking about "freedom" involves far too many different problems and perspectives. Asking such questions as "Is freedom of action compatible with scientific determinism?" or "Can there be freedom in a socialist state?" gives your thinking a specific orientation and way of proceeding.

2. Be clear about the difficulties you face in tackling the question. Are the terms of the question clear? It is not always necessary or possible to define terms at the start of your essay. Indeed, defining the key term may be the basic and most difficult conclusion you reach. Also, it is often a poor idea to depend on a dictionary (even a good one) for clarifying your question. Dictionaries are not written by philosophers and generally reflect popular usage—which may include just such philosophical misunderstandings as you are attempting to correct.

3. Clarify the position you are arguing. Do not force the reader (your instructor) to guess where you are going. When you are clear about the question you ask, it will help you clarify the answer you intend to give, and vice versa. In fact, you may well change your mind—about both the question and the answer—several times while you are writing; this is the real danger of attempting a one-draft-the-night-before approach to essay writing.

4. Argue your case. Demonstrate why you hold the position you do. The most frequent criticism of student papers is "This is your assertion: Where is the argument?" When an exam question asks you to discuss an idea or a quotation "critically," this does not mean that you must attack it or find fault with it but, rather, that you need to consider the merits and possible inadequacies, consider the reasons given, and give your own reasons for what you say.

5. Anticipate objections to your position and to your arguments and take the offensive against rival positions. If you do not know what your position is opposed to, it is doubtful that you are clear about what your own position is. If you cannot imagine how anyone could possibly disagree with you, you probably have not thought through your position carefully.

6. Do not be afraid to be yourself, to be humorous, charming, sincere, or personal. The most powerful philosophical writings, those that have endured for centuries, often reflect the author's deepest concerns and attitudes toward life. However, remember that no philosophical writing can be just humorous, charming, sincere, or personal. Make sure that everything you write—including a joke—is relevant to the topic at hand. What makes your writing philosophical is that it involves general concerns and careful arguments while attempting to prove an important point and answer one of the age-old questions.

History of Philosophy

3000 B.C.E.

The Epic of Gilgamesh **(2700 B.C.E.)**

2000 B.C.E.

Abraham **(ca. 1900)**

1500 B.C.E. Hindu Vedas **(ca. 1500)**

Moses **(fl. 1220-1200)**

Trojan War **(1185 B.C.E.)**

1000 B.C.E. Chinese develop gunpowder **(1000 B.C.E.)**

Homer **(9th-8th century)**

First Olympic Games **776 B.C.E.**

Rome is founded **753 B.C.E.**

Pythagoras **ca. 581-507 B.C.E.**

Laozi **570-510 B.C.E.**

Buddha (Siddhartha Gautama) **566-486 B.C.E.**

500 B.C.E.

Aesop's *Fables* **ca. 550 B.C.E.**

Confucius **551-479 B.C.E.**

Heraclitus **ca. 535-470 B.C.E.**

Confucian *Analects* compiled **ca. 475-221 B.C.E.**

Socrates **469-399 B.C.E.**

Parthenon is completed **433 B.C.E.**

Plato **427-347 B.C.E.**

400 B.C.E. Job **ca. 400 B.C.E.**

Pentateuch established **ca. 400 B.C.E.**

Plato's *The Symposium* **ca. 385-380 B.C.E.**

Aristotle **384-322 B.C.E.**

Plato's *The Republic* **ca. 380 B.C.E.**

Mencius **372-289 B.C.E.**

Alexander the Great conquers Egypt **332 B.C.E.**

300 B.C.E.

Julius Caesar assassinated **44 B.C.E.**

Jesus Christ **ca. 5 B.C.E.-30 C.E.**

1 B.C.E.

St. Paul **ca. 10-65**

St. Augustine **354-430**

St. Augustine's *Confessions* **397-398**

C.E. 500

Muhammad **ca. 570-632**

1000   *Beowulf* **ca. 1000**

St. Anselm **ca. 1033-1109**

Al-Ghazali **1058-1111**

The first crusade captures Jerusalem **1099**

1100

Oxford University founded **1149**

1200

The Magna Carta is signed **1215**

St. Thomas Aquinas **1225-1274**

Aquinas' *Summa Theologica* **1265-1274**

Marco Polo returns from China **1275**

Farsighted eyeglasses are invented **1285**

1300   Gunpowder used for the first time in Europe **1300**

Dante's *Divine Comedy* **1310**

The Bubonic Plague **1348-1375**

Chaucer's *Canterbury Tales* **1386**

1400

First documented black slaves arrive in Europe **1441**

Christian Constantinople falls to the Muslims **1453**

Johannes Gutenberg invents the printing press **1455**

Columbus and Spanish exploration and colonization of the Americas
and Caribbean **1492-1520**

1500   Northern European Renaissance begins **1500**

High Renaissance in Italy **1500-1530**

Niccolo Machiavelli's *The Prince* **1513**

Copernican Revolution **1514**

Martin Luther's 95 Theses **1517**

Protestant Reformation **1517-1541**

830,000 killed in massive earthquake in China **1556**

Thomas Hobbes **1588-1679**

René Descartes **1596-1650**

1600

Shakespeare's *Hamlet* **1601**

Miguel de Cervantes Saavedra's *Don Quixote* **1605**

King James Bible **1611**

Thirty Years War **1618-1648**

Pilgrims arrive at Plymouth **1620**

Blaise Pascal **1623-1662**

Benedictus de Spinoza **1632-1677**

John Locke **1632-1704**

Descartes' *Discourse on Method* **1637**

Descartes' *Meditations on First Philosophy* **1641**

Isaac Newton **1642-1727**

Gottfried Wilhelm von Leibniz **1646-1716**

1650

Hobbes' *Leviathan* **1651**

John Milton's *Paradise Lost* **1667**

Pascal's *Pensées* **1670**
Spinoza's *Ethics* **1677**
Bishop George Berkeley **1685–1753**
Newton's *Principles of Mathematics* 1687
Locke's *An Essay Concerning Human Understanding* **1690**

1700

Berkeley's *A Treatise Concerning the Principles of Human Knowledge* 1710
David Hume **1711–1776**
Jean-Jacques Rousseau **1712–1778**
Leibniz's *The Monadology* **1714**
Immanuel Kant **1724–1804**
Agricultural revolution in Western Europe 1730–1850
Benjamin Franklin's *Poor Richard's Almanac* **1732**
Hume's *A Treatise of Human Nature* **1739**
Jeremy Bentham **1748–1832**
Hume's *An Enquiry Concerning Human Understanding* **1748**
Voltaire's *Candide* **1759**
Rousseau's *Emile* **1762**
Rousseau's *The Social Contract* **1762**
Leibniz's *New Essays on Human Understanding* **1765**
Georg Wilhelm Friedrich Hegel **1770–1831**
Boston Tea Party 1773
The American colonies declare independence 1776
Adam Smith's *Wealth of Nations* **1776**
Kant's *Critique of Pure Reason* **1781**
Kant's *Prolegomena to any Future Metaphysics* **1783**
Arthur Schopenhauer **1788–1860**
Kant's *Critique of Practical Reason* **1788**
French Revolution begins 1789
Mary Wollstonecraft's *A Vindication of the Rights of Women* **1792**
Reign of Terror in France 1793
Kant's *Metaphysics of Morals* **1797**

1800

Napoleon crowned emperor of France 1804
John Stuart Mill **1806–1873**
Harriet Taylor **1807–1858**
Hegel's *Phemonenology of Spirit* **1807**
Charles Darwin 1809–1882
Søren Kierkegaard **1813–1855**
The Battle at Waterloo 1815
Frederick Douglass **1817–1895**
Henry David Thoreau **1817–1862**
Karl Marx **1818–1883**
Schopenhauer's *The World as Will and Representation* **1818**
Mary Shelley's *Frankenstein* 1818
Fyodor Dostoyevsky **1821–1881**
England outlaws slavery 1833
Ralph Waldo Emerson's "Nature" **1836**
William James **1842–1910**

Friedrich Nietzsche **1844-1900**

The Potato Famine 1845-1848

Karl Marx and Friedrich Engel's *The Communist Manifesto* **1848**

1850

Herman Melville's *Moby Dick* 1851

Thoreau's *Walden* **1854**

Sigmund Freud **1856-1939**

Edmund Husserl **1859-1938**

John Dewey **1859-1952**

Darwin's *Origin of Species* 1859

Mill's *Utilitarianism* **1863**

Emancipation Proclamation 1863

Lewis Carroll's *Alice's Adventures in Wonderland* **1865**

Telegraph cable connects the United States and Europe 1866

Mahatma Gandhi **1868-1948**

Louisa May Alcott's *Little Women* 1868

Bertrand Russell **1872-1970**

Global economic depression 1873-1877

Leo Tolstoy's *Anna Karenina* 1875

Albert Einstein **1879-1955**

Dostoyevsky's *The Brother's Karamazov* **1880**

Karl Jaspers **1883-1969**

Ludwig Wittgenstein **1889-1951**

Martin Heidegger **1889-1976**

1900

Gilbert Ryle **1900-1976**

Keiji Nishitani **1900-1990**

W. E. B. DuBois's *The Souls of Black Folks* **1903**

John Wisdom **1904-1993**

Jean-Paul Sartre **1905-1980**

Upton Sinclair's *The Jungle* 1906

Maurice Merleau-Ponty **1908-1961**

Simone de Beauvoir **1908-1986**

NCAAP established 1909

1910

Nationalist Revolution in China 1911

Russell's *The Problems of Philosophy* **1912**

Titanic sinks 1912

Albert Camus **1913-1960**

World War I 1914-1918

Russian Revolution 1917

Influenza epidemic kills 20 million people 1918

1920

John Rawls **1921-2002**

James Joyce's *Ulysses* 1922

John Scopes indicted for teaching evolution 1925

Malcolm X **1925-1965**

Kafka's *The Trial* 1925

Michel Foucault **1926-1984**

Virginia Woolf's *To the Lighthouse* 1927

U.S. stock market crash **1929**
William Faulkner's *The Sound and the Fury* **1929**
Worldwide economic depression **1929-1939**
Martin Luther King, Jr. 1929-1968

1930 Rise of Nazis in Germany **1930**
Jacques Derrida 1930-2004
Richard Rorty 1931-2007
Zora Neale Hurston's *Their Eyes Were Watching God* **1937**
John Steinbeck's *Grapes of Wrath* **1939**
World War II **1939-1945**

1940
The Japanese attack Pearl Harbor **1941**
Merleau-Ponty's *The Structure of Behavior* 1942
Camus's *The Stranger* 1942
The Shoah (Holocaust) **1942-1945**
Sartre's *Being and Nothingness* 1943
Formation of the United Nations **1945**
George Orwell's *Animal Farm* **1945**
The atomic bomb attack on Hiroshima **1945**
India gains independence from Britain; Pakistan is created **1947**
Israel is created **1948**
Marshall Plan **1948**
Arthur Miller's *Death of a Salesman* **1949**
Beauvoir's *The Second Sex* 1949
Communist victory in China, Mao Tse-tung **1949**

1950
J. D. Salinger's *Catcher in the Rye* **1951**
Samuel Beckett's *Waiting for Godot* **1952**
Ralph Ellison's *Invisible Man* **1952**
Brown v Board of Education **1954**
The Vietnam War **1955-1975**

1960 Harper Lee's *To Kill a Mockingbird* **1960**
Cuban Missile Crisis **1962**
Betty Friedan's *The Feminine Mystique* **1963**
John Fitzgerald Kennedy is assassinated **1963**
The Civil Rights Act is passed in the United States **1964**
Cultural Revolution in China **1965-1973**
Gabriel Garcia Márquez's *One Hundred Years of Solitude* **1967**
Dr. Martin Luther King, Jr., is assassinated **1968**
Woodstock Music Festival **1969**

1970
Rawls's *Theory of Justice* 1971
Robert Nozick's *Anarchy, State, and Utopia* 1974
Lebanese Civil War **1975**
Ronald Dworkin's *Taking Rights Seriously* 1977
Rorty's *Philosophy and the Mirror of Nature* 1979
Thomas Nagel's *Mortal Questions* 1979

1980 Rise of Ronald Reagan and conservatism in the United States **1980**
Jacques Derrida's *Margins of Philosophy* 1982

XXVIII | HISTORY OF PHILOSOPHY

Apple's Macintosh computers are released **1984**
Glasnost (openness) and *perestroika* (restructuring) policies
in Soviet Union **1985**
Toni Morrison's *Beloved* **1987**
Berlin Wall falls **1989**

1990   Internet introduced to the general public **1990**
Soviet Union dissolved **1991**
Hilary Putnam's *Renewing Philosophy* 1992
First democratic elections in South Africa **1994**
**Charles Taylor's *Multiculturalism: Examining the Politics
of Recognition* 1994**
Genocide in Rwanda **1995**

2000

September 11, **2001**
Iraq War begins **2003**
Barack Obama becomes president of the Unites States **2009**

Introduction

The unexamined life is not worth living.

SOCRATES

A. Socrates

He was not the first philosopher, but he was, and is still, the ideal of philosophers. Once assured by the oracle at Delphi that he was the wisest man in Athens, **Socrates** (470-399 B.C.E.) borrowed his view of life from the inscription at Delphi, "Know Thyself." Mixing humility with arrogance, he boasted that his superiority lay in his awareness of his own ignorance, and he spent the rest of his life making fools of the self-proclaimed "wise men" of Athens.

In the opinion of Socrates and other critics of the time, the government of Athens was corrupt and notoriously bumbling, in marked contrast to the "Golden Age" of Pericles a few years before. Philosophical arguments had become all cleverness and demagoguery, rhetorical tricks to win arguments and legal cases; political ambition replaced justice and the search for the good life. Socrates believed that the people of Athens held their principles glibly, like banners at a football game, but rarely lived up to them and even more rarely examined them. Against this, he developed a technique of asking seemingly innocent questions, trapping his audience in their own confusions and hypocrisies, exploding the pretensions of his times. And against their easy certainties, he taught that "the unexamined life is not worth living." He referred to himself as a "gadfly" (an obnoxious insect with a painful bite), keeping his fellow citizens from ever becoming as smug and self-righteous as they would like to have been. Accordingly, he made many enemies and was satirized by Aristophanes in his play *The Clouds*.

FIG. I.1 A traditional image of Socrates *(Image © kmiragaya, 2011. Used under license from Shutterstock.com)*

Socrates (470-399 B.C.E.)

An Athenian philosopher with a gift for rhetoric and debating. He had a notoriously poor marriage, had several children, and lived in poverty most of his life. Socrates began his studies in the physical sciences but soon turned to the study of human nature, morality, and politics. He became famous debating with the many "sophists" who wandered about giving practical training in argument and persuasion (the ancient equivalent of law school). Socrates found their general skepticism intolerable and urged a return to the absolute ideals of wisdom, virtue, justice, and the good life. In his philosophy, he approached these questions as matters of finding the exact definitions of these concepts in order to clarify our pursuit of them. In doing so, he developed a brilliant technique of dialogue or "dialectic" in which he would discover these definitions by constant debating, forcing his opponents or students to advance various theories, which he, in turn, would knock down. In the process, the correct definition would slowly emerge. In his not always tactful search for truth, however, Socrates made many enemies, who eventually had him condemned to death, a cruel and unfair verdict that he accepted with dignity.

 FROM *The Clouds*
BY **Aristophanes**[1]

STUDENT OF SOCRATES: Socrates asked Chaerephon how many of its own feet a flea could jump—one had bitten Chaerephon's brow and then jumped to Socrates' head.

STREPSIADES: And how did he measure the jump?

STUDENT: Most ingeniously. He melted wax, caught the flea, dipped its feet, and the hardened wax made Persian slippers. Unfastening these, he found their size.

STREPSIADES: Royal Zeus! What an acute intellect!

STUDENT: But yesterday a high thought was lost through a lizard.

STREPSIADES: How so? Tell me.

STUDENT: As he gaped up at the moon, investigating her paths and turnings, from off the roof a lizard befouled him.

In the play, Aristophanes made Socrates and his students look utterly ridiculous, and the Athenian public enjoyed Aristophanes' sarcasm as a mild form of vengeance for Socrates' constant criticisms. Aristophanes' "clouds" refer to that confusion which we mean when we talk of someone "having his head in the clouds." Aristophanes probably expressed the general public opinion when he described Socrates as "shiftless" and merely a master at verbal trickery.

Socrates' students, however, virtually worshiped him. They described him as "the bravest, most wise and most upright man of our times" and perceived him as a martyr for the truth in a corrupted society. The price of his criticism was not merely the satire of the playwrights. Because he had been such a continual nuisance, the government arranged to have Socrates brought to trial for "corrupting the youth of Athens" and "not believing in the gods of the city." And for these trumped-up "crimes," Socrates was condemned to death. But at his trial, he once again became a gadfly to those who condemned him.

FROM The *Apology*
BY **Plato**[2]

He assesses the penalty at death. So be it. What counterassessment should I propose to you, gentlemen of the jury? Clearly it should be a penalty I deserve, and what do I deserve to suffer or to pay because I have deliberately not led a quiet life but have neglected what occupies most people: wealth, household affairs, the position of general or public orator or the other offices, the political clubs and factions that exist in the city? I thought myself too honest to survive if I occupied myself with those things. I did not follow that path that would have made me of no use either to you or to myself, but I went to each of you privately and conferred upon him what I say is the greatest benefit, by persuading him not to care for any of his belongings before

---

caring that he himself should be as good and as wise as possible, not to care for the city's possessions more than for the city itself, and to care for other things in the same way. What do I deserve for being such a man? Some good, gentlemen of the jury, if I must truly make an assessment according to my deserts, and something suitable.

Socrates here suggests that the state should give him a pension, rather than a punishment, for being a public benefactor and urging his students to be virtuous.

It is for the sake of a short time, gentlemen of the jury, that you will acquire the reputation and the guilt, in the eyes of those who want to denigrate the city, of having killed Socrates, a wise man, for they will say that I am wise even if I am not. If you had waited but a little while, this would have happened of its own accord. You see my age, that I am already advanced in years and close to death. I am saying this not to all of you but to those who condemned me to death, and to these same jurors I say: Perhaps you think that I was convicted for lack of such words as might have convinced you, if I thought I should say or do all I could to avoid my sentence. Far from it. I was convicted because I lacked not words but boldness and shamelessness and the willingness to say to you what you would most gladly have heard from me, lamentations and tears and my saying and doing many things that I say are unworthy of me but that you are accustomed to hear from others. I did not think then that the danger I ran should make me do anything mean, nor do I now regret the nature of my defense. I would much rather die after this kind of defense than live after making the other kind. Neither I nor any other man should, on trial or in war, contrive to avoid death at any cost. Indeed it is often obvious in battle that one could escape death by throwing away one's weapons and by turning to supplicate one's pursuers, and there are many ways to avoid death in every kind of danger if one will venture to do or say anything to avoid it. It is not difficult to avoid death, gentlemen of the jury, it is much more difficult to avoid wickedness, for it runs faster than death. Slow and elderly as I am, I have been caught by the slower pursuer, whereas my accusers, being clever and sharp, have been caught by the quicker, wickedness. I leave you now, condemned to death by you, but they are condemned by truth to wickedness and injustice. So I maintain my assessment, and they maintain theirs. This perhaps had to happen, and I think it is as it should be.

Now I want to prophesy to those who convicted me, for I am at the point when men prophesy most, when they are about to die. I say gentlemen, to those who voted to kill me, that vengeance will come upon you immediately after my death, a vengeance much harder to bear than that which you took in killing me. You did this in the belief that you would avoid giving an account of your life, but I maintain that quite the opposite will happen to you. There will be more people to test you, whom I now held back, but you did not notice it. They will be more difficult to deal with as they will be younger and you will resent them more. You are wrong if you believe that by killing people you will prevent anyone from reproaching you for not living in the right way. To escape such tests is neither possible nor good, but it is best and easiest not to discredit others but to prepare oneself to be as good as possible. With this prophecy to you who convicted me, I part from you.

> "It is not difficult to avoid death, gentlemen of the jury, it is much more difficult to avoid wickedness, for it runs faster than death."
> – PLATO'S SOCRATES

In prison, he was given the opportunity to escape. He refused it. He had always taught that "the really important thing is not to live, but to live well." And to "live well" meant, along with the more enjoyable things in life, to live according to your principles. When his friend

Crito tried to persuade him otherwise, Socrates countered his pleas and arguments with powerful arguments of his own. Look carefully at the structure of these arguments and judge for yourself their soundness.

 FROM **The Crito**
BY **Plato**[3]

SOCRATES: My good Crito, why should we care so much for what the majority think? The most reasonable people, to whom one should pay more attention, will believe that things were done as they were done.

CRITO: You see, Socrates, that one must also pay attention to the opinion of the majority. Your present situation makes clear that the majority can inflict not the least but pretty well the greatest evils if one is slandered among them.

SOCRATES: Would that the majority could inflict the greatest evils, for they would then be capable of the greatest good, and that would be fine, but now they cannot do either. They cannot make a man either wise or foolish, but they inflict things haphazardly.

CRITO: That may be so. But tell me this, Socrates, are you anticipating that I and your other friends would have trouble with the informers if you escape from here, as having stolen you away, and that we should be compelled to lose all our property or pay heavy fines and suffer other punishment besides? If you have any such fear, forget it. We would be justified in running this risk to save you, and worse, if necessary. Do follow my advice, and do not act differently.

SOCRATES: I do have these things in mind, Crito, and also many others.

CRITO: Have no such fear. It is not much money that some people require to save you and get you out of here. . . .

Besides, Socrates, I do not think that what you are doing is right, to give up your life when you can save it, and to hasten your fate as your enemies would hasten it, and indeed have hastened it in their wish to destroy you.

. . .

SOCRATES: My dear Crito, your eagerness is worth much if it should have some right aim; if not, then the greater your keenness the more difficult it is to deal with. We must therefore examine whether we should act in this way or not, as not only now but at all times I am the kind of man who listens only to the argument that on reflection seems best to me. I cannot, now that this fate has come upon me, discard the arguments I used; they seem to me much the same. I value and respect the same principles as before, and if we have no better arguments to bring up at this moment, be sure that I shall not agree with you, not even if the power of the majority were to frighten us with more bogeys, as if we were children, with threats of incarcerations and executions and confiscation of property. How should we examine this matter more reasonably? Would it be by taking up first your argument about the opinions of men, whether it is sound in every case that one should pay attention to some opinions, but not to others? Or was that well-spoken before the necessity to die came upon me, but now it is clear that this was said in vain for the sake of argument,

3 Plato, *The Crito*, in *The Trial and Death of Socrates*, 2nd ed., trans. G. M. A. Grube. Copyright © 1975 by Hackett Publishing Company. Reprinted with permission.

that it was in truth play and nonsense? I am eager to examine together with you, Crito, whether this argument will appear in any way different to me in my present circumstances, or whether it remains the same, whether we are to abandon it or believe it. It was said on every occasion that one should greatly value some opinions, but not others. Does that seem to you a sound statement? . . . Examine the following statement in turn as to whether it stays the same or not, that the most important thing is not life, but the good life.

CRITO: It stays the same.

SOCRATES: And that the good life, the beautiful life, and the just life are the same; does that still hold, or not?

CRITO: It does hold.

SOCRATES: As we have agreed so far, we must examine next whether it is right for me to try to get out of here when the Athenians have not acquitted me. If it is seen to be right, we will try to do so; if it is not, we will abandon the idea. As for those questions you raise about money, reputation, the upbringing of children, Crito, those considerations in truth belong to those people who easily put men to death and would bring them to life again

FIG. 1.2 The name "Plato" literally means "broad shoulders." (Image © pseudolongino, 2011. Used under license from Shutterstock.com)

Plato (427–347 B.C.E.)

Plato was born into a family of wealth and political power. But in Athens, he fell under the influence of Socrates and turned his talents to philosophy. He conceived of a "philosopher-king," the ideal wise ruler, who certainly did not exist in Athens. He was disillusioned by Socrates' execution and devoted his life to continuing Socrates' work. Plato set up the Academy for this purpose and spent the rest of his life teaching there. He first set down his reminiscences of Socrates' life and death, and, using the dialogue form with Socrates as his mouthpiece, he extended Socrates' thought into entirely new areas, notably, metaphysics and the theory of knowledge. Plato incorporated a theory of morality into his metaphysics and politics, particularly in *The Republic*. Like all Greeks, he saw ethics as part of politics and the good life for the individual in terms of the strength and harmony of the society. In *The Republic*, accordingly, Socrates argues against the various views of selfishness and hedonism that would interfere with such a conception. Virtue, he argues, is the harmony of the individual soul as well as the harmony of the individual within the society. It is still difficult to know, since we have nothing from Socrates himself, how much is original Plato and how much is transcribed Socrates.

if they could, without thinking; I mean the majority of men. For us, however, since our argument leads to this, the only valid consideration, as we were saying just now, is whether we should be acting rightly in giving money and gratitude to those who will lead me out of here, and ourselves helping with the escape, or whether in truth we shall do wrong in doing all this. If it appears that we shall be acting unjustly, then we have no need at all to take into account whether we shall have to die, if we stay here and keep quiet, or suffer in another way, rather than do wrong.

CRITO: I think you put that beautifully, Socrates, but see what we should do.

SOCRATES: Let us examine the question together, my dear friend, and if you can make any objection while I am speaking, make it and I will listen to you, but if you have no objection to make, my dear Crito, then stop now from saying the same thing so often, that I must leave here against the will of the Athenians. I think it important to persuade you before I act, and not to act against your wishes. . . .

SOCRATES: Then . . . I ask you: when one has come to an agreement that is just with someone, should one fulfill it or cheat on it?

CRITO: One should fulfill it.

SOCRATES: See what follows from this: If we leave here without the city's permission, are we injuring people whom we should least injure? And are we sticking to a just agreement, or not?

"Not only now but at all times I am the kind of man who listens only to the argument that on reflection seems best to me."

– PLATO'S SOCRATES

CRITO: I cannot answer your question, Socrates, I do not know.

SOCRATES: Look at it this way. If, as we were planning to run away from here, or whatever one should call it, the laws and the state came and confronted us and asked: "Tell me, Socrates, what are you intending to do? Do you not by this action you are attempting intend to destroy us, the laws, and indeed the whole city, as far as you are concerned? Or do you think it possible for a city not to be destroyed if the verdicts of its courts have no force but are nullified and set at naught by private individuals?" What shall we answer to this and other such arguments? For many things could be said, especially by an orator on behalf of this law we are destroying, which orders that the judgments of the courts shall be carried out. Shall we say in answer, "The city wronged me, and its decision was not right." Shall we say that, or what?

CRITO: Yes, by Zeus, Socrates, that is our answer.

SOCRATES: Then what if the laws said, "Was that the agreement between us, Socrates, or was it to respect the judgments that the city came to?" And if we wondered at their words, they would perhaps add: "Socrates, do not wonder at what we say but answer, since you are accustomed to proceed by question and answer. Come now, what accusation do you bring against us and the city, that you should try to destroy us? Did we not, first, bring you to birth, and was it not through us that your father married your mother and begat you? Tell us, do you find anything to criticize in those of us who are concerned with marriage?" And I would say that I do not criticize them. "Or in those of us concerned with the nurture of babies and the education that you too received? Were those assigned to that subject not right to instruct your father to educate you in the arts and in physical culture?" And I would say that they were right. "Very well," they would continue, "and after you were born and nurtured and educated, could you, in the first place, deny that you are our offspring and servant, both you and your forefathers? If that is so, do you think that we are on an equal footing as regards the right, and that whatever we do to you it is right for you to do to us? You were not on an equal footing with your father as regards the right, nor with your master if you had one, so as to retaliate for anything they did to you, to revile them if they reviled you, to beat them if they beat you, and so with many other things. Do you think you have this right to retaliation against your country and its laws? That if we undertake to destroy you and think it right to do so, you can undertake to destroy us, as far as you can, in return? And will you say that you are right to do so, you who truly care for virtue? Is your wisdom such as not to realize that your country is to be honoured more than your mother, your father, and all your ancestors, that it is more to be revered and more sacred, and that it counts for more among the gods and sensible men, that you must worship it, yield to it and placate its anger more than your father's? You must either persuade it or obey its orders, and endure in silence whatever it instructs you to endure, whether blows or bonds, and if it leads you into war to be wounded or killed, you must obey. To do so is right, and one must not give way or retreat or leave one's post, but both in war and in courts and everywhere else, one must obey the commands of one's city and country, or persuade it as to the nature of justice. It is impious to bring violence to bear against your mother or father, it is much more so to use it against your country." What shall we say in reply, Crito, that the laws speak the truth, or not?

CRITO: I think they do.

SOCRATES: "Reflect now, Socrates," the laws might say, "that if what we say is true, you are not treating us rightly by planning to do what you are planning. . . .

"So decisively did you choose us and agree to be a citizen under us. Also, you have had children in this city, thus showing that it was congenial to you. Then at your trial you could have assessed your penalty at exile if you wished, and you are now attempting to do against the city's wishes what you could then have done with her consent. Then you prided yourself that you did not resent death, but you chose, as you said, death in preference to exile. Now, however, those words do not make you ashamed, and you pay no heed to us, the laws, as you plan to destroy us, and you act like the meanest type of slave by trying to run away, contrary to your undertakings and your agreement to live as a citizen under us. First then, answer us on this very point, whether we speak the truth when we say that you agreed, not only in words but by your deeds, to live in accordance with us." What are we to say to that, Crito? Must we not agree?

CRITO: We must, Socrates.

SOCRATES: "Surely," they might say, "you are breaking the undertakings and agreements that you made with us without compulsion or deceit, and under no pressure of time for deliberation. You have had seventy years during which you could have gone away if you did not like us, and if you thought our agreements unjust. You did not choose to go to Sparta or to Crete, which you are always saying are well governed, nor to any other city, Greek or foreign. You have been away from Athens less than the lame or the blind or other handicapped people. It is clear that the city has been outstandingly more congenial to you than to other Athenians, and so have we, the laws, for what city can please if its laws do not? Will you then not now stick to our agreements? You will, Socrates, if we can persuade you, and not make yourself a laughingstock by leaving the city.

"Be persuaded by us who have brought you up, Socrates. Do not value either your children or your life or anything else more than goodness, in order that you may have all this as your defense before rulers there. If you do this deed, you will not think it better or more just or more pious, nor will any one of your friends, nor will it be better for you when you arrive yonder. As it is, you depart, if you depart, after being wronged not by us, the laws, but by men; but if you depart after shamefully returning wrong for wrong and injury for injury, after breaking your agreement and contract with us, after injuring those you should injure least—yourself, your friends, your country and us—we shall be angry with you while you are

FIG. 1.3 *Socrates in Prison* (1785) by Johann Heinrich Tischbein the Elder
(Bildarchiv Preussischer Kulturbesitz / Art Resource, NY)

still alive, and our brothers, the laws of the underworld, will not receive [you] kindly, knowing that you tried to destroy us as far as you could. Do not let Crito persuade you, rather than we, to do what he says."

. . .

CRITO: I have nothing to say, Socrates.

SOCRATES: Let it be then, Crito, and let us act in this way, since this is the way the god is leading us.

> • By choosing to go on living in the city, Socrates has agreed with Athens to obey its laws. Therefore, even if he is wrongly condemned by the same laws, he has the duty to stay and accept his punishment. Do you agree that he has made such a tacit agreement? Do you agree that he has the duty to stay and accept punishment even if he was wrongly condemned? Have *you* entered into such an agreement with your community? Your country? What would you do if you were Socrates?

Socrates believed that the good of his "soul" was far more important than the transient pleasures of life. Accordingly, he preferred to die for his ideas than live as a hypocrite. An idea worth living for may be an idea worth dying for as well.

 FROM **The *Phaedo***
BY **Plato**[4]

And while he was saying this, he was holding the cup, and then drained it calmly and easily. Most of us had been able to hold back our tears reasonably well up till then, but when we saw him drinking it and after he drank it, we could hold them back no longer; my own tears came in floods against my will. So I covered my face. I was weeping for myself—not for him, but for my misfortune in being deprived of such a comrade. Even before me, Crito was unable to restrain his tears and got up. Apollodorus had not ceased from weeping before, and at this moment his noisy tears and anger made everybody present break down, except Socrates, "What is this," he said, "you strange fellows. It is mainly for this reason that I sent the women away, to avoid such unseemliness, for I am told one should die in good omened silence. So keep quiet and control yourselves. . . ."

Such was the end of our comrade, Echecrates, a man who, we would say, was of all those we have known the best, and also the wisest and the most upright.

Is there anything that you believe so passionately that you would die for it? Is there anything that you believe so passionately that it really makes your life worth living? For most people, now as always, life is rather a matter of "getting by." One of the more popular phrases of self-praise these days is "I'm a survivor." But, ironically, a person who is not willing to die for anything (for example, his or her own freedom) is thereby more vulnerable to threats and corruption. To be willing to die—as Socrates was—is to have a considerable advantage over someone for whom "life is everything."

---

4 Plato, *The Phaedo*, in *The Trial and Death of Socrates*, 2nd ed., trans. G. M. A. Grube. Copyright © 1975 by Hackett Publishing Company, Inc. Reprinted by permission. All rights reserved.

FIG. I.4 *The Death of Socrates* (1787) by Jacques Louis David *(Image copyright © The Metropolitan Museum of Art / Art Resource, NY)*

If you look closely at your life, not only at your proclaimed ideals and principles but your desires and ambitions as well, do the facts of your life add up to its best intentions? Or are you too just drifting with the times, dissatisfied with ultimately meaningless jobs and mindless joyless entertainments, concerned with the price of tuition and some recent stupidity of your government, the petty competitions of school and society, the hassles of chores and assignments, car troubles and occasional social embarrassments, interrupted only by all too rare and too quickly passing pleasures and distractions? What we learn from Socrates is how to rise above all of this. Not that we should give up worldly pleasures—good food and fun, sex, sports and entertainment—and put our heads in the "clouds"; but we should see them in perspective and examine for ourselves that jungle of confused reactions and conditioned responses that we have unthinkingly inherited from our parents and borrowed from our peers. The point is not to give up what we have learned or to turn against our culture. Rather, the lesson to be learned from Socrates is that thinking about our lives and clarifying our ideals can turn it from a dreary series of tasks and distractions into a self-conscious adventure, one even worth dying for and certainly worth living for. It is a special kind of **abstract** thinking, rising above petty concerns and transforming our existence into a bold experiment in living. This special kind of thinking is called philosophy.

"We shall rightly call a philosopher the man who is easily willing to learn every kind of knowledge."

– PLATO'S SOCRATES

 FROM **The *Republic*** BY **Plato**[5]

SOCRATES: Do you agree, or not, that when we say that a man has a passion for something, we shall say that he desires that whole kind of thing, not just one part of it and not the other?

GLAUCON: Yes, the whole of it.

SOCRATES: The lover of wisdom, we shall say, has a passion for wisdom, not for this kind of wisdom and not that, but for every kind of wisdom?

GLAUCON: True.

SOCRATES: As for one who is choosy about what he learns, especially if he is young and cannot yet give a reasoned account of what is useful and what is not, we shall not call him a lover of learning or a philosopher, just as we shall not say that a man who is difficult about his food is hungry or has an appetite for food. We shall not call him a lover of food but a bad feeder.

GLAUCON: And we should be right.

SOCRATES: But we shall rightly call a philosopher the man who is easily willing to learn every kind of knowledge, gladly turns to learning things, and is unsatiable in this respect. Is that not so?

B. What Is Philosophy?

Philosophy is not like any other academic subject; rather it is a critical approach to all subjects, the comprehensive vision within which all other subjects are contained. Philosophy is a style of life, a life of ideas or the life of **reason**, which a person like Socrates lives all of the time, which many of us live only a few hours a week. It is thinking, about everything and anything. But mainly, it is living thoughtfully. **Aristotle**, the student of **Plato**, who was the student of Socrates, called this "contemplative" or philosophical life the ideal life for humankind. He did not mean, however, that one should sit and think all of the time without doing anything. Aristotle, like the other Greek philosophers, was not one to abstain from pleasure or from political and social involvement for the sake of isolated thinking. Philosophy need not, as commonly believed, put our heads in the clouds, out of touch with everyday reality. Quite to the contrary, philosophy takes our heads out of the clouds, enlarging our view of ourselves and our knowledge of the world, allowing us to break out of prejudices and harmful habits that we have held since we were too young or too naive to know better. To say that philosophy is "critical" is not to say that it is negative or nihilistic; it is only to say that it is *reflective*. It looks at and thinks about ideas carefully, instead of unthinkingly accepting them.

Philosophy puts our lives and our beliefs in perspective by enabling us to see afresh the ways in which we view the world, to see what we assume, what we **infer**, and what we know for certain. It also allows us to appreciate *other* views of the world. It encourages us to see the consequences of our views and sometimes their hopeless inconsistencies. It allows us to see the justification (or lack of it) for our most treasured beliefs, and to separate what we will

5 Plato, *The Republic*, Bk. V, trans. G. M. A. Grube, Indianapolis, IN: Hackett, 1974.

continue to believe with confidence from what we should consider doubtful or reject. It allows us the option of considering alternatives. Philosophy gives us the intellectual strength to defend what we do and what we believe to others and to ourselves. It forces us to be clear about the limits as well as the warrants for our acts and beliefs. Consequently, it gives us the intellectual strength to understand, tolerate, and even sympathize with or adopt views very different from our own.

Philosophy is first and foremost a discipline that teaches us how to articulate, hold, and defend beliefs that, perhaps, we have always held, but without having spelled them out and argued for them. For example, suppose you have been brought up in a deeply religious home; you have been taught respect for God and church, but you have never had to learn to justify or argue for your beliefs. You know that, although there are people who would disagree with you, your belief is a righteous and necessary one, but you have never had to explain this to anyone, nor have you tried to explain it to yourself. But now you enter college and immediately you are confronted by fellow students, some of whom you consider close friends and admire in many ways, who are openly skeptical about religion. Others accept very different doctrines and beliefs, and vociferously defend these. Your first reactions may be almost physical; you feel weak, flushed, and anxious. You refuse to listen, and if you respond at all, it is with

Aristotle (384-322 B.C.E.)

One of the greatest Western philosophers, Aristotle was born in northern Greece (Stagira). His father was the physician to Philip, king of Macedonia, and he himself was to become the tutor to Philip's son, Alexander the Great. For eighteen years, Aristotle was a student in Plato's Academy in Athens, where he learned and parted from Plato's views. After Plato's death, he turned to the study of biology, and many of his theories ruled Western science until the Renaissance. Aristotle was with Alexander until 335 B.C.E., when he returned to Athens to set up his own school, the Lyceum. After Alexander's death, the anti-Macedonian sentiment in Athens forced Aristotle to flee (commenting that the Athenians would not sin twice against philosophy). In addition to his biological studies, Aristotle virtually created the sciences of logic and linguistics; developed extravagant theories in physics and astronomy; and made significant contributions to metaphysics, ethics, politics, and aesthetics. His *Metaphysics* is still a basic text on the subject, and *Nicomachean Ethics* codified ancient Greek morality. This latter work stresses individual virtue and excellence for a small elite of Greek citizens. The best life of all, according to Aristotle, is the life of contemplation, that is, the life of a philosopher, for it is the most self-contained and the "closest to the gods." But such contemplation must be together with the pleasures of life, honor, wealth, and virtuous action.

FIG. I.5 Aristotle is sometimes referred to as "The Philosopher." *(Image © Dhoxax, 2011. Used under license from Shutterstock.com)*

a tinge of hysteria. You may get into fights as well as arguments. You feel as if some foundation of your life, one of its main supports, is slipping away. But slowly you gain some confidence; you begin to listen. You give yourself enough distance so that you will consider arguments about religion in just the same way you would consider arguments about some scientific or political dispute. You ask yourself *why* your friends don't believe what you believe. Are their arguments persuasive, their **reasons** *good* reasons? You begin asking yourself how you came to believe in your religion in the first place, and you may well come up with the answer (many freshmen do) that you were "conditioned" by your parents and by society in general. Consequently, you may, perhaps for a time, perhaps for a lifetime, question or reject the ideas you had once "naturally" accepted. Or you may reaffirm your faith with new commitment, determined that, whatever the source, your beliefs are right or, at least, right for you. But after further consideration and argument, perhaps with some new religious experience, you come to see both sides of the arguments. For the first time, you can weigh their merits and demerits against each other without defensively holding onto one and attacking the other. You may remain a believer; you may become an atheist or an agnostic (a person who admits not knowing whether there is a God or not). Some people convert to another faith. Or one can adopt a position in which he or she gives all religions (and nonreligion) equal weight, continuing to believe but not insisting that one belief is the only correct one or that a person is necessarily superior because of it. But whatever you decide, your position will no longer be naive and unthinking. You know the arguments, both for and against. You know how to defend yourself. And, most importantly, you have confidence that your position is

"Philosophy is to be studied, not for the sake of any definite answers to its questions, since no definite answers can, as a rule, be known to be true, but rather for the sake of the questions themselves; because these questions enlarge our conception of what is possible, enrich our intellectual imagination and diminish the dogmatic assurance which closes the mind against speculation; but above all because through the greatness of the universe which philosophy contemplates, the mind also is rendered great, and becomes capable of that union with the universe which constitutes its highest good."

Bertrand Russell, *from* **The Problems of Philosophy**

secure, that you have considered its objections, and that you have mastered its strengths. So it is with all philosophical problems and positions. Philosophy does not pull us away from our lives; it clarifies them. It secures them on intellectual ground in place of the fragile supports provided by inherited prejudices, fragments of parental advice, and mindless slogans borrowed from television commercials.

"Philosophy" sounds like a new and mysterious discipline, unlike anything you have ever encountered. But the basic ideas of philosophy are familiar to all of us, even if we have not yet formally confronted the problems. In this sense, we are all philosophers already. Watch yourself in a crisis, or listen to yourself in an argument with a friend. Notice how quickly abstract concepts like "freedom," "mankind," "self-identity," "nature" and "natural," "relative," "reality," "illusion," and "truth" enter our thoughts and our conversations. Notice how certain basic philosophical principles—whether conservative or radical, pragmatic or idealistic, confident or skeptical, pedestrian or heroic—enter into our arguments and our thinking as well as our actions. We all have some opinions about God, about morality and its principles, about the nature of man and the nature of the universe. But because we haven't questioned them, they are merely the **assumptions** of our thinking. We believe many things without having thought about them, merely assuming them, sometimes without evidence or good reasons. What the study of philosophy does for us is to make our ideas explicit, to give us the means of defending our **presuppositions**, and to make alternative suppositions available to us as well. Where once we merely assumed a point of view, passively and for lack of alternatives, we now can argue for it with confidence, knowing that our acceptance is active and critical, systematic rather than merely a collection of borrowed beliefs (who knows from where). To be **critical** means to examine carefully and cautiously, willing, if necessary, to change one's own beliefs. It does not need to be nasty or destructive. There is "constructive criticism" as well. And to "argue" does not mean to "have a fight"; an **argument** is nothing less than an attempt to justify our beliefs, to back them up with good reasons.

So what is philosophy? Literally, from the Greek (*philein, sophia*), it is "the love of wisdom."[6] It is an attitude of critical and systematic thoughtfulness rather than a particular subject matter. This makes matters very difficult for the beginner, who would like a definition of philosophy of the same kind received when he or she began biology, as "the study of living organisms." But the nature of philosophy is itself among the most bitter disputes in philosophy. Many philosophers say that it is a science, in fact, the "queen of the sciences," the womb in which physics, chemistry, mathematics, astronomy, biology, and psychology began their development before being born into their own distinguished worlds and separate university departments. Historically, this is certainly true. (Thus, in almost any scientific field, the highest degree is "doctor of philosophy" ["Ph.D."].) Insofar as one says that philosophy is the road to reality and that the goal of philosophy is truth, that would seem to make it the ultimate science as well.

But it has also been argued, as far back as Socrates, that the main business of philosophy is a matter of definitions—finding clear meanings for such important ideas as truth, justice, wisdom, knowledge, and happiness. Accordingly, many philosophers have taken advantage of the increasingly sophisticated tools of logic and linguistics in their attempts to

---

6 The word was invented by Pythagoras. When he was asked if he was already a wise man, he answered, "No, I am not wise, but I am a *lover* of wisdom."

find such definitions. Other philosophers, however, would insist that philosophy is rather closer to morality and religion, its purpose to give meaning to our lives and lead us down "the right path" to "the good life." Still others insist that philosophy is an art, the art of criticism and argumentation as well as the art of conceptual **system** building or, perhaps, the art of creating comprehensive and edifying visions, dazzling metaphors, new ways of thinking. So considered, philosophy may be akin to storytelling or mythology. Some philosophers place strong emphasis upon **proof** and argument; others place their trust in intuition and insight. Some philosophers reduce all philosophizing to the study of experience; other philosophers take it as a matter of principle not to trust experience. Also, some philosophers insist on being practical, in fact, insist that there are no other considerations but practicality; and then there are others who insist on the purity of the life of ideas, divorced from any practical considerations. But philosophy cannot, without distortion, be reduced to any one of these preferences. All enter into that constantly redefined critical and creative life of ideas that Socrates was willing to die for. In fact, Socrates himself insisted that it is the *seeking* of wisdom that is the essence of philosophy and that anyone who is sure that he or she has wisdom already is undoubtedly wrong. In *The Apology*, for example, he makes this famous disclaimer:

 FROM **The *Apology***
BY **Plato**[7]

The effect of these investigations of mine, gentlemen, has been to arouse against me a great deal of hostility, and hostility of a particularly bitter and persistent kind, which has resulted in various malicious suggestions, including the description of me as a professor of wisdom. This is due to the fact that whenever I succeed in disproving another person's claim to wisdom in a given subject, the bystanders assume that I know everything about that subject myself. But the truth of the matter, gentlemen, is pretty certainly this: that real wisdom is the property of God, and this oracle is his way of telling us that human wisdom has little or no value. It seems to me that he is not referring literally to Socrates, but has merely taken my name as an example, as if he would say to us "The wisest of you men is he who has realized, like Socrates, that in respect of wisdom he is really worthless."

That is why I still go about seeking and searching in obedience to the divine command, if I think that anyone is wise, whether citizen or stranger; and when I think that any person is not wise, I try to help the cause of God by proving that he is not. This occupation has kept me too busy to do much either in politics or in my own affairs; in fact, my service to God has reduced me to extreme poverty.

———————————————————————

In the West (that is, Europe, North America, and those parts of the world most influenced by them), Socrates remains a pivotal figure. But philosophy did not begin in Greece. It is a three-thousand-year-old conversation, or, rather, many conversations, that began in many different places, all around the globe.

The oldest philosophical texts we know are from South Asia, in what is now India, dating from more than a thousand years before Socrates—three thousand years ago. A remarkable series of texts, the *Vedas*, became a source for many of the great religions of the world, beginning with what came to be called Hinduism (which for many centuries referred only to

---

[7] Plato, *The Last Days of Socrates*, trans. Hugh Tredennick, Harmondsworth, Middlesex: Penguin, 1954.

a very loose collection of local religious beliefs and practices) and then providing the philosophical foundations for Buddhism. Before Socrates, too, in China, a modest teacher named Kong Fuzi ("Confucius") started a very different philosophical tradition, in parallel with another Chinese philosophy called Daoism (sometimes spelled "Taoism"). And in the Middle East, of course, there was a great deal of philosophical activity, in ancient Persia as well as in the religious cauldron of Jerusalem. Moreover, there had been philosophers in Greece for several centuries by the time Socrates came on the scene, so that the world was already steeped in philosophy. The twentieth-century philosopher Karl Jaspers describes this as "The Axial Period," and says that it was the turning point of civilization.

FROM "The 'Axial Period'" BY Karl Jaspers[8]

It would seem that this axis of history is to be found in the period around 500 B.C.E., in the spiritual process that occurred between 800 and 200 B.C.E. It is there that we meet with the most deep-cut dividing line in history. Man, as we know him today, came into being. For short we may style this the "Axial Period."

The most extraordinary events are concentrated in this period. Confucius and Lao-Tzu were living in China, all the directions of Chinese philosophy came into being, including those of Mo-ti, Chuang-tse, Lieh-tsu, and a host of others; India produced the Upanishads and Buddha, and, like China, ran the whole gamut of philosophical possibilities down to skepticism, to materialism, sophism and nihilism; in Iran Zarathustra taught the challenging view of the world as a struggle between good and evil; in Palestine the prophets made their appearance, from Elijah, by way of Isaiah and Jeremiah, to Deutero-Isaiah; Greece witnessed the appearance of Homer, of the philosophers—Parmenides, Heraclitus, and Plato—of the tragedians, of Thucydides, and of Archimedes. Everything that is merely intimated by these names developed during these few centuries almost simultaneously in China, India, and the Occident without any one of these knowing of the others.

What is new about this age, in all three of these worlds, is that man becomes aware of Being as a whole, of himself and his limitations. He experiences the terrible nature of the world and his own impotence. He asks radical questions. Face to face with the void he strives for liberation and redemption. By consciously recognizing his limits he sets himself the highest goals. He experiences unconditionality in the depth of selfhood and in the clarity of transcendence.

- Why might it be a good thing to have one's head in "the clouds"?
- Why does Socrates think it is more difficult to avoid wickedness than death? Why does he think that one shouldn't avoid death at any cost?
- How does Socrates respond to Crito's attempt to persuade him to escape? What are his reasons and arguments for staying in jail? What would you do?
- What makes reason a good reason?
- Is philosophy more like an art or a science?
- Which requires explanation: the fact that things change (like your body) or the fact that some things seem eternal (like 2+2 = 4)?

---

8 From Karl Jaspers, *Basic Philosophical Writings–Selections*, edited, translated, and with introductions by Edith Ehrlich, Leonard H. Ehrlich, and George B. Pepper, Athens, OH: Ohio University Press, 1986, pp. 382-387.

Although this book is grounded in the Western tradition since Socrates, it is important to keep in mind the traditions from Asia as well. It would be utterly foolish to try to summarize the differences between "East and West," as too many commentators try to do, especially since the Western tradition is thought to include both the reason-oriented legacy of the Greeks and the faith-oriented religions of the Hebrews and Christians, and eventually Islam, too. Furthermore, the diversity of ideas in Asia is colossal, between the "all is One" philosophy of the ancient Vedas to the world- and self-as-illusion philosophy of Buddhism and the **Dao-**("the Way-") oriented philosophy of the Chinese. But it might be worth making a few rather simplified comments about similarities and differences. The first concerns the remarkable affinities between the philosophies that arose in Greece and the Middle East ("Asia minor") and the ancient Vedic philosophies, particularly in their mutual fascination with unified explanation. (Think of the "unity of science," evident even in the earliest Greek philosophies, and monotheism, which pretty much defined the three great "Western" religions.)

Second, there is a dramatic contrast between the Greek notion of *logos*, suggesting "logic" and eternal truth (it also serves a central function in Christianity, as in "in the beginning was the *logos*"), and the Chinese conception of the Dao, which is more oriented toward change, movement, and process. Closely related to this is the Western affection for polarities and oppositions (good versus evil, reality versus appearance, the sacred versus the secular) and the Chinese insistence on *yin/yang*, the interrelatedness of such seeming opposites. Of equal importance, Western thought over the past two thousand years has been pretty much defined by its attempts to come to grips with the idea of the One God. (Atheists, too, are caught up in the arguments concerning God's nature and existence.) Much of Eastern thought, by contrast, has no such concern, or it is a very different kind of concern, although the notion of spirituality plays a central role in many Asian religions.

But while admitting that these very general characterizations brush over a wealth of interesting differences, it is worth insisting that the inclusion of Asian and other voices in the text that follows should not be treated as exotic spice added to the substance of philosophy, nor should it be thought of as mere echoes of Western ideas. Rather, it is an attempt to open windows to a number of very different perspectives, sometimes in contrast, sometimes as unexpected support. But philosophy has many faces and voices, and as one learns to appreciate the profundity of philosophical inquiries it is necessary to appreciate its diversity as well.

With diversity in mind, we can bring this section to a close with a very different description of philosophy from the ancient Chinese Daoist philosopher Laozi in the texts of the *Dao De Jing*.[9]

 FROM ***Dao De Jing***
BY **Laozi**[10]

14
Look for it, and it can't be seen.
Listen for it, and it can't be heard.
Grasp for it, and it can't be caught.
These three cannot be further described,
so we treat them as The One.

---

[9] The philosopher and his text are sometimes referred to in the classic Wade-Giles transliteration as Lao-Tzu and the *Tao Te Ching*. The modern pinyin style is now much preferred, and we use it throughout this edition to refer to all Chinese names.

[10] From Lao-Tzu, *Tao Te Ching*, trans. J. H. McDonald, 1996 (for the public domain).

FIG. I.6 Laozi is supposed to have delivered the *Dao De Jing* to an official and then disappeared, riding an ox. *(© iStockphoto.com/ HultonArchive)*

Laozi

Laozi likely flourished in the fourth century B.C.E., and is generally believed to be the author of the *Dao De Jing,* the founding and most important text for all Taoist thought. Laozi is an honorific title, which can be roughly translated as "the Old Master" or "the Old Child." Laozi and Confucius are said to have met in the Imperial Library of the Zhou Dynasty court. The older Laozi likely had a great influence on the younger Confucius's thought. Laozi believed in Dao or "the Way," which is the flowing reality that encompasses everything, with which we should try to attune our lives. Following the Dao means adopting the principle of *wu-wei,* or action through inaction. To follow the Dao is to be like a river: it is not that one does not move or engage in action, but that the action is a kind of effortlessness; it does not involve striving. The *Dao De Jing* covers many of the traditional areas of philosophy, but the text is more poetic than many philosophical texts and is difficult to read straightforwardly. It is often viewed as falling within the mystical tradition of philosophical writing.

Its highest is not bright.
Its depths are not dark.
Unending, unnameable, it returns to nothingness.
Formless forms, and imageless images,
subtle, beyond all understanding.

Approach it and you will not see a beginning;
follow it and there will be no end.
When we grasp the Tao of the ancient ones,
we can use it to direct our life today.
To know the ancient origin of Tao:
this is the beginning of wisdom.

17
The best leaders are those the people hardly know exist.
The next best is a leader who is loved and praised.
Next comes the one who is feared.
The worst one is the leader that is despised.
If you don't trust the people,
they will become untrustworthy.

The best leaders value their words, and use them
    sparingly.
When she has accomplished her task,
the people say, "Amazing:
we did it, all by ourselves!"

C. A Modern Approach to Philosophy

The orientation to philosophy in this book is, inevitably, essentially a modern Western approach in which criticism plays a predominant role. Historically, modern European philosophy has its origins in the rise of science and technology. (As you shall see, philosophy and science both emerged in ancient Greece and Asia Minor and, about the same time, in South and East Asia.) We should understand science, however, not just as a particular discipline or subject matter, but rather as a state of mind, a way of looking at the world. In the European tradition, this means that the world is understandable and every event in the world is explainable. It sees the universe as *rational*—operating according to universal laws. And it sees the human mind as rational, too—in the sense that it can grasp and formulate these laws for itself. European philosophy and science also put enormous emphasis on the mind of the individual and the ability of human beings to learn the truth about reality.

Although science is essentially a team effort, requiring the labor and thinking of thousands of men and women, the great breakthroughs in science have often been the insights of one man or woman alone. The most famous modern example of this individual genius is the British philosopher-scientist **Isaac Newton**. In the eyes of his contemporaries and followers, he single-mindedly mastered the laws of the universe, while sitting (so the story goes) under an apple tree. The ideal of modern Western philosophy is, in a phrase, *thinking for yourself*. That is, philosophy is thinking for yourself about basic questions—about life, knowledge, religion, and what to do with yourself. It is *using* the rationality built into your brain to comprehend the rationality (or lack of it) in the world around you. In some cultures, however, the emphasis lies on the group or community, and thinking for yourself is not as important as maintaining group harmony and cohesiveness. In India and China, for example, it is the elusiveness of scientific knowledge that defines much of philosophy. In many of these traditions enlightenment rather than scientific knowledge is the main goal of philosophy. It is important to keep this difference in mind.

In much of Western tradition, the central demand of modern philosophy is *the autonomy of the individual person*. This means that each of us must be credited with the ability to ascertain what is true and what is right, through our own thinking and experience, without just depending upon outside authority: parents, teachers, popes, kings, or a majority of peers. This does not mean that you should not listen to or, where appropriate, obey other people. Nor does it mean that whatever you think is true or right, even "for you." What it means is that whether you believe in God or not, for example, must be decided by you, by appeal to your own reason and arguments that you can formulate and examine by yourself. Whether you accept a scientific theory, a doctor's diagnosis, a television network's version of the news, or the legitimacy of a new law are also matters to be decided by you on the basis of evidence, your evaluation of the testimony or authority of others, principles that you can accept, and arguments that you acknowledge as valid. Nevertheless, all of this—the evidence, your evaluation, testimony, and principles—must be subject to examination by other people and other standards than just your own. The truth is not whatever you believe but how you come to understand and justify the truth is nevertheless your responsibility. This stress on individual **autonomy** stands at the very foundation of contemporary Western thought. We might say that it is our most basic assumption. (Accordingly, we shall have to examine it as well; but the obvious place to begin is to assume that we are—each of us—capable of carrying out the **reflection** and criticism that philosophy demands of us.)

Historically, the position of individual autonomy can be found most famously in Socrates, who went against the popular opinions of his day and, consequently, sacrificed his life for the "Laws" and principles he believed to be right. It also appears in many medieval philosophers, some of whom also faced grave danger in their partial rejection or questioning of the authority of the Church. It can also be found in those philosophers who, like the **Buddha**, struck out from established society to find a new way. The stress on individual autonomy comes to dominate Western thinking in that intellectually brilliant period of history called the **Enlightenment** (sometimes called "the Age of Reason"), which began in the late seventeenth century and continued through the French Revolution (1789). It appeared in different countries with varying speed and intensity, but ultimately it influenced the thinking of Europe, from England and France to Spain and Russia, and became the ideology of young America, which used Enlightenment doctrines in the formulation of a "Declaration of Independence," a war for its own autonomy, and a new government established on Enlightenment principles. Those principles were, whatever the variations from one country or party to another, the autonomy of the individual and each person's

FIG. I.7 A nineteenth-century engraving of Isaac Newton. *(© iStockphoto.com/ Georgios Kollidas)*

Isaac Newton (1643–1727)

One of the most formidable intellectual figures in history. Newton was an innovator in multiple areas. His contributions include the theory of universal gravitation and the basic laws of classical mechanics, the theory of the calculus (independently developed by Gottfried Leibniz), and the reflective telescope. Newton also wrote extensively on religious topics. He found the intricate organization of nature to be evidence of a divine Creator who had organized the world according to principles that human reason could apprehend.

right to choose and to speak his[11] own religious, political, moral, and philosophical beliefs, to "pursue happiness" in his own way, and to lead the life that he, as a reasonable person, sees as right.

If these principles have often been abused, creating confusion and sometimes anarchy and encouraging ruthlessness in politics and strife in a mixed society, they are principles that can be challenged only with great difficulty and a sense of imminent danger. Once the individual's right or ability to decide such matters for himself or herself is denied, who shall decide? Society no longer agrees on any single unambiguous set of instructions from the Scriptures. Those in power are no longer trusted. We are rightfully suspicious of those who attack the individual, because it is not clear what else they have in mind. Whatever the abuses, and whatever political, social, or economic systems might be required to support them, philosophical autonomy is the starting point. Even in the most authority-minded societies, autonomy and the ability to think beyond prescribed limits remain essential.

The metaphor of enlightenment is common to many cultures. The comparison of clear thinking with illumination is to be found in ancient, Christian, and Eastern thought as well as in modern philosophy and comic-book symbolism (e.g., the cartoon lightbulb over a character's head). The seventeenth-century French philosopher **René Descartes** (1596-1650) was one of the founders of the Enlightenment, and he was particularly fond of the "illumination" metaphor. He is generally recognized as the father of modern philosophy. Like Socrates two thousand years before him, Descartes believed that each person was capable of ascertaining what beliefs were true and what actions were right. But whereas Socrates searched for the truth through dialogue and discussion, Descartes searched in the solitude of his own thinking. With considerable risk to his safety, he challenged the authority of the French government and the Catholic Church. He insisted that he would accept as true only those ideas that were demonstrably true to him. Against what he considered were obscure teachings of the Church and often opaque commands of his government, Descartes insisted upon "clear and distinct ideas" and arguments based upon "the light of reason." The modern philosophy of individual autonomy began with Descartes. As a matter of fact, his results were quite conservative. He retained much of his medieval teachings: he continued to believe in God and the Church, and he made it his first "moral maxim" to "obey the laws and customs of my country." His challenge to authority was rather his **method**, which signified one of the greatest revolutions in Western thought. From Descartes on, the ultimate authority was to be found in man's own thinking and experience, nowhere else.

None of this is meant to deny authority as such, nor is it to deny the "objectivity" of truth. Appeals are still made to authority, but authorities are never to be taken as absolutes. For example, none of us would particularly like to go out and establish on our own the figures of the 2010 census of the U.S. population. But it is up to the individual whether or not to ac-

---

René Descartes (1596-1650)

The French philosopher who is usually considered the "father of modern philosophy." Descartes was raised in the French aristocracy and educated at the excellent Jesuit College of La Flèche. He became skilled in the classics, law, and medicine; however, he decided that they fell far short of proper knowledge, so he turned to modern science and mathematics. His first book was a defense of Copernicus, which he prudently did not publish. Descartes discovered, while still a young man, the connections between algebra and geometry (developing the field we now call "analytic geometry") and used this discovery as a model for the rest of his career. Basing the principles of philosophy and theology on a similar mathematical basis, he was able to develop a method in philosophy that could be carried through according to individual reason and no longer depended upon an appeal to authorities whose insights and methods were questionable. In *Discourse on Method* (1637), he set out these basic principles, which he had already used in *Meditations on First Philosophy* (not published until 1641), to reexamine the foundations of philosophy. Descartes sought a basic premise from which, as in a geometric proof, he could deduce all the principles that could be known with certainty.

---

[11] Not, at that point in history, *hers* as well. The concept of a woman's autonomy and right to choose is a late nineteenth-century idea that has only recently become accepted.

cept the official "authoritative" figures, to question, if necessary, the integrity or motivation of the authorities, and to appeal, if necessary, to alternative sources of information. Nevertheless, the true figures do exist, whether we or anyone else ever discovers them. Intellectual autonomy and integrity do not demand that we give up the search for truth but rather that we should be continually critical—of both ourselves and others—in the pursuit of it.

For anyone beginning to study philosophy today, Descartes is a pivotal figure. His method is both easy to follow and very much in accord with our own independent temperaments. Descartes proceeded by means of logical arguments, giving his readers a long monologue of presentations and proofs of his philosophical doubts and beliefs. Like Socrates before him, Descartes used his philosophy to cut through the clouds of prejudice and unreliable opinions. He was concerned with their truth, no matter how many people already believed them—or, how few. Descartes' arguments were his tools for finding this truth and distinguishing it from falsehood and mere opinion.

Philosophy has always been concerned with truth and mankind's knowledge of reality. Not coincidentally, Descartes' new philosophy developed in the age of Galileo and the rise of modern science. In ancient Greece, the origins of philosophy and the birth of Greek science were one and the same. The truth, however, is not always what most people believe at any given time. (Most people once believed that the earth was flat and stationary, for example.) But, at the same time that they simply refuse to accept "common sense," philosophers try not to say things that common sense finds absurd. For example, a philosopher who in a public speech really denied that anyone existed besides himself would clearly be absurd. So too, the philosopher who argued that he knew that nobody ever knows anything. Nevertheless, philosophers often take such claims very seriously, if only to refute them and show us *why* they are absurd.

Accordingly, two of the most important challenges in the philosopher's search for truth are (1) skepticism and (2) paradox. In **skepticism**, the philosopher finds himself or herself unable to justify what every sane person knows to be the case; for example, that we are not merely dreaming all of the time. In Eastern as well as Western philosophy, skepticism has provided a valuable probe for our everyday presumptions of knowledge, and it sometimes becomes a philosophy in its own right. In a **paradox**, an absurd conclusion seems to

FIG. 1.8 This detail from *Dreaming of Immortality in a Thatched Cottage* by Tang Yin (1470-1524) reflects the Daoist ideal of free and easy mental wandering. *(© Art Archive, The / SuperStock)*

result from perfectly acceptable ways of thinking. For example, there is the familiar paradox of Epimenides the Cretan, who claimed that "all Cretans are liars." (That sounds reasonable enough.) But if what he said was true, then he was lying and what he said, accordingly, was false. But how can the same statement be both true and false? What Epimenides said was true only if it was false at the same time. That is a paradox, and whenever a philosophical argument ends in paradox we can be sure that something has gone wrong. Again, in both East and West, philosophers have always been intrigued by paradoxes and have often been prompted by them to strike out in bold new directions in search of a resolution.

Skepticism begins with **doubt**. The philosopher considers the possibility that something that everyone believes is possibly mistaken. Some doubt is a healthy sign of intellectual autonomy, but excessive doubting becomes skepticism, which is no longer healthy. It has its obvious dangers: if you doubt whether you are ever awake or not, you might well do things that wouldn't have serious consequences in a dream but would be fatal in real life (jumping out of a plane, for example). Philosophers who have doubts about the most ordinary and seemingly unquestionable beliefs are called *skeptics*. For example, there was the Chinese philosopher who, when he once dreamed that he was a butterfly, started wondering whether he really were a butterfly—dreaming that he was a philosopher. But however challenging skeptics may be as philosophers, in practice their skepticism is impossible. Accordingly, one of the main drives in philosophy has been to refute the skeptic and return philosophy to common sense (to prove, for example, that we are *not* dreaming all of the time). Opposed to skepticism is an ancient philosophical ideal, the ideal of **certainty**, the ability to prove beyond a doubt that what we believe is true. Socrates and Descartes, in their very different ways, tried to provide precisely this certainty for the most important beliefs, and thus refute the skeptics of their own times.

In Western philosophy, the precision of mathematics has long served as an ideal of knowledge. In mathematics, we believe, we can be *certain*. For Descartes, certainty is the **criterion**, that is, the test according to which beliefs are to be evaluated. But do we ever find such certainty? It seems that we do, at least in one discipline Descartes suggested—mathematics. Who can doubt that two plus two equals four or that the interior angles of a triangle total 180 degrees? Using mathematics as his model, Descartes (and many generations of philosophers following him) attempted to apply a similar method in philosophy. First, he had to find, as in Euclidean geometry, a small set of "**first principles**" or **axioms** that were obvious or **self-evident**. They had to be assumed without proof or be so fundamental that they seemed not to allow any proof. These would serve as premises or starting points for the *arguments* that would take a person from the self-evident axioms to other principles that might not be self-evident at all. But if they could be deduced from other principles that were already certain, like the theorems of geometry, then they would share the certainty of the principles from which they had been derived.

Descartes was a scientist and a mathematician as well as a philosopher. With that in mind, we can understand his *Discourse on Method*. Descartes set out four basic rules that would define philosophy for many years:

FROM *Discourse on Method*
BY **René Descartes**[12]

The first of these was to accept nothing as true which I did not clearly recognise to be so; that is to say, carefully to avoid precipitation and prejudice in judgments, and to accept in them nothing more than what was presented to my mind so clearly and distinctly that I could have no occasion to doubt it.

The second was to divide up each of the difficulties which I examined into as many parts as possible, and as seemed requisite in order that it might be resolved in the best manner possible.

The third was to carry on my reflections in due order, commencing with objects that were the most simple and easy to understand, in order to rise little by little, or by degrees, to knowledge of the most complex, assuming an order, even if a fictitious one, among those which do not follow a natural sequence relatively to one another.

The last was in all cases to make enumerations so complete and reviews so general that I should be certain of having omitted nothing.

One might say that the essence of these rules is to be cautious and to think for oneself. The premises, upon which all else depends, must be utterly beyond doubt, "perfectly certain," otherwise all else is futile. The test or criterion of such a premise is that it be "a clear and distinct idea," self-evident, and "springing from the light of reason alone."

You will see much more of Descartes in the following chapters. Descartes' technique for assuring the certainty of his premises will be what he called the **method of doubt** (or *methodological doubt*). In order to make sure that he did not accept any principle too quickly ("too precipitously") before being convinced of its "perfect certainty," he resolved to doubt every belief until he could prove it true beyond question, and to show that the very act of doubting this belief led to an intolerable paradox. The point of this kind of argument is not to become a skeptic, but, quite the contrary, to find those premises that even the skeptic cannot doubt. From those premises, Descartes and many generations of philosophers who have followed him have attempted and will attempt to prove that we do indeed know what we think we know. Like Socrates, Descartes begins by questioning what no one but a philosopher would doubt and ends up changing the way we think about ourselves and our knowledge for several centuries. In other cultures too, entire societies have been dramatically altered by philosophers who challenged what seemed to be obvious; sometimes they challenged reality itself.

Finally, two contemporary philosophers sum up their views of philosophy. The first is by the great English philosopher Bertrand Russell. The second one is by Mary Midgley:

> But further, if we are not to fail in our endeavour to determine the value of philosophy, we must first free our minds from the prejudices of what are wrongly called "practical" men. The "practical" man, as this word is often used, is one who recognises only material needs, who realises that men must have food for the body, but is oblivious of the necessity of providing food for the mind. If all men were well off, if poverty and disease had been reduced to their lowest possible point, there would still remain much to be done to produce a valuable society; and even in the existing world

> "The first of [my rules] was to accept . . . nothing more than what was presented to my mind so clearly and distinctly that I could have no occasion to doubt it."
>
> – RENÉ DESCARTES

12 Excerpt from *Discourse on Method* by René Descartes, trans. Elizabeth S. Haldane and G. R. T. Ross, 1911. Reprinted with the permission of Cambridge University Press.

FIG. I.9 Philosopher Bertrand Russell *(AP Photo)*

Bertrand Russell (1872-1970)

One of the greatest philosophers of the twentieth century. As a young man, Russell wrote, with Alfred North Whitehead, a book called *Principia Mathematica* (1903), which set the stage for modern logic and foundations of mathematics and gave logic a central role as a philosophical tool. He wrote an enormous number of philosophical books on virtually every topic, including several notorious polemics in favor of atheism and what was branded "free love." Russell was a persistent and harsh critic of religion in general and Christianity in particular, as a source of what he called superstition and legitimized murder. He was a committed pacifist during World War I and wrote at least one of his most famous books while sitting in prison for his anti-war activities. Like his famous predecessor, David Hume (with whom he has much in common), Russell was too controversial for most universities, and a famous court case prevented him from teaching at the City College of New York. He won the Nobel prize for literature in 1950.

the goods of the mind are at least as important as the goods of the body. It is exclusively among the goods of the mind that the value of philosophy is to be found; and only those who are not indifferent to these goods can be persuaded that the study of philosophy is not a waste of time.

Is philosophy like plumbing?

Plumbing and philosophy are both activities that arise because elaborate cultures like ours have, beneath their surface, a fairly complex system which is usually unnoticed, but which sometimes goes wrong. In both cases, this can have serious consequences. Each system supplies vital needs for those who live above it. Each is hard to repair when it does go wrong, because neither of them was ever consciously planned as a whole. There have been many ambitious attempts to reshape both of them, but existing complications are usually too widespread to allow a completely new start.

Neither system ever had a single designer who knew exactly what needs it would have to meet. Instead, both have grown imperceptibly over the centuries, and are constantly being altered piecemeal to suit changing demands, as the ways of life above them have branched out. Both are therefore now very intricate. When trouble arises, specialized skill is needed if there is to be any hope of locating it and putting it right.

Here, however, we run into the first striking difference between the two cases. About plumbing, everybody accepts this need for specialists with painfully acquired technical knowledge. About philosophy, people—especially British people—not only doubt the need, they are often skeptical about whether the underlying system even exists at all. It is much more deeply hidden. When the concepts we are living by function badly, they do not usually drip audibly through the ceiling or swamp the kitchen floor. They just quietly distort and obstruct our thinking.[13]

· · ·

Socrates lived, as we do, in a society that was highly articulate and self-conscious—indeed, strongly hooked on words. It may well be that other cultures, less committed to talking, find different routes to salvation, that they pursue a less word-bound form of wisdom. But wisdom itself matters everywhere, and everybody must start from where they are. I think it might well pay us to be less impressed with what philosophy can do for our dignity, and more aware of the shocking malfunctions for which it is an essential remedy.

Mary Midgley (1919-)

A moral philosopher and animal rights advocate. Midgley is a noteworthy critic of the view that science is a sufficient basis for understanding ourselves and the world.

---

[13] Mary Midgley, from "Water and Thought" in *Utopias, Dolphins, and Computers; Problems of Philosophical Plumbing.* London: Routledge, 2006, pp. 1–2. Reproduced by permission of Taylor & Francis Books UK.

- Why is doubt important to philosophy?
- Why not simply rely on our senses for certainty?
- List a few differences between Eastern Philosophy and Western Philosophy.
- Do you have "a philosophy"? What is it?
- What does philosophy deal with?
- How does philosophy begin?
- What is the meaning of life? (Extra bonus points if you can answer this one.)
- Why does Socrates insist on the importance of good reasons?

D. A Brief Introduction to Logic

Descartes' strategy, and the technique of many philosophers, is to present arguments for what they believe. In Plato's *Crito*, Socrates and Crito offer arguments for their views, and Socrates wins because his arguments are better. An argument is a verbal attempt to get other people to accept a belief or opinion by providing reasons why they should accept it. We usually think of an argument as a confrontation between two people. When they try to convince each other, they usually resort to certain verbal means, and it is with these means that a philosopher is concerned. Of course, there are other ways of getting people to agree with you—tricks, bribes, brainwashing, and threats of physical force. But the use of arguments is the most durable and trustworthy, as well as the most respectable, way of getting others to agree. Freedom of speech is the cornerstone of democracy (and the bane of totalitarianism) just because of our faith in the ability of arguments to determine the best among competing opinions. On the other hand, one should not think of an argument as a political weapon whose purpose is to shut down conversation or put other people and their opinions on the defensive. It is always reasonable to ask for arguments, but it may not be reasonable to push a person for arguments that he or she cannot provide. To fail to argue for a position is not necessarily to give up on it, and to refute the arguments for a position is not necessarily to reject the position.

You don't have to be arguing with anyone in particular in order to construct an argument. Editorials in newspapers, for example, argue for a position, but not necessarily against anyone. But whether your argument is a letter to a magazine, in which you are trying to convince the entire American population of your views, or a personal letter, in which you are trying to convince a friend not to do something foolhardy, the main point of argument is to demonstrate or establish a point of view. A scientist describing an experiment tries to demonstrate to other scientists the truth of his or her theory. A politician tries to demonstrate to his or her constituency the need for higher taxes. A philosopher tries to demonstrate to us the value of a certain view of life, a certain view of reality, a certain view of ourselves. In each case, these people try to give as many reasons as possible why other people should accept their view of things; in short, they use arguments to persuade others.

Argument involves at least two components: **logic** and **rhetoric**. Logic concerns those reasons that should hold for anyone, anywhere, without appealing to personal feelings, sympathies, or prejudices. Rhetoric, on the other hand, does involve such personal appeals. Personal charm may be part of rhetoric, in a writer as well as in a public speaker. Jokes may be part of rhetoric. Personal pleas are effective rhetorical tools; so is trying to be sympathetic to readers or playing off their fears. None of these personal tactics are part of logic, however. Logic is impersonal, and for this reason logic may be less flamboyant and personally exciting; but it has the advantage of being applicable to everyone. A logical argument goes beyond rhetorical appeal. But it is important to understand that logic and rhetoric virtually always function together. Although it is possible to be persuasive through pure rhetoric without being at all logical, such efforts often disappear as soon as readers have had a chance to think again about how they have been persuaded. One can also be logical without attention to rhetoric, but such arguments will be dry and unattractive, even if they do convince anyone who would take the time to read them. However, logic and rhetoric in combination can be very persuasive and are rarely separable in any great work of philosophy. In all of the readings of this book, you will notice the combination of impersonal logic and personal appeal, all aimed at getting the reader to agree with the author's point of view.

There are good arguments and there are bad arguments. Just as the success of a logically inadequate argument may depend upon the passing mood of a reader or the fact that he or she has not yet heard the other side, so a good argument must survive passing moods, reflection, and criticism. This requires good logic as well as effective rhetoric, and so it is important to master the basic rules of argument, as well as to be aware of the all too common pitfalls that lie in wait for those who ignore the rules. Knowing these rules and warnings will not only help you avoid what are called **fallacies**—it will allow you to criticize effectively other people's arguments as well. Have you ever heard someone say, "Well, there's something wrong with that argument, but I'm not sure what it is"? Knowing a little logic may help you see clearly what is wrong with an argument.

Standard logic textbooks emphasize two primary forms of logical argument:

1. **Deductive arguments** reason from one statement to another by means of accepted logical rules; anyone who accepts the premises is bound logically to accept the conclusion.

2. **Inductive arguments** infer one statement from another, but it is possible for the conclusion to be false even if all of the premises are true. The most familiar example of an inductive argument is a **generalization** from a set of particular observations to a general statement called a "hypothesis."

1. Deductive Arguments

A deductive argument is **valid** when it correctly conforms to the rules of deduction, when it is impossible for the premise(s) to be true and the conclusion false. In this sense, the premise(s) *guarantee* the truth of the conclusion. The following are some examples of the most familiar rules:

1. It was either Phyllis or Fred. (It was Phyllis *or* it was Fred.)
   It wasn't Phyllis.
   Therefore it was Fred.

2. Both Tom and Jerry went to the circus last night. (Tom went to the circus last night *and* Jerry went to the circus last night.)
   Therefore Tom went to the circus last night.

3. *If* Carol did that all by herself, *then* she's courageous.
   Carol did it all by herself.
   Therefore Carol is courageous.

It is important to emphasize that whether or not an argument is valid depends only on the form of the argument. A valid argument—one in the correct form—can still have a conclusion that is false. Consider this:

4. If Carol did that all by herself, then elephants can fly.
   Carol did it all by herself.
   Therefore elephants can fly.

Notice that example 4 is identical in form to example 3. The conclusion is patently false, but the argument is still valid.

But what good is a deductive argument if its conclusion can be false? The answer is that if the initial statements are true, then the truth of the conclusion is guaranteed. The initial statements are called **premises**, and if the premises are true, then the conclusion must be true if the argument form is valid. It is important to remember that a deductive argument cannot prove its own premises. To be effective, you must be sure of the premises before beginning the deductive argument. Thus the following argument, although it is valid, is an appallingly bad argument.

5. If someone argues for socialized medicine, then he or she is a communist.
   Communists want to kill people.
   Therefore if someone is for socialized medicine, he or she wants to kill people.

This argument has the valid form:

5'. If p then q.
   If q then r.
   Therefore if p then r.

But although the argument is valid, its premises are not true, and therefore they provide no guarantee that the conclusion is true. A valid argument guarantees the truth of the conclusion only if the premises are true. Therefore, in using or evaluating any deductive argument, you must always ask yourself two things:

   a. Are the premises true?
   b. Is the argument valid?

If the answer to both of these is yes, then the argument is said to be **sound**.

An argument in an essay may not appear exactly in the form provided by the rules of deduction. This does not mean that the argument is invalid. In example 5, the second premise, "Communists want to kill people," must be restated in "If . . . then . . ." form. In fact, straightforward copying of the rules of deduction in an essay makes boring reading, so arguments usually must be restated in order to fit these forms exactly. When you are writing an argument, it is necessary to pay attention both to the validity of the argument and to the degree of interest with which it is stated. Sometimes it is permissible to leave out one of the premises, if it is so obvious to every reader that actually stating it would seem absurd. For example,

6. Men can't give birth.
   Therefore Robert can't give birth.

The missing premise, of course, is

   Robert is a man.

But it would be unnecessary in most contexts to say this. When using deductive arguments effectively, rhetorical considerations are important too.

One of the best-known forms of deductive reasoning is called the **syllogism**. It refers to one kind in

---

TRUTH, VALIDITY, AND SOUNDNESS

"If I say 'Today's Tuesday' and it's Tuesday, then what I said is true. On Wednesday or Sunday, it's not. If I say 'If today's Tuesday, then I have a philosophy paper due' and it's true that today's Tuesday, then I can soundly conclude that 'I have a philosophy paper due.' If I say 'If today's Tuesday, then I have a philosophy paper due' and then I lie and say 'It's Tuesday' when it's not, then I can validly conclude that 'I have a philosophy paper due,' but this conclusion is unsound because I lied about it's being Tuesday."

George Gale, Olson Professor of Philosophy, University of Missouri-Kansas City

particular: deductive arguments, with two premises and a conclusion, usually involving membership in groups, and using the terms *all*, *some*, and *none*. The best-known example is

7. All men are mortal.
   Socrates is a man.
   Therefore Socrates is mortal.

The first statement, "All men are mortal," is called the *major premise;* the second statement, "Socrates is a man," is called the *minor premise*. The final statement, following from the other two, is the *conclusion* and is generally preceded by the word "therefore." In this example, the words "men" and "man" are called the *middle term*, the word "mortal" is called the **predicate**, and the name "Socrates" is called the *subject*. The middle term serves to link the subject and the predicate, both of which are joined in the conclusion. The form of this syllogism is

7′. All A's are B's.
    C is an A.
    Therefore C is a B.

Any nouns can be substituted for the A, B, and C in this deductive form. For example,

8. All cows are pigeons.
   George Washington is a cow.
   Therefore George Washington is a pigeon.

Argument 8 is valid, although its conclusion is false. The reason, of course, is that the premises are false. Again, a valid argument does not guarantee a true conclusion unless the premises are true. So always be certain that you have adequately defended the premises before beginning your deduction.

Valid arguments sometimes proceed from negative premises as well as positive **assertions**. For example,

9. No woman has ever been president.
   Eleanor Roosevelt was a woman.
   Therefore Eleanor Roosevelt was not president.

The form is

9′. No A's are B's.
    C is an A.
    Therefore C is not a B.

Another common argument is

FIG. I.10 *(Image © Viorel Sima, 2011. Used under license from Shutterstock.com)*

FIG. I.11 *(© iStockphoto.com/savas keskiner)*

FIG. I.12 *(Image © pandapaw, 2011. Used under license from Shutterstock.com)*

10. Some elephants weigh more than two thousand pounds.
    Elephants are animals.
    Therefore some animals weigh more than two thousand pounds.

The form, with a little rephrasing, is

10′. Some A's are B's. (Some elephants are more than two thousand pounds in weight.)
    All A's are C's. (All elephants are animals. The "all" is implicit.)
    Therefore, some C's are B's. (Some animals are more than two thousand pounds in weight.)

Not all deductive arguments are syllogisms in this traditional sense. For example, the following is a valid deductive argument, but not a syllogism:

11. Jones is an idiot, and he (Jones) is also the luckiest man alive.
    Therefore Jones is an idiot.

The form of this argument is

11′. p and q.
    Therefore p.

In the discussion that follows, therefore, we will talk about deductive arguments in general and not worry whether they are properly to be called "syllogisms" or not.

It is impossible in this introduction to list all of the correct forms of deduction. We will, however, describe some of the most dangerous *fallacies*, mistakes in deductive form. The following example is one, for it looks dangerously like example 10′:

12. Some elephants are domesticated.
    Some camels are domesticated.
    Therefore some elephants are camels.

This form

12′. Some A's are B's.
    Some C's are B's.
    Therefore some A's are C's.

is **invalid** (not valid), and is thus a fallacy. This fallacy often appears in political arguments. For example,

13. We all know that some influential Republicans are corrupt.
    And we all know that at least some Communists are corrupt.
    Therefore we know that at least some Republicans are Communists.

When stated so simply, the fallacy is obvious. But when this argument is spread through a long-winded speech, such fallacies are often accepted as valid arguments. Using the logician's symbolic forms to analyze a complex speech or essay will often make clear the validity or invalidity of an argument.

Another common fallacy closely resembles the deductive form in example 3:

14. If this antidote works then the patient will live.
    The patient lived.
    Therefore the antidote works.

This looks valid at first glance, but it is not. The patient may have recovered on his or her own, proving nothing about the antidote. The form of this argument is

14′. If p then q.

    q.

    Therefore p.

The correct deductive form of example 3 was

    If p then q.

    p.

    Therefore q.

Be particularly careful of the difference between these two.

    "If . . . then . . ." statements are often used in another pair of arguments, one valid, one invalid. The valid one is

15. If this antidote works then the patient will live.

    The patient didn't live.

    Therefore the antidote did not work.

The form is

15′. If p then q.

    Not q.

    Therefore not p.

This is valid, although one might insist on adding an explicit qualification to the first premise. The qualification is, "for nothing else whatever can save the patient," since one might argue that something else, perhaps a miracle, might save the patient rather than the antidote. Notice that this qualification doesn't save the invalid argument in example 14, however, nor does it save the invalid argument in the following example:

16. If this antidote doesn't work, then the patient will die.

    The antidote works.

    Therefore the patient won't die.

Again, the patient might very well die of other causes, despite the antidote. The form

16′. If p then q.

    Not p.

    Therefore not q.

is invalid.

    Most valid and invalid deductive argument forms are a matter of common sense. What makes fallacies so common is not ignorance of logic so often as sloppy thinking or writing, or talking faster than one can organize thoughts in valid form. Most important, therefore, are careful thinking and writing. Yet even the greatest philosophers commit fallacies, and you will see some of them.

2. Inductive Arguments

In deduction, the conclusion never states more than the premises. (It is often said that the conclusion is already "contained in" the premises.) In an inductive argument, the conclusion *always* states more than the premises. It is, therefore, a less certain form of argument, but that does not mean that it is any less important. Many of the premises in deductive arguments will come from inductive ones, and most of our knowledge and almost all of science depend upon induction. Induction takes various forms and defies rigid characterization. One general form of an inductive argument is

Every A we have observed is a B.
Therefore A is a B.

The argument, in other words, is from an observed set of things to an entire class of things. For example

17. Every crow we have observed in the past twenty years is black.
    Therefore all crows are black.

But induction, unlike deduction, does not guarantee the truth of the conclusion, even if we know that the observations are all correct. So the conclusion of example 17 should properly read

It is probable that all crows are black.

This tentative conclusion is called a **hypothesis**. A hypothesis is an educated guess on the basis of the evidence collected thus far. It is always possible, when we are using induction, that a new piece of evidence will turn up that will refute the hypothesis. This new piece of evidence is called a **counterexample**. Inductive arguments must always be ready for such counterexamples because no inductive argument guarantees certainty. There is always the possibility that a counterexample will be found, or that a better hypothesis will be formulated. This is not to say, however, that we should not accept such arguments. Human beings have observed millions of rabbits, and never has a rabbit weighed more than two thousand pounds. This does not mean that it is impossible to find a two-thousand-pound rabbit, but neither does it mean that we should therefore hesitate to believe that no rabbits weigh more than two thousand pounds. Induction is never certain, but, on the basis of the evidence, we can nevertheless agree on the best hypothesis. It is worth noting, however, that some philosophers, following David Hume (see Chapter 2), have claimed that induction is without rational justification, no matter how undeniably useful it may be.

FIG. I.13 "Just then flew down a monstrous crow, as black as a tar-barrel!" *(Lewis Carroll,* Through the Looking Glass*) (Image © Anton Harder, 2011. Used under license from Shutterstock.com)*

There are good (sound) and bad (**unsound**) inductive arguments. The most familiar reason why an inductive argument may be called unsound is generalization on the basis of too few examples. For instance, the following is clearly unsound:

18. Every U.S. president from the state of Pennsylvania has been a Democrat.
    Therefore we can suppose that every U.S. president from the state of Pennsylvania will be a Democrat.

There has only been one president from Pennsylvania, and the intricacies of politics are clearly such that the next president from Pennsylvania could as likely be a Republican as a Democrat. Similarly,

19. The driver of every Italian bus we rode had a beard.
    Therefore all Italian bus drivers have beards.

is unsound. Although the sampling involves more than one example, this is still not sufficient to make a sound inductive generalization. How many examples are required? It varies with the case. If a chemist, conducting an experiment, adds chemical g to chemical h and gets j, that in itself will probably warrant a hypothesis that

$$g + h \rightarrow j,$$

although this hypothesis, like all hypotheses, will have to be tested by further experiments and observations. (Deductions, on the contrary, do not have to be tested, assuming the truth of their premises.) A chemist can usually assume that one set of pure chemicals will react like any other set of the same chemicals. But when the hypothesis is about people, generalizations should be made with extreme caution, especially when writing about such a sensitive subject as "national character." For example, "Italians are . . . ," "Russians tend to be . . . ," "Americans are too . . ." require extreme care. But caution does not mean that it is impossible to write about such subjects. It has often been done brilliantly, and you might even agree that a person who refuses to see the general differences between different peoples and societies is even more foolish than someone who generalizes too quickly and carelessly. But all generalizations (even this one) must be made with care for the context and the subject matter.

A different kind of inductive unsoundness comes from generalizing to a hypothesis that goes too far beyond what the evidence will support. For example,

20. Every graduate we know of from Delmonico High School is an excellent athlete.

Therefore we can suppose that the physical education teachers there must be very good.

The problem here is not too small a sampling; in fact, we might even look at *every* graduate of Delmonico High School. The problem is that this kind of evidence isn't sufficient to prove anything about the teachers. The students might come from athletic homes. Or the food in the student cafeteria might be loaded with extra vitamins and protein. Or the students may enjoy playing sports outside of school, even though their gym classes are badly taught. It is important to be sure that the hypothesis you defend is supported by the right kind of evidence. In this case, we need evidence about the physical education teachers, not just about the students.

Not every inductive argument proceeds from evidence to a generalization. For example, detectives use inductive arguments in moving from the evidence to the indictment of a particular individual. (What Sherlock Holmes refers to as his "powers of deduction" is in fact his remarkable ability with induction.) It is worth noting that not every philosopher thinks that induction is so important for knowledge. For example, the contemporary British philosopher Karl Popper believes that the logic of science (and police investigations) proceeds not by way of induction but by way of the *disconfirmation* of proposed hypotheses with counterexamples. In other words, knowledge proceeds from hypothesis to hypothesis, not from evidence to hypothesis by way of induction. But whatever one thinks of the justifiability of induction and its importance, it is essential not to think of induction as occurring in a vacuum. Inductive reasoning always goes on against a background of other hypotheses, theories, and scientific viewpoints as well as an abundance of other evidence that is taken for granted, built into the hypothesis itself or, perhaps, ignored as irrelevant, undependable, or unimportant. Because of its formality, deduction can deal with isolated arguments. But induction, even when subjected to the formal rigors of probability theory, can never be so understood out of context. Background conditions and the state of knowledge at the moment are always in some sense presupposed. Because of this informal (if not chaotic) complexity, induction is just as much a matter of insight as logic.

A very different kind of problem arises for induction when the hypothesis is *self-confirming*. A self-confirming hypothesis creates its own confirmation or, alternatively, blocks all possible counterexamples from the start. Two familiar examples: a policeman (in uniform) tries to evaluate the driving patterns of the cars that pass him, making sure that they all drive at the legal speed. Of course they do! But the same sort of self-confirmation often goes on in subtle ways in science, for example, where the equipment itself is designed to present precisely the evidence it is supposed to be looking for. The other example is the paranoid, who advances the hypothesis that "they're all out to get me." Given that way of looking at the world, indeed they are. Not only does the paranoid systematically interpret other people's behavior in a hostile way, he also behaves in such a way that people really do become wary of him, if not hostile to him. But again, this extreme case has thousands of more everyday instances; persons who feel friendless may easily work on a mild version of the paranoid hypothesis and confirm their own thesis. A person who entertains the hypothesis that "all people are basically selfish" will have little trouble finding what he or she is looking for, and, within that investigation, some selfish motive can always be found (for example, "in order not to feel guilty") for even the most generous and unselfish behavior. (We might note that there are also *self-defeating* hypotheses; the policeman may hypothesize that everyone breaks the law and go out, in uniform, to catch them, thereby undermining his own hypothesis.)

3. Argument by Analogy

A form of inductive argument that is sometimes controversial is *argument by analogy*. An argument by analogy defends the similarity between some aspect of two things on the basis of their similarity in other respects. For example, a politician defends the need for more efficient government and fewer unnecessary jobs on the basis of an argument by analogy between government and business. A government is like a business, the politician argues. It has a certain product to turn out, namely, services to the people, and receives a certain income from the sale of that product, namely, taxes. It employs a certain number of people, whose job it is to turn out that product and who are paid with that income. Their business is to produce the product as cheaply but as well as possible, to keep the cost down, and make a profit in order to be able to offer new and better services. Thus, the politician argues, the more efficiently it is run and the fewer unnecessary employees it must support, the better a government will be.

Such an argument is valuable in getting people to see similarities and in clarifying complex and confusing issues. The danger, and the reason why many logicians reject arguments by analogy altogether, is that no two things are similar in every respect. (Otherwise, they would be the same.) And just because two things are similar in certain respects, it doesn't follow that they will be similar in others. But this objection is too strong. If two things are similar in several respects, it is at least plausible to suggest that they will be similar in others. For example, running the government is like running a business. Both involve managing an organization. Both require skill in handling money. The success of both depends on the quality of the products and services they produce. Therefore, the way to handle the city transportation problem, for instance, is to ask which plan will give the most service for the least money.

Arguments by analogy may employ both deductive and inductive arguments; insofar as *A* (government) is like *B* (a business) deductions appropriate in discussing *A* will be appropriate in discussing *B* as well. And if *A* and *B* are similar in so many ways, then it is inductively plausible that they will be similar in other ways as well. So arguments by analogy are at least a valuable form of reasoning, if not always a reliable form of proof. It is important, however, to pay careful attention to each particular analogy, to make sure that the two things compared are significantly similar and, most importantly, that the aspect that is argued about is significantly similar in both cases. Arguments by analogy are extremely valuable, but they must always be used with care. In traditional Western philosophy, analogies and metaphors play an enormous but often unappreciated role in the great

FIG. I.14 How often do analogies compare apples and oranges? *(Image © Gunnar Pippel, 2011. Used under license from Shutterstock.com)*

philosophical classics. The assumption, or at least the expectation, is that these analogies and metaphors can be recast in terms of deductive and inductive arguments. But not all philosophical traditions make this assumption. In Chinese philosophy, for example, analogical reasoning is far more central to philosophical disputation than deductive arguments. What the philosopher does, in certain traditions, is to provide new ways of seeing things—a particular virtue of arguments by analogy. So, too, in many folk philosophies around the world, the use of myth and metaphor has not yet been replaced—and probably cannot be replaced—by the standard logics of Western reasoning. The place of logic itself can be an important philosophical problem.

The three kinds of arguments discussed here—deductive, inductive, and argument by analogy—attempt to defend a view or an opinion. But part of almost every argument is an attack on alternative views and opinions. In general, someone else's position can be questioned by asking the following:

a. What is he or she arguing? Is the position clear?

b. What are the arguments? Are they deductive? Inductive? Or by analogy?

> If deductive:
>> What are the premises and are they all true?
>> Are the deductive arguments valid?

If the answer to either of these questions is no, a good counter-argument exists to show that the adversary has not given us a reason for accepting his or her view.

> If inductive:
>> Is there enough evidence to support the hypothesis?
>> Does the evidence support the hypothesis?
>> Is the hypothesis sufficiently clear?
>> Is this the best hypothesis to explain the evidence?

If the answer to any of these is no, a good counter-argument exists to show that the adversary has not defended his or her general claim.

If argument by analogy:
>Are the things compared similar?
>Are the things similar in the relevant respects in question?

If the answer to either of these is no, a good argument exists to show that the opponent's analogy is not a good one.

c. Does the conclusion mean what the opponent says it means?

4. Necessary and Sufficient Conditions, "Logical Possibility," and Arguments by Counterexample

Two concepts that will be of considerable importance in understanding the arguments of the great philosophers are the concepts of "necessary and sufficient conditions" and "logical possibility." A is a necessary condition for B when B can't happen without A. So B requires A; if A doesn't happen then B can't happen; or necessarily if B then A. A is a sufficient condition for B when A is enough to guarantee B, so A implies B, or necessarily if A then B. Consequently A is necessary and sufficient for B when A is both required for B and enough to guarantee B ("A if and only if B"). When this happens, A and B necessarily go together—you can't have one without the other.

A definition supposedly supplies necessary and sufficient conditions. Thus, a way of challenging a philosophical definition or theory put forward, for example, a definition or theory of "justice" or "freedom," is to show that it is logically possible to have an A without B, or a B without A. What you have supplied are counterexamples, not to an inductive argument or hypothesis, but to a philosophical claim. Since definitions or philosophical claims or theories give necessary and sufficient conditions, the person who has thus defined A in terms of B has to go back to the drawing board.

One need not actually find a counterexample in order to challenge a philosophical definition. Insofar as definitions claim to provide *logically* necessary and sufficient conditions, it is enough that you can merely *imagine* a possible counterexample. That is to say, since a definition proffers logically necessary and sufficient conditions that cover all *possible* cases, the mere logical possibility of a counterexample suffices to challenge the definition. Whenever a philosopher makes a general or a universal claim, it is possible to challenge it with a counterexample.

In Section 2, we mentioned counterexamples with respect to inductive generalizations. A counterexample that refutes a hypothesis, such as "here is an *a* that is not *b*," will always give trouble to someone who argues that "all *a*'s are *b*'s." For example, if a bigot says, "All people from Poland are naturally unintelligent," the single counterexample of Copernicus, a Pole, is sufficient to undermine that claim. Counterexamples may also work in the face of deductively defended claims, however. Consider a common philosophical argument (which we shall discuss in Chapter 8):

21. All events in nature are determined by physical forces (gravity, chemistry, electromagnetic forces, and so on).
All human actions are events in nature.
Therefore all human actions are determined by physical forces.

This syllogism is a valid argument, of the form

21'. All A's are B's.
All C's are A's.
Therefore all C's are B's.

FIG. I.15 What would it take to convince you that Martians actually exist? *(© iStockphoto.com/joaquin croxatto)*

One way to attack this valid argument, even if you don't see any reasons to reject the premises as such, is to use the method of counterexamples: "Look. I decided to come to this college of my own free will. I thought about it for a few days, and I remember the exact moment when I made my decision—while eating pizza at Harry's restaurant. Now I made that decision. It wasn't caused in me by physical forces. Therefore, I reject your conclusion."

What has happened here is this: On the one hand, if we accept the premises as true and the argument as valid, it would seem that we have to accept the conclusion. But what the counterexample does in this case is force the person who has argued the syllogism to clarify what is meant by "determined by physical forces" in both the premise and the conclusion. Does this mean only that *some* forces must be present? If so, the argument is not nearly so interesting as we thought, for everyone will admit that when a person makes a decision there is an electrical charge or a chemical change in the brain. Does it mean rather that there are *only* physical causes present, in which case "free will" is indeed excluded? But what then of the counterexample (your college decision)? The burden of proof is on the person who argued the syllogism; he or she is forced to explain how it seems that you made a decision of your own free will when in fact there is no such thing as free will. You can see how this philosophical argument could become very complicated, but we only want to make a simple point. A single, well-placed counterexample can open up a whole new discussion, even when it might seem as if the matter had already been settled.

A general comment is necessary here. It might seem to you as if arguments are conclusive, one way or the other. In fact, this is almost never the case. An argument can be convincing and persuasive, but there is always room for further argument if someone is stubborn or persistent enough. A good counterexample can always be explained away, and even a large number of counterexamples might be explained away if one is willing to adjust other aspects of the theory, by refining definitions, for example. What ultimately sinks a bad hypothesis or general claim is the weight of the extra explanations it needs. For example, someone argues that there are Martians currently living on the Earth. You point out that no one has ever seen a Martian. Your opponent explains this away by suggesting that the Martians are invisible to the human eye. You argue that the atmosphere on Earth would not support Martian life. Your opponent argues that they are a different form of life, different from any that we can understand. You ask your opponent what these Martians do and how we might come to test his or her view. He or she says that the Martians don't want us to know that they are here, so they are careful not to do anything that would let us discover their presence. At this point, you will probably walk away in disgust. You have not silenced your opponent. In fact, he or she might go on inventing new ways out of your arguments forever. But, at a certain point, your opponent's explanations will have become so obviously self-serving and defensive that you and everyone else will be completely justified in ignoring him or her. The point of argument, remember, is to persuade. Absolute proof is impossible. But this means too that persuading some people is also impossible. There are limits to argument—at least, practical limits.

5. Reductio ad Absurdum

One last argument deserves mention. It is usually called by its Latin name, **reductio ad absurdum**, and is a form of deductive argument. It is, however, an "indirect" argument. It consists of taking your opponent's view and showing that it has intolerable or **contradictory** consequences. For example, someone argues that one can never know whether minds exist other than one's own. You counter by pointing out that the very act of arguing this with you contradicts his point. He replies, no doubt, that he can't *know* that you exist. You show that he cannot even know that *he* exists. What you have done is reduce your opponent's view to absurdity, showing that it leads to consequences that no one could accept, in this case, the idea that he cannot have self-knowledge at all. A reductio ad absurdum argument, like a good counterexample, is often an excellent way of forcing other people to clarify their positions and explain more carefully exactly what they mean to argue.

6. The Most Insidious Kinds of Fallacies

No brief survey of logic would be adequate without identifying other fallacies, more general and more tempting than those we discussed previously under deductive arguments. Whatever kinds of arguments you employ, be careful when you are tempted to use the following:

MERE ASSERTION The fact that you accept a position is not sufficient for anyone else to believe it. Stating your view is not an argument for it, and unless you are just answering a public opinion survey, every opinion always deserves a supporting argument. There are statements, of course, that everyone would accept at face value, and you need not argue those. But that does not mean that they cannot be argued, for even the most obvious facts of common sense must be argued when challenged—this is what much of philosophy is about.

BEGGING THE QUESTION Another fallacy is something that looks like an argument but simply accepts as a premise what is supposed to be argued for as a conclusion. For example, suppose you are arguing that one ought to be a Christian, and your reason is that the Bible tells you so. This may, in fact, be conclusive for you, but if you are trying to convince someone who doesn't believe in Christ, he or she will probably not believe what the Bible says either. As an argument for becoming a Christian, therefore, referring to the Bible begs the question. Question begging often consists of a reworded conclusion, as in "this book will improve your grades because it will help you to do better in your courses."

VICIOUS CIRCLE **Begging the question** is similar to another error, which is often called arguing in a "**vicious circle.**" Consider a more elaborate version of the above fallacy. A person claims to know God exists because she has had a religious vision. Asked how she knows that the vision was religious rather than just the effect of something she ate, she replies that such an elaborate and powerful experience could not have been caused by anyone or anything but God. Asked how she knows this, she replies that God Himself told her—in the vision. Or, "he must be guilty because of the look on his face." "How do you know that he looks guilty rather than frightened or sad?" "Because he's the one who did it, that's why!" If you argue A because of B, and B because of C, but then C because of A, you have argued in a vicious circle. It is vicious because, as in begging the question, you have assumed just what you want to prove. But the following is worth remembering: Ultimately, all positions may come full circle, depending upon certain beliefs that can be defended only if you accept the rest of a great many beliefs. Debates between religious people and atheists are often like this, or arguments between free marketeers and Marxists, where many hours of argument show quite

FIG. I.16 An example of an irrelevancy *(Image © VisibleMind, 2011. Used under license from Shutterstock.com)*

clearly that each person accepts a large system of beliefs, all of which depend on the others. Some logicians call this a "virtuous circle," but this does not mean that there are no vicious circles. A virtuous circle is the development of an entire world view, and it requires a great deal of thinking and organizing. Vicious circles, like begging the question, are usually shortcuts to nowhere that result from careless thinking.

IRRELEVANCIES You have seen people who argue a point by arguing everything else, throwing up charts of statistics and complaining about the state of the universe and telling jokes—everything but getting to the point. This may be a technique of wearing out your opponent; it is not a way of persuading him or her to agree with you. No matter how brilliant an argument may be, it is no good to you unless it is relevant to the point you want to defend.

AD HOMINEM ARGUMENTS The most distasteful kind of irrelevancy is an attack on your opponent personally instead of arguing against his or her position. It may well be that the person you are arguing against is a liar, a sloppy dresser, bald and ugly, too young to vote or too old to work, but the only question is whether what he or she says is to be accepted. Harping on the appearance, reputation, manners, intelligence, friends, or possessions of your opponent may sometimes give your readers insight into why he or she holds a certain position, but it does not prove or disprove the position itself. As insight into an opponent's motives, personal considerations may, in small doses, be appropriate. But more than a very small dose is usually offensive, and it will usually weigh more against you than against your opponent. Whenever possible, avoid this kind of argument completely. It usually indicates that you don't have any good arguments yourself.

UNCLEAR OR SHIFTING CONCLUSIONS One of the most frustrating arguments to read is an argument that has a vague conclusion or that shifts conclusions with every paragraph. If something is worth defending at all, it is worth stating clearly and sticking with. If you argue that drug users should be punished, but aren't clear whether you mean people who traffic in heroin or people who take aspirin, you are not worth listening to. If you say that you mean illegal drug offenders, don't argue that drugs are bad for your body, since this is equally true for both legal and illegal drugs. If you say that you mean amphetamine users, then don't switch to talking about the illegality of drugs when someone explains to you the several medical uses of amphetamines. Know what you are arguing, or your arguments will have no point.

CHANGING MEANINGS It is easy to miss a fallacy when the words seem to form a valid argument. For example, consider this:

> *People are free as long as they can think for themselves.*
> *Prisoners in jail are free to think for themselves.*
> *Therefore, prisoners in jail are free.*

This paradoxical conclusion is due to the ambiguity of "free," first used to refer to a kind of mental freedom, second to refer to physical freedom. An interesting example is the argument often attributed to the famous British philosopher John Stuart Mill: "Whatever people desire, that is what is desirable." But notice that this argument plays with an ambiguity in the English language. Not everything that is in fact desired *should* be desired (for example, alcohol by alcoholics), so the argument is deductively invalid. (Mill makes the case, however, that the only evidence that x is desirable is that people in fact desire it.) Be careful that the key terms in your argument keep the same meaning throughout.

DISTRACTION Another familiar form of fallacy is the "red herring," the sometimes long-winded pursuit of an argument leading away from the point at issue. For example, in the middle of an argument about the relation between the mind and the brain, a neurologist may well enjoy telling you, in impressive detail, any number of odd facts about neurology, about brain operations he or she has performed, about silly theories that neurology-ignorant philosophers have defended in the past. But if these do not bear on the issue at hand, they are only pleasant ways of spending the afternoon, not steps to settling a difference of opinion. Distraction is a fallacy that is especially advantageous when the time for argument is limited. (For this reason, it is particularly prevalent in the classroom.)

FIG. I.17 "Red herring" refers to something so surprising that it can distract people from making good arguments. *(Image © TonisPan, 2011. Used under license from Shutterstock.com)*

PSEUDO-QUESTIONS Sometimes fallacious reasoning begins with the very question being asked. For example, some philosophers have argued that asking such questions as "How is the mind related to the body?" or "Could God create a mountain so heavy that even He could not move it?" are pseudo-questions; that is, they look like real questions—even profound questions—but are ultimately unanswerable because they are based on some hidden piece of nonsense. (In these two cases, it has been suggested that there is no legitimate distinction between mind and body, and therefore any question about how they are "related" is pointless; the second question presumes that God is "omnipotent" in the sense that He can do the logically impossible, which is absurd.) Pseudo-questions, like distractions, lead us down a lengthy path going nowhere, except that, with pseudo-questions, we start from nowhere as well.

DUBIOUS AUTHORITY We mentioned earlier that modern philosophy is based on the assumption that we have a right—and sometimes a duty—to question authority. Yet, most of our knowledge and opinions are based on appeals to authorities—whether scientists or "the people" are particularly wise or not. It would be extremely foolish, if not fatal, not to so appeal to authorities, especially in a world that has grown so technologically and socially complicated. We ask an economist what will happen if interest rates fall. We ask Miss Manners which fork to use for the salad. The fallacy of dubious authority arises when we ask the *wrong* person, when we appeal to an expert who is not in fact an expert in the area of concern. For example, when physicians are asked questions about nuclear policy or physicists are asked questions about high school education, their expertise in one field does not necessarily transfer to the other. Appealing to opinions in books and newspapers depends on the authority of the authors and publications in question. What is in print is not necessarily authoritative.

SLIPPERY SLOPE Metaphors often pervade arguments. One of the more common metaphors is the "slippery slope," the greased incline that, once trod, inevitably carries us to the bottom. (In politics, it is sometimes called "the chilling effect" or "the domino theory.") For example,

FIG. I.18 When we attack a straw man, we've been taken in by a scarecrow. *(Image © Joao Virissimo, 2011. Used under license from Shutterstock.com)*

it is argued that any interference with free speech whatsoever, even forbidding someone to scream "fire" in a crowded auditorium, will sooner or later lead to the eradication of free speech of every kind, including informed, responsible political discussion. But is it the case that, by attacking an extreme instance, we thereby endanger an entire institution? Sometimes, this may be so. But more often than not, the slippery slope metaphor leads us to think that there is such inevitability when in fact there is no such thing.

ATTACKING A STRAW MAN Real opponents with real arguments and objections are sometimes difficult to refute, and so the easy way out is to attack an unreal opponent with easily refutable arguments and objections. This unreal fellow is called a "straw man," and he provides us with the extra advantage of not fighting back. For example, a writer of religion attacks those who have suggested that Muhammed never existed, when in fact his opponents have only questioned a particular interpretation of his being a prophet. A writer discussing the mind-body problem lampoons those who believe that there is *no* possible correlation between mental events and some (perhaps unknown) physical events—a position that has been argued by virtually no one.

PITY (AND OTHER EMOTIONAL APPEALS) Some forms of fallacy appeal to the better parts of us, even as they challenge our fragile logical abilities. The appeal to pity has always been such an argument. Photographs of suffering people may well be an incentive to social action, but the connection between our pity—which is an undeniable virtue—and the social action in question is not yet an argument. The appeal to pity—and all appeals to emotion—have a perfectly legitimate place in philosophical argument, but such appeals are not yet themselves arguments for any particular position. An orator may make us angry, but what we are to do about the problem must be the product of further argument.

APPEAL TO FORCE Physical might never makes philosophical right. Sometimes a person can be intimidated, but he or she is not thus refuted. Sometimes one has to back up a philosophical conviction with force, but it is never the force that justifies the conviction.

INAPPROPRIATE ARGUMENTS The last fallacy we will mention has to do with choice of methods. To insist on deductive arguments when there are powerful inductive arguments against you is a fallacy, too—not a fallacious argument, perhaps, but a mistake in logic all the same. For example, if you are arguing deductively that there cannot be any torture going on in a certain country, since Mr. Q rules the country and Mr. Q is a good man (where the implicit premise is that "good men don't allow torture in their country"), you had better be willing to give up the argument when dozens of trustworthy eyewitnesses publicly describe the tortures they have seen or experienced. To continue with your deduction in the face of such information is foolish. This may not tell you where your argument has gone wrong: Perhaps Mr. Q is not such a good man. Or perhaps he has been overpowered. Or perhaps good men can't prevent torture if they aren't told about it. But in any case, the argument must now be given up.

The same may be true the other way around. Certain abstract questions seem to be answerable only by deduction. When arguing about religious questions, for example, looking for evidence upon which to build an inductive argument may be foolish. What is at stake are your basic concepts of religion and their **implications**. Evidence, in the sense of looking around for pertinent facts, may be irrelevant. Very abstract questions often require deductive arguments only.

To be caught in one of these fallacies is almost always embarrassing and damaging to your overall argument. If you have a case to make, then make it in the most powerfully persuasive way. An intelligent combination of deductive and inductive arguments, coupled with analogies and proper criticisms of alternative positions, is the most effective persuasion available. If you think your opinions are important, then they deserve nothing less than the best supporting arguments you can put together.

As you proceed with your course, you will have the opportunity to use many of these logical forms, not only on the great philosophers of the past but on your own thinking as well. You will find that philosophical criticism is a powerful tool in the arguments you have with your friends and the debates you carry on, whatever the topic. Most importantly, philosophy is a valuable aid to getting together your own thoughts about things, about the problems of philosophy that you will encounter in this book, and about life in general.

But then again, why should we assume that the truth is all that **coherent** or logical? As Ralph Waldo Emerson once wrote:

A foolish consistency is the hobgoblin of little minds, adored by little statesmen and philosophers and divines. With consistency a great soul has simply nothing to do. He may as well concern himself with his shadow on the wall. Speak what you think now in hard words and to-morrow speak what to-morrow thinks in hard words again, though it contradict every thing you said to-day.—"Ah, so you shall be sure to be misunderstood."— Is it so bad then to be misunderstood? Pythagoras was misunderstood, and Socrates and Jesus, and Luther, and Copernicus, and Galileo, and Newton, and every pure and wise spirit that ever took flesh. To be great is to be misunderstood.[14]

Ralph Waldo Emerson (1803–1882)

The founder of American transcendentalism, a philosophical movement that defended the idea of an intuitively accessible spiritual reality. This spiritual realm is more fundamental than the material world. Emerson wrote essays on such topics as self-reliance, fate, and the virtue of cultivating one's individual character and avoiding conformity.

FIG. I.19 American transcendentalist Ralph Waldo Emerson *(Art Resource, NY)*

Nevertheless, it would be prudent to advise: do not contradict yourself. Even if you are "great" it is unpleasant to be misunderstood, especially by your instructor. A prudent consistency is the salvation of most students.

---

[14] Ralph Waldo Emerson, "Self Reliance," New York: Wise, 1929, pp. 143–44.

KEY TERMS

abstract	deductive argument	predicate
ad hominem argument	dialectic	premise
aphorism	doubt	presupposition
argument	Enlightenment	proof
asceticism	fallacy	proposition
assertion	first principles	reason
assumption	formal logic	reasons
autonomy	generalization	reductio ad absurdum
axiom	hypothesis	reflection
begging the question	implication	rhetoric
Buddha	incoherent	rule of inference
Cartesianism	inconsistent	self-contradictory
certainty	inductive argument	self-evident
coherence	inference	skepticism
consistent	invalid	sound
contradiction	logic	syllogism
counterexample	method (sometimes,	system
criterion	methodology)	trivial
critical	method of doubt (or	unsound
Dao	methodological doubt)	valid
declarative sentence	paradox	vicious circle

BIBLIOGRAPHY AND FURTHER READING

The trial, imprisonment, and death of Socrates are recounted by Plato in the dialogues *Apology*, *Crito*, and *Phaedo* in *The Trial and Death of Socrates*, 3rd ed., trans. G. M. A. Grube (Indianapolis: Hackett, 2001).

Excellent accounts of Socrates' life are A. E. Taylor, *Socrates* (New York: Doubleday, 1959), and, with a more contemporary focus, Alexander Nehamas, "Socratic Reflections" in *The Art of Living* (Berkeley: University of California Press, 1998).

The best single book on the Enlightenment is Peter Gay, *The Enlightenment* (New York: Norton, 1995); and a philosophical anthology of the period is Isaac Kramnick, *The Portable Enlightenment Reader* (New York: Penguin, 1995).

A standard introduction to logic is Graham Priest, *Logic: A Very Short Introduction* (New York: Oxford University Press, 2001).

The World and Beyond

1 | Religion

The age-old efforts of metaphysicians to know the way the world really is have rarely been motivated by curiosity or the scientific spirit alone. Most often, metaphysics and philosophy in general have been motivated by religious devotion. The search for truth and the concern with what we can know and how we ought to behave have often been tied to concern about the nature of the divine and its relationship to us. For many thoughtful people, there is no more powerful an experience than religious experience, and they have no more important beliefs than their religious beliefs. Religion defines their lives, and their religious views define reality. Although the issues of religion are philosophically within the domain of metaphysics, epistemology, and ethics, the importance of religion demands special attention. Religion involves experiences of a kind that are not common to other ontological and cosmological concerns. Religious beliefs involve emotions that are not relevant to the technical concerns with substance and science. It is this emotional involvement in religion that has inspired some of the greatest art, the bloodiest wars, the kindest actions, and the most brilliant philosophy in history.

A. What Is Religion?

Religion has played an important role in the history of philosophy. Indeed, many scholars would claim that philosophy grew out of religion and only occasionally has turned against its religious heritage. But there have been many different religions. Some differ so drastically from one another that it is hard to say what they have in common. For instance, you may be inclined to cite "belief in God or gods" as a criterion for calling something a religion. But one of the biggest religious followings in the world—Buddhism—has no such concept. Or you may cite as a criterion some sort of social organization, a church, or a prayer gathering. But there are Christian Protestant sects who believe that religion is ultimately a private affair for which no congregation is necessary.

Although many philosophical schools share their beginnings with religions, we would not necessarily want to call a Methodist minister a philosopher. Nor would we want to call a

FIG. 1.1 Symbols associated with (clockwise starting at left) the Jewish, Sikh, Islamic, Christian, Hindu, Daoist, Baha'i, Buddhist, Jain, Shinto, Confucian, and Native American religions. *(Image © justincaas, 2011. Used under license from Shutterstock.com)*

college teacher who assigns the works of Maimonides (an important Jewish philosopher and theologian) a rabbi. Although religion and philosophy are intimately linked, we hesitate to identify them. Central to both, however, is religious belief. A person who believes in a single, independent being, **God**, who is the creator of the universe, is a **theist**, a believer, whether Jewish, Catholic, Protestant, or Muslim. (To refuse to believe in God is to be an **atheist**. To admit one's ignorance, and simply accept the fact that one does not know and perhaps has no way of knowing whether there is such a being or not is to be an **agnostic**. We discuss some atheistic and agnostic claims, as well as several different religious traditions, later in this chapter.)

Before we investigate specific religious-philosophical debates, however, let us take a look at how some philosophers have answered a preliminary question: What is religion? Twentieth-century philosopher John Wisdom, a student of **Ludwig Wittgenstein**, claims that the essential feature of religious belief is a certain "attitude" that the religious person has toward his or her surroundings and that the gap between the religious "attitude" and that of the philosopher or scientist who is interested in explanation is unbridgeable.

 FROM **"Gods"**
BY **John Wisdom**[1]

Two people return to their long neglected garden and find among the weeds a few of the old plants surprisingly vigorous. One says to the other "It must be that a gardener has been coming and doing something about these plants." Upon inquiry they find that no neighbor has ever seen anyone at work in their garden. The first man says to the other "He must have worked while people slept." The other says "No, someone would have heard him and besides, anybody who cared about the plants would have kept down these weeds." The first man says "Look at the way these are arranged. There is purpose and a feeling for beauty here. I believe that someone comes, someone invisible to mortal eyes. I believe that the more carefully we look the more we shall find confirmation of this." They examine the garden ever so carefully and sometimes they come on new things suggesting the contrary and even that a malicious person has been at work. Besides examining the garden carefully they also study what happens to gardens left without attention. Each learns all the other learns about this and about the garden. Consequently, when after all this, one says "I still believe a gardener comes" while the other says "I don't" their different words now reflect no difference as to what they have found in the garden, no difference as to what they would find in the garden if they looked further, and no difference about how fast untended gardens fall into disorder. At this stage, in this context, the gardener hypothesis has ceased to be experimental; the difference between one who accepts and one who rejects it is

John Wisdom (1904-1993)

Wisdom was part of the analytic movement in philosophy. He taught at Cambridge University and the University of Oregon and worked primarily in philosophy of mind and metaphysics.

now not a matter of the one expecting something the other does not expect. What is the difference between them? The one says: "A gardener comes unseen and unheard. He is manifested only in his works with which we are all familiar." The other says "There is no gardener." And with this difference in what they say about the gardener goes a difference in how they feel toward the garden, in spite of the fact that neither expects anything of it which the other does not expect.

But is this the whole difference between them—that the one calls the garden by one name and feels one way toward it, while the other calls it by another name and feels in another way toward it? And if this is what the difference has become, then is it any longer appropriate to ask "Which is right?" or "Which is reasonable?"

For Wisdom, religious belief is obviously different from the scientific quest for causal explanation. Since the scientific revolution of the sixteenth to eighteenth centuries, many philosophers have tried to define religion and science in contrast to one another, and many have tried to cast their lots with science. But there is plenty of resistance to such a move. Many scientists are deeply religious people, and many religious thinkers accept the authority of science without compromising their religious **faith**. No less a scientist than Albert Einstein, for example, argued that it is this religious awe and appreciation for the complex regularities of nature that has spawned the great efforts of science to understand it. Indeed, he says, science itself inspires a "cosmic religious feeling."

> "The one says: 'A gardener comes unseen and unheard. He is manifested only in his works with which we are all familiar.' The other says 'There is no gardener.'"
>
> – JOHN WISDOM

FIG. 1.2 John Wisdom observes that people may agree completely in their descriptions of a garden without agreeing about whether there is a gardener. *(Image © Tischenko Irina, 2011. Used under license from Shutterstock.com)*

> "I maintain that the cosmic religious feeling is the strongest and noblest motive for scientific research."
>
> – ALBERT EINSTEIN

On the Design of the Universe
BY Albert Einstein[2]

It is easy to see why the churches have always fought science and persecuted its devotees. On the other hand, I maintain that the cosmic religious feeling is the strongest and noblest motive for scientific research. Only those who realize the immense efforts and, above all, the devotion without which pioneer work in theoretical science cannot be achieved are able to grasp the strength of the emotion out of which alone such work, remote as it is from the immediate realities of life, can issue. What a deep conviction of the rationality of the universe and what a yearning to understand, were it but a feeble reflection of the mind revealed in this world, Kepler and Newton must have had to enable them to spend years of solitary labor in disentangling the principles of celestial mechanics! Those whose acquaintance with scientific research is derived chiefly from its practical results easily develop a completely false notion of the mentality of the men who, surrounded by a skeptical world, have shown the way to kindred spirits scattered wide through the world and the centuries. Only one who has devoted his life to similar ends can have a vivid realization of what has inspired these men and given them the strength to remain true to their purpose in spite of countless failures. It is cosmic religious feeling that gives a man such strength. A contemporary has said, not unjustly, that in this materialistic age of ours the serious scientific workers are the only profoundly religious people.

Albert Einstein (1879-1955)

A German physicist who made many groundbreaking contributions to theoretical physics, most notably the theory of relativity. He sought to develop a unified field theory, a theory that would unify the basic concepts within physics. He received the Nobel Prize in physics in 1921.

FIG. 1.3 According to Einstein, a cosmic religious feeling has prompted scientific investigation into such matters as the design of the universe and the details of celestial mechanics. *(Image © Ventura, 2011. Used under license from Shutterstock.com)*

Einstein's statement of scientific faith is particularly important in times when science and religion seem once again at each other's throats. Current controversies over "Creation" versus "evolution," for example, have made it seem as if science and religion are utterly irreconcilable, with completely opposed visions of the world. But consider this response from **Keiji Nishitani**, a Japanese philosopher conversant in both Christianity and Buddhism. Nishitani claims that the distinguishing feature of religion is the "personal/impersonal," or, in other words, the deeply personal recognition that each of us must give to the amazing existence that we share with all other things in the universe. This recognition involves our stepping outside ourselves to consider the world and ourselves from an impersonal perspective. Nishitani calls this perspective "personal **nihility**." It is an intimate and unique activity, but also a necessary one. Everyone, whether consciously or unconsciously, must engage in it at some point in his or her life, when our circumstances prompt the question of why we exist.

2 Albert Einstein, "Religion and Science," in *Ideas and Opinions*, trans. Sonia Bargmann, New York: Crown, 1954.

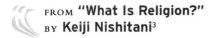 FROM **"What Is Religion?"** BY **Keiji Nishitani**[3]

Keiji Nishitani (1900-1990)

A Japanese philosopher, representative of the "Kyoto school," founded by Kitaro Nishida (1870-1945). The work of this school was devoted to incorporating Western thought, especially existentialism, into Buddhism.

"What is religion?" we ask ourselves, or, looking at it the other way around, "What is the purpose of religion for us? Why do we need it?" Though the question about the need for religion may be a familiar one, it already contains a problem. In one sense, for the person who poses the question, religion does not seem to be something he needs. The fact that he asks the question at all amounts to an admission that religion has not yet become a necessity for him. In another sense, however, it is surely in the nature of religion to be necessary for just such a person. Wherever questioning individuals like this are to be found, the need for religion is there as well. In short, the relationship we have to religion is a contradictory one: those for whom religion is *not* a necessity are, for that reason, the very ones for whom religion *is* a necessity. There is no other thing of which the same can be said.

When asked, "Why do we need learning and the arts?" we might try to explain in reply that such things are necessary for the advancement of mankind, for human happiness, for the cultivation of the individual, and so forth. Yet even if we can say why we need such things, this does not imply that we cannot get along without them. Somehow life would still go on. Learning and the arts may be indispensable to living well, but they are not indispensable to living. In that sense, they can be considered a kind of luxury.

Food, on the other hand, is essential to life. Nobody would turn to somebody else and ask him why he eats. Well, maybe an angel or some other celestial being who has no need to eat might ask such questions, but men do not. Religion, to judge from current conditions in which many people are in fact getting along without it, is clearly not the kind of necessity that food is. Yet this does not mean that it is merely something we need to live *well*. Religion has to do with life itself. Whether the life we are living will end up in extinction or in the attainment of eternal life is a matter of the utmost importance for life itself. In no sense is religion to be called a luxury. Indeed, this is why religion is an indispensable necessity for those very people who fail to see the need for it. Herein lies the distinctive feature of religion that sets it apart from the mere life of "nature" and from culture. Therefore, to say that we need religion for example, for the sake of social order, or human welfare, or public morals is a mistake, or at least a confusion of priorities. Religion must not be considered from the viewpoint of its *utility*, any more than life should. A religion concerned primarily with its own utility bears witness to its own degeneration. One can ask about the utility of things like eating for the natural life, or of things like learning and the arts for culture. In fact, in such matters the question of utility should be of constant concern. Our ordinary mode of being is restricted to these levels of natural or cultural life. But it is in breaking through that ordinary mode of being and overturning it from the ground up, in pressing us back to the elemental source of life where life itself is seen as useless, that religion becomes something we need—a *must* for human life.

Two points should be noted from what has just been said. First, religion is at all times the individual affair of each individual. This sets it apart from things like culture,

3 Keiji Nishitani, "What Is Religion?" from *Religion and Nothingness*, ed. and trans. Jan Van Bragt. Copyright © 1982 by Keiji Nishitani. Published by University of California Press.

which, while related to the individual, do not need to concern each individual. Accordingly, we cannot understand what religion is from the outside. The religious quest alone is the key to understanding it; there is no other way. This is the most important point to be made regarding the essence of religion.

Second, from the standpoint of the essence of religion, it is a mistake to ask "What is the purpose of religion for us?" and one that clearly betrays an attitude of trying to understand religion apart from the religious quest. It is a question that must be broken through by another question coming from within the person who asks it. There is no other road that can lead to an understanding of what religion is and what purpose it serves. The counterquestion that achieves this breakthrough is one that asks, "For what purpose do I myself exist?" Of everything else we can ask its purpose for us, but not of religion. With regard to everything else we can make a *telos* of ourselves as individuals, as man, or as mankind, and evaluate those things in relation to our life and existence. We put ourselves as individuals/man/mankind at the center and weigh the significance of everything as the *contents* of our lives as individuals/man/mankind. But religion upsets the posture from which we think of ourselves as *telos* and center for all things. Instead, religion poses as a starting point the question: "For what purpose do I exist?"

We become aware of religion as a need, as a must for life, only at the level of life at which everything else loses its necessity and its utility. Why do we exist at all? Is not our very existence and human life ultimately meaningless? Or, if there is a meaning or significance to it all, where do we find it? When we come to doubt the meaning of our existence in this way, when we have become a question to ourselves, the religious quest awakens within us. These questions and the quest they give rise to show up when the mode of looking at and thinking about everything in terms of how it relates to *us* is broken through, where the mode of living that puts us at the center of everything is overturned. This is why the question of religion in the form, "Why do we need religion?" obscures the way to its own answer from the very start. It blocks our becoming a question to ourselves.

The point at which the ordinarily necessary things of life, including learning and the arts, all lose their necessity and utility is found at those times when death, nihility, or sin—or any of those situations that entail a fundamental negation of our life, existence, and ideals, that undermine the roothold of our existence and bring the meaning of life into question—become pressing personal problems for us. This can occur through an illness that brings one face-to-face with death, or through some turn of events that robs one of what had made life worth living. . . .

Nihility refers to that which renders meaningless the meaning of life. When we become a question to ourselves and when the problem of why we exist arises, this means that nihility has emerged from the ground of our existence and that our very existence has turned into a question mark. The appearance of this nihility signals nothing less than that one's awareness of self-existence has penetrated to an extraordinary depth.

Normally we proceed through life, on and on, with our eye fixed on something or other, always caught up with something within or without ourselves. It is these engagements that prevent the deepening of awareness. They block off the way to an opening up of that horizon on which nihility appears and self-being becomes a question. This is even the case with learning and the arts and the whole range of other cultural engagements. But when this horizon does open up at the bottom of those engagements that keep life moving continually on and on, something seems to halt and linger before us. This something is the meaninglessness that lies in wait at the bottom of those very engagements that bring meaning to life. This is the point at which that sense of nihility, that sense that "everything is the same" we find in Nietzsche and Dostoevski, brings the restless, forward-advancing pace of life to a halt and makes it take a step back. In the Zen phrase, it "turns the light to what is directly underfoot."

In the forward progress of everyday life, the ground beneath our feet always falls behind as we move steadily ahead; we overlook it. Taking a step back to shed light on what is underfoot of the self—"stepping back to come to the self," as another ancient Zen phrase has it—marks a conversion in life itself. This fundamental conversion in life is occasioned by the opening up of the horizon of nihility at the ground of life. It is nothing less than a con-

FIG. 1.4 A Zen rock garden invites contemplation on the mysterious fact of existence, the "being real" that we share with rocks.
(Ryoanji Rock Garden © iStockphoto.com/Stanislav Komogorov)

version from the self-centered (or man-centered) mode of being, which always asks what *use* things have for us (or for man), to an attitude that asks for what *purpose* we ourselves (or man) exist. Only when we stand at this turning point does the question "What is religion?" really become our own.

- How would you decide whether there is a gardener or not?
- Do you think that belief is necessary for religion? If so, belief in what?
- Is the belief in God's existence the same sort of belief as the belief that it is raining outside? Do you think that there is scientific evidence for God's existence? Does there need to be?
- What does Nishitani mean when he says, "[T]hose for whom religion is not a necessity are, for that reason, the very ones for whom religion is a necessity"?
- What kind of answer might one give to the question, "For what do I exist?"

B. The Western Religions

Among the world religions, Judaism, Christianity, and Islam bear a special relationship to each other and to philosophy. They may be called the **"Abrahamic" religions** because all three trace their roots to Abraham of the Old Testament. Thus, the God worshiped in all three of these religions is the "God of Abraham." We may also call them the three "Western" religions, in that they all originated among peoples living west of the Indus River (one traditional dividing line between the East and the West).

Judaism, Christianity, and Islam are closely associated with each other and with the West for another reason as well. The early religious thinking of all three was heavily influenced by the Greek philosophy of Plato and Aristotle. Although some other religions make use of Greek philosophy, its influence in other faiths does not approach the status it holds in Christian, Jewish, and Muslim thought.

Yet the God who appears in the Old Testament is not readily understood in either Platonic or Aristotelian terms. (You may look ahead at our discussions of Plato and Aristotle

FIG. 1.5 Many artists have depicted God with human characteristics. Most philosophers would describe God (or the idea of God) in more abstract terms, such as omniscience and omnipotence, but these traits, too, are understood by comparison with our own capacities. (© iStockphoto.com/nicoolay)

in earlier chapters and see if you can find anything akin to the Judeo-Christian God described there.) Therefore, early thinkers, particularly in the Middle Ages, had their work cut out for them in offering defenses of their beliefs or in arriving at rational religious beliefs using the Greeks as their model. The medieval philosophers' attempts to do so are among the most monumental efforts in the history of philosophy, with some of the most provocative and widely influential results.

In many cases, philosophy played a crucial role in the conversions of individuals and of whole countries to one of these religions. In others, philosophical disputes were the primary cause of sectarian secessions. In all cases, philosophical arguments were a vital ingredient in the development of the doctrines that have come down to us today.

1. The Traditional Conception of God

The principal issues for all three of these great monotheisms, of course, are the existence and character of God. The God of Judaism, Christianity, and Islam has many characteristics that must be identified for our understanding. Most important, it is generally believed that God is an independent being, the Creator of the universe, and distinct from the universe He created. It is generally agreed that God is the supremely rational and moral being with concern for human justice and human suffering. It is agreed that He is all-powerful (**omnipotent**) and all-knowing (**omniscient**) and that He is everywhere at once (**omnipresent**). In the Old Testament, it is made evident that God has emotions; for example, we read of God as "a jealous God," and we hear of the "wrath of God." It is the attempt to understand the being who has these characteristics that defines Western theology and a great deal of Western metaphysics.

To insist that God is an independent being, the creator of the universe but distinct from that universe, is of the utmost importance for Western religion. When people try to reinterpret God so that He is nothing other than some universal quality, as in "God is love," or "God is the ultimate force," or "God is life," or "God is the universe," there is a real possibility that God's existence as an independent being is being denied. One can say "God is love" as shorthand for "God loves us and wants us to love each other" without this danger. But if one believes that God simply is identical to people loving one another, then it is evident that this belief is no different from that of a person who may not believe in God at all but just believes in love. Similarly, it is one thing to believe that God is a "force," among other things, who created the universe, but if you believe that God is nothing other than a force that created the universe, without consciousness or concern, then your belief does not differ from that of someone who also believes that some force created the universe but does not believe in God.

In Judaism, Christianity, and Islam, the independence of God from the universe He created is an all-important belief. Philosophers and theologians refer to this independence as the **transcendence** of God. We say that God "transcends" the universe and humankind. We also say that He "transcends" all human experience. It is this notion of transcendence that raises an immediate epistemological problem. If God transcends our experience, how can we know that He exists at all? If He is outside our every possible experience—if we cannot see, hear, or touch Him—what possible evidence can we have for His existence, and how can we have any way of knowing what He must be like?

In some ancient religions, gods and goddesses were very much like human beings. They were usually stronger and perhaps smarter. The Greek and Roman gods, for example, were like this. Although they were immortal, they often misbehaved and became jealous or furious at one another. Philosophers use the word **anthropomorphism** when they refer to the perception of gods as being more or less human. It is natural, when people try to envision their deities, that they should endow them with those characteristics they understand best—human characteristics.

The Greek philosopher **Xenophanes** criticized popular Greek religion around 500 B.C.E. by noting that "if cows, horses, and lions had hands, or could draw and work like men with their hands, horses would draw gods in the shape of horses, etc." He also noted that "Ethiopians make their gods black and snub-nosed, Thracians give them red hair and gray eyes." There is one God, he concluded, but he is "in no way like mortals in body and mind."

The God of Judaism, Christianity, and Islam is much less anthropomorphic than the gods and goddesses of ancient Greece and Rome. But it would be a mistake to deny that God is conceived in certain anthropomorphic ways as well. The God of the Hebrews frequently took their side in battle in the Old Testament, helping them to fell the walls of Jericho, keeping the sun still for extra hours, and holding apart the waters of the Red Sea. The God of the Old Testament has many human emotions: He becomes jealous or angry when His commands are not carried out, having people swallowed by whales and sometimes destroying whole cities. Even the notion that God is a loving God carries with it anthropomorphism. It is often said that these are mere approximations, based on the idea that we can never really know or understand what God is like. (For example, it is said that we cannot understand divine love and that we use our all-too-human conception of love as the only

FIG. 1.6 Xenophanes
(Image © Jozef Sedmak, 2011. Used under license from Shutterstock.com)

example we can find.) But it must also be said that seeing our characterizations of God as anthropomorphic projections does not amount to an objection to belief in God; it is only to be expected that people will try to understand religion in those terms that they know best.

The scriptural emphasis on God's sense of justice and His concern for humankind also demonstrates anthropomorphic characteristics, even if it is true, as we are so often told, that God's conception of justice may be different from our own. These characteristics are so important that if a person does not believe that God is a merciful and concerned being with a strong sense of justice, then that person probably does not believe in God at all. (For example, Aristotle's "prime mover," despite the Western theologians' marvelous adaptation of the concept to their religions, is not on the face of it very much like the Judeo-Christian God.) Prayer is meaningful only on the assumption that God listens to us and understands us; confidence in God is intelligible only on the assumption that God cares about us. Without these characteristics, God would probably not be a moral force in our lives.

Some sophisticated theists and theologians have tried to purge the idea of God of all anthropomorphic characteristics, speaking, for example, only of "Being Itself," rather than the usual characterization of God as "Him." Still, although we may not actually believe that God, like Zeus, resembles some superhuman immortal being, it is clear that our traditional conception of God is far more anthropocentric than some theologians would prefer.

The Western religions' conception of God has been varied in so many ways that we cannot even begin to consider them. The differences between the God of the Old Testament and the God of the New Testament have often been discussed. Then there are the obvious differences between the views of the various sects of Judaism, Christianity, and Islam. And the differences between the Abrahamic God and other gods (Zeus, Krishna, Isis) are so enormous that traditional Christians, Jews, and Muslims would hesitate to call these dieties "God."

- If God is transcendent and independent from creation, then how do we know that God has the qualities that we ascribe to him (e.g., omniscient, good, omnipotent)?
- Do you think anything would be lost or gained by trying to avoid anthropomorphism in our thinking about God?

C. Proving God: The Ontological Argument

It is one thing to be taught that there is a God; it is another to believe in God for good reason, rationally, and to know what one believes. Of course, many people have insisted that belief in God is not a matter of rationality or knowledge at all but only of faith. But the turn to faith logically comes after attempts to know. So before we examine other philosophical questions raised by religious belief, let us ask whether or not we can know that God exists.

The problem is a familiar one. Since God by definition transcends our experience, how can we have evidence for His existence? There are people who claim to have been direct witnesses to miracles or to have heard God's own voice. But assuming that none of us is one of them, our problem remains: Should we believe their reports? Might they have been victims of imagination or hallucination? Is there any evidence in our experience that would allow us to know of God's existence? If not, what reasons can we give for a belief in God?

In the long history of Western theology, three major sets of "proofs" have emerged as attempts to demonstrate God's existence. Each has received various formulations, and all are still being discussed today. They are called (1) the **ontological argument**, (2) the **cosmological argument**, and (3) the **teleological argument**.

THE ONTOLOGICAL ARGUMENT This is the most difficult, for it is a purely logical proof; it attempts to argue from the idea of God to His necessary existence. Descartes used this argument in his *Meditations* to prove God's existence. Similar arguments were to be found in both Spinoza and Leibniz. But the man who is generally credited with the first clear formulation of the argument is an eleventh-century monk named **St. Anselm**. Because the argument depends wholly on the idea of God's existence, it is called *ontological*. Here is how Anselm presents it:

 On The Ontological Argument
BY **St. Anselm**[4]

Some time ago, at the urgent request of some of my brethren, I published a brief work, as an example of meditation on the grounds of faith. I wrote it in the role of one who seeks, by silent reasoning with himself, to learn what he does not know. But when I reflected on this little book, and saw that it was put together as a long chain of arguments, I began to ask myself whether *one* argument might possibly be found, resting on no other argument for its proof, but sufficient in itself to prove that God truly exists, and that he is the supreme good, needing nothing outside himself, but needful for the being and well-being of all things. I often turned

4 St. Anselm, *Proslogion*, in *A Scholastic Miscellany*, Vol. 10, The Library of Christian Classics, ed. and trans. Eugene R. Fairweather, 1956. Used by permission of Westminster John Knox Press.

my earnest attention to this problem, and at times I believed that I could put my finger on what I was looking for, but at other times it completely escaped my mind's eye, until finally, in despair, I decided to give up searching for something that seemed impossible to find. But when I tried to put the whole question out of my mind, so as to avoid crowding out other matters, with which I might make some progress, by this useless preoccupation, then, despite my unwillingness and resistance, it began to force itself on me more persistently than ever. Then, one day when I was worn out by my vigorous resistance to the obsession, the solution I had ceased to hope for presented itself to me, in the very turmoil of my thoughts, so that I enthusiastically embraced the idea which in my disquiet, I had spurned.

FIG. 1.7 St. Anselm (1033-1109) is depicted in this nineteenth-century artist's rendering as reluctantly accepting the position of Archbishop of Canterbury in 1093. *(HIP / Art Resource, NY)*

St. Anselm (1033-1109)

The archbishop of Canterbury and a proponent of the ontological argument for God's existence. He was one of the main defenders of the intellect and "understanding" against the then-current anti-intellectualism of the church. He is best known for his *Monologion* and *Proslogion*, in which the ontological argument is developed.

. . .

GOD TRULY IS

And so, O Lord, since thou givest understanding to faith, give me to understanding—as far as thou knowest it to be good for me—that thou dost exist, as we believe, and that thou art what we believe thee to be. Now we believe that thou art a being than which none greater can be thought. Or can it be that there is no such being, since "the fool hath said in his heart, 'There is no God'"? But when this same fool hears what I am saying—"A being than which none greater can be thought"—he understands what he hears, and what he understands is in his understanding, even if he does not understand that it exists. For it is one thing for an object to be in the understanding, and another thing to understand that it exists. When a painter considers beforehand what he is going to paint, he has it in his understanding, but he does not suppose that what he has not yet painted already exists. But when he has painted it, he both has it in his understanding and understands that what he has now produced exists. Even the fool, then, must be convinced that a being than which none greater can be thought exists at least in his understanding, since when he hears this he understands it, and whatever is understood is in the understanding. But clearly that than which a greater cannot be thought cannot exist in the understanding alone. For if it is actually in the understanding alone, it can be thought of as existing also in reality, and this is greater. Therefore, if that than which a greater cannot be thought is in the understanding alone, this same thing than which a greater cannot be thought is that than which a greater can be thought. But obviously this is impossible. Without doubt, therefore, there exists, both in the understanding and in reality, something than which a greater cannot be thought.

GOD CANNOT BE THOUGHT OF AS NONEXISTENT

And certainly it exists so truly that it cannot be thought of as nonexistent. For something *can* be thought of as existing, which cannot be thought of as not existing, and this is greater than that which can be thought of as not existing. Thus, if that than which a greater cannot be thought can be thought of as not existing, this very

"For God is that than which a greater cannot be thought, and whoever understands this rightly must understand that he exists in such a way that he cannot be nonexistent even in thought."

– ST. ANSELM

FIG. 1.8 St. Anselm argues that while it is in his power to imagine or not imagine a winged horse, such as the mythical Pegasus, it is not in his power to imagine God without existence. *(© iStockphoto.com/Steven Wynn)*

thing than which a greater cannot be thought is *not* that than which a greater cannot be thought. But this is contradictory. So, then, there truly is a being than which a greater cannot be thought—so truly that it cannot even be thought of as not existing.

And *thou* art this being, O Lord our God. Thou so truly are, then, O Lord my God, that thou canst not even be thought of as not existing. And this is right. For if some mind could think of something better than thou, the creature would rise above the Creator and judge its Creator; but this is altogether absurd. And indeed, whatever is, except thyself alone, can be thought of as not existing. Thou alone, therefore, of all beings, has being in the truest and highest sense, since no other being so truly exists, and thus every other being has less being. Why, then, has "the fool said in his heart, 'There is no God,'" when it is so obvious to the rational mind that, of all beings, thou dost exist supremely? Why indeed, unless it is that he is a stupid fool?

HOW THE FOOL HAS SAID IN HIS HEART WHAT CANNOT BE THOUGHT

But how did he manage to say in his heart what he could not think? Or how is it that he was unable to think what he said in his heart? After all, to say in one's heart and to think are the same thing. Now if it is true—or, rather, since it is true—that he thought it, because he said it in his heart, but did not say it in his heart, since he could not think it, it is clear that something can be said in one's heart or thought in more than one way. For we think of a thing, in one sense, when we think of the word that signifies it, and in another sense, when we understand the very thing itself. Thus, in the first sense God can be thought of as nonexistent, but in the second sense this is quite impossible. For no one who understands what God is can think that God does not exist, even though he says these words in his heart—perhaps without any meaning, perhaps with some quite extraneous meaning. For God is that than which a greater cannot be thought, and whoever understands this rightly must understand that he exists in such a way that he cannot be nonexistent even in thought. He, therefore, who understands that God thus exists cannot think of him as nonexistent.

Thanks be to thee, good Lord, thanks be to thee, because I now understand by thy light what I formerly believed thy gift, so that even if I were to refuse to believe in thy existence, I could not fail to understand its truth.

The logic of the argument is deceptively simple: The concept of "God" is defined, innocently enough, as "a being greater than which none can be thought." Then, Anselm asks, "which would be greater, a being who is merely thought, or a being who actually exists?" The answer, of course, is a being who actually exists. But since God is, by definition, the greatest being who can be thought, He must therefore exist. "God cannot be nonexistent even in thought." Anselm goes on to argue that the idea of an eternal being who either does not yet exist or no longer exists is self-contradictory, so that the very idea we have of such a being requires existence. It is worth noting that while formulating the ontological argument, Anselm was also putting into place some of the final ingredients in the Christian conception of God as not only a perfect or even the most perfect being but, rather, as the greatest (most perfect) *conceivable* being.

The argument has had a long, influential history, and logicians are still arguing about it. The argument was not seriously altered for five centuries, when Descartes took up Anselm's argument and gave it its modern formulation. In the seventeenth century, Descartes (in his *Meditations*) made explicit the presupposition of the argument, that existence is a property that, like color, shape, weight, and charm, a thing may either have or not have. Some properties, however, are essential to a thing: three angles are essential to a triangle, spots are essential to a Dalmatian. So, too, Descartes suggests, perfection is essential to the most perfect being, and existence is a perfection. One can no more conceive of a most perfect being without existence than one can conceive of a triangle without three angles or a Dalmatian without spots.

On the Ontological Argument
BY René Descartes[5]

But now, if just because I can draw the idea of something from my thought, it follows that all which I know clearly and distinctly as pertaining to this object does really belong to it, may I not derive from this an argument demonstrating the existence of God? It is certain that I no less find the idea of God, that is to say, the idea of a supremely perfect Being, in me, than that of any figure or number whatever it is; and I do not know any less clearly and distinctly that an [actual and] eternal existence pertains to this nature than I know that all that which I am able to demonstrate of some figure or number truly pertains to the nature of this figure or number, and therefore, although all that I concluded in the preceding Meditations were found to be false, the existence of God would pass with me as at least as certain as I have ever held the truths of mathematics (which concern only numbers and figures) to be.

This indeed is not at first manifest, since it would seem to present some appearance of being a sophism. For being accustomed in all other things to make a distinction between existence and essence, I easily persuade myself that the existence can be separated from the essence of God, and that we can thus conceive God as not actually existing. But, nevertheless, when I think of it with more attention, I clearly see that existence can no more be separated from the essence of God than can its having its three angles equal to two right angles be separated from the essence of a [rectilinear] triangle, or the idea of a mountain from the idea of a valley; and so there is not any less repugnance to our conceiving a God (that is, a Being supremely perfect) to whom existence is lacking (that is to say, to whom a certain perfection is lacking), than to conceive of a mountain which has no valley.

5 René Descartes, "Meditation IV," in *Meditations on First Philosophy*, in *The Philosophical Works of Descartes*, trans. Elizabeth S. Haldane and G. R. T. Ross, 1911. Reprinted with the permission of Cambridge University Press.

"From the fact that I cannot conceive God without existence, it follows that existence is inseparable from Him, and hence that He really exists."

– RENÉ DESCARTES

But although I cannot really conceive of a God without existence any more than a mountain without a valley, still from the fact that I conceive a mountain with a valley, it does not follow that there is such a mountain in the world; similarly although I conceive of God as possessing existence, it would seem that it does not follow that there is a God which exists; for my thought does not impose any necessity upon things, and just as I may imagine a winged horse, although no horse with wings exists, so I could perhaps attribute existence to God, although no God existed.

But a sophism is concealed in this objection; for from the fact that I cannot conceive a mountain without a valley, it does not follow that there is any mountain or any valley in existence, but only that the mountain and the valley, whether they exist or do not exist, cannot in any way be separated one from the other. While from the fact that I cannot conceive God without existence, it follows that existence is inseparable from Him, and hence that He really exists; not that my thought can bring this to pass, or impose any necessity on things, but, on the contrary, because the necessity which lies in the thing itself, i.e., the necessity of the existence of God determines me to think in this way. For it is not within my power to think of God without existence (that is of a supremely perfect Being devoid of a supreme perfection) though it is in my power to imagine a horse either with wings or without wings.

And we must not here object that it is in truth necessary for me to assert that God exists after having presupposed that He possesses every sort of perfection, since existence is one of these, but that as a matter of fact my original supposition was not necessary, just as it is not necessary to consider that all quadrilateral figures can be inscribed in the circle; for supposing I thought of this, I should be constrained to admit that the rhombus might be inscribed in the circle since it is a quadrilateral figure, which, however, is manifestly false. Although it is not necessary that I should at any time entertain the notion of God, nevertheless whenever it happens that I think of a first and a sovereign Being, and, so to speak, derive the idea of Him from the storehouse of my mind, it is necessary that I should attribute to Him every sort of perfection, although I do not get so far as to enumerate them all, or to apply my mind to each one in particular. And this necessity suffices to make me conclude (after having recognised that existence is a perfection) that this first and sovereign Being really exists; just as though it is not necessary for me ever to imagine any triangle, yet, whenever I wish to consider a rectilinear figure composed only of three angles, it is absolutely essential that I should attribute to it all those properties which serve to bring about the conclusion that its three angles are not greater than two right angles, even although I may not then be considering this point in particular. But when I consider which figures are capable of being inscribed in the circle, it is in no way necessary that I should think that all quadrilateral figures are of this number; on the contrary, I cannot even pretend that this is the case, so long as I do not desire to accept anything which I cannot conceive clearly and distinctly. And in consequence there is a great difference between the false suppositions such as this, and the true ideas born within me, the first and principal of which is that of God. For really I discern in many ways that this idea is not something factitious, and depending solely on my thought, but that it is the image of a true and immutable nature; first of all, because I cannot conceive anything but God himself to whose essence existence [necessarily] pertains; in the second place because it is not possible for me to conceive two or more Gods in this same position; and, granted that there is one such God who now exists, I see clearly that it is necessary that He should have existed from all eternity and that He must exist eternally; and finally, because I know an infinitude of other properties in God, none of which I can either diminish or change.

Descartes' version of the ontological argument is

> *I cannot conceive of a God without the property of existence.*
> *("His existence cannot be separated from His essence.")*
> *Therefore, God exists.*

Then he adds,

> *My conception of God is such that He has every sort of perfection.*
> *Existence is a perfection.*
> *Therefore, God necessarily exists.*

These arguments are valid as stated, but are they also sound? Consider the following argument, which has been proposed in the same form as the foregoing arguments. Define a "grenlin" as "the greenest imaginable creature." Now, which is greener, a green creature that does exist or one that does not? Obviously the one that exists. Therefore, at least one grenlin exists.

It is worth noting that this objection had been raised against Anselm, too, by Gaunilo of Marmoutier, who suggested the existence of an island more perfect than any other, on the same grounds that it would be contradictory for the most perfect island not to exist. Anselm replied that the argument cannot be applied to islands (or grenlins) or anything else whose nonexistence is conceivable. The question, then, is what it means for nonexistence to be conceivable or for existence to be a necessary property of a thing.

Descartes faced a similar challenge to his formulation when a critic attacked his analogy with triangles and insisted that, while it may be true that *if* a triangle exists, then it must have three angles, it does not follow that triangles must exist or that any in fact do exist. Descartes' answer is similar to Anselm's response to his critic: The essence of triangle does not include the perfection of existence, as God's surely does.

The ontological argument makes a special case for God because He is the only "greatest conceivable" or "most perfect" being. Nevertheless, the argument has made many believers uneasy and has been dismissed as a clever trick by nonbelievers. But whatever our unease, the argument is clearly valid.

The argument is a straightforward syllogism of the "All men are mortal/Socrates is a man/Socrates is mortal" type, the only real (but significant) difference being that although there can be any number of men, there can be only one God, one "most perfect" being. But what we have so far taken for granted in the foregoing presentations of the argument is the presupposition that existence is a property like a color or shape. One way of attacking the logic of the argument, even while accepting its validity, is to challenge this presupposition and thus the soundness of the argument. Is "exists" really a predicate like "barks" and "is green"? Or is it rather a quantifier like "all" and "none" and "some" (and usable in formulations such as "there exists at least one . . .")? The objection that "existence is not a predicate" was formulated against the ontological argument by **Immanuel Kant**.

The great philosopher Kant suggested that the problem lies in the central idea, shared by the ontological argument and the unacceptable arguments that follow the same form, that existence is one of the essential properties, that is, part of the definition of a thing. But existence, Kant argues, is not a property and cannot be part of a definition. In an often-quoted passage of his *Critique of Pure Reason*, he presents this argument:

Against the Ontological Argument
BY Immanuel Kant[6]

I answer:—Even in introducing into the concept of a thing, which you wish to think in its possibility only, the concept of its existence, under whatever disguise it may be, you have been guilty of a contradiction. If you were allowed to do this, you would apparently have carried your point; but in reality you have achieved nothing, but have only committed a tautology. I simply ask you, whether the proposition, that *this* or *that thing* (which, whatever it may be, I grant you as possible) *exists*, is an analytical or a synthetical proposition? If the former, then by its existence you add nothing to your thought of the thing; but in that case, either the thought within you would be the thing itself, or you have presupposed existence, as belonging to possibility, and have according to your own showing deducted existence from internal possibility, which is nothing but a miserable tautology. The mere word *reality*, which in the concept of a thing sounds different from existence in the concept of the predicate, can make no difference. For if you call all accepting or positing (without determining what it is) reality, you have placed a thing, with all its predicates, within the concept of the subject, and accepted it as real, and you do nothing but repeat it in the predicate. If, on the contrary, you admit, as every sensible man must do, that every proposition involving existence is synthetical, how can you say that the predicate of existence does not admit of removal without contradiction, a distinguishing property which is peculiar to analytical propositions only, the very character of which depends on it?

I might have hoped to put an end to this subtle argumentation, without many words, and simply by an accurate definition of the concept of existence, if I had not seen that the illusion, in mistaking a logical predicate for a real one (that is the predicate which determines a thing), resists all correction. Everything can become a *logical predicate*, even the subject itself may be predicated of itself, because logic makes no account of any contents of concepts. *Determination*, however, is a predicate, added to the concept of the subject, and enlarging it, and it must not therefore be contained in it.

Being is evidently not a real predicate, or a concept of something that can be added to the concept of a thing. It is merely the admission of a thing, and of certain determinations in it. Logically, it is merely the copula of a judgment. The proposition, *God is almighty*, contains two concepts, each having its object, namely, God and almightiness. The small word *is*, is not an

FIG. 1.9 Immanuel Kant (1724–1804), who made important contributions to virtually every area in philosophy, is commemorated by this German stamp.
(© iStockphoto.com/Hüseyin HIDIR)

Immanuel Kant (1724–1804)

A German philosopher, probably the greatest Western philosopher since Plato and Aristotle, who lived his entire life in a small town in East Prussia (Königsburg). He was a professor at the university there for more than thirty years; he never married, and his neighbors said that his habits were so regular that they could set their clocks by him. (A later German poet said, "It is hard to write about Kant's life, for he had no life.") Yet, from a safe distance, he was one of the most persistent defenders of the French Revolution and, in philosophy, created no less a revolution himself. His philosophical system, embodied in three huge volumes called *Critique of Pure Reason* (1781), *Critique of Practical Reason* (1788), and *Critique of Judgment* (1790), changed the thinking of philosophers as much as the revolution changed France. His central thesis was the defense of what he called "synthetic a priori" judgments (and their moral and religious equivalents) by showing their necessity for all human experience. (Synthetic a priori judgments can be verified independently of experience.) In this way, he escaped from Hume's skepticism and avoided the dead-end intuitionism of his rational predecessors.

6 Immanuel Kant, *The Critique of Pure Reason*, rev. 2nd ed., trans. Max Müller, London: Macmillan, 1927.

additional predicate, but only serves to put the predicate *in relation* to the subject. If, then, I take the subject (God) with all its predicates (including that of almightiness), and say, *God is,* or there is a God, I do not put a new predicate to the concept of God, but I only put the subject by itself, with all its predicates, in relation to my concept, as its object. Both must contain exactly the same kind of thing, and nothing can have been added to the concept, which expresses possibility only, by my thinking its object as simply given and saying it is. And thus the real does not contain more than the possible. A hundred real dollars do not contain a penny more than a hundred possible dollars. For as the latter signify the concept, the former the object and its position by itself, it is clear that, in case the former contained more than the latter, my concept would not express the whole object, and would not therefore be its adequate concept. In my financial position no doubt there exists more by one hundred real dollars, than by their concept only (that is their possibility), because in reality the object is not only contained analytically in my concept, but is added to my concept (which is a determination of my state), synthetically; but the conceived hundred dollars are not in the least increased through the existence which is outside my concept.

> "*Being* is evidently not a real predicate, or a concept of something that can be added to the concept of a thing."
>
> – IMMANUEL KANT

What Kant is arguing is that the existence of a thing can never be merely a matter of logic. (This is what he means when he says that the proposition that a thing exists cannot be analytic.) "Existence" or "being," he argues, isn't a "real predicate" (although it is a grammatical predicate) because it does not tell us anything more about whatever is said to have existence or being. In other words, there is something odd about the statement, "this apple is red, round, ripe, and exists." What is odd is that "exists" does not give a characteristic of the apple but rather says that there is an apple with these characteristics. The proper characterization of God, therefore, includes the various characteristics we discussed earlier in this chapter, but it should not include, according to Kant, any characteristic that implies God's existence. It is one thing to say that God, if He exists, has such-and-such characteristics; it is something more to say that such a God exists. (This is what Kant means by his example about the one hundred real versus one hundred possible dollars; they both have exactly the same number of cents, but only the one hundred real dollars are worth anything.)

Whether or not the argument succeeds in anything like its classical form, it can be understood in another way, which clearly distinguishes it from all the absurd arguments that apparently have the same form. If you believe in God, then the argument may be taken in a different way, not as a "proof" but as an attempt to articulate your belief. The theologian Karl Barth argued that this is what Anselm's argument really tries to do, and as you read over his argument a second or third time, it becomes clear that he is expressing his faith as much as he is offering a logical proof. In general, the "proofs" of God's existence have been such articulations and expressions as well as proper logical arguments. Even if they fail as proofs, they often succeed in this other, and perhaps more important, function. Descartes' and Anselm's argument is, ultimately, that we cannot think about God and at the same time doubt His existence.

It is clear that considered simply as a logical argument, the ontological argument does not have the power to convert nonbelievers into believers. Or if you are a believer, it is clear that an objection to the "proof" is not going to shake your faith in any way whatsoever. So the significance of the proof is ambiguous: as a logical exercise, it is brilliant; as an expression of faith, it may be edifying; but as an actual proof that God exists or as a means of converting atheists, it seems to have no power at all.

- Do any of our ideas about God (for example, the idea that nothing is greater than God) accurately reflect God's nature? Are we in a position to know whether they do?
- What does it mean to say that a "proof" for God's existence is not really a proof at all, but an articulation of belief?

D. God as Creator: Intelligence and Design

The ontological argument is a fascinating exercise in logic and rationality, but critics often object that it does not seem to say anything about the all-important role of God as creator. Other arguments, however, take creation as their central focus, either by arguing the necessity of a creator or by paying attention to the detailed design of the world that was created. The "cosmological argument" is actually a series of arguments, all of which involve something like Aristotle's premise that there must be a first cause ("a prime mover"), some ultimate explanation for the existence and nature of the universe. If there were no such first cause or ultimate explanation, that would suggest an infinite regress (arguing backward forever), which Aristotle and most Western logicians until modern times considered unacceptable. In the next selection, St. Thomas Aquinas presents several of the best-known formulations of the cosmological argument in the first four of what he calls the "five ways" of proving God's existence.

 ### On the Cosmological Argument
BY **St. Thomas Aquinas**[7]

The first and more manifest way is the argument from motion. It is certain, and evident to our senses, that in the world some things are in motion. Now whatever is moved is moved by another, for nothing can be moved except it is in potentiality to that towards which it is moved whereas a thing moves inasmuch as it is in act. For motion is nothing else than the reduction of something from potentiality to actuality. But nothing can be reduced from potentiality to actuality, except by something in a state of actuality. Thus that which is actually hot, as fire, makes wood, which is potentially hot, to be actually hot, and thereby moves and changes it. Now it is not possible that the same thing should be at once in actuality and potentiality in the same respect, but only in different respects. For what is actually hot cannot simultaneously be potentially hot; but it is simultaneously potentially cold. It is therefore impossible that in the same respect and in the same way a thing should be both mover and moved, i.e., that it should move itself. Therefore, whatever is moved must be moved by another. If that by which it is moved be itself moved, then this also must needs be moved by another, and that by another again. But this cannot go on to infinity, because then there would be no first mover, and consequently, no other mover, seeing that subsequent movers move only inasmuch as they are moved by the first mover, as the staff moves only because it is moved by the hand. Therefore, it is necessary to arrive at a first mover, moved by no other; and this everyone understands to be God.

The second way is from the nature of efficient cause.[8] In the world of sensible things we find there is an order of efficient causes. There is no case known (nei-

> "We cannot but admit the existence of some being having of itself its own necessity, and not receiving it from another, but rather causing in others their necessity."
>
> — ST. THOMAS AQUINAS

---

7 St. Thomas Aquinas, *Summa Theologica*, trans. Fathers of the English Dominican Province, New York: Benziger, Bruce & Glencoe, 1948.

8 An efficient cause is an event (or an agent) that brings something about. The term comes from Aristotle. See "cause" in the glossary.

ther is it, indeed, possible) in which a thing is found to be the efficient cause of itself; for so it would be prior to itself, which is impossible. Now in efficient causes it is not possible to go on to infinity, because in all efficient causes following in order, the first is the cause of the intermediate cause, and the intermediate is the cause of the ultimate cause, whether the intermediate cause be several, or one only. Now to take away the cause is to take away the effect. Therefore, if there be no first cause among efficient causes, there will be no ultimate, nor any intermediate cause. But if in efficient causes it is possible to go on to infinity, there will be no first efficient cause, neither will there be an ultimate effect, nor any intermediate efficient causes; all of which is plainly false. Therefore it is necessary to admit a first efficient cause, to which everyone gives the name of God.

St. Thomas Aquinas (1225-1274)

The architect of the most comprehensive theological structure of the Roman Catholic Church, the *Summa Theologica*, which has long been recognized as the "official" statement of orthodox Christian beliefs by many theologians. Aquinas drew many of his arguments from Aristotle, as can be seen in his "five ways" of demonstrating the existence of God.

FIG. 1.10 The "five ways" of Thomas Aquinas (1225-1274) are the classical statement of the cosmological and teleological arguments for the existence of God. (*Réunion des Musées Nationaux / Art Resource, NY*)

The third way is taken from possibility and necessity, and runs thus. We find in nature things that are possible to be and not to be, since they are found to be generated, and to be corrupted, and consequently, it is possible for them to be and not to be. But it is impossible for these always to exist, for that which can not-be at some time is not. Therefore, if everything can not-be, then at one time there was nothing in existence. Now if this were true, even now there would be nothing in existence, because that which does not exist begins to exist only through something already existing. Therefore, if at one time nothing was in existence, it would have been impossible for anything to have begun to exist; and thus even now nothing would be in existence—which is absurd. Therefore, not all beings are merely possible, but there must exist something the existence of which is necessary. But every necessary thing either has its necessity caused by another, or not. Now it is impossible to go on to infinity in necessary things which have their necessity caused by another, as has been already proved in regard to efficient causes. Therefore we cannot but admit the existence of some being having of itself its own necessity, and not receiving it from another, but rather causing in others their necessity. This all men speak of as God.

In his "fourth way," Aquinas combines the form of cosmological argument with some of the ideas from the ontological argument:

The fourth way is taken from the gradation to be found in things. Among beings there are some *more* and some *less* good, true, noble, and the like. But more and less are predicated of different things according as they resemble in their different ways something which is the maximum, as a thing is said to be hotter according as it more nearly resembles that which is hottest; so that there is something which is truest, something best, something noblest, and, consequently, something which is most being, for those things that are greatest in truth are greatest in being, as it is written in [Aristotle's] *Metaphysics*. . . . Now the maximum in any genus is the cause of all in that genus, as fire, which is the maximum of heat, is the cause of all hot things, as is said in the same book. Therefore, there must also be something which is to all beings the cause of their being, goodness, and every other perfection; and this we call God.

The cosmological argument, in all these versions, is also both an attempt at "proof" and an expression of one's belief in God. Accordingly, it must be appreciated for its role in articulating the concept of God in traditional Christianity as well as being evaluated as a logical argument. As a logical argument, two modern objections seem to have considerable weight. First, even if the argument is formally valid, it proves only that there is some "first mover" or "first cause" or "necessary being." It does not prove that this being has all the other attributes that allow us to recognize God. (Aquinas' fourth "way," however, includes moral attributes of perfection as well.) Taken at face value, the first three versions of the cosmological argument are similar to Aristotle's argument for the "prime mover" (see Chapter 2) except that Aquinas takes the "first cause" to be an "efficient" as well as "final" cause, that is, as the creator as well as the meaning of the universe.

Furthermore, Aristotle (in his *Physics*) allows that there may be several unmoved movers, while Aquinas is clear that there can be only one. Nevertheless, one may accept the argument and believe only in a "first cause" and deny the existence of God. Or if it is accepted that there must be a first cause, why could the universe itself not be its own cause? In current physics, scientists would argue that this idea is just as plausible as the idea that there must have been something else that caused our universe to exist. This argument leads us to the second objection, which would have been unthinkable to Aquinas (or Aristotle) but is generally accepted today. The idea of an infinite regress, that the universe did not have a beginning but has always existed, seemed like an obvious absurdity to most Western thinkers until the nineteenth century. But now, even though scientists and mathematicians talk about the beginning of the universe

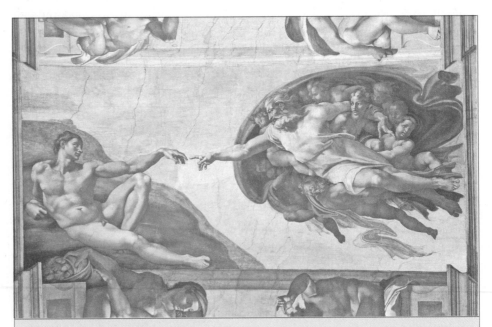

FIG. 1.11 The cosmological and teleological arguments for God's existence both emphasize God's role as creator, a role that Michelangelo artistically presented in his fresco on the ceiling of the Sistine Chapel. *(Erich Lessing / Art Resource, NY)*

and the relativity of time, they no longer consider an infinite regress as necessarily impossible. Without the idea that every infinite regress is an absurdity, the cosmological argument loses its main premise.

In fact, Aquinas admits that there is no valid argument against the claim that God and the universe existed for all eternity, but he has another argument to help him here. He says that the beginning of the universe required an *act*, which means that the universe could not have been the cause of itself. Furthermore, even if the universe existed eternally, it would still require a prime mover to keep it in motion. Therefore, he concludes, God must exist even if the infinite regress argument by itself does not prove God's existence.

The most familiar "proof" of God's existence has been much in the news in the past several years. It is more of an empirical proof, an inference to the best explanation, not of the sheer existence of the world,

FIG. 1.12 The cosmological argument presupposes that an initial force must have caused the movement or energy that is present within the universe. *(© iStockphoto.com/Don Bayley)*

but of its magnificent details, especially the miracle of life. It is often called the **argument from design**, although lately it has taken on the more explicit title of "intelligent design." Some proselytizers have even presented it as a theory in science, that is, "creation science," as opposed to the generally accepted scientific accounts of Darwinian evolution (the succession of one species after another based on the principles of natural selection). It is quite controversial whether the argument from design can properly be understood as a scientific argument and whether there is any solid evidence that could count for or against it. But whether or not it is scientific, the strategy of the argument is clear enough: how could the world be as complex and intricate as it is (a question shared by Darwinians as well as by defenders of intelligent design)? At this point, the Darwinians argue for random mutation and natural selection. The intelligent design theorists insist that such mechanisms could not possibly explain the complexity of the world. But we need not enter into the convoluted arguments against Darwin to appreciate the appeal of the argument, which evokes as much our emotional sense of wonder as our rationality and scientific curiosity.

Immanuel Kant called the argument from design the "teleological argument" because it attributes purpose to the creation of the world. We have already seen a version of the teleological argument in John Wisdom's discussion of the religious attitude. The argument was accessibly and charmingly presented by a Christian minister, William Paley, in the eighteenth century:

 FROM **"The Watch and the Watchmaker"**
BY **William Paley**[9]

STATE OF THE ARGUMENT

In crossing a heath, suppose I pitched my foot against a *stone*, and were asked how the stone came to be there, I might possibly answer, that for any thing I knew to the contrary it had lain there for ever; nor would it, perhaps, be very easy to show the absurdity of this answer. But suppose I had found a watch upon the ground, and it should be inquired how the watch happened to be in that place, I should hardly think of

---

[9] Paley, William, "The Teleological Argument" from *Natural Theology and the Horae Pauline*, New York: American Tract Society, 1852.

William Paley (1743-1805)

A British Christian apologist, philosopher, and utilitarian. He is best known for his exposition of the teleological argument for the existence of God in his work *Natural Theology*.

the answer which I had before given, that for any thing I knew the watch might have always been there. Yet why should not this answer serve for the watch as well as for the stone; why is it not as admissible in the second case as in the first? For this reason, and for no other, namely, that when we come to inspect the watch, we perceive—what we could not discover in the stone—that its several parts are framed and put together for a purpose, *e.g.* that they are so formed and adjusted as to produce motion, and that motion so regulated as to point out the hour of the day; that if the different parts had been differently shaped from what they are, or placed after any other manner or in any other order than that in which they are placed, either no motion at all would have been carried on in the machine, or none which would have answered the use that is now served by it. To reckon up a few of the plainest of these parts and of their offices, all tending to one result: We see a cylindrical box containing a coiled elastic spring, which, by its endeavor to relax itself, turns round the box. We next observe a flexible chain—artificially wrought for the sake of flexure—communicating the action of the spring from the box to the fusee. We then find a series of wheels, the teeth of which catch in and apply to each other, conducting the motion from the fusee to the balance and from the balance to the pointer, and at the same time, by the size and shape of those wheels, so regulating that motion as to terminate in causing an index, by an equable and measured progression, to pass over a given space in a given time. We take notice that the wheels are made of brass, in order to keep them from rust; the springs of steel, no other metal being so elastic; that over the face of the watch there is placed a glass, a material employed in no other part of the work, but in the room of which, if there had been any other than a transparent substance, the hour could not be seen without opening the case. This mechanism being observed—it requires indeed an examination of the instrument, and perhaps some previous knowledge of the subject, to perceive and understand it; but being once, as we have said, observed and understood, the inference we think is inevitable, that the watch must have had a maker—that there must have existed, at some time and at some place or other, an artificer or artificers who formed it for the purpose which we find it actually to answer, who comprehended its construction and designed its use.

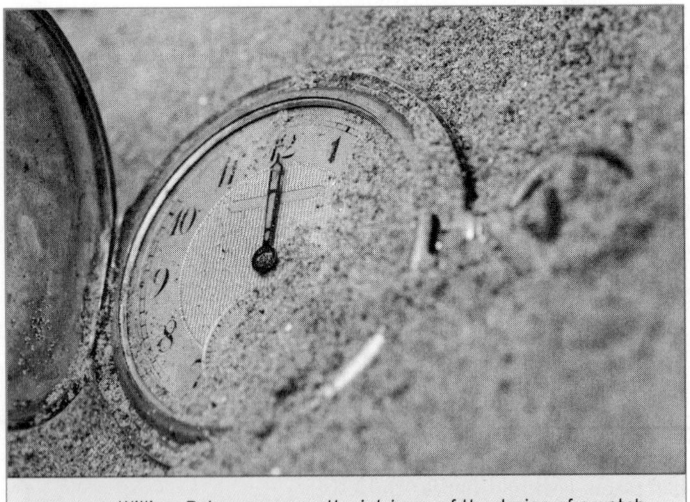

FIG. 1.13 William Paley compares the intricacy of the design of a watch we may find on a beach to the intricacy of the design we observe in nature. *(Image © viki2win, 2011. Used under license from Shutterstock.com)*

I. Nor would it, I apprehend, weaken the conclusion, that we had never seen a watch made—that we had never known an artist capable of making one—that we were altogether incapable of executing such a piece of workmanship ourselves, or of understanding in what manner it was performed; all this being no more than what is true of some exquisite remains of ancient art, of some lost arts, and, to the generality of mankind, of the more curious productions of modern manufacture. Does one man in a million know how oval frames are turned? Ignorance of this kind exalts our opinion of the unseen and unknown, but raises no doubt in our minds of the existence and agency of such an artist, at some former time and in some place or other. Nor can I perceive that it varies at all the inference, whether the question arise concerning a human agent or concerning an agent of a different species, or an agent possessing in some respects a different nature.

II. Neither, secondly, would it invalidate our conclusion, that the watch sometimes went wrong, or that it seldom went exactly right. The purpose of the machinery, the design, and the designer might be evident, and in the case supposed, would be evident in whatever way we accounted for the irregularity of the movement, or whether we could account for it or not. It is not necessary that a machine be perfect, in order to show with what design it was made: still less necessary, where the only question is whether it were made with any design at all.

III. Nor, thirdly, would it bring any uncertainty into the argument, if there were a few parts of the watch, concerning which we could not discover or had not yet discovered in what manner they conduced to the general effect; or even some parts, concerning which we could not ascertain whether they conduced to that effect in any manner whatever. For, as to the first branch of the case if by the loss, or disorder, or decay of the parts in question, the movement of the watch were found in fact to be stopped, or disturbed, or retarded, no doubt would remain in our minds as to the utility or intention of these parts, although we should be unable to investigate the manner according to which, or the connection by which, the ultimate effect depended upon their action or assistance; and the more complex the machine, the more likely is this obscurity to arise. Then, as to the second thing supposed, namely, that there were parts which might be spared without prejudice to the movement of the watch, and that we had proved this by experiment, these superfluous parts, even if we were completely assured that they were such, would not vacate the reasoning which we had instituted concerning other parts. The indication of contrivance remained, with respect to them, nearly as it was before.

IV. Nor, fourthly, would any man in his senses think the existence of the watch with its various machinery accounted for, by being told that it was one out of possible combinations of material forms; that whatever he had found in the place where he found the watch, must have contained some internal configuration or other; and that this configuration might be the structure now exhibited, namely, of the works of a watch, as well as a different structure.

V. Nor, fifthly, would it yield his inquiry more satisfaction, to be answered that there existed in things a principle of order, which had disposed the parts of the watch into their present form and situation. He never knew a watch made by the principle of order; nor can he even form to himself an idea of what is meant by a principle of order, distinct from the intelligence of the watchmaker.

VI. Sixthly, he would be surprised to hear that the mechanism of the watch was no proof of contrivance, only a motive to induce the mind to think so.

VII. And not less surprised to be informed, that the watch in his hand was nothing more than the result of the laws of *metallic* nature. It is a perversion of language to assign any law as the efficient, operative cause of any thing. A law presupposes an agent; for it is only the mode according to which an agent proceeds: it implies a power; for it is the order according to which that power acts. Without this agent, without this power, which are both distinct from itself, the *law* does nothing, is nothing. The expression, "the law of metallic nature," may sound strange and harsh to a philosophic ear; but it seems quite as justifiable as some others which are more familiar to him such as "the law of vegetable nature," "the law of animal nature," or, indeed, as "the law of nature" in general, when assigned as the cause of phenomena, in exclusion of agency and power, or when it is substituted into the place of these.

VIII. Neither, lastly, would our observer be driven out of his conclusion or from his confidence in its truth, by being told that he know nothing at all about the matter. He knows enough for his argument; he knows the utility of the end; he knows the subserviency and adaptation of the means to the end. These points being known, his ignorance of other points, affect not the certainty of his reasoning. The consciousness of knowing little need not beget a distrust of that which he does know. . . .

APPLICATION OF THE ARGUMENT

Every indication of contrivance, every manifestation of design which existed in the watch, exists in the works of nature, with the difference on the side of nature of being greater and more, and that in a degree which exceeds all computation. I mean, that the contrivances of nature surpass the contrivances of art, in the complexity, subtilty, and curiosity of the mechanism; and still more, if possible, do they go beyond them in number and variety; yet, in a multitude of cases, are not less evidently mechanical, not less evidently contrivances, not less evidently accommodated to their end or suited to their office, than are the most perfect productions of human ingenuity. . . .

St. Thomas Aquinas' "fifth way" is a classical statement of the argument from design (also called "the teleological argument"):

On the "Fifth Way"
BY **St. Thomas Aquinas**[10]

The fifth way is taken from the governance of the world. We see that things which lack knowledge, such as natural bodies, act for an end, and this is evident from their acting always, or nearly always in the same way, so as to obtain the best result. Hence it is plain that they achieve their end, not fortuitously, but designedly. Now whatever lacks knowledge cannot move towards an end, unless it be directed by some being endowed with knowledge and intelligence; as the arrow is directed by the archer. Therefore some intelligent being exists by whom all natural things are directed to their end; and this being we call God.

The argument is powerful psychologically, but it has its problems. Like the earlier two arguments, it may prove much less about God than the theist needs to have proved. The God who has rationally designed the universe need not have the slightest concern for humankind, for example. He may well consider us just one of those little curiosities of evolution that, for a few thousand years, interfered with His other interests. But there are other problems peculiar to this argument. It is easily mocked, and Voltaire, who was around when the argument was most popular, parodied its logic in *Candide* (by suggesting that, among other things, it

10 St. Thomas Aquinas, *Summa Theologica*, trans. Fathers of the English Dominican Province, New York: Benziger, Bruce & Glencoe, 1948.

was marvelous that God gave us noses so that we can wear eyeglasses). A Leibnizian philosopher, Dr. Pangloss, dismisses all the horrible tragedies that befall young Candide and his wife Cunegund on the grounds that this is, he keeps repeating, "the best of all possible worlds." (A contemporary version of *Candide*, an opera by Leonard Bernstein, uses the following refrain: "Once one dismisses the rest of all possible worlds, one finds that this is the best of all possible worlds.")

Perhaps the "design" in nature appears as such only to one who is already predisposed to believe in a designer. This is most powerfully presented by David Hume in his blasphemous (and therefore posthumous) *Dialogues on Natural Religion:*

> "This world, for aught he knows, ... was only the first rude essay of some infant deity who afterwards abandoned it."
>
> – DAVID HUME

 FROM *Dialogues on Natural Religion* BY **David Hume**[11]

In a word, Cleanthes, a man who follows your hypothesis is able, perhaps, to assert or conjecture that the universe sometime arose from something like design; but beyond that position he cannot ascertain one single circumstance and is left afterwards to fix every point of his theology by the utmost license of fancy and hypothesis. This world, for aught he knows, is very faulty and imperfect compared to a superior standard and was only the first rude essay of some infant deity who afterwards abandoned it, ashamed of his lame performance; it is the work only of some dependent, inferior deity and is the object of derision to his superiors; it is the production of old age and dotage in some superannuated deity and, ever since his death, has run on at adventures from the first impulse and active force which it received from him.

Hume's argument is, quite simply, that this is not a perfect world, which means that the God who supposedly designed it cannot be perfect either. One can even wonder whether a universe that was so badly designed was designed at all. But Cleanthes replies that he rejects both the suppositions and the tone of these sarcastic remarks and even insists that the argument that the universe is badly designed presupposes a designer. There are more powerful replies, however: that the world is in fact designed as well as it could possibly be, or else that it is a design that has not yet been fully realized and has not yet come to see full perfection.

Hume goes on to argue that if the world is designed, its character suggests that God is either less powerful or less good than the traditional conception allows.

FIG. 1.14 David Hume, shown in this engraving of 1854, held views so contrary to religious orthodoxy that he allowed his *Dialogues Concerning Natural Religion* to be published only posthumously. (© iStockphoto.com/Duncan Walker)

David Hume (1711-1776)

Often admired as the outstanding genius of British philosophy. Born in Scotland (Edinburgh), where he spent much of his life, Hume often traveled to London and Paris. After a vacation in France, he wrote the *Treatise of Human Nature* (1739). He achieved notoriety as well as literary fame in his lifetime, was involved in scandals, and was often at odds with church authorities. Hume was refused professorships at the leading universities for his "heresies." Yet he was, by all accounts, a delightful man who never lost his sense of humor. He was "the life of the party" in London, Edinburgh, and Paris, and he has long set the standard of the ideal thinker for British philosophers. Hume's *Enquiry Concerning the Principles of Morals* (1751) created as much of a stir in the intellectual world as his *Enquiry Concerning Human Understanding* (1748). Like the latter book, the book on morality was a rewriting of his youthful *Treatise*, which never received the attention it deserved. Hume's thesis in moral philosophy was as skeptical and shocking as his thesis in epistemology: There is no knowledge of right and wrong and no rational defense of moral principles. Morality is based upon sentiment or feeling and, as such, cannot be defended by argument.

[11] David Hume, *Dialogues on Natural Religion*, ed. Norman Kemp Smith, Oxford: Oxford University Press, 1935.

FIG. 1.15 Hume thought that the imperfections of our world are evidence against the idea of a perfect, benevolent designer. *(© iStockphoto.com/Ian McDonnell)*

On the concurrence, then, of these *four* circumstances does all or the greatest part of natural evil depend. Were all living creatures incapable of pain, or were the world administered by particular volitions, evil never could have found access into the universe; and were animals endowed with a large stock of powers and faculties, beyond what strict necessity requires, or were the several springs and principles of the universe so accurately framed as to preserve always the just temperament and medium, there must have been very little ill in comparison of what we feel at present. What then shall we pronounce on this occasion? Shall we say that these circumstances are not necessary, and that they might easily have been altered in the contrivance of the universe? This decision seems too presumptuous for creatures so blind and ignorant. Let us be more modest in our conclusions. Let us allow that, if the goodness of the Deity (I mean a goodness like the human) could be established on any tolerable reasons *a priori*, these phenomena, however untoward, would not be sufficient to subvert that principle, but might easily, in some unknown manner, be reconcilable to it. But let us still assert that, as this goodness is not antecedently established but must be inferred from the phenomena, there can be no grounds for such an inference while there are so many ills in the universe, and while these ills might so easily have been remedied, as far as human understanding can be allowed to judge on such a subject.

The credibility of the argument from design has suffered enormously (but perhaps needlessly) from the shock of Darwin's theory of evolution. Accordingly, numerous Christian leaders have combatted the latter with all the resources at their command. But the battle has been largely unnecessary and, if anything, has falsely overemphasized the conflict between science and religion, weakening the credibility of the church. For evolution need not deny the argument from design. It only changes the argument from the traditional idea that God created the universe all at once (although even in Genesis, He spread it out over several days) to the idea that He created it over a long period, using natural selection as one of His tools.

But the logic of evolution does undermine the appeal of the argument from design in a more subtle way. The power of the argument is, boiled down to essentials, "Isn't it marvelous that things are as they are!" But our "marvel" depends on our putting some premium on "the way things are." We place a high premium on "the way things are" because, according to the laws of probability (or chance), the odds against this way are enormous. Now consider the following analogy: You are playing cards, stud poker, and the dealer gives you excellent hands twice in a row. You would be suspicious. The odds are against it. And, particularly if you lose both times, you will be certain that some "design" (namely, the dealer's) is behind it. But now, why would you not have the same suspicions, given any two consecutive hands, for the odds are exactly the same against any combination of cards? (The odds against receiving any hand of the same five cards twice consecutively are 2.6 million to 1.) The answer, of course, has nothing to do with the "likelihood" of getting one set of hands rather than another, but with the significance you place on the one combination rather than the other. So, too, with the argument from design.

Evolution has given the world many different "ways that things are" and will give it many more. The reason for our marveling at this particular "way that things are" is that we suppose that the odds against it are uniquely high. But they are not. They are equally high against every other possible "way that things are," so this "way" seems to deserve no special explanation. This does not deny "design," of course; it only emphasizes the importance of a certain way of seeing the world, a way shared by science and nature lovers as well as theists. Wittgenstein summed up this view toward the argument from design in a phrase: "What is remarkable is not how things are, but that they are at all." (This statement turns us back to the cosmological argument.)

FIG. 1.16 The detractors of Charles Darwin have often taken offense at his theory, which does not treat human beings as fundamentally different in nature from other animals. This stamp from Rwanda pokes fun at Darwin by depicting him as an ape. *(Image © akva, 2011. Used under license from Shutterstock.com)*

- Is an infinite regress absurd? Do you find the idea of an uncaused cause any less absurd?
- Do you think that one must believe either in God or in evolution? Can one consistently believe in both?
- Do you think that any of the arguments for God's existence establish the existence of the traditional God with all His qualities? Do you think that any argument could?

E. Religion, Morality, and Evil

The three traditional forms of "proof" do not seem to be adequate as literal proofs. To accept any of them, it looks as if one has to *begin* by believing in God. Moreover, what each of them proves is not the existence of *God*, but at most the existence of something—something that is defined by its existence, something that is a first cause, or something that is an intelligent "designer." But a very different view of God is defended, for example, by Immanuel Kant. According to this view, the most important attribute of the traditional Western God—the reason why men and women have worshiped Him, prayed to Him, feared Him, fought wars, and died for Him—is their belief in God's divine justice. Thus the most important attributes of God in Western religion are His moral qualities. Without them, our belief in God would be very different than it is.

According to this view, the importance of God in Western thought is His role as the source of our moral laws, as the judge of our actions and feelings, and as the sanction that stands behind those laws and judgments. The preceding "proofs" of God's existence are not wholly convincing, even if they are valid, just because they leave out this all-important moral aspect of belief in God. Accordingly, the question of God's existence has a distinctly moral dimension. The conception of the human good, for believers, depends on a conception of God.

1. Religion and "Practical Reason"

Immanuel Kant, after attempting to refute all three of the traditional arguments of God's existence, offered one of his own. He no longer tried to "prove" God's existence as such and even said that, strictly speaking, we could have no knowledge of God at all, since God, as transcendent, cannot be the object of any possible experience. So Kant, following a long tradition in Christianity, said that belief in God is a matter of faith. But this does not mean, as people so often take it to mean, that it is an irrational belief. Quite to the contrary, Kant insisted that it is the most rational belief of all. For without it, we would not have the anchor for our morality, nor would we have any reason to suppose that our good deeds would eventually be rewarded or our evil deeds would be punished. It was obvious to Kant, as it has been to every person with his or her eyes open since ancient times, that justice is not always delivered in this life. Innocent children are butchered in wars; evil men live grand lives well into old age. Nevertheless, according to Kant, it was rational to believe in God, rational to have faith, even if faith was not, strictly speaking, a matter of knowledge. It is, he says, a "Postulate of Practical Reason."

 **On God and Morality**
BY **Immanuel Kant**[12]

The moral law led, in the foregoing analysis, to a practical problem which is assigned solely by pure reason and without any concurrence of sensuous incentives. It is the problem of the completeness of the first and principal part of the highest good, viz., morality; since this problem can be solved only in eternity, it led to the postulate of immortality. The same law must also lead us to affirm the possibility of the second element of the highest good, i.e., happiness proportional to that morality; it must do so just as disinterestedly as heretofore, by a purely impartial reason. This it can do on the supposition of the existence of a cause adequate to this effect, i.e., it must postulate the existence of God as necessarily belonging to the possibility of the highest good (the object of our will which is necessarily connected with moral legislation of pure reason). We proceed to exhibit this connection in a convincing manner.

Happiness is the condition of a rational being in the world. In whose whole existence everything goes according to wish and will. It thus rests on the harmony of nature with his entire end and with the essential determining ground of his will. But the moral law commands as a law of freedom through motives wholly independent of nature and of its harmony with our faculty of desire (as incentives). Still, the acting rational being in the world is not at the same time the cause of

[12] Immanuel Kant, *The Critique of Practical Reason*, trans. Lewis White Beck. Copyright © 1993, pp. 130–132. Reprinted by permission of Prentice-Hall, Inc., Upper Saddle River, NJ.

the world and of nature itself. Hence there is not the slightest ground in the moral law for a necessary connection between the morality and proportionate happiness of a being which belongs to the world as one of its parts and as thus dependent on it. Not being nature's cause, his will cannot by its own strength bring nature, as it touches on his happiness, into complete harmony with his practical principles. Nevertheless, in the practical task of pure reason, i.e., in the necessary endeavor after the highest good, such a connection is postulated as necessary: we *should* seek to further the highest good (which therefore must be at least possible). Therefore also the existence is postulated of a cause of the whole of nature, itself distinct from nature, which contains the ground of the exact coincidence of happiness with morality. This supreme cause, however, must contain the ground of the agreement of nature not merely with a law of the will of rational beings but with the idea of this law so far as they make it the supreme ground of determination of the will. Thus it contains the ground of the agreement of nature not merely with actions moral in their form but also with their morality as the motives to such actions, i.e., with their moral intention. Therefore, the highest good is possible in the world only on the supposition of a supreme cause of nature which has a causality corresponding to the moral intention. Now a being which is capable of actions by the idea of laws is an intelligence (a rational being), and the causality of such a being according to this idea of laws is his will. Therefore, the supreme cause of nature, in so far as it must be presupposed for the highest good, is a being which is the cause (and consequently the author) of nature through understanding and will, i.e., God. As a consequence, the postulate of the possibility of a highest derived good (the best world) is at the same time the postulate of the reality of a highest original good, namely, the existence of God. Now it was our duty to promote the highest good; and it is not merely our privilege but a necessity connected with duty as a requisite to presuppose the possibility of this highest good. This presupposition is made only under the condition of the existence of God, and this condition inseparably connects this supposition with duty. Therefore, it is morally necessary to assume the existence of God.

The key to Kant's argument is the obvious fact that good deeds are not always rewarded in this life and evil deeds are often not punished. Why then, he asks, should a person be moral and do what is right? If we are to decide rationally to be moral, we must also believe that happiness and morality will be in harmony (what Kant calls "the highest good"), that good people will be rewarded with happiness and evil people will be punished. But if this does not happen in this life, then we must believe that it happens in another life ("this problem can be solved only in eternity"). Furthermore, we must believe in some ultimate source of justice, a divine judge who will weigh good against evil and make certain that eternal happiness and punishment are meted out fairly. This argument is at one and the same time a defense of the Christian belief in the immortality of the human soul and in God. It is necessary to believe in both, according to Kant, to sustain our willingness to be moral. "Therefore, it is morally necessary to assume the existence of God."

A similar position was argued more recently by the pragmatist William James. James's position is a "pragmatic" one; that is, believing in God is "rational" insofar as it does not conflict with our other beliefs (for example, our belief in science, a matter that Kant also stressed) and if it tends to make us lead better lives. James argues the following:

FROM "The Will to Believe" BY William James[13]

Science says things are; morality says some things are better than other things; and religion says essentially two things.

First, she says that the best things are the more eternal things, the overlapping things, the things in the universe that throw the last stone, so to speak, and say the final word. "Perfection is eternal"—this phrase of Charles Secrétan seems a good way of putting this first affirmation of religion, an affirmation which obviously cannot yet be verified scientifically at all.

The second affirmation of religion is that we are better off even now if we believe her first affirmation to be true.

Now, let us consider what the logical elements of this situation are *in case the religious hypothesis in both its branches be really true.* (Of course, we must admit that possibility at the onset. If we are to discuss the question at all, it must involve a living option. If for any of you religion be a hypothesis that cannot, by any living possibility be true, then you need go no farther. I speak to the "saving remnant" alone.) So proceeding, we see, first, that religion offers itself as a *momentous* option. We are supposed to gain, even now, by our belief, and to lose by our nonbelief, a certain vital good. Secondly, religion is a *forced* option, so far as that good goes. We cannot escape the issue by remaining sceptical and waiting for more light, because, although we do avoid error in that way *if religion be untrue*, we lose the good, *if it be true*, just as certainly as if we positively chose to disbelieve. It is as if a man should hesitate indefinitely to ask a certain woman to marry him because he was not perfectly sure that she would prove an angel after he brought her home. Would he not cut himself off from that particular angel-possibility as decisively as if he went and married someone else? Scepticism, then, is not avoidance of option; it is option of a certain particular kind of risk. *Better risk loss of truth than chance of error*—that is your faith-vetoer's exact position. He is actively playing his stake as much as the believer is; he is backing the field against the religious hypothesis, just as the believer is backing the religious hypothesis against the field. To preach scepticism to us as a duty until "sufficient evidence" for religion be found, is tantamount therefore to telling us, when in presence of the religious hypothesis, that to yield to our fear of its being error is wiser and better than to yield to our hope that it may be true. It is not intellect against all passions, then; it is only intellect with one passion laying down its law. And by what, forsooth, is the supreme wisdom of this passion warranted? Dup-

FIG. 1.17 Philosopher and psychologist William James defended mystical states as legitimate sources of knowledge, a knowledge deeper than what we gain through rationality. *(© Bettmann/CORBIS)*

William James (1842–1910)

Perhaps the greatest American philosopher (and psychologist) to this day. He developed the particularly American philosophy of pragmatism from the brilliant but obscure formulations of his colleague at Harvard, Charles Sanders Peirce, into a popular and still-powerful intellectual force. James was born in New York City and graduated from Harvard, with a medical degree, but he decided to teach (at Harvard), rather than to practice medicine. His best-known work in philosophy, besides his work called *Pragmatism: A New Name for Some Old Ways of Thinking* (1907), is *The Varieties of Religious Experience* (1902). James also established himself as one of the fathers of modern psychology with his *Principles of Psychology* (1890).

[13] William James, "The Will to Believe," in *The Will to Believe and Other Essays in Popular Philosophy*, New York: Longmans, Green, 1896.

ery for dupery, what proof is there that dupery through hope is so much worse than dupery through fear? I, for one, can see no proof; and I simply refuse obedience to the scientist's command to imitate his kind of option, in a case where my own stake is important enough to give me the right to choose my own form of risk. If religion be true and the evidence for it be still insufficient, I do not wish, by putting your extinguisher upon my nature (which feels to me as if it had after all some business in this matter), to forfeit my sole chance in life of getting upon the winning side—that chance depending, of course, on my willingness to run the risk of acting as if my passional need of taking the world religiously might be prophetic and right.

FIG. 1.18 The shrine at Chimayó, New Mexico, testifies to many believers' confidence in God's intervention in their lives. *(© Kathleen M. Higgins)*

All this is on the supposition that it really may be prophetic and right, and that, even to us who are discussing the matter, religion is a live hypothesis which may be true. Now, to most of us religion comes in a still further way that makes a veto on our active faith even more illogical. The more perfect and more eternal aspect of the universe is represented in our religions as having personal form. The universe is no longer a mere *It* to us, but a *Thou*, if we are religious; and any relation that may be possible from person to person might be possible here. For instance, although in one sense we are passive portions of the universe, in another we show a curious autonomy, as if we were small active centres on our own account. We feel, too, as if the appeal of religion to us were made to our own active good-will, as if evidence might be forever withheld from us unless we met the hypothesis half-way. To take a trivial illustration: just as a man who in a company of gentlemen made no advances, asked a warrant for every concession, and believed no one's word without proof, would cut himself off by such churlishness from all the social rewards that a more trusting spirit would earn—so here, one who should shut himself up in snarling logicality and try to make the gods extort his recognition willy-nilly, or not get it at all, might cut himself off forever from his only opportunity of making the gods' acquaintance. This feeling, forced on us we know not whence, that by obstinately believing that there are gods (although not to do so would be so easy both for our logic and our life) we are doing the universe the deepest service we can, seems part of the living essence of the religious hypothesis. If the hypothesis *were* true in all its parts, including this one, then pure intellectualism, with its veto on our making willing advances, would be an absurdity; and some participation of our sympathetic nature would be logically required. I, therefore, for one, cannot see my way to accepting the agnostic rules of truth-seeking, or willfully agree to keep my willing nature out of the game. I cannot do so for this plain reason, that *a rule of thinking which would absolutely prevent me from acknowledging certain kinds of truth if those kinds of truth were really there, would be an irrational rule*. That for me is the long and short of the formal logic of the situation, no matter what the kinds of truth might materially be.

"The universe is no longer a mere It to us, but a Thou, if we are religious; and any relation that may be possible from person to person might be possible here."

– WILLIAM JAMES

Blaise Pascal (1623–1669)

A French scientist and philosopher with mildly mystical tendencies. He stressed confidence in the "heart," rather than in reason, and many of his best-known writings are concerned with the problems of religious faith. However, Pascal was also one of the inventors of the computer and a famous mathematician. His best-known work is *Pensées* ("Thoughts") (1669).

FIG. 1.19 A mathematical genius as well as a religious thinker, Pascal argued that in the face of uncertainty, religious faith is a better bet than atheism.

This "practical" argument for belief in God ruled philosophy from the time of Kant until the present century. It has its origins in a short but brilliant argument by the French philosopher **Blaise Pascal**. Pascal offered an argument that he called a wager, literally a bet about God. It is not a proof of God's existence in any sense; in fact, one of its explicit terms is the fact that we cannot know whether God exists or not. But then, Pascal says, if God exists, and we believe in Him, we are entitled to an infinite reward. If He exists and we do not believe in Him, on the other hand, we are really in for it—eternal damnation. Even if God does not exist, we are still better off believing in Him because of the qualities faith brings to life in us. In support of the decision to believe, Pascal asks:

> Now, what harm will befall you in taking this side? You will be faithful, honest, humble, grateful, generous, a sincere friend, truthful. Certainly you will not have those poisonous pleasures, glory and luxury; but will you not have others? I will tell you that you will thereby gain in this life, and that, at each step you take on this road, you will see so great certainty of gain, so much nothingness in what you risk, that you will at last recognize that you have wagered for something certain and infinite, for which you have given nothing.[14]

So, if we treat this as a betting situation, in which our option is simply to believe or not believe, our betting odds look like this:

"PASCAL'S WAGER"

	AND GOD EXISTS	AND GOD DOESN'T EXIST
IF WE BELIEVE	Eternal reward.	We've wasted a little piety but perhaps been better people.
IF WE DON'T BELIEVE	Eternal damnation.	No reward, no punishment.

Looking at the odds as a betting person, it is obvious which option we ought to choose. The risk of eternal damnation overwhelms the promise of a few "poisonous" pleasures, and the promise of eternal reward is well worth the risk that we may be wrong, considering what is gained even in this life. The conclusion, then, on strictly practical grounds, is that we ought to believe in God.

All three of these arguments by Kant, James, and Pascal are based on the same all-important assumption that God is just. On the basis of this assumption, they then argue that it is rational to believe in God, even if it is not possible to prove (or even know) that He exists. Accordingly, belief in God is a matter of faith, but this faith can be argued and justified as rational belief. Just because it is faith and not knowledge, it does not follow that it is "blind faith" or irrational, beyond argument or arbitrary. To insist that belief in God is a matter of faith, therefore, is not to say that it is beyond the reach of philosophy or rational consideration.

---

[14] Blaise Pascal, *Pensées, no. 233*, New York: Modern Library, 1941.

- Can you will yourself to believe something? Is will sufficient to counter religious doubt?
- Do you think our need for justice is a good ground for believing in God?
- What does Pascal's wager fail to capture about religious belief or devotion?

2. The Problem of Evil

These "moral" arguments for believing in God are sound only as long as we accept the assumption that God is just. There have been few sophisticated theists who have actually denied this assumption, of course, but there have been a great many, particularly in modern times, who have worried about it considerably. The problem is called **the problem of evil**. It can be stated simply, but the solution, if you believe in God, is not simple at all. The problem is this: If God is all-powerful (omnipotent), all-knowing (omniscient), and just, then how is it possible that there is so much unearned suffering and unpunished wickedness in the world? Or simply, if God exists, how can the world be so full of evil? It cannot be that He does not know of these misfortunes, for He is all-knowing. Nor can it be that He is unable to do anything about them, for He is all-powerful. And if He is just and has concern for human beings, then He must care about protecting the innocent and punishing or preventing evil.

The problem of evil is a problem because few believers in any religion are willing to give up their faith in the power of nature or of its Creator, its innate goodness, or the belief that there is real justice. The clearest and most widely known characterization of the problem of evil for the religious belief is probably still the one found in the biblical Book of Job, in which Job, deeply pious yet undeservedly suffering, struggles to keep his faith:

> Then his wife said to him, "Are you still unshaken in your integrity? Curse God and die!" But he answered, ". . . If we accept good from God, shall we not accept evil?" (2:9-10)

But eventually, Job asks God:

> "Why should the sufferer be born to see the light?
> Why is life given to men who find it so bitter?" (3:20)

The most common solution to the problem of evil is offered to Job by his friend Eliphaz:

> "Mischief does not grow out of the soil
> nor trouble spring from the earth;
> man is born to trouble,
> as surely as birds fly upwards." (Job 5:6,
>   New English Bible)

In other words, Eliphaz suggests that man has been created by God with the kind of nature that brings with it its own creation of troubles.

This has often been the solution offered by philosophers and theologians to the problem of evil. There are

FIG. 1.20 The story of Job (depicted in this engraving by Gustave Doré) suggests that suffering is not necessarily the result of previous wrongdoing. (© iStockphoto.com/Duncan Walker)

several versions even of this solution (that human beings have "free will"). The version most influential in Christianity was offered by St. Augustine. In his youth, Augustine had come under the influence of a religion called Manichaeism. Manichaeism was branded as heresy by all the great monotheisms (including, at that time, the Persian religion, Zoroastrianism) precisely because of the explanation of evil that it espoused. The Manichaeans claimed that there were two equally powerful gods, one of which was good and one evil. The good god ruled the spirit and mind, and the evil god ruled the body. According to the Manichaeans, then, neither god was all-powerful, and human beings were not free, but rather at the mercy of one or the other of the gods. Only at death, claimed the Manichaeans, when the soul is separated forever from the body, could human beings achieve real moral goodness.

Augustine abandoned Manichaeism and embraced Christianity. As a Christian, he wrote eloquently about the freedom of the will and the ability of human beings to observe the moral obligations to which God has commanded them.

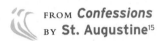

FROM *Confessions*
BY **St. Augustine**[15]

But although I declared and firmly believed that you, our Lord God, the true God who made not only our souls but also our bodies and not only our souls and bodies but all things, living and inanimate, as well, although I believed that you were free from corruption or mutation or any degree of change, I still could not find a clear explanation, without complications, of the cause of evil. Whatever the cause might be, I saw that it was not to be found in any theory that would oblige me to believe that the immutable God was mutable. If I believed this, I should myself become a cause of evil, the very thing which I was trying to discover. So I continued the search with some sense of relief, because I was quite sure that the theories of the Manichees were wrong. I repudiated these people with all my heart, because I could see that while they were inquiring into the origin of evil they were full of evil themselves, since they preferred to think that yours was a substance that could suffer evil rather than that theirs was capable of committing it.

I was told that we do evil because we choose to do so of our own free will, and suffer it because your justice rightly demands that we should. I did my best to understand this, but I could not see it clearly. I tried to raise my mental perceptions out of the abyss which engulfed them, but I sank back into it once more. Again and again I tried, but always I sank back. One thing lifted me up into the light of your day. It was that I knew that I had a will, as surely as I knew that there was life in me. When I chose to do something or not to do it, I was quite certain that it was my own self, and not some other person, who made this act of will, so that I was on the point of understanding that herein lay the cause of my sin. If I did anything against my will, it seemed to me to be something which happened to me rather than something which I did, and I looked upon it not as a fault, but as a punishment. And because I thought of you as a just God, I admitted at once that your punishments were not unjust.

But then I would ask myself once more: "Who made me? Surely it was my God, who is not only good but Goodness itself. How, then, do I come to possess a will that can choose to do wrong and refuse to do good, thereby providing a just reason why I should be punished? Who put this will into me? Who sowed this seed of bitterness in

[15] St. Augustine, *Confessions*, Bk. VII, trans. R. S. Pine-Coffin. Copyright © 1961 by R. S. Pine-Coffin. Penguin Classics, 1961, pp. 136–149. Reprinted by permission of Penguin Books, Ltd.

me, when all that I am was made by my God, who is Sweetness itself? If it was the devil who put it there, who made the devil? If he was a good angel who became a devil because of his own wicked will, how did he come to possess the wicked will which made him a devil, when the Creator, who is entirely good, made him a good angel and nothing else?"

These thoughts swept me back again into the gulf where I was being stifled. But I did not sink as far as that hell of error where no one confesses to you his own guilt, choosing to believe that you suffer evil rather than that man does it.

. . .

"Where then is evil? What is its origin? How did it steal into the world? What is the root or stem from which it grew? Can it be that there simply is no evil? If so, why do we fear and guard against something which is not there? If our fear is unfounded, it is itself an evil, because it stabs and wrings our hearts for nothing. In fact the evil is all the greater if we are afraid when there is nothing to fear. Therefore, either there is evil and we fear it, or the fear itself is evil.

St. Augustine (354-430)

The main figure in the development of medieval Christian thought from its roots in classical Greece and Rome. Augustine was born in North Africa and lived during the decline of the Roman Empire. After exploring various pagan beliefs, he was converted to Christianity and became bishop of Hippo in North Africa. He is best known for his theological treatise *The City of God* and for his very personal *Confessions*.

FIG. 1.21 St. Augustine, who once believed that the world was a battleground for the warring forces of good and evil, came to believe that evil is only the absence of good.
(© Marka / SuperStock)

"Where then does evil come from, if God made all things and, because he is good, made them good too? It is true that he is the supreme Good, that he is himself a greater Good than these lesser goods which he created. But the Creator and all his creation are both good. Where then does evil come from?

"Can it be that there was something evil in the matter from which he made the universe? When he shaped this matter and fitted it to his purpose, did he leave in it some part which he did not convert to good? But why should he have done this? Are we to believe that, although he is omnipotent, he had not the power to convert the whole of this matter to good and change it so that no evil remained in it? Why, indeed, did he will to make anything of it at all? Why did he not instead, by this same omnipotence, destroy it utterly and entirely? Could it have existed against his will? If it had existed from eternity, why did he allow it to exist in that state through the infinite ages of the past and then, after so long a time, decide to make something of it? If he suddenly determined to act, would it not be more likely that he would use his almighty power to abolish this evil matter, so that nothing should exist besides himself, the total, true, supreme, and infinite Good? Or, if it was not good that a God who was good should not also create and establish something good, could he not have removed and annihilated the evil matter and replaced it with good, of which he could create all things? For he would not be omnipotent if he could not create something good without the help of matter which he had not created himself."

These were the thoughts which I turned over and over in my unhappy mind, and my anxiety was all the more galling for the fear that death might come before I had found the truth. But my heart clung firmly to the faith in Christ your Son, our

> "Whatever is, is good; and evil . . . is not a substance, because if it were a substance, it would be good."
>
> – ST. AUGUSTINE

Lord and Saviour, which it had received in the Catholic Church. There were many questions on which my beliefs were still indefinite and wavered from the strict rule of doctrine, yet my mind never relinquished the faith but drank it in more deeply day by day.

. . .

12

It was made clear to me also that even those things which are subject to decay are good. If they were of the supreme order of goodness, they could not become corrupt; but neither could they become corrupt unless they were in some way good. For if they were supremely good, it would not be possible for them to be corrupted. On the other hand, if they were entirely without good, there would be nothing in them that could become corrupt. For corruption is harmful, but unless it diminished what is good, it could do no harm. The conclusion then must be either that corruption does no harm—which is not possible; or that everything which is corrupted is deprived of good—which is beyond doubt. But if they are deprived of all good, they will not exist at all. For if they still exist but can no longer be corrupted, they will be better than they were before, because they now continue their existence in an incorruptible state. But could anything be more preposterous than to say that things are made better by being deprived of all good?

So we must conclude that if things are deprived of all good, they cease altogether to be; and this means that as long as they are, they are good. Therefore, whatever is, is good; and evil, the origin of which I was trying to find, is not a substance, because if it were a substance, it would be good. For either it would be an incorruptible substance of the supreme order of goodness, or it would be a corruptible substance which would not be corruptible unless it were good. So it became obvious to me that all that you have made is good, and that there are no substances whatsoever that were not made by you. And because you did not make them all equal, each single thing is good and collectively they are very good, for our God made his whole creation *very good*.

13

For you evil does not exist, and not only for you but for the whole of your creation as well, because there is nothing outside it which could invade it and break down the order which you have imposed on it. Yet in the separate parts of your creation there are some things which we think of as evil because they are at variance with other things. But there are other things again with which they are in accord, and then they are good. In themselves, too, they are good. And all these things which are at variance with one another are in accord with the lower part of creation which we call the earth. The sky, which is cloudy and windy, suits the earth to which it belongs. So it would be wrong for me to wish that these earthly things did not exist, for even if I saw nothing but them, I might wish for something better, but still I ought to praise you for them alone. For all things *give praise to the Lord on earth, monsters of the sea and all its depths; fire and hail, snow and mist; and the storm-wind that executes his decree; all you mountains and hills, all you fruit trees and cedars; all you wild beasts and cattle, creeping things and birds that fly in air; all you kings and peoples of the world, all you that are princes and judges on earth; young men and maids, old men and boys together; let them all give praise to the Lord's name.* The heavens, too, ring with your praises, O God, for you are the god of us all. *Give praise to the Lord in heaven; praise him, all that dwells on high. Praise him, all you angels of his, praise him, all his armies. Praise him, sun and moon; praise him, every star that shines. Praise him, you highest heavens, you waters beyond the heavens. Let all these praise the Lord.* And since this is so, I no longer wished for a better world, because I was thinking of the whole creation, and in the light of this clearer discernment I had come to see that though the higher things are better than the lower, the sum of all creation is better than the higher things alone.

The problem arises once again, however, if we ask, How could God have given people free will, knowing—as He must have—that they would misuse it so badly? Would everyone be much better off if we had a bit less "free will," or at least if we would have more desires to do good and fewer impulses to cause trouble and suffering?

There are several traditional responses to this question. One is that God has allowed us moral latitude to provide a test of our virtue, for if we were all "naturally" good, there would be little question of good versus evil or salvation versus damnation. But it is open to question whether these distinctions are themselves desirable; wouldn't it have been better for humanity to have stayed in the Garden of Eden? Why did God have to create temptation, and what would have been lost from the world if Adam and Eve had been created with a bit more fortitude and obedience?

Then there is the familiar defense, "but doesn't the world need some evil so that we recognize the good?" But it isn't at all obvious that we need anything like the amount of evil and suffering we have in the world to recognize what is good. And even if we were to agree on this "free will" defense of the traditional conception of God as omnipotent, omniscient, and perfectly just, laying the blame for suffering on people's own choices, that would not solve the problem of evil. This is why we said that this line of free will defense is, at best, a partial solution. For not all human hardships and sufferings seem to be our own doing. Much of the evil in the world does not seem to depend on human action in any way.

Even if we accept the claim that we cause evil through free choice, we still need to explain how the effects of our choices can seem so unrelated to the actions that are supposedly their cause. The Western religions' concept of "original sin" offers one such explanation, and it, too, finds its first expression in the Book of Job. When Job insists that he has done nothing to warrant his suffering, his friend Bildad suggests: "Inquire now of older generations and consider the experience of their fathers" (8:8), implying that the "sins of the fathers," the original sin of the whole human race, justifies Job's punishment. The punishment by God of any individual person, so goes the claim, is just, even though that particular individual did nothing to deserve it. Thus, God remains both just and good.

But this solution, rejected by Job himself, undermines our hopes that right action will be rewarded, and so again

FIG. 1.22 Augustine argued that much of the suffering in the world is a product of free human choices. *(© iStockphoto.com /Ivan Burmistrov)*

FIG. 1.23 In the late eighteenth century, French intellectuals were abandoning most Christian doctrines beyond belief in a creator God and defending Enlightenment thought and the French Revolution. This famous work by Jacques Louis David memorializes Jean Paul Marat, a physician, social theorist, and orator who was assassinated in his bathtub in 1793 for his role in defending the Revolution and inspiring violence against counterrevolutionaries. *(Erich Lessing / Art Resource, NY)*

Voltaire (the pen name of François Marie Arouet) (1694-1778).

Voltaire was an adroit satirist, and his wit got him into trouble (both imprisonment and exile). An influential Enlightenment figure and prolific writer, he defended a reliance on reason, religious tolerance, and social reform.

FIG. 1.24 Voltaire was a deist, who held that God initially caused the world, but no longer intervenes in it. *(© iStockphoto.com /pictore)*

it belies the moral force that God is supposed to play in our lives. For if we were destined to suffer anyway for sins committed by others, then God would not appear to be just, and there would be little incentive for us to be faithful and follow God's commandments.

Some philosophers answered the problem of evil in a different way, by denying one of the main tenets of traditional theistic thinking, namely, the idea that God is good. For example, Spinoza's **pantheism** was one of these many attempts to save belief in God while maintaining a rational picture of nature. More radical versions of pantheism deny that God is just and that He has any moral characteristics at all. In Spinoza's theory, however, which has often been compared to that of the Eastern religions, God is identical to the universe. He is not its creator. He is not a moral agent, so He has neither concern nor the ability to rectify the misfortunes and suffering of the world. If one defends an extreme determinism in which no one—not even God—has "free will," questions of moral responsibility, reward, and punishment become irrelevant, a matter of human vanity, nothing more. It is not surprising that Spinoza, although devout, was long branded an atheist, and his books were proscribed.

The German philosophers Johann Fichte and G. W. F. Hegel also defended versions of pantheism in which God was immanent (instead of transcendent) and identical to the one universe as "Spirit" as well as Spinoza's substance. They, too, fought off accusations of atheism in their careers (and Fichte was actually fired in a great scandal over this). In France, the anticlerical Enlightenment was trying to replace the increasingly dubious authority of the church with rationality, but this often meant gutting religion (Christianity, in particular) of much of its content, especially most of its rituals and its "superstitions." Jean-Jacques Rousseau and his devoted followers in the French Revolution (for example, the Robespierre brothers) advocated belief in a "Supreme Being," but jettisoned most other Christian beliefs. Foremost in this fight was Voltaire, who also held onto his belief in God but sheared Him of all His moral attributes, thus avoiding the problem of evil by denying God His attribute of "justice." "It makes no more sense to say that God is just or unjust than it does to say that he is blue or green."

For Voltaire, God was just a "hypothesis," the creator who turned on the giant Newtonian machine but then left it to go on its own. This peculiarly truncated version of theism is usually called **deism**. Deism includes a belief in God, but this "God" is not much of one. It is essentially an appeal to the cosmological argument, and it is satisfied with a minimal deity, which stops far short of our traditional conception of God. (Most of the American Founding Fathers, by the way, were deists.) As we have seen, Voltaire also despised the "argument from design," with all of its hidden moralizing. The world is full of evil, Voltaire insisted, and there is no denying it. And since there is evil, there cannot be an all-powerful, all-knowing God who is also just, and there can be no appeal to His "mysterious ways." He has no "mysterious ways." In fact, He has no "ways" at all. Thus Voltaire made his point against Leibniz and his "best of all possible worlds" hypothesis in *Candide*, lampooning the Leibnizian Dr. Pangloss. By saving rationality of faith in this way, the French philosophers lost a great deal of the religion. But the question for many believers would be the following: is the deist God God at all?

- What attributes of God are necessary for there to be a "problem" of evil?
- Do you think free will resolves the problem of evil? What about the evil in the world that is not humanly caused?
- Do you think that we must be convinced that good deeds must be rewarded and bad deeds punished to sustain a confidence in morality?
- What are the limitations to a purely rationalist view of faith?
- What does it mean to say God is a "hypothesis"?
- Does deism solve the problem of evil?
- Do you think that the deist God is God?

3. *Hinduism, Buddhism, Karma, and Compassion*

The difficulties stemming from the "free will" solution to the problem of evil may indicate to some that the Western religions' conceptions of God and of human nature are just not adequate. The Western religions characterize human beings as so limited in our understanding of God's justice that we can never predict the ultimate evil or good effects of our actions. But if this is so, how can we have any meaningful moral theory at all? How do we know whether an action is evil or good? Similarly, these religions claim that the wrongdoings we engage in during our short lives here on Earth are punished eternally by God and that our occasional good actions are rewarded eternally. The view that each and every human lifetime belongs to a unique eternal soul would seem to make all God's rewards and punishments intrinsically unjust—way out of proportion to the insignificant actions that are supposedly their cause.

One interesting alternative to these conceptions of humans and God is offered by the Hindu religion, whose solution to the problem of evil is unique in its use of the notion of **karma**.

Hinduism is not actually a single religion. At best it is a family of religious beliefs and practices united, among other things, by a belief in the notion of social caste and a shared lineage from the Indic religions, such as Upanishadism, which we will consider in the following chapter. There are no identifiable "core" Hindu *beliefs*—beyond a reverence for the Veda, although it is rarely read, and a participation in a social organization. Nevertheless, one may speak of "scriptures" and of ideas that have, over the centuries, been more at the center of Hindu culture than others. In general, a theistic worldview has, more than any other, dominated Hindu belief and guided religious practices. However, the Hindu conception of God is radically different from that shared by Judaism, Christianity, and Islam. Theistic Hinduism acknowledges a plurality of gods, even though many Hindus believe that they are all manifestations of the same divine reality (a view called "henotheism"). The Hindu notion of human nature also radically differs from the Western notion. Most Hindus believe that human beings have free will. However, the free exercise of that will *changes* the human being. This is the doctrine of karma, which claims that any course of action that one undertakes

FIG. 1.25 When Arjuna hesitates to give the order to begin a battle, Krishna tells him that it is his duty and assures him that death is not complete destruction, but only a transformation. *(Bildarchiv Preussischer Kulturbesitz / Art Resource, NY)*

creates a psychological tendency to repeat it. One's free will thus becomes limited by one's own dispositions to action, or habits. These dispositions, according to much ancient Indian thought, continue even into a new birth. The inveterate smoker, for instance, may be drawn to the taste of tobacco at a young age in her next incarnation.

Of all the many, many "scriptures" and sacred texts that have moved the hearts of the faithful in India over the centuries, the ***Bhagavadgītā*** (or "***Gītā***"), the "Song of God" (ca. 200 B.C.E.), clearly stands out as the most important. The *Gītā* is a small portion of a long epic poem, the *Mahābhārata*. The central theme of the passages presented here is the unique Hindu response to the problem of evil. The warrior **Krishna** is the ruler of a neighboring state. Throughout most of the long poem, Krishna is an ordinary person although an able, just, clever, and politically astute one. The key event of the entire epic is a battle over political succession. The political issues involved are complex; only one side of the warring family has a just claim. Five brothers are the principal representatives of the just family (although many noble and venerable sages and heroes fight against them). Krishna joins the battle line as charioteer for the third of the five brothers, a champion archer named Arjuna. The *Gītā* is a dialogue between Krishna and Arjuna that occurs just minutes before the battle begins. In the dialogue, Krishna ceases to be a mere mortal and reveals Himself to Arjuna as God incarnate. So his advice to Arjuna, at least according to Hindu theists, is not simply the encouragement of a friend or the wise teachings of a guru; His words are the voice of God speaking to a human being in a time of personal moral crisis. Arjuna insists that it cannot be the morally right thing to do to fight and kill his kinsmen, teachers, friends, and loved ones who face him on the far side of the field of Kuruksetra. Krishna challenges this perspective.

 FROM **The Bhagavadgītā**[16]

"No good do I see in killing my own family in battle. I desire not victory, nor rule, nor pleasures, Krishna; what is power to us, enjoyments, or life, Govinda? Those who make rulership desirable for us, and enjoyments and pleasures, it is they that are arrayed in battle (against us), abandoning life and wealth. Teachers, fathers, sons, grandfathers, uncles, inlaws—these I do not wish to kill even if it means that I must die, Krishna—not even to rule the three worlds, why then for the earth?"

Despite the passion and sincerity of moral feeling that Arjuna expresses, Krishna insists that the right thing to do in the circumstances is to fight, to kill the opposing warriors, and to win the battle.

There are several dimensions of Krishna's explanation why fighting is the right course of action for Arjuna, and more commentary has probably been elicited by His response to Arjuna's plea for guidance than by any other comparably brief text, except perhaps the Torah and the Gospels. In the verses that follow (part of Krishna's reply), Krishna first explains the cosmic foundations of human action. Next He states His own motive as God for assuming mortal birth. Krishna goes on to talk again about human action and closes with a refrain recurring throughout the *Gītā*–the injunction to practice yoga (i.e., spiritual "discipline"). Through the practices of self-discipline–whether *karmayoga* (the yoga of devoting one's actions to God), *jāñayoga* (the yoga of knowledge and meditation), or *bhaktiyoga*, (the yoga of love and devotion)–Krishna lays out the three "paths" by which one may live a spiritually transformed life.

[Krishna:] Without personal attachment undertake action, Arjuna, for just one purpose, for the purpose of sacrifice. From work undertaken for purposes other than sacrifice, this world is bound to the law of karma. Having loosed forth creatures along with sacrifice, the Creator said of old, "With this may you bring forth fruit, let it be your horn-of-plenty.[17] Make the gods flourish with this and may the gods make you flourish. Mutually fostering one another, you will attain the supreme good. For made to flourish by sacrifice, the gods will give you the enjoyments you desire. One who not giving to them enjoys their gifts is nothing but a thief." . . . Know action to have its origin in the Absolute, Brahman, and Brahman to have its foundation in the Immutable. Therefore is the omnipresent Brahman established through all time in sacrifice. . . . Although I exist as the unborn, the imperishable self (*ātmān*), and although I exist as the Lord of beings, resorting to and controlling my own nature I come into (phenomenal) being by my own magical power of self-delimitation. Whenever there is a crisis of *dharma* [righteousness, the good, the cosmic direction], Arjuna, and a rising up of *adharma*, then I loose myself forth. For the protection of good people and for the destruction of evil-doers, for the establishment of *dharma*, I take birth age after age. . . . Just in the ways in which I am approached, so do I receive to my love. People on all sides follow the path that is mine, Arjuna. . . . Actions do not stain me; nor do I have desire for the fruits of works. The person who recognizes me as this way is himself not bound by dispositions of action. So knowing, very ancient seekers of liberation and enlightenment carried out works. Therefore simply do actions as were done of old

---

[16] The following texts are from Bhagavadgītā 1.31b-35, 3.9-12, 3.15, 4.6-8, 4.11, 4.14-19, 4.22-24, 4.31-33, 4.36-37, and 4.42b. Trans. Steve Phillips.

[17] Literally, "wish-fulfilling cow."

by the ancients. What action is (and all its implications), and what inaction, even the seer-sages are confused on this score. To you I will explain that kind of action which when understood you will be free from the untoward and evil.... For action must be understood, and wrong action as well; inaction must be understood—deep, dark, and dense is the nature of action. Were one to see inaction in action and action in inaction, that person among mortals would be the one with wisdom; he, spiritually disciplined, would be the agent of all works. One whose instigations and undertakings are all free from the motive of personal desire, the wise see that person as the truly learned, as one whose personal dispositions have been burned up in the fire of knowledge.... Satisfied with whatever gain comes by him, passed beyond oppositions and dualities, untouched by jealousy, equal-minded and balanced in the face of both success and failure, such a person though he acts is not bound (by karmic dispositions). All dispositions dissolve and wash away when a person is free from attachment, "liberated," and has his mind firmly fixed in knowledge—acting in a spirit of sacrifice.... This world does not belong to one who fails to sacrifice, so how could the next, Arjuna? In this way, numerous diverse sacrifices are spread wide in the mouth of Brahman.

Know them all as born in action. Thus knowing, you will be "liberated" and enlightened. The sacrifice that is knowledge, O you who are a great warrior, is superior to any sacrifice involving material things. All work and action in its entirety, Arjuna, culminates and is fulfilled in (spiritual) knowledge.... Even if of all sinners you are now the very worst evil-doer, once in the boat of knowledge you will safely cross over the crookedness of evil. As a fire kindled reduces its fuel to ashes, Arjuna, so the fire of knowledge makes ashes all *karma*.... In yoga, in "spiritual discipline," take your stand; son of Bharata, stand up and fight.

FIG. 1.26 Many Buddhists in East Asia believe that the bodhisattva Guanyin is so compassionate that she hears the prayers of Buddhists and non-Buddhists alike. *(Image © Hung Chung Chih, 2011. Used under license from Shutterstock.com)*

Yet another approach to religion and the problem of evil is offered in Buddhism, whose Indian roots spread throughout Asia. In Buddhism, the theistic problem of evil is avoided entirely, since Buddhism abandons any conception of an anthropomorphic God. Yet Buddhism retains a belief in moral obligation. A Buddhist answer to "the problem of evil" is *compassion*, confronting the evil of suffering by helping those who suffer. This is the approach, in particular, of the northern, or Mahāyāna, school of Buddhism. Against the Theravada Buddhists, who encourage a course of spiritual discipline toward personal enlightenment, the Mahāyāna argue that this effort falls short of the highest end. Mahāyānists seek not only personal enlightenment, but the deliverance of all sentient beings from suffering and ignorance. A follower of this path attempts to acquire the moral, intellectual, and spiritual perfections (*paramitā*) possessed by Siddhārtha Gautama, who, in this conception, is less "the Buddha" than a *bodhisattva*. A bodhisattva has one foot, so to speak, in the bliss of *nirvāna*, but is motivated by compassion to further the welfare of all beings. Thus Mahāyāna is more world-affirming than Theravada Buddhism in that the goal is not an extinction of individuality and personality in an other-worldly bliss. Instead, one does not aim at extinction of individual form; one needs individual form and body as a medium with which to help others.

The six personal perfections (*pāramitā*) sought by Mahāyānists are liberality or charity, good moral character, patience or peace in the face of anger or desires, energy (energy to strive for the good), the ability to maintain deep meditation, and, most important, insight or wisdom (*prajñā*). The Mahāyānists do not view the natural world as an evil place to be abandoned, but as the "Body of the Buddha," the *dharmakāya*. Even though nature comes to be viewed in such a positive way, however, Buddhist philosophy throughout the long history of Mahāyāna tends to be thoroughly "idealistic." The answer to evil lies not in the world but in us.

- What is karma, and how is it related to free will?
- Do you think it is necessary to believe in reincarnation to accept some notion of karma? Why or why not?
- Do you think that spiritual liberation depends on an attitude of detachment?
- The Mahayana Buddhists advocate adopting the stance of the bodhisattva, who is committed to delivering all sentient beings from ignorance and suffering. Do you think the problem of evil can be resolved by taking this practical approach?

F. Beyond Reason: Faith and Irrationality

Whenever you can defend your belief rationally, it is obviously desirable to do so. The move from rationality to irrationality in the defense of religion, therefore, is a serious step. Kant, who defended the belief in God as a matter of faith, nevertheless defended this belief as rational. But there have always been religious people who have defended faith against reason, emphasizing the impossibility of rational justification and the irrelevance of the usual forms of understanding and knowledge where religion is concerned. In some cases, particularly in modern times, this step away from rationality may be a convenient escape from arguments and doubts that have become too overpowering. But it is not always, or even usually, taken for this reason. As we have seen, there has always been an enthusiastic movement within the sometimes overly formal confines of all the organized religions and dogmas to emphasize the experience of religious belief, called "**mysticism**." Such experiences may well be indescribable and incommunicable. (Philosophers would thereby say it is **ineffable**.) But it is precisely the fact that they defy description and contradict our everyday rational beliefs that makes such experiences so important to those who have had them.

1. God as Experience

Elsewhere in the text we will discuss the rationalist notion of intuition, a special kind of experience that allows us to know some things for certain without argument and without abstraction from experience in the usual sense. According to the rationalists, we know the basic principles

FIG. 1.27 The lyrical work of the great Persian poet Hafiz (1315–1390) is often appreciated for its mystical overtones. *(Image © nadi555, 2011. Used under license from Shutterstock.com)*

of logic and arithmetic in this way, and perhaps the basic principles of metaphysics as well. Not everyone, however, believes that intuition is part of rationality. Some deny that rationality is essential for insight. There may also be, according to most religious mystics, extra-rational or even irrational insight. Their epistemology is often ambiguous at this point. On the one hand, mystics want to deny the rational nature of their intuitions. But at the same time, they want to insist that what they experience is true.

You can see how this can generate considerable confusion. When the mystic insists that his experience is true, he or she has made a claim that is on a par with the rationalist's claim (whether they agree or disagree in their conclusions). If they disagree, that is, if the mystic insists that there is a God (perhaps he has even "seen" Him) and the rationalist denies it, it should be obvious that little room for constructive argument exists. The mystic considers the rationalist's arguments irrelevant; the rationalist considers the mystic obstinate and unwilling to argue rationally. At this point, assuming the discussion does not degenerate into name-calling and fisticuffs, the rationalist will probably storm out of the room in frustration and the mystic, like a Zen master, may just shrug his or her shoulders. In such a case, that is probably the most rational response for both of them.

Mystics need not argue that what they have experienced is true, however. They may insist only that what they have "seen" is extremely important to them personally. In this case mystics need have no disagreement whatsoever with rationalists, either in conclusions or in methods. Their views are different, of course, but they are not at odds. Or the mystics could argue, as the Islamic mystics (or **Sufis**) from al-Ghazali on have done, that rationalist and mystical experience lead to the same truths by different "paths." But whether the mystical experience is an intuition of the (more or less) traditional Judeo-Christian God, whether it is a vision of the Virgin Mary or simply a "feeling of oneness with the universe," whether the experience is the result of twenty years of prayer and meditation or induced in an evening with peyote or mescaline, the philosophical question that follows is always one of interpretation. Without denying the reality of the experience, the question is always whether one ought to interpret the experience as knowledge of reality. Is it just an experience—perhaps beautiful, worth repeating, even worth building your life around? Or—a very different to claim—is the experience true, a breakthrough beyond our normal perceptions (or, perhaps, our everyday **illusions**) to the reality behind them? None of this is to say that the mystic must be wrong. It is only to say that given the impossibility of argument, there is no rational means for deciding the issue.

FIG. 1.28 From the ninth century C.E., the Islamic tradition has fostered the development of science, philosophy, and scholarly inquiry generally. The philosophical tradition of the West is greatly indebted to medieval Arabic thought. *(Bildarchiv Preussischer Kulturbesitz / Art Resource, NY)*

Following the Enlightenment, particularly in Germany, religion took a dramatic swing to the subjective. Attempts at rational defense were given up entirely. The German Romantic philosopher Friedrich Schleiermacher insisted that religion was simply a matter of intense feelings of dependence, nothing more. (His contemporary, Hegel, wryly retorted that this would make a dog a better Christian than most of us.) Other philosophers turned to modernized mysticism, including contemporary experiments with drug-induced experiences, in an attempt to save their religion from rational criticism. The American philosopher William James, for example, writes about mysticism in his book *The Varieties of Religious Experience* and defended the idea that personal religious experience has a central place in religion and that mysticism is the root of such experience. He too insists that mystical experiences are essentially "ineffable," that is, impossible to describe to anyone else, and he compares this experience with the experience of listening to a symphony or being in love. But he also insists that mystical experiences provide us with knowledge, "states of insight into depths of truth unplumbed by the discursive intellect." James concludes that "the existence of mystical states absolutely overthrows the pretension of non-mystical states to be the sole and ultimate dictators of what we may believe." "The mystic," he writes, "is *invulnerable*, and must be left, whether we like it or not, in undisturbed enjoyment of his creed."[18] The Sufi philosopher **Mohammad al-Ghazali**, a medieval mystic, similarly insists that rationality cannot properly evaluate mysticism, which can be fathomed only through direct experience:

 FROM ***The Deliverance from Error***
BY **Mohammad al-Ghazali**[19]

When I had finished with [philosophy and theology], I next turned with set purpose to the method of mysticism (or Sufism). I knew that the complete mystic "way" includes both intellectual belief and practical activity; the latter consists in getting rid of the obstacles in the self and in stripping off its base characteristics and vicious morals, so that the heart may attain to freedom from what is not God and to constant recollection of Him.

The intellectual belief was easier to me than the practical activity. I began to acquaint myself with their belief by reading their books. . . . I thus comprehended their fundamental teachings on the intellectual side, and progressed, as far as is possible by study and oral instruction, in the knowledge of mysticism. It became clear to me, however, that what is most distinctive of mysticism is something which cannot be apprehended by study, but only by immediate experience (*dhawq*—literally "tasting"), by ecstasy and by a moral change. What a difference there is between *knowing* the definition of health and satiety, together with their causes and presuppositions, and *being* healthy and satisfied! What a difference between being acquainted with the definition of drunkenness—namely, that it designates a state arising from the domination of the seat of the intellect by vapours arising from the stomach—and being drunk! Indeed, the drunken man while in that condition does not know the definition of drunkenness nor the scientific account of it; he has not the very least scientific knowledge of it. The sober man, on the other hand, knows the definition of drunkenness and its basis, yet he is not drunk in the very least. Again the

Mohammad al-Ghazali (1058–1111)

An Islamic philosopher and theologian, known especially for his criticisms of Aristotelianism and Avicenna. His most famous work was called *The Incoherence of the Philosophers*.

18 William James, "The Varieties of Religious Experience," in *The Writings of William James*, ed. John J. McDermott, New York: Random House, 1967.

19 Mohammad al-Ghazali, *The Deliverance from Error*, from *The Faith and Practice of al-Ghazali*, trans. William Montgomery Watt, London: Allen & Unwin, 1953.

"What is most distinctive of mysticism is something which cannot be apprehended by study, but only by immediate experience . . . by ecstasy and by a moral change."

– MOHAMMAD AL-GHAZALI

doctor, when he is himself ill, knows the definition and causes of health and the remedies which restore it, and yet is lacking in health. Similarly there is a difference between knowing the true nature and causes and conditions of the ascetic life and actually leading such a life and forsaking the world.

I apprehended clearly that the mystics were men who had real experiences, not men of words, and that I had already progressed as far as was possible by way of intellectual apprehension. What remained for me was not to be attained by oral instruction and study but only by immediate experience and by walking in the mystic way.

2. The Leap of Faith

An eccentric Danish philosopher, **Søren Kierkegaard**, is often claimed as the father of both the "new" Christianity and that nonreligious philosophy called existentialism. Kierkegaard was born into a society in which everyone was a Christian; they all believed the same dogmas, without thinking about them. They all went to the same (Lutheran) churches for Sunday services and Friday afternoon bingo games and enjoyed these social gatherings immensely. They were all entitled to call themselves "Christians" just by virtue of the fact that they had been born of certain parents, brought as children to certain churches, and continued to mouth certain doctrines that they did not understand or care to understand in the slightest. What they all lacked was passion. Their religion and they themselves, according to Kierkegaard, were boring through and through. Whatever happened to the phrase "the fear of God in their hearts"? These people felt no "fear," just the security of a comfortable and self-righteous society and warm swill of beer in their bellies, he complained. Kierkegaard, who had been brought up in an unusually devout Lutheran home, was disgusted with them. This is not Christianity, he insisted, and the sophisticated disputes over doctrine and dogma had nothing more to do with being religious than the calculations of an accountant at tax time.

FIG. 1.29 Kierkegaard argued that religion is a matter of personal passion, not proof. *(Snark / Art Resource, NY)*

Søren Kierkegaard (1813-1855)

A Danish philosopher and theologian who is generally recognized as the father of existentialism and the founder of many varieties of contemporary religious irrationalism. Kierkegaard dedicated himself to religious writing after a short and not altogether successful attempt at the wild life and a brief engagement, which he broke off to devote himself to his work. The basic tenet of Kierkegaard's philosophy was the need for each individual to choose his own way of life. Christianity could not be considered anything other than just such a choice, a passionate choice, which had nothing to do with doctrines, churches, social groups, and ceremonies.

Accordingly Kierkegaard offered his alternative—a new (in fact, very old) way of seeing oneself as a Christian. Rational argument was irrelevant. The doctrines of Christianity, he admitted, were absolutely absurd. But that did not matter. In fact, it was the very absurdity of these beliefs that made the passion of Christianity possible. After all, if it were simply a matter of accepting some proposition, why should we feel anything? And "proofs" of God's existence, needless to say, were as irrelevant—in fact, offensive—as you could imagine. "Christianity is passion!" he insisted. "Religion is feeling and commitment." No talk of "truth"—unless you mean simply **subjective truth**, truth for me alone. No talk of "proof" and no talk of "rationality." There is simply, to use his most famous phrase, *the leap of faith*, across the borders of rationality and thinking to the passion-filled life of old-fashioned Christian fear and awe of God. "My only analogy is Socrates. My task is a Socratic task—to revise the conception of what it means to be a Christian."

Kierkegaard's move away from rationality is characterized as a rejection of "objectivity." Being a Christian, he says, is not a matter of "objective faith" (consisting of reason, doctrines, and "proofs") but of subjectivity, passion, and "inwardness."

On Subjective Truth
BY **Søren Kierkegaard**[20]

"Suppose Christianity is . . . inwardness, and . . . also the paradox, . . . for the existing individual in the inwardness of his existence."

— SØREN KIERKEGAARD

Objective faith: what does that mean? It means a sum of dogmas. But suppose Christianity is nothing of the kind; suppose, on the contrary, it is inwardness, and therefore also the paradox, so as to push away objectively; and thus to acquire significance for the existing individual in the inwardness of his existence, in order to place him more decisively than any judge can place the accused, between time and eternity in time, between heaven and hell in the time of salvation. Objective faith: it is as if Christianity had also been heralded as a kind of little system, although not quite so good as the Hegelian system; it is as if Christ—yes, no offense intended—it is as if Christ were a professor, and as if the Apostles had formed a little professional society. Truly, if it was once no easy thing to become a Christian, I believe now it becomes more difficult every year, because by now it has become so easy to become one—one finds a little competition only in becoming a speculative philosopher. And yet the speculative philosopher is perhaps most removed from Christianity, and perhaps it is far preferable to be an offended individual who nonetheless continually relates himself to Christianity, than to be a speculative philosopher who supposes he has understood it.

· · ·

Suppose, however, that subjectivity is truth, and that subjectivity is the existing subjectivity, then, to put it this way, Christianity is an exact fit. Subjectivity culminates in passion, Christianity is paradox, paradox and passion fit one another exactly, and paradox exactly fits one whose situation is in the extremity of existence. Yes, in the wide world there could not be found two lovers so well fitted for one another as paradox and passion, and their argument is like a lovers' argument, when they argue whether he first aroused her passion, or she his. So it is here: by means of the paradox itself, the existing person has been situated in the extremity of existence. And what is more delightful for lovers than that they are allowed a long time together without any change in the relationship between them, except that it becomes more intensive in inwardness?

Religion is a confrontation with the unknown, not something knowable.

But what is this unknown thing, with which reason in its paradoxical passion is affronted, and which even upsets for man his self-knowledge? It is the Unknown. But it is certainly something human, insofar as we know what it is to be human, nor is it some other thing humans know. Let us call this unknown something: *the God*. That is merely the name we give to it. To want to prove that this unknown something (the God) exists could hardly occur to reason. For of course if God does not exist, it would be impossible to prove it, but if God does exist, it would be folly to try to prove it; for, in the very moment I began my proof, I would have presupposed it, not as dubious but as certain (a presupposition is never dubious, just because it is a

[20] The first and third readings are from Søren Kierkegaard, *Concluding Unscientific Postscript,* and the second reading is from Søren Kierkegaard, *Philosophical Fragments.* All three were translated from the Danish by Clancy Martin and reprinted with his permission.

"If God does not exist, it would be impossible to prove it, but if God does exist, it would be folly to try to prove it."

– SØREN KIERKEGAARD

presupposition); since otherwise I would never begin, understanding that the whole would be impossible if he did not exist. But if when I speak of proving God's existence I mean that I propose to prove that the Unknown, which exists, is God, then I express myself less fortunately; for then I prove nothing, least of all existence, but merely develop the content of a concept. In general, to try to prove that something exists is a difficult matter, and what is still worse for the bold who would attempt it, the difficulty is of a kind that will not bring fame to those who occupy themselves with it. The whole proof always turns into something entirely different, turns into an additional development of the consequences that come from my having assumed that the object in question exists. Thus I continually deduce not toward existence, but I deduce from existence, whether I exert myself indeed in the world I can grasp with my hands or in thought. So I do not prove that a stone exists, but that something which exists is a stone; a court of justice does not prove that a criminal exists, but that the accused, who certainly exists, is a criminal. Whether one calls existence an *accessorium* [a predicate] or the eternal *prius* [first given], it can never be proven. Let us take our time; for us there is no reason to hurry, as there is for those, who from concern for themselves or for God or for some other thing, must hurry to show they exist. When it is so, there is indeed excellent reason to hurry, especially if the prover sincerely tries to appreciate the danger that he himself or the thing in question may not exist until the proof is complete, and does not secretly entertain the thought that it exists whether he succeeds in proving it or not.

So if from Napoleon's actions one tried to prove Napoleon's existence, would it not be of the greatest peculiarity, since *his* existence very well explains his actions, but actions cannot prove his existence, unless I have already understood the word "his" such that I assume that he exists. But Napoleon is only an individual, and insofar there is no absolute relationship between him and his actions; after all, another person may have performed the same actions. Perhaps this is why I cannot deduce from actions to existence. If I call these actions the actions of Napoleon, then the proof is superfluous, since I have already named him; if I ignore this, I can never prove from the actions that they are Napoleon's, but (purely ideally) prove that such actions are the actions of a great general, etc. But between God and his works there is an absolute relationship, God is not a name, but a concept, and perhaps it follows from that, that his *essentia involvit existentiam* [essence entails existence]. God's works can only be done by God; quite right, but where then are the works of God? The works from which I would deduce his existence are not immediately given. Or does the wisdom in nature, the goodness, the wisdom in the governance of the world, reside on the very face of things? Are we not here confronted with the most terrible temptations to doubt, and is it not impossible finally to dispose of those doubts? But from such an order of things I will certainly not prove God's existence, and even if I began I would never finish, and furthermore would live constantly *in suspenso* [in suspense], that something terrible should suddenly happen that would demolish my little proof. So, from what works will I prove it? From the works as apprehended through an ideal interpretation, i.e., such as they do not immediately reveal themselves. But in that case it is not from the works that I prove it, but I develop only the ideality I have presupposed; because of my confidence in *this* I boldly defy all objections, even those that have not yet been made. As soon as I begin I have presupposed the ideal interpretation, and presuppose that I will be successful in carrying it through; but this is just to presuppose that God exists, and that in confidence in him is how I am actually beginning.

You can see how little Kierkegaard thinks of the ingenious "proofs" of God's existence, as well as all attempts to "know" Him. The point of religion, he says, is precisely not to know, but rather to feel. It is the absurdity and the irrationality of Christian doctrines, he insists, that makes this rare intensity of feeling possible.

> Precisely its objective repulsion, the absurd is the measure of the intensity of faith in inwardness. There is a man who wants to have faith, well, let the comedy begin. He wants to have faith, but he also wants to ensure himself with the help of an objective inquiry and its approximation-process. What happens? With the help of the approximation-process, the absurd becomes something else; it becomes probable, it becomes more probable, it becomes extremely and exceedingly probable. Now he is prepared to believe it, and he boldly supposes that he does not believe as shoemakers and tailors and simple folk do, but only after long consideration. Now he is prepared to believe it, but lo and behold, now it has become impossible to believe it. The almost probable, the very probable, the extremely and exceedingly probable: that he can almost know, or as good as know, to a greater degree and exceedingly almost *know*—but *believe* it, that is impossible, for the absurd is precisely the object of faith, and only that can be believed.

Christianity, Kierkegaard concludes, involves suffering, the suffering that comes with the anticipation of our own death and our feeling of smallness and insignificance when we consider the eternal order of things. For those who try to minimize this suffering through professional "understanding" and knowledge, Kierkegaard has little but sarcasm: *"The two ways.* One is to suffer; the other is to become a professor of the fact that another suffered."

In his journals, Kierkegaard wrote the following:

> What I really lack is to be clear in my mind what I am to do, not what I am to know, except insofar as a kind of understanding must precede every action. The thing is to understand myself, to see what God truly wishes me to do; the thing is to find a truth which is true for me, to find the idea I can live and die for. What would be the use of discovering so-called objective truth, of mastering all the systems of philosophy and of being able, if required, to discuss them all and reveal the inconsistencies within each; what good would it do me to be able to develop a theory of the state and synthesize all details into one whole, and so to create a world I did not live in, but only held up for others to see; what good would it do me to be able to explain the meaning of Christianity if it had no deeper significance for me and for my life; what good would it do me if truth herself stood before me, cold and naked, not caring whether I recognized her or not, and producing in me a shudder of terror rather than a trusting devotion? Indeed I do not deny that I yet acknowledge an imperative of understanding and that with it one can control men, but it must be taken up into my life, and that is what I now recognize as the most important thing.[21]

3. God as the Ultimate Concern

Following Kierkegaard, Christian "irrationalism" changed the complexion of Western religion and gave faith a meaning that is not vulnerable to rational arguments. **Paul Tillich** proposed an extremely powerful form of Christianity that also gives up the traditional view of God and

"This is just to presuppose that God exists, and that in confidence in him is how I am actually beginning."

— SØREN KIERKEGAARD

---

[21] Trans. Clancy Martin.

moves the focus of the religion to purely personal concerns and commitments. These are what our religion amounts to, and we do not need anything more.

On the Ultimate Concern
BY Paul Tillich[22]

We have discussed the meaning of symbols generally because, as we said, man's ultimate concern must be expressed symbolically! One may ask: Why can it not be expressed directly and properly? If money, success, or the nation is someone's ultimate concern, can this not be said in a direct way without symbolic language? Is it not only in those cases in which the content of the ultimate concern is called "God" that we are in the realm of symbols? The answer is that everything which is a matter of unconditional concern is made into a god. If the nation is someone's ultimate concern, the name of the nation becomes a sacred name and the nation receives divine qualities which far surpass the reality of the being and functioning of the nation. The nation then stands for and symbolizes the true ultimate, but in an idolatrous way. Success as ultimate concern is not the natural desire of actualizing potentialities, but its readiness to sacrifice all other values of life for the sake of a position of power and social predominance. The anxiety about not being a success is an idolatrous form of the anxiety about divine condemnation. Success is grace; lack of success, ultimate judgment. In this way concepts designating ordinary realities become idolatrous symbols of ultimate concern.

The reason for this transformation of concepts into symbols is the character of ultimacy and the nature of faith. That which is the true ultimate transcends the realm of finite reality infinitely. Therefore, no finite reality can express it directly and properly. Religiously speaking, God transcends his own name. This is why the use of his name easily becomes an abuse or a blasphemy. Whatever we say about that which concerns us ultimately, whether or not we call it God, has a symbolic meaning. It points beyond itself while participating in that to which it points. In no other way can faith express itself adequately. The language of faith is the language of symbols. If faith were what we have shown that it is not, such an assertion could not be made. But faith, understood as the state of being ultimately concerned, has no language other than symbols. When saying this I always expect the question: Only a symbol? He who asks this question shows that he has not understood the difference between signs and symbols nor the power of symbolic language, which surpasses in quality and strength the power of any nonsymbolic language. One should never say "only a symbol," but one should say "not less than a symbol." With this in mind we can now describe the different kinds of symbols of faith.

The fundamental symbol of our ultimate concern is God. It is always present in any act of faith, even if the act of faith includes the denial of God. Where there is ultimate concern, God can be denied only in the name of God. One God can deny the other one. Ultimate concern cannot

Paul Tillich (1886-1965)

A German-born philosopher who spent many of his later years teaching in the United States. Tillich is among the best known of those modern theologians who, like the Romantics of the 19th century, place the emphasis on emotion and "concern," rather than on reason in religion. In his theology, God is no longer the transcendent judge of the scriptures, but simply the symbol of our "ultimate concern." Tillich is the author of *Systematic Theology* (1953-63), *The Dynamics of Faith* (1957), and *The Courage to Be* (1952).

22 "Religious Symbols" from "Symbols of Faith," pp. 50-55 in *The Dynamics of Faith* by Paul Tillich. Copyright © 1957 by Paul Tillich, renewed 1985 by Hannah Tillich. Reprinted by permission of HarperCollins Publishers.

deny its own character as ultimate. Therefore, it affirms what is meant by the word "God." Atheism, consequently, can only mean the attempt to remove any ultimate concern—to remain unconcerned about the meaning of one's existence. Indifference toward the ultimate question is the only imaginable form of atheism. Whether it is possible is a problem which must remain unsolved at this point. In any case, he who denies God as matter of ultimate concern affirms God, because he affirms ultimacy in his concern. God is the fundamental symbol for what concerns us ultimately. Again, it would be completely wrong to ask: So God is nothing but a symbol? Because the next question has to be: A symbol for what? And then the answer would be: For God! God is symbol for God. This means that in the person of God we must distinguish two elements: the element of ultimacy, which is a matter of immediate experience and not symbolic in itself, and the element of concreteness, which is taken from our ordinary experience and symbolically applied to God. The man whose ultimate concern is a sacred tree has both the ultimacy of concern and the concreteness of the tree which symbolizes his relation to the ultimate. The man who adores Apollo is ultimately concerned, but not in an abstract way. His ultimate concern is symbolized in the divine figure of Apollo. The man who glorifies Jahweh, the God of the Old Testament, has both an ultimate concern and a concrete image of what concerns him ultimately. This is the meaning of the seemingly cryptic statement that God is the symbol of God. In this qualified sense God is the fundamental and universal content of faith.

It is obvious that such an understanding of the meaning of God makes the discussions about the existence or nonexistence of God meaningless. It is meaningless to question the ultimacy of an ultimate concern. This element in the idea of God is in itself certain. The symbolic expression of this element varies endlessly through the whole history of mankind. Here again it would be meaningless to ask whether one or another of the figures in which an ultimate concern is symbolized does "exist." If "existence" refers to something which can be found within the whole of reality, no divine being exists. The question is not this, but: Which of the innumerable symbols of faith is most adequate to the meaning of faith? In other words, which symbol of ultimacy expresses the ultimate without idolatrous elements? This is the problem, and not the so-called "existence of God"—which is in itself an impossible combination of words. God as the ultimate in man's ultimate concern is more certain than any other certainty, even that of oneself. God as symbolized in a divine figure is a matter of daring faith, of courage and risk.

God is the basic symbol of faith, but not the only one. All the qualities we attribute to him, power, love, justice, are taken from finite experiences and applied symbolically to that which is beyond finitude and infinity. If faith calls God "almighty," it uses the human experience of power in order to symbolize the content of its infinite concern, but it does not describe a highest being who can do as he pleases. So it is with all the other qualities and with all the actions, past, present, and future, which men attribute to God. They are symbols taken from our daily experience, and not information about what God did once upon a time or will do sometime in the future. Faith is not the belief in such stories, but it is the acceptance of symbols that express our ultimate concern in terms of divine actions.

Another group of symbols of faith are manifestations of the divine in things and events, in persons and communities, in words and documents. This whole realm of sacred objects is a treasure of symbols. Holy things are not holy in themselves, but they point beyond themselves to the source of all holiness, that which is of ultimate concern.

> "God as the ultimate in man's ultimate concern is more certain than any other certainty, even that of oneself."
>
> – PAUL TILLICH

Notice how far Tillich has moved from the traditional Judeo-Christian-Islamic conception of God, although he is still a theist and a Christian. Yet it is not clear that "God" means the same for Tillich as it does in the Old and New Testaments. God is a symbol of "ultimate concern." Nevertheless, is this symbol God as Christians are supposed to think of Him? The belief in God is now expanded to represent the fact that one finds his or her life meaningful. Tillich says that this "makes the discussions about the existence or nonexistence of God meaningless." It also undercuts the Western idea that God is a single kind of being with the characteristics we discussed earlier. This brings Tillich's theism close to the *general* idea of religion, which Nishitani described in the passage presented earlier. God is whatever concerns us ultimately, whatever is most important in our lives. This is even true, Tillich says, when one denies the existence of God. "Where there is ultimate concern, God can be denied only in the name of God."

- How does subjectivism differ from mysticism?
- Do you think having an experience that is ineffable (i.e., it cannot be described or communicated to others) is a form of knowledge?
- Why does Kierkegaard claim that absurdity or paradox is the essence of faith?
- For Tillich, what is "an ultimate concern"? Why does it make the question of God's existence "meaningless"?
- How is God a symbol of "the ultimate concern?" Can you have an ultimate concern and not believe in God?

G. Doubts about Religion

It is often said that religion is a matter of personal belief and faith, suggesting that the objects of religious belief are beyond criticism and no one's business but one's own. But it is a questionable slide from this view—which is amiably suited to promoting tolerance among believers of different faiths—to the idea that true faith is immune to doubt, or, for that matter, to criticisms of a very different kind. On the one hand, religious belief may necessarily involve doubts; indeed, it may be argued that the dogmatic certainty sought by many believers is something less than real faith. Such a view is implied by Kierkegaard, for example, and his insistence on passionate commitment arises precisely to confront the "objective uncertainty" of faith. An even more profound doubt *within* the bonds of faith was expressed by the great Russian author, Fyodor Dostoyevsky. Dostoyevsky was a devout Christian whose faith was shaken many times, not least by the cruelty he often witnessed (and of which he was sometimes the victim) in feudal Tsarist Russia. In his novel *The Brothers Karamazov*, brother Alyosha is a devout but still naive religious novice, whereas his brother Ivan is entertaining serious doubts about the justification for belief in a good God. (The author clearly recognized himself in both brothers.) In a conversation between the two of them, Ivan presents us with a vivid and horrible picture of human evil challenging his faith.

FROM *The Brothers Karamazov*
BY **Fyodor Dostoyevsky**[23]

"One picture, only one more, because it's so curious, so characteristic, and I have only just read it in some collection of Russian antiquities. I've forgotten the name. I must look it up. It was in the darkest days of serfdom at the beginning of the century, and long live the Liberator of the People! There was in those days a general of aristocratic connections, the owner of great estates, one of those men—somewhat exceptional, I believe, even then—who, retiring from the service into a life of leisure, are convinced that they've earned absolute power over the lives of their subjects. There were such men then. So our general, settled on his property of two thousand souls, lives in pomp, and domineers over his poor neighbors as though they were dependents and buffoons. He has kennels of hundreds of hounds and nearly a hundred dog boys—all mounted and in uniform. One day a serf boy, a little child of eight, threw a stone in play and hurt the paw of the general's favorite hound. 'Why is my favorite dog lame?' He is told that the boy threw a stone that hurt the dog's paw. 'So you did it.' The general looked the child up and down. 'Take him.' He was taken—taken from his mother and kept shut up all night. Early that morning the general comes out on horseback, with the hounds, his dependents, dog boys, and huntsmen, all mounted around him in full hunting parade. The servants are summoned for their edification, and in front of them all stands the mother of the child. The child is brought from the lockup. It's a gloomy, cold, foggy autumn day, a capital day for hunting. The general orders the child to be undressed; the child is

A Russian novelist and essayist. His works are noteworthy for their psychological and philosophical depth. Dostoyevsky is often mentioned as a precursor of the existentialist movement because of his explorations of the darker sides of the human psyche in such works as *Notes from Underground* and *The Brothers Karamazov*.

FIG. 1.30 Vasilij Perov, *Portrait of Fyodor Dostoyevsky* (1872). Dostoyevsky displays the conflict between religious conviction and religious doubt in the interactions of two of the brothers in his literary masterpiece, *The Brothers Karamozov*. *(Scala / Art Resource, NY)*

stripped naked. He shivers, numb with terror, not daring to cry. . . . 'Make him run,' commands the general. 'Run! run!' shout the dog boys. The boy runs. . . . 'At him!' yells the general, and he sets the whole pack of hounds on the child. The hounds catch him, and tear him to pieces before his mother's eyes! . . . I believe the general was afterwards declared incapable of administering his estates. Well—what did he deserve? To be shot? To be shot for the satisfaction of our moral feelings? Speak, Alyosha!"

"To be shot," murmured Alyosha, lifting his eyes to Ivan with a pale, twisted smile.

"Bravo!" cried Ivan delighted. "If even you say so . . . You're a pretty monk! So there is a little devil sitting in your heart, Alyosha Karamazov!"

"What I said was absurd, but—"

"That's just the point, that 'but'!" cried Ivan. "Let me tell you, novice, that the absurd is only too necessary on earth. The world stands on absurdities, and perhaps nothing would have come to pass in it without them. We know what we know!"

23 Fyodor Dostoyevsky, *The Brothers Karamazov*, trans. Constance Barnett, New York: Modern Library, 1929.

FIG. 1.31 Dostoevsky challenges belief in God's justice, asking how a good and just God could have created a world in which human brutality (such as that shown in Francisco Goya's *The Third of May*, 1808) is possible. *(Erich Lessing / Art Resource, NY)*

"What do you know?"

"I understand nothing," Ivan went on, as though in a delirium. "I don't want to understand anything now. I want to stick to the fact. I made up my mind long ago not to understand. If I try to understand anything, I shall be false to the fact, and I have determined to stick to the fact."

"Why are you trying me?" Alyosha cried, with sudden distress. "Will you say what you mean at last?"

"Of course, I will; that's what I've been leading up to. You are dear to me. I don't want to let you go, and I won't give you up to your Zossima."

Ivan for a minute was silent; his face became all at once very sad.

"Listen! I took the case of children only to make my case clearer. Of the other tears of humanity with which the earth is soaked from its crust to its center, I will say nothing. I have narrowed my subject on purpose. I am a bug, and I recognize in all humility that I cannot understand why the world is arranged as it is. Men are themselves to blame, I suppose; they were given paradise, they wanted freedom, and stole fire from heaven, though they knew they would become unhappy, so there is no need to pity them. With my pitiful, earthly, Euclidian understanding, all I know is that there is suffering and that there are none guilty; that effect follows cause, simply and directly; that everything flows and finds it level—but that's only Euclidian nonsense, I know that, and I can't consent to live by it! What comfort is it to me that there are none guilty and that effect follows cause simply and directly, and that I know it—I must have justice, or I will destroy myself. And not justice in some remote infinite time and space, but here on earth, and that I could see myself. I have believed in it. I want to see it, and if I am dead by then, let me rise again, for if it all happens without me, it will be too unfair. Surely I haven't suffered, simply that I, my crimes and my sufferings, may manure the soil of the future harmony for somebody else. I want to see with my own eyes the hind lie down with the lion and the victim rise up and embrace his murderer. I want to be there when everyone suddenly understands what it has all been for. All the religions of the world are built on this longing, and I am a believer. But then there are the children, and what am I to do about them? That's a question I can't answer. For the hundredth time I repeat, there are numbers of questions, but I've only taken the children, because in their case what I mean is so unanswerably clear. Listen! If all must suffer to pay for the eternal harmony, what have children to do with it, tell me, please? It's beyond all comprehension why they should suffer, and why they should pay for the harmony. Why should they, too, furnish material to enrich the soil for the harmony of the future? I understand solidarity in sin among men. I understand solidarity in retribution, too; but there can be no such solidarity with children. And if it is really true that they must share responsibility for all their fathers' crimes, such a truth is not of this world and is beyond my comprehension. Some jester will say, perhaps, that the child would have grown up and have sinned, but you see he didn't grow up, he was torn to pieces by the dogs, at eight years old. Oh, Alyosha, I am not blaspheming! I understand, of course, what an upheaval of the universe it will be, when everything in heaven and earth blends in one hymn of praise and everything that lives and has lived cries aloud: 'Thou art just, O Lord, for Thy ways are revealed.' When the mother embraces the fiend who threw her child to the dogs, and all three cry aloud with tears, 'Thou art just, O Lord!' then, of course, the crown of knowledge will be reached and all will be made clear. But what pulls me up here is that I can't accept that harmony. And while I am on earth, I make haste to take my own measures. You see, Alyosha, perhaps it really may happen that if I live to that moment, or rise again to see it, I, too, perhaps, may cry aloud with the rest, looking at the mother embracing the child's torturer, 'Thou art just, O Lord!' But I don't want to cry aloud then. While there is still time, I hasten to protect myself, and so I renounce the higher harmony altogether. It's not worth the tears of that one tortured child who beat itself on the breast with its little fist and prayed in its stinking outhouse, with its unexpiated tears to 'dear, kind God'! It's not worth it, because those tears are unatoned for. They must be atoned for, or there can be no harmony. But how? How are you going to atone for them? Is it possible? By their being avenged? But what do I care for avenging them? What do I care for a hell for oppressors? What good can hell do, since those children have already been tortured? And what becomes of harmony, if there is hell? I want to forgive. I want to embrace. I don't want more suffering. And if the sufferings of children go to swell the sum of sufferings which was necessary to pay for truth, then I protest that the truth is not worth such a price. I don't want the mother to embrace the oppressor who threw her son to the dogs! She dare not forgive him! Let her forgive him for herself, if she will, let her forgive the torturer for the immeasurable suffering of her mother's heart. But the sufferings of her tortured child she has no right to forgive; she dare not forgive the torturer, even if the child were to forgive him! And if that is so, if they dare not forgive, what becomes of harmony? Is there in the whole world a being who would have the right to forgive and could forgive? I don't want harmony. From love for humanity I don't want it. I would rather be left with the unavenged suffering. I would rather remain with my unavenged suffering and unsatisfied indignation, *even if I were wrong*. Besides, too high a price is asked for harmony; it's beyond our means to pay so much to enter on it. And so I hasten to give back my entrance ticket, and if I am an honest man I am bound to give it back as soon as possible. And that I am doing. It's not God that I don't accept, Alyosha, only I most respectfully return Him the ticket."

> "It's not God that I don't accept, Alyosha, only I most respectfully return Him the ticket."
>
> – IVAN KARAMOZOV (in Fyodor Dostoyevsky's *The Brothers Karamazov*)

Doubt, however, is not limited to those of faith, and the more vicious attacks on the Judeo-Christian tradition challenge not only the theology of religion but its underlying motivation. It could be that religious faith is a perfectly understandable expression of hope for a better world or an appeal for some justice that transcends what we witness here in secular life. But it has been charged that religion is something more problematic than this, an escape from worldly responsibilities, an irresponsible reaction to a world we cannot cope with, or perhaps a childish unwillingness to give up an illusion of security that we ought to have outgrown in adolescence. These various views have been forcefully argued by Karl Marx, Friedrich Nietzsche, and Sigmund Freud.

Karl Marx is often quoted for his incisive critique of religion. His point is simple, and he makes it powerfully. Humans invent religion to escape their intolerable social conditions. And once we see this, we should reject religion as an escape and turn instead to the correction of those conditions that make such an escape necessary.

FROM *Critique of Hegel's Philosophy of Right* BY **Karl Marx**[24]

The basis of irreligious criticism is this: *man makes religion;* religion does not make man. Religion is indeed man's self-consciousness and self-awareness so long as he has not found himself or has lost himself again. But *man* is not an abstract being, squatting outside the world. Man *is the human world*, a state, society. This state, this society, produce religion which is an *inverted world consciousness*, because they are an *inverted world*. Religion is the general theory of this world, its encyclopedic compendium, its logic in popular form, its spiritual *point d'honneur*, its enthusiasm, its moral sanction, its solemn complement, its general basis of consolation and justification. It is *the fantastic realization* of the *human being* inasmuch as the human being possesses no true reality. The struggle against religion is, therefore, indirectly a struggle against *that world* whose spiritual *aroma* is religion.

Religious suffering is at the same time an *expression* of real suffering and a *protest* against real suffering. Religion is the sigh of the oppressed creature, the sentiment of a heartless world, and the soul of soulless conditions. It is the *opium* of the people.

The abolition of religion as the *illusory* happiness of men, is a demand for their *real* happiness. The call to abandon their illusions about their condition is a *call to abandon a condition which requires illusions*. The criticism of religion is, therefore, *the embryonic criticism of this vale of tears* of which religion is the *halo*.

Criticism has plucked the imaginary flowers from the chain, not in order that man shall bear the chain without caprice or consolation but so that he shall cast off the chain and pluck the living flower. The criticism of religion disillusions man so that he will think, act and fashion his reality as a man who has lost his illusions and regained his reason; so that he will revolve about himself as his own true sun. Religion is only the illusory sun about which man revolves so long as he does not revolve about himself.

. . .

It is clear that the arm of criticism cannot replace the criticism of arms. Material force can only be overthrown by material force; but theory itself becomes a material force when it has seized the masses. Theory is capable of seizing the masses when it demonstrates ad hominem, and it demonstrates ad hominem as soon as it becomes radical. To be radical is to grasp things by the root. But for man the root is man himself. What proves beyond doubt the radicalism of German theory, and thus its practical energy, is that it begins from the resolute *positive* abolition of religion. The criticism of religion ends with the doctrine that *man is the supreme being for man*. It

Karl Marx (1818-1883)

A German philosopher and social theorist who formulated the philosophical basis for one of the most cataclysmic political ideologies of the twentieth century. He received a doctorate in philosophy but could not teach in Germany because of his radical views. He spent most of his life abroad, in Paris, Brussels, and London, developing his theories and writing for various journals and newspapers (including the *New York Herald Tribune*). His savage attacks on established beliefs and advocacy of revolution were constant throughout his life and forced him into exile. As a young man, he wrote a devastating critique of G. W. F. Hegel, whom he had studied and followed as a young student and whose concept of "dialectic" he used in developing a powerful social-political philosophy of class conflict and economic determination.

FIG. 1.32 Marx thought that religion encouraged people to acquiesce in injustice in this world by convincing them that justice would be meted out in the next life.
(© SuperStock / SuperStock)

ends, therefore, with the *categorical imperative to overthrow all those conditions* in which man is an abased, enslaved, abandoned, contemptible being—conditions which can hardly be better described than in the exclamation of the Frenchman on the occasion of a proposed tax upon dogs: "Wretched dogs! They want to treat you like men!"

Fifty years later, **Friedrich Nietzsche** opened an even more blistering attack on religion in general and on Christianity in particular. Christianity is accused of being nothing other than rationalizations for impotence, an expression of everything that is most contemptible in human nature.

FROM *Beyond Good and Evil*
BY **Friedrich Nietzsche**[25]

The Jewish "Old Testament," the book of divine justice, has people, things, and speeches in such grand style that Greek and Indian literature have nothing to set beside it. One stands in awe and trembling before this monstrous vestige of what humanity once was, and has sorrowful thoughts about old Asia and its protruding little peninsula Europe, which would like to stand out over and against Asia as the "progress of humanity." To be sure: there will be nothing in these ruins to astonish or distress anyone who is just a wretched tame house pet himself and understands only house pet needs (like our

Friedrich Nietzsche (1844-1900)
A German philosopher who declared himself the archenemy of traditional morality and Christianity and spent much of his life writing polemics against them. His most sustained and vicious attack (partly included in the text) is in one of his last books, *Antichrist* (1888). Although Nietzsche is generally known as an immoralist (a name he chose for himself), his moral philosophy is actually an attack on one conception of morality in order to replace it with another. The morality he attacked was the morality of traditional Christianity as defined by Kant. The morality he sought to defend was the ancient morality of personal excellence, as defined by Aristotle. Nietzsche referred to the first as "slave morality," suggesting that it was suitable only for the weak and servile, and to the latter as "master morality," suggesting that it was the morality of the strong and independent few.

cultured people of today, including the Christians of "cultured" Christianity)—the taste for the Old Testament is a touchstone for the "great" and the "small"—perhaps he will find the New Testament, the book of mercy, more to his taste (it is full of the true delicate musty odor of devotee and petty soul). To have glued this New Testament, a kind of rococo of taste in every respect, on to the Old Testament to make a single book, a "Bible," a "book in itself": this is perhaps the greatest piece of temerity and "sin against the spirit" that literary Europe has on its conscience.

FROM *The Antichrist*
BY **Friedrich Nietzsche**[26]

Christianity should not be prettified and ornamented: it has waged deadly war against the higher type of human being; it has raised an edict against all the basic instincts . . . and out of these instincts it has distilled evil and the Evil One: the strong as the characteristically reprehensible, the "reprobate." Christianity takes sides with everything weak and base, with every failure; it has made an ideal of what *contradicts* the instinct of strong life to maintain itself; it has corrupted the reason of even the strongest in

[25] Friedrich Nietzsche, *Beyond Good and Evil*, trans. Clancy Martin.
[26] Friedrich Nietzsche, *The Antichrist*, trans. Clancy Martin.

FIG. 1.33 Casfar David Friedrich, *Wanderer–Above a Sea of Fog* (ca. 1817). Nietzsche believed that traditional Christianity has undermined believers' psychological well-being; consequently, he thought that a cultural turn toward atheism could represent a move toward greater spiritual health. *(Bildarchiv Preussischer Kulturbesitz / Art Resource, NY)*

spirit . . . in its fear of them it has bred the opposite sort: —the house pet, the herd animal, the sick human animal: —the Christian. As long as the priest is considered a *higher* type of human—this *career* refuter, slanderer, and poisoner of life—there is no answer to the question: what is truth? For truth has been stood on her head when the conscious proponent of nothingness and negation is welcomed as the representative of "truth." In Christianity, morality and religion do not have even a single point of contact with reality.

. . .

This world of *pure fiction* is greatly inferior to the world of dreams, so far as the latter *mirrors* reality, and the former falsifies, devalues, and negates reality. . . . Who alone has good cause to lie his way out of reality? One who suffers from it!

. . .

The Christian concept of God—God as god of the sick, God as a spider, God as spirit—is among the most corrupt concepts of the divine the world has ever accepted. It may well represent the low-water mark in the descending development of divine kinds.

. . .

This pitiful god of Christian monotonotheism! This hybrid creation of decay, this mix of zero, concept and contradiction, in which every instinct of decadence, every timorousness and exhaustion of the soul, finds its justification!

FROM *The Gay Science*
BY **Friedrich Nietzsche**[27]

The meaning of our cheerfulness.—The greatest recent event—that "God is dead," that belief in the Christian god has become unbelievable—is even now beginning to cast its first shadows over Europe. At least for the few, whose eyes—in whose eyes the *suspicion* is strong and fine enough for this spectacle, some sun seems to have set and some ancient deep trust has been transformed into doubt; to them our old world with every day looks more like evening: more mistrustful, stranger, "older." But in general one may say: the event itself is much too great, too distant, too removed from the capacity of the many for understanding, for even its harbingers to be supposed as having *arrived* yet. One should suppose all the less that many people yet know *what*

[27] Friedrich Nietzsche, *The Gay Science*, trans. Clancy Martin.

this event truly means—and how much must collapse now that this belief has been undermined, because it is built on the foundation of this belief, is supported by it, has developed on it: for example, our entire European morality. This long abundance and succession of collapse, destruction, ruin and disaster that is now upon us—who today could guess enough of it to feel the need to play the teacher and first prophet of this monstrous logic of horror, the proclaimer of a darkness and an eclipse of the sun the like of which has probably yet to occur on earth?

· · ·

The first consequences, the consequences for *us*, are just the opposite of what one might expect: they are not at all sad and dark but rather like a new barely describable sort of light, happiness, relief, exhilaration, encouragement, daybreak. Indeed, we philosophers and "free spirits" feel, when we hear the news that "the old god is dead," as if a new dawn shines on us; our hearts over flow with gratitude, astonishment, presentiments, expectations. At long last the horizon looks free to us once more, even if it is not bright; at long last our ships may venture out once more, venture out to brave any risk; all the daring of the lover of knowledge is allowed once more; the sea, *our* sea, lies open once more; perhaps never yet has there been such an "open sea."

Finally, in the twentieth century, the attack was given a psychoanalytic foundation by **Sigmund Freud**, who also reduces the grand aspirations of religion to mere illusions, but, even worse, the illusions of an insecure child who has never properly grown up.

 FROM *The Future of an Illusion*
BY **Sigmund Freud**[28]

...the psychical origin of religious ideas. These, which are given out as teachings, are not precipitates of experience or end results of thinking: they are illusions, fulfilments of the oldest, strongest and most urgent wishes of mankind. The secret of their strength lies in the strength of those wishes. As we already know, the terrifying impression of helplessness in childhood aroused the need for protection—for protection through love—which was provided by the father; and the recognition that this helplessness lasts throughout life made it necessary to cling to the existence of a father, but this time a more powerful one. Thus the benevolent rule of a divine Providence allays our fear of the dangers of life; the establishment of a moral world-order ensures the fulfilment of the demands of justice, which have so often remained unfulfilled in human civilization; and the prolongation of earthly existence in a future life provides the local and temporal framework in which these wish-fulfilments shall take place. Answers to the riddles that tempt the curiosity of man, such as how the universe began or what the relation is between body and mind, are developed in conformity with the underlying assumptions of this system. It is an enormous relief to the individual psyche if the conflicts of its childhood arising from the father-complex—conflicts which it has never wholly overcome—are removed from it and brought to a solution which is universally accepted.

When I say that these things are all illusions, I must define the meaning of the word. An illusion is not the same thing as an error; nor is it necessarily an error. Aristotle's belief that vermin are developed out of dung (a belief to which ignorant people

"Illusions need not necessarily be false—that is to say, unrealizable or in contradiction of reality."

– SIGMUND FREUD

28 From *The Future of an Illusion* by Sigmund Freud, trans. James Strachey. Translation Copyright © 1961 by James Strachey, renewed 1989 by Alix Strachey. Reprinted by permission of W. W. Norton & Company, Inc.

Sigmund Freud (1856–1939)

An Austrian psychiatrist and neurologist and founder of the psychoanalytic school of psychology.

FIG. 1.34 Freud contended that religion offers illusory wish fulfillment that indulges immaturity. *(Adoc-photos / Art Resource, NY)*

still cling) was an error; so was the belief of a former generation of doctors that *tabes dorsalis* is the result of sexual excess. It would be incorrect to call these errors illusions. On the other hand, it was an illusion of Columbus's that he had discovered a new searoute to the Indies. The part played by his wish in this error is very clear. One may describe as an illusion the assertion made by certain nationalists that the Indo-Germanic race is the only one capable of civilization; or the belief, which was only destroyed by psychoanalysis, that children are creatures without sexuality. What is characteristic of illusions is that they are derived from human wishes. In this respect they come near to psychiatric delusions. But they differ from them, too, apart from the more complicated structure of delusions. In the case of delusions, we emphasize as essential their being in contradiction with reality. Illusions need not necessarily be false—that is to say, unrealizable or in contradiction of reality. . . . Thus we call a belief an illusion when a wish-fulfilment is a prominent factor in its motivation, and in doing so we disregard its relations to reality, just as the illusion itself sets no store by verification.

In conclusion, Freud agrees with Marx and Nietzsche that the only proper concern of man is humanity. But is this necessarily an indictment of religion? Freud was fascinated by Jewish mysticism, and Nietzsche offered extravagant praise of Buddhism. For many people, religion is an emotional support without which they could not even function as human beings. Many Christians, Muslims, and Jews have used their religion as a metaphysical basis for concerted social activism and humanism—but also for "holy" wars. And therein lies a problem. No one can deny that there have been thousands of atrocities—to both spirit and body—in the name of religion. But is such cruelty essential to religion? Most believers would deny this. And no one has demonstrated that religion is as easily dispensable as some of its critics have suggested. (Even Nietzsche had his serious doubts.)

- Explain Marx's remark that religion is "the opium of the people."
- What are the human characteristics that religion emphasizes, and why does Nietzsche find them so contemptible?
- What does Freud mean when he says that the religious person is like a child?

SUMMARY AND CONCLUSION

Religion is one of the most important, and therefore one of the most controversial and sensitive, parts of our lives. It is therefore also one of the most important, controversial, and sensitive areas of philosophy. Initially, religion seems to be part of metaphysics, an examination of the way the world really is. But we have seen that religion is much more than a search for knowledge; it is also a search for meaning, for morality, for ultimate justice, and for a type of experience that is like no other. Philosophy of religion begins as a metaphysical discipline, often attempting to define a supreme entity of a certain type (God) and to demonstrate His existence through rational arguments and proofs. But many philosophers and religious people deny that such a metaphysical approach is either possible or appropriate. Some philosophers deny that we can *know* God but insist that it is necessary to have faith. And while some philosophers interpret this faith as a form of rationality, others claim that it is strictly an emotional commitment beyond the domain of rational argument and understanding.

These various approaches to the philosophy of religion are all very much alive, and so, too, are the doubts that accompany each approach. Those who believe that we can know God are at odds with those who deny that we can know Him. Those who insist on faith disagree among themselves whether this faith can be or ought to be justified. There are those who want to believe in God but find that certain problems (for example, the problem of evil) make it difficult or impossible for them to do so. There are those who see belief in God as an outmoded belief, left over from the inadequate science and metaphysics of previous centuries. And there are those who attack religion as not only outmoded, but as insidious, as a symptom of decadence, weakness, or immaturity. But in the face of these various doubts and attacks, the world's religious traditions continue to develop their responses and to raise new questions. Religion is humanity's oldest philosophy, and it is still the most controversial area of philosophical concern.

CHAPTER REVIEW QUESTIONS

1. Give Anselm's version of the ontological argument for the existence of God and Descartes' revision of that argument. Then explain Kant's attack on the argument. Do you agree with Kant that existence is not a predicate? Can you think of any other apparent predicates that are not actual predicates? If existence is a special case, why?

2. Hume argues that if God built the universe, he was not a very good architect. Some theists respond that the universe was built as well as it could be and that any changes would only make it worse. Do you find this response convincing? The poet Wallace Stevens once wrote a letter to his wife claiming that "with a wishing lamp and a bucket of sand I could make a world better than this one." Do you agree with Stevens? Can you imagine a better world? What would you change?

3. Explain how Freud's attack on Christianity developed from Marx's and Nietzsche's critiques. What does Freud mean by the word *illusion*? Are illusions always bad? Could Christianity and other forms of religion be good, helpful illusions? How would Nietzsche respond to your answer?

4. What are the differences between the rationalist and irrationalist views of faith? Which do you find convincing?

5. How would you characterize the pragmatic argument for God's existence? What are its weaknesses, if any? Do you think that it undermines belief in God?

6. What is the problem of evil and what are the theists' responses to it? Which of their arguments do you find convincing, if any?

KEY TERMS

Abrahamic religions
agnostic
anthropomorphic

argument from design
atheist
Bhagavadgītā ("Gītā")

Brahma ("Brahman")
Buddha
cosmological argument

KEY TERMS *cont'd*

Deism	Krishna	pantheism
Dharma	mysticism	problem of evil
faith	nihility	subjective truth
Four Noble Truths	omnipotent	Sufism
God	omnipresent	teleological argument
illusion	omniscient	theist
ineffable	ontological argument	transcendence
karma		

BIBLIOGRAPHY AND FURTHER READING

Some good general collections on religion and the philosophy of religion are Willard G. Oxtoby, *World Religion*, 2 vols. (New York: Oxford University Press, 1996); Stephen Phillips, *Philosophy of Religion: A Global Approach* (Belmont, CA: Wadsworth, 1995); Steven M. Cahn, ed., *Ten Essential Texts in the Philosophy of Religion* (New York: Oxford University Press, 2004); Louis S. Pojman and Michael Rea, eds., *Philosophy of Religion: An Anthology*, 5th ed. (Belmont, CA: Wadsworth, 2007); Charles Taliaferro and Paul J. Griffiths, eds., *Philosophy of Religion: An Anthology* (New York: Wiley-Blackwell, 2003); and William J. Wainwright, *Philosophy of Religion*, 2nd ed. (Belmont, CA: Wadsworth Press, 1998).

A general discussion of religious issues is J. Hick, *Faith and Knowledge*, 2nd ed. (Ithaca, NY: Cornell University Press, 1966).

A good series of lectures on the problem of evil is Peter Van Inwagen, *The Problem of Evil* (New York: Oxford University Press, 2008).

David Hume's *Dialogues on Natural Religion* 2nd ed. (Indianapolis, IN: Hackett, 1998) makes excellent and provocative reading.

A convenient collection of Søren Kierkegaard's writings is W. H. Auden, *The Living Thoughts of Kierkegaard* (New York: New York Review of Books Classics, 1999).

Two useful studies of Kierkegaard are John D. Caputo and Simon Critchley, *How to Read Kierkegaard* (New York: W. W. Norton, 2008); and Louis Mackey, *Kierkegaard: A Kind of Poet* (Philadelphia: University of Pennsylvania Press, 1972).

The selections from Karl Marx, Friedrich Nietzsche, and Sigmund Freud are developed in Karl Marx, *Early Writings*, trans. T. Bottomore (New York: McGraw-Hill, 1963); Friedrich Nietzsche, "The Antichrist" in *The Viking Portable Nietzsche*, trans. Walter Kaufmann (New York: Viking, 1976); and Sigmund Freud, *The Future of an Illusion*, trans. W. D. Robson-Scott, rev. ed. by James Strachey (Garden City, NY: Doubleday, 1964).

On medieval religions, see A. Hyman and J. Walsh, *Philosophy in the Middle Ages*, 3rd ed. (Indianapolis, IN: Hackett, 2010).

For more on Nishitani's perspective, see Nishitani Keiji, *Religion and Nothingness* (Berkeley: University of California Press, 1982). See also D. T. Suzuki, *Zen Buddhism* (New York: Doubleday, 1956).

2 | Reality

Well over three thousand years ago, philosophers in India, in the *Rg Veda* (the oldest of those holy books called the *Vedas*), contemplated the nature and origins of the whole of reality ("Brahman"), concluding, with considerable skepticism, that reality as such was not, or at least not normally, known by us, and perhaps it could not be known at all. Now, at the beginning of the twenty-first century, some philosophers and some of our best-known physicists have come to believe that ultimate reality, those evasive particles that seem to multiply as the experiments get more sophisticated and the origin of everything ("the big bang") gets more and more (rather than less and less) mysterious, and some theorists even suggest that we *create* reality through our observation of it and there is no independent reality at all.

These two questions about the ultimate nature of reality and the origins of the universe (or, from the Greek *cosmos*, thus, **cosmology** the nature of the universe, and **cosmogony**, the origins of the universe) have defined much of philosophy from most ancient times until today. (And we have no reason to suppose that the questions are getting any easier.) The way the question is asked, of course, varies considerably with the growth of science and among various religious and cultural contexts, but they are, in one sense, the most fundamental of philosophical questions.

A. "The Way the World Really Is"

Because it was a Greek who coined the term *philosophy* and in Greece where philosophy was first recognized as a formal discipline, Western philosophers today often refer to the first Greek thinkers as the first "philosophers." Philosophy in this sense is said to begin with a seemingly odd claim made by the Greek philosopher **Thales** on the coast of Turkey sometime around 580 B.C.E. He suggested that the source of everything was water. The earth floats upon water, and it and all things on it are made of water. Aristotle later called his theory "childish," but he also acknowledged that his was the "oldest view that has been transmitted to us" (in his essay "On the Heavens"). In his *Metaphysics*, **Aristotle** went on to consider Thales' view in some detail:

> "There must be some nature—either one or more than one—from which the other things come into being."
>
> – ARISTOTLE

FROM *Metaphysics* BY **Aristotle**[1]

Most of the first philosophers thought that principles in the form of matter were the only principles of all things. For they say that the element and first principle of the things that exist is that from which they all are and from which they first come into being and into which they are finally destroyed, its substance remaining and its properties changing. . . . There must be some nature—either one or more than one—from which the other things come into being, it being preserved. But as to the number and form of this sort of principle, they do not all agree. Thales, the founder of this kind of philosophy, says that it is water (that is why he declares that the earth rests on water). He perhaps came to acquire this belief from seeing that the nourishment of everything is moist and that heat itself comes from this and lives by this (for that from which anything comes into being is its first principle)—he came to his belief both for this reason and because the seeds of everything have a moist nature, and water is the natural principle of moist things.

Thales (6th century B.C.E.)

The first known Greek philosopher, who taught that all things are ultimately composed of water.

So too, the commentator Simplicius suggested that "Thales was the first to introduce the study of nature to the Greeks." His seemingly simple claim, that the world rests on water, was in fact one of the most remarkable claims of the ancient world, not because it is so

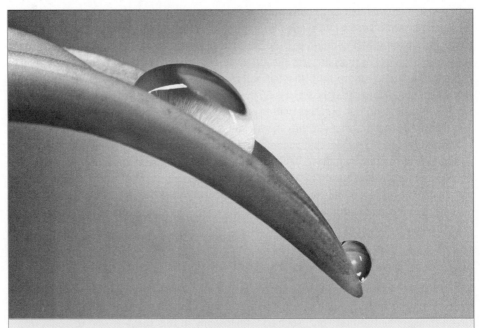

FIG. 2.1 Is it so implausible that water is the source of all things? *(Image © Constant, 2011. Used under license from Shutterstock.com)*

[1] Reprinted by permission of the publishers and the Loeb Classical Library from *Aristotle: Metaphysics, Volume XVII*, trans. H. Tredennick, Cambridge, MA: Harvard University Press, 1933.

implausible (as his own students pointed out to him) but because it was one of the first recorded attempts to describe "the way the world really is," beyond all appearances and day-to-day opinions. Accordingly, Thales' theory marks the beginning of Western science as well as philosophy. He was the first Greek thinker to break with common sense and religion and offer a general theory about the ultimate nature of reality. In place of mythological accounts of nature and human behavior in terms of divine agencies (gods, goddesses, and spirits), he and other thinkers of the period provided explanations in terms of laws and abstract generalizations. Knowledge became an end in itself, one of the noblest pursuits of humanity.

- Do you consider Thales' theory that the source of everything is water "childish"? How would you make his theory more plausible?
- In what ways are contemporary physicists' theories that subatomic particles are the basis of the physical world anticipated by Thales?

B. The First Greek Philosophers

We are all aware that the way the world really is may not correspond to our everyday views of the world, the way it seems to be. For example, we casually talk of "sunrises" and "sunsets," and surely it does seem as if the sun goes "up" and "down," while we and our earth stay in place. It took several thousand years for people in general to recognize that, despite appearances, our earth actually moves around the sun. We now accept that without question, even if there is little in our everyday experience to support it. Similarly, consider the chair on which you are sitting: Does it seem to you that it is composed mostly of empty space and tiny electrically charged colorless particles whirling about at fantastic speeds? Of course not, but modern science has taught you that "solid" objects are indeed made up of just such spaces and particles. The world is not as it seems, and the beginnings of both philosophy and science were the first attempts of men and women to see beyond their "commonsense" views of things and try to find the reality behind them.

Although the pre-Socratic Greeks were the first thinkers to call themselves "philosophers," we can look back from our modern vantage point to many ancient traditions we might want to call "philosophical," in the sense that they looked beyond ordinary experience for an understanding of "reality." The ancient philosophers did not have the advantage of either our scientific sophistication or a long history of philosophical thinking to give them support. Yet, there were lots of new and profoundly thoughtful opinions offered by the ancients about reality, whatever the differences in the ways different thinkers from different places thought about the world. The first investigations into the ultimate nature of reality, among which we include Thales' account, appeared in the middle of the first millennium B.C.E.

What is this "Being"? What is the way the world really is? How do you answer that question? Very likely you will appeal to the authority of modern science, and that is probably a reasonable beginning. But you know that the "science" of one generation is seen as the superstitions of another. (Once people believed that the earth was flat.) You have probably, at least once in your school career, caught one of the "authorities"—perhaps a teacher, perhaps even a noted scientist—in a mistake. Can we simply accept what scientists tell us without question, any more than Descartes could accept the teachings of his teachers without question? Have you ever examined the evidence for the theory that the earth goes around the sun? If not, why should you believe it? Or, to take a very different example, scientists are generally agreed that some version of Darwin's theory of evolution is true. Does that mean that you have to believe it? Many people do not, because it seems to contradict the story of creation in the Bible. You have to decide which to believe. Even within science there are always disagreements and debates. There are different theories to answer the same questions, and you have to decide. Which are you to believe?

Your view of reality is influenced by modern science but it is also influenced by twenty-five hundred years of philosophy, even if you've never studied it before. We can say, with some confidence, that we know much more about the world than the ancient philosophers. But we must not be too confident. Not only are there still many scientific problems unsolved, there are and always will be conflicting views of how we are to see our world in more general terms. How much faith should we have in religion? How much should we see the world as a world of people and how much as a world of physical objects? How much should we accept "common sense" (which changes all the time) and how much should we indulge in scientific and philosophical speculation (which changes all the time also)?

1. The Ionian Naturalists

Thales' approach was somewhat different from that of the thinkers of other early traditions; he is rightly credited with being the first in the line of philosophers of which Socrates was the culmination (called the "pre-Socratics"). Thales' answer, that ultimate reality is water, should not surprise nearly so much as the fact that he attempted such a theory at all. Indeed, we should be impressed by the fact that he even asked "What is the world really like?" because as far as we know, no one had attempted to ask such a question in such a way before him.

Thales was not willing to accept the opinions and mythologies that had been handed down for generations. He insisted, instead, on observing the world for himself, on thinking out his own answer, and on discussing it with his friends and neighbors, many of whom, no doubt, thought that he was slightly peculiar. (It is also said, however, that his cosmic speculations helped him to make a fortune in the olive oil business. No doubt his neighbors respected that.)

Anaximander (611–547? B.C.E.)

A pre-Socratic philosopher who taught that reality is ultimately composed of an indeterminate something (the *apeiron*) that we can never know directly through experience.

FIG. 2.2 The pre-Socratic philosopher Anaximander demonstrates the use of a sundial on this clock by Antoine Beranger (1785–1867). *(Réunion des Musées Nationaux / Art Resource, NY)*

Thales was the first of a group of philosophers—or rather, the first of several groups of philosophers—scattered around the various Greek islands and the coasts of Asia Minor, or Ionia, who lived in the sixth and fifth centuries B.C.E., just before the time of Socrates. Accordingly, they are called Ionians, one group of the pre-Socratics. Their opinions varied greatly. Among them they developed a wide range of systematic views of the universe and the ultimate nature of reality. Unlike Socrates and most later philosophers, they were not very concerned with questions of method. They went straight to the heart of the question, to the nature of the universe itself. As we shall see, some of them came strikingly close to our modern scientific conceptions.

The idea that everything was water did not satisfy Thales' friends and students. They appreciated his attempt to find the "One Reality," but they thought that it must be something else. Thales' first student, named **Anaximander**, argued against his teacher that some things, for example, the dry, dusty cliffs of Asia Minor, could not possibly be made of water, which was naturally wet and never dry. Anaximander was the first recorded student to talk back to his teacher (which in philosophy, unlike most other subjects, is considered a virtue rather than a discourtesy). Thales had made the first gigantic step, rejecting the "obvious" answers of common sense and trying to find out "the way the world really is." But notice that Thales' answer to that question still appeals to a commonsense ingredient, water, which is so familiar to us. Thales' defense of his thesis also depended on some very commonsensical claims: for example, the idea that if you dig deep enough into the earth, you will eventually hit water.

Once Thales had made the break with common sense and said that the way the world really is need not be at all like the way it seems to us, it was no longer necessary to suppose that reality was anything like our experiences. Anaximander, consequently, argued that ultimate reality could not be composed of any of the then-known elements—earth, air, fire, or water—since these were each so different from the others. They might be mixed together, as when earth and water are mixed to make mud or clay, but it made no sense to suppose that any of them might really be made up of any of the others. So Anaximander suggested that the ultimate nature of reality was something else—let us simply call it "primordial stuff"—that is not like anything we could ever experience.

The word Anaximander actually used was the **apeiron**, which is sometimes translated as "the indefinite" or "the unlimited." The *apeiron*, or "primordial stuff," was a chaos or void, which yielded the variety of things in the world. This notion of "stuff" was a second major step in philosophy and science. Today, we feel comfortable with the idea that things are made of "stuff" (atoms and molecules) that we never experience in everyday life. But in the ancient world, this suggestion must have seemed extremely exciting.

Anaximander's student, **Anaximenes**, thought his teacher's notion of "stuff" was too mysterious, but he also rejected Thales' theory and replaced it with the idea that air is the basic "stuff." Just as our soul, which is air, integrates us, so breath and air surround the whole cosmos. Air

FIG. 2.3 Where does the water end and the air begin? *(Image © Marko5, 2011. Used under license from Shutterstock.com)*

Anaximenes (6th century B.C.E.)

A pre-Socratic philosopher who taught that the basic element of reality is air and that all things in the universe are different forms of air.

makes up the other elements and the various things of the world by becoming thicker and thinner. (Think of steam condensing to form water and then ice.) Anaximenes thus introduced the idea that changes in the quantity of basic elements can produce changes in quality as well–a key principle of modern science.

- How is Anaximander's theory that "primordial stuff" is the ultimate reality an improvement on Thales' theory? In what ways is it more problematic?
- To what extent must you reject "common sense" when trying to explain reality? What are the limitations to such speculation and theorizing?

2. Monism, Materialism, and Immaterial "Stuff"

The attempt to reduce all of the varied things in the world to one kind of thing as Thales and his students did with water, air, and *apeiron*, is called **monism**. It is the search for ultimate reality, which might be very different from the appearance of everyday life, that has motivated philosophy and science for twenty-five hundred years. So the debate began: Was the world really made of water? Perhaps, thought Thales' students, it is some other kind of "stuff." Today, the debate continues: Is everything made up of matter, or energy, or matter-energy? Are there basic particles that cannot be reduced to anything else? Scientists once thought that atoms were such particles; then they discovered electrons, protons, and neutrons that made up atoms. Since then, they have discovered dozens of other particles, and today they are debating a mysterious particle called a quark, which physicists now think may provide the ultimate answer to Thales' ancient question. But notice that all of these views are strictly physical. That is, they are concerned about basic questions of what we now call physics and chemistry, concerned about the material "stuff" of which all things are composed. This was true of Thales; and it is still true of modern "quark" theorists. Accordingly, the philosophies of all of these thinkers can be called **materialism**, the view that reality is ultimately composed of some kind of material "stuff." (In this context, "materialism" does not mean concern about the material things in life–money, cars, jewelry, or getting a new garbage disposal every year.)

If you think like a physical scientist, the idea that the universe is made up of some kind of material "stuff" sounds very plausible. In fact, you might wonder, what else could it be made of? Consider this: There are some things in the universe that could not plausibly be made of material "stuff." For example, what about your thoughts and feelings? Are they simply bits of matter, or are they composed of some entirely different kind of "stuff," perhaps some kind of mental or spiritual "stuff"? Some early philosophers, particularly in Asia, claimed that reality was not made of just physical elements, like water, air, or even the *apeiron*, but rather that reality was inherently spiritual. Many of these thinkers claimed that

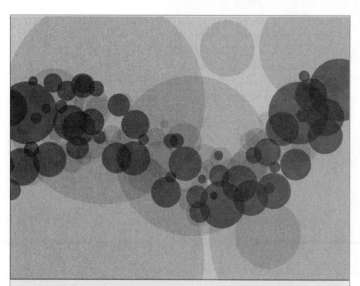

FIG. 2.4 The idea that the universe is made of atoms traces back to the pre-Socratics. *(Image © Alekksall, 2011. Used under license from Shutterstock.com)*

the primordial "stuff" was divine, or godly. We will see that in Greece as well, the pre-Socratic philosopher **Heraclitus** was already groping for a conception of an immaterial "stuff," something which was not material but rather spiritual or nonphysical. ("Immaterial," in a philosophical context, does not mean, as it does in law, "irrelevant.")

3. Heraclitus

Back in Greece, another pre-Socratic philosopher of the same period, named Heraclitus, quite independently defended the idea that fire was the fundamental "stuff" of reality. For Heraclitus, however, "fire" seemed to connote both the "natural element" it was for the Ionians and a "spiritual power." Heraclitus' philosophy was cryptically expressed, and his contemporaries and commentators did not understand him very well, calling him such things as "riddler." Indeed, Heraclitus seems to have been a very cynical person, hardly interested in sharing his thoughts with others. Nonetheless, Heraclitus' profound and provocative claims have been an inspiration to many philosophers since, especially during the nineteenth century.

Heraclitus (5th century B.C.E.)

A pre-Socratic philosopher who taught that the basic element of reality is fire and that all things are in constant flux but yet are unified by an underlying logic or *logos*.

FIG. 2.5 *Heraclitus* by Johann Heinrich Tischbein the Elder *(Bildarchiv Preussischer Kulturbesitz / Art Resource, NY)*

Although Heraclitus claimed that everything in the world was a manifestation of fire, he did not understand fire as an eternal and unchanging origin. Quite the opposite; he claimed that everything that exists is fleeting and changeable. Fire was the element that best explained, or at least represented, the constant flux which Heraclitus claimed underlay nature. "It is in changing that things find repose," [23][2] he stated, indicating that the only thing in the world which is constant is change. "You cannot step into the same river, for other waters are continually flowing on," [21] he claimed. The fact that we refer to "the" river at all, however, shows that something is constant—the very change and flow itself.

"This world that is the same for all," one fragment of his work reads, ". . . ever was and is and shall be ever-living fire that kindles in regular measures and goes out by regular measures." [B 30] This fire, or on the other hand, the fluxuating flow of the river, itself seems to have measure, a rhythm, underlying it. Although the world never stops changing, the measure with which it does so can be understood. So, Heraclitus claimed, our ever-changing reality has a *form* that remains the same, which he called the *Logos*. The *Logos* is the deeper "nature" behind natural, changing things, but you cannot see it, or hear it, or touch it. Thus, "nature loves to hide" [17] beneath the constant flux of the ordinary world we perceive.

Heraclitus' doctrines were provocative, confusing, and sometimes maddening, as the following fragments indicate:

1. Man's character is his fate.

2. Wisdom is one thing: to understand the *logos* by which all things are guided through all things.

3. The sun will not overstep his measures; if he does, the Erinyes [furies], the handmaids of justice, will find him out.

---

[2] This and the following fragments of Heraclitus were translated by John Burnet.

4. You cannot step twice into the same rivers; for fresh waters are ever flowing in upon you.

5. The sea is the purest and the impurest water. Fish can drink it, and it is good for them; to men it is undrinkable and destructive.

6. Good and ill are one.

7. To God all things are fair and good and right, but men hold some things wrong and some right.

8. We must know that war is common to all and strife is justice, and that all things come into being and pass away.

9. The way up and the way down is one and the same.

- How does Heraclitus' view improve upon the materialism/immaterialism debate? (How does Heraclitus bridge the materialism/immaterialism divide?)
- Why does fire seem to be the appropriate element for Heraclitus?
- How can an ever-changing reality or "flux" have form (a logos)?
- What does Heraclitus mean when he says that you can't step into the same river twice?

---

4. Democritus, Atoms, and Pluralism

Not all materialists thought that there was only one ultimate component of reality. A number of philosophers appeared in the ancient world who believed in **pluralism**, that is, that more than one basic "stuff" made up the universe. The best known of the pluralists was **Democritus**, who suggested that the universe was made up of tiny bits of "stuff" that he called *atoms*. These combined together to form the many different things and qualities of the world. (The soul, he suggested, consists of smooth, round, unusually mobile atoms, disposed throughout the body.) Other pluralists stressed the idea that these different bits of "stuff" were very different in kind as well, so that the bits of "stuff" that composed water, for example, would be very different from those that composed fire. You can appreciate how modern these concepts are, given our current ideas in chemistry and physics. These ancient Greek issues and answers have not become obsolete; they have changed and become more refined. Some have been more in favor at one time and others at other times. But they are still very much with us.

Democritus (5th century B.C.E.**)**

A pre-Socratic philosopher who taught that reality is divisible into small "atoms" that combine to make up all things but which themselves are eternal and indivisible.

FIG. 2.6 *Democritus* by Johann Heinrich Tischbein the Elder *(Bildarchiv Preussischer Kulturbesitz / Art Resource, NY)*

5. Animism

These ancient attempts to find out the way the world really is should not be thought of as clumsy attempts to find out the things that modern scientists now know. All the theories of "stuff" were indeed the precursors of modern physics and chemistry. But you can already see that these philosophers were also concerned with what we would call the mental and the spiritual aspects of the world. Even the most materialistic among them, for example, Thales, did not believe that the basic matter of the universe was cold and lifeless "stuff." All of these philosophers believed that the universe itself, as well as everything in it, was alive in at least some limited way. That is, they all believed in **animism**, the doctrine that everything, volcanoes and stones as well as elephants and flowers, are living things. Furthermore, animism has not disappeared because of the advances of science, though in certain periods (like our own) it has been treated less favorably than in others. As recently as the nineteenth century, when physics and chemistry were making some of their most spectacular advances, animism was an extremely popular doctrine, even among scientists. A great many people today still accept a modified version of it. So don't think that the problems discussed by these ancient philosophers have been solved by science or simply gone away. The place of mind and spirit in a world of matter and energy is still among our basic problems. The ancient search for the way the world really is is still very much with us.

- Is Democritus' "atomic" view appealing just because it seems to anticipate modern physics? What are its merits in its own terms?
- What, if anything, is problematic about the claim that reality is made of individual "atoms"?
- How is animism alive today?

FIG. 2.7 Others besides animists may see hints of life in this rock formation. *(Image © javarman, 2011. Used under license from Shutterstock.com)*

6. Pythagoras

Another Greek pre-Socratic philosopher, **Pythagoras**, also attempted to defend a view of the world that did not depend upon the usual kinds of material "stuff." He believed, however, that numbers were the real nature of things, and he taught his students to worship the mathematical order of the universe. He was particularly inspired by new Greek discoveries in music and harmony, and he saw the universe itself as a grand *harmony*. (The term "the music of the spheres" was part of his teachings.) Unlike the other pre-Socratic Greek philosophers we have met, Pythagoras was much more of a religious figure. He was a **mystic** and the leader of a powerful underground cult that believed in reincarnation and the **immortality** of the soul, which he understood as that part of man which is capable of abstract thought, such as mathematics. In accordance with his religion, he gave the mind and the soul a much more prominent place in his view of the world than did other pre-Socratic philosophers.

Despite the sometimes mysterious views of Pythagoras and his cult, he is still recognized as one of the most important thinkers of the ancient world. With Heraclitus, he was one of the first Greeks to defend a view of reality that depended more on logic and thought than purely material "stuff." (The

FIG. 2.8 Pythagoras *(© iStockphoto.com/ HultonArchive)*

Pythagoras (6th–5th century B.C.E.)

A religious mystic who believed that numbers are the essence of all things. One of the pre-Socratics.

"Pythagorean theorem" that students learn in high school is named after him.) It was his discovery and proof.

- How is modern science still very much in the spirit of Pythagoras?
- Why is it necessary, in studying physics or engineering, to know a lot of math?

7. The Appearance/Reality Distinction

All of the thinkers we have considered so far, whatever their differing views and outlooks, have espoused an underlying reality that is different from the way the world appears in one's ordinary experiences. Many, as you will recall, claimed that this underlying reality was One: others claimed that it was diverse and changing. In Greece, the profound discrepancy between the way the world seems and the way it really must be grew wider and wider. The problem has come to be called, not surprisingly, the "appearance/reality distinction."

For Thales, water was the eternal and unchanging element, although the forms it took might be very different and change constantly. For Democritus, atoms were unchanging and indestructible, although the things they combined to compose might change and be destroyed.

Heraclitus' *Logos* and Pythagoras' notion of the immortal "soul" were right on the edge of an investigation into how the world can be both one and many, both changing and stable. Because he believed that the nature of reality was firelike, Heraclitus appreciated the importance of change, as in the flickering of a flame. But he insisted that the *logos*, or logic, underlay the constant changes in the world. We shall see that the presupposition that reality cannot change, however much things seem to change, will remain one of the most important beliefs in Western culture. (In Christianity, for example, the eternal and unchanging nature of God and the human soul are built upon the same philosophical foundation.)

None of the early thinkers, however, offered an explanation as to why the world should appear so different to people than their philosophical investigations led them to believe it really was. Nor did these thinkers present any convincing argument that this should be so. The conflict finally came to a head, and the argument was finally offered. The philosopher who brought it out most clearly was a pre-Socratic Greek, **Parmenides**.

8. Parmenides

Parmenides was an accomplished mathematician who thought far more of the eternal certainties of arithmetic than he did the transient things of everyday experience. He, too, was a monist and believed in a single reality, "the One." Because he shared the assumption that reality must be eternal and unchanging, he came to an astonishing conclusion: This world, the world of our experience, cannot be real! Our world is constantly changing: Objects are created and destroyed; organisms live and die; people grow old, change their appearance, and move from place to place. So this world, with all its changes, could not be the real world, nor could we ever know the real world, since we are as inconstant and changing as the other things of our experience. We are, at best, living in a kind of illusion, not in reality at all!

Parmenides gave us what is sometimes postulated to be the first full-scale philosophical argument.

"It is right that what is for saying and knowing should *be,* for it can be; but nothing can *not be.*"

– PARMENIDES

FROM *Fragments* BY **Parmenides**[3]

(The goddess addresses the young philosopher) Come, I will tell you—and you, take the story when you have heard it—about the only routes there are for seeking to know: One says is and that there is no not being; this is the path of Persuasion (for she goes the way of Truth). The other says is not, and that not being is right. This I point out to you is an utterly ignorant footway. For you could not either get to know that which is not (for it is not attainable) or point to it.

. . . because the same thing is for knowing (or "thinking about") that is for being.

It is right that what is for saying and knowing should *be*, for it can be; but nothing can *not be*.

. . . what is is unborn and imperishable, a whole of a single kind, unshakable and not incomplete. It neither was nor will be, because it is now, all of it together, one cohesive. For what birth will you seek for it? From what would it have grown? I will not let you say or think that it came from what is not. For "is not" cannot be said or thought.

FIG. 2.9 Bust of Parmenides *(Scala / Art Resource, NY)*

Parmenides (5th century B.C.E.)
A pre-Socratic philosopher who taught that reality is eternal and unchanging and that therefore we cannot know it as such.

The argument is: What really is cannot have come to be, for there is nothing outside of reality (what really is) that could have been its source. It is an argument that is the source of much of Western metaphysics. Naturally, no two scholars agree about what it means. But all agree on the main point: that philosophers should be interested only in *what is* in the fullest sense, and not in what is not, or in what sometimes is and sometimes is not. This means that philosophers should not be interested in anything that changes. The weather in Austin is cold one day, and not cold the next. Because it sometimes *is not* cold, it is not a proper subject for the pure philosopher. What is, according to Parmenides, is *unchanging and eternal*.

A simple way to understand the root of this argument is this: We cannot put nonexistent apples in a sack or nonexistent dollars in our wallet. By the same token, Parmenides assumes, we cannot put things that do not exist in our mind; we can only truly think about or know things that *are*. Moreover, only one kind of thought really contains knowledge

THE TORTOISE AND THE HARE

Suppose the tortoise gets a head start of ten feet in a hundred foot race. By the time the hare covers that same ten feet, the tortoise will have walked another foot. But by the time the hare hops that foot, the tortoise will have traveled another inch or two. And by the time the hare travels that inch or two, the tortoise will have walked. . . . How can the hare ever catch the tortoise?

FIG. 2.10 Can the tortoise actually win the race? *(Image © James Steidl, 2011. Used under license from Shutterstock.com)*

---

[3] Parmenides, *Fragments* (B2; B3; B6, ll 1-2; B8, ll 3-9), trans. Paul Woodruff.

of the thing we are thinking about. Suppose we are thinking about beer. It is no use thinking about all the things beer is not—like wine and orange juice. Really thinking about beer is thinking about what beer really is.

Since thinking about change involves thinking about things that are not always the same, it involves thinking, in a sense, about things that are not (as the weather is not cold today). But this, according to the Parmenides assumption, is impossible: We can only think about what is.

Since Thales, the main achievement of philosophy had been to break away from common sense and ordinary experience in order to find out the way the world really is. But now we can see how far away from common sense and ordinary experience this breaking away can lead us. In Parmenides' philosophy, if the results of his logic are incompatible with common sense and ordinary experience, so much the worse for common sense and ordinary experience. The followers of Parmenides, particularly the mathematician **Zeno of Elea**, carried these bizarre conclusions even further. Zeno argued, by means of a series of famous paradoxes, that all motion and change is nothing but an illusion.

- How do you understand the claim that what is cannot have come to be?
- Is it helpful when explaining what something is to explain what it is not? Is it necessary?

9. The Sophists

The following generation of philosophers, who called themselves **sophists** (who have ever since given "sophistry" a bad name because of their rhetorical debating tricks), went even further. They argued that there is no reality, and even if there were, we couldn't know anything about it anyway. (So argued the sophist Gorgias.) The teaching of Protagoras, another sophist, is still well known today; he said, "Man is the measure of all things," which means that there is no reality except for what we take to be reality. We shall later see that the sophists, despite their bad reputation, anticipated many of the most important philosophical concerns of the twentieth century. In particular, they stressed *practical* questions rather than abstract questions, and thus anticipated our own American *pragmatists*. In suggesting that truth is *relative* to people, they anticipated the much-disputed question of *relativism*, the idea that truth might be different at different times for different people. Wandering around the countryside, giving lessons in debating and rhetoric, the sophists used the accomplishments of the earlier philosophers to ridicule philosophy and make fools of practically everyone. That is, until they met Socrates, whose arguments against them changed the course of philosophy and Western thought in general.

- How do you understand the claim that "man is the measure of all things"? What does this mean?
- How might you defend the position that man is the measure of all things?

10. Metaphysics

These various theories about the way the world really is have a proper name. They are called metaphysical doctrines, and the attempt to develop such doctrines, in which we have been taking part for these past pages, is called **metaphysics**. The business of metaphysics is to ask and attempt to answer the most basic questions about the universe, its composition and the "stuff" of which it is composed, the rule of man and mind, and the nature of the immaterial aspects of the universe as well as its physical nature. But now that we are about to discuss metaphysics in its maturity, with Plato and Aristotle, let us also give "stuff" its proper name. It is called (first by Aristotle) **substance**. Accordingly, metaphysics, the study of "the way the world really is," begins with the answers to a series of questions about substance and how it is manifested in particular things (such as people and trees).

1. How many substances are there? (Monism versus pluralism.)

2. What are they? (Water, air, fire, numbers, something unknown, minds, spirit, atoms?)

3. How are individual things composed? (And how do we tell them apart, identify them, reidentify them?)

4. How do different things and (if there is more than one) different substances interact?

5. How did substance come into being? (Created by God? Or has it always been there?)

6. Are substances "in" space and time? Are space and time substances? (If not, what are they?)

The first four questions are usually referred to as **ontology**, the study of being as such. The last questions are referred to as cosmology, the study of the universe. (For the pre-Socratics, these were the same.) Cosmological questions are necessarily shared between philosophers, physicists, and astronomers, and it is impossible for us to give them more than a cursory review within a strictly philosophical book. Ontology, on the other hand, is still considered by many philosophers to be the heart of metaphysics. Therefore, the rest of this chapter will be primarily concerned with ontology.

- How would a materialist understand thoughts and feelings, which seem immaterial? How would a materialist understand numbers (not numerals)?
- Why have philosophers and scientists tried so hard to find the basic "stuff" of the universe? Why not just say "everything is what it is and is not another thing"?

C. Ultimate Reality in the East: India, Persia, and China

1. Reality as One: The Upanishads

While the Ionian Naturalists were pursuing their protoscientific inquiries in Greece, sages in India were developing their own doctrines about the nature of reality which were essentially religious. The earliest articulation of a single ultimate reality appears in the ancient Indian Vedic literature, especially in the appendages called **Upanishads**, "secret doctrines," from which later Eastern religious and spiritual notions emerged. In addition to the innumerable sects and divisions of religious belief and practice traditionally termed Hindu or Buddhist, other Indic religions, such as Jainism and Sikhism, also owe a conceptual debt to the early Upanishads.

"He who experiences all things in the Self and the Self in all things . . . does not fear."

– UPANISHADS

A passage from one of the oldest Upanishads (ca. 800 B.C.E.) relates to the spiritual aspiration that sets the tone for much Upanishadic teaching (whom or what is invoked in this passage is not clear):

 FROM **Upanishads**[4]

From non-being (*asat*) to true being (*sat*) lead me.
From darkness to light lead me.
From death to immortality lead me.

The "seeking" expressed in the early Upanishads centers on "**Brahman**," considered the ultimate reality both of ourselves and of the universe. The Upanishadic notion of Brahman is of a Unity underlying all individual selves and things.

An ocean, a single seer without duality becomes he whose world [of vision] is *brahman*. This is his supreme attainment. This is his highest fulfillment. This is his best world. This is his supreme bliss. Other creatures subsist on a small bit of this bliss.

This "Absolute" is considered to have a peculiar "nature" unlike that of everyday, finite, physical things. Brahman is the source of the universe and the inner reality within everything, yet it is transcendent of "names and forms." In other words, it is transcendent of everything finite. All opposites coincide in Birahman. Although Brahman cannot be understood through thought, it can be discovered through mystical experience.

Not moving the One is swifter than the mind. The gods do not reach That running [always] before. . . . That moves; That moves not. It is far, and It is near. It is within all this; It indeed is outside all this. He who experiences all things in the Self and the Self in all things thereupon does not fear.

Om. That is the Full. This is the Full. From the Full, the Full proceeds. Taking away the Full of the Full, it is just the Full that remains.

The Upanishadic conception of reality is sometimes interpreted as a form of "pantheism," an identification of God and Nature. Whether the following passage illustrates pantheism or not, it reveals a doctrine of divine immanence, of divine *indwelling* in all things. It also suggests an Inner Controller, the Self, who is thought to be "other" than the things, and particular selves, in which it indwells.

Who standing in the earth is other than the earth, whom the earth knows not, whose body the earth is, who within controls the earth, that is this, the Self, the Inner Controller, the Immortal. Who standing in the waters is other than the waters, whom the waters know not, whose body the waters are, that is this, the Self, the Inner Controller. . . . Who standing in the wind is other than the wind, whom the wind knows not, whose body the wind is, who within controls the wind, that is this, the Self, the Inner Controller, the Immortal. . . . Who standing in all beings is other than all beings, whom all beings know not, whose body all beings are, that is this, the Self, the Inner Controller, the Immortal. . . . Who standing in the eye is other than the eye, whom the eye knows not, whose body the eye is, who within controls the

---

[4] These five passages are taken from *Brhadāranyaka* 1.3.28, *Brhadāranyaka* 4.3.32, *Īśā Upanisad* 4-6, *Brhadāranyaka* 5.1.1, *Brhadāranyaka* 3.7.3-3.7.23 passim. *Chāndogya* 6.11, and *Katha* 1.25-27, 2.11-12, and 2.20-23. Unless noted otherwise, all passages were translated by Stephen Phillips.

eye, that is this, the Self, the Inner Controller, the Immortal. Who standing in the ear is other than the ear, whom the ear knows not, whose body the ear is, that is this, the Self, the Inner Controller, the Immortal. . . . Who standing in the understanding is other than the understanding, whom the understanding knows not, whose body the understanding is, who within controls the understanding, that is this, the Self, the Inner Controller, the Immortal. . . . Who standing in the seed of generation is other than the seed of generation, whom the seed of generation knows not, whose body the seed of generation is, that is this, the Self, the Inner Controller, the Immortal. Unseen, the seer, unheard, the hearer, unthought, the thinker, unknown, the knower; there is no other seer than this, no other hearer than this, no other thinker than this, no other knower than this. That is this, the Self, the Inner Controller, the Immortal; valueless is anything other.

The passage above—one that is quoted repeatedly over centuries of commentary and discussion—illustrates a "spiritually monist" view that has enjoyed substantial prominence in India, a view that finds the "self" (or ātman) as the key to life and reality. Clearly the "self" referred to here is not the individual, personal self. It is rather the "self" of all reality, an all-encompassing spiritual reality that includes us all. Indian spirituality in the Upanishads recognizes the small worth of worldly desires and attachments in the light of inevitable death and the possibility of an extraordinary knowledge, or experience, that can carry us beyond this great fear.

"Were someone to hack the root of this large tree, dear child, it would bleed but live; were someone to hack its trunk, it would bleed but live; were someone to hack its tops, it would bleed but live. Pervaded by the living self (ātman), it stands continually drinking and exulting. If life were to leave one branch, then that branch would dry up; if a second, then that would dry up; a third, then that would dry up; if the whole, then the whole would dry up. Just in this way indeed, dear child," he [Śvetaketu's teacher] said, "understand: this endowed most surely with life dies; life does not die. That which is this, this is the most subtle, everything here has that as its soul (ātma). That is the reality; that is the self (ātman); you are that O Śvetaketu." "Please, sir, instruct me even further." "Alright, dear one," he said. . . .

[Yama, "Death":] "Whatever desires, (even) the most difficult to win in the world of mortals, have them all at your demand. Delightful females with chariots, with music—none like these may be won by mortal men—be entertained by them, O Naciketas, given by me. Do not inquire into dying." [Naciketas:] Existing only until tomorrow are such desires of a mortal, and, O Bringer-of-the-end, they wear away the splendor and vigor of every sense and power one has. Even all that is alive is of small worth indeed. Yours alone are the chariots; yours the dancing and the singing. A person is not to be satisfied with wealth. Are we to have wealth once we have seen you? But the boon that I wish to choose is this (answer this question): 'Will we continue to exist while you rule?' " . . . [Death:] Having seen in your grasp, O Naciketas, the fulfillment of desire and the foundation of the world and an infinity of power, of self-will, and the safe shore of fearlessness, and great fame sung far and wide, you wisely let it all go. A person who is wise and steadfast, discerning the God through spiritual discipline and study—the one that is difficult to experience, who has plunged deep into the hidden and is established in the secret place, standing in the cavern, the ancient— leaves joy and sorrow behind. . . . Subtler than the subtle, grander than the grand, the self is set in the secret heart of the creature. One who is without self-will experiences this (and becomes) free of sorrow; through his clearness and purity towards material things [or, "through the grace of the Creator"[5]], one experiences the self's greatness and breadth. Seated he travels far; lying down he goes everywhere. Who other than I is fit to know this God, the one that has both maddening pleasure and freedom from maddening pleasure? The wise person, recognizing the bodiless in bodies, the settled in things unsettled, the great and pervasive self (*ātma*), does not grieve nor suffer. This the self is not to be won by eloquent instruction, nor by intelligence, nor by much study. Just that person whom this chooses, by such a person is this to be won; to such a person this the self reveals, uncovers its very own form and body.

- How can "Emptiness" or nothing be "Fullness" or "Oneness"? Does this make sense to you?
- How do you understand the idea of a "Self" that is different from things, but nonetheless inhabits all things and is unknown?
- Do you think the inevitability of death diminishes or augments the worth of worldly goods?

---

2. Reality, Good, and Evil: Zarathustra

In the sixth century B.C.E., a Persian reformer named **Zarathustra** broke away from the Indic peoples who were the progenitors of the Upanishads. He preached a **monotheism** over and against the early Indian **polytheism**. Zarathustra claimed that his god—called **Ahura Mazda**— was not just spiritual or divine nature, but a creator, the one origin of all that existed. Ahura Mazda was a personal and all-good god, who created all natural things. Thus, Zarathustra and the religion he began (called **Zoroastrianism**) were extremely influential on the later monotheistic religions of Christianity, Judaism, and Islam.

Zarathustra was the first to recognize and formulate a doctrine regarding the existence and origin of good and evil in the universe. Ahura Mazda, the One Lord, created first among all things two twin spirits, lower sorts of divinities. The character of the first, called **Spenta Mainyush**, drew him and everything that followed him to goodness and good acts. The character of the other, called **Angra Mainyush**, led him and everything in his service to do evil. The twins are described in this passage from the *Gathas* (the original portion of the **Zend-Avesta**, the scripture of Zoroastrianism).

 FROM **Zend-Avesta**[6]

Thus are the primeval spirits who as a pair (combining their opposite strivings), and (yet each) independent in his action, have been famed (of old). (They are) a better thing, they two, and a worse, as to thought, word, and as to deed. And between these two let the wisely acting choose right. (Yasna, XLV:2)

Although Angra Mainyush and Spenta Mainyush are born with natural tendencies toward evil and good, respectively, they choose quite freely to express it in action. Thus,

---

[5] The Sanskrit text is ambiguous between these two meanings; the first suggests Buddhist doctrines, and the alternative suggests Hindu theism.

[6] All passages from the Yasna are taken from the Zend-Avesta, Part III, trans. L. H. Mills; part of the series,*The Sacred Books of the East*, ed. F. Max Muller, Westport, CT: Greenwood Press, 1972 (Oxford, 1887). All passages from the Yashts are taken from the Zend-Avesta, Part II, trans. James Darmesteter; part of the series, *The Sacred Books of the East*, ed. F. Max Muller, Motilal Banarsidass: Delhi, 1965 (Oxford, 1883).

while Ahura Mazda is responsible for the creation of everything, Angra Mainyush is responsible for unleashing evil, whose forms are deceit, destructiveness, and death. The natural world, according to Zoroastrianism, is set against itself like two armies, in an eternal battle between good and evil. Everything that exists freely chooses its alliance in accordance with its tendencies. Human beings, however, are free and conscious decision makers, and so have more choice about their moral alliances than do other creatures.

It followed that all natural entities were things either to be worshiped or reviled. Fire, which represented the "Beneficent Immortal" spirit, **Asha** or "Righteousness," was especially to be worshiped, as the best of the "good creation." In fact, in their own time, Zoroastrians were referred to as "fire worshipers."

Zarathustra (Zoroaster)
(6th century B.C.E.)

An ancient Persian reformer and prophet of what is considered the first monotheistic religion, Zoroastrianism.

FIG. 2.11 A Zoroastrian high priest engaged in a fire ceremony.
(HIP / Art Resource, NY)

In the following passage, also from the *Gathas*, Ahura Mazda despairs for his creation, should Asha find no good guardian for it.

> Upon this the creator of the Kine (the holy herds) asked of Righteousness: How (was) thy guardian for the Kine (appointed) by thee when, as having power (over all her fate), ye made her? ... Whom did ye select as her (life's) master who might hurl back the fury of the wicked?
>
> Asha: ... (Great was our perplexity); a chieftain who was capable of smiting back (their fury), and who was himself without hate (was not to be obtained by us).

Zarathustra freely takes initiative on behalf of the herd. Recognizing his worthiness, God names Zarathustra its guardian. Zarathustra, then, takes a profoundly spiritual perspective on the question of the underlying nature of reality.

Although Zoroastrianism originally had no full-blown notion of "immaterial stuff," or thought, as the essential nature of reality, Zarathustra's Ahura Mazda is an immortal, conscious entity that creates from thought, and it is the human's ability to think, according to Zarathustra, that gives humankind its unique moral capacity. In addition, Zoroastrianism had a notion of eternity—of which our time here on earth is only a part. At the end of our time, so it was claimed, the evil creation would be eternally vanquished.

- How do you think that Zarathustra influences the monotheistic religions of Christianity, Judaism, and Islam?

3. Confucius

In its earlier form in China, philosophy was not so concerned with the questions we have called "protoscientific," but rather with human beings, their relationships, and their actions. This focus is particularly evident in one Chinese thinker of the sixth century B.C.E., Confucius, who set the forms for Chinese society for millennia afterward. "Reality" for the Confucians, unlike the ontologies of the West, was primarily *human* reality. Confucius and his followers claimed that human beings were divided within themselves, and among

"He who learns,
but does not think,
is lost."

– CONFUCIUS

themselves, because their passions, ambitions, and confused loyalties distracted them from their moral duty. Through conscious and attentive adherence to propriety, the Confucians claimed, human beings could overcome their selfish desires and develop into exemplary people. Confucius did not think that many people were sufficiently committed to this goal, as these passages from *The Analects* (a compendium of Confucius' teachings) attest:

 FROM **The Confucian Analects**[7]

The Master [Confucius] said, [in response to the saying] "He who thinks but does not learn, is in grave danger." (XI:5)

The Master said, I have never yet seen anyone whose desire to build up his moral power was as strong as sexual desire. (IX:17)

The Master said, I have never yet seen a man who was truly steadfast. Someone answered, "Shen Ch'eng." The Master said, Ch'eng! He is at the mercy of his desires. How can he be called steadfast? (V:10)

Confucius (6th–5th century B.C.E.)

An ancient Chinese sage and founder of the Confucian religion. His doctrine sought "gentlemanly conduct," which was to be achieved through adherence to ritual.

FIG. 2.12 Kongfuzi ("the honorable Master Kong") became known as "Confucius" in the West. *(Image © fotohunter, 2011. Used under license from Shutterstock.com)*

Confucius encouraged society to return to ritual forms of behavior that had been abandoned during times of warfare and social turmoil. Whether in the context of grand ceremonies or everyday etiquette, ritual results in non-coercive social harmony that is the consequence of everyone's cooperative efforts. Each individual has an impact on the well-being of society by fulfilling his or her roles in relation to other people. Hence, Confucius says that a father should be a father, a son a son, a ruler a ruler, and so on. The exemplary person is one whose behavior is always appropriate, both to the role he or she is playing and to the situation. Confucius refers to this exemplary way of life as the "Way" (or *Dao*).

Wealth and rank are what every man desires; but if they can only be retained to the detriment of the Way he possesses, he must relinquish them. . . . The gentleman who ever parts company with goodness does not fulfill that name. Never for a moment does a gentleman quit the way of Goodness. (IV:5)

The goal for society, according to Confucius, was the achievement of interpersonal harmony at every level, beginning with the family. The family is particularly important in Confucian thought because it is the basis on which everyone learns to relate to other people. Confucius considers the harmony attained in music as a model for that which ideally prevails among family members and members of the community at large. To attain this, he encouraged his disciples to cultivate themselves through study and adherence to ritual.

[B]oth small matters and great depend upon it [harmony]. If things go amiss, he who knows the harmony will be able to attune them. But if harmony itself is not modulated by ritual, things will go amiss. (I:12)

---

[7] Confucius, *The Analects of Confucius*, translated and annotated by Arthur Waley, New York: Vintage, 1938.

- Do you think our passions and ambitions distract us from our moral duty? Is this always so?
- Why is etiquette or acting in socially appropriate ways important?

4. Laozi, or the Poets of the Dao De Jing

In China during Confucius' own lifetime, or so the story goes, a religious mystic named Laozi espoused a doctrine that rebelled against the powerful Chinese dynasty and the ancient heroes whom Confucius revered. This radical doctrine, which developed into the religion Daoism, also rejected the Confucian faith in ritual, or the exterior expression of moral goodness. More likely, the poems attributed to Laozi, called the poems of the *Dao De Jing* (or "Way of Life"), were composed by several authors who shared Confucius' frustration with unethical behavior and political corruption, but responded in a radically different way. They were mystic recluses who claimed that there was a nature of reality, called the **Dao**, or "Way," which they understood quite differently from Confucius. They claimed that the *Dao* could not be taught or understood through discourse or rules, nor mimicked through the constancy of gentlemanly conduct. Rather, they claimed, the *Dao* could be known only through direct acquaintance with it. The seeker after the *Dao* could only be prepared for its revelation to him through meditation—not ever through ritual. Thus, the poets of the *Dao De Jing* shared Confucius' primarily practical and moral focus, including the impersonality of goodness. They believed, however, that "impersonal goodness" could be neither sought nor expressed in any visible, speakable, observable way. They claimed the *Dao* was "**ineffable**" and could not be known through words or thought.

 FROM *Dao De Jing*
BY **Laozi**[8]

Existence is beyond the power of words
To define:
Terms may be used
But are none of them absolute.
When people lost sight of the way to live
Came codes of love and harmony,
Learning came, charity came,
Hypocrisy took charge; . . .

Thus, these mystics were monists. They believed that the nature of reality is one, and that this One is, in a sense, alive. But they did not go the way of the scientific and animistic doctrines of Greece. It was certainly not one of the physical elements, nor could it be known by way of the rules set down by our ancestors.

What we look for beyond seeing
And call the unseen
Listen for beyond hearing,

---

[8] From Lao-Tzu, *Tao Te Ching*, trans. J. H. McDonald, 1996 (for the public domain).

And call the unheard,
Grasp for beyond reaching
And call the withheld,
Merge beyond understanding
In a oneness. . . .

Knowledge studies others,
Wisdom is self-known; . . .

A realm is governed by ordinary acts,
A battle is governed by extraordinary acts,
The world is governed by no acts at all.

- How can one follow or seek the Dao if it is beyond description?
- How can one act without acting?

5. Buddha

Buddhism's historical founder, Siddhārtha Gautama of the Śākya clan, was born a prince in India (or perhaps what is now southern Nepal) near the year 560 B.C.E. The **Buddha** (the Sanskrit term *buddha* means literally "the awakened one") did not write anything himself. Records of his teachings and sermons apparently were kept by his disciples.

Through the centuries—first in India and then in almost every Asian country east of India—Buddhist doctrines and practices evolved; in each culture and epoch in which Buddhism prospered, local customs and indigenous religious beliefs were assimilated, giving the religion everywhere a unique form and expression.

As a young prince, the Buddha-to-be led a life of pleasure and enjoyment. His father, fearing the prophecy that his son would become a religious mendicant, tried to protect him from the sight of anything unpleasant or evil. However, one day the young prince journeyed some distance from the royal enclave and encountered first a diseased person, then a wrinkled and decrepit old man, and then a corpse. Inquiring about each of these and being told that all persons are subject to such infirmities, the prince renounced his life of enjoyments and vowed to search tirelessly for the origin and cause of these evils—and for the power to root them up. Buddha's experience of enlightenment did not occur immediately, however; he had to try various paths before arriving at the "Middle Way," a way of life he later proclaimed to his disciples. Eventually, after a long ordeal of meditation under a Bodhi tree, Buddha achieved the *summum bonum*, "nibbana" (the Sanskrit "nirvāna"), an extinction of evil at its roots. The remainder of his life, Buddha spent traveling and preaching—helping others to reach this supreme good and developing a picture of reality to support this conception.

Buddha (6th century B.C.E.)

The "Awakened One," a name for the founder of the Buddhist religion; the ancient Indian prince, Siddharta Gautama, after his enlightenment.

FIG. 2.13 The Great Buddha, Kamakura, Japan (© iStockphoto .com/Burak Demir)

Among the most important of Buddha's teachings are the **Four Noble Truths:**

1. All is suffering (and transitory).

2. The root of suffering is desire, attachment, and personal clinging.

3. There is a way to eliminate desire, and thereby eliminate suffering, namely *nibbana*.

4. The way to this supreme good is The Eightfold Noble Path: right thought, right resolve, right speech, right conduct, right livelihood, right effort, right mindfulness, and right concentration or meditation.

The Buddhist vision of the universe was, in one sense, much like Parmenides', in that the world as we know it must be understood as *illusion*. But, like the Hindus of the *Upanishads*, the underlying reality was One, except that the Buddhists called this "emptiness" or "noth-ingness." Also like the Hindus, the Buddha proclaimed the "wheel of becoming." However, according to the Buddhists, the wheel of becoming shows the connectedness between life, craving, rebirth (rebirth seems never to have been doubted by the Buddha), and the causal interdependence of all things, their insubstantiality, and similarly the insubstantiality of the self or soul—there is "no soul" according to the Buddha.[9] Although each of these doctrines and others received much elaboration in later years, Buddhism is primarily practical, em-phasizing meditation and compassion. What follows is one of the most famous of the many hundreds of sermons and discourses attributed to the Buddha.

 FROM **"Fire-Sermon"**
ATTRIBUTED TO **Buddha**[10]

And there The Blessed One addressed the priests:

"All things, O priests, are on fire. And what, O priests, are all these things which are on fire?

"The eye, O priests, is on fire; forms are on fire; eye-consciousness is on fire; impressions received by the eye are on fire; and whatever sensation, pleasant, unpleas-ant, or indifferent, originates in dependence on impressions received by the eye, that also is on fire.

"And with what are these on fire?

"With the fire of passion, say I, with the fire of hatred, with the fire of infatua-tion; with birth, old age, death, sorrow, lamentation, misery, grief, and despair are they on fire.

"The ear is on fire; sounds are on fire; . . . the nose is on fire; odors are on fire; . . . the tongue is on fire; tastes are on fire; . . . the body is on fire; things tangible are on fire; . . . the mind is on fire; ideas are on fire; . . . mind-consciousness is on fire; impres-sions received by the mind are on fire; and whatever sensation, pleasant, unpleasant, or indifferent, originates in dependence on impressions received by the mind, that also is on fire.

---

9 Some of these doctrines clearly have forerunners in the Upanishads; it is noteworthy that the Buddha upholds certain lines of continuity between his and previous spiritual perceptors' teachings. Others are distinctively Buddhist, in particu-lar the "insubstantiality" doctrines.

10 "Fire-Sermon," from *Mahā-Vagga*. Reprinted by permission of the publishers from *Buddhism in Translation: Passages Selected from the Buddhist Sacred Texts and Translated from the Original Pali into English* by Henry Clark Warren, Stu-dent's Edition, Harvard Oriental Series 3, pp. 351-353. Cambridge, MA: Harvard University Press, 1896, 1922. Copyright © 1953 by the President and Fellows of Harvard College.

> "The learned and noble disciple . . . becomes divested of passion, and by the absence of passion he becomes free."
>
> – THE BUDDHA

"And with what are these on fire?

"With the fire of passion, say I, with the fire of hatred, with the fire of infatuation; with birth, old age, death, sorrow, lamentation, misery, grief, and despair are they on fire.

"Perceiving this, O priests, the learned and noble disciple conceives an aversion for the eye, conceives an aversion for forms, conceives an aversion for eye-consciousness, conceives an aversion for the impressions received by the eye; and whatever sensation, pleasant, unpleasant, or indifferent, originates in dependence on impressions received by the eye, for that also he conceives an aversion. Conceives an aversion for the ear, conceives an aversion for sounds, . . . conceives an aversion for the nose, conceives an aversion for odors, . . . conceives an aversion for the tongue, conceives an aversion for tastes, . . . conceives an aversion for the body, conceives an aversion for things tangible, . . . conceives an aversion for the mind, conceives an aversion for ideas, conceives an aversion for mind-consciousness, conceives an aversion for the impressions received by the mind; and whatever sensation, pleasant, unpleasant, or indifferent, originates in dependence on impressions received by the mind, for this also he conceives an aversion. And in conceiving this aversion, he becomes divested of passion, and by the absence of passion he becomes free, and when he is free he becomes aware that he is free; and he knows that rebirth is exhausted, that he has lived the holy life, that he has done what it behooved him to do, and that he is no more for this world."

Now while this exposition was being delivered, the minds of the thousand priests became free from attachment and delivered from the depravities.

- Buddha claimed that attachment or desire is the root of suffering. Is there a difference between attachment and desire? How might either cause us to suffer?
- Does one become free from suffering when one becomes devoid of passion?

D. Two Kinds of Metaphysics: Plato and Aristotle

The term *metaphysics* is relatively new (from about 70 B.C.E. or so), but it is generally agreed that the first great systematic metaphysicians were Plato (427-347 B.C.E.) and Aristotle (384-322 B.C.E.). Plato had been a student of Socrates and his most faithful recorder. (Almost all that we have of Socrates' teachings comes to us through Plato.) Yet Socrates was a moralist, not a metaphysician, and most of the metaphysical doctrines that Plato discusses using Socrates as his mouthpiece are probably Plato's own. Aristotle never tried to be a faithful disciple of Plato, and he became his teacher's harshest and most famous critic. It has been said of each of them that the history of philosophy is nothing more than a series of footnotes to their brilliant dialogues and treatises of twenty-four hundred years ago.

Metaphysics is what Aristotle called "first philosophy," the investigation of "Being as Being," or ultimate reality. What does it mean for something to exist? What is it for something to change? What makes one thing like another? Sometimes these questions, or at least the answers to these questions, are presupposed in our everyday thinking, whether we actually think about them or not. For example, we "naturally" believe that a tree continues to exist when we aren't looking at it. But why do we believe this? Even when such questions are the creations of philosophers, they outline views of the world that nonphilosophers share with them. The problem is, as we shall see, that people disagree violently about these issues, even from one generation to the next (for example, from Plato to Aristotle). What seems to be clear and obvious to one philosopher will seem obscure, merely metaphorical, or downright paradoxical to another. But as we watch the warring history of metaphysics, we too should be humbled by it, for it cannot be that all of those geniuses got it wrong while we now have it right. We too, whether explicitly or not, have metaphysical views, and we too may have to be ready to give them up as we think more about them and face further arguments.

With Plato and Aristotle, metaphysics becomes a cautious consuming enterprise, producing monumental systems of many volumes that require a lifetime of study to master. All we can do here is present a thumbnail sketch, with some brief selections of Plato's metaphysics and a very brief introduction to Aristotle's philosophy, which seems, at first glance, to be primarily a refutation of Plato. But like so many philosophers who seem to be attacking each other from completely opposed viewpoints, Plato and Aristotle have much in common. Both attempted to resolve the problems they inherited from the pre-Socratics: to find the ultimate substance of the universe, to understand what was eternal and unchanging, to understand change, and to show that the universe as a whole is intelligible to human understanding. Plato, following Parmenides and the other pre-Socratics who trusted their reason more than common sense, gave **reason** a grander position in human life and in the universe in general than it had ever received before. Aristotle, although he too defended reason, insisted that philosophy return to common sense and have a respect for ordinary opinion, which many of the Greek philosophers seemed to have lost. But whatever their differences, it is the shared grandeur of their enterprise that should impress us most about Plato and Aristotle. Between them, they established what we today call "philosophy." And between them, they also laid the intellectual foundations for Christian theology. **St. Augustine**, for example, was very much a Platonist, and **St. Thomas Aquinas** was thoroughly indebted to Aristotle.

1. Plato

The most important single feature of Plato's philosophy is his theory of **Forms**. (The Greek word is *Eidos*.) Plato's Forms are sometimes referred to as **Ideas**, but Plato does not mean "ideas" in a person's mind, but rather *ideal forms* or perfect examples—the perfect circle or perfect beauty. To avoid confusion, we shall use, not the word "Ideas," but "Forms."

Forms are the ultimate reality. Things change, people grow old and die, but Forms are eternal and unchanging. Thus Plato could agree with Heraclitus that the world of our experience is constantly changing; but he could also agree with Parmenides, who insisted that the real world, the eternal and unchanging world, was not the same as the world of our experience. According to Plato, it was a *world of Forms*, a world of eternal truths. There were, in other words, two worlds: (1) the world in which we live, a world of constant change or a *world of Becoming*, and (2) a world of Forms, an unchanging world, the real world or the *world of Being*. We can see here Plato's close connection with Parmenides, holding that ultimate reality (the Forms) must be changeless and eternal. Furthermore, also in accordance with Parmenides, it is only such changeless and eternal things that truly can be known. Our only access to this latter world, the real world, is through our reason, our capacity for intellectual thought. Plato's "two-worlds" view was to have a direct and obvious influence on Christian theology. It would also affect philosophers, mathematicians, mystics, poets, and romantics of all kinds until the present day. But in his own time it had a more immediate importance; it allowed him to reconcile Heraclitus and Parmenides, to resolve the problems of the pre-Socratics, and to finally give ideas their proper place in human thought.

Plato thought of the Forms as having the special features of *what is* according to Parmenides. The most exciting Form for Plato was the Form of beauty. Plato thought a person could get to know beauty by falling in love in the right way and by realizing that the excitement of love is really aimed not at the personality of the person loved but at the link between that person and eternal beauty.

FROM **The Symposium**
BY **Plato**[11]

You see, the man who has been thus far guided in matters of Love, who has beheld beautiful things in the right order and correctly, is coming now to the goal of Loving: All of a sudden he will catch sight of something wonderfully beautiful in its nature; that, Socrates, is the reason for all his earlier labors: First, [Beauty] always is, and neither comes to be nor passes away, neither waxes nor wanes. Second, it is not beautiful this way and ugly that way, nor beautiful at one time and ugly at another; nor beautiful in relation to one thing and ugly in relation to another; nor is it beautiful here but ugly there, as it would be if it were beautiful for some people and ugly for others.

Nor will the beautiful appear to him in the guise of a face or hands or anything else that belongs to the body. It will not appear to him as one idea or one kind of knowledge. It is not anywhere in another thing, as in an animal, or in earth, or in heaven, or in anything else, but itself by itself with itself, it is always one in form; and all the other beautiful things share in that, in such a way that when those others come to be or pass away, this does not become the least bit smaller or greater nor suffer any change.

For Plato, it is the world of Forms, the world of being, that is real. But this is not to say (as Parmenides had argued) that the world we live in, the world of becoming, is unreal. It is, however, less than real, not an illusion, but without those qualities of eternity and necessity that are the marks of true reality. This might seem like a verbal trick; it is not. The idea of a hierarchy of realities was already familiar in religions that antedated Plato's philosophy by centuries. We still use such notions in our own thinking, comparing, for example, the world of film and novels to "the real world," or the dreary humdrum of working-day life to "really living." But the best illustration of Plato's two-worlds view is his own, which he offers us in a parable called the Myth of the Cave.

It is a parable about bringing people from the less real to the really real. Indeed, one of the most striking features of Plato's philosophy (and much of Greek philosophy in general) is its emphasis on the *love* of wisdom, the irresistibility of reality; and what is too easily lost in translation is the very erotic imagery Plato uses to describe our passion

FIG. 2.14 Plato's Myth of the Cave describes the shock of moving from darkness into light. *(© iStockphoto.com/Michael Utech)*

for the truth. The Myth of the Cave not only illustrates two kinds of knowledge, two kinds of worlds; it is also a parable about human timidity, the difficulties we have in facing the truth, and our resistance to the dazzling light of truth itself.

FROM **The *Republic***
BY **Plato**[12]

SOCRATES: Imagine men to be living in an underground cavelike dwelling place, which has a way up to the light along its whole width, but the entrance is a long way up. The men have been there from childhood, with their neck and legs in fetters, so that they remain in the same place and can only see ahead of them, as their bonds prevent them turning their heads. Light is provided by a fire burning some way behind them, and on a higher ground, there is a path across the cave and along this a low wall has been built, like the screen at a puppet show in front of the performers who show their puppets above it.

GLAUCON: I see it.

SOCRATES: See then also men carrying along that wall, so that they overtop it, all kinds of artifacts, statues of men, reproductions of other animals in stone or wood fashioned in all sorts of ways, and, as is likely, some of the carriers are talking while others are silent.

GLAUCON: This is a strange picture, and strange prisoners.

SOCRATES: They are like us, I said. Do you think, in the first place, that such men could see anything of themselves and each other except the shadows which the fire casts upon the wall of the cave in front of them?

GLAUCON: How could they, if they have to keep their heads still throughout life?

SOCRATES: And is not the same true of the objects carried along the wall?

GLAUCON: Quite.

SOCRATES: If they could converse with one another, do you not think that they would consider these shadows to be the real things?

GLAUCON: Necessarily.

SOCRATES: What if their prison had an echo which reached them from in front of them? Whenever one of the carriers passing behind the wall spoke, would they not think that it was the shadow passing in front of them which was talking? Do you agree?

GLAUCON: By Zeus, I do.

SOCRATES: Altogether then, I said, such men would believe the truth to be nothing else than the shadows of the artifacts?

GLAUCON: They must believe that.

SOCRATES: Consider then what deliverance from their bonds and the curing of their ignorance would be if something like this naturally happened to them. Whenever one of them was freed, had to stand up suddenly, turn his head, walk, and look up toward the light, doing all that would give him pain, the flash of the fire would make it impossible for him to see the objects of which he had earlier seen the shadows. What do you

[12] Plato, *The Republic*, Bk. VII, trans. G. M. A. Grube. Copyright © 1974 by Hackett Publishing Company. Reprinted with permission. All rights reserved.

think he would say if he was told that what he saw was foolishness, that he was now somewhat closer to reality and turned to things that existed more fully, that he saw more correctly? If one then pointed to each of the objects passing by, asked him what each was, and forced him to answer, do you not think he would be at a loss and believe that the things which he saw earlier were truer than the things now pointed out to him?

GLAUCON: Much truer.

SOCRATES: If one then compelled him to look at the fire itself, his eyes would hurt, he would turn round and flee toward those things which he could see, and think that they were in fact clearer than those now shown to him.

GLAUCON: Quite so.

SOCRATES: And if one were to drag him thence by force up the rough and steep path, and did not let him go before he was dragged into the sunlight, would he not be in physical pain and angry as he was dragged along? When he came into the light, with the sunlight filling his eyes, he would not be able to see a single one of the things which are now said to be true.

GLAUCON: Not at once, certainly.

SOCRATES: I think he would need time to get adjusted before he could see things in the world above; at first he would see shadows most easily, then reflections of men and other things in water, then the things themselves. After this he would see objects in the sky and the sky itself more easily at night, the light of the stars and the moon more easily than the sun and the light of the sun during the day.

GLAUCON: Of course.

SOCRATES: Then, at last, he would be able to see the sun, not images of it in water or in some alien place, but the sun itself in its own place, and be able to contemplate it.

GLAUCON: That must be so.

SOCRATES: After this he would reflect that it is the sun which provides the seasons and the years, which governs everything in the visible world, and is also in some way the cause of those other things which he used to see.

GLAUCON: Clearly that would be the next stage.

SOCRATES: What then? As he reminds himself of his first dwelling place, of the wisdom there and of his fellow prisoners, would he not reckon himself happy for the change, and pity them?

GLAUCON: Surely.

SOCRATES: And if the men below had praise and honours from each other, and prizes for the man who saw most clearly the shadows that passed before them, and who could best remember which usually came earlier and which later, and which came together and thus could most ably prophesy the future, do you think our man would desire those rewards and envy those who were honoured and held power among the prisoners, or would he feel, as Homer put it, that he certainly wished to be "serf to another man without possessions upon the earth"[13] and go through any suffering, rather than share their opinions and live as they do?

---

13 *The Odyssey* 11, 489-90, where Achilles says to Odysseus, on the latter's visit to the underworld, that he would rather be a servant to a poor man on earth than king among the dead [trans. note].

GLAUCON: Quite so, I think he would rather suffer anything.

SOCRATES: Reflect on this too. If this man went down into the cave again and sat down in the same seat, would his eyes not be filled with darkness, coming suddenly out of the sunlight?

GLAUCON: They certainly would.

SOCRATES: And if he had to contend again with those who had remained prisoners in recognizing those shadows while his sight was affected and his eyes had not settled down—and the time for this adjustment would not be short—would he not be ridiculed? Would it not be said that he had returned from his upward journey with his eyesight spoiled, and that it was not worthwhile even to attempt to travel upward? As for the man who tried to free them and lead them upward, if they would somehow lay their hands on him and kill him, they would do so.

GLAUCON: They certainly would.

SOCRATES: This whole image, my dear Glaucon, must be related to what we said before. The realm of the visible should be compared to the prison dwelling, and the fire inside it to the power of the sun. If you interpret the upward journey and the contemplation of things above as the upward journey of the soul to the intelligible realm, you will grasp what I surmise since you were keen to hear it. Whether it is true or not only the god knows, but this is how I see it, namely that in the intelligible world the Form of the Good is the last to be seen, and with difficulty; when seen it must be reckoned to be for all the cause of all that is right and beautiful, to have produced in the visible world both the light and the fount of light, while in the intelligible world it is itself that which produces and controls truth and intelligence, and he who is to act intelligently in public or in private must see it.

GLAUCON: I share your thought as far as I am able.

SOCRATES: Come then, share with me this thought also: do not be surprised that those who have reached this point are unwilling to occupy themselves with human affairs, and that their souls are always pressing upward to spend their time there, for this is natural if things are as our parable indicates.

GLAUCON: That is very likely.

SOCRATES: Further, do you think it at all surprising that anyone coming to the evils of human life from the contemplation of the divine behaves awkwardly and appears very ridiculous while his eyes are still dazzled and before he is sufficiently adjusted to the darkness around him, if he is compelled to contend in court or some other place about the shadows of justice or the objects of which they are shadows, and to carry through the contest about these in the way these things are understood by those who have never seen Justice itself?

GLAUCON: That is not surprising at all.

SOCRATES: Anyone with intelligence would remember that the eyes may be confused in two ways and from two causes, coming from light into darkness as well as from darkness into light. Realizing that the same applies to the soul, whenever he sees a soul disturbed and unable to see something, he will not laugh mindlessly but will consider whether it has come from a brighter life and is dimmed because unadjusted, or has come from greater ignorance into greater light and is filled with a brighter dazzlement. The former he would declare happy in its life and experience,

> "One must turn one's whole soul from the world of becoming until it can endure to contemplate reality, and the brightest of realities, which we say is the Good."
>
> – PLATO'S SOCRATES

the latter he would pity, and if he should wish to laugh at it, his laughter would be less ridiculous than if he laughed at the soul that has come from the light above.

GLAUCON: What you say is very reasonable.

SOCRATES: We must then, if these things are true, think something like this about them, namely that education is not what some declare it to be; they say that knowledge is not present in the soul and that they put it in, like putting sight into blind eyes.

GLAUCON: They surely say that.

SOCRATES: Our present argument shows that the capacity to learn and the organ with which to do so are present in every person's soul. It is as if it were not possible to turn the eye from darkness to light without turning the whole body; so one must turn one's whole soul from the world of becoming until it can endure to contemplate reality, and the brightest of realities, which we say is the Good.

GLAUCON: Yes.

SOCRATES: Education then is the art of doing this very thing, this turning around, the knowledge of how the soul can most easily and most effectively be turned around; it is not the art of putting the capacity of sight into the soul; the soul possesses that already but it is not turned the right way or looking where it should. This is what education has to deal with.

GLAUCON: That seems likely.

Our world is like a set of shadows of the real world; that does not make it an illusion, but it does make it a mere imitation of the bright originals. Notice, too, the savior-like role of the philosopher that Plato is setting up here. (His famous argument that philosophers should be kings, and kings philosophers, is included here too.) Like Pythagoras, Plato believed that knowledge of pure Forms, knowledge of the world of "Being," is a person's only hope for salvation and the "good life."

- Do you see any similarities between Plato's Forms and ideas in Eastern philosophy?
- In what sense is ignorance like being imprisoned in a cave? What are the shadows in Socrates' story?

Socrates had taught his students, Plato among them, that the truth, if we can know it at all, must be in us. Plato (using his teacher as his literary spokesman) gives this revelation a new twist. It begins with a puzzle. How is it possible to learn anything? If we don't already know it, how will we recognize it when we find it? And if we already do know it, it makes no sense to say that we "learn it." Now this puzzle sounds like nonsense if we think only of examples such as "what is the beer consumption rate in Omaha, Nebraska?" To answer such questions, obviously we can't simply "look into ourselves"; we have to go out into the world and get information. But Plato insists that he is after much bigger game than "information"; he wants Knowledge (with a capital *K*), knowledge of reality, to which we have access only through thinking. That world, unlike the world of change and "information" in which we live, is characterized by the fact that everything in it is eternal and necessary. In this eternal world, reality is not discoverable merely through observation and experience. For example, consider the simple truth, 2 + 2 = 4; it never changes—no experience is necessary to know it; it is one of those eternal truths that deserves its place in Plato's world of Being.

Perhaps the best way to understand Plato's exciting but somewhat mysterious notion of the Forms is to think of them in terms of *definitions*. The Forms are what different things of the same kind have in common and what make them things of the same kind. For example, two horses have in common the Form horse, and you recognize a horse, Plato would say, because of its Form. Suppose that you've never seen a horse before. Is it possible for you to know what a horse is? The answer is, "of course." It is enough that you have learned what a horse is (from pictures or descriptions) even if you've never seen one. But how is such learning possible? According to Plato, it is possible because we know a definition and thus recognize the Form of a horse, like the ideal Form of a triangle, and with it we are able to know what a horse is, even if we have never seen one, and we recognize horses when we do see them. In Plato's terms, we can recognize all horses, no matter what their age, shape, color, or peculiarities, just because they "participate" in the Form horse. For Plato, the Form horse has even more reality than particular, flesh-and-blood horses.

The concept of Form allows Plato to explain what it is that one comes to understand when one learns that two or more things are of the same kind. But for Plato the notion of Form serves another purpose as well. In addition to what we know about things from experience, we also know some things independent of experience, and we know these things with certainty (the same certainty Descartes sought in our introduction). For example, we know that every horse is an animal. We know that not simply because every horse that we have seen has turned out to be an animal, but because we know, apart from any particular experiences with horses, that the very Form horse includes the Form animal. (In our times, we would say that the meaning of the English word "horse" already includes the concept of "being an animal"; accordingly, philosophers refer to this kind of truth as **conceptual truth**. But this term was not available to Plato.)

Definitions are essential because without them it is difficult to know exactly what one is talking about. But this quest for definitions should not be confused with the high school debating technique of asking your opponent to "define [your] terms." Rather, a definition is the *conclusion* of a philosophical argument—and it is very hard to come by. In his dialogue *The Meno*, Plato has Socrates push for a definition of "virtue"; his arguments here are a good illustration of the Socratic pursuit of the Forms as definitions.

 FROM **The *Meno***
BY **Plato**[14]

MENO: Can you tell me, Socrates, can virtue be taught? Or is it not teachable but the result of practice, or is it neither of these, but men possess it by nature or in some other way?

SOCRATES: Before now, Meno, Thessalians had a high reputation among the Greeks and were admired for their horsemanship and their wealth, but now, it seems to me, they are also admired for their wisdom, not least the fellow citizens of your friend Aristippus of Larissa. The responsibility for this reputation of yours lies with Gorgias, for when he came to your city he found that the leading Aleuadae, your lover Aristippus among them, loved him for his wisdom, and so did the other leading

Thessalians. In particular, he accustomed you to give a bold and grand answer to any question you may be asked, as experts are likely to do. Indeed, he himself was ready to answer any Greek who wished to question him, and every question was answered. But here in Athens, my dear Meno, the opposite is the case, as if there were a dearth of wisdom, and wisdom seems to have departed hence to go to you. If then you want to ask one of us that sort of question, everyone will laugh and say: "Good stranger, you must think me happy indeed if you think I know whether virtue can be taught or how it comes to be; I am so far from knowing whether virtue can be taught or not that I do not even have any knowledge of what virtue itself is."

I myself, Meno, am as poor as my fellow citizens in this matter, and I blame myself for my complete ignorance about virtue. If I do not know what something is, how could I know what qualities it possesses? Or do you think that someone who does not know at all who Meno is could know whether he is good-looking or rich or well-born, or the opposite of these? Do you think that is possible?

MENO: I do not; but, Socrates, do you really not know what virtue is? Are we to report this to the folk back home about you?

SOCRATES: Not only that, my friend, but also that, as I believe, I have never yet met anyone else who did know.

MENO: How so? Did you not meet Gorgias when he was here?

SOCRATES: I did.

MENO: Did you then not think that he knew?

SOCRATES: I do not altogether remember, Meno, so that I cannot tell you now what I thought then. Perhaps he does know; you know what he used to say, so you remind me of what he said. You tell me yourself, if you are willing, for surely you share his views.

FIG. 2.15 Ptolemy and Strabo in *School of Athens* by Raphael. Plato suggests that reason, which can solve complex mathematical puzzles, is innate in all human beings, even an illiterate slave boy. (© iStockphoto.com/estelle75)

MENO: I do.

SOCRATES: Let us leave Gorgias out of it, since he is not here. But, Meno, by the gods, what do you yourself say that virtue is? Speak and do not begrudge us, so that I may have spoken a most unfortunate untruth when I said that I had never met anyone who knew, if you and Gorgias are shown to know.

MENO: It is not hard to tell you, Socrates. First, if you want the virtue of a man, it is easy to say that a man's virtue consists of being able to manage public affairs and in so doing to benefit his friends and harm his enemies and to be careful that no harm comes to himself; if you want the virtue of a woman, it is not difficult to describe: she must manage the home well, preserve its possessions, and be submissive to her husband; the virtue of a child, whether male or female, is different again, and so is that of an elderly man, if you want that, or if you want that of a free man or a slave. And there are very many other virtues, so that one is not at a loss to say what virtue is. There is virtue for every action and every age, for every task of ours and every one of us—and Socrates, the same is true for wickedness.

SOCRATES: I seem to be in great luck, Meno; while I am looking for one virtue, I have found you to have a whole swarm of them. But, Meno, to follow up the image of swarms, if I were asking you what is the nature of bees, and you said that they are many and of all kinds, what would you answer if I asked you: "Do you mean that they are many and varied and different from one another in so far as they are bees? Or are they no different in that regard, but in some other respect, in their beauty, for example, or their size or in some other such way?" Tell me, what would you answer if thus questioned?

MENO: I would say that they do not differ from one another in being bees.

SOCRATES: If I went on to say: "Tell me, what is this very thing, Meno, in which they are all the same and do not differ from one another?" Would you be able to tell me?

MENO: I would.

Meno continues to try to satisfy Socrates with a definition of virtue, but every time he either contradicts himself or argues in a circle. So how does one know a definition? The answer, according to Plato, is that we recognize the Forms. We know what a horse is because we recognize the Form of a horse. We recognize that $2 + 2 = 4$ because we know the Forms. But how do we *know* the Forms? If we do not and cannot learn of them from experience (the changing world of Becoming in everyday life), then how do we know them at all? The answer, according to Plato, is that they already are "in us."

The second principle of Plato's metaphysics, our bridge between the two worlds, is the immortality and immateriality of the human soul. Our souls contain knowledge of the world of Being that is already in us at birth. Such knowledge and ideas are called **innate**. Experience only triggers them off and allows us to "remember" them. Here is the extravagant answer to Plato's puzzle, "How is it possible to learn a truth about the world of Being?" The answer is: We already "know" it; it's just a matter of recalling it. Consider his famous illustration of this second doctrine in *The Meno*:

MENO: How will you look for it, Socrates, when you do not know at all what it is? How will you aim to search for something you do not know at all? If you should meet with it, how will you know that this is the thing that you did not know?

SOCRATES: I know what you want to say, Meno. Do you realize what a debater's argument you are bringing up, that a man cannot search either for what he knows or

"...There is no teaching but recollection, in order to show me up at once as contradicting myself."

– PLATO'S SOCRATES

for what he does not know? He cannot search for what he knows—since he knows it, there is no need to search—nor for what he does not know, for he does not know what to look for.

MENO: Does that argument not seem sound to you, Socrates?

SOCRATES: Not to me.

MENO: Can you tell me why?

SOCRATES: I can. I have heard wise men and women talk about divine matters....

MENO: What did they say?

SOCRATES: What was, I thought, both true and beautiful.

MENO: What was it, and who were they?

SOCRATES: The speakers were among the priests and priestesses whose care it is to be able to give an account of their practices. Pindar too says it, and many others of the divine among our poets. What they say is this; see whether you think they speak the truth: They say that the human soul is immortal; at times it comes to an end, which they call dying, at times it is reborn, but it is never destroyed, and one must therefore live one's life as piously as possible:

> Persephone will return to the sun above in the ninth year the souls of those from whom she will exact punishment for old miseries, and from these come noble kings, mighty in strength and greatest in wisdom, and for the rest of time men will call them sacred heroes.

As the soul is immortal, has been born often and has seen all things here and in the underworld, there is nothing which it has not learned; so it is in no way surprising that it can recollect the things it knew before, both about virtue and other things. As the whole of nature is akin, and the soul has learned everything, nothing prevents a man, after recalling one thing only—a process men call learning—discovering everything else for himself, if he is brave and does not tire of the search, for searching and learning are, as a whole, recollection. We must, therefore, not believe that debater's argument, for it would make us idle, and fainthearted men like to hear it, whereas my argument makes them energetic and keen on the search. I trust that this is true, and I want to inquire along with you into the nature of virtue.

MENO: Yes, Socrates, but how do you mean that we do not learn, but that what we call learning is recollection? Can you teach me that this is so?

SOCRATES: As I said just now, Meno, you are a rascal. You now ask me if I can teach you, when I say there is no teaching but recollection, in order to show me up at once as contradicting myself.

MENO: No, by Zeus, Socrates, that was not my intention when I spoke, but just a habit. If you can somehow show me that things are as you say, please do so.

At this dramatic point in the dialogue, Socrates calls over an illiterate, uneducated slave boy and with minimal instructions leads him to discover an elementary geometrical proof. What is crucial is that Socrates does not tell the boy the answer but "draws it out of him." But then the question becomes, where was this answer "in him," and how did he recognize it? After the demonstration, Socrates draws his conclusions:

SOCRATES: What do you think, Meno? Has he, in his answers, expressed any opinion that was not his own?

MENO: No, they were all his own.

SOCRATES: And yet, as we said, he did not know a short time ago?

MENO: That is true.

SOCRATES: So these opinions were in him, were they not?

MENO: Yes.

SOCRATES: So the man who does not know has within himself true opinions about the things that he does not know?

MENO: So it appears.

SOCRATES: These opinions have now just been stirred up like a dream, but if he were repeatedly asked these same questions in various ways, you know that in the end his knowledge about these things would be as accurate as anyone's.

MENO: It is likely.

SOCRATES: And he will know it without having been taught but only questioned, and find the knowledge within himself?

MENO: Yes.

SOCRATES: And is not finding knowledge within oneself recollection?

MENO: Certainly.

SOCRATES: Must he not either have at some time acquired the knowledge he now possesses, or else have always possessed it?

MENO: Yes.

SOCRATES: If he always had it, he would always have known. If he acquired it, he cannot have done so in his present life. Or has someone taught him geometry? For he will perform in the same way about all geometry, and all other knowledge. Has

FIG. 2.16 The ancient Egyptians built architectural tributes to the belief in human immortality.
(© iStockphoto.com/Luke Daniek)

someone taught him everything? You should know, especially as he has been born and brought up in your house.

MENO: But I know that no one has taught him.

SOCRATES: Yet he has these opinions, or doesn't he?

MENO: That seems indisputable, Socrates.

SOCRATES: If he has not acquired them in his present life, is it not clear that he had them and had learned them at some other time?

MENO: It seems so.

SOCRATES: Then that was the time when he was not a human being?

MENO: Yes.

SOCRATES: If then, during the time he exists and is not a human being he will have true opinions which, when stirred by questioning, become knowledge, will not his soul have learned during all time? For it is clear that during all time he exists either as a man or not.

MENO: So it seems.

SOCRATES: Then if the truth about reality is always in our soul, the soul would be immortal so that you should always confidently try to seek out and recollect what you do not know at present—that is, what you do not recollect?

MENO: Somehow, Socrates, I think that what you say is right.

SOCRATES: I think so too, Meno.

The doctrine of the immortality of the soul did not originate with Plato, of course. The ancient Egyptians believed in it many centuries before the first Greek philosophers, and Pythagoras had taught it to his students. But Plato's doctrine had more than religious significance; it was his answer to the skeptics and our bridge to the eternal world of Being. Of course, as a student of Socrates, he also appreciated the advantages of believing in an afterlife. Socrates could face death so calmly, he told his students, just because he believed in life after death. But for Plato it signified something more; it provided us with knowledge in this life as well as continued existence in another.

Plato's doctrines of the world of Being and the immortality of the soul introduce a clearly immaterialist conception of reality, as opposed to all of the more or less materialist conceptions we have encountered so far (the world as "stuff"). Even Pythagoras' numbers and Heraclitus' *logos* had their materialistic foundations, for neither philosopher was willing to grant these things independent existence, independent, that is, of the material things of this world. The things of Plato's world of Being can exist apart from them.

What is in this "other world," this world of Being? We have already met one of its inhabitants: the simple truth, 2 + 2 = 4. Its inhabitants are Forms. Consider the following familiar example: Your geometry teacher asks you to prove that the internal angles of a triangle total 180°. Simple enough. You remember how: You extend the base of the triangle, draw a line parallel to the base through the apex, and then proceed with your proof. But now, how do you know that you have not only shown that the internal angles of *this* triangle total 180°? As a matter of fact, it is pretty obvious that what you have drawn isn't even a triangle; the sides sag, one of the angles is broken, and the lines are fat (after all, a real line has no width at all). But yet you claim to have proved something about all triangles. Well, it is clear that you needn't do the proof even twice, much less an infinite number of times, to make your claim. How come? Because, you will answer, what you have been working with is not this particular poorly drawn triangle in your notebook but an ideal triangle, the form of all and any triangles. And there it is—Plato's Form of a triangle. It is not identical to any particular triangle. (How could it be, for it would have to be acute, isosceles, right, and nonright all at the same time!) It is their ideal Form, which each particular triangle approximates, that has its own existence in the world of Being. Plato says that every triangle that we can draw participates in the ideal Form and that it is only through reason, not through observation of particular triangles, that we come into contact with these ideal Forms.

To know a Platonic Form is not just to "see" something. It is to fall in love with it; in fact, it is to fall madly in love. So Socrates, in nearly all of Plato's dialogues, repeats the claim that a philosopher is a kind of lover. Indeed, he says that to know the Forms is to want to reproduce, to propagate, to teach everyone else to see them and to love them too. The Myth of the Cave and the metaphor of the Sun and shadows have two sides. The first is that the changing world of our everyday experience is only a shadow, an imitation of reality. But the second side is that the world of our everyday experience is also an image of the divine and ultimate reality, and so in the things of everyday life we get at least a glimpse of perfection.

Among the Forms are those ideals of human perfection that we should not only recognize but try to realize here in the world of Becoming: Wisdom, Justice, Beauty, and Goodness. To these ideals of perfection each of us aspires, and it is the definition of these ideals that is the task of every philosopher. His or her job (Socrates' main task in all of Plato's dialogues) is to sort out the common confusions about such vital matters. The business of the philosopher, in short, is to make others recognize eternal Forms and make it possible to achieve that heroic wisdom to which Plato's teacher, Socrates, had devoted his life.

I hope that you can appreciate, even from this brief sketch, the power of the metaphysical doctrines Plato has developed. You may also be aware of some of their difficulties. Most importantly, the gap between our world and the real world makes us exceedingly uncomfortable; none of us likes to think of ourselves living merely in the shadows. (As Plato himself warns, "wouldn't the prisoners who had never been released . . . laugh at him and even . . . kill" the philosopher who thus instructs them?) The connection between the world of Being and our own world of Becoming is not at all clear. Plato does say that the things of this latter world "participate" in the Forms of the former, but one thing that we shall have to learn right away in philosophy (and in every other discipline) is that the words that pretend to be explanations are often only cosmetic cover-ups. It looks as if we have a theory when in fact we have only a word. This is particularly true of Plato's word "participates" (*methexis*), and he himself raises serious doubts about it in his later dialogues. But the real attack comes, as it should come in philosophy, from his own students, and in particular, from one, perhaps the greatest of them all, Aristotle.

- How does the slave boy discover the proof without being told? Do you find Socrates' explanation at all plausible?
- How otherwise might the slave boy discover mathematical truth?

2. Aristotle

Aristotle claimed that he did not understand Plato's concept of "**participation**." (When a philosopher claims "not to understand" something, it means that he is pushing for a better account of it, that he is not at all satisfied so far. Aristotle probably understood Plato as well as anybody ever has.) Aristotle's objection was, essentially, that Plato had failed to explain the relationship between the Forms and particular things, and that the word "participation" was no more than "a mere empty phrase and a poetic metaphor."[15] Furthermore, Plato's emphasis on the Forms made it impossible to appreciate the full reality of particular things, and the eternal permanence of the Forms made them useless for understanding how particular things could change. Indeed, the question "How do things change?" becomes the central theme of Aristotle's philosophy.

Aristotle also wanted to determine the nature of reality. But Plato had argued that reality was something other than the world of our experience. Aristotle, a practical man of the earth, a great biologist, physicist, and worldly tutor to Alexander the Great, would have none of this. This world, our world, is reality. He agreed with Plato that knowledge must be universal and concerned with what things have in common, but he rejected Plato's idea that these common universal ingredients—the Forms of things—could be separated from particular things. But this meant that Aristotle also rejected Plato's separation of the human soul from the body, and Aristotle, unlike Plato, saw human beings entirely as creatures of nature, "rational animals"—but still animals. Metaphysics, for Aristotle, was not the study of another world, recollected in our eternal souls; metaphysics was simply the study of nature (*physis*) and, as importantly, the study of ourselves. Accordingly, he brought metaphysics "back home." But it must not be thought that he made it any simpler. The beginning student of Aristotle—as well as the trained scholar—will attest to the fact that he is among the most difficult authors in philosophy.

FROM *Metaphysics*
BY **Aristotle**[16]

There is a branch of knowledge that studies being qua being, and the attributes that belong to it in virtue of its own nature. Now this is not the same as any of the so-called special sciences, since none of these enquires universally about being *qua* being. They cut off some part of it and study the attributes of this part—that is what the mathematical sciences do, for instance. But since we are seeking the first principles, the highest causes, it is of being qua being that we must grasp the first causes.

The study of being *qua* being is metaphysics, which Aristotle was the first to isolate from other branches of philosophy. It is, first of all, the study of the different ways the word *be* can be used. This leads Aristotle to his famous theory of categories:

There are several senses in which a thing may be said to "be." In one sense the "being" meant is "what a thing is" or a "this," while in another sense it means a quality or a quantity or one of the other things that are predicated as these are. While "being" has all these senses, the primary type of being is obviously the "what," which indicates the substance of the thing. For when we say of what quality something is, we say that it is good or bad, not that it is six feet long or that it is a man; but when we say what it is, we do not say "white" or "hot" or "six feet long," but "a man" or "a god." All other things are said to be because they are quantities of that which is in this primary sense, or qualities of it, or in some other way characteristics of it.

---

[15] Aristotle, *Metaphysics*, trans. W. D. Ross, Oxford: Oxford University Press, 1924.

[16] Aristotle, *Metaphysics*, T.1.1003a21, Z.1.1028a10, trans. W. D. Ross, Oxford: Oxford University Press, 1924.

The primary use of "be" is to tell us what something *really is*, what it is in an unqualified sense: We are, in this sense, a certain individual human being. We are also a certain number of inches tall; but that fact is secondary, it is something *about* us, which could change without changing what we *are*, first and foremost, and belongs to the category of *quantity*. We may also be pale or dark; that fact also is secondary and belongs to the category of *quality*. The primary category is that of *substance*. "Substance," as Aristotle defines it, is "that which stands alone." In other words, "substance" is *independent* being. You would exist, for instance, even if you didn't have hair. But *your* hair could not exist without you, and so it is not a substance. Substances are the basic elements in Aristotle's metaphysics. A horse, a tree, and a butterfly are substances.

Tables and chairs are not primary beings for Aristotle, because he thinks of primary beings as having their own natures. Something made by a human being, such as a table, can only exist *along with* human beings. It cannot move or fulfill its nature—in this case, holding our foot—by itself. Our nature is what we will do if nothing stops us. A human being grows up and leads a human life, if nothing stops him; that's his nature. But a wooden table will inevitably rot if no one stops it, since that is the nature of the wood it is made of. Wood has a nature, tables do not. For that reason, Aristotle treats artifacts (things we make) as having a lower level of being than we do ourselves.

 FROM *Physics*
BY **Aristotle**[17]

Some people think that the nature and real being of a natural object is the primary material in it (material in itself unformed)—in a bed it would be the wood, in a statue the bronze. It is an indication of this, according to Antiphon, that if you bury a bed, and the rotting wood becomes able to send up a shoot, what comes up will not be a bed, but wood—suggesting that the arrangement in accordance with the rules of the art belongs only incidentally, and that the reality—what the thing really is—is what actually persists through all those changes.

· · ·

But there is another way of speaking, according to which the nature of a thing is its shape or form as given in its definition . . . and this rather than its matter is a thing's nature. For (i) each thing is called whatever it is, when it is that thing actually rather than just potentially [the wood or the seed, the matter, is not a table or a lettuce—though it may have the potentiality of being one—until it has actually been put together or has actually germinated and grown]. Further, (ii) men come to be from men, but not beds from beds. That is precisely why people say that the nature of a bed is not the shape but the wood; if it sprouts it is not a bed but wood that comes up. But if this shows that the wood is nature, form too is nature; for men come to be from men.

The doctrines of Aristotle's metaphysics sound as simple as they could be. This world, the world of our experience, is reality; there is no other world. The ultimate things of reality, which he calls substances, are individual things—people, horses, trees, and butterflies. Change is real and much of reality is subject to change. Forms are real, but cannot exist separately from the particular substances whose forms they are. This is not as radical a departure from Plato as it may seem. Aristotle did believe that the highest level of reality was not subject to

[17] Aristotle, *Physics*, II.1.193a9; II.1.193, I.8.191a24, trans. W. D. Ross, Oxford: Oxford University Press, 1936.

change. Gods, the heavens, and even the forms of biological species were changeless in his system. Aristotle did not believe in any form of evolution.

For Aristotle, the primary substances are individual things; secondary substances (less real than individuals) are what he called the "species" and the "genus" to which a thing belongs. To return to our equestrian example, this particular horse, for Aristotle, is the primary substance. The species, "horse," and the even broader genus, "animal," are less real than the horse itself. Aristotle, like Plato, has a hierarchy of reality. But he turns Plato's hierarchy upside down. Plato holds that the more abstract things are the more real; Aristotle argues that the more concrete things, individuals, are the more real. For Aristotle, as in common sense, the more tangible things are considered to be the most real things.

What is a substance? Aristotle spends many pages giving a number of definitions, enough to keep the philosophers of the Middle Ages busy for a thousand years sorting them out. For our purposes, it will be enough to mention three different descriptions of substance, each of which is important for Aristotle and for later philosophy. The first characterization of substance is presented in terms of grammar. Aristotle says, "a substance is that which is neither predictable of a subject nor present in a subject; for instance, the individual man or horse."[18] More simply, a substance is the thing referred to by a noun, which is the subject of a sentence; for example, "the man is . . ." or "Socrates is . . ." or "the horse is. . . ." (This characterization would have been less confusing in Greek.) A more ontological way of saying this, but unfortunately very confusing too, is to say that a substance is independent of anything else. (We shall see how important this becomes in the modern metaphysics of Spinoza and Leibniz.) Other things might depend upon a substance, but a substance does not depend upon them. This is an awkward way of saying, perhaps, that the color of a horse could not exist without the horse; indeed, nothing could be true of a horse if it did not exist.

A second way of characterizing substance is to say that substance is what underlies all of the properties and changes in something. In this sense, you can say that you are the same person (that is, the same substance) that you were ten years ago, despite the fact that you are, quite obviously, very different in a great many ways. (Aristotle says, "Substance, while remaining the same, is capable of admitting contrary properties.") Combining these two characterizations, we can say that a substance is whatever is most basic to reality, like the pre-Socratic philosophers' notion of "stuff." It is the concrete individual thing, which remains constant despite the fact that it changes and has different properties at different times. You are the same person before and after you've gotten a haircut, tried on a new suit of clothes, or had your appendix removed.

The third characterization of substance requires the introduction of another new term, which became a central concern of philosophers before this century. A substance can be defined in terms of what is *essential*. An **essence** (or an essential **property**) is that aspect of an individual that identifies it as a particular individual. For example, it is part of the essence of being Socrates that he is a human being, that he lived in the fourth century B.C.E., and that he was wise. Anything that does not have these properties could not possibly be Socrates. There are other properties that Socrates has, of course; for example, the fact that he had a wart on his nose. But this is not an essential property. (Aristotle calls it an *accident* or an *accidental property*.) Socrates still would have been Socrates without it. But Socrates could not have been a centipede, for it is part of his essence to be human.

A substance is a combination of form and matter. Aristotle's "form" is roughly the same as Plato's Form, except that for Aristotle, it does not exist apart from the individual things that have it; it is always *informing* some matter. Matter is a discovery of Aristotle's. It is, basi-

---

[18] Aristotle, *Categories*, trans. J. L. Ackrill, Oxford: Oxford University Press, 1963.

cally, what things are made out of; it is what is given shape and structure by the form. The matter of a boat is wood; its form is the design that the boatbuilder realized in the wood. (Notice that "form" is written with a small *f* here, although Aristotle uses the same word as Plato, *eidos*. His word for the matter is *hylē*.)

This enabled Aristotle to explain change. Earlier philosophers, he thought, believed only in matter that by itself would stay the same. Plato believed only in Forms that are eternally unchanging. But Aristotle believed in things that *combined* matter and form in a variety of ways. Substantial change, the "coming to be and passing away" of a substance, takes place when matter is given a new form.

With both concepts available, Aristotle thinks he can avoid the mistakes of his predecessors, especially the mistake of Parmenides, which he blames on inexperience:

> The first people to philosophise about the nature and truth of things got side-tracked and driven off course by inexperience. They said that nothing comes to be or passes away, because whatever comes to be must do so either from what is, or from what is not—and neither of these is possible. For what is cannot come to be, since it is already; and nothing can come to be from what is *not*, since there must [in all change and coming into being] be something underlying.

The essence of a thing cannot change (or it would no longer be the same thing), and it is of little metaphysical importance if accidents change. So what does change?

Form and matter, Aristotle says, cannot exist separately, but they can be *distinguished* everywhere in nature. The best examples can be found in human craftsmanship. One can take a lump of clay, for example, and make it into a bowl of any number of shapes. Or one can take a piece of silver and make it into a fork, a spoon, a bracelet, or a couple of rings. The clay or the silver is the matter; the shape and the function define the form. Aristotle also says that the matter itself can be analyzed in terms of form and matter. The matter of the clay and the silver would be the basic elements—earth, air, fire, and water. The form would be the shape and proportion these elements assume to make clay or silver. Indeed, Aristotle even holds that the basic elements themselves can be analyzed in terms of more primitive matter—hotness, coldness, dryness, and wetness—which combine to give the form of the elements. It is the form of things that we can know and explain, according to Aristotle, never the matter. Thus, we can *talk* about form and matter separately, and so *understand* change. His predecessor, he thought, mistook the way we talk about reality for the way it is. The form, *by itself*, can never change, nor can the matter, but the way they combine can change. By changing their form, caterpillars turn into butterflies and seeds into fruits and flowers. Thus, Aristotle explains both change and stability.

You may already anticipate certain troubles that will plague later philosophers. How much can we change a person, for example, and still have him or her be the same? Provide a haircut? A college education? A ten-year jail sentence? A sex-change operation?

FIG. 2.17 Are these all pictures of the same man?
(© iStockphoto.com/knape)

But before we worry about such problems, let us appreciate the importance of this notion of essence in Aristotle's philosophy. With it, he can do everything that Plato wanted to do with his special notion of Forms, but without invoking anything otherworldly. According to Aristotle, we can know that Socrates is a man, for instance, just because the essence of Socrates includes the property of being a man. We can know that a horse is an animal because the essence of being a horse includes the property of being an animal. In Plato, a conceptual truth of this kind was a truth about eternal Forms; for Aristotle, it is the form that changes, and a conceptual truth is rather a statement about essences.

In both medieval and modern philosophy, the concepts of substance and essence will take on a particularly important role in debates about God and his relation to his creations as well as in the continuing controversies in ontology that accompanied the rise of modern science. But Aristotle's ontology, much more than the philosophy of his predecessors, was linked up with an exciting prescientific cosmology, an account of the nature and purpose of the universe. In the Middle Ages, these theories profoundly inspired the great Christian theologian St. Thomas Aquinas, who would refer to Aristotle as simply "The Philosopher."

> • What are the three definitions of substance that Aristotle gives? How are they all expressions of the same thing? Give an example of how the form-matter combination explains change.

To understand Aristotle's cosmology, we have to begin with a notion that is extremely foreign to people today; it is that the universe as a whole, and all things in it, have a purpose, a goal. The Greek word for "purpose" or "goal" is *telos*, and Aristotle's view is called **teleology**. Teleology can be directly contrasted with our modern scientific view of reality, which is primarily a *causal* view. Teleology explains something by looking for its purpose, goal, or end; causal explanations seek to understand *how* something came about, not *why* it came about. If you were asked why a frog has a heart, for example, the teleological answer would be "in order to keep it alive, by pumping the blood through its body." The causal answer, on the other hand, would be an explanation of the genetics, the evolutionary process, the development of the frog. If you were asked why a plant turns its leaves toward the sunlight, the teleological answer would be "in order to face the sun." The causal explanation, instead, would refer you to the fact that the cells grow faster on one side of the stem and that certain light-sensitive chemicals do such-and-such, and so on. In modern science, a causal answer is always preferable, and if a teleological answer is allowed at all it is always with the qualification that either there is an underlying causal explanation or we do not yet have (but someday will have) an adequate causal explanation. In Aristotle's metaphysics, on the other hand, one does not have an explanation at all unless one knows what purpose a thing or an event serves. "Nature does nothing in vain" is the motto of the teleologist.[19]

Aristotle believed that every substance, every individual thing whether human, animal, vegetable, or mineral, had its own nature, its own internal principles, certain tendencies that were part of its essence. This was, for example, the basis of his famous theory of falling objects: Every object has its "place," and if that object is moved, it will return to its rightful place on its own power. That means that any object of sufficient size, whose place is on (or under) the ground, will fall toward the earth immediately if it is lifted into the air. And larger objects, which are not slowed down by the air's resistance, will fall faster than smaller ones. Indeed, this

---

[19] Aristotle rejected a theory of natural selection argued by Empedocles twenty-three hundred years before Darwin because it was not a teleological theory.

seemed so inherently reasonable to Aristotle and everyone around him that it never occurred to them to test it under experimental conditions. But gravitation, which Newton would not discover for another two millennia, is essentially a causal concept. Aristotle's explanation was a teleological one, which the Greeks found far more convincing. Moreover, even if they had had the equipment for a test, which they did not, the Greeks still might not have believed the answer. Aristotle could not understand how causation could possibly operate at a distance. Thus, Aristotle thought that the cause of an object falling had to be in the object and not in the earth.

A reader who begins Aristotle may be initially confused by his use of the word *cause* (*aition*) to include not only what we have been calling causal explanation but teleological accounts as well. In fact, Aristotle lists four different kinds of **cause**, all of which together explain why a thing is as it is at any given time. The first of these is the matter that makes it up, the *material cause*, the silver in the spoon or the flesh and blood that make up our bodies. The second is the principle or law by which it is made, the *formal cause*, the architect's blueprint or the craftsman's model. The third is what we would call "the cause," which Aristotle calls the *efficient cause*, the person or event that actually makes something happen by doing something—pushing a button, causing an explosion, calling the person in charge. Fourth, there is the purpose of the thing, its *final cause*, its *telos*. Now notice that Aristotle's four causes are better suited for explaining human activities than giving what we would call scientific explanations about things that happen in nature. But this is indeed Aristotle's paradigm, and he even says in *Physics*, "If purpose is present in art, it must also be present in nature." It is the final cause that provides us with the most important explanation.

We can understand this without any difficulty when we are explaining human activities. We want to know, first of all, what purpose a person has in doing something. But when it comes to nature, we do not generally ask about purpose, but we are more likely to ask about (efficient) causes. We might ask of an animal, what purpose is served by a long neck, or certain features in its feet, or some kind of fur, but we are less likely to ask that of a plant and would find such a question unintelligible with reference to rocks, clouds, and stars. Aristotle and his fellow Greeks would not find this unintelligible at all. Indeed, he believed (and thousands of scientists followed him until the seventeenth century) that everything that existed had to be accounted for in terms of its inner purposes and the overall purpose it served in nature. Thus a magnet literally "attracts" little pieces of metal, and the stars really do have a purpose in their heavenly wanderings. Not only do all the things and creatures of the universe have their purposes, but the universe itself has its purpose too. Indeed, it is this ultimate purpose of the universe that gives all the particular things their significance. Indeed, for Aristotle, the idea that the universe as a whole might *not* have a purpose would have been absurd. One of his most famous arguments is aimed at showing why there must be an ultimate purpose, a "first (Final) cause," or what he calls, "the **prime mover**."

 FROM *Metaphysics*
BY **Aristotle**[20]

Moreover, it is obvious that there is some first principle, and that the causes of things are not infinitely many either in a direct sequence or in kind. For the material generation of one thing from another cannot go on in an infinite progression (e.g., flesh from earth, earth from air, air from fire, and so on without a stop); nor can the source of motion (e.g., man be moved by air, air by the sun, the sun by Strife, with no limit to the series). In the same way neither can the Final Cause

[20] Aristotle, *Metaphysics*, trans. Hugh Tredennick, Cambridge, MA: Harvard University Press, 1933.

FIG. 2.18 An infinite regress goes on forever. *(Image © Ykh, 2011. Used under license from Shutterstock.com)*

[that is, purposes] recede to infinity—walking having health for its object, and health happiness, and happiness something else: one thing always being done for the sake of another. And it is just the same with the Formal Cause [that is, the essence]. For in the case of all intermediate terms of a series which are contained between a first and last term, the prior term is necessarily the cause of those which follow it; because if we had to say which of the three is the cause, we should say "the first." At any rate it is not the last term, because what comes at the end is not the cause of anything. Neither, again, is the intermediate term, which is only the cause of one (and it makes no difference whether there is one intermediate term or several, nor whether they are infinite or limited in number). But of series which are infinite in this way, and in general of the infinite, all the parts are equally intermediate, down to the present moment. Thus if there is no first term, there is no cause at all.

The argument, simply stated, is that teleological explanations cannot go on forever, or what philosophers sometimes call an **infinite regress**. For Aristotle, if *x* exists for the purpose of *y* and *y* exists for the purpose of *z*, there must be some ultimate purpose that will explain them all. A similar argument can be made with regard to efficient causes, that if *p* makes *q* happen and *r* makes *p* happen and so on, there must be an end to the "and so on," and so too with the material cause and the formal cause. But the most exciting aspect of this infinite regress argument is the idea that the universe itself must have a purpose, a Final cause, a "prime mover" that Aristotle characterizes as "pure thought, thinking about itself." It is an obscure but intriguing idea, which was taken up by Christian theology as an apt characterization of the Christian God (see Chapter 4). But Aristotle's prime mover has few of the characteristics of the Judeo-Christian-Islamic God; he (it) did not create the universe and has no special concern for man. The prime mover is more of a metaphysical necessity than a proper object of worship. But it is not too far-fetched to say that Aristotle, like most of the Greeks, viewed the universe as something like a cosmic organism, with an ultimate purpose, whose ultimate goal was thinking itself.

We can appreciate how this cosmology would become a source of inspiration for a great many philosophers, poets, and religious people. In more recent centuries, for example, it was used as a welcome alternative to the nuts and bolts materialism of modern Newtonian science (as we shall see in Leibniz). Tied to the technical details of Aristotle's ontology is an extremely imaginative cosmology: the picture of a purposeful universe, developing according to its own goals and principles. It is a fascinating picture and still an attractive alternative to the lifeless picture of the physical universe that is so central to our modern scientific outlook.

- What is teleology? To what extent do we still rely on teleological explanations?

E. Modern Metaphysics

Throughout the Middle Ages, philosophers and theologians developed elaborate systems of metaphysics, many of them derived directly or indirectly from the thoughts and theories of Plato and Aristotle. Inherent in all such systems was the confidence that the world is ultimately intelligible, and that the truths that reason can discern about reality are not only true, but necessarily true. Throughout this rich millennium of philosophy (from the later days of the Roman Empire through the Renaissance and Reformation), philosophy and theology in Europe became pretty much a single subject, until the rise of the "new" science in the sixteenth and seventeenth centuries. At that time a series of revolutions took place that justify a discussion about the beginning of the "modern" era of philosophy. What distinguished these revolutions was not a separation from religion and theology (most of these philosophers were pious theists whose God played a central role in their thinking), but rather a new boldness of thought, often in contradiction with church authority and strikingly original in its form. The father of these revolutions was René Descartes (whom we met earlier in the Introduction), whose philosophy represented a radically new turn in some very old ways of metaphysical thinking. (We should remind ourselves that no thinker, however bold or brilliant, carries off a revolution all alone. Generations paved the way for Descartes' revolution.)

Descartes' metaphysics was derived from ancient concerns, and in particular from the Aristotelian notion of *substance* as it had developed through the intervening centuries of Judeo-Christian and Arabic-Islamic theology during the Middle Ages. It was also a product of modern science, which was rapidly developing under the guidance of such geniuses as Copernicus and Galileo, and soon, under Sir Isaac Newton. And as with Aristotle, one of Descartes' central concerns was teleology, the purposiveness of the world, but in the new religious climate the question of purposiveness was focused wholly on the Being through whom all purposes were to be ultimately explained, the Judeo-Christian-Islamic God. But this sense of purpose (or final causality) started to run counter to the notions of efficient and material causality that had already come to rule modern science. With the birth of modern science and the modern world, the clash between the teleological visions of faith and the causal explanations of science became inevitable.

The most dramatic new ingredient in modern metaphysics, however, was a concept that played virtually no role in ancient metaphysics at all, and that was the notion of *mind* or *consciousness*. To be sure, the Greeks talked about their own psychological states. (Aristotle wrote long discussions of such emotions as anger, for example. Homer often described the psychology of his heroes, but almost always in physiological terms.) But the idea of a mind as a self-contained arena—what the contemporary philosopher Daniel Dennett has dubbed "the Cartesian theater"—is distinctively new. One can trace its development through the centuries by way of the ever-increasing Christian emphasis on the soul and inner personal experience, but it is only in modern metaphysics that we get the full-blown view that what the world is made of, the ultimate reality of things, is the mind. This view, in general, is called **idealism**. For a few eccentric philosophers, this might be taken to mean that the reality of the world is a function of one's individual mind, but most idealists had something much grander in mind, as we shall see. Deriving their views from medieval Christianity, for example, some philosophers suggested that there is ultimately only one mind, or one supreme mind, and that is the mind of God. Others suggested that mind pervades everything, both God and everything else. In one sense, this view is plausible: we realize that we know about the things of reality only by way of their effects (direct or indirect) on our minds. But whether they exist only because of our minds is a much more radical proposition, and whether our minds are "free" to conceive of things and determine our actions, in the light of modern science, will become one of the most pressing concerns of philosophy.

Descartes' metaphysical system was an amalgam of the latest theories in science and mathematics (some of which he discovered), established theology, and the new science of psychology. The method itself (discussed briefly in the Introduction) was based on the model of mathematical proof, starting with premises that were self-evident and arguing deductively to conclusions that were therefore equally certain. We consider Descartes' contributions to knowledge—and the famous arguments beginning with his *Cogito* ("I think, therefore I am")—in the following chapter. Here we consider Descartes' equally famous metaphysical model of the world, one which has set the stage for much of philosophy ever since. (The basic idea that mind and body are distinct is still referred to as Cartesian dualism.) Next we look at Descartes' two most famous and brilliant followers, who developed elaborate metaphysical systems quite different from—and in opposition to—his own. The first is a Jewish philosopher, excommunicated for his heresies, who lived his life in poverty on the outskirts of Amsterdam. He is **Benedictus**[21] **de Spinoza** (1632-1677). The second is his slightly younger contemporary, **Gottfried Wilhelm von Leibniz** (1646-1716), Germany's first, great, modern philosopher. Together, they present us with the classics in modern Western metaphysics, three very different speculations on the nature of the world.

1. René Descartes

Modern metaphysics begins with Descartes' insistence upon perfect certainty and mathematical deduction as the legitimate methodology. But methodology aside, metaphysics is a continuous enterprise from the Greeks through medieval philosophy, with Descartes its direct heir. We should not be surprised, for example, to find that the central concept of Descartes' metaphysics is *substance*, and that his definition of it (and the term itself) comes straight from Aristotle: "a thing existing in such a manner that it has need of no other thing in order to exist." (Both Spinoza and Leibniz follow Descartes in taking substance as their central concept, and they follow him also in their method. The three philosophers are usually grouped together as a single school of thought called *Rationalism*.)

Descartes' metaphysics can be understood best in terms of a monumental historical conflict between the "new" science (developed by Galileo and others) and the established authority of the Roman Catholic Church. Descartes, like many of the most important philosophers to follow him, was both an enthusiast of the new science—in fact he was an important contributor to both science and its mathematical foundations—and a religious man. He could not tolerate the idea that science should replace the orderly, meaningful worldview of Christianity with a Godless, amoral universe of mere "matter in motion." Neither could Descartes ever agree that science should reduce human existence—in particular, the thinking self—to another mere machine. (It is often noted that Descartes did think that animals were mere machines: What we too generously attribute to them by way of learning and responding to the environment is in fact nothing but a mechanical adjustment.) Accordingly, his metaphysics divides the world into three sorts of "substances": God; the mind, or self; and physical, material being. The latter two sorts of substances are, of course, created by and dependent on God. Indeed, Descartes begins all his studies with a proof of the existence of the world (and one's knowledge of it) that rests on the presumption of God's goodness. Because God is rational and good, we can trust (within limits) our own limited knowledge of the world. (We examine some of these proofs and arguments in the following chapter.) But because the world (of minds and matter) depends on God, there is no danger that science should leave us with a Godless, meaningless, mechanical universe. In Aristotelian terms, the ultimate causes

FIG. 2.19
René Descartes

---

[21] Born Baruch, he changed his name after he was excommunicated from the Jewish faith.

in the universe are "final" (or purposive) causes, not "efficient" (or mechanical) causes. The physical world is God's creation; and though it must be understood by science according to causal mechanisms, it is, nevertheless, within the domain of God's providence.

Within the domain of nature there are two (sorts of) substances, mind and body. Because these are substances, they are utterly distinct and independent. One immediate advantage of this "Cartesian dualism" is that the science of mind and the science of physical bodies (like theology and science) do not and cannot contradict one another. There is a science of the self and a science of physics, and there is no reason to suppose that science will deny the freedom of the self anymore than there is reason to fear that science will ultimately conflict with theology. What is true of physical bodies is not what is true of minds, and vice versa. Bodies may be wholly constrained by the laws of physics, but minds are free.

What is substance, according to Descartes? He delineates three different kinds:

On Substance
BY René Descartes[22]

PRINCIPLE LI

What substance is, and that it is a name which we cannot attribute in the same sense to God and to His creatures.

As regards these matters which we consider as being things or modes of things, it is necessary that we should examine them here one by one. By substance, we can understand nothing else than a thing which so exists that it needs no other thing in order to exist. And in fact only one single substance can be understood which clearly needs nothing else, namely, God. We perceive that all other things can exist only by the help of the concourse of God. That is why the word substance does not pertain *univoce* to God and to other things, as they say in the Schools, that is, no common signification for this appellation which will apply equally to God and to them can be distinctly understood.

PRINCIPLE LII

That it may be attributed univocally to the soul and to body, and how we know substance.

Created substances, however, whether corporeal or thinking, may be conceived under this common concept; for they are things which need only the concurrence of God in order to exist. But yet substance cannot be first discovered merely from the fact that it is a thing that exists, for that fact alone is not observed by us. We may, however, easily discover it by means of any one of its attributes because it is a common notion that nothing is possessed of no attributes, properties, or qualities. For this reason, when we perceive any attribute, we therefore conclude that some existing thing or substance to which it may be attributed, is necessarily present.

PRINCIPLE LIII

That each substance has a principal attribute, and that the attribute of the mind is thought, while that of body is extension.

But although any one attribute is sufficient to give us a knowledge of substance, there is always one principal property of substance which constitutes its nature and essence, and on which all the others depend. Thus extension in length, breadth and

22 René Descartes, *Principles of Philosophy*, in *The Philosophical Works of Descartes*, ed. E. Haldane and G. R. T. Ross, 1911. Reprinted with the permission of Cambridge University Press.

FIG. 2.20 The body is extended in space, but the mind seems almost limitless. *(Image © Redshinestudio, 2011. Used under license from Shutterstock.com)*

depth, constitutes the nature of corporeal substance; and thought constitutes the nature of thinking substance. For all else that may be attributed to body presupposes extension, and is but a mode of this extended thing; as everything that we find in mind is but so many diverse forms of thinking. Thus, for example, we cannot conceive figure but as an extended thing, nor movement but as in an extended space; so imagination, feeling, and will only exist in a thinking thing. But, on the other hand, we can conceive extension without figure or action, and thinking without imagination or sensation, and so on with the rest; as is quite clear to anyone who attends to the matter.

This is to say, following Aristotle, everything is either a substance or an attribute of substance, and a substance (as opposed to an attribute) can be thought of independently and can exist independently. Strictly speaking, this is true only of God. But we can also so define physical and mental substances. What defines physical substance, Descartes tells us, is its *extension in space*. Mind, by contrast, is unextended; that is, a thought does not have (in the sense that a wooden box has) a location in the physical dimensions of space.

PRINCIPLE LIV

That the nature of body consists . . . in . . . extension alone.

The nature of matter or of body in its universal aspect, does not consist in its being hard, or heavy, or coloured, or one that affects our senses in some other way, but solely in the fact that it is a substance extended in length, breadth and depth. . . . If, whenever we moved our hands in some direction, all the bodies in that part retreated with the same velocity as our hands approached them, we should never feel hardness; and yet we have no reason to believe that the bodies which recede in this way would on this account lose what makes them bodies. It follows from this that the nature of body does not consist in hardness. The same reason shows us that weight, colour, and all the other qualities of the kind that is perceived in corporeal matter, may be taken from it, it remaining meanwhile entire: it thus follows that the nature of body depends on none of these.

PRINCIPLE XIII

What external place is . . .

The words place and space signify nothing different from the body which is said to be in a place, and merely designate its magnitude, figure, and situation as regards other bodies. . . . For example, if we consider a man seated at the stern of a vessel when it is carried out to sea, he may be said to be in one place if we regard the parts of the vessel . . . : and yet he will be found continually to change his position, if regard be paid to the neighbouring shores. . . . But if at length we are persuaded that there are no points in the universe that are really immovable, as will presently be shown to be probable, we shall conclude that there is nothing that has a permanent place except in so far as it is fixed by our thought.

Although physical nature is ruled by mechanical, causal laws, mental substance (the mind, the self) is defined by its freedom.

PRINCIPLE XXXIX

That freedom of the will is self-evident.

Finally it is so evident that we are possessed of a free will that can give or withhold its assent, that this may be counted as one of the first and most ordinary notions

"Extension in length, breadth and depth, constitutes the nature of corporeal substance; and thought constitutes the nature of thinking substance."

– RENÉ DESCARTES

that are found innately in us. We had before a very clear proof of this, for at the same time as we tried to doubt all things and even supposed that He who created us employed His unlimited powers in deceiving us in every way, we perceived in ourselves a liberty such that we were able to abstain from believing what was not perfectly certain and indubitable. But that of which we could not doubt at such a time is as self-evident and clear as anything we can ever know.

FIG. 2.21 *(© iStockphoto.com/Franky De Meyer)*

But the mind not only "wills"; it also understands. We perceive the world and come to know its objects. But since the physical world and the mind are two distinct substances, how can there be a link between the two? The answer is that we have *ideas*, which are states of mind but nevertheless represent objects in the world that are their causes. However, this raises a number of ancient and more modern problems. Descartes, like Plato and Aristotle, has far more faith in reason and its favorite methods (e.g., mathematics) than he does in perception and the information gleaned from the senses. The senses can fool us, and we tend to rush to judgment prematurely on the basis of sensory experience. For instance:

 FROM **"Meditation VI"**
BY **René Descartes**[23]

When I feel pain in my foot, my knowledge of physics teaches me that this sensation is communicated by means of nerves dispersed through the foot, which, being extended like cords from there to the brain, when they are contracted in the foot, at the same time contract the inmost portions of the brain which is their extremity and place of origin, and then excite a certain movement which nature has established in order to cause the mind to be affected by a sensation of pain represented as existing in the foot. But because these nerves must pass through the tibia, the thigh, the loins, the back and the neck, in order to reach from the leg to the brain, it may happen that although their extremities which are in the foot are not affected, but only certain ones of their intervening parts, this action will excite the same movement in the brain that might have been excited there by a hurt received in the foot, in consequence of which the mind will necessarily feel in the foot the same pain as if it had received a hurt. And the same holds good of all the other perceptions of our senses.

. . .

From this it is quite clear that, notwithstanding the supreme goodness of God, the nature of man, inasmuch as it is composed of mind and body, cannot be otherwise than sometimes a source of deception.

[23] René Descartes, *Meditations on First Philosophy*, in *The Philosophical Works of Descartes*, trans. Elizabeth S. Haldane and G. R. T. Ross, 1911. Reprinted with the permission of Cambridge University Press.

John Locke (1632-1704)

Generally credited as not only the founder of British empiricism, but the father of modern political liberalism. Locke spent his early life in the English countryside, including many years at Oxford, where he taught philosophy and the classics until he earned a medical degree and turned to medicine. Much of his mature life, however, was spent in politics, and Locke joined a more or less revolutionary group that was fighting for the overthrow of the government. He was forced to flee England in 1683 and lived in Holland until the Glorious Revolution of 1688. For his part in the struggle, Locke received a governmental position, although he spent most of his time writing his two *Treatises on Government* (1689) to justify the revolution and its political principles and defending his *Essay Concerning Human Understanding* (1690), which he had written while in exile.

FIG. 2.22 John Locke
(HIP / Art Resource, NY)

But there is another source of ideas in addition to those caused in us by perception. There are also *innate* ideas, those implanted in us by God. Because of innate ideas we can know certain propositions to be true *for certain* (e.g., the propositions of geometry, as Plato also had argued). It is because of innate ideas that we are able to *reason* and, in particular, to do philosophy, to know God, to know universal truths. But even here a dramatic difference must be noted between Descartes and his ancient predecessors. Plato and Aristotle would have claimed to know reality itself (whether this consisted of Forms or essences). But Descartes ultimately claims that we know only the ideas. There is always that gap between the mind and the world that the ancients never allowed and never entertained. Thus the doctrine of innate ideas might be said to play an even more essential role in Descartes' philosophy than in Plato's. Nevertheless, in his time Descartes was accused by the Roman Catholic Church of overreaching our claim to knowledge: His claim that the human mind has access to the truth through innate ideas was still a challenge to the church's claim to being the sole authority in all ultimate matters.

The most difficult problem facing Descartes' philosophy, however, was the relationship between the various substances. How could God create a substance if that so-called substance were then dependent on God? For example, how could one substance interact with another as physical objects must do if they are to cause in us a perception? In general, how do the mind and the body interact, as surely they must, on Descartes' account? By definition substances are distinct and independent; interaction would seem to be interdependence and not logically possible. These are the questions that most bothered Locke, Spinoza, and Leibniz—the questions that would define much of philosophy for years to come.

 FROM *An Essay Concerning Human Understanding* (1690) BY **John Locke**

CHAPTER XXIII
OF OUR COMPLEX IDEAS OF SUBSTANCES

1. *Ideas of particular Substances, how made.* The mind being, as I have declared, furnished with a great number of the simple ideas, conveyed in by the senses as they are found in exterior things, or by reflection on its own operations, takes notice also that a certain number of these simple ideas go constantly together; which being presumed to belong to one thing, and words being suited to common apprehensions, and made use of for quick dispatch, are called, so united in one subject, by one name; which, by inadvertency, we are apt afterward to talk of and consider as one simple idea, which indeed is a complication of many ideas together: because, as I have said, not imagining how these simple ideas *can* subsist by themselves, we accustom ourselves to suppose some *substratum* wherein they do subsist, and from which they do result, which therefore we call *substance*.

2. *Our obscure Idea of Substance is general.* So that if any one will examine himself concerning his notion of pure substance in general, he will find he has no other idea of it at all, but only a supposition of he knows not what *support* of such qualities which are capable of producing simple ideas in us; which qualities are commonly called accidents. If any one should be asked, what is the subject wherein colour or weight inheres, he would have nothing to say, but the solid extended parts; and if he were demanded, what is it that solidity and extension adhere in, he would not be in a much better case than the Indian before mentioned who, saying that the world was supported by a great elephant, was asked what the elephant rested on; to which his answer was—a great tortoise: but being again pressed to know what gave support to the broad-backed tortoise, replied—*something, he knew not what.* And thus here, as in all other cases where we use words without having clear and distinct ideas, we talk like children: who, being questioned what such a thing is, which they know not, readily give this satisfactory answer, that it is *something:* which in truth signifies no more, when so used, either by children or men, but that they know not what; and that the thing they pretend to know, and talk of, is what they have no distinct idea of at all, and so are perfectly ignorant of it, and in the dark. The idea then we have, to which we give the *general* name substance, being nothing but the supposed, but unknown, support of those qualities we find existing, which we imagine cannot subsist *sine re substante*, without something to support them, we call that support *substantia*; which, according to the true import of the word, is, in plain English, standing under or upholding.

3. *Of the Sorts of Substances.* An obscure and relative idea of *substance in general* being thus made we come to have the ideas of *particular sorts of substances*, by collecting *such* combinations of simple ideas as are, by experience and observation of men's senses, taken notice of to exist together; and are therefore supposed to flow from the particular internal constitution, or unknown essence of that substance. Thus we come to have the ideas of a man, horse, gold, water, &c.; of which substances, whether any one has any other *clear* idea, further than of certain simple ideas coexistent together, I appeal to every one's own experience. It is the ordinary qualities observable in iron, or a diamond, put together, that make the true complex idea of those substances, which a smith or a jeweller commonly knows better than a philosopher; who, whatever *substantial forms* he may talk of, has no other idea of those substances, than what is framed by a collection of those simple ideas which are to be found in them: only we must take notice, that our complex ideas of substances, besides all those simple ideas they are made up of, have always the confused idea of something to which they belong, and in which they subsist: and therefore when we speak of any sort of substance, we say it is a thing having such or such qualities; as body is a thing that is extended, figured, and capable of motion; spirit, a thing capable of thinking; and so hardness, friability, and power to draw iron, we say, are qualities to be found in a loadstone. These, and the like fashions of speaking, intimate that the substance is supposed always *something besides* the extension, figure, solidity, motion, thinking, or other observable ideas, though we know not what it is.

4. *No clear or distinct idea of Substance in general.* Hence, when we talk or think of any particular sort of corporeal substances, as horse, stone, &c., though the idea we have of either of them be but the complication or collection of those several simple ideas of sensible qualities, which we used to find united in the thing called horse or stone; yet, *because we cannot conceive how they should subsist alone, nor one in another,* we suppose

them existing in and supported by some common subject; which support we denote by the name substance, though it be certain we have no clear or distinct idea of that thing we suppose a support.

5. *As clear an Idea of spiritual substance as of corporeal substance.* The same thing happens concerning the operations of the mind, viz. thinking, reasoning, fearing, &c., which we concluding not to subsist of themselves, nor apprehending how they can belong to body, or be produced by it, we are apt to think these the actions of some other *substance*, which we call *spirit*; whereby yet it is evident that, having no other idea or notion of matter, but something wherein those many sensible qualities which affect our senses do subsist; by supposing a substance wherein thinking, knowing, doubting, and a power of moving, &c., do subsist, we have as clear a notion of the substance of spirit, as we have of body; the one being supposed to be (without knowing what it is) the *substratum* to those simple ideas we have from without; and the other supposed (with a like ignorance of what it is) to be the *substratum* to those operations we experiment in ourselves within. It is plain then, that the idea of *corporeal substance* in matter is as remote from our conceptions and apprehensions, as that of *spiritual substance*, or spirit: and therefore, from our not having any notion of the substance of spirit, we can no more conclude its non-existence, than we can, for the same reason, deny the existence of body; it being as rational to affirm there is no body, because we have no clear and distinct idea of the substance of matter, as to say there is no spirit, because we have no clear and distinct idea of the substance of a spirit.

6. *Our ideas of particular Sorts of Substances.* Whatever therefore be the secret abstract nature of substance in general, all the ideas we have of particular distinct sorts of substances are nothing but several combinations of simple ideas, co-existing in such, though unknown, cause of their union, as makes the whole subsist of itself. It is by such combinations of simple ideas, and nothing else, that we represent particular sorts of substances to ourselves; such are the ideas we have of their several species in our minds; and such only do we, by their specific names, signify to others, v.g. man, horse, sun, water, iron: upon hearing which words, every one who understands the language, frames in his mind a combination of those several simple ideas which he has usually observed, or fancied to exist together under that denomination; all which he supposes to rest in and be, as it were, adherent to that unknown common subject, which inheres not in anything else. Though, in the meantime, it be manifest, and every one, upon inquiry into his own thoughts, will find, that he has no other idea of any substance, v.g. let it be gold, horse, iron, man, vitriol, bread, but what he has barely of those sensible qualities, which he supposes to inhere; with a supposition of such a *substratum* as gives, as it were, a support to those qualities or simple ideas, which he has observed to exist united together. Thus, the idea of the sun,—what is it but an aggregate of those several simple ideas, bright, hot, roundish, having a constant regular motion, at a certain distance from us, and perhaps some other: as he who thinks and discourses of the sun has been more or less accurate in observing those sensible qualities, ideas, or properties, which are in that thing which he calls the sun. . . .

9. *Three sorts of Ideas make our complex ones of Corporeal Substances.* The ideas that make our complex ones of corporeal substances, are of these three sorts. First, the ideas of the primary qualities of things, which are discovered by our senses, and are in them even when we perceive them not; such are the bulk, figure, number, situation, and motion of the parts of bodies; which are really in them, whether we take notice of them or not. Secondly, the sensible secondary qualities, which, depending on these,

E. MODERN METAPHYSICS | 155

are nothing but the powers those substances have to produce several ideas in us by our senses; which ideas are not in the things themselves, otherwise than as anything in its cause. Thirdly, the aptness we consider in any substance, to give or receive such alterations of primary qualities, as that the substance so altered should produce in us different ideas from what it did before; these are called active and passive powers: all which powers, as far as we have any notice or notion of them, terminate only in sensible simple ideas. For whatever alteration a loadstone has the power to make in the minute particles of iron, we should have no notion of any power it had at all to operate on iron, did not its sensible motion discover it: and I doubt not, but there are a thousand changes, that bodies we daily handle have a power to cause in one another, which we never suspect, because they never appear in sensible effects.

10. *Powers thus make a great Part of our complex Ideas of particular Substances. Powers* therefore justly make a great part of our complex ideas of substances. He that will examine his complex idea of gold, will find several of its ideas that make it up to be only powers; as the power of being melted, but of not spending itself in the fire; of being dissolved in *aqua regia*, are ideas as necessary to make up our complex idea of gold, as its colour and weight: which, if duly considered, are also nothing but different powers. For, to speak truly, yellowness is not actually in gold, but is a power in gold to produce that idea in us by our eyes, when placed in a due light: and the heat, which we cannot leave out of our ideas of the sun, is no more really in the sun, than the white colour it introduced into wax. These are both equally powers in the sun, operating, by the motion and figure of its sensible parts, so on a man, as to make him have the idea of heat; and so on wax, as to make it capable to produce in a man the idea of white.

11. *The now secondary Qualities of Bodies would disappear, if we could discover the primary ones of their minute Parts.* Had we senses acute enough to discern the minute particles of bodies, and the real constitution on which their sensible qualities depend, I doubt not but they would produce quite different ideas in us: and that which is now the yellow colour of gold, would then disappear, and instead of it we should see an admirable texture of parts, of a certain size and figure. This microscopes plainly discover to us; for what to our naked eyes produces a certain colour, is, by thus augmenting the acuteness of our senses, discovered to be quite a different thing; and the thus altering, as it were, the proportion of the bulk of the minute parts of a coloured object to our usual sight, produces different ideas from what it did before. Thus, sand or pounded glass, which is opaque, and white to the naked eye, is pellucid in a microscope; and a hair seen in this way, loses its former colour, and is, in a great measure, pellucid, with a mixture of some bright sparkling colours, such as appear from the refraction of diamonds, and other pellucid bodies. Blood, to the naked eye, appears all red; but by a good microscope, wherein its lesser parts appear, shows only some few globules of red, swimming in a pellucid liquor, and how these red globules would appear, if glasses could be found that could yet magnify them a thousand or ten thousand times more, is uncertain. . . .

14. *Our specific Ideas of Substances.* But to return to the matter in hand,—the ideas we have of substances, and the ways we come by them. I say, our *specific* ideas of substances are nothing else but *a collection of a certain number of simple ideas, considered as united in one thing.* These ideas of substances, though they are commonly simple apprehensions, and the names of them simple terms, yet in effect are complex and compounded. Thus the idea which an Englishman signifies by the name swan, is white colour, long neck, red beak, black legs, and whole feet, and all these of a certain

size, with a power of swimming in the water, and making a certain kind of noise, and perhaps, to a man who has long observed this kind of birds, some other properties: which all terminate in sensible simple ideas, all united in one common subject.

15. *Our Ideas of spiritual Substances, as clear as of bodily Substances.* Besides the complex ideas we have of material sensible substances, of which I have last spoken,—by the simple ideas we have taken from those operations of our own minds, which we experiment daily in ourselves, as thinking, understanding, willing, knowing, and power of beginning motion, &c., co-existing in some substance, we are able to frame the *complex idea of an immaterial spirit.* And thus, by putting together the ideas of thinking, perceiving, liberty, and power of moving themselves and other things, we have as clear a perception and notion of immaterial substances as we have of material. For putting together the ideas of thinking and willing, or the power of moving or quieting corporeal motion, joined to substance, of which we have no distinct idea, we have the idea of an immaterial spirit; and by putting together the ideas of coherent solid parts, and a power of being moved, joined with substance, of which likewise we have no positive idea, we have the idea of matter. The one is as clear and distinct an idea as the other: the idea of thinking, and moving a body, being as clear and distinct ideas as the ideas of extension, solidity, and being moved. For our idea of substance is equally obscure, or none at all, in both: it is but a supposed I know not what, to support those ideas we call accidents. It is for want of reflection that we are apt to think that our senses show us nothing but material things. Every act of sensation, when duly considered, gives us an equal view of both parts of nature, the corporeal and spiritual. For whilst I know, by seeing or hearing, &c., that there is some corporeal being without me, the object of that sensation, I do more certainly know, that there is some spiritual being within me that sees and hears. This, I must be convinced, cannot be the action of bare insensible matter; nor ever could be, without an immaterial thinking being.

16. *No Idea of abstract Substance either in Body or Spirit.* By the complex idea of extended, figured, coloured, and all other sensible qualities, which is all that we know of it, we are as far from the idea of the substance of body, as if we knew nothing at all: nor after all the acquaintance and familiarity which we imagine we have with matter, and the many qualities men assure themselves they perceive and know in bodies, will it perhaps upon examination be found, that they have any more or clearer primary ideas belonging to body, than they have belonging to immaterial spirit.

17. *Cohesion of solid parts and Impulse, the primary ideas peculiar to Body.* The primary ideas we have *peculiar to body,* as contradistinguished to spirit, are the *cohesion of solid, and consequently separable, parts,* and a *power of communicating motion by impulse.* These, I think, are the original ideas proper and peculiar to body; for figure is but the consequence of finite extension.

18. *Thinking and Motivity, the primary ideas peculiar to spirit.* The ideas we have belonging and *peculiar to spirit,* are *thinking,* and *will,* or *a power of putting body into motion by thought, and, which is consequent to it, liberty.* For, as body cannot but communicate its motion by impulse to another body, which it meets with at rest, so the mind can put bodies into motion, or forbear to do so, as it pleases. The ideas of *existence, duration,* and *mobility,* are common to them both. . . .

37. *Recapitulation.* And thus we have seen what kind of ideas we have of *substances of all kinds,* wherein they consist, and how we came by them. From whence, I think, it is very evident,

First, That all our ideas of the several *sorts* of substances are nothing but collections of simple ideas: with a supposition of *something* to which they belong, and in which they subsist: though of this supposed something we have no clear distinct idea at all.

Secondly, That all the simple ideas, that thus united in one common *substratum*, make up our complex ideas of several *sorts* of substances, are no other but such as we have received from sensation or reflection. So that even in those which we think we are most intimately acquainted with, and that come nearest the comprehension of our most enlarged conceptions, we cannot go beyond those simple ideas. And even in those which seem most remote from all we have to do with, and do infinitely surpass anything we can perceive in ourselves by reflection; or discover by sensation in other things, we can attain to nothing but those simple ideas, which we originally received from sensation or reflection; as is evident in the complex ideas we have of angels, and particularly of God himself.

Thirdly, That most of the simple ideas that make up our complex ideas of substances, when truly considered, are only *powers*, however we are apt to take them for positive qualities; v.g. the greatest part of the ideas that make our complex idea of *gold* are yellowness, great weight, ductility, fusibility, and solubility in *aqua regia*, &c., all united together in an unknown *substratum*: all which ideas are nothing else but so many relations to other substances; and are not really in the gold, considered barely in itself, though they depend on those real and primary qualities of its internal constitution, whereby it has a fitness differently to operate, and be operated on by several other substances.

With the rise of modern science, it became the generally accepted view that the universe was a giant machine, perhaps set up by God, but in any case a well-coordinated and predictable mechanism. Isaac Newton's discovery of the causal laws of motion and gravity only brought to a climax a scientific worldview that had been in the making for centuries. And though ancient animism was still alive and belief in God and spirituality was still virtually universal, the modern mechanical view of reality was an absolutely unavoidable consideration for any metaphysician.

Both Spinoza and Leibniz fully appreciated this modern scientific view, although they interpreted it very differently. They were both religious men. (Spinoza, ironically, was branded an atheist and his philosophy banned from most of Europe.) They both accepted Descartes' "rationalist," deductive method and both developed their thinking along the lines of a geometrical system. They both began by considering the concept of substance. Yet Spinoza emerged as a monist, Leibniz as a pluralist. In viewing their impressive systems of thought, it is important to keep in mind the long history we have quickly reviewed, the powerful influences of Christianity and science, and, most importantly, the various metaphysical problems to which we were introduced in the preceding chapter.

- What are the similarities between Cartesian dualism and Plato's view of reality?
- Do we perceive substances, according to Descartes? If not, what do we perceive?
- Why does Descartes think that the body is a source of deception? Give evidence from your own experience that supports this claim.
- How does Locke's view of the relationship between minds and bodies compare with Descartes'?

Benedictus de Spinoza (1632-1677)

Spinoza was born Baruch ben Michael, the son of Jewish refugees from the Spanish Inquisition. He was born and grew up in Amsterdam, a relative haven of toleration in a world still dangerous because of religious hatreds. Spinoza studied to be a rabbi, making himself familiar with Christian theology as well. He was always a recluse, who wandered about the country making a living by grinding lenses, and he was later ostracized by his fellow Jews for his heretical beliefs. His best-known book is *Ethics* (1677); it is a radical reinterpretation of God as identical to the universe (pantheism) and a protracted argument concerning the uselessness of human struggle in the face of a thoroughly determined universe.

FIG. 2.23
Baruch Spinoza

2. Benedictus de Spinoza

Spinoza's *Ethics* is one of the few modern works that is accepted as an unqualified classic by virtually everyone in philosophy. It is the author's only major work. Spinoza was an avid political reformer, particularly on the issue of religious toleration, and even in liberal Amsterdam that made him a dangerous person to know. The following work, which, as you will see, is much more than a study in ethics, was his most forceful contribution to the issue of tolerance. Spinoza introduced a shockingly radical reinterpretation of God and His relation to the universe. He also gave an equally shocking theory of our roles in the universe. So while you are attempting to comprehend these difficult statements and proofs about "substance," keep your mind open for the dramatic changes in the way Spinoza teaches us to look at our world and for his radical rethinking of Judaism.

Spinoza begins with a set of definitions:

FROM *Ethics*
BY **Benedictus de Spinoza**[24]

DEFINITIONS

I. By that which is *self-caused*, I mean that of which the essence involves existence, or that of which the nature is only conceivable as existent.

II. A thing is called *finite after its kind*, when it can be limited by another thing of the same nature; for instance, a body is called finite because we always conceive another greater body. So, also, a thought is limited by another thought, but a body is not limited by thought, nor a thought by body.

III. By *substance*, I mean that which is in itself, and is conceived through itself: in other words, that of which a conception can be formed independently of any other conception.

IV. By *attribute*, I mean that which the intellect perceives as constituting the essence of substance.

V. By *mode*, I mean the modifications of substance, or that which exists in, and is conceived through, something other than itself.

VI. By *God*, I mean a being absolutely infinite—that is, a substance consisting in infinite attributes, in which each expresses eternal and infinite essentiality.

VII. That thing is called free, which exists solely by the necessity of its own nature, and of which the action is determined by itself alone. On the other hand, that thing is necessary, or rather constrained, which is determined by something external to itself to a fixed and definite method of existence or action.

VIII. By *eternity*, I mean existence itself, in so far as it is conceived necessarily to follow solely from the definition of that which is eternal.

24 Benedictus de Spinoza, from *Ethics*, in *The Rationalists*, trans. R. H. M. Elwes, New York: Doubleday, 1960.

These definitions sound much more forbidding than they really are. Notice first how many of these terms and definitions are familiar to us from Aristotle: for example, the definition of substance as the basic "stuff" that has various properties but is dependent only on itself and can be thought of without thinking of anything else. **Attributes** and **modes**, on the other hand, are properties: attributes consist of essential characteristics of a substance; modes are modifications of attributes. (For example, having a body is an attribute of substance; being blond and blue-eyed are merely modes.) The **cause-of-itself** is like Aristotle's prime mover, but with some very important differences. Spinoza's "mover" turns out to be identical to the universe, and Spinoza's "God" is much more than "thought thinking itself," as in Aristotle. But the basic starting point of the entire system, as summarized in these definitions and axioms, is the Aristotelian notion of substance. Like the ancient metaphysicians, Spinoza insists that whatever really exists, exists eternally (Definition VIII). But that also means—there can be no Creation and no Creator!

As in geometry, the definitions are followed by a set of *axioms*, that is, principles that are so obvious that they need no defense. In plane geometry, such an axiom would be "the shortest distance between two points is a straight line." Spinoza's axioms may not seem quite so obvious at first glance, partly because of the unfamiliarity of his metaphysical terminology.

AXIOMS

I. Everything which exists, exists either in itself or in something else.

II. That which cannot be conceived through anything else must be conceived through itself.

III. From a given definite cause an effect necessarily follows, and, on the other hand, if no definite cause be granted, it is impossible that an effect can follow.

IV. The knowledge of an effect depends on and involves the knowledge of a cause.

V. Things which have nothing in common cannot be understood, the one by means of the other; the conception of one does not involve the conception of the other.

VI. A true idea must correspond with its ideate or object.

VII. If a thing can be conceived as non-existing, its essence does not involve existence.

You can see that the axioms follow approximately the same sequence as the definitions, and the axioms in most cases are based on the definitions, although they do not strictly follow from them. For example, Axiom I, like Definition I, concerns the idea that everything has an explanation. Definition I, although stated in terms of "cause" ("self-caused"), concerns that which must exist if it can just be thought of. Axiom I says that everything must either be explainable through itself (that is, "self-caused") or through something else.

Similarly, Definition II uses a technical term ("finite after its kind") to talk about things that can be explained only by reference to something greater, while Axiom II says that anything that cannot be so explained must be explained simply in terms of itself ("self-caused" again). Axioms III and IV outline the basic principles of cause and effect; that is, that a cause makes its effect happen necessarily, and without the cause, there would be no effect, and that the knowledge of the effect depends on knowing the cause. (These principles have had a long and important history in both metaphysics and theories of science and knowledge. They will play a key role in Spinoza's theory of determinism [the idea that everything happens necessarily because of its causes] and in "deterministic" theories generally. These will be discussed in Chapter 6 in detail.) Axioms V–VII return to the central theme of explanation begun in Axioms I and II; Axiom V insists that one thing can be explained in terms of another only if

"Everything which exists, exists either in itself or in something else."

– BENEDICTUS DE SPINOZA

they have "something in common." Thus you explain one physical event in terms of another physical event (since they have in common certain physical properties). Axiom VI repeats the important assumption we made explicit at the end of the introduction, namely, that our ideas are capable of grasping reality. (This axiom also states a seemingly innocent theory of truth, often called "the correspondence theory of truth," which says that "a true idea corresponds with some actual fact [*ideate* or *object*] in the world.") Axiom VII returns to the idea of "essence involving existence," in other words, that which is self-caused, or substance or God. Axiom VII is stated negatively, however, and says that if we can think of something as not existing (for example, we can imagine what it would be like to live in a world without freeways, or without stars, or even without other people), then "its essence does not involve existence." That is, existing is not one of its essential characteristics and it is not "self-caused."

The general theme of the axioms is that everything has an explanation for its existence, either by reference to something else or because it is "self-caused" or self-explanatory, that is, its "essence involves its existence" or it is entirely "in itself and conceived through itself." This last phrase is from the definition of "substance" (Def. III), so you can see how, even in his axioms and definitions, Spinoza is setting up his main thesis—that there can only be one substance.

Starting with these definitions and axioms, which he takes to be unobjectionable, Spinoza begins the "proofs" of his "propositions," which follow like the theorems of Euclidean geometry from the definitions of terms such as "line," "point," and "parallel." Again, these look forbidding, but their philosophical relevance should be clear.

PROPOSITIONS

PROP. I. *Substance is by nature prior to its modifications.*

Proof.—This is clear from Def. iii. and v.

PROP. II. *Two substances, whose attributes are different, have nothing in common.*

Proof.—Also evident from Def. iii. For each must exist in itself, and be conceived through itself; in other words, the conception of one does not imply the conception of the other.

PROP. III. *Things which have nothing in common cannot be one the cause of the other.*

Proof.—If they have nothing in common, it follows that one cannot be apprehended by means of the other (Ax. v.), and, therefore, one cannot be the cause of the other (Ax. iv.). Q.E.D. [Latin, *quod erat demonstrandum*, a phrase used in traditional logic meaning "thus it is proven."]

PROP. IV. *Two or more distinct things are distinguished one from the other either by the difference of the attributes of the substances, or by the difference of their modifications.*

Proof.—Everything which exists, exists either in itself or in something else (Ax. i.),—that is (by Def. iii. and v.), nothing is granted in addition to the understanding, except substance and its modifications. Nothing is, therefore, given besides the understanding, by which several things may be distinguished one from the other, except the substances, or, in other words (see Ax. iv.), their attributes and modifications. Q.E.D.

PROP. V. *There cannot exist in the universe two or more substances having the same nature or attribute.*

Proof.—If several distinct substances be granted, they must be distinguished one from the other, either by the difference of their attributes, or by the difference of their modifications (Prop. iv.). If only by the difference of their attributes, it will be granted that there cannot be more than one with an identical attribute. If by the difference of their modifications—as substance is naturally prior to its modifications

(Prop. i.),—it follows that setting the modifications aside, and considering substance in itself, that is truly (Deff. iii. and vi.), there cannot be conceived one substance different from another,—that is (by Prop. iv.), there cannot be granted several substances, but one substance only. *Q.E.D.*

PROP. VI. *One substance cannot be produced by another substance.*

Proof.—It is impossible that there should be in the universe two substances with an identical attribute, *i.e.*, which have anything common to them both (Prop. ii.), and, therefore (Prop. iii.), one cannot be the cause of another, neither can one be produced by the other. *Q.E.D.*

So far, the main point is quite simple: if there is more than one substance, the substances could have no possible relation to each other. Therefore, by a kind of *reductio ad absurdum* argument, there can only be one substance. In the propositions that follow (and especially the note to Prop. VIII) this is demonstrated again:

PROP. VII. *Existence belongs to the nature of substance.*

Proof.—Substance cannot be produced by anything external (Corollary, Prop. vi.), it must, therefore, be its own cause—that is, its essence necessarily involves existence, or existence belongs to its nature.

PROP. VIII. *Every substance is necessarily infinite.*

Proof.—There can only be one substance with an identical attribute, and existence follows from its nature (Prop. vii.); its nature, therefore, involves existence, either as finite or infinite. It does not exist as finite, for (by Def. ii.) it would then be limited by something else of the same kind, which would also necessarily exist (Prop. vii.); and there would be two substances with an identical attribute, which is absurd (Prop. v.). It therefore exists as infinite. *Q.E.D.*

Note.—No doubt it will be difficult for those who think about things loosely, and have not been accustomed to know them by their primary causes, to comprehend the demonstration of Prop. vii.: for such persons make no distinction between the modifications of substances and the substances themselves, and are ignorant of the manner in which things are produced; hence they attribute to substances the beginning which they observe in natural objects. Those who are ignorant of true causes, make complete confusion—think that trees might talk just as well as men—that men might be formed from stones as well as from seed; and imagine that any form might be changed into any other. So, also, those who confuse the two natures, divine and human, readily attribute human passions to the deity, especially so long as they do not know how passions originate in the mind. But, if people would consider the nature of substance, they would have no doubt about the truth of Prop. vii. In fact, this proposition would be a universal axiom, and accounted a truism. For, by substance, would be understood that which is in itself, and is conceived through itself—that is, something of which the conception requires not the conception of anything else; whereas modifications exist in something external to themselves, and a conception of them is formed by means of a conception of the thing in which they exist. Therefore, we may have true ideas of non-existent modifications; for, although they may have no *actual* existence apart from the conceiving intellect, yet their essence is so involved in something external to themselves that they may through it be conceived. Whereas the only truth substances can have, external to the intellect, must consist in their existence, because they are conceived through themselves. Therefore, for a person to say that he has a clear and distinct—that is, a true—idea of a substance, but that he is not sure whether such substance exists, would be the same as if he said that he had a true idea, but was not sure whether or not it was false (a little consid-eration will make this plain); or if anyone affirmed that substance is created, it would be the same as saying that a false idea was true—in short, the height of absurdity. It must, then, necessarily be admitted that the existence of substance as its essence is an eternal truth. And we can hence conclude by another process of reasoning—that there is but one such substance.

This last phrase summarizes the key doctrine of the entire *Ethics*, that there can be but one substance. The argument in this note, which insists that the essence of substance includes its existence, was a very popular argument throughout the Middle Ages. It means, quite simply, that if you can even imagine something whose essence includes existence, then you know that thing necessarily exists. In a further digression (but it is the digressions that often contain the most philosophy), Spinoza adopts Aristotle's insistence (see p. 145) that everything (or every event) must have its cause:

There is necessarily for each individual existent thing a cause why it should exist.
This cause of existence must either be contained in the nature and definition of the thing defined, or must be postulated apart from such definition.

Such an assertion gives Aristotle the basis for his "prime mover" argument. But Spinoza, unlike Aristotle, has no qualms about the idea of an "infinite regress"; in his view, the universe extends back in time forever, has always existed, and at no time ever came into existence.
What then follows is the working-out of the notion that there is one substance:

PROP. IX. *The more reality or being a thing has, the greater the number of its attributes* (Def. iv.).
PROP. X. *Each particular attribute of the one substance must be conceived through itself.*
Proof.—An attribute is that which the intellect perceives of substance, as consti-tuting its essence (Def. iv.), and, therefore, must be conceived through itself (Def. iii.). Q.E.D.

Spinoza goes on to explain that, although we might think of different attributes separately (for example, think of minds and bodies as totally different from each other), we must not conclude that they are different substances. They are rather separate properties of one and the same substance. He then concludes:

Consequently it is abundantly clear, that an absolutely infinite being must necessar-ily be defined as consisting in infinite attributes, each of which expresses a certain eternal and infinite essence.
If anyone now ask, by what sign shall he be able to distinguish different sub-stances, let him read the following propositions, which show that there is but one substance in the universe, and that it is absolutely infinite, wherefore such a sign would be sought for in vain.

Now this looks complicated, but we can appreciate its straightforward significance by look-ing at it through our earlier questions in ontology and cosmology (pp. 52-62): first, "How many substances does Spinoza say that there are (and must be)?" Only one—he is a monist, like the earliest pre-Socratics. Descartes, Spinoza's immediate predecessor, had argued that there are three kinds of substance: bodies, minds, and God. Spinoza, however, argues that the very defi-nition of substance makes it necessary that there be only one substance and that bodies and minds are attributes of this one substance, not substances themselves.
So the answer to our second ontological question, "What kind of substances?" is "one infinite substance," the full nature of which we cannot know. But at least we know two of

its properties, namely body and mind. Now notice that this gets around a problem that will plague Descartes (see Chapter 5): How can different substances, which by definition are independent, interact with one another (our fourth question)? If mind and body are separate substances, then how can they come together to form a person? For Spinoza, since there is only one substance, this problem does not arise. With regard to our third question, "How do we distinguish different things (attributes, bodies, and minds)?" Spinoza's answer is fantastic; there is ultimately only one body, namely the physical universe, and one mind, namely all of the thinking in the universe (which in turn are different attributes of the one substance). This means that distinctions between our bodies ("my" body and "your" body) and between our bodies and the rest of the physical universe are ultimately unwarranted, a humanistic pretension that has no basis in reality. But even more surprising is the idea that there is but a single mind and that our individual minds are somehow only "part of it" (that is, particular modes) but not individual minds at all! Your pride in your "individuality," therefore, has no foundation in reality. You are only a part of that one cosmic substance, the universe.

But the universe is also God. Here is where the innocent-looking obscurity of Spinoza's system becomes the heresy that was banned throughout Europe. By Proposition X, Spinoza has proved that God, substance, and the cause-of-itself are all identical. In the next few propositions, he proves that God necessarily exists (offering a version of the ontological proof we considered in Chapter 1). Then, Proposition XIV: "*Besides God, no substance can be granted or conceived.*" This means that God and the universe are one and the same. This position, called **pantheism** (literally, "everything is God"), was considered sacrilege, even in liberal Amsterdam. It means, against all traditional Judeo-Christian teachings, that God has no existence independent of the universe and that He therefore cannot be its Creator. Look again at the explanation to Definition VIII and then at Proposition XV and those that follow:

> PROP. XV. *Whatsoever is, is in God, and without God nothing can be, or be conceived.*
> PROP. XVI. *From the necessity of the divine nature must follow an infinite number of things in infinite ways—that is, all things which can fall within the sphere of infinite intellect.*

FIG. 2.24 Causality in action. *(Image © Anthony Hall, 2011. Used under license from Shutterstock.com)*

PROP. XVII. *God acts solely by the laws of his own nature, and is not constrained by anyone.*

PROP. XVIII. *God is the indwelling and not the transient cause of all things.*

PROP. XIX. *God, and all the attributes of God, are eternal.*

PROP. XX. *The existence of God and his essence are one and the same.*

PROP. XXI. *All things which follow from the absolute nature of any attribute of God must always exist and be infinite, or, in other words, are eternal and infinite through the said attribute.*

PROP. XXII. *Whatever follows from any attribute of God, in so far as it is modified by a modification, which exists necessarily and as infinite, through the said attribute, must also exist necessarily and as infinite.*

PROP. XXIII. *Every mode which exists both necessarily and as infinite must necessarily follow either from the absolute nature of some attribute of God, or from an attribute modified by a modification which exists necessarily and as infinite.*

PROP. XXIV. *The essence of things produced by God does not involve existence.*

PROP. XXV. *God is the efficient cause not only of the existence of things, but also of their essence.*

Yes, Spinoza believes in God. But God is nothing other than the universe. He has few of the characteristics traditionally attributed to Him and worshiped in Him. For example, Spinoza goes on to argue, on the basis of what he has said already, that God has no will, that He doesn't do anything, and, ultimately, He doesn't care about anything either, including humanity. Here is a scientific worldview that is so unrelenting that even Newton himself would be shocked by it. This does not mean that Spinoza is a materialist; quite to the contrary, the importance of his constant insistence upon "the infinite attributes of God," of which we are capable of knowing only two (could you imagine what some of the others might be like?) is to say that God has not only physical existence but (at least) mental existence as well.

But where the scientific outlook becomes most dramatic is in Spinoza's defense of the doctrine we shall call **determinism**, the thesis that every event in the universe necessarily occurs as the result of its cause. The ultimate cause is God, which is to say, the universe itself. Once again, the terms come from Aristotle, but it is therefore important to insist that Spinoza does not believe—with either Aristotle or Christendom—that the universe has any purpose whatsoever. Nor does he believe that the universe or God has any beginning or end, thus answering our two sets of cosmological questions with a single necessary truth, once again, derived directly from the definition of substance.

The ultimate meaning of Spinoza's arguments for determinism is that no action, whether of man or God, is ever free. Everything in the universe, according to Spinoza, is exactly as it must be; the universe couldn't be any other way. Nothing is so pointless as struggling against a universe in which everything, including our own natures and actions, is already determined.

PROP. XXVI. *A thing which is conditioned to act in a particular manner has necessarily been thus conditioned by God; and that which has not been conditioned by God cannot condition itself to act.*

PROP. XXVII. *A thing, which has been conditioned by God to act in a particular way, cannot render itself unconditioned.*

PROP. XXVIII. *Every individual thing, or everything which is finite and has a conditioned existence, cannot exist or be conditioned to act, unless it be conditioned for existence and action by a cause other than itself, which also is finite and has a conditioned existence; and likewise this cause cannot in its turn exist or be conditioned to act, unless it be conditioned for existence and action by another cause, which also is finite and has a conditioned existence, and so on to infinity.*

PROP. XXIX. *Nothing in the universe is contingent, but all things are conditioned to exist and operate in a particular manner by the necessity of the divine nature.*[25]

PROP. XXX. *Intellect, in function finite, or in function infinite, must comprehend the attributes of God and the modifications of God, and nothing else.*

PROP. XXXI. *The intellect in function, whether finite or infinite, as will, desire, love, & c., should be referred to passive nature and not to active nature.*

PROP. XXXII. *Will cannot be called a free cause, but only a necessary cause.*

PROP. XXXIII. *Things could not have been brought into being by God in any manner or in any order different from that which has in fact obtained. [God is determined too.]*

PROP. XXXIV. *God's power is identical with his essence.*

PROP. XXXV. *Whatsoever we conceive to be in the power of God, necessarily exists.*

PROP. XXXVI. *There is no cause from whose nature some effect does not follow.*

Part II of the *Ethics* discusses "the Nature and Origin of the Mind." It begins with a further set of definitions and axioms, most importantly, the definition of body as "**extended** thing," that is, extended in space (which Spinoza got directly from Descartes and the medieval philosophers) and idea, "the mental conception which is formed by the mind as a thinking thing." Mind, unlike body, is defined as **unextended** (that is, it has no spatial dimensions). It is in this part that Spinoza argues those surprising doctrines that we have already summarized: Mind and body are each one of an infinite number of attributes of God, not substance themselves (as they were for Descartes), and our individual minds are really indistinguishable modifications of the one Great Mind of the One Substance. And Spinoza joins with all of his metaphysical colleagues in insisting that "the order and connection of ideas is the same as the order and connection of things" (Prop. VII). Here again is Spinoza's affirmation of his confidence in thought to grasp reality. (Remember Heraclitus, "thought is Being.")

The upshot of Part II, and the subject that dominates the *Ethics* for the remaining three parts, is Spinoza's determinism.

PROP. XLVIII. *In the mind there is no absolute or free will; but the mind is determined to wish this or that by a cause, which has been determined by another cause, and this last by another cause, and so on to infinity.*

Spinoza has none of Aristotle's fears of an "infinite regress," and if he believes in a "cause-of-itself" that is not the same as a "first cause," for there is no such thing. We shall talk more about this "free will and determinism" problem in Chapter 6; but it is worth noting, as a way of summing up, Spinoza's drastic answer to the problem. As an unyielding determinist, he rejects every attempt to save some space for freedom of human action. But he assures us that we can, with heroic effort (Prop. XLVII), understand the nature of this determinism, and accept it gracefully. The folly is in the fighting, he tells us. The remainder of the *Ethics* is given over to the attempt to draw out the logical consequences of this stoic conclusion.

Part III is a long argument against emotions and what we would call "emotional involvement" as the needless cause of suffering and vice. Against them, Spinoza argues the virtues of human reason, which penetrates the useless involvements of the emotions and allows us

---

[25] We are all determined by the nature of God or the universe. But then, here is a problem: Are we not then compelled to struggle and can't help doing so? If so, what is the point of Spinoza's urging us not to?

FIG. 2.25 Gottfried Wilhelm von Leibniz

Gottfried Wilhelm von Leibniz (1646-1716)

Leibniz has been called "the last of the universal geniuses." He was one of the inventors of the calculus; the father of modern formal linguistics; the inventor of a primitive computer; a military strategist (who may have influenced Napoleon); a physicist who, in his own time, was thought to be the rival of Newton; and, most of all, a great philosopher. He grew up in Leipzig but traveled considerably (to Paris and Amsterdam and all over Germany). Leibniz spoke personally with most of the great philosophers of his time and debated with them constantly. His metaphysics is a curious combination of traditional theology and a radical alternative to the physical doctrines of Newton, to whose philosophy he had once been attracted but later gave up as "absurd." His short *Monadology* (1714) is a summary of his mature metaphysical theories.

to understand the causes of our actions and feelings. To understand an emotion, Spinoza believes, is to change and eliminate it. For example, to understand why one is angry, according to Spinoza, is sufficient to let us get rid of our anger. To realize that we are unable to change, according to Spinoza, is the only freedom we can really be said to have.

What you have just seen is modern metaphysics at its most brilliant. The geometrical method, however, is no longer fashionable, and much of Spinoza's language is, to us, antiquated and unnatural. But the intricacies of his system, the way he ties so many different ideas together, the answers he gave to ancient philosophical problems, and the boldness with which he sets out a new vision of the universe, have made Spinoza's philosophy widely appreciated despite his difficult style. What you are about to read, though, is no less astonishing, no less brilliant, and its author no less remarkable a genius. The work from which these excerpts come is a very short work (of about ninety paragraphs) written by Leibniz, who begins with much the same concepts and definitions as Spinoza but ends up with a wholly different metaphysical system. (Leibniz and Spinoza met several times and discussed these issues. But Leibniz found Spinoza's opinions too shocking and acquaintanceship with him too dangerous.)

- How does Spinoza "solve" the problem of interaction among substances?
- What is the essence of God, according to Spinoza?

3. Gottfried Wilhelm von Leibniz

Leibniz begins with the same technical notion of substance, and from it he draws an entirely different but equally fantastic picture of the universe. Where Spinoza's universe was mechanical and wholly dependent upon causes, Leibniz's universe is very much alive, and everything happens for a purpose (as in Aristotle's ancient teleology). The guiding principle of Leibniz's philosophy is called the "**Principle of Sufficient Reason**," which says, simply, that there must be a reason for everything. Even God, on this account, cannot act capriciously but must have a reason for whatever He has created. We shall see that this principle is among the most important guidelines to Leibniz's philosophy. From it, he develops a radical alternative to Isaac Newton's physics and a spectacularly optimistic view that, because God acts according to this principle, this world that He created must be "the **best of all possible worlds**."

Where Spinoza argues that there can be at most one substance, Leibniz argues that there are many. He calls them **monads**. Every monad is different from every other, and God (who is something of a supermonad and the only "uncreated monad") has created them all. The work presented here, accordingly, is called the *Monadology* ("the study of monads"), written in 1714. It is a very condensed summary of Leibniz's metaphysics:

FROM *Monadology*
BY **Gottfried Wilhelm von Leibniz**[26]

1. The Monad, of which we will speak here, is nothing else than a simple substance, which goes to make up composites; by simple, we mean without parts.

2. There must be simple substances because there are composites; for a composite is nothing else than a collection or *aggregatum* of simple substances.

A simple substance is one that cannot be divided. The argument is curious: any "composite" is obviously divisible. That means that every composite must be "composed" of some simple substances that make it up. (There is a hidden infinite regress argument here: If there weren't ultimately simple substances, then we could go on dividing things forever.) But if the simple substances were extended in space, then they too would be further divisible, for anything that has length, for example, no matter how small, can be cut in two (at least in theory). Therefore, Leibniz concludes, these basic simple substances or monads must be immaterial and have no extension. They can have neither parts, nor extension, nor divisibility:

3. Now, where there are no constituent parts there is possible neither extension, nor form, nor divisibility. These Monads are the true Atoms of nature, and, in fact, the Elements of things.

Here, in Leibniz's first three propositions, are the answers to our first two ontological questions: "How many substances are there?" Many. This answer makes Leibniz a pluralist. "What kind of substances are they?" Simple and immaterial substances, which makes Leibniz an *immaterialist*. (Don't be misled by the term "atoms": we are used to thinking of atoms as the smallest material substances, but Leibniz's atoms are *im*material.) Now, in three more propositions, Leibniz answers our first cosmological question: "Are these substances eternal, or do they come into being at some time? How do they come into being? Are they destructible?"

4. This dissolution, therefore, is not to be feared and there is no way conceivable by which a simple substance can perish through natural means.

5. For the same reason there is no way conceivable by which a simple substance might, through natural means, come into existence, since it cannot be formed by composition.

6. We may say then, that the existence of Monads can begin or end only all at once, that is to say, the Monad can begin only through creation and end only through annihilation. Composites, however, begin or end gradually.

Spinoza had argued that the one substance could neither be created nor destroyed; it had neither beginning nor end. Leibniz's substances, or "monads," can be created or destroyed, but not by any "natural" means. They can be created or destroyed only "all at once." Anticipating later propositions, we can guess that Leibniz will have God (who is something of a supermonad) create them. But notice that compounds of monads, for example, "material objects," can be created and destroyed "naturally."

Now our third question, "How do we distinguish different substances or monads?"

[26] Gottfried Wilhelm von Leibniz, from *Monadology*, in *The Rationalists*, trans. George Montgomery, New York: Doubleday, 1968.

FIG. 2.26 According to Leibniz, identical twins are not identical. *(© iStockphoto.com/Franky De Meyer)*

8. Still Monads must have some qualities, otherwise they would not even be existences. And if simple substances did not differ at all in their qualities, there would be no means of perceiving any change in things. Whatever is in a composite can come into it only through its simple elements and the Monads, if they were without qualities, since they do not differ at all in quantity, would be indistinguishable one from another. For instance, if we imagine *a plenum* or completely filled space, where each part receives only the equivalent of its own previous motion, one state of things would not be distinguishable from another.

9. Each Monad, indeed, must be different from every other. For there are never in nature two beings which are exactly alike, and in which it is not possible to find a difference either internal or based on an intrinsic property.

Only God could actually know everything about every monad in order to compare and contrast them. But even God can distinguish different monads only because they in fact have differences between them. This leads Leibniz to suggest one of his most controversial principles, the so-called "Principle of the **Identity of Indiscernibles**": no two monads can have the same properties (Prop. 9). Why is this? According to the "Principle of Sufficient Reason" (Prop. 32) nothing can be without good reason. Even God, therefore, would have no good reason for duplicating any monad. If two monads were identical, Leibniz argues, God could have no reason for putting one in one place and the other in another place, or for creating them both in the first place. Therefore, no two monads could be exactly alike. A strange kind of argument, but very much at the heart of Leibniz's philosophy, as we shall see later.

How does a monad, which is by definition "simple," alter or combine with other monads to form the changing and familiar universe of our experience? (Here you should be reminded of the similar problems that faced the ancient pre-Socratics and Plato.) Here is our fourth question, and the most difficult Leibniz has to answer: "How do substances interact?" By definition, monads cannot literally "interact." So Leibniz's answer is extremely speculative and imaginative:

7. There is also no way of explaining how a Monad can be altered or changed in its inner being by any other created thing, since there is no possibility of transposition within it, nor can we conceive of any internal movement which can be produced, directed, increased or diminished there within the substance, such as can take place in the case of composites where a change can occur among the parts. The Monads have no windows through which anything may come in or go out.

The problem is that different substances, by definition, are independent and cannot, therefore, have anything to do with one another. Descartes, as we shall see in Chapter 5, had a terrible time getting together his two substances of mind and body. Spinoza, as a monist, solved the problem in the simplest possible way; since there is only one substance, no question of "interaction" is applicable. But Leibniz is a pluralist; there are many substances. They cannot interact as such. They cannot even perceive each other in the usual sense. They "have no windows," in his peculiar but now famous expression; "nothing can come in or go out." Unlike the ancient (and modern) materialist atomists, Leibniz cannot have his monads simply combine and recombine to form new compounds in any usual sense. They cannot, in Leibniz's words, "be altered or changed in [their] inner being by any other created thing." So, how do monads change? They must have all changes already created (by God) within themselves.

Remember the animism that was so prevalent in the ancient Greek philosophers. For them, the phenomenon of life was the model for metaphysics. The idea of Newtonian mechanics would have been incomprehensible to them. Leibniz, we may now say, was vehemently anti-Newton. He was, we may also say, one of the outstanding modern animists. A monad is as different as can be from a Newtonian material atom; a monad is alive, and its changes come from within, never from without. (Except, that is, for its initial creation.) Think of a monad as a living being, "programmed" (to use a modern word) with all of the information and experiences it needs to develop in a certain way, like an acorn developing into an oak tree. Thus the changes in the monad are all internal, programmed by God at the creation. Now keep in mind that a monad is immaterial, and so its "growth" cannot be thought of as a development in the physical world. The growth too, therefore, must be internal, and the apparent interaction between monads must really be changes in the perceptions of the monads themselves.

10. I assume it as admitted that every created being, and consequently the created Monad, is subject to change, and indeed that this change is continuous in each.

11. It follows from what has just been said, that the natural changes of the Monad come from an internal principle, because an external cause can have no influence upon its inner being.

12. Now besides this principle of change there must also be in the Monad a manifoldness which changes. This manifoldness constitutes, so to speak, the specific nature and the variety of the simple substances.

13. This manifoldness must involve a multiplicity in the unity or in that which is simple. For since every natural change takes place by degrees, there must be something which changes and something which remains unchanged, and consequently there must be in the simple substance a plurality of conditions and relations, even though it has no parts.

14. The passing condition which involves and represents a multiplicity in the unity, or in the simple substance, is nothing else than what is called Perception. This should be carefully distinguished from Consciousness.

Leibniz argues that what we are really describing when we talk about a squirrel climbing a particular tree at a particular moment in time is ourselves. The perception of the squirrel is a permanent part of one unchanging monad—our perception as a whole. The apparent differences between parts of a monad are really changes in perception. Leibniz is arguing that the sense in which material things seem to exist in space is as different perceptions or experiences of a perceiving monad. What is ultimately real, therefore, is the perceiving monad. Perceptions change, within each monad, to create the appearance of a moving and changing material world. Notice that Leibniz carefully distinguishes "Perception" from what he calls "Consciousness." Perception is experience, in general, and is present, in some degree, in every monad. Consciousness, on the other hand, is a very special kind of experience, reflective and articulate, and is to be found only in a few monads. (It is worth noting that, with this distinction, Leibniz precociously introduces the concept of "the unconscious" into German philosophy two hundred years before Freud.)

Here is the attack on Newton's more materialist view of the universe. Such a view, Leibniz complains, cannot account for experience (perception), in other words, the immaterial aspects of the universe.

17. It must be confessed, however, that Perception, and that which depends upon it, are inexplicable by mechanical causes, that is to say, by figures and motions. Supposing that there were a machine whose structure produced thought, sensation, and perception, we could conceive of it as increased in size with the same proportions until one was able to enter into its interior, as he would into a mill. Now, on going into it he would find only pieces working upon one another, but never would he find anything to explain Perception.

It is accordingly in the simple substance, and not in the composite nor in a machine that the Perception is to be sought. Furthermore, there is nothing besides perceptions and their changes to be found in the simple substance. And it is in these alone that all the internal activities of the simple substance can consist.

18. All simple substances or created Monads may be called Entelechies, because they have in themselves a certain perfection. There is in them a sufficiency which makes them the source of their internal activities, and renders them, so to speak, incorporeal Automations. [In other words, every monad is alive, to a certain extent.]

19. If we wish to designate as soul everything which has perceptions and desires in the general sense that I have just explained, all simple substances or created Monads could be called souls. But since feeling is something more than a mere perception I think that the general name of Monad or Entelechy should suffice for simple substances which have only perception, while we may reserve the term Soul for those whose perception is more distinct and is accompanied by memory. [Again, Leibniz insists that "Perception" is most primitive and is common to all monads.]

20. We experience in ourselves a state where we remember nothing and where we have no distinct perception, as in periods of fainting, or when we are overcome by a profound, dreamless sleep. In such a state the soul does not sensibly differ at all from a simple Monad. As this state, however, is not permanent and the soul can recover from it, the soul is something more.

21. Nevertheless it does not follow at all that the simple substance is in such a state without perception. This is so because of the reasons given above; for it cannot perish, nor on the other hand would it exist without some affection and the affection is nothing else than its perception. When, however, there are a great number of weak perceptions where nothing stands out distinctively, we are stunned; as when one turns around and around in the same direction, a dizziness comes on, which makes

him swoon and makes him able to distinguish nothing. Among animals, death can occasion this state for quite a period.

22. Every present state of a simple substance is a natural consequence of its preceding state, in such a way that its present is pregnant with its future. [Here is Leibniz's version of the thesis that one cause necessarily follows another.]

23. Therefore, since on awakening after a period of unconsciousness we become conscious of our perceptions, we must, without having been conscious of them, have had perceptions immediately before; for one perception can come in a natural way only from another perception, just as a motion can come in a natural way only from a motion.

. . .

29. It is the knowledge of eternal and necessary truths that distinguishes us from mere animals and gives us reason and the sciences, thus raising us to a knowledge of ourselves and of God. This is what is called in us the Rational Soul or the Mind.

30. It is also through the knowledge of necessary truths and through abstractions from them that we come to perform Reflective Acts, which cause us to think of what is called the I, and to decide that this or that is within us. It is thus, that in thinking upon ourselves we think of *being*, of *substance*, of the *simple* and *composite*, of a *material* thing and of *God* himself, conceiving that what is limited in us is in him without limits. These Reflective Acts furnish the principal objects of our reasonings.

As we have seen, the answer to our fourth question is, "Monads don't interact." Each is locked into itself and contains within itself its own view of the universe as a whole.

56. Now this interconnection, relationship, or this adaptation of all things to each particular one, and of each one to all the rest, brings it about that every simple substance has relations which express all the others and that it is consequently a perpetual living mirror of the universe.

57. And as the same city regarded from different sides appears entirely different, and is, as it were multiplied respectively, so, because of the infinite number of simple substances, there are a similar infinite number of universes which are, nevertheless, only the aspects of a single one as seen from the special point of view of each monad.

But, of course, the perspective of any one monad is extremely one-sided and confused.

60. Besides, in what has just been seen can be seen the a priori reasons why things cannot be otherwise than they are. It is because God, in ordering the whole, has had regard to every part and in particular to each monad; and since the Monad is by its very nature *representative*, nothing can limit it to represent merely a part of things. It is nevertheless true that this representation is, as regards the details of the whole universe, only a confused representation, and is distinct only as regards a small part of them, that is to say, as regards those things which are nearest or greatest in relation to each Monad. If the representation were distinct as to the details of the entire universe, each Monad would be a Deity. It is not in the object represented that the Monads are limited, but in the modifications of their knowledge of the object. In a confused way they reach out to infinity or to the whole, but are limited and differentiated in the degree of their distinct perceptions.

Now Leibniz has an alternative to Newton: bodies (composite monads) only seem to interact; in fact, it all happens within each monad, programmed and created by God in **"preestablished harmony."**

> "Every present state of a simple substance is a natural consequence of its preceding state, in such a way that its present is pregnant with its future."
>
> – GOTTFRIED WILHELM VON LEIBNIZ

61. In this respect composites are like simple substances, for all space is filled up; therefore, all matter is connected. And in a plenum or filled space every movement has an effect upon bodies in proportion to this distance, so that not only is every body affected by those which are in contact with it and responds in some way to whatever happens to them, but also by means of them the body responds to those bodies adjoining them, and their intercommunication reaches to any distance whatsoever. Consequently every body responds to all that happens in the universe, so that he who saw all could read in each one what is happening everywhere, and even what has happened and what will happen.

62. Thus although each created Monad represents the whole universe, it represents more distinctly the body which specially pertains to it and of which it constitutes the entelechy. And as this body expresses all the universe through the interconnection of all matter in the plenum, the soul also represents the whole universe in representing this body, which belongs to it in a particular way.

Every monad develops as a reflection of the development of all the other monads in the universe as well. If, for example, we are watching a squirrel climb around a tree, Leibniz's view is that the reality of the squirrel climbing around the tree is actually our perception of this. But you can see that this alone is not sufficient; we might simply dream or hallucinate this view, and it would then not be "real" at all. The difference between the dream and the reality is the changes in the other monads, for instance, the monads that constitute the squirrel and any other observers of the same scene, including God. Reality is composed of the totality of all monads, each perceiving from its own perspective (although God, Leibniz insists, perceives from all perspectives at once). The "preestablished harmony" guarantees that all of these views from all of these perspectives are in agreement, so that our view of the squirrel, for example, is matched by the squirrel's view of us.

This view of the preestablished harmony between monads allows Leibniz to give a surprising answer to our fourth question, "How do different substances interact?" By definition, substances cannot interact as such. But they can seem to interact if their perceptions are coordinated. Thus, the collision of two billiard balls is in fact a harmony of perceptions about the collision of two billiard balls. Two people fighting is in fact a harmony of perceptions by each of the two people (and anyone else who is watching) about those two people fighting. This answer may seem to be extreme, but given Leibniz's conception of the universe as composed of a great number of immaterial substances, it is an answer that is necessary for his philosophy to be consistent. It is an answer that is also necessary, however, to enable him to reject Newton's cosmology, which he and many of his contemporaries found even more extreme and difficult to understand than Leibniz's own strange view of interaction.

The last of our initial set of questions about substance and our second cosmological question is, "Are space and time themselves substances?" According to Leibniz, the answer to this question is an emphatic no. It is on this question that Leibniz makes his sharpest break with Newton's physics. Are monads "in" space? Leibniz would have said no. But he also seems to give the surprising answer that not only are monads not "in" space (since they are immaterial), they are, strictly speaking, not "in" time either. The monad does not change in time, but rather, time is in the monad. That is, time is a relation between experiences of the monad. It is not something independent. These views of space and time are intimately tied to Leibniz's analysis of the only seeming "interaction" between monads. Both are rejections of Newton's theory and an attempt to offer an alternative.

To our way of thinking, Leibniz's views seem bizarre, compared to the almost common-sense character of Newton's theory. Newton had argued that the universe was the motion of (material) atoms in empty space, acting against each other according to the laws of motion, force, and gravity that he had so elegantly formulated. But Newton's theories, which seem almost quaintly obvious to us now, contained what most people of his and Leibniz's time—including Newton himself—considered to be manifest absurdities. One, relating to our fourth ontological question, was the idea of **action-at-a-distance**, the idea that one object could affect another although the two were not even in contact. (For example, the idea that the moon and the earth have gravitational attraction for each other.) Thus Leibniz's conception of windowless monads, each seeming to interact with others but in fact only developing within itself, would have seemed to his contemporaries no more absurd than Newton's view of causality. Leibniz didn't need causality; he had his "preestablished harmony." Newton, meanwhile, had a great deal of trouble reconciling his mechanistic theories with the traditional ideas of God and Creation, which he continued to hold for the rest of his life.

The most famous disagreement between Leibniz and Newton concerns the nature of space and time, a topic that is still being debated because of the impact of Einstein's theory of relativity at the beginning of the twentieth century. Newton's mechanical theory seemed to presuppose the existence of some permanent container, namely space, in which the material atoms of his theory could mutually attract and bounce against each other. This container, which could exist independently of its contents, is called **absolute space**. In itself, this sounds entirely reasonable; we talk about things "moving in space" and "taking up space." But then, can we also talk about the entire universe being "in" space, the way a basketball can be said to be "in" the basket? This idea has some absurd consequences that led Leibniz and many of his contemporaries to reject it. The idea that space could exist apart from all things in it, perhaps even entirely empty (or what many philosophers called the **void**), would mean that it makes sense to talk about movement or location in space even when there isn't anything in space, not even points and rulers with which to measure distances or dimensions. **Bertrand Russell**, one of Leibniz's most famous followers, pointed out the absurdity of this idea by asking, "If space is absolute, then wouldn't it make sense to suggest that the universe might have doubled in size last night?" But what would it mean to say that the universe has gotten larger? An elephant or a planet or even a galaxy can get larger, but only in comparison to some measuring stick and a frame of reference. It is only by such comparisons that such "size" talk makes sense. But to say that the universe doubles in size is to say that our measuring stick, and we ourselves, double in size also. So all comparisons remain the same. Similarly, what would it mean to say that the universe in its entirety moved one foot to the left? All of the one-foot measurements are in the universe. There is no way to talk about the universe itself moving. On the basis of such considerations, Leibniz rejected Newton's idea of absolute space as absurd. In its place, he insisted that space is relative, that is, relative to measurements and things that are measured. There is no absolute space; there is only space relative to the various positions of the monads, that is, to observers.

The same is true of time. Newton believed in **absolute time** also, time as existing apart from anything happening "in" it. But the same consequences follow this initially reasonable idea. If time is absolute, it seems to make sense to ask, "When did the universe begin?" (In fact, astronomers are again asking this question.) But what could this "when" refer to? It can't refer to any measurement in the universe (clocks, the age of rocks or stars) for it is the universe itself that is being measured, and there aren't any measures of time outside of the universe. Consequently, Leibniz rejected absolute time along with absolute space. Both are relative to the monads and have no possible existence of their own. This means, among other things, that there could be no void or empty space, nor could there be any sense of time in which literally nothing happened. Space and time, according to Leibniz, are relative to our own perceptions.

Now I said many pages ago that such cosmological issues were never the domain of philosophy alone, and you are well aware that current physics and astronomy are still very much involved with these questions. Both alternatives, from Newton and from Leibniz, are still very much alive. Scientists do indeed still talk about the beginning of the universe, and with awesome sophistication; of course, they also talk in strictly relativistic terms, like Leibniz, but now à la Einstein. To delve into these issues any further, therefore, we should have to leave eighteenth-century metaphysics and move into twentieth- and twenty-first-century physics. What is often relevant to these philosophical debates are the new and sometimes strange experimental findings that are always emerging from the sciences. Recently, for example, experiments with the speed of light have brought about startling changes in our views of space and time. One consequence of this changed view is the idea that we cannot talk intelligibly about two events happening "at the same time" if they are a sufficiently great distance apart, say several billion light years. The discovery of radiation from outer space and the expansion of galaxies has raised old issues about creation in a new way: whether the universe was created all at once and then started to expand and change (the "big-bang theory") or whether there is continuous creation going on even now (the "steady-state theory"). Because of recent theories in science, philosophers are now willing to say things that would have seemed like utter nonsense to both Newton and Leibniz—for example, that "space is curved."

These are not issues to be settled by scientists alone, however; it is philosophical theories that give structure and meaning to the scientific experiments. But neither can philosophers simply cut themselves off from science and pretend that they can solve these problems "just in their heads." At the outer reaches of science, you will find philosophy, just as, at the beginnings of philosophy, you will find the unanswered problems of science.

In an earlier chapter, we stressed the importance of a basic assumption of all metaphysics, that the universe is intelligible. In Leibniz's philosophy, this assumption is presented as one of the basic presuppositions of all thinking; he calls it

> 32. . . . *the Principle of Sufficient Reason*, in virtue of which we believe that no fact can be real and no statement true unless it has a sufficient reason why it should be thus and not otherwise. Most frequently, however, these reasons cannot be known to us.

They can, however, be known to God, who knows everything. It is on the basis of this principle, for example, that Leibniz defends the claim he made in Proposition 9, that two monads can never be identical ("the identity of indiscernibles"). The reasoning is this: Since God is the supremely rational Being (monad), He must have a reason for all that He does. But Leibniz also argues (Prop. 58) that God must have created the universe "with the greatest possible variety together with the greatest order that may be." Here is the reason why God would not have created any two monads alike. But the Principle of Sufficient Reason has a further implication; it also serves as a principle of divine ethics. Among the various possible worlds (that is, among the infinitely many ways in which the world might have been), God chooses the most perfect, that is, "the best of all possible worlds." Here is the doctrine of cosmic optimism that Voltaire so brilliantly lampooned in his novel *Candide*. But Leibniz took this concept of "the best of all possible worlds" very seriously. In the next century, it was to provide a foundation for much of the optimism of the Enlightenment. And in Leibniz's own metaphysics, it provides the concluding propositions of *Monadology*, a joyous optimism that creates as close to a happy ending as one can expect to find in a serious philosophical treatise.

> 85. Whence it is easy to conclude that the totality of all spirits must compose the city of God, that is to say, the most perfect state that is possible under the most perfect monarch.

. . .

90. Finally, under this perfect government, there will be no good action unrewarded and no evil action unpunished; everything must turn out for the well-being of the good; that is to say, of those who are not disaffected in this great state, who, after having done their duty, trust in Providence and who love and imitate, as is meet, the Author of all Good, delighting in the contemplation of his perfections according to the nature of that genuine, pure love which finds pleasure in the happiness of those who are loved. It is for this reason that wise and virtuous persons work in behalf of everything which seems conformable to presumptive or antecedent will of God, and are, nevertheless, content with what God actually brings to pass through his secret, consequent and determining will, recognizing that if we were able to understand sufficiently well the order of the universe, we should find that it surpasses all the desires of the wisest of us, and that it is impossible to render it better than it is, not only for all in general, but also for each one of us in particular, provided that we have the proper attachment for the author of all, not only as the Architect and the efficient cause of our being [our Creator] but also as our Lord and the Final Cause [purpose of our existence] who ought to be the whole goal of our will, and who alone can make us happy.

> "It is easy to conclude that the totality of all spirits must compose the city of God, that is to say, the most perfect state that is possible under the most perfect monarch."
>
> – GOTTFRIED WILHELM VON LEIBNIZ

This theological "happy ending" is not an afterthought for Leibniz; it is the heart of his philosophy. Like his older contemporary Spinoza, his involvement in metaphysics is ultimately a very personal concern for religion and for his own view of himself and his place in the world. From this perspective, it is revealing to see the vast differences between the two philosophers. Spinoza's view of humanity is extremely anti-individualistic, and each individual is wholly submerged in the concept of the one substance. In Leibniz, however, his pluralism reinforces the view that each individual is a world in himself or herself, and his idealism places an emphasis on mind and thought that is in sharp contrast with Spinoza's balance between thought and body (although many critics have charged Spinoza with emphasizing body to an alarming degree). Spinoza's determinism and his view that ultimately we can do nothing but understand is surely a gloomy view compared to Leibniz's happy confidence that this is the "best of all possible worlds." Of course, Spinoza's heretical view of God as the one substance (sometimes called *pantheism*) is very different from Leibniz's more traditional and pious view.

But these considerations are far from being merely coincidental or curious implications of Descartes', Spinoza's, and Leibniz's metaphysical views. These religious concerns lie at the heart of their philosophical concerns, and one might well say that their metaphysics is constructed as an ingenious form of support for their religious convictions. Indeed, for most of the past two thousand years, and until very recently, the Judeo-Christian-Islamic religious tradition has provided much of the motivation and the structure of philosophy.

More recently, however, questions about God have receded in philosophy and metaphysics (although the philosophy of religion has become an important specialized topic in philosophy). The questions of metaphysics have moved away from speculative questions about the ultimate nature of reality and have turned more toward a descriptive analysis of reality as it appears to human beings. (This turn is largely due to the doubts about metaphysics that preoccupied philosophers in the mid-twentieth century, when an important group of philosophers called "**logical positivists**" rejected the very idea of metaphysical speculation in favor of the concreteness of science.) But this turn to descriptive analysis took two very different directions in European and Anglo-American philosophies, and it has once again become a rich source of philosophical engagement. In Europe, it tended to follow a philosophical method called *phenomenology* (see Chapter 3, pp. 251-253), which explicitly appealed to the structures of human experience to describe the way the world must be. One of the most famous and most difficult authors in this tradition is a German named Martin Heidegger, whose mammoth tome *Being and Time* set up a grand scheme for analyzing the nature of *Being* from the perspective of human experience. The selection that follows is drawn from Heidegger's essay, "The Fundamental Question of Metaphysics."

FROM "The Fundamental Question of Metaphysics" BY Martin Heidegger[27]

Why are there essents [things that exist] rather than nothing? That is the question. Clearly it is no ordinary question. "Why are there essents, why is there anything at all, rather than nothing?"—obviously this is the first of all questions, though not in a chronological sense. Individuals and peoples ask a good many questions in the course of their historical passage through time. They examine, explore, and test a good many things before they run into the question "Why are there essents rather than nothing?" Many men never encounter this question, if by encounter we mean not merely to hear and read about it as an interrogative formulation but to ask the question, that is, to bring it about, to raise it, to feel its inevitability.

And yet each of us is grazed at least once, perhaps more than once, by the hidden power of this question, even if he is not aware of what is happening to him. The question looms in moments of great despair, when things tend to lose all their weight and all meaning becomes obscured. Perhaps it will strike but once like a muffled bell that rings into our life and gradually dies away. It is present in moments of rejoicing, when all the things around us are transfigured and seem to be there for the first time, as if it might be easier to think they are not than to understand that they are and are as they are. The question is upon us in boredom, when we are equally removed from despair and joy, and everything about us seems so hopelessly commonplace that we no longer care whether anything is or is not—and with this the question "Why are there essents rather than nothing?" is evoked in a particular form.

But this question may be asked expressly, or, unrecognized as a question, it may merely pass through our lives like a brief gust of wind; it may press hard upon us, or, under one pretext or another, we may thrust it away from us and silence it. In any case it is never the question that we ask first in point of time.

But it is the first question in another sense—in regard to rank. This may be clarified in three ways. The question "Why are there essents rather than nothing?" is first in rank for us first because

FIG. 2.27 Twentieth-century German philosopher Martin Heidegger. (© *Estate of Fred Stein / Art Resource, NY / Artists Rights Society (ARS), New York*)

Martin Heidegger (1889-1976)

A German phenomenologist and student of Edmund Husserl, whose rebellion against his teacher began the "existential" movement in phenomenology. His best-known work is *Being and Time* (1927). Although focusing on metaphysics and phenomenology, this work is also one of the first existentialist studies of "human nature."

---

[27] From *An Introduction to Metaphysics* by Martin Heidegger, translated by Ralph Manbeim (1959) for Yale University Press, Inc. Reprinted by permission of Yale University Press, Inc.

it is the most far reaching, second because it is the deepest, and finally because it is the most fundamental of all questions.

Philosophy is one of the few autonomous creative possibilities and at times necessities of man's historical being-there [Dasein]. The current misinterpretations of philosophy, all of which have some truth about them, are legion. Here we shall mention only two, which are important because of the light they throw on the present and future situation of philosophy. The first misinterpretation asks too much of philosophy. The second distorts its function.

Roughly speaking, philosophy always aims at the first and last grounds of the essent, with particular emphasis on man himself and on the meaning and goals of human being-there. This might suggest that philosophy can and must provide a foundation on which a nation will build its historical life and culture. But this is beyond the power of philosophy. As a rule such excessive demands take the form of a belittling of philosophy. It is said, for example: Because metaphysics did nothing to pave the way for the revolution it should be rejected. This is no cleverer than saying that because the carpenter's bench is useless for flying it should be abolished. Philosophy can never *directly* supply the energies and create the opportunities and methods that bring about a historical change; for one thing, because philosophy is always the concern of the few. Which few? The creators, those who initiate profound transformation. It spreads only indirectly, by devious paths that can never be laid out in advance, until at last, at some future date, it sinks to the level of a commonplace; but by then it has long been forgotten as original philosophy.

What philosophy essentially can and must be is this: a thinking that breaks the paths and opens the perspectives of the knowledge that sets the norms and hierarchies, of the knowledge in which and by which a people fulfills itself historically and culturally, the knowledge that kindles and necessitates all inquiries and thereby threatens all values.

The second misinterpretation involves a distortion of the function of philosophy. Even if philosophy can provide no foundation for a culture, the argument goes, it is nevertheless a cultural force, whether because it gives us an overall, systematic view of what is, supplying a useful chart by which we may find our way amid the various possible things and realms of things, or because it relieves the sciences of their work by reflecting on their premises, basic concepts, and principles. Philosophy is expected to promote and even to accelerate—to make easier as it were—the practical and technical business of culture.

But—it is in the very nature of philosophy never to make things easier but only more difficult. And this not merely because its language strikes the everyday understanding as strange if not insane. Rather, it is the authentic function of philosophy to challenge historical being-there and hence, in the last analysis, being pure and simple. It restores to things, to the essents, their weight (being). How so? Because the challenge is one of the essential prerequisites for the birth of all greatness, and in speaking of greatness we are referring primarily to the works and destinies of nations. We can speak of historical destiny only where an authentic knowledge of things dominates man's being-there. And it is philosophy that opens up the paths and perspectives of such knowledge.

Even supposed observations assail you unawares. Such judgments are often disarming, precisely because they seem so natural. You hear remarks such as "Philosophy leads to nothing," "You can't do anything with philosophy," and readily imagine that they confirm an expression of your own. There is no denying the soundness of these two phrases, particularly common among scientists and teachers of science. Any attempt to refute them by proving that after all it does "lead to something" merely strengthens the prevailing misinterpretation to the effect that the everyday standards by which we judge bicycles or sulphur baths are applicable to philosophy.

It is absolutely correct and proper to say that "You can't do anything with philosophy." It is only wrong to suppose that this is the last word on philosophy. For the rejoinder imposes itself; granted that *we* cannot do anything with philosophy, might not philosophy, if we concern ourselves with it, do something *with us*? So much for what philosophy is not.

- What does Leibniz mean by preestablished harmony, and how does this notion solve the problem of interaction among substances?
- What is a monad, and how do we distinguish among them? What is the "Principle of the Identity of Indiscernibles"?
- If even God must act for a reason, as Leibniz claims, can God be said to be free? Is this the best of all possible worlds?
- What is the difference, according to Heidegger, between things that exist and Being as such?

SUMMARY AND CONCLUSION

Metaphysics is the study of ultimate reality, the attempt to find out the way the world really is. The first recognized metaphysical theory in Western philosophy is Thales' suggestion that everything is ultimately made of water. After Thales, a number of schools of metaphysics suggested alternative theories, all of them depending on the speculative powers of human reason and diverging in various and important ways from "common sense." But these thinkers were not only the first significant Western philosophers; they were also the first theoretical scientists, anticipating in many ways some of the most sophisticated theories of contemporary physics, astronomy, and chemistry.

The first turning point in Western metaphysics came with Socrates, although Socrates himself was more interested in moral issues than in metaphysics as such. Socrates' student Plato and his student Aristotle in turn became the first great systematic metaphysicians, and philosophy ever since has been deeply indebted to them. Plato introduced an elaborate theory in which ultimate reality consisted of Forms, in contrast to the particular and changing things of everyday life. To support this "two-worlds" theory of Forms versus individual things, he offered a theory of learning, a "theory of recollection," in which he argued that the human soul is immortal and that each of us already knows, in some sense, what we appear to learn in our lives. Aristotle argues instead that only individual things deserve the ultimate claim to reality, for these individual things are the primary substances. Since Aristotle, metaphysicians have typically used the term *substance* as the name of the basic entities that compose reality.

We have also summarized the thought of some of the greatest metaphysical thinkers of modern times. In Europe, they begin from the concept of "substance" and attempt to use deduction as a method for proving the ultimate nature of reality. Their answers are extremely different. Spinoza argues that there can only be one substance; Leibniz argues that there are many. For Spinoza, God is identical to the universe, to the one substance; for Leibniz, God is distinct from all other substances, which He created. For Spinoza, mind and body are but two of an infinite number of attributes of God, the only two that we can know; for Leibniz, all substances are ultimately immaterial. But beneath these technical concerns is a struggle by both philosophers to answer the most important problems of human existence: the nature of God and proper religion, the place of man and woman in the universe, and the role and foundations of science.

CHAPTER REVIEW QUESTIONS

1. What similarities do you find among modern philosophy (Descartes, Leibniz, Spinoza), the pre-Socratics, and Eastern thought (Upanishads, Confucianism, Daoism, Buddhism) and their attempt to explain the ultimate reality?

2. What pre-Socratic influences can you identify in Plato? (Be specific: e.g., "Plato, like Parmenides, believes that . . .")

3. How do you still think about metaphysical issues today? What problems are still very much alive for you?

4. Which modern theories about the nature of reality are materialist? Which are immaterialist?

5. How is Plato responding to the pre-Socratics with the theory of Forms? What is Aristotle's response to Plato's theory of Forms?

6. Explain the problem of substances interacting with each other. Provide a detailed account of the ways that Descartes, Leibniz, and Spinoza solve this problem. Further, could any of these solutions help Plato solve the problem of participation? Are there any similarities between participation and substance interaction? Why or why not?

7. What is the value of talking about different "possible worlds" in Leibniz? Are these literally different worlds?

KEY TERMS

absolute space
absolute time
action-at-a-distance
Ahura Mazda
Analects, The
Angra Mainyush
animism
apeiron
Asha
attribute
Becoming (in Plato)
Being (in Plato)
best of all possible worlds
Brahman
Buddha
cause
cause-of-itself (causa sui)
conceptual truth
cosmogony
cosmology
Dao
determinism
divine preordination

essence (or an essential property)
extended
extended (substance)
Form (in Plato)
Four Noble Truths
freedom of the will
idea
idealism
Identity of Indiscernibles
immaterialism
immortality
ineffable
infinite regress
innate (ideas)
materialism
metaphysics
modes (in Spinoza)
monad (in Leibniz)
monism
monotheism
mysticism

naturalism
ontology
pantheism
participation
pluralism
polytheism
preestablished harmony
prime mover (in Aristotle)
Principle of Sufficient Reason (in Leibniz)
property
reason
sophists
Spenta Mainyush
substance
substance (in Descartes)
teleology (teleological)
unextended
Upanishads
void
Zend-Avesta
Zoroastrianism

BIBLIOGRAPHY AND FURTHER READING

General surveys of ancient Greek philosophy can be found in J. Burnet, *Early Greek Philosophy* (London: Black, 1958), and W. K. C. Guthrie, *The Greek Philosophers: From Thales to Aristotle* (New York: Harper & Row, 1960).

The most important texts from the pre-Socratics are in G. S. Kirk and J. E. Raven, *The Presocratic Philosophers* (Cambridge: Cambridge University Press, 1957).

Plato's dialogues are collected in *Plato, Dialogues*, 4th ed., trans. Benjamin Jowett (Oxford: Oxford University Press, 1953); a helpful survey of his work is A.E. Taylor, *Plato: The Man and His Work* (New York: Dial, 1936).

Aristotle's works are collected in R. McKeon, ed., *The Basic Works of Aristotle* (New York: Random House, 1941).

An excellent survey of all Aristotle's works is W. D. Ross, *Aristotle* (New York: Meridian, 1959).

Brief surveys of the pre-Socratics, Socrates, Plato, and Aristotle are D. J. O'Connor, ed., *A Critical History of Western Philosophy* (New York: Free Press, 1964) and P. Edwards, ed., *The Encyclopedia of Philosophy* (New York: Macmillan, 1967).

Benedictus de Spinoza's *Ethics* is in *The Rationalists* (New York: Doubleday, 1960); an excellent account of Spinoza's philosophy is St. Hampshire, *Spinoza* (London: Penguin, 1951).

A convenient collection of Gottfried W. von Leibniz's major works is Philip Wiener, ed., *Leibniz, Selections* (New York: Charles Scribner's Sons, 1951).

Two recent studies of Leibniz are Hidé Ishiguro, *Leibniz's Philosophy of Logic and Language* (Ithaca, NY: Cornell University Press, 1972) and Robert Merrihew Adams, *Leibniz: Determinist, Theist, Idealist* (New York: Oxford University Press, 1994).

An important but biased study is Bertrand Russell, *A Critical Exposition of the Philosophy of Leibniz* (London: George Allen and Unwin, 1937).

To study more recent metaphysical systems, see A. Lovejoy, *The Great Chain of Being* (Cambridge, MA: Harvard University Press, 1936); Jacques Maritain, *A Preface to Metaphysics* (London: Sheed, 1948); Henri Bergson, *An Introduction to Metaphysics*, trans. T. E. Hulme (New York: Bobbs-Merrill, 1949); Martin Heidegger, *An Introduction to Metaphysics*, trans. Ralph Manheim (New Haven, CT: Yale University Press, 1959); Richard Taylor, *Metaphysics* (Englewood Cliffs, NJ: Prentice-Hall, 1963); D. F. Pears, ed., *The Nature of Metaphysics* (London: Macmillan, 1957); Simon Blackburn, *Thinking* (New York: Oxford University Press, 1999); Peter Van Inwagen, *Metaphysics* (Boulder, Co: Westview Press, 1993); Richard Gale, *Blackwell Guide to Metaphysics* (Oxford: Blackwell Press, 2002); and E. J. Lowe, *A Survey of Metaphysics* (New York: Oxford University Press, 2002).

For a discussion of medieval philosophy, see A. Hyman and J. Walsh, *Philosophy in the Middle Ages* (Indianapolis: Hackett, 1973).

A broad selection of sources from non-Western cultures is found in R. Solomon and K. Higgins, *World Philosophy* (New York: McGraw-Hill, 1995).

3 | Knowledge

Once upon a time, I, Chuang Tzu, dreamt I was a butterfly, fluttering hither and thither, to all intents and purposes a butterfly. I was conscious only of following my fancies as a butterfly, and was unconscious of my individuality as a man. Suddenly, I waked, and there I lay, myself again. Now I do not know whether I was then a man dreaming I was a butterfly, or whether I am now a butterfly dreaming I am a man.

ZHUANGZI[1]

After an evening of heated but fruitless metaphysical debate with a number of his friends, the British physician **John Locke** turned to them and asked, "Shouldn't we first determine whether we are capable of answering such questions?" They agreed. Perhaps you are thinking much the same thing. These great metaphysical systems are surely monuments to human intelligence. But do they achieve what they are intended to? Do they tell us "the way the world really is"? Since each of the contending systems claims that it does, how can it be that they disagree? Which is right? And how can we decide?

In 1690 Locke took philosophy around a sharp turn, one that had been suggested by Descartes a half century before. But Descartes had broached the question, "What can we know?" only as a preface to his metaphysics. Locke, on the other hand, decided to put questions about reality on the shelf until he could develop an adequate theory of human knowledge. Accordingly, his great book is not primarily an inquiry into **substance** or reality or God or truth (although all of these enter in); it is *An Essay Concerning Human Understanding*. From metaphysics, the study of ultimate reality, we now turn to **epistemology**, the study of human knowledge—how we get it, what it is, whether we have it, or why we don't.

Even before Plato, Parmenides had seen that between a false belief and knowledge of reality are many opinions and **appearances** of reality, which might be very different from the reality itself. Plato's "Myth of the Cave" is a graphic illustration of this distinction. Descartes, although he distrusted his senses and wasn't certain that they gave accurate representations of reality, at least could be certain of the appearances themselves—he could not be mistaken

---

[1] From Herbert A. Giles, trans., *Chuang-Tzu: Taoist Philosopher and Chinese Mystic*, London: George Allen and Unwin, 1961 [1889], p. 47.

about them. And here is the problem that has defined epistemology, the seeming abyss between reality and mere appearance. Perhaps we know the appearances of things, but how can we know that we know the reality "behind" them?

Let us return for a moment to the central idea of traditional metaphysics, that of substance. Substance is that which underlies all of the various properties of a thing (or things); and it is the properties, never the substance itself, that are experienced by us. Now, presumably, there can be no properties unless they are properties of something. That seems to be a platitude. But yet, we cannot experience the nature of the substance itself. And here begins the embarrassment of metaphysics.

The problem was stated succinctly by the best-known British philosopher of this century, Bertrand Russell, in a little volume called *The Problems of Philosophy*, in which he says the following:

 FROM *The Problems of Philosophy*
BY **Bertrand Russell** [2]

In daily life, we assume as certain many things which, on a closer scrutiny, are found to be so full of apparent contradictions that only a great amount of thought enables us to know what it is that we really may believe. In the search for certainty, it is natural to begin with our present experiences, and in some sense, no doubt, knowledge is to be derived from them. But any statement as to what it is that our immediate experiences make us know is very likely to be wrong. It seems to me that I am now sitting in a chair, at a table of a certain shape, on which I see sheets of paper with writing or print. By turning my head I see out of the window buildings and clouds and the sun. I believe that the sun is about ninety-three million miles from the earth; that it is a hot globe many times bigger than the earth; that, owing to the earth's rotation, it rises every morning, and will continue to do so for an indefinite time in the future. I believe that, if any other normal person comes into my room, he will see the same chairs and tables and books and papers as I see, and that the table which I see is the same as the table which I feel pressing against my arm. All this seems to be so evident as to be hardly worth stating, except in answer to a man who doubts whether I know anything. Yet all this may be reasonably doubted, and all of it requires much careful discussion before we can be sure that we have stated it in a form that is wholly true.

To make our difficulties plain, let us concentrate attention on the table. To the eye it is oblong, brown and shiny, to the touch it is smooth and cool and hard; when I tap it, it gives out a wooden sound. Any one else who sees and feels and hears the table will agree with this description, so that it might seem as if no difficulty would arise; but as soon as we try to be more precise our troubles begin. Although I believe that the table is "really" of the same colour all over, the parts that reflect the light look much brighter than the other parts, and some parts look white because of reflected light. I know that, if I move, the parts that reflect the light will be different,

FIG. 3.1 How do we know if we are dreaming? *(Image © Holger W., 2011. Used under license from Shutterstock.com)*

2 Bertrand Russell, *The Problems of Philosophy*, Oxford: Oxford University Press, 1912.

so that the apparent distribution of colours on the table will change. It follows that if several people are looking at the table at the same moment, no two of them will see exactly the same distribution of colours, because no two can see it from exactly the same point of view, and any change in the point of view makes some change in the way the light is reflected.

For most practical purposes the differences are unimportant, but to the painter they are all-important: the painter has to unlearn the habit of thinking that things seem to have the colour which common sense says they "really" have, and to learn the habit of seeing things as they appear. Here we have already the beginning of one of the distinctions that cause most trouble in philosophy—the distinction between "appearance" and "reality," between what things seem to be and what they are. The painter wants to know what things seem to be, the practical man and the philosopher want to know what they are; but the philosopher's wish to know this is stronger than the practical man's, and is more troubled by knowledge as to the difficulties of answering the question.

To return to the table. It is evident from what we have found, that there is no colour which preeminently appears to be *the* colour of the table, or even of any one particular part of the table—it appears to be of different colours from different points of view, and there is no reason for regarding some of these as more really its colour than others. And we know that even from a given point of view the colour will seem different by artificial light, or to a colour-blind man, or to a man wearing blue spectacles, while in the dark there will be no colour at all, though to touch and hearing the table will be unchanged. This colour is not something which is inherent in the table, but something depending upon the table and the spectator and the way the light falls on the table. When, in ordinary life, we speak of *the* colour of the table, we only mean the sort of colour which it will seem to have to a normal spectator from an ordinary point of view under usual conditions of light. But the other colours which appear under other conditions have just as good a right to be considered real; and therefore, to avoid favouritism, we are compelled to deny that, in itself, the table has any one particular colour.

The same thing applies to the texture. With the naked eye one can see the grain, but otherwise the table looks smooth and even. If we looked at it through a microscope, we should see roughnesses and hills and valleys, and all sorts of differences that are imperceptible to the naked eye. Which of these is the "real" table? We are naturally tempted to say that what we see through the microscope is more real, but that in turn would be changed by a still more powerful microscope. If, then, we cannot trust what we see with the naked eye, why should we trust what we see through a microscope? Thus, again, the confidence in our sense with which we began deserts us.

The *shape* of the table is not better. We are all in the habit of judging as to the "real" shapes of things, and we do this so unreflectingly that we come to think we actually see the real shapes. But, in fact, as we all have to learn if we try to draw, a given thing looks different in shape from every different point of view. If our table is "really" rectangular, it will look, from almost all points of view, as if it had two acute angles and two obtuse angles. If opposite sides are parallel, they will look as if they converged to a point away from the spectator; if they are of equal length, they will look as if the nearer side were longer. All these things are not commonly noticed in looking at

FIG. 3.2 What does a table really look like? *(Image © Simon Krzic, 2011. Used under license from Shutterstock.com)*

> "The real table, if there is one, is not *immediately* known to us at all, but must be an inference from what is immediately known."
>
> – BERTRAND RUSSELL

a table, because experience has taught us to construct the "real" shape from the apparent shape, and the "real" shape is what interests us as practical men. But the "real" shape is not what we see; it is something inferred from what we see. And what we see is constantly changing in shape as we move about the room; so that here again the senses seem not to give us the truth about the table itself, but only about the appearance of the table.

Similar difficulties arise when we consider the sense of touch. It is true that the table always gives us a sensation of hardness, and we feel that it resists pressure. But the sensation we obtain depends upon how hard we press the table and also upon what part of the body we press with; thus the various sensations due to various pressures or various parts of the body cannot be supposed to reveal *directly* any definite property of the table, but at most to be *signs* of some property, which *causes* all the sensations, but is not actually apparent in any of them. And the same applies still more obviously to the sounds which can be elicited by rapping the table.

Thus it becomes evident that the real table, if there is one, is not the same as what we immediately experience by sight or touch or hearing. The real table, if there is one, is not *immediately* known to us at all, but must be an inference from what is immediately known. Hence, two very difficult questions at once arise; namely, (1) Is there a real table at all? (2) If so, what sort of object can it be?

In these few pages, Russell succeeds in summarizing the problems that have dominated British philosophy since Locke's original epistemological studies. But why say "British philosophy"? Why should this problem have been more serious there than on the continent of Europe, where most of the great metaphysicians were working? Why should it have had more impact on Locke and his followers than on Descartes, Spinoza, Leibniz, and their latter-day followers? Because of a single profound difference, which has always created a general gap in understanding between British-American philosophy and European philosophy. Descartes, Spinoza, and Leibniz retained their faith in human **reason's** ability to give us knowledge of reality, despite the fact that reality was beyond our every possible experience. Because of their confidence in the powers of reason, they are usually called **rationalists**. Because it happens that all three were Europeans (Descartes was French; Spinoza, Dutch; and Leibniz, German), they are often called *continental rationalists*. The movement developed by John Locke, on the other hand, is generally called **empiricism**, because of its insistence upon the data of experience (or *empirical* data) as the source of all knowledge. (A **datum** [plural, *data*] is a bit of "given" information; modern empiricist philosophers sometimes talk of **sense-data**, that is, the information immediately given by the senses.) Also included in this group of empiricists are **Bishop George Berkeley**[3] and **David Hume**, whom we shall also meet in this chapter. Because they were all from Great Britain, they are often called *British empiricists*. (Berkeley was Irish; Hume, Scottish; Russell is generally considered a more contemporary member of this same movement.)

- What problem does Russell suggest lies at the heart of epistemology? What problem does the "appearance/reality distinction" pose?
- Is there a "problem of knowledge"? What is it?

---

[3] Bishop Berkeley traveled to the United States. Berkeley, California, is named after him.

Although epistemology received a renewed attention and a new kind of treatment in the era after Descartes, the rift between the claims of rationalists and those of empiricists was not new. The basics of the debate were laid out by Plato, in his dialogue *Theatetus:*

FROM *Theatetus*
BY **Plato**[4]

SOCRATES: But the question you were asked, Theatetus, was not, what are the objects of knowledge, nor yet how many sorts of knowledge there are. We did not want to count them, but to find out what the thing itself—knowledge—is. . . . Perception, you say, is knowledge?

THEATETUS: Yes.

SOCRATES: The account you give of the nature of knowledge is not, by any means, to be despised. It is the same that was given by Protagoras, though he stated it in a somewhat different way. He says, you will remember, that "man is the measure of all things—alike of the being of things that are and of the not-being of things that are not." No doubt you have read that.

THEATETUS: Yes, often.

SOCRATES: He puts it in this sort of way, doesn't he, that any given thing "is to me such as it appears to me and is to you such as it appears to you," you and I being men?

THEATETUS: Yes, that is how he puts it.

SOCRATES: Well, what a wise man says is not likely to be nonsense. So let us follow his meaning. Sometimes, when the same wind is blowing, one of us feels chilly, the other does not, or one may feel slightly chilly, the other quite cold.

THEATETUS: Certainly.

SOCRATES: Well, in that case are we to say that the wind in itself is cold or not cold? Or shall we agree with Protagoras that it is cold to the one who feels chilly and not to the other? . . . [I]ndeed the doctrine is a remarkable one. It declares that nothing is *one* thing just by itself, nor can you rightly call it by one definite name, nor even say it is of any definite sort.

In this way, Socrates claims that the empiricist cannot have any knowledge at all. He defends the rationalist's claim earlier in the dialogue:

SOCRATES: You do not suppose a man can understand the name of a thing when he does not know what the thing is?

THEATETUS: Certainly not.

SOCRATES: Then, if he has no idea of knowledge, "knowledge about shoes" conveys nothing to him?

THEATETUS: No.

SOCRATES: "Cobblery" in fact, or the name of any other art has no meaning for anyone who has no conception of knowledge.

4 Plato, from *Theatetus*, trans. F. M. Cornford, reprinted in *The Collected Dialogues of Plato*, ed. Edith Hamilton and Huntington Cairnes, Bollingen Series, Princeton: Princeton University Press, 1980, p. 61.

FIG. 3.3 Author Robert C. Solomon in the wind—can we tell if he is chilly?
(© Kathleen M. Higgins)

Russell, like Theatetus, associates knowledge with **perception**, or "sense-data." Thus, he had assumed that any notion of "substance" we might have must be *derived* from our perceptions. Socrates claimed that our varied perceptions can never give us a notion of substance. All we would be able to get out of a bunch of differing perceptions is a bunch of differing perceptions. Since we *have* a notion of substance, however (in Russell's example, for instance, of a "table"), we must have gotten it from something other than our perceptions. Knowledge, concludes Socrates, must be something other than perception. The continental rationalists in a sense, agreed with Socrates on this point and claimed that the nonperceptual source of knowledge must be "reason" itself. The British empiricists went the other way, claiming that there simply wasn't any other source of ideas other than perception. ("Perception" actually can mean both "sense-data" and "understanding." We mean the first sense here.)

So, how are we to know reality? By retaining confidence in our own powers of abstract reason? Or by appeal to experience, which carries with it the threat that we may never know reality beyond our experience at all? In the pages that follow, you will see one of the most vigorous and long-lasting dialogues in philosophy, not only between the rationalists and the empiricists but (as we saw in the juxtaposition of Spinoza and Leibniz in Chapter 2) between various rationalists and empiricists as well.

Is the choice between reason and experience a "false dilemma" (a kind of pseudo-question)? Among the issues in dispute are not only the emphasis on and faith in reason versus experience but also the nature of reason and the nature of experience. What is an idea that can be known to be true by reasons alone—a **"truth of reason"**? How can we infer from the nature of our private experience what the world "outside" is like? How do we even know that there *is* an "external" world? How is it possible to have "abstract" ideas, that is, ideas that are not simply based on the concrete particulars of experience, such as *this* dog, *this* table, *that* star over there to the left of the Big Dipper? How do we get the idea, for example, of "dog" in general, not this dog or that dog or big dog or little dog or Chihuahua or German Shepherd but just "dog," which includes all of them?

The question of *substance* comes up again and again; what is a substance? How do we know of substances? So does the notion of **cause**. Is an idea *caused* by an object of which it is the idea, or do we make the idea up, and so "cause" it ourselves? And, a more specific set of questions: What aspects of a thing are *in it*? What aspects of a thing are rather *in us*, that is, in the way we perceive it, in the mental apparatus that we use in our knowledge? But beneath the welter of questions and debates, there is a singular shared concern. All of the rationalists and empiricists are men of science who appreciate the advances of modern physics and its kindred disciplines, who think of knowledge as one of the highest human attributes, and who want to understand knowledge and its foundations as a way of justifying their faith in science. At the bottom of all of these disputes, in other words, is that basic admiration and concern for knowledge as such, as the question "How is this knowledge possible?" is itself an extension of that same admiration and concern.

A. The Rationalist's Confidence: Descartes

Let's return to the philosopher who began the modern emphasis on methodology, René Descartes. We have already mentioned his "method of doubt," but the goal of this method is not to defend the doubts but, quite to the contrary, to move from doubt to knowledge and certainty. Descartes' doubt is intended only to separate what is doubtful from what is not. He never doubted, nor did his followers, that he would be able to find beliefs about reality. These beliefs would be "clear and distinct" and "perfectly certain." (Spinoza refers to such ideas as "adequate ideas"; Leibniz calls them "truths of reason.") Once Descartes had found even one such belief, he could use it as a premise from which he could deduce all of his other beliefs about reality. And none of this depends upon the data of experience; it is entirely a process of reason, of examining the clarity of his beliefs and the logical connections between them.

Once again, it is important to remind ourselves that these problems and their some-times radical complications and solutions do not appear in a vacuum. Descartes lived in the time of Galileo, and Galileo's new science is always in the background of Descartes' method of doubt. In undermining the traditional science of Aristotle and the Middle Ages, Galileo raised the doubt that what we think that we see we might not really see at all. Col-ors, for example, seemed to be more in the minds of men and women than in the objects themselves. But if we could be mistaken about something so seemingly certain as the color of objects, Descartes reasons, could we not be mistaken about much else besides? Indeed, could we not be mistaken in our perceptions *in general*? For this reason Descartes appeals to reason rather than to experience (although, as we shall see, he dangerously calls reason into question as well). We might also add that, although he was a devout Catholic, Descartes could not help but be affected by Martin Luther's challenge to church authority the century before. Thus the insistence of resolving these doubts for oneself, instead of appealing to established authority, was very much a part of the radical tempera-ment of the time.

In six famous "meditations," Descartes begins with the resolve to doubt everything that he believes, that is, until he can find a first premise that is beyond doubt, from which he can then argue for the truth of other beliefs, which he can then use as premises to prove more beliefs, and so on. In the first meditation, he states his method of doubt and begins to elimi-nate all of those beliefs about which he could possibly be mistaken. He doubts his senses; could they not mislead him, as they do in an optical illusion or a hallucination? He examines his belief in God; could it be that his Jesuit teachers had been fooling him? He even doubts the existence of the world; is it not conceivable that he is merely dreaming? Here is the first of the meditations.

> "I was convinced that I must . . . build anew from the foundation."
>
> – RENÉ DESCARTES

FROM "Meditation I" BY René Descartes[5]

OF THE THINGS WHICH MAY BE BROUGHT WITHIN THE SPHERE OF THE DOUBTFUL

It is now some years since I detected how many were the false beliefs that I had from my earliest youth admitted as true, and how doubtful was ev-erything I had since constructed on this basis; and from that time I was convinced that I must once and for all seriously undertake to rid myself of all the opinions which I had formerly accepted, and commence to build anew from the foundation, if I wanted to establish any firm and permanent struc-ture in the sciences.

FIG. 3.4 Descartes employs a method of radical doubt. *(© iStockphoto.com/Naomi Hasegawa)*

---

5 René Descartes, *Meditations on First Philosophy*, in *The Philosophical Works of Descartes*, trans. Elizabeth S. Haldane and G. R. T. Ross, 1911. Reprinted with the permission of Cambridge University Press.

In order to "build anew" his system of beliefs and eliminate his false beliefs, Descartes resolves to doubt everything that he believes. But this does not mean that he has to list every belief he has; that might take forever. Instead, it is necessary only for him to examine those "first principles" upon which all of his other beliefs are based.

> Now for this object it is not necessary that I should show that all of these are false—I shall perhaps never arrive at this end. But inasmuch as reason already persuades me that I ought no less carefully to withhold my assent from matters which are not entirely certain and indubitable than from those which appear to me manifestly to be false, if I am able to find in each one some reason to doubt, this will suffice to justify my rejecting the whole. And for that end it will not be requisite that I should examine each in particular, which would be an endless undertaking; for owing to the fact that the destruction of the foundations of necessity brings with it the downfall of the rest of the edifice, I shall only in the first place attack those principles upon which all my former opinions rested.

The first set of principles to be doubted is that "commonsense" set of beliefs that relies upon the senses: seeing, hearing, tasting, smelling, and touching. Descartes argues that, despite our commonsense reliance on these, it is nevertheless possible that we could be deceived by our senses.

> All that up to the present time I have accepted as most true and certain I have learned either from the senses or through the senses; but it is sometimes proved to me that these senses are deceptive, and it is wiser not to trust entirely to any thing by which we have once been deceived.
>
> But it may be that although the senses sometimes deceive us concerning things which are hardly perceptible, or very far away, there are yet many others to be met with as to which we cannot reasonably have any doubt, although we recognise them by their means. For example, there is the fact that I am here, seated by the fire, attired in a dressing gown, having this paper in my hands and other similar matters. And how could I deny that these hands and this body are mine, were it not perhaps that I compare myself to certain persons, devoid of sense, whose cerebella are so troubled and clouded by the violent vapours of black bile, that they constantly assure us that they think they are kings when they are really quite poor, or that they are clothed in purple when they are really without covering, or who imagine that they have an earthenware head or are nothing but pumpkins or are made of glass. But they are mad, and I should not be any the less insane were I to follow examples so extravagant.

Now Descartes makes one of his most famous philosophical moves: He wonders whether he could possibly be dreaming all of his experience; for in a dream, as we all know, it is possible that everything can still seem perfectly real, as if we were actually awake:

> At the same time I must remember that I am a man, and that consequently I am in the habit of sleeping, and in my dreams representing to myself the same things or sometimes even less probable things, than do those who are insane in their waking moments. How often has it happened to me that in the night I dreamt that I found myself in this particular place, that I was dressed and seated near the fire, whilst in reality I was lying undressed in bed! At this moment it does indeed seem to me that it is with eyes awake that I am looking at this paper; that this head which I move is not asleep, that it is deliberately and of set purpose that I extend my hand and perceive it; what happens in sleep does not appear so clear nor so distinct as does all

this. But in thinking over this I remind myself that on many occasions I have in sleep been deceived by similar illusions, and in dwelling carefully on this reflection I see so manifestly that there are no certain indications by which we may clearly distinguish wakefulness from sleep that I am lost in astonishment. And my astonishment is such that it is almost capable of persuading me that I now dream.

Thus Descartes has brought himself to the point where he doubts the existence of the whole of nature, even the existence of his own body. After all, one can dream that one's body has changed grotesquely, and on rare occasions it is even possible to dream that one leaves one's body altogether. So isn't it possible, according to this strict method of doubt, to wonder whether one does indeed have a body, just as it is possible to wonder how one knows of the existence of the "external world" in general?

But there is one sphere of knowledge that would seem to be immune even to Descartes' radical doubting—the principles of arithmetic and geometry:

> **Euclid [300 B.C.E.]**
>
> A mathematician who founded a school in Alexandria. He is the author of *Elements*, a systematic compendium of mathematical knowledge that was the standard text in geometry for more than two thousand years. In this text Euclid shows that the basic principles of geometry could be proved by assuming only a small set of axioms.

Arithmetic, Geometry and other sciences of that kind which only treat of things that are very simple and very general, without taking great trouble to ascertain whether they are actually existent or not, contain some measure of certainty and an element of the indubitable. For whether I am awake or asleep, two and three together always form five, and the square can never have more than four sides, and it does not seem possible that truths so clear and apparent can be suspected of any falsity [or uncertainty].

But these can be doubted, too. To do so, Descartes turns his attention to God, his Creator, and asks whether God might be able to deceive him, even about these apparently certain principles:

Nevertheless I have long had fixed in my mind the belief that an all-powerful God existed by whom I have been created such as I am. But how do I know that He has not brought it to pass that there is no earth, no heaven, no extended body, no magnitude, no place, and that nevertheless [I possess the perceptions of all these things and that] they seem to me to exist just exactly as I now see them? And, besides, as I sometimes imagine that others deceive themselves in the things which they think they know best, how do I know that I am not deceived every time that I add two and three, or count the sides of a square, or judge of things yet simpler, if anything simpler can be imagined? But possibly God has not desired that I should be thus deceived, for He is said to be supremely good. If, however, it is contrary to His goodness to have made me such that I constantly deceive myself, it would also appear to be contrary to His goodness to permit me to be sometimes deceived, and nevertheless I cannot doubt that He does permit this.

Descartes' argument, which he will use again later in his *Meditations*, is that God is good and would not deceive him. But suppose, just suppose, that God did not exist:

There may indeed be those who would prefer to deny the existence of a God so powerful, rather than believe that all other things are uncertain. But let us not oppose them for the present, and grant that all that is here said of a God is a fable; nevertheless in whatever way they suppose that I have arrived at the state of being that I have reached—whether they attribute it to fate or to accident, or make out that it is by a continual succession of antecedents, or by some other method—since to err and deceive oneself is a defect, it is clear that the greater will be the probability of my being so imperfect as to deceive myself ever, as is the Author to whom they assign my origin the less powerful. To these reasons I have certainly nothing to reply, but at the end I feel constrained to confess that there is nothing in all that I formerly believed to be true, of which I cannot in some measure doubt, and that not merely through want of thought or through levity, but for reasons which are very powerful and maturely considered; so that henceforth I ought not the less carefully to refrain from giving credence to these opinions than to that which is manifestly false, if I desire to arrive at any certainty [in the sciences].

To bring his method to its extreme conclusion, Descartes now introduces a drastic supposition, namely, that not a good God but an evil genius, a malicious demon, is constantly deceiving him, even about those things of which he seems to be most certain:

FIG. 3.5 Could an evil genius deceive us about everything? *(© iStockphoto.com/Olena Chernenko)*

I shall then suppose, not that God who is supremely good and the fountain of truth, but some evil genius not less powerful than deceitful, has employed his whole energies in deceiving me; I shall consider that the heavens, the earth, colours, figures, sound, and all other external things are nought but the illusions and dreams of which this genius has availed himself in order to lay traps for my credulity; I shall consider myself as having no hands, no eyes, no flesh, no blood, nor any senses, yet falsely believing myself to possess all these things; I shall remain obstinately attached to this idea, and if by this means it is not in my power to arrive at the knowledge of any truth, I may at least do what is in my power [i.e., suspend my judgment], and with firm purpose avoid giving credence to any false thing, or being imposed upon by this arch deceiver, however powerful and deceptive he may be. But this task is a laborious one, and insensibly a certain lassitude leads me into the course of my ordinary life. And just as a captive who in sleep enjoys an imaginary liberty, when he begins to suspect that this liberty is but a dream, fears to awaken, and conspires with these agreeable illusions that the deception may be prolonged, so insensibly of my own accord I fall back into my former opinions, and I dread awakening from this slumber, lest the laborious wakefulness which would follow the tranquility of this repose should have to be spent not in daylight, but in the excessive darkness of the difficulties which have just been discussed.

Descartes has taken his doubt as far as he can possibly go; he now doubts everything, until, that is, he finds the one principle that is beyond all doubt and perfectly certain. That principle is the fact of his own existence. That he cannot doubt, for if he doubts it, he still knows that he must exist to doubt. Thus, he can be certain of one thing, at least, that he himself exists. From this first principle, Descartes proceeds, through the "Meditations" that follow, to reestablish his confidence in other things he believes as well—the existence of God, the existence of the "external world," and the existence of his own body.

- Why does Descartes undertake his enterprise of "methodological doubt"? What does he hope to get out of it?
- What does Descartes' dream argument demonstrate? Why does he introduce the idea of an evil genius? What does the possibility of the evil genius allow us to doubt?
- What, according to Descartes, is indubitable (beyond doubt)? How can we be certain of anything if we assume that we are being deceived?

Many philosophers have challenged the extremity of Descartes' method and have often objected that once you begin to doubt things so thoroughly, you will never again be able to argue your way back to certainty. One way of making this objection is to ask, how can Descartes possibly get rid of an "evil genius" who is deceiving him about everything once he has introduced this possibility? Indeed, the supposition of an evil genius was so extreme that even Descartes, in the years that followed the publication and many disputes about his *Meditations*, insisted that no one should take his argument too seriously. But in the "Meditations" themselves he tried to show that we could indeed get rid of the evil genius. Having watched Descartes work his way into the depth of Plato's cave, let us now watch him work his way out again.

 FROM **"Meditation II"**
BY **René Descartes**[6]

OF THE NATURE OF THE HUMAN MIND;
AND THAT IT IS MORE EASILY KNOWN THAN THE BODY

The Meditation of yesterday filled my mind with so many doubts that it is no longer in my power to forget them. And yet I do not see in what manner I can resolve them; and, just as if I had all of a sudden fallen into very deep water, I am so disconcerted that I can neither make certain of setting my feet on the bottom, nor can I swim and so support myself on the surface. I shall nevertheless make an effort and follow anew the same path as that on which I yesterday entered, i.e. I shall proceed by setting aside all that in which the least doubt could be supposed to exist, just as if I had discovered that it was absolutely false; and I shall ever follow in this road until I have met with something which is certain, or at least, if I can do nothing else, until I have learned for certain that there is nothing in the world that is certain. Archimedes, in order that he might draw the terrestrial globe out of its place, and transport it elsewhere, demanded only that one point should be fixed and immovable; in the same way I shall have the right to conceive high hopes if I am happy enough to discover one thing only which is certain and indubitable.

I suppose, then, that all the things that I see are false; I persuade myself that nothing has ever existed of all that my fallacious memory represents to me. I consider that I possess no senses; I imagine that body, figure, extension, movement and place are but the fictions of my mind. What, then, can be esteemed as true? Perhaps nothing at all, unless that there is nothing in the world that is certain.

But how can I know there is not something different from those things that I have just considered, of which one cannot have the slightest doubt? Is there not some

---

6 René Descartes, *Meditations on First Philosophy*, in *The Philosophical Works of Descartes*, trans. Elizabeth S. Haldane and G. R. T. Ross, 1911. Reprinted with the permission of Cambridge University Press.

"I am, I exist, is necessarily true each time that I pronounce it, or that I mentally conceive it."

— RENÉ DESCARTES

God, or some other being by whatever name we call it, who puts these reflections into my mind? That is not necessary, for is it not possible that I am capable of producing them myself? I myself, am I not at least something? But I have already denied that I had senses and body. Yet I hesitate, for what follows from that? Am I so dependent on body and senses that I cannot exist without these? But I was persuaded that there was nothing in all the world, that there was no heaven, no earth, that there were no minds, nor any bodies; was I not then likewise persuaded that I did not exist? Not at all; of a surety I myself did exist since I persuaded myself of something [or merely because I thought of something]. But there is some deceiver or other, very powerful and very cunning, who ever employs his ingenuity in deceiving me. Then without doubt I exist also if he deceives me, and let him deceive me as much as he will, he can never cause me to be nothing so long as I think that I am something. So that after having reflected well and carefully examined all things, we must come to the definite conclusion that this proposition: I am, I exist, is necessarily true each time that I pronounce it, or that I mentally conceive it.

Here it is, the one, certain truth that Descartes needs to start his argument. The more famous formulation of this truth, **cogito, ergo sum**, "I think, therefore I am," occurs in his earlier *Discourse on Method* (1637). (A similar argument appears in St. Augustine, more than one thousand years earlier.)

But now that Descartes knows that he exists, what is he? His answer: "a thing which thinks."

But I do not yet know clearly enough what I am, I who am certain that I am; and hence I must be careful to see that I do not imprudently take some other object in place of myself, and thus that I do not go astray in respect of this knowledge that I hold to be the most certain and most evident of all that I have formerly learned. That is why I shall now consider anew what I believed myself to be before I embarked upon these last reflections; and of my former opinions I shall withdraw all that might even in a small degree be invalidated by the reasons which I have just brought forward, in order that there may be nothing at all left beyond what is absolutely certain and indubitable.

What then did I formerly believe myself to be? Undoubtedly I believed myself to be a man. But what is a man? Shall I say a reasonable animal? Certainly not; for then I should have to inquire what an animal is, and what is reasonable; and thus from a single question I should insensibly fall into an infinitude of others more difficult; and I should not wish to waste the little time and leisure remaining to me in trying to unravel subtleties like these. But I shall rather stop here to consider the thoughts which of themselves spring up in my mind, and which were not inspired by anything beyond my own nature alone when I applied myself to the consideration of my being. In the first place, then, I considered myself as having a face, hands, arms, and all that system of members composed of bones and flesh as seen in a corpse which I designated by the name of body. In addition to this I considered that I was nourished, that I walked, that I felt, and that I thought, and I referred all these actions to the soul: but I did not stop to consider what the soul was, or if I did stop, I imagined that it was something extremely rare and subtle like a wind, a flame, or an ether, which was spread throughout my grosser parts. As to body I had no manner of doubt about its nature, but thought I had a very clear knowledge of it; and if I had desired to explain it according to the notions that I had then formed of it, I should have described it thus: By the body I understand all that which can be defined by a certain figure: something which can be confined in a certain place, and which can fill a given space in such a way that every other body will be excluded from it; which can be perceived either by touch, or by sight, or by hearing, or by taste, or by smell: which can be moved in many ways not, in truth, by itself, but by something which is foreign to it, by which it is touched [and from which it receives impressions]: for to have the power of self-movement, as also of feeling or of thinking, I did not consider to appertain to the nature of body: on the contrary, I was rather astonished to find that faculties similar to them existed in some bodies.

But what am I, now that I suppose that there is a certain genius which is extremely powerful, and, if I may say so, malicious, who employs all his power in deceiving me? Can I affirm that I possess the least of all those things which I have just said pertain to the nature of body? I pause to consider, I revolve all these things in my mind, and I find none of which I can say that it pertains to me. It would be tedious to stop to enumerate them. Let us pass to the attributes of soul and see if there is any one which is in

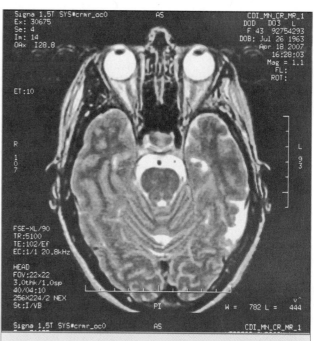

FIG. 3.6 The mind, not the body, is a thing that thinks, according to Descartes. (© iStockphoto.com/Allison Herreid)

me? What of nutrition or walking [the first mentioned]? But if it is so that I have no body it is also true that I can neither walk nor take nourishment. Another attribute is sensation. But one cannot feel without body, and besides I have thought I perceived many things during sleep that I recognized in my waking moments as not having been experienced at all. What of thinking? I find here that thought is an attribute that belongs to me; it alone cannot be separated from me. I am, I exist, that is certain. But how often? Just when I think; for it might possibly be the case if I ceased entirely to think, that I should likewise cease altogether to exist. I do not now admit anything which is not necessarily true: to speak accurately I am not more than a thing which thinks, that is to say a mind or a soul, or an understanding, or a reason, which are terms whose significance was formerly unknown to me. I am, however, a real thing and really exist; but what thing? I have answered: a thing which thinks. . . . What is a thing which thinks? It is a thing which doubts, understands, [conceives], affirms, denies, wills, refuses, which also imagines and feels.

In other words, Descartes cannot know for certain that he has a body, much less a particular kind of body, since the evil genius could fool him about that. The only thing that the evil genius could not possibly fool him about is his own thinking, and therefore, the "I" that he knows to exist can only be a thinking "I," not a person or a man in the more usual sense. Later on, this will cause Descartes to raise a gigantic problem, namely, how to explain the connection between this thinking self and the body with which it is associated. But for now, we are more interested in the way he will use his discovery of a single, certain truth. (His discussion of the "mind-body" connection occurs in "Meditation VI," which we shall discuss in Chapter 5, pp. 333-336.)

Descartes has his premise, the fact of his own existence as a "thinking thing." What must follow, then, is the use of this premise in an argument that will "prove" the beliefs he began by doubting: the existence of his own body, the existence of the "external" world, and the existence of God. Finally, he must somehow get rid of his tentative supposition of the evil demon. But first, he raises once again the old metaphysical question of substance. In a famous example from "Meditation II" he argues:

Let us begin by considering the commonest matters, those which we believe to be the most distinctly comprehended, to wit, the bodies which we touch and see; not indeed bodies in general, for these general ideas are usually a little more confused, but let us consider one body in particular. Let us take, for example, this piece of wax: it has been taken quite freshly from the hive, and it has not yet lost the sweetness of the odour of the honey which it contains; it still retains somewhat of the odour of the flowers from which it has been culled; its colour, its figure, its size are apparent; it is hard, cold, easily handled, and if you strike it with the finger, it will emit a sound. Finally all the things which are requisite to cause us distinctly to recognize a body, are met with in it. But notice that while I speak and approach the fire what remained of the taste is exhaled, the smell evaporates, the colour alters, the figure is destroyed, the size increases, it becomes liquid, it heats, scarcely can one handle it, and when one strikes it, no sound is emitted. Does the same wax remain after this change? We must confess that it remains; none would judge otherwise. What then did I know so distinctly in this piece of wax? It could certainly be nothing of all that the senses brought to my notice, since all these things which fall under taste, smell, sight, touch and hearing, are found to be changed, and yet the same wax remains.

Perhaps it was what I now think, viz. that this wax was not that sweetness of honey, nor that agreeable scent of flowers, nor that particular whiteness, nor that figure, nor that sound, but simply a body which a little while before appeared to me as perceptible under these forms, and which is now perceptible under others. But what, precisely, is it that I imagine when I form such conceptions? Let us attentively consider this, and, abstracting from all that does not belong to the wax, let us see what remains. Certainly nothing remains excepting a certain extended thing which is flexible and movable. But what is the meaning of flexible and movable? Is it not that I imagine that this piece of wax being round is capable of becoming square and of passing from a square to a triangular figure? No, certainly it is not that, since I imagine it admits of an infinitude of similar changes, and I nevertheless do not know how to compass the infinitude of my imagination, and consequently this conception which I have of the wax is not brought about by the faculty of imagination. What now is this extension? Is it not also unknown? For it becomes greater when the wax is melted, greater when it is boiled, and greater still when the heat increases; and I should not conceive [clearly] according to truth what wax is, if I did not think that even this piece that we are considering is capable of receiving more variations in extension than I have ever imagined. We must then grant that I could not even understand through the imagination what this piece of wax is, and that it is my mind alone which perceives it. I say this piece of wax in particular, for as to wax in general it is yet clearer. But what is this piece

FIG. 3.7 The same substance can exhibit varying properties. *(© iStockphoto.com/James Brey)*

of wax which cannot be understood excepting by the [understanding or] mind? It is certainly the same that I see, touch, imagine, and finally it is the same which I have always believed it to be from the beginning. But what must particularly be observed is that its perception is neither an act of vision, nor of touch, nor of imagination, and has never been such although it may have appeared formerly to be so, but only an intuition of the mind, which may be imperfect and confused as it was formerly, or clear and distinct as it is at present, according as my attention is more or less directed to the elements which are found in it, and of which it is composed.

This "intuition of mind" is the key to all rationalist thinking. **Intuition** is where the rationalist obtains his premises, from which he argues to all other conclusions. The difference between the rationalist and the empiricist, at least in what they say that they are doing, is the rationalist's heavy reliance on nonempirical intuition. Both would agree on the legitimacy of the deductions that follow; it is the source of the premises that is in dispute. And intuition, according to the rationalists, has its source in reason alone. (Notice that "reason" refers not only to the activity of reasoning but to unreasoned intuitions and insights as well.) Accordingly it is this source of intuition that will be the center of the dispute rather than the actual arguments that Descartes then uses to "prove" his other beliefs. The strategy of Descartes' argument is as follows. First, there is the premise, which you have seen:

I exist *(as a thinking thing).*

Then (in "Meditation III"), Descartes uses this premise to prove the existence of God. This is the second key move in the argument. (The first is the establishment of the premise, "I exist.") The argument itself is a version of two arguments called "the cosmological argument" and "the ontological argument for God's existence." We discussed them in detail in Chapter 1 ("Religion"), but the basic logic of both arguments is this: If a finite, dependent, and merely contingent being like myself can even think of an infinite, independent, and necessary being, then such a being must exist. The details of these arguments, however, are not so much the concern of epistemology or the theory of knowledge as they are of the special logical considerations necessary when talking about the Supreme Being. For now, therefore, let us simply grant Descartes his second step, with the promissory note that the proofs will be explained in the later chapter on the philosophy of religion. So, we have

I exist *(as a thinking thing). (premise)*
God exists *(because I could not exist without Him).*

Now we can say that, by His very nature (another intuition), God is good, in fact, perfectly good. So, as Descartes says in "Meditation VI,"

 FROM **"Meditation VI"**
BY **René Descartes**[7]

Since He has given me a very strong inclination to believe that these ideas (of trees, houses, etc.) arise from corporeal objects, I do not see how he could be vindicated from the charge of deceit, if in truth they proceeded from any other source, or were produced by other causes than corporeal things? (For example, by the evil demon, or in dreams.)

---

7 René Descartes, *Meditations on First Philosophy*, in *The Philosophical Works of Descartes*, trans. Elizabeth S. Haldane and G. R. T. Ross, 1911. Reprinted with the permission of Cambridge University Press.

Therefore,

> We *cannot be deceived* [whether by the evil demon or whatever else]. . . . I cannot doubt but that there is in me a certain passive faculty of perception, that is, of receiving and taking knowledge of the ideas of sensible things; but this would be useless to me, if there did not also exist in me, or in some other thing, another active faculty capable of forming and producing those ideas. But this active faculty cannot be in me [in as far as I am but a thinking thing], seeing that it does not presuppose thought, and also that those ideas are frequently produced in my mind without my contributing to it in any way, and even frequently contrary to my will. This faculty must therefore exist in some substance different from me, in which all the objective reality of the ideas that are produced by this faculty is contained formally or eminently, as I before re-marked: and this substance is either a body, that is to say, a corporeal nature in which is contained formally [and in effect] all that is objectively [and by representation] in those ideas; or it is God himself, or some other creature, of a rank superior to body, in which the same is contained eminently. But as God is no deceiver, it is manifest that he does not of himself and immediately communicate those ideas to me, nor even by the intervention of any creature in which their objective reality is not formally, but only eminently, contained. For as he has given me no faculty whereby I can discover this to be the case, but, on the contrary, a very strong inclination to believe that those ideas arise from corporeal objects, I do not see how he could be vindicated from the charge of deceit, if in truth they proceeded from any other source, or were produced by other causes than corporeal things: and accordingly it must be concluded, that corporeal objects exist. Nevertheless they are not perhaps exactly such as we per-ceive by the senses, for their comprehension by the senses is, in many instances, very obscure and confused; but it is at least necessary to admit that all which I clearly and distinctly conceive as in them, that is, generally speaking, all that is comprehended in the object of speculative geometry, really exists external to me.

The argument is not convincing, as Descartes' critics were quick to point out. Where does Descartes get his confidence in reason to begin with, such that he feels confident in his own abilities to prove God's existence? Descartes' answer is that we get that confidence from God Himself. But with this answer he has begged the question; that is, he has presumed the existence of God in order to get the confidence with which he then proves God's existence. (This circularity of argument is often called "the Cartesian Circle.") Another way of criticizing the same strategy is to say that, having once introduced the evil demon, Descartes has no way of getting rid of him, since that supposition undermines his confidence in his own reason just as thoroughly as his confidence in God bolsters it.

- Why is Descartes considered a "rationalist"? What does this designation mean?
- What is the "Cartesian Circle"? Why is it a problem?

Our primary concern, however, is with Descartes' claim that certain beliefs are self-evident or "clear and distinct" on the basis of intuition and reason alone. These are beliefs that we don't have to learn—in fact, couldn't learn—from experience. It is not just Descartes' "I exist" premise that is such a belief; all of the **rules of inference**, which he uses in his argu-ments, are also beliefs of this kind. Ultimately, his confidence in reason itself is one, too. But how does one defend these beliefs, for not every philosopher agrees with them. In particular, John Locke, in his disillusionment with metaphysics, begins his philosophy with an assault on the very idea of knowledge that is independent of experience. Thus he begins with an attack on the heart of the rationalist methodology.

B. Innate Ideas Concerning Human Understanding: John Locke

Regarding metaphysics, John Locke is reported to have commented to a friend, "you and I have had enough of this kind of fiddling." Against the sometimes fantastic claims of the metaphysicians, Locke sought a restoration of common sense.[8] Just as Aristotle had acted as a critic of Plato's extravagant two-worlds view, Locke acted as a corrective to the metaphysical enthusiasm of the medieval and modern worlds. He accepted Descartes' method of tentative **skepticism**, but he questioned his French predecessor's urge to metaphysics as well as his confidence in the insights of pure reason. He rejected the unsupportable "intuitions" that provided Descartes with his rules and his premises, and he turned instead to the data of experience as the ultimate source of all knowledge. He therefore rejected Descartes' exclusively deductive method and supplanted it with a method appropriate to **generalizations from experience**, or **induction**. In inductive reasoning, the conclusion always goes beyond the premises and therefore, unlike deductions, is always less certain than they are. (For example, from the observed fact that all the philosophy professors that you have met have been absent-minded [the premise] you conclude by **inductive generalization** that all philosophy professors are probably absent-minded.) Accordingly, Locke also modified Descartes' demand for "perfect certainty" and allowed for probability and "degrees of assent." But it must not be thought that Locke therefore rejected reason as such. He still accepted the certainty of mathematical reasoning and the validity of deductive inferences; but he also expanded the concept of rationality to include inductive reasoning and probability as well as deduction and certainty.

FIG. 3.8 Locke disagrees with Descartes over whether any of our ideas are innate. *(Image © Bruce Rolff, 2011. Used under license from Shutterstock.com)*

- What is induction? (You can refer back to pages 28–31.) Give an example of inductive reasoning. How does induction differ from deduction?

Locke's *An Essay Concerning Human Understanding* (1689) is built on a single premise, namely, that all our knowledge comes from experience. This means, in his view, that there cannot possibly be ideas that are prior to experience, ideas that are "born into us," as suggested so vividly by Plato. In other words, Locke refuses to accept the notion of **innate ideas**, by which he means not only those ideas that are literally "born into us" but all ideas that

---

[8] British empiricism traditionally has considered itself the defender of "common sense" against the excesses of metaphysics. This was even true of Berkeley and Hume, who reached conclusions more outrageous than any metaphysician. It is also true of Bertrand Russell and G. E. Moore in the twentieth century.

are derived without appeal to experience. This includes, in his opinion, Descartes' "clear and distinct ideas," Spinoza's "adequate ideas," and Leibniz's "truths of reason."

 FROM *An Essay Concerning Human Understanding*
BY **John Locke**[9]

1. *The way shown how we come by any knowledge, sufficient to prove it not innate.*—It is an established opinion among some men, that there are in the understanding certain innate principles; some primary notions, κοιναίέννοιαι, characters, as it were, stamped upon the mind of man which the soul receives in its very first being, and brings into the world with it. It would be sufficient to convince unprejudiced readers of the falseness of this supposition, if I should only show (as I hope I shall in the following parts of this discourse) how men, barely by the use of their natural faculties, may attain to all the knowledge they have, without the help of any innate impressions, and may arrive at certainty, without any such original notions or principles. . . .

2. *General Assent the great Argument.*—There is nothing more commonly taken for granted, than that there are certain principles, both speculative and practical (for they speak of both), universally agreed upon by all mankind, which therefore, they argue, must needs be constant impressions which the souls of men receive in their first beings, and which they bring into the world with them, as necessarily and really as they do any of their inherent faculties.

3. *Universal Consent proves nothing innate.*—This argument, drawn from universal consent, has this misfortune in it, that if it were true in matter of fact that there were certain truths wherein all mankind agreed, it would not prove them innate, if there can be any other way shown how men may come to that universal agreement in the things they do consent in, which I presume may be done.

4. *"What is, is," and "it is impossible for the same Thing to be and not to be," not universally assented to.*—But, which is worse, this argument of universal consent, which is made use of to prove innate principles, seems to me a demonstration that there are none such; because there are none to which all mankind give an universal assent. I shall begin with the speculative, and instance in those magnified principles of demonstration, "Whatsoever is, is" and "It is impossible for the same thing to be, and not to be"; which, of all others, I think, have the most allowed title to innate. These have so settled a reputation of maxims universally received that it will no doubt be thought strange if anyone should seem to question it. But yet I take liberty to say that these propositions are so far from having an universal assent that there are a great part of mankind to whom they are not so much as known.

5. *Not on the Mind naturally imprinted, because not known to Children, Idiots, &c.*—For, first, it is evident that all children and idiots have not the least apprehension or thought of them; and the want of that is enough to destroy that universal assent which must needs be the necessary concomitant of all innate truths: it seeming to me near a contradiction to say that there are truths imprinted on the soul which it perceives or understands not; imprinting, if it signify anything, being nothing else but the making certain truths to be perceived. For to imprint anything on the mind without the mind's perceiving it, seems to me hardly intelligible. If therefore children and idiots have souls, have minds, with those impressions upon them, they must unavoid-

---

9 John Locke, *An Essay Concerning Human Understanding*, ed. A. C. Fraser, Oxford: Clarendon Press, 1894.

ably perceive them, and necessarily know and assent to these truths; which since they do not, it is evident that there are no such impressions. For if they are not notions naturally imprinted, how can they be innate, and if they are notions imprinted, how can they be unknown? To say a notion is imprinted on the mind, and yet at the same time to say that the mind is ignorant of it, and never yet took notice of it, is to make this impression nothing. No proposition can be said to be in the mind which it never yet knew, which it was never yet conscious of.

The argument is straightforward; there is, in fact, no universal agreement regarding supposedly "innate" principles, and even if there were, that would not prove their "innateness." Rather, Locke argues:

FIG. 3.9 According to Locke, our minds are blank tablets until experience writes on them. (© iStockphoto.com/blackred)

Let us suppose the mind to be, as we say, a blank tablet *(tabula rasa)* of white paper, void of all characters, without any ideas; how comes it to be furnished? Whence comes it by that vast store, which the busy and boundless fancy of man has painted on it with almost endless variety? Whence has it all the materials of reason and knowledge? To this I answer in one word, from *experience:* in that all our knowledge is founded, and from that it ultimately derives itself.

> • What does Locke mean when he says that the mind is like a blank tablet *(tabula rasa)* of white paper? What is he arguing against?

It is this premise that Locke is concerned to defend and use, and his attack on innate ideas is by way of introduction. But Locke fails to prove that the human mind does not have inborn potentials and limitations, and more importantly, he fails to recognize that inference from experience might itself require principles that are not drawn from experience. In fact, Leibniz, one of the chief targets of Locke's attack, was not long in providing what we might call "the rationalist's reply." Turning Locke against himself, Leibniz argued that, by his own principles, he could not attack the concept of innate ideas.

 FROM *New Essays on Human Understanding*
BY **Gottfried Wilhelm von Leibniz**[10]

The question at issue is whether the soul in itself is entirely empty, like the tablet upon which nothing has yet been written (tabula rasa), as is the view of Aristotle and the author of the *Essay* (Locke), and whether all that is traced on it comes solely from the senses and from experience; or whether the soul contains originally the principles of various notions and doctrines which external objects merely awaken from time to time, as I believe, with Plato and even with the Schoolmen, and with

> "No proposition can be said to be in the mind which it never yet knew, which it was never yet conscious of."
>
> – JOHN LOCKE

[10] "Leibniz's Rebuttal," from *New Essays on Human Understanding*, by Gottfried Wilhelm von Leibniz, trans. A. G. Langley. Reprinted by permission of Open Court Publishing Company, a division of Carus Publishing Company, Peru, IL. Copyright © 1949 by Open Court Publishing.

all those who take in this sense the passage of St. Paul (Romans, 2:15) where he re-marks that the law of God is written in the heart. . . . From this there arises another question, whether all truths depend on experience, that is to say, on induction and examples, or whether there are some that have some other basis. For if some events can be foreseen before any trial has been made of them, it is clear that we must here contribute something of our own. The senses, although necessary for all our actual knowledge, are not sufficient to give us the whole of it, since the senses never give anything except examples, that is to say, particular or individual truths. All examples which confirm a general truth, however numerous they may be, are not enough to establish the universal necessity of this same truth; for it does not follow that what has happened will happen again in the same way.

. . .

It would seem that necessary truths, such as are found in pure mathematics, and especially in arithmetic and in geometry, must have principles the proof of which does not depend on examples, nor, consequently, on the testimony of the senses, although without the senses it would never have occurred to us to think of them. This ought to be well recognised; Euclid has so well understood it that he often demonstrates by reason what is obvious enough through experience and by sensible images. Logic also, together with metaphysics and ethics, one of which forms natural theology and the other natural jurisprudence, are full of such truths; and consequently their proof can only come from internal principles, which are called innate. It is true that we must not imagine that these eternal laws of the reason can be read in the soul as in an open book, as the edict of the praetor can be read in his *album* without difficulty or research; but it is enough that they can be discovered in us by dint of attention, for which opportunities are given by the senses. The success of experiments serves also as confirmation of the reason, very much as proofs serve in arithmetic for better avoiding error of reckoning when the reasoning is long.

. . .

It seems that our able author claims that there is nothing potential in us and nothing even of which we are not at any time actually conscious; but he cannot mean this strictly, or his opinion would be too paradoxical; for acquired habits and the contents of our memory are not always consciously perceived and do not even always come to our aid at need, although we often easily bring them back to mind on some slight occasion which makes us remember them, just as we need only the beginning of a song to remember the song. Also he modifies his assertion in other places by saying that there is nothing in us of which we have not been at least for-merly conscious. But besides the fact that no one can be sure by reason alone how far our past apperceptions, which we may have forgotten, may have gone, especially in view of the Platonic doctrine of reminiscence, which, mythical as it is, is not, in part at least, incompatible with bare reason; in addition to this, I say, why is it nec-essary that everything should be acquired by us through the perceptions of exter-nal things, and that nothing can be unearthed in ourselves? Is our soul, then, such a blank that, besides the images borrowed from without, it is nothing? . . . [T]here are a thousand indications that lead us to think that there are at every moment numberless perceptions in us, but without apperception and without reflections; that is to say, changes in the soul itself of which we are not conscious, because the impressions are either too slight and too numerous, or too even, so that they have nothing sufficient to distinguish them one from the other; but, joined to others, they do not fail to produce their effect and to make themselves felt at least confusedly in the mass.

> • How does Locke rebute the notion that "whatsoever is, is" and "It is impossible for the same thing to be, and not to be" are innate ideas? What kind of allegedly innate truths does Leibniz cite in response?

Locke himself did not continue the debate; he was already convinced of his position and had more urgent problems to worry about (the political chaos in London following the "Glorious Revolution" of 1688). But the debate continued in different forms. The rise of anthropology in the nineteenth century, with the discoveries of societies whose basic ideas were radically different from our own, seemed to support Locke's claim that no one will believe in innate universal principles if they "ever look beyond the smoke of their own chimneys." But in the nineteenth century a great many philosophers still argued for the existence of universal principles not learned through experience. (Immanuel Kant did so in a very powerful set of arguments that we will view in the next several chapters.) In the early twentieth century, opinion was in general accord with Locke, but recently it has taken another swing back to Leibniz, this time, ironically, supported by anthropology. A major movement in the social sciences, usually called structuralism (whose main proponent is Claude Lévi-Strauss in France), has argued that underneath the many superficial differences between very different societies there are certain basic "structures" that are universal and innate. In America, the notion of innate ideas has appeared once again in the work of the well-known linguist Noam Chomsky. According to Chomsky, certain capacities for language are built into us from birth, and this allows him to explain not only the similarities of human thinking (which was the view that Locke attacked) but also the enormous capacity for learning different languages quickly. (The average three year old learns a language in six months.) The Locke-Leibniz debate is still very much alive.

Noam Chomsky (1928-)
American philosopher and linguist. Chomsky is also a prominent figure in the campaign for international rights.

FIG. 3.10 Philosopher and linguist Noam Chomsky *(AP Photo/ Mohammad Abu Ghosh)*

C. Two Empiricist Theories of Knowledge

Leaving aside those special concerns that involve only "the relations between ideas" (as in mathematics, logic, and trivial **conceptual truths** such as "a horse is an animal"), all of our ideas are derived from experience. Epistemology (and philosophy in general) now became a kind of psychology (indeed, the two disciplines were not yet distinguished), a study of the history of our common experiences in order to discover where we get our ideas, particularly such ideas as substance, God, and our various conceptions of reality. In his theory, Locke uses three familiar terms: **sensation** (or what more modern empiricists call sense-data), **ideas** (not in the Platonic sense but simply "the immediate object of perception, thought, or understanding"), and **quality** (or what we have so far been calling property, for example, being red, being round, being heavy).

John Locke

FROM *An Essay Concerning Human Understanding* BY John Locke[11]

1. Concerning the simple ideas of Sensation, it is to be considered—that whatsoever is so constituted in nature as to be able, by affecting our senses, to cause any perception in the mind, doth thereby produce in the understanding a simple idea; which, whatever be the external cause of it, when it comes to be taken notice of by our discerning faculty, it is by the mind looked on and considered there to be a real positive idea in the understanding, as much as any other whatsoever; though, perhaps, the cause of it be but a privation of the subject.

2. Thus the ideas of heat and cold, light and darkness, white and black, motion and rest, are equally clear and positive ideas in the mind; though perhaps, some of the causes which produce them are barely privations, in those subjects from whence our senses derive those ideas. These the understanding, in its view of them, considers all as distinct positive ideas, without taking notice of the causes that produce them: which is an inquiry not belonging to the idea, as it is in the understanding, but to the nature of the things existing without us. These are two very different things, and carefully to be distinguished; it being one thing to perceive and know the idea of white or black, and quite another to examine what kind of particles they must be, and how ranged in the superficies, to make any object appear white or black.

. . .

7. To discover the nature of our *ideas* the better, and to discourse of them intelligibly, it will be convenient to distinguish them *as they are ideas or perceptions in our minds;* and *as they are modifications of matter in the bodies that cause such perceptions in us:* that so we may not think (as perhaps usually is done) that they are exactly the images and resemblances of something inherent in the subject; most of those of sensation being in the mind no more the likeness of something existing without us, than the names that stand for them are the likeness of our ideas, which yet upon hearing they are apt to excite in us.

8. Whatsoever the mind perceives *in itself*, or is the immediate object of perception, thought, or understanding, that I call *idea;* and the power to produce any idea in our mind, I call *quality* of the subject wherein that power is. Thus a snowball having the power to produce in us the ideas of white, cold, and round—the power

FIG. 3.11 A snowball's quality, such as cold, is its power to produce an idea in us, for example, the idea of cold. *(Image © 2011. Used under license from Shutterstock.com)*

---

[11] John Locke, *An Essay Concerning Human Understanding*, ed. A. C. Fraser, Oxford: Clarendon Press, 1894.

to produce those ideas in us, as they are in the snowball, I call qualities; and as they are sensations or perceptions in our understanding, I call them ideas; which *ideas*, if I speak of sometimes as in the things themselves, I should be understood to mean those qualities in the objects which produce them in us.

Notice that the basis of Locke's theory is the "commonsense" distinction between physical objects in the world and sensations and ideas in our minds. Accordingly, we may talk of the qualities or properties inherent in the objects in the world, such as size and shape, and the qualities or properties they merely appear to have, such as color or texture, but they do not exist independently of the objects' effects on our sense organs. Locke refers to those properties of the objects themselves as **primary qualities;** he calls those "properties" of the objects that we merely see them as having **secondary qualities**.

PRIMARY QUALITIES:

Qualities thus considered in bodies are, *First*, such as are utterly inseparable from the body, in what state soever it be; and such as in all the alterations and changes it suffers, all the force can be used upon it, it constantly keeps; and such as sense constantly finds in every particle of matter which has bulk enough to be perceived; and the mind finds inseparable from every particle of matter, though less than to make itself singly be perceived by our senses: e.g. Take a grain of wheat, divide it into two parts; each part has still solidity, extension, figure, and mobility: divide it again, and it retains still the same qualities; and so divide it on, till the parts become insensible; they must retain still each of them all those qualities. For division (which is all that a mill, or pestle, or any other body, does upon another, in reducing it to insensible parts) can never take away either solidity, extension, figure, or mobility from any body, but only makes two or more distinct separate masses of matter, of that which was but one before; all which distinct masses, reckoned as so many distinct bodies; after division, make a certain number. These I call *original* or *primary qualities* of body, which I think we may observe to produce simple ideas in us, viz. solidity, extension, figure, motion or rest, and number.

· · ·

SECONDARY QUALITIES:

Secondly, such qualities which in truth are nothing in the objects themselves but powers to produce various sensations in us by their primary qualities, i.e., by the bulk, figure, texture, and motion of their insensible parts, as colours, sounds, tastes, &c. These I call *secondary qualities*. To these might be added a *third* sort, which are allowed to be barely powers; though they are as much real qualities in the subject as those which I, to comply with the common way of speaking, call qualities, but for distinction, secondary qualities. For the power in fire to produce a new colour, or consistency, in *wax* or *clay*—by its primary qualities, is as much a quality in fire, as the power it has to produce in *me* a new idea or sensation of warmth or burning, which I felt not before—by the same primary qualities, viz. the bulk, texture, and motion of its insensible parts.

FIG. 3.12 We can keep dividing a grain of wheat, but its parts still take up space. *(Image © David Dohnal, 2011. Used under license from Shutterstock.com)*

The question, then, is how physical objects cause us to have sensations and ideas. Locke's answer (which, like his theory as a whole, is very strongly influenced by the physical theories of his contemporary Isaac Newton) is, by impulse. This might not seem illuminating until you try to think of the Newtonian theory of force as a product of particles and masses in motion. It is on this model that Locke develops what is now called his "**Causal Theory of Perception.**" First, for the primary qualities:

> If then external objects be not united to our minds when they produce ideas therein; and yet we perceive these *original* qualities in such of them as singly fall under our senses, it is evident that some motion must be thence continued by our nerves, or animal spirits, by some parts of our bodies, to the brains or the seat of sensation, there to produce in our minds the particular ideas we have of them. And since the extension, figure, number, and motion of bodies of an observable bigness, may be perceived at a distance by the sight, it is evident some singly imperceptible bodies must come from them to the eyes, and thereby convey to the brain some motion; which produces these ideas which we have of them in us.

Then, for secondary qualities:

> After the same manner that the ideas of these original qualities are produced in us, we may conceive that the ideas of *secondary* qualities are also produced, viz. by the operation of insensible particles on our senses. For, it being manifest that there are bodies and good store of bodies, each whereof are so small, that we cannot by any of our senses discover either their bulk, figure, or motion—as is evident in those particles of the air and water, and others extremely smaller than those; perhaps as much smaller than the particles of air and water, as the particles of air and water are smaller than peas or hail-stones;—let us suppose at present that the different motions and figures, bulk and number, of such particles, affecting the several organs of our senses, produce in us those different sensations which we have from the colours and smells of bodies; e.g. that a violet, by the impulse of such insensible particles of matter, of peculiar figures and bulks, and in different degrees and modifications of their motions, causes the ideas of the blue colour, and sweet scent of that flower to be produced in our minds. It being no more impossible to conceive that God should annex such ideas to such motions, with which they have no similitude, than that he should annex the idea of pain to the motion of a piece of steel dividing our flesh, with which that idea hath no resemblance.
>
> What I have said concerning colours and smells may be understood also of tastes and sounds, and other the like sensible qualities; which, whatever reality we by mistake attribute to them, are in truth nothing in the objects themselves, but powers to produce various sensations in us; and depend on those primary qualities, viz. bulk, figure, texture, and motion of parts [as I have said].

Therefore,

> I think it easy to draw this observation—that the ideas of primary qualities of bodies are resemblances of them, and their patterns do really exist in the bodies themselves, but the ideas produced in us by these secondary qualities have no resemblance of them at all. There is nothing like our ideas, existing in the bodies themselves. They are, in the bodies we denominate from them, only a power to produce those sensations in us: and what is sweet, blue, or warm in idea, is but the certain bulk, figure, and motion of the insensible parts, in the bodies themselves, which we call so.

"The ideas of primary qualities of bodies are resemblances of them, and their patterns do really exist in the bodies themselves, but the ideas produced in us by these secondary qualities have no resemblance of them at all."

– JOHN LOCKE

Flame is denominated hot and light; snow, white and cold; and manna, white and sweet, from the ideas they produce in us. Which qualities are commonly thought to be the same in those bodies that those ideas are in us, the one the perfect resemblance of the other, as they are in a mirror, and it would by most men be judged very extravagant if one should say otherwise. And yet he that will consider that the same fire that, at one distance produces in us the sensation of warmth, does, at a nearer approach, produce in us the far different sensation of pain, ought to bethink himself what reason he has to say—that this idea of warmth, which was produced in him by fire, is *actually in the fire;* and his idea of pain, which the same fire produced in him the same way, is *not* in the fire. Why are whiteness and coldness in snow, and pain not, when it produces the one and the other idea in us; and can do neither, but by the bulk, figure, number, and motion of its solid parts?

FIG. 3.13 For Locke, heat is no more "in the fire" than pain is in the fire. *(© iStockphoto.com/Monika Lewandowska)*

The particular bulk, number, figure, and motion of the parts of fire or snow are really in them—whether any one's senses perceive them or no: and therefore they may be called *real* qualities, because they really exist in those bodies. But light, heat, whiteness, or coldness, are no more really in them than sickness or pain is in manna. Take away the sensation of them; let not the eyes see light or colours, nor the ears hear sounds; let the palate not taste, nor the nose smell, and all colours, tastes, odours, and sounds, *as they are such particular ideas*, vanish and cease, and are reduced to their causes, i.e., bulk, figure, and motion of parts.

- What does Locke mean by "primary qualities"? Give an example.
- What does Locke mean by "secondary qualities"? Give an example.

This is the basic empiricist theory as Locke presented it. The logical consequences of empiricism, as we shall see when we study Berkeley and Hume, are not nearly so palatable. But how does the "causal theory of perception" allow Locke to approach the traditional questions of metaphysics? Significantly, the first two steps in the argument are identical with those we traced in Descartes—one's own existence and the existence of God—and Locke even includes the problematic notion of "intuition."

1. The knowledge of our own being we have by intuition. The existence of God, reason clearly makes known to us.

But then, the strict empiricist reemerges and insists:

The knowledge of the existence of *any other thing* we can have only by *sensation:* for there being no necessary connexion of real existence with any *idea* a man hath in his memory; nor of any other existence but that of God with the existence of any particular man: no particular man can know the existence of any other being, but only when, by actual operating upon him, it makes itself perceived by him. For, the having the idea of anything in our mind, no more proves the existence of that thing, than the picture of a man evidences his being in the world, or the visions of a dream make thereby a true history.

FIG. 3.14 While he writes, Locke cannot doubt that he is writing. As you read this, can you doubt that you are reading? (© iStockphoto.com/nicoolay)

2. It is therefore the *actual receiving* of ideas from without that gives us notice of the existence of other things, and makes us know, that something doth exist at that time without us, which causes that idea in us; though perhaps we neither know nor consider how it does it. For it takes not from the certainty of our senses, and the ideas we receive by them, that we know not the manner wherein they are produced: e.g. whilst I write this, I have, by the paper affecting my eyes, that idea produced in my mind, which, whatever object causes, I call *white;* by which I know that that quality or accident (i.e. whose appearance before my eyes always causes that idea) doth really exist, and hath a being without me. And of this, the greatest assurance I can possibly have, and to which my faculties can attain, is the testimony of my eyes, which are the proper and sole judges of this thing; whose testimony I have reason to rely on as so certain, that I can no more doubt, whilst I write this, that I see white and black, and that something really exists that causes that sensation in me, than that I write or move my hand; which is a certainty as great as human nature is capable of, concerning the existence of anything, but a man's self alone, and of God.

Here Locke asserts his alternative to the strict Cartesian limitation of knowledge to matters of certainty and deduction:

3. The notice we have by our senses of the existing of things without us, though it be not altogether so certain as our intuitive knowledge, or the deductions of our reason employed about the clear abstract ideas of our own minds; yet it is an assurance that deserves the name of *knowledge.* If we persuade ourselves that our faculties act and inform us right concerning the existence of those objects that affect them, it cannot pass for an ill-grounded confidence: for I think nobody can, in earnest, be so sceptical as to be uncertain of the existence of those things which he sees and feels. At least, he that can doubt so far, (whatever he may have with his own thoughts,) will never have any controversy with me; since he can never be sure I say anything contrary to his own opinion. As to myself, I think God has given me assurance enough of the existence of things without me: since, by their different application, I can produce in myself both pleasure and pain, which is one great concernment of my present state. This is certain: the confidence that our faculties do not herein deceive us, is the greatest assurance we are capable of concerning the existence of material beings. For we cannot act anything but by our faculties; nor talk of knowledge itself, but by the help of those faculties which are fitted to apprehend even what knowledge is.

Locke then answers Descartes:

8. But yet, if after all this any one will be so sceptical as to distrust his senses, and to affirm all that we see and hear, feel and taste, think and do, during our whole being, is but the series and deluding appearance of a long dream, whereof there is no reality; and therefore will question the existence of all things, or our knowledge of anything: I must desire him to consider, that, if all be a dream, then he doth but dream that he makes the question, and so it is not much matter that a waking man should answer him. But yet, if he pleases, he may dream that I make him this an-

swer, that the certainty of things existing in *rerum natura* when we have the testimony of our senses for it is not only as great as our frame can attain to, but as our condition needs. For, our faculties being suited not to the full extent of being, nor to a perfect, clear, comprehensive knowledge of things free from all doubt and scruple; but to the preservation of us, in whom they are; and accommodated to the use of life: they serve to our purpose well enough, if they will but give us certain notice of those things, which are convenient or inconvenient to us. For he that sees a candle burning, and hath experimented the force of its flame by putting his finger in it, will little doubt that this is something existing without him, which does him harm, and puts him to great pain: which is assurance enough, when no man requires greater certainty to govern his actions by than what is as certain as his actions themselves. And if our dreamer pleases to try whether the glowing heat of a glass furnace be barely a wandering imagination in a drowsy man's fancy, by putting

FIG. 3.15 *(Image © sharpner, 2011. Used under license from Shutterstock.com)*

his hand into it, he may perhaps be wakened into a certainty greater than he could wish, that it is something more than bare imagination. So that this evidence is as great as we can desire, being as certain to us as our pleasure or pain, i.e., happiness or misery; beyond which we have no concernment, either of knowing or being. Such an assurance of the existence of things without us is sufficient to direct us in the attaining the good and avoiding the evil which is caused by them, which is the important concernment we have of being made acquainted with them.

9. In summary, then, when our senses do actually convey into our understanding any idea, we cannot but be satisfied that there doth something *at that time* really exist without us, which doth affect our senses, and by them give notice of itself to our apprehensive faculties, and actually produce that idea which we then perceive.

We are now ready to return to the traditional metaphysical notion of substance—that which underlies both the primary and the secondary qualities of a thing.

1. *Ideas of Substances, how made.*—The mind being, as I have declared, furnished with a great number of the simple ideas conveyed in by the senses, as they are found in exterior things, or by reflection on its own operations, takes notice, also, that a certain number of these simple ideas go constantly together; which being presumed to belong to one thing, and words being suited to common apprehensions, and made use of for quick dispatch, are called, so united in one subject, by one name; which, by inadvertency, we are apt afterward to talk of and consider as one simple idea, which indeed is a complication of many ideas together: because, as I have said, not imagining how these simple ideas can subsist by themselves, we accustom ourselves to suppose some substratum wherein they do subsist, and from which they do result; which therefore we call "substance."

2. *Our Ideas of Substance in general.*—So that if anyone will examine himself concerning his notion of pure substance in general, he will find he has no other idea of it at

all, but only a supposition of he knows not what support of such qualities which are capable of producing simple ideas in us; which qualities are commonly called "accidents." If anyone should be asked, "What is the subject wherein colour or weight inheres?" he would have nothing to say but, "The solid extended parts." And if he were demanded, "what is it that solidity and extension inhere in?" he would not be in a much better case than the Indian . . . who, saying that the world was supported by a great elephant, was asked what the elephant rested on? to which his answer was, "a great tortoise"; but being again pressed to know what gave support to the broad-backed tortoise, replied—something, he knew not what. And thus here, as in all other cases where we use words without having clear and distinct ideas, we talk like children, who, being questioned what such a thing is which they know not, readily give this satisfactory answer, that it is something, which in truth signifies no more, when so used, either by children or men, but that they know not what; and that the thing they pretend to know and talk of is what they have no distinct idea of at all, and so are perfectly ignorant of it, and in the dark. The idea, then, we have, to which we give the general name "substance" being nothing but the supposed, but unknown, support of those qualities we find existing, which we imagine cannot subsist *sine re substante*, "without something to support them," we call that support *substantia;* which, according to the true import of the word, is, in plain English, "standing under," or "upholding."

. . .

Hence, when we talk or think of any particular sort of corporeal substances, as horse, stone, &c., though the idea we have of either of them be but the complication or collection of those several simple ideas of sensible qualities which we used to find united in the thing called "horse" or "stone"; yet because we cannot conceive how they should subsist alone, nor one in another, we suppose them existing in, and supported by some common subject; which support we denote by the name "substance," though it be certain we have no clear or distinct idea of that thing we suppose a support.

• Why does Locke claim that substance is "we know not what"? Is this conclusion reason to say that we don't know what substance (a thing in itself) is?

Substance is "we know not what." Yet Locke hesitates to reject the notions, for he cannot escape the suspicion that talk of "qualities" makes no sense unless the qualities are the qualities of something. But this suspicion is dispensable according to Locke's own principles. So, it turns out, is his central distinction between primary and secondary qualities, as Bishop Berkeley is soon to point out. The consequence of these simple, technical moves will be shocking, to say the least.

Bishop George Berkeley

Beginning from John Locke's "commonsense" philosophy, Bishop Berkeley developed the most provocative thesis in all philosophy. Berkeley's thesis is called **subjective idealism**. It is the doctrine that there are no material substances, no physical objects, only minds and ideas in mind. (His concept of "idea" comes directly from Locke.) This surprising position emerges directly from Locke's thesis by three simple steps. First, it accepts the argument that we have no idea whatsoever what a substance might be, and it agrees that all that we can ever know of a thing are its sensible properties (or "qualities"). Second, it is shown that the distinction between primary and secondary qualities cannot be, as Locke had argued, a

FIG. 3.16 George Berkeley *(© Bettmann/CORBIS)*

distinction between properties inherent in the objects themselves as opposed to properties that the objects simply cause in us. Third, once one has agreed that all knowledge of the world (except for knowledge of one's own existence and of God) must be based upon experience, the question becomes why we should ever think that there is anything other than our experiences. Locke had argued that our experiences were caused by the physical objects; but how could this claim be justified by experience? Since we have no experience of either the objects themselves or their causation, but only of their effects (that is, the ideas they cause in us), a consistent empiricist must give up not only the causal theory of perception but the notion of physical objects as well.

Berkeley is an exceptionally clear writer, and the following excerpts from his *Treatise Concerning the Principles of Human Knowledge* (1710) should not be difficult to understand:

 FROM *Treatise Concerning the Principles of Human Knowledge* BY **Bishop George Berkeley**[12]

§ 1. It is evident to any one who takes a survey of the objects of human knowledge, that they are either ideas actually imprinted on the senses, or else such as are perceiv'd by attending to the passions and operations of the mind, or lastly ideas formed by help of memory and imagination; either compounding, dividing, or barely representing those originally perceiv'd in the aforesaid ways. By sight I have the ideas of light and colours with their several degrees and variations. By touch I perceive hard and soft, heat and cold, motion and resistance, and of all these more and less either as to quantity or degree. Smelling furnishes me with odors; the palate with tastes, and hearing conveys sounds to the mind in all their variety of tone and composition. And as several of these are observ'd to accompany each other, they come to be marked by one name, and so to be reputed as one thing. Thus, for example, a certain colour, taste, smell, figure and consistence having been observ'd to go together, are accounted one distinct thing, signified by the name *apple*. Other collections of ideas constitute a stone, a tree, a book and the like sensible things; which as they are pleasing or disagreeable excite the passions of love, hatred, joy, grief, etc.

§ 2. But besides all that endless variety of ideas or objects of knowledge, there is likewise something which knows or perceives them, and exercises divers operations, as willing, imagining, remembering about them. This perceiving, active being is what I call *mind, spirit, soul* or *my self*. By which words I do not denote any one of my ideas, but a thing intirely distinct from them, wherein they exist, or, which is the same thing, whereby they are perceiv'd, for the existence of an idea consists in being perceiv'd.

§ 3. That neither our thoughts, nor passions, nor ideas formed by the imagination, exist without the mind, is what every body will allow. And to me it is no less evident that the various sensations or ideas imprinted on the sense, however blended or combin'd together (that is whatever objects they compose) cannot exist otherwise than in a mind perceiving them. I think an intuitive knowledge may be obtain'd of this, by any one that shall attend to what is meant by the term *exist* when apply'd to sensible things. The table I write on, I say, exists, i.e. I see and feel it, and if I were out of my study I should say it existed, meaning thereby that if I was in my study I might perceive it, or that some other spirit actually does perceive it. There was an odor, i.e.

12 Bishop George Berkeley, *Treatise Concerning the Principles of Human Knowledge*, London: Brown & Sons, 1907.

"There was an odor, i.e. it was smelt; there was a sound, i.e. it was heard; a colour or figure and it was perceiv'd by sight or touch. . . . Their *esse* is *percipi*."

– GEORGE BERKELEY

it was smelt; there was a sound, i.e. it was heard; a colour or figure and it was perceiv'd by sight or touch. This is all that I can understand by these and the like expressions. For as to what is said of the absolute existence of unthinking things without any relation to their being perceiv'd, that is to me perfectly unintelligible. Their *esse* is *percipi*, (to be is to be perceived) nor is it possible they shou'd have any existence, out of the minds or thinking things which perceive them.

§ 4. It is indeed an opinion strangely prevailing amongst men, that houses, mountains, rivers and in a word all sensible objects have an existence natural or real, distinct from their being perceiv'd by the understanding. But with how great an assurance and acquiescence soever, this principle may be entertained in the world: yet whoever shall find in his heart to call it in question may, if I mistake not, perceive it to involve a manifest contradiction. For what are the foremention'd objects but the things we perceive by sense, and what, do we perceive besides our own ideas or sensations, and is it not plainly repugnant that any one of these or any combination of them shou'd exist unperceiv'd.?

This is Berkeley's central thesis—that "to be is to be perceived" (*esse est percipi*). In what follows, Berkeley argues that there is nothing other than these perceptions, or "ideas," and it is nonsense to suppose that there are things outside of the mind "like" our ideas—for "nothing is like an idea but another idea."

§ 6. Some truths there are so near and obvious to the mind that a man need only open his eyes to see 'em. Such I take this important one to be, viz. that all the choir of heaven and furniture of the earth, in a word all those bodies which compose the mighty frame of the world, have not any subsistence without a mind, that their *being* is to be perceiv'd or known; that consequently so long as they are not actually perceiv'd by me, or do not exist in my mind or that of any other created spirit, they must either have no existence at all, or else subsist in the mind of some eternal spirit: it being perfectly unintelligible and involving all the absurdity of abstraction, to attribute to any single part of them an existence independent of a spirit. To make this appear with all the light and evidence of an axiom, it seems sufficient if I can but awaken the reflexion of the reader, that he may take an impartial view of his own meaning, and turn his thoughts upon the subject itself, free and disengaged from all embarras of words and prepossession in favour of received mistakes.

§ 7. From what has been said, 'tis evident, there is not any other substance than *spirit* or that which perceives. But for the fuller demonstration of this point, let it be consider'd, the sensible qualities are colour, figure, motion, smell, taste, etc. the ideas perceiv'd by sense. Now for an idea to exist in an unperceiving thing is a manifest contradiction, for to have an idea is all one as to perceive, that therefore wherein colour, figure, etc. exist must perceive them; hence 'tis clear there can be no unthinking substance or *substratum* of those ideas.

§ 8. But say you, though the ideas themselves do not exist without the mind, yet there may be things like them whereof they are copies or resemblances, which things exist without the mind, in an unthinking substance. I answer an idea can be like nothing but an idea, a colour, or figure, can be like nothing but another colour or figure. If we look but never so little into our thoughts, we shall find it impossible for us to conceive a likeness except only between our ideas. Again, I ask whether those suppos'd originals or external things, of which our ideas are the pictures or representations, be themselves perceivable or no? If they are, then they are ideas and we have gain'd our point; but if you say they are not, I appeal to any one whether it be sense, to assert a colour is like something which is invisible; hard or soft, like something which is intangible, and so of the rest.

At this point Berkeley takes up Locke's distinction between "primary and secondary qualities," and maintains that the arguments Locke put forward regarding the latter also can be applied to the former. Primary qualities too can be ideas only, and not properties of matter.

§ 9. Some there are who make a distinction betwixt *primary* and *secondary* qualities: by the former, they mean extension, figure, motion, rest, solidity or impenetrability and number: by the latter they denote all other sensible qualities as colours, sounds, tastes, etc. The ideas we have of these they acknowlege not to be the resemblances, of any thing existing without the mind or unperceiv'd, but they will have our ideas of the primary qualities to be patterns or images of things which exist without the mind, in an unthinking substance which they call *matter*. By matter, therefore, we are to understand an inert, senseless substance, in which extension, figure, motion, etc. do actually subsist, but it is evident from what we have already shewn, that extension, figure and motion are only ideas existing in the mind, and that an idea can be like nothing but another idea, and that consequently neither they nor their archetypes can exist in an unperceiving substance. Hence it is plain, that the very notion of what is called *matter* or *corporeal substance*, involves a contradiction in it.

. . .

§ 10. They who assert that figure, motion, and the rest of the primary or original qualities do exist without the mind, in unthinking substances, do at the same time acknowlege that colours, sounds, heat, cold, do not, which they tell us are sensations existing in the mind alone, that depend on and are occasion'd by the different size, texture, motion, of the minute particles of matter. This they take for an undoubted truth, which they can demonstrate beyond all exception. Now if it be certain, that those original qualities are inseparably united with the other sensible qualities, and not, even in thought, capable of being abstracted from them, it plainly follows that they exist only in the mind. But I desire any one to reflect and try, whether he can by any abstraction of thought, conceive the extension and motion of a body, without all other sensible qualities. For my own part, I see evidently that it is not in my power to frame an idea of a body extended and moving, but I must withal give it some colour or other sensible quality which is acknowleg'd to exist only in the mind. (In short, extension, figure, and motion, abstracted from all other qualities, are inconceivable. Where therefore the other sensible qualities are, there must these be also, i.e. in the mind and no where else.)

. . .

§ 14. I shall farther add, that after the same manner, as modern philosophers prove colours, tastes, to have no existence in matter, or without the mind, the same thing may be likewise prov'd of all other sensible qualities whatsoever. Thus, for instance, it is said that heat and cold, are affections only of the mind, and not at all patterns of real beings, existing in the corporeal substances which excite them, for that the same body which appears cold to one hand, seems warm to another. Now why may we not as well argue that figure and extension, are not patterns or resemblances of qualities existing in matter, because to the same eye at different stations, or eyes of a different texture at the same station, they appear various, and cannot therefore be the images of any thing settled and determinate without the mind? Again, 'tis prov'd that sweetness is not really in the sapid thing, because the thing remaining unalter'd the sweetness is changed into bitter, as in case of a fever or otherwise vitiated palate. Is it not as reasonable to say, that motion is not without the mind, since if the succession of ideas in the mind become swifter, the motion, it is acknowledg'd, shall appear slower without any external alteration.

§ 15. In short, let any one consider those arguments, which are thought manifestly to prove that colours, tastes, exist only in the mind, and he shall find they may with equal force, be brought to prove the same thing of extension, figure, and motion. Though it must be confess'd this method of arguing does not so much prove that there is no extension, colour, in an outward object, as that we do not know by sense which is the true extension or colour of the object. But the arguments foregoing plainly shew it to be impossible that any colour or extension at all, or other sensible quality whatsoever, shou'd exist in an unthinking subject without the mind, or in truth, that there shou'd be any such thing as an outward object.

Must there be substances apart from the mind? Berkeley asks. It is true that we are somehow "affected," but it does not follow that there must be material objects. How would we know of any such objects?

§ 18. But though it were possible that solid, figur'd moveable substances may exist without the mind, corresponding to the ideas we have of bodies, yet how is it possible for us to know this? Either we must know it by sense or by reason. As for our senses, by them we have the knowledge only of our sensations, ideas, or those things that are immediately perceiv'd by sense, call 'em what you will: but they do not inform us that things exist without the mind, or unperceiv'd, like to those which are perceiv'd. This the materialists themselves acknowlege. It remains therefore that if we have any knowlege at all of external things, it must be by reason, inferring their existence from what is immediately perceiv'd by sense. But I do not see what reason can induce us to believe the existence of bodies without the mind, from what we perceive, since the very patrons of matter themselves do not pretend, there is any necessary connexion betwixt them and our ideas. I say it is granted on all hands (and what happens in dreams, frenzys and the like puts it beyond dispute) that it is possible we might be affected with all the ideas we have now, though there were no bodies existing without resembling them. Hence it is evident the supposition of external bodies is not necessary for the producing our ideas: since it is granted they are produced sometimes, and might possibly be produced always in the same order, we see them in at present, without their concurrence.

§ 19. But, though we might possibly have all our sensations without them, yet perhaps it may be thought easier to conceive and explain the manner of their production, by supposing external bodies in their likeness rather than otherwise, and so it might be at least probable there are such things as bodies that excite their ideas in our minds. But neither can this be said, for though we give the materialists their external bodies, they by their own confession are never the nearer knowing how our ideas are produced: since they own themselves unable to comprehend in what manner body can act upon spirit, or how it is possible it shou'd imprint any idea in the mind. Hence it is evident the production of ideas or sensations in our minds, can be no reason why we shou'd suppose matter or corporeal substances, since that is acknowleg'd to remain equally inexplicable with, or without this supposition. If therefore it were possible for bodies to exist without the mind, yet to hold they do so, must needs be a very precarious opinion; since it is to suppose, without any reason at all, that God has created innumerable beings that are intirely useless, and serve to no manner of purpose.

§ 20. In short, though there were external bodies, 'tis impossible we shou'd ever come to know it; and if there were not, we might have the very same reasons to think there were that we have now. Suppose, what no one can deny possible, an intelligence without the help of external bodies to be affected with the same train of sensations or ideas that you are, imprinted in the same order and with like vividness in his mind. I ask whether that intelligence hath not all the reason to believe the existence of corporeal substances, represented by his ideas, and exciting them in his mind, that you can possibly have for believing the same thing? Of this there can be no question, which one consideration were enough to make any reasonable person, suspect the strength of whatever arguments he may think himself to have, for the existence of bodies without the mind.

§ 21. Were it necessary to add any farther proof against the existence of matter, after what has been said, I cou'd instance several of those errours and difficulties (not to mention impieties) which have sprung from that tenent. It has occasion'd numberless controversies and disputes in philosophy, and not a few of far greater moment in religion. But I shall not enter into the detail of them in this place, as well because I think, arguments a posteriori are unnecessary for confirming what has been, if I mistake not, sufficiently demonstrated a priori, as because I shall hereafter find occasion to speak somewhat of them.

§ 22. I am affraid I have given cause to think, I am needlessly prolix in handling this subject. For to what purpose is it to dilate on that which may be demonstrated with the utmost evidence in a line or two, to any one that's capable of the least reflexion? It is but looking into your own thoughts, and so trying whether you can conceive it possible for a sound, or figure, or motion, or colour to exist without the mind, or unperceiv'd. This easy trial may make you see, that what you contend for, is a downright contradiction. Insomuch that I am content to put the whole upon this issue; if you can but conceive it possible for one extended, moveable substance, or in general, for any one idea or any thing like an idea to exist otherwise than in a mind perceiving it, I shall readily give up the cause: and as for all that *compages* of external bodies you contend for, I shall grant you its existence, though you cannot either give me any reason why you believe it exists, or assign any use to it when it is supposed to exist. I say, the bare possibility of your opinions being true, shall pass for an argument that it is so.

§ 23. But say you, surely there's nothing easier than to imagine trees, for instance, in a park, or books existing in a closet, and no body by to perceive them. I answer you may so, there is no difficulty in it: but what is all this, I beseech you, more than framing in your mind certain ideas which you call *books* and *trees*, and at the same time omitting to frame the idea of any one that may perceive them?

FIG. 3.17 When we say there are books and trees, we have ideas of books and trees in our minds. (© iStockphoto.com/Aldo Murillo)

"But whatever power I may have over my own thoughts, I find the ideas actually perceiv'd by sense . . . are not creatures of my will. There is therefore some other will or spirit that produces them."

– GEORGE BERKELEY

But do not you your self perceive or think of them all the while? This therefore is nothing to the purpose: it only shews you have the power of imagining or forming ideas in your mind; but it does not shew that you can conceive it possible, the objects of your thought may exist without the mind; to make out this, it is necessary that you conceive them existing unconceiv'd or unthought of, which is a manifest repugnancy. When we do our utmost to conceive the existence of external bodies, we are all the while only contemplating our own ideas. But the mind taking no notice of it self, is deluded to think it can and does conceive bodies existing unthought of or without the mind; though at the same time they are apprehended by or exist in it self.

- • What is subjective idealism? How does Berkeley argue that Locke's view leads to subjective idealism?
- • What is Berkeley's argument against the distinction between primary and secondary qualities?

But what, then, can explain the fact that we cannot simply "think" things into existence by imagining them? And how can we say that a thing exists when no one is there to perceive it? ("If a tree falls in the forest, and there's no one there to hear it, does it make a sound?") It is here that God enters the picture as a matter of necessity.

§ 29. But whatever power I may have over my own thoughts, I find the ideas actually perceiv'd by sense have not a like dependence on my will. When in broad day-light I open my eyes, 'tis not in my power to chuse whether I shall see or no, or to determine what particular objects shall present themselves to my view; and so likewise as to the hearing and other senses, the ideas imprinted on them are not creatures of my will. There is therefore some other will or spirit that produces them.

§ 30. The ideas of sense are more strong, lively and distinct than those of the imagination, they have likewise a steddiness, order and coherence, and are not excited at random, as those which are the effects of human wills often are, but in a regular train or series, the admirable connexion whereof sufficiently testifies the wisdom and benevolence of its author. Now the set rules or establish'd methods, wherein the mind we depend on excites in us the ideas of sense, are called the *laws of nature:* and these we learn by experience, which teaches us that such and such ideas are attended with such and such other ideas, in the ordinary course of things.

§ 31. This gives us a sort of foresight, which enables us to regulate our actions for the benefit of life. And without this we shou'd be eternally at a loss, we cou'd not know how to act any thing that might procure us the least pleasure, or remove the least pain of sense. That food nourishes, sleep refreshes, and fire warms us; that to sow in the seed-time is the way to reap in the harvest, and, in general, that to obtain such or such ends, such or such means are conducive, all this we know, not by discovering any necessary connexion between our ideas, but only by the observation of the settled laws of nature, without which we shou'd be all in uncertainty and confusion, and a grown man no more know how to manage himself in the affairs of life, than an infant just born.

. . .

§ 33. The ideas imprinted on the senses by the Author of nature are called *real things*, and those excited in the imagination being less regular, vivid and constant, are more properly termed *ideas*, or *images of things*, which they copy and represent. But then our sensations, be they never so vivid and distinct, are nevertheless *ideas*, i.e. they exist in the mind, or are perceived by it, as truly as the ideas of its own framing. The ideas of sense are allow'd to have more reality in them, i.e. to be more strong, orderly and coherent than the creatures of the mind; but this is no argument that they exist without the mind. They are also less dependent on the spirit, or thinking substance which perceives them, in that they are excited by the will of another and more powerful spirit: yet still they are *ideas*, and certainly no *idea*, whether faint or strong, can exist otherwise than in a mind perceiving it.

This final formulation, that the things of the world are nothing other than ideas in the mind of God, is the subject of a limerick by Ronald Knox, quoted for us by Bertrand Russell:

> There was a young man who said, "God
> Must think it exceedingly odd
>   If he finds that this tree
>   Continues to be
> When there's no one about in the Quad."

> REPLY

> Dear Sir:
>   Your astonishment's odd:
> I am always about in the Quad.
>   And that's why the tree
>   Will continue to be,
> Since observed by
>   *Yours faithfully,*
>   GOD.

- Do the objects in your bedroom cease to exist when you are not there to perceive them, according to Berkeley?
- Why is God so important for Berkeley's idealism?

Finally, the defense against common sense:

§ 38. But after all, say you, it sounds very harsh to say we eat and drink ideas, and are clothed with ideas. I acknowledge it does so; the word "idea" not being used in common discourse to signify the several combinations of sensible qualities which are called "things"; and it is certain that any expression which varies from the familiar use of language will seem harsh and ridiculous. But this doth not concern the truth of the proposition, which in other words is no more than to say, we are fed and clothed with those things which we perceive immediately by our senses.

§ 39. If it be demanded why I make use of the word "idea," and do not rather in compliance with custom call them "thing"; I answer, I do it for two reasons—first, because the term "thing" in contradistinction to "idea," is generally supposed to denote somewhat existing without the mind; secondly, because "thing" hath a more comprehensive signification than "idea," including spirit or thinking things as well as ideas. Since therefore the objects of sense exist only in the mind, and are withal thoughtless and inactive, I chose to mark them by the word "idea," which implies those properties.

Is this where Locke was leading us? If so, it looks as if the "new metaphysics" is every bit as fantastic as the old ones. But the controversial development of Locke's empiricism has still another step to go.

D. The Congenial Skeptic: David Hume

It isn't very far from Berkeley's subjective idealism to David Hume's outrageous, but seemingly irrefutable, skepticism. Russell, writing about Hume two hundred years later (1945), says,

> To refute him has been, ever since he wrote, a favorite pastime among metaphysicians. For my part, I find none of their refutations convincing; nevertheless, I cannot but hope that something less skeptical than Hume's system may be discoverable.

And

> Hume's skeptical conclusions . . . are equally difficult to refute and to accept. The result was a challenge to philosophers, which, in my opinion, has still not been adequately met.[13]

There have been philosophers who have said—or feared—that Hume's skepticism is the last word in philosophy. In any case, it is one of those positions that no philosophy student can avoid taking seriously.

Hume's *Treatise of Human Nature* (1739) was written when he was in his early twenties; his ambition was no less than to be the Isaac Newton of philosophy and psychology, following but outdoing John Locke. The book failed to attract much attention (he said "it fell stillborn from the press"), and Hume turned his attention to other matters, making himself famous as a historian. Later, in 1748, he wrote a more popular version of his earlier *Treatise*, which he called *An Enquiry Concerning Human Understanding*. It was extremely successful, and Hume became widely known as a "devil's advocate" during his lifetime, a position he generally enjoyed. Both the *Treatise* and the *Enquiry* are firmly committed to Locke's empiricist methodology, but where Locke was generous with doubtful ideas with no clear experiential basis (notably, substance and God), Hume was ruthless. In a famous threatening passage, he bellowed

FIG. 3.18 The term *devil's advocate* comes from canonization hearings in the Catholic Church. The devil's advocate advances reasons why a person should not be canonized. *(Image © Igor Zakowski, 2011. Used under license from Shutterstock.com)*

> When we run over libraries, persuaded of these [empiricist] principles, what havoc must we make? If we take in our hand any volume of divinity or school metaphysics, for instance, let us ask, Does it contain any abstract reasoning concerning quantity or number? No. Does it contain any experimental reasoning concerning matter of fact and existence? No, Commit it to the flames, for it can contain nothing but sophistry and illusion.[14]

[13] Bertrand Russell, *A History of Western Philosophy*, New York: Simon and Schuster, 1945.

[14] David Hume, *An Enquiry Concerning Human Understanding*, 2nd ed., ed. L. A. Selby-Bigge, Oxford: Oxford University Press, 1902.

In this unveiled threat to traditional metaphysics we can see in a glance Hume's formidable tactics—the insistence that every justifiable belief must be either a "relation of ideas," for example, a statement of mathematics, logic, or a trivial conceptual truth, or a "matter of fact," which can be confirmed by appeal to our experience. (This "either-or" is sometimes called "**Hume's fork**.") Of course, most of the modern philosophers we have discussed shared this insistence upon justifiability either by reason ("relation of ideas") or by experience. But it is only Hume who realizes the severity of this demand and the embarrassing number of our fundamental beliefs that do not allow **justification** either by reason or experience.

Like his empiricist predecessor, Hume insists that all knowledge begins with basic units of sensory experience. Hume's "**impressions**" (Locke's "sensations") are these basic units (what we would still call "sensations" or "sense-data").

FIG. 3.19 *(© iStockphoto.com/David H. Lewis)*

FROM *A Treatise of Human Nature*
BY **David Hume**[15]

All the perceptions of the human mind resolve themselves into two distinct kinds, which I shall call *impressions* and *ideas*. The difference betwixt these consists in the degrees of force and liveliness with which they strike upon the mind, and make their way into our thought or consciousness. Those perceptions, which enter with most force and violence, we may name *impressions;* and under this name I comprehend all our sensations, passions and emotions, as they make their first appearance in the soul. By *ideas* I mean the faint images of these in thinking and reasoning; such as, for instance, are all the perceptions excited by the present discourse, excepting only, those which arise from the sight and touch, and excepting the immediate pleasure or uneasiness it may occasion. I believe it will not be very necessary to employ many words in explaining this distinction. Every one of himself will readily perceive the difference betwixt feeling and thinking. The common degrees of these are easily distinguished; tho' it is not impossible but in particular instances they may very nearly approach to each other. Thus in sleep, in a fever, in madness, or in any very violent emotions of soul, our ideas may approach to our impressions: As on the other hand it sometimes happens, that our impressions are so faint and low, that we cannot distinguish them from our ideas. But notwithstanding this near resemblance in a few instances, they are in general so very different, that no-one can make a scruple to rank them under distinct heads, and assign to each a peculiar name to mark the difference.

There is another division of our perceptions, which it will be convenient to observe, and which extends itself both to our impressions and ideas. This division is into *simple* and *complex*. Simple perceptions or impressions and ideas are such as admit of no distinction nor separation. The complex are the contrary to these, and may be distinguished into parts. Tho' a particular colour, taste, and smell are qualities

[15] David Hume, *A Treatise of Human Nature*, ed. L. A. Selby-Bigge, Oxford: Oxford University Press, 1888.

> "That idea of red, which we form in the dark, and that impression, which strikes our eyes in sun-shine, differ only in degree, not in nature."
>
> —DAVID HUME

all united together in this apple, 'tis easy to perceive they are not the same, but are at least distinguishable from each other.

Having by these divisions given an order and arrangement to our objects, we may now apply ourselves to consider with the more accuracy their qualities and relations. The first circumstance, that strikes my eye, is the great resemblance betwixt our impressions and ideas in every other particular, except their degree of force and vivacity. The one seems to be in a manner the reflexion of the other; so that all the perceptions of the mind are double, and appear both as impressions and ideas. When I shut my eyes and think of my chamber, the ideas I form are exact representations of the impressions I felt, nor is there any circumstance of the one, which is not to be found in the other. In running over my other perceptions, I find still the same resemblance and representation. Ideas and impressions appear always to correspond to each other. This circumstance seems to me remarkable, and engages my attention for a moment.

Upon a more accurate survey I find I have been carried away too far by the first appearance, and that I must make use of the distinction of perceptions into *simple and complex*, to limit this general decision, *that all our ideas and impressions are resembling.* I observe, that many of our complex ideas never had impressions, that corresponded to them, and that many of our complex impressions never are exactly copied in ideas. I can imagine to myself such a city as the *New Jerusalem*, whose pavement is gold and walls are rubies, tho' I never saw any such. I have seen *Paris;* but shall I affirm I can form such an idea of that city, as will perfectly represent all its streets and houses in their real and just proportions?

I perceive, therefore, that tho' there is in general a great resemblance betwixt our *complex* impressions and ideas, yet the rule is not universally true, that they are ex-

FIG. 3.20 We can imagine many things that we have never seen.
(© iStockphoto.com/bubaone)

act copies of each other. We may next consider how the case stands with our *simple* perceptions. After the most accurate examination, of which I am capable, I venture to affirm, that the rule here holds without any exception, and that every simple idea has a simple impression, which resembles it; and every simple impression a correspondent idea. That idea of red, which we form in the dark, and that impression, which strikes our eyes in sun-shine, differ only in degree, not in nature. That the case is the same with all our simple impressions and ideas, 'tis impossible to prove by a particular enumeration of them. Every one may satisfy himself in this point by running over as many as he pleases. But if any one should deny this universal resemblance, I know of no way of convincing him, but by desiring him to show a simple impression that has not a correspondent idea, or a simple idea, that has not a correspondent impression. If he does not answer this challenge, as 'tis certain he cannot, we may from his silence and our own observation establish our conclusion.

Thus we find, that all simple ideas and impressions resemble each other; and as the complex are formed from them, we may affirm in general, that these two species of perception are exactly correspondent. Having discover'd this relation, which requires no farther examination, I am curious to find some other of their qualities. Let us consider how they stand with regard to their existence, and which of the impressions and ideas are causes, and which effects.

The *full* examination of this question is the subject of the present treatise; and therefore we shall here content ourselves with establishing one general proposition. *That all our simple ideas in their first appearance are deriv'd from simple impressions, which are correspondent to them, and which they exactly represent.*

- What is the difference between "impressions" and "ideas"?

According to Hume, simple ideas are derived from simple impressions. A simple idea would be something like a red, round image; the simple impression would be seeing a red, round image. More complex ideas, for example, the idea of an apple, are complex arrangements and associations of simple ideas. To justify a belief as knowledge, therefore, we must break up its complex ideas into simple ideas and then find the impressions upon which those ideas are based. If I claim to see an apple, for example, I analyze my experience; my idea that there is an apple out there depends upon my seeing several red, round images from different angles, feeling something smooth, tasting something fruity and tart, and so on. If I claim that there are objects of a certain kind (apples, for example), I must identify the simple ideas and impressions upon which my supposed knowledge is based. And if I make a metaphysical claim, about the existence of God or substances, I must either be preapproved to identify the ideas and impressions upon which such a claim is based, or I must show that it is nothing other than a "relation of ideas"; otherwise, the claim cannot be justified ("commit it to the flames").

But, to the embarrassment of most metaphysical doctrines, they cannot be defended by either of the methods allowed by Hume. They are, by their very nature, about things beyond everyday experience (for example, God, substance) and so are not based upon "impression"; nor are they "**relations of ideas**" that can be demonstrated by a simple logical or mathematical proof. Therefore, they cannot be justified. The problem, however, is that the same argument extends far beyond the debatable claims of metaphysics and undermines some of the beliefs that are most essential to our everyday experiences as well.

In Hume's philosophy, three such beliefs in particular are singled out for analysis. On the one hand, they are so fundamental to our daily experience and common knowledge that no sane man or woman could possibly doubt them; on the other hand, they are completely without justification. As Hume argues, first, there is our idea of **causation** (or causality), of one event bringing about or causing another event.

FIG. 3.21 Is it simply crazy to argue that the sun may not rise tomorrow? It is extraordinarily unlikely, yes, but are we absolutely certain? What is our defense of the claim that the sun will rise tomorrow? *(© iStockphoto.com/Jonny Kristoffersson)*

From this idea, which provides what Hume calls "the strongest connections" of our experience and, elsewhere, "the cement of the universe," we derive a most important principle, the **principle of universal causation**, which states that every event has its cause (or causes). It is evident that we invoke such a principle every time we explain anything; for example, the car won't start. We search for the cause, but everything seems to check out—the carburetor, the electrical system, and so on. Now we might search for hours without finding the cause, but there is one thing that we know for certain and that is that there must be a cause somewhere—even if it is a very complex cause. What is not possible is that there be no cause. Presupposed in our everyday thinking is this principle, that every event has its cause. (You may recognize this principle as a version of Leibniz's Principle of Sufficient Reason, which substitutes the more Newtonian notion of "cause" for the notion of "reason.")

Second, because of our presupposed belief in causation and its universal applicability, we are able to think beyond our immediate "ideas" and predict the future and explain the past. But to do so, we must also believe that our observations of the present will have some relevance in the future, that we can in fact draw valid inductive generalizations from our experience. Of course, we do so all of the time; for example, when I wake up at 6:00 in the morning, I expect the sun to rise within the hour. Why? Because it has always done so, and because it is February 26 and the almanac says it will. In making every such prediction, we presuppose a **principle of induction**, that is, that the laws of nature that have always held in the past will continue to hold in the future. The principle of induction is sometimes summarized as "the future will be like the past," which is all right only so long as it is not taken too literally; for of course the future is never just like the past—you are now fifteen seconds older, for example, you have added a whole expression to your knowledge, and (unless you are eating while you read) you have lost a tiny bit of weight as well. But the laws of nature, at least, do not change from moment to moment.

Third, there is our belief in the "external world," that is, a physical or material world that exists independently of our impressions and ideas, which it presumably causes in us. Bishop Berkeley had already done Hume's work for him here. Hume, following Berkeley, also rejects all notions of substance as unintelligible, including even that minimal "we know not what" of John Locke. But where Berkeley turned the rejection of matter and substance into a metaphysics (namely, his subjective idealism) and used it to defend the existence of God, Hume rejects this idealist metaphysics as well and remains wholly skeptical, refusing to accept the existence of God. He remains firm in his insistence that our belief in the existence of anything is no different from "the idea of what we conceive to be existent."

We can see that these three basic beliefs are intimately tied together; the notion of cause supports the principle of induction,[16] and the causal theory of perception supports our belief in the "external world." Accordingly, Hume takes causation to be the central idea of all reasoning,[17] that is, all attempts to connect separate ideas together in a single belief. Hume's arguments are both elegant and simple to follow. He refutes both the principle of universal causation and the principle of induction by showing that neither can be defended either as a "relation of ideas" or as a "**matter of fact**." He begins with a statement that all human knowledge must be one or the other, explains what he means by "relations of ideas" and

[16] Modern philosophers have given a great deal of attention to inductive inferences that are not based upon any obvious causes, for example, statistical probabilities (as in genetics or gambling).

[17] It is important to remember that Hume, like Locke, models his philosophy-psychology after Newton's physics. So even if he rejects Locke's "causal theory of perception," the Newtonian model, in which causality is central, remains at the heart of his theories.

"matters of fact," shows how it is that "cause and effect" are the basis of all reasoning, and then proceeds to show that such reasoning can be neither a relation of ideas nor a simple matter of fact.

 FROM *An Enquiry Concerning Human Understanding* BY **David Hume**[18]

All the objects of human reason or enquiry may naturally be divided into two kinds, to wit, *Relations of Ideas*, and *Matters of Fact*. Of the first kind are the sciences of Geometry, Algebra, and Arithmetic; and in short, every affirmation which is either intuitively or demonstratively certain. *That the square of the hypotenuse is equal to the square of the two sides*, is a proposition which expresses a relation between these figures. *That three times five is equal to the half of thirty*, expresses a relation between these numbers. Propositions of this kind are discoverable by the mere operation of thought, without dependence on what is anywhere existent in the universe. Though there never were a circle or triangle in nature, the truths demonstrated by Euclid would for ever retain their certainty and evidence.

Matters of fact, which are the second objects of human reason, are not ascertained in the same manner; nor is our evidence of their truth, however great, of a like nature with the foregoing. The contrary of every matter of fact is still possible; because it can never imply a contradiction, and is conceived by the mind with the same facility and distinctness, as if ever so conformable to reality. *That the sun will not rise tomorrow* is no less intelligible a proposition, and implies no more contradiction than the affirmation, *that it will rise*. We should in vain, therefore, attempt to demonstrate its falsehood. Were it demonstratively false, it would imply a contradiction, and could never be distinctly conceived by the mind.

It may, therefore, be a subject worthy of curiosity, to enquire what is the nature of that evidence which assures us of any real existence and matter of fact, beyond the present testimony of our senses, or the records of our memory. This part of philosophy, it is observable, has been little cultivated, either by the ancients or moderns; and therefore our doubts and errors, in the prosecution of so important an enquiry, may be the more excusable; while we march through such difficult paths without any guide or direction. They may even prove useful, by exciting curiosity, and destroying that implicit faith and security, which is the bane of all reasoning and free enquiry. The discovery of defects in the common philosophy, if any such there be, will not, I presume, be a discouragement, but rather an incitement, as is usual, to attempt something more full and satisfactory than has yet been proposed to the public.

All reasonings concerning matter of fact seem to be founded on the relations of *Cause and Effect*. By means of that relation alone we can go beyond the evidence of our memory and senses. If you were to ask a man, why he believes any matter of fact, which is absent; for instance, that his friend is in the country, or in France; he would give you a reason; and this reason would be some other fact; as a letter received from him, or the knowledge of his former resolutions and promises. A man finding a watch or any other machine in a desert island, would conclude that there had once been men in that island. All our reasonings concerning fact are of the same nature. And here it is constantly supposed that there is a connexion between the present fact

[18] David Hume, *An Enquiry Concerning Human Understanding*, 2nd ed., ed. L. A. Selby-Bigge, Oxford: Oxford University Press, 1902.

and that which is inferred from it. Were there nothing to bind them together, the inference would be entirely precarious. The hearing of an articulate voice and rational discourse in the dark assures us of the presence of some person: Why? because these are the effects of the human make and fabric, and closely connected with it. If we anatomize all the other reasonings of this nature, we shall find that they are founded on the relation of cause and effect, and that this relation is either near or remote, direct or collateral. Heat and light are collateral effects of fire, and the one effect may justly be inferred from the other.

Hume's argument, which we shall see again and again, is that we explain our experiences and events by appeal to other experiences and events. If I burn my finger and wonder how, I look down and see that I have just placed my hand too near the stove-top burner. I explain that the heat of the burner is the cause and the burn is the effect of the hot burner. Indeed, we are perplexed whenever we cannot find some causal **explanation**, and the suggestion that there might not be one ("there was no cause; you just burned yourself, that's all") is all but unintelligible to us. But now, Hume asks, where do we get this knowledge of causes and effects?

If we would satisfy ourselves, therefore, concerning the nature of that evidence, which assures us of matters of fact, we must enquire how we arrive at the knowledge of cause and effect.

I shall venture to affirm, as a general proposition, which admits of no exception, that the knowledge of this relation is not, in any instance, attained by reasonings a priori; but arises entirely from experience, when we find that any particular objects are constantly conjoined with each other. Let an object be presented to a man of ever so strong natural reason and abilities; if that object be entirely new to him, he will not be able, by the most accurate examination of its sensible qualities, to discover any of its causes or effects. Adam, though his rational faculties be supposed, at the very first, entirely perfect, could not have inferred from the fluidity and transparency of water that it would suffocate him, or from the light and warmth of fire that it would consume him. No object ever discovers, by the qualities which appear to the senses, either the causes which produced it, or the effects which will arise from it; nor can our reason, unassisted by experience, ever draw any inference concerning real existence and matter of fact.

This proposition, *that causes and effects are discoverable, not by reason but by experience*, will readily be admitted with regard to such objects, as we remember to have once been altogether unknown to us; since we must be conscious of the utter inability, which we then lay under, of foretelling what would arise from them. Present two smooth pieces of marble to a man who has no tincture of natural philosophy; he will never discover that they will adhere together in such a manner as to require great force to separate them in a direct line, while they make so small a resistance to lateral pressure. Such events, as bear little analogy to the common course of nature, are also readily confessed to be known only by experience; nor does any man imagine that the explosion of gunpowder, or the attraction of a lodestone, could ever be discovered by arguments a priori. In like manner, when an effect is supposed to depend upon an intricate machinery or secret structure of parts, we make no difficulty in attributing all our knowledge of it to experience. Who will assert that he can give the ultimate reason, why milk or bread is proper nourishment for a man, not for a lion or a tiger?

But the same truth may not appear, at first sight, to have the same evidence with regard to events, which have become familiar to us from our first appearance in the

"The mind can never possibly find the effect in the supposed cause. . . . For the effect is totally different from the cause, and consequently can never be discovered in it."

– DAVID HUME

world, which bear a close analogy to the whole course of nature, and which are supposed to depend on the simple qualities of objects, without any secret structure of parts. We are apt to imagine that we could discover these effects by the mere operation of our reason, without experience. We fancy, that were we brought on a sudden into this world, we could at first have inferred that one Billiard-ball would communicate motion to another upon impulse; and that we needed not to have waited for the event, in order to pronounce with certainty concerning it. Such is the influence of custom, that, where it is strongest, it not only covers our natural ignorance, but even conceals itself, and seems not to take place, merely because it is found in the highest degree.

FIG. 3.22 *(© iStockphoto.com/Drazen Vukelic)*

But to convince us that all the laws of nature, and all the operations of bodies without exception, are known only by experience, the following reflections may, perhaps, suffice. Were any object presented to us, and were we required to pronounce concerning the effect, which will result from it, without consulting past observation; after what manner, I beseech you, must the mind proceed in this operation? It must invent or imagine some event, which it ascribes to the object as its effect; and it is plain that this invention must be entirely arbitrary. The mind can never possibly find the effect in the supposed cause, by the most accurate scrutiny and examination. For the effect is totally different from the cause, and consequently can never be discovered in it. Motion in the second Billiard-ball is a quite distinct event from motion in the first; nor is there anything in the one to suggest the smallest hint of the other. A stone or piece of metal raised into the air, and left without any support, immediately falls: but to consider the matter a priori, is there anything we discover in this situation which can beget the idea of a downward, rather than an upward, or any other motion in the stone or metal?

And as the first imagination or invention of a particular effect, in all natural operations, is arbitrary, where we consult not experience; so must we also esteem the supposed tie or connexion between the cause and effect, which binds them together, and renders it impossible that any other effect could result from the operation of that cause. When I see, for instance, a Billiard-ball moving in a straight line towards another; even suppose motion in the second ball should by accident be suggested to me, as the result of their contact or impulse; may I not conceive, that a hundred different events might as well follow from that cause? May not both these balls remain at absolute rest? May not the first ball return in a straight line, or leap off from the second in any line or direction? All these suppositions are consistent and conceivable. Why then should we give the preference to one, which is no more consistent or conceivable than the rest? All our reasonings a priori will never be able to show us any foundations for this preference.

Hume's argument so far is that we do not know particular causes and effects through reason, but only through experience. Because you have seen it so many times, you know that a billiard ball moving toward and striking another billiard ball sets the second in motion on a predictable path. But if you had never seen anything like it before—perhaps if you were Adam or Eve (pool tables were not created until the eighth day of creation)—you would not have any idea of what to expect. Both balls might stop dead. Both might explode. The second might start a lawsuit. Prediction of cause and effect, in other words, depends upon prior experience, and no amount of mere reasoning will suffice by itself.

> In a word, then, every effect is a distinct event from its cause. It could not, there-fore, be discovered in the cause, and the first invention or conception of it, a priori, must be entirely arbitrary. And even after it is suggested, the conjunction of it with the cause must appear equally arbitrary; since there are always many other effects, which, to reason, must seem fully as consistent and natural. In vain, therefore, should we pretend to determine any single event, or infer any cause or effect, without the assistance of observation and experience.

. . .

> When we reason a priori, and consider merely any object or cause, as it appears to the mind, independent of all observation, it never could suggest to us the notion of any distinct object, such as its effect; much less, show us the inseparable and invio-lable connexion between them. A man must be very sagacious who could discover by reasoning that crystal is the effect of heat, and ice of cold, without being previ-ously acquainted with the operations of these qualities.

In this argument, we see Hume applying the first half of his "fork" to the idea of causa-tion. The idea of cause and effect cannot be a relation of ideas, because, for example, no matter how closely we examine the idea of fire, we will never discover the idea of its causing gunpowder to explode. Reasoning alone cannot reveal the causes or effects of particular events. At the outset of this argument, Hume also suggests that the idea of causation is not discoverable through perception either: Although we perceive many different qualities of fire, we never perceive its power to cause gunpowder to explode. Hume concludes that the idea of cause and effect must be derived from our experience of the constant conjunction of two events. We observe, for example, that every time we set a match to gunpowder it ex-plodes; and because we expect the future to be like the past, we infer that the application of fire is the cause of the gunpowder's exploding. In short, our knowledge of causes is arrived at through induction from past experiences.

Hume's argument against induction, and in particular against the inductive principle that the future will be like the past, takes exactly the same form. Again he begins with his "fork" between "relations of ideas" and "matters of fact," and again he proves that one of the basic assumptions of all our thinking, the principle of induction, cannot be established either way:

> But we have not yet attained any tolerable satisfaction with regard to the ques-tion first proposed. Each solution still gives rise to a new question as difficult as the foregoing, and leads us on to further enquiries. When it is asked, *What is the nature of all our reasonings concerning matter of fact?* the proper answer seems to be, that they are founded on the relation of cause and effect. When again it is asked, *What is the founda-tion of all our reasonings and conclusions concerning that relation?* it may be replied in one word, Experience. But if we still carry on our shifting humour, and ask, *What is the foundation of all conclusions from experience?* this implies a new question, which may be of more difficult solution and explication. Philosophers, that give themselves airs of superior wisdom and sufficiency, have a hard task when they encounter persons of inquisitive dispositions, who push them from every corner to which they retreat,

and who are sure at last to bring them to some dangerous dilemma. The best expedient to prevent this confusion, is to be modest in our pretensions; and even to discover the difficulty ourselves before it is objected to us. By this means, we may make a kind of merit of our very ignorance.

I shall content myself, in this section, with an easy task, and shall pretend only to give a negative answer to the question here proposed. I say then, that, even after we have experience of the operations of cause and effect, our conclusions from that experience are *not* founded on reasoning, or any process of the understanding. This answer we must endeavour both to explain and to defend.

It must certainly be allowed, that nature has kept us at a great distance from all her secrets, and has afforded us only the knowledge of a few superficial qualities of objects; while she conceals from us those powers and principles on which the influence of those objects entirely depends. Our senses inform us of the colour, weight, and consistence of bread; but neither sense nor reason can ever inform us of those qualities which fit it for the nourishment and support of a human body. Sight or feeling conveys an idea of the actual motion of bodies; but as to that wonderful force or power, which would carry on a moving body for ever in a continued change of place, and which bodies never lose but by communicating it to others; of this we cannot form the most distant conception. But notwithstanding this

FIG. 3.23 We know it is bread because of how it smells, feels, and tastes. *(© iStockphoto.com/Carmen Martínez Banús)*

ignorance of natural powers and principles, we always presume, when we see like sensible qualities, that they have like secret powers, and expect that effects, similar to those which we have experienced, will follow from them. If a body of like colour and consistence with that bread, which we have formerly eat, be presented to us, we make no scruple of repeating the experiment, and foresee, with certainty, like nourishment and support. Now this is a process of the mind or thought, of which I would willingly know the foundation. It is allowed on all hands that there is no known connexion between the sensible qualities and the secret powers; and consequently, that the mind is not led to form such a conclusion concerning their constant and regular conjunction, by anything which it knows of their nature. As to past *Experience*, it can be allowed to give *direct* and *certain* information of those precise objects only, and that precise period of time, which fell under its cognizance: but why this experience should be extended to future times, and to other objects, which for aught we know, may be only in appearance similar; this is the main question on which I would insist. The bread, which I formerly eat, nourished me; that is, a body of such sensible qualities was, at that time, endued with such secret powers: but does it follow, that other bread must also nourish me at another time, and that like sensible qualities must always be attended with like secret powers? The consequence seems nowise necessary. At least, it must be acknowledged that there is here a consequence drawn by the mind; that there is a certain step taken; a process of thought, and an inference, which wants to be explained. These two propositions are far from being the same, *I have found that such an object has always been attended with such an effect*, and *I foresee, that other objects, which are, in appearance, similar, will be attended with similar effects.*

The argument so far is just like the argument regarding cause and effect, namely, that it is only from experience that we know the properties and effects of things and events, that moving bodies cause others to move, for instance, or that eating bread gives me nourishment. But now Hume distinguishes two propositions: (1) I have recognized a certain cause-and-effect relationship in my past experience, and (2) I predict that a similar cause-and-effect relationship will hold in the future also. The reference is surely reasonable, Hume says, but again he forces us to say why such an inference is reasonable, and he argues that we cannot do so.

I shall allow, if you please, that the one proposition may justly be inferred from the other: I know, in fact, that it always is inferred. But if you insist that the inference is made by a chain of reasoning, I desire you to produce the reasoning. The connexion between these propositions is not intuitive. There is required a medium, which may enable the mind to draw such an inference, if indeed it be drawn by reasoning and argument. What that medium is, I must confess, passes my comprehension; and it is incumbent on those to produce it, who assert that it really exists, and is the origin of all our conclusions concerning matter of fact.

This negative argument must certainly, in process of time, become altogether convincing, if many penetrating and able philosophers shall turn their enquiries this way and no one be ever able to discover any connecting proposition or intermediate step, which supports the understanding in this conclusion. But as the question is yet new, every reader may not trust so far to his own penetration, as to conclude, because an argument escapes his enquiry, that therefore it does not really exist. For this reason it may be requisite to venture upon a more difficult task; and enumerating all the branches of human knowledge, endeavour to show that none of them can afford such an argument.

FIG. 3.24 Reasoning and argument are like a good detective. *(© iStockphoto.com/Tom Chiarolini)*

Here is "Hume's fork": the division of all knowledge into reasoning about relations of ideas (which he here calls "demonstrative") and reasoning about matters of fact (which he here calls "moral"). He says that it is clear from the above arguments that no demonstrative reasoning is available to justify our predictions of the future. But then he goes on to argue that no reasoning about matters of fact—no appeal to experience—can justify our propensity to make predictions either. For in order to justify our belief that the future will resemble the past on the basis of our experience, we would in effect be arguing that we know that the future will be like the past because in the past the future has always been like the past, and this is "begging the question" and a "vicious circle," in which one defends a proposition by referring it back to itself. (Like asking a suspected liar, "Are you lying to me?") Therefore our propensity for predicting can't be justified by appealing to experience either, which leaves us without any justification at all.

- What is "Hume's fork"? Which three beliefs does he claim are unjustified as a result?
- How does Hume undermine our ability to make predictions?

All reasonings may be divided into two kinds, namely, demonstrative reasoning, or that concerning relations of ideas, and moral reasoning, or that concerning matters of fact and existence. That there are no demonstrative arguments in the case seems evident; since it implies no contradiction that the course of nature may change, and that an object, seemingly like those which we have experienced, may be attended with different or contrary effects. May I not clearly and distinctly conceive that a body, falling from the clouds, and which, in all other respects, resembles snow, has yet the taste of salt or feeling of fire? Is there any more intelligible proposition than to affirm, that all the trees will flourish in December and January, and decay in May and June? Now whatever is intelligible, and can be distinctly conceived, implies no contradiction, and can never be proved false by any demonstrative argument or abstract reasoning a priori.

If we be, therefore, engaged by arguments to put trust in past experience, and make it the standard of our future judgement, these arguments must be probable only, or such as regard matter of fact and real existence, according to the division above mentioned. But that there is no argument of this kind, must appear, if our explication of that species of reasoning be admitted as solid and satisfactory. We have said that all arguments concerning existence are founded on the relation of cause and effect; that our knowledge of that relation is derived entirely from experience; and that all our experimental conclusions proceed upon the supposition that the future will be conformable to the past. To endeavour, therefore, the proof of this last supposition by probable arguments, or arguments regarding existence, must be evidently going in a circle, and taking that for granted, which is the very point in question.

· · ·

When a man says, *I have found, in all past instances, such sensible qualities conjoined with such secret powers:* And when he says, *Similar sensible qualities will always be conjoined with similar secret powers*, he is not guilty of tautology, nor are these propositions in any respect the same. You say that the one proposition is an inference from the other. But you must confess that the inference is not intuitive; neither is it demonstrative: Of what nature is it, then? To say it is experimental, is begging the question. For all inferences from experience suppose, as their foundation, that the future will resemble the past, and that similar powers will be conjoined with similar sensible qualities. If there be any suspicion that the course of nature may change, and that the past may be no rule for the future, all experience becomes useless, and can give rise to no inference or conclusion. It is impossible, therefore, that any arguments from experience can prove this resemblance of the past to the future; since all these arguments are founded on the supposition of that resemblance. Let the source of things be allowed hitherto ever so regular; that alone, without some new argument or inference, proves not that, for the future, it will continue so. In vain do you pretend to have learned the nature of bodies from your past experience. Their secret nature, and consequently all their effects and influence may change, without any change in their sensible qualities. This happens sometimes, and with regard to some objects: Why may it not happen always, and with regard to all objects? What logic, what process of argument secures you against this position? My practice, you say, refutes my doubts. But you mistake the purport of my question. As an agent, I am quite satisfied in the point; but as a philosopher, who has some share of curiosity, I will not say scepticism, I want to learn the foundation of this inference. No reading, no enquiry has yet been able to remove my difficulty, or give me satisfaction in a matter of such importance. Can I do better than propose the difficulty to the public, even though, perhaps, I have small hopes of obtaining a solution? We shall at least, by this means, be sensible of our ignorance, if we do not augment our knowledge.

Hume's arguments against the principle of universal causation and the principle of induction are also arguments against **rationalism** in general. What he is saying is that reasoning alone, without information from experience, cannot tell us anything whatever about the world. Reasoning **a priori**, that is, thinking without any appeal to experience, is incapable of proving any of those theorems so important to the rationalists, such as the existence of substances, a God, and causes, as well as the conformity of future events to past ones. His arguments are at the same time skeptical ones, since he reasons that even an appeal to experience cannot prove the reality of any of these things.

What is the solution to these skeptical doubts? If we seek a justification or defense, there is none, according to Hume. But in everyday life, such philosophical doubts need have no effect at all, for though there is no justification of our beliefs, we can yet remain confident that at least there is an explanation for them.

Suppose a person, though endowed with the strongest faculties of reason and reflection, to be brought on a sudden into this world; he would, indeed, immediately observe a continual succession of objects and one event following another, but he would not be able to discover anything further. He would not at first, by any reasoning, be able to reach the idea of cause and effect, since the particular powers by which all natural operations are performed never appear to the senses; nor is it reasonable to conclude, merely because one event in one instance precedes another, that therefore the one is the cause, the other the effect. The conjunction may be arbitrary and casual. There may be no reason to infer the existence of one from the appearance of the other: and, in a word, such a person without more experience could never employ his conjecture or reasoning concerning any matter of fact or be assured of anything beyond what was immediately present to his memory or senses.

Suppose again that he has acquired more experience and has lived so long in the world as to have observed similar objects or events to be constantly conjoined together—what is the consequence of this experience? He immediately infers the existence of one object from the appearance of the other, yet he has not, by all his experience, acquired any idea or knowledge of the secret power by which the one object produces the other, nor is it by any process of reasoning he is engaged to draw this inference; but still he finds himself determined to draw it, and though he should be convinced that his understanding has no part in the operation, he would nevertheless continue in the same course of thinking. There is some other principle which determines him to form such a conclusion.

This principle is *custom* or *habit*. For wherever the repetition of any particular act or operation produces a propensity to renew the same act or operation without being impelled by any reasoning or process of the understanding, we always say that this propensity is the effect of *custom*. By employing that word we pretend not to have given the ultimate reason of such a propensity. We only point out a principle of human nature which is universally acknowledged, and which is well known by its effects. Perhaps we can push our inquiries no further or pretend to give the cause of this cause, but must rest contented with it as the ultimate principle which we can assign of all our conclusions from experience. It is sufficient satisfaction that we can go so far without repining at the narrowness of our faculties, because they will carry us no further. And it is certain we here advance a very intelligible proposition at least, if not a true one, when we assert that after the constant conjunction of two objects, heat and flame, for instance, weight and solidity, we are determined by custom alone to expect the one from the appearance of the other. This hypothesis seems even the only one which explains the difficulty why we draw from a thousand instances an inference which we are not able to draw from one instance that is in no respect different from them. Reason is incapable of any such variation. The conclusions which it draws from considering one circle are the same which it would form upon surveying all the circles in the universe. But no man, having seen only one body move after being impelled by another, could infer that every other body will move after a like impulse. All inferences from experience, therefore, are effects of custom, not of reasoning.

> "All inferences from experience . . . are effects of custom, not of reasoning."
> – DAVID HUME

In other words, there is no "solution to these skeptical doubts," but, at most, what Hume calls "a skeptical solution." It means an end, not only to philosophy, but to all **rational** inquiry and all claims that we can know anything (even that the sun will rise tomorrow, or that there is a textbook now in front of you). You might think that such conclusions would have driven Hume mad or caused him such confusion that he would have been incapable of coping with the most everyday chores. Yet we know that he was the most practical and jolliest sort of fellow. As a philosopher, he has been driven right up against the wall of Plato's Cave. But he remains unperturbed. In a famous passage at the end of the *Treatise*, he simply remarks:

> Most fortunately it happens, that since reason is incapable of dispelling these clouds, nature herself suffices to that purpose, and cures me of this philosophical melancholy and delirium, either by relaxing this bent of mind, or by some avocation, and lively impression of my senses, which obliterate all these chimeras. I dine, I play a game of backgammon, I converse, and am merry with my friends; and when after three or four hours' amusement, I wou'd return to these speculations, they appear so cold, and strain'd, and ridiculous, that I cannot find in my heart to enter into them any farther.[19]

• Why does Hume think that rationality alone is unable to give us knowledge? Why does he think empiricism alone is unable to give us knowledge? What is Hume's "solution" to this problem?

Perhaps you too find "these speculations cold, strained and ridiculous." If so, however, this is not the time to run off to dinner and an evening of games and conversation. Something has gone very wrong. The empiricist attempt to restore common sense to philosophy has ended in the least commonsensical philosophy imaginable. A person who really believed that there might be no material world or that the future will not resemble the past (and therefore, having been hit by a truck last week, steps into the street convinced that it will not happen

[19] David Hume, *A Treatise of Human Nature*, ed. L. A. Selby-Bigge, Oxford: Oxford University Press, 1888.

again) would be crazy! How can our intellects be so out of joint with our experience or our philosophy so far away from practical life? How serious is Hume's skepticism?

E. Kant's Revolution

Immanuel Kant is considered by a great many philosophers to be the greatest thinker since Plato and Aristotle. He stands at the beginning of almost every modern movement in philosophy in the United States and Europe, as an inspiration and as a kind of founder. Existentialism would not be possible without him; nor would phenomenology, **pragmatism**, or many of the varieties of linguistic philosophy that dominated English and American philosophy for most of the twentieth century. He brings together the often opposed threads of rationalism and empiricism and weaves them into a single monumental philosophical system, which he published primarily in three "critiques" (*The Critique of Pure Reason*, *The Critique of Practical Reason*, and *The Critique of Judgment*) in the last two decades of the eighteenth century. His writing is notoriously difficult, but it is possible for even a beginning philosophy student to appreciate the main theme of his self-proclaimed "revolution" in philosophy. It is, in one sense, a total reorientation of what we mean when we talk about reality and knowledge.

FIG. 3.25 What, for Kant, is the hardware, and what is the software? *(© iStockphoto.com/Leigh Schindler)*

Ever since the ancient Greeks, almost all philosophers had accepted the idea that there is a reality "out there," which we could come to know through reason, through experience, or perhaps which we could not come to know at all, according to a skeptic such as David Hume. The idea of an "external world" seemed innocent enough, until metaphysicians began to find that their contradictory views about this world could not be reconciled. This dilemma prompted John Locke to turn away from metaphysics and pay more attention to the way we acquire knowledge. The shift of attention to knowledge led Hume to argue that we couldn't even know that the sun would rise tomorrow, or that one billiard ball in fact causes the movement of another, or that there is indeed a world outside of our own ideas.

This skeptical conclusion seemed utterly absurd to Kant, who was, in his own words, "awakened from his dogmatic slumbers" by Hume. Kant had been a metaphysician (a follower of Leibniz), but reading Hume convinced him that there was a serious problem, not only for metaphysics, but for our claims to know the world at all. And Kant, who was also a scientist and an enthusiastic supporter of Isaac Newton and the new physics, saw that he had to refute Hume if he was going to keep claiming that scientists (and everyone else) could know anything at all. But the problem, as he diagnosed it, turned out to be the unquestioned idea that there was a distinction to be made between our beliefs and experience of the world, on the one hand, and the world itself, Reality or Truth, on the other.

What Kant suspected, and what many philosophers believe today, is that our "ideas"—our concepts and our language—do not just correspond to reality but in some sense shape and "set up" the world, impose upon the world the structures we experience. We see material objects instead of just patterns of light and colors (as seen perhaps by a newborn baby), and this is our contribution to experience. We experience events in a cause-and-effect relationship, instead of as mere sequences of events, and this is not because of experience alone, but because we *make* our experience conform to causal rules. We expect certain events in the future on the basis of what we have experienced in the past; and this too is not mere habit, but a set of rules we impose necessarily on every experience. According to Kant, space and time do not exist "out there," independent of our experience; we impose the forms of three-dimensional space and one-dimensional time on our experience, and through these forms come to know the world. So too, Kant argues, all of our knowledge of the world is in part a product of the various forms and rules that we impose upon, or use to "set up," our experience. The word Kant uses for "set up" is "constitutes." A "constitution" sets up a government, provides it with its rules and structures. We **constitute** our own experience in the sense that we provide the rules and structures according to which we experience objects, as objects in space and time, as governed by the laws of nature and the relations of cause and effect. Kant writes, "the understanding does not derive its laws from, but prescribes them to, nature."

According to Kant's philosophy, reality has no existence that we can understand except as we constitute it through our basic concepts. Kant took these concepts—or what he called "**categories**"—to be the basic rules of the human mind as such, common to all peoples in all places at all times. Today, many philosophers would rather say that these concepts through which we constitute the world are part of a language, which raises the intriguing but controversial possibility that the world might be quite different for people who speak different languages. (Kant himself did not believe this.) Truth and Knowledge, in other words, are a function of our concepts. Kant's revolution rejects the very idea of an external Reality and instead looks to the concepts through which we "constitute" Reality. Thus there is no point to wondering whether our concepts match up to Reality, since there would be no Reality without our concepts. Our concepts not only cohere with each other; they "set up" a corresponding reality as well. Of course those concepts "work"—it is as if someone were to wonder how it is that a ceramic mold exactly fits a piece of jewelry, when the mold gave shape to the jewelry in the first place.

Previous philosophers had asked, "How can we know that our ideas correspond with the way the world really is?" Kant rejected that question. Instead, he asked, *"How do our ideas constitute the world?"* "What is the structure and what are the rules (the *concepts* or *categories*) of the human mind according to which we 'set up' our world, the world of our experience?"

- What does Kant mean that we "constitute" our world? Are there other ways to "constitute" the world according to Kant?
- How does Kant answer Hume's skeptical challenge? Does he succeed?

The project of Kant's *The Critique of Pure Reason* is to analyze and prove the **necessity** of these concepts, which we can know a priori—independently of all experience and with certainty, just because they are the rules within which all of our knowledge is possible. Think of it this way: You take a number of pieces of wood and a checkerboard and "set up" the game by making up rules about what can be moved where, how, and when. Then, within the game, you are free to make any number of moves, some brilliant, some stupid, but you are always bound by the rules that you yourself have "set up." And since you yourself have established these rules, it would be absurd to wonder whether or not they are "true."

Kant's revolution changed our conception of reality, our conception of knowledge, and, most importantly, our conception of ourselves. Truth is no longer correspondence between our ideas and reality, but our own system of rules (concepts or categories) by which we constitute our reality. Knowledge, accordingly, is no longer the comprehending of a reality beyond our experience, but knowledge of our experience. But this does not mean knowledge of experience, distinct from knowledge of objects, for the objects of our experience are all there is to reality. Moreover, in making this move, Kant gives the philosophers something which they thought they had lost, a renewed ideal of certainty, for, he argued, we can be certain of the rules of our own experience. Kant defended the necessity of the truths of arithmetic and geometry as those rules that have to do with the a priori forms of our intuitions of space and time. According to Kant's philosophy in general, reality is the world of our experience, as we constitute it through the concepts of our understanding. Therefore, we can know it with certainty, for truth, in general, is our own construction.

You might at first think that there is some trick here, as if Kant is saying, "Well, if we can't have knowledge in the hard sense, then I'll simply redefine the words *knowledge, reality,* and *truth*." But what he has done is to point to the difficulty of the picture that other philosophers had accepted; he has shown that what we normally mean by "truth," "knowledge," and "reality" is not an insatiable appeal to a world beyond our experience. Underneath Kant's spectacular pronouncements there is, once again, a return to common sense. This world, the one I stand in, touch, and see, is the real world. But what makes it real, according to Kant, is not just that I stand in, touch, and see it, but that I actively constitute it as the way it is, apply my own rules for understanding it, and structure it through my own experience.

Kant gives us a general way of giving an account of all those truths that metaphysicians have always argued about. Using Kant's terminology, we can say they are forms of **synthetic a priori knowledge**. Such knowledge is, briefly characterized, knowledge of our own rules with which we (necessarily) constitute reality. If a truth is not true because of our experiences, nor is it true because of the grammar or meanings of the sentences of our language, how else could it be defended? This was Hume's dilemma, and with this two-test system of justification, he eliminated many of our most important beliefs as "unjustifiable," as neither "truths of reason" nor "matters of fact." But now, we have our third way: A belief can be true, necessarily true, if it is one of those rules that we impose to constitute our experience. Thus we saw that Kant defended the truths of arithmetic and geometry by showing that they were the "(a priori) forms of intuition," the ways in which we must experience our world. So too will he defend all of those truths that Hume had claimed to be unjustifiable.

The principle of universal causation is neither a generalization from experience nor an **analytic** truth, but rather a *rule* for "setting up" our world. That rule is, "Always look for regular (or 'lawlike') connections between events, so that you can explain an event as an *effect* of previous events, and therefore predict future events as well." Like a rule in chess, this is not a move within the game but one of those rules that defines the game. So too with the principle of **induction**; it is neither based upon experience nor a trivial truth but a rule with which we govern all of our experience. So too for our belief in the "external" or material world, which Berkeley and Hume found so problematic. Our experience alone will not tell us whether we are dreaming or not, and the idea of the material ("external") world is not a **tautology** or a conceptual truth. It too is one of the rules that we use to constitute our experience, namely, that we shall *always* interpret our experience of objects in space as external to us and as material or *substantial*. But notice, our metaphysical notion of substance is no longer that which is, by definition, outside of our experience. It is now part of the rules by which we set up our experience.

FROM *The Critique of Pure Reason*
BY **Immanuel Kant**[20]

THE DISTINCTION BETWEEN PURE (A PRIORI) AND EMPIRICAL (A POSTERIORI) KNOWLEDGE

That all our knowledge begins with experience there can be no doubt. For how should the faculty of knowledge be called into activity, if not by objects which affect our senses, and which either produce representations by themselves, or rouse the activity of our understanding to compare, or connect, or to separate them, and thus to convert the raw material of our sensuous impressions into a knowledge of objects, which we call experience? In respect of time, therefore, no knowledge within us is antecedent to experience, but all knowledge begins with it.

But although all our knowledge begins with experience, it does not follow that it arises from experience. For it is quite possible that even our empirical experience is a compound of that which we receive through impressions, and of that which our own faculty of knowledge (incited only by sensuous impressions), supplies from itself, a supplement which we do not distinguish from that raw material, until long practice has roused our attention and rendered us capable of separating one from the other.

It is therefore a question which deserves at least closer investigation, and cannot be disposed of at first sight, whether there exists a knowledge independent of experience, and even of all impressions of the senses? Such *knowledge* is called a priori, and distinguished from *empirical* knowledge, which has its source a posteriori, that is, in experience.

FROM *Prolegomena to Any Future Metaphysics*
BY **Immanuel Kant**[21]

My purpose is to persuade all those who think metaphysics worth studying that it is absolutely necessary to pause a moment and, regarding all that has been done as though undone, to propose first the preliminary question, "Whether such a thing as metaphysics can be even possible at all?"

If it be science, how is it that it cannot, like other sciences, obtain universal and lasting recognition? If no, how can it maintain its pretensions and keep the human mind in suspense with hopes never ceasing, yet never fulfilled? Whether then we demonstrate our knowledge or our ignorance in this field, we must come one and for all to a definite conclusion respecting the nature of this so-called science, which cannot possibly remain on its present footing. It seems almost ridiculous, while every other science is continually advancing, that in this, which pretends to be wisdom incarnate, for whose oracle everyone inquires, we should constantly move round the same spot, without gaining a single step. And so its votaries having melted away, we do not find men confident of their ability to shine in other sciences venturing their reputation here, where everybody, however ignorant in other matters, presumes

> "My purpose is to persuade all those who think metaphysics worth studying that it is absolutely necessary to . . . propose first the preliminary question, 'Whether such a thing as metaphysics can be even possible at all?'"
>
> – IMMANUEL KANT

---

[20] Immanuel Kant, *The Critique of Pure Reason*, rev. 2nd ed., trans. Max Müller, London: Macmillan, 1927.

[21] Immanuel Kant, *Prolegomena to Any Future Metaphysics*, trans. Lewis White Beck. Copyright © 1959. Reprinted by permission of Pearson Education, Inc., Upper Saddle River, NJ.

to deliver a final verdict, because in this domain there is actually as yet no standard weight and measure to distinguish sound knowledge from shallow talk.

· · ·

Hume started chiefly from a single but important concept in metaphysics, namely, that of the connection of cause and effect (including its derivatives force and action, and so on). He challenged reason, which pretends to have given birth to this concept of herself, to answer him by what right she thinks anything could be so constituted that if that thing be posited, something else also must necessarily be posited; for this is the meaning of the concept of cause. He demonstrated irrefutably that it was perfectly impossible for reason to think a priori and by means of concepts such a combination, for it implies necessity. We cannot at all see why, in consequence of the existence of one thing, another must necessarily exist or how the concept of such a combination can arise a priori. Hence he inferred that reason was altogether deluded with reference to this concept, which she erroneously considered as one of her own children, whereas in reality it was nothing but a bastard of imagination, impregnated by experience, which subsumed certain representations under the law of association and mistook a subjective necessity (habit) for an objective necessity arising from insight. Hence he inferred that reason had no power to think such combinations, even in general, because her concepts would then be purely fictitious and all her pretended a priori cognitions nothing but common experiences marked with a false stamp. In plain language, this means that there is not and cannot be any such thing as metaphysics at all.

· · ·

I openly confess my recollection of David Hume was the very thing which many years ago interrupted my dogmatic slumber and gave my investigations in the

FIG. 3.26 For Kant, there is a wall beyond which reason cannot go. What is that wall? *(© iStockphoto .com/Jean Thirion)*

field of speculative philosophy a quite new direction. I was far from following him in the conclusions at which he arrived by regarding, not the whole of his problem, but a part, which by itself can give us no information. If we start from a well-founded, but undeveloped, thought which another has bequeathed to us, we may well hope by continued reflection to advance farther than the acute man to whom we owe the first spark of light.

I therefore first tried whether Hume's objection could not be put into a general form, and soon found that the concept of the connection of cause and effect was by no means the only concept by which the understanding thinks the connection of things a priori, but rather that metaphysics consists altogether of such concepts. I sought to ascertain their number; and when I had satisfactorily succeeded in this by starting from a single principle, I proceeded to the deduction of these concepts, which I was now certain were not derived from experience, as Hume had attempted to derive them, but sprang from the pure understanding. This deduction (which seemed impossible to my acute predecessor, which had never even occurred to anyone else, though no one had hesitated to use the concepts without investigating the basis of their objective validity) was the most difficult task which ever could have been undertaken in the service of metaphysics; and the worst was that metaphysics, such as it is, could not assist me in the least because this deduction alone can render metaphysics possible. But as soon as I had succeeded in solving Hume's problem, not merely in a particular case, but with respect to the whole faculty of pure reason, I could proceed safely, though slowly, to determine the whole sphere of pure reason completely and from universal principles, in its boundaries as well as in its contents. This was required for metaphysics in order to construct its system according to a safe plan.

Kant gives us a way of resolving the age-old disputes of metaphysics—questions concerning reality as such. Since the claims of the metaphysicians are all synthetic a priori, Kant provides us with the following policy:

1. Those claims that are rules by which we must interpret our experience are true—necessarily true.

2. Those claims that contradict rules by which we must interpret our experience are false—necessarily false.

3. Those that are not rules by which we must interpret our experience are either analytic, contingently true, or contingently false.

4. Finally, those claims that cannot be decided by appeal to the rules of our experiences and make no difference to our experience one way or the other are to be rejected as possible topics of knowledge.

The logical positivists in the twentieth century took this last part of Kant's policy as a program for a devastating attack on metaphysics in general. Although the logical positivists, as empiricists in the tradition of David Hume, did not accept much of Kant's theory, they wholeheartedly endorsed his rejection of claims that made no difference whatever to our experience. They said that any claim that makes no difference to our experience—that cannot be tested in any way—is meaningless.

Some of the metaphysician's claims will be upheld. For example, Kant saves Newton's (and Spinoza's) determinism in his rule of causality, thus rejecting Leibniz's "pre-established harmony" view as necessarily false. With some revisions, he accepts a large part of Leibniz's view of space and time as relative, that is, relative to our experience. He saves the notion of substance because he says that one of the most important rules of our experience is that we see objects as substantial (that is, as "real"). But he does not accept the view that substance is something independent of human experience, for such a view, by definition, means that substance would be irrelevant to our experience. Nor does he accept the central dispute between Spinoza and Leibniz, whether there is but one substance or many, for no rule of our experience is concerned one way or another. It makes no difference to our experience. It is a metaphysician's game and not a possible topic for knowledge.

Kant's revolution is the elimination of "reality" and "truth" as external to ourselves. Since Kant, many philosophers no longer view human knowledge as the passive reception of sensations or intuitions. And, needless to say, the problems of philosophy have become radically changed.

Kant destroyed the old problems, resolved the old disputes, and answered Hume's skepticism, at least for a while. In rejecting the **correspondence theory of truth** and the idea of an "external" reality, he eliminated the basis of those problems, disputes, and doubts. But I expect that you can already see a new and even more virulent version of those problems, disputes, and doubts on the horizon. By denying us our anchor in reality, Kant launches philosophy in a bold new direction, and he creates the dilemma that still defines philosophy today: If we supply our own rules for experience, is there any uniquely correct way of describing the way the world is?

The basis of Kant's theory is that we supply the rules according to which we constitute our experience. Truth can be talked about only within our experience and according to those rules. But you can see what happens when we raise the following question: What about people (or creatures) who are very different from us? Will they use the same rules? Will they have the same experiences? And, if we do differ from them, who is "right"? Whose rules are "better"? Whose experience is "true"? You can see here the problems of the **coherence theory of truth** coming to haunt Kant's philosophy. Suppose there are two (or more) sets of rules, equally coherent? Can they both be "true"? And the problems of the **semantic theory**, too: What if there are different languages with different basic concepts or categories, constituting different "facts"? Are they all "true"? You can appreciate how easily the German Romantic philosophers who immediately followed Kant replaced his notion of "constitution" with the more exciting notion of "creation." We create our realities, they announced. We are all artists, building our worlds. Notice the words reali*ties*" and "worlds"; there is no longer confidence, much less a guarantee, that there is only one reality or one world.

Kant's most immediate follower, a German named **Johann Gottlieb Fichte**, used the **pragmatic theory of truth** to come to the same conclusion; the truth is, according to him, that which is most practical, most conducive to the good life, and the evaluation of different realities depends wholly on the practical consequences. (He said, in his most famous dictum: "The kind of philosophy a man chooses depends upon the kind of man he is.") With Kant's revolution, the Truth seems destined to be replaced by many truths, our knowledge with the possibility of different kinds of knowledge.

But before we go on to explore these intriguing complications, let us make it clear that Kant himself

Johann Gottlieb Fichte (1762-1814)

A German philosopher, student of Immanuel Kant, who turned Kant's "transcendental" philosophy into a practically oriented and relativistic "ethical idealism." He taught that "the kind of philosophy a man chooses depends upon the kind of man he is." One of the first German nationalists.

FIG. 3.27 Johann Gottlieb Fichte *(© PIXTAL / SUPERSTOCK)*

never accepted a word of all this. According to him, there was still but one possible set of rules and therefore only one way of constituting our experience, whoever we are, wherever we're from, and no matter what kind of conscious creature we happen to be. This means: one world, one science, one reality, and one truth. Kant tries to prove this in the central section of *The Critique of Pure Reason* in a formidable argument that he calls a "**transcendental deduction**."

Like so much philosophical jargon, Kant's term is easily explained and is used often enough to make it worth explaining. You already know that a deduction is an inference from one statement to another according to a set of rules of inference. In this case, Kant attempts to infer from various statements that we believe, the basic rules (concepts, categories) of human experience. This is what "**transcendental**" means, the basic rules of human experience. But a transcendental deduction is not satisfied with simply deducing some such rules; it also proves that they are the *only* rules that we are able to use to constitute our experience. That is why it is so important to Kant. It allows him his revolution without its anarchist consequences.

The argument itself is enormously complicated and scholars who have studied it for half their lives still do not agree what it is or whether it is a valid argument. So, obviously, we won't try to summarize it for you here. What can and must be said is this, however: Kant believed that such a transcendental deduction would prove that, although it is we ourselves who supply the rules of our experience and determine what can be true for us, we don't have a choice in the matter. There is still only one truth for all of us.

Philosophers are still arguing whether any such transcendental argument (Kant's or not) might succeed. If one does, then people must, in their basic rules, all agree. (Of course, they will always disagree about particular matters; no two chess players make all the same moves.) But if there is no successful transcendental argument, then there need be no such universal agreement. It then makes sense to talk about different truths for different people. This, we may say, is the dominant battle of twentieth-century philosophy in the United States and in Europe. But obviously, it is not new to the twentieth century. Those who believe that there is only one set of rules and one truth are often called **absolutists** (though many philosophers find that name repulsive because it sounds so dogmatic). Others, who believe that there are different rules for different people and therefore different "truths," are called **relativists**. You have probably already figured out that Plato, and Descartes, for example, were absolutists and that Protagoras and the Sophists were relativists. Kant was an absolutist. Most of his followers were relativists. (This is obscured by the confusing fact that many of them talked about "the Absolute" all the time. But, they were still relativists, and to avoid confusion, we shall not talk about "the Absolute" at all in this book.)

- What consequences do you see following from the difference between relativism and absolutism on questions of knowledge?

F. The Battle in Europe After Kant: Relativism and Absolutism

The story of philosophy in Europe since Kant is largely the story of a war between **relativism** and **absolutism**, in which even the politics and arts of the times play a continuing role. The philosophers immediately following Kant, as we have already mentioned, pursued relativism with relish, developing alternative systems of philosophy as fast as they could find publishers. The philosopher Friedrich Schelling, for example, produced about one system a year at the turn of the century. He became the best-known "Romantic" philosopher of a large group of

"Romantic" intellectuals, poets, and critics throughout Europe who turned to the virtual worship of individual "genius" and competed for the most extravagant and creative views of the world. The virtually undisputed winner of this contest, however, was not Schelling but one of his schoolmates, **Georg Wilhelm Friedrich Hegel**.

1. Hegel

Hegel was in college (Tübingen Lutheran seminary) when the French Revolution was raging just across the border. He was just starting to put together his mature philosophy when Napoleon was attempting to take over all of Europe. This international turmoil helps us understand the global reach of Hegel's philosophy and his bold effort to proclaim an "absolute" position with reference to knowledge. Like many young German intellectuals in that exciting period, he was trying to get outside his provincial perspective and to understand the world from a larger, even a "divine" point of view. Accordingly, Hegel's theory of truth is part and parcel of his all-embracing system of thought.

Hegel begins by rejecting many key metaphors that have ruled modern philosophy, especially all the "correspondence" metaphors in which the world in itself (or "the Absolute") is on one side and our knowledge (beliefs, sentences, utterances) are on the other, separated by some distorting filter (our senses) or actively altered by the machinery of our understanding. In place of such metaphors (and the skepticism they inevitably engender), Hegel suggests a holistic worldview in which consciousness and the world are not separate but inseparably integrated. In traditional terms, this means that there is no world, no reality-in-itself apart from consciousness.

It also means that we must give up our view of consciousness and the self as self-enclosed and, in some sense, "inside" us. Indeed, Hegel also suggests that we give up the view that the self is essentially a feature of the individual: the self—or "Spirit"—is shared by all of us; or rather, in more Platonic language, we all "participate" in Spirit. Not surprisingly, Hegel was familiar with some Oriental thinkers and incorporated some Eastern views into his notion of truth. However, the truth, according to Hegel, "is the whole"—that is, the unity of all our consciousnesses and the world. This means that there is no saying (and no point in attempting to say) what the world might be apart from our conceptions of it. But neither is this to invite skepticism, for the world is nothing but the synthesis of all our possible conceptions of it.

Hegel, like Kant, is an idealist. He calls himself an "absolute idealist" (in contrast to Kant's "transcendental idealism"). This means, simply stated, that reality is the product of mind (not individual minds, of course)—the cosmic mind, "Spirit." Yet this opens the way for the most radical departure from Kant, who argued at great length that there could be but one possible way of conceiving the world—that is, one a priori set of forms of intuition (space and time) and one set of categories (substance, causality, etc.). Hegel's predecessor (Kant's immediate successor) Fichte had already argued that there are at least two basically different ways of envisioning the world—the scientific, objective ("dogmatic") way and the practical, moral, activist ("idealist") way—

Georg Wilhelm Friedrich Hegel (1770-1831)

A German philosopher who, during the age of Napoleon, wrote his *Phenomenology of Spirit* (1807), which was the single most powerful influence on European philosophy—after Kant's works—for the next hundred years. Hegel argued that there were many different views of the world, that none of them should be thought to be wholly correct or incorrect in exclusion of the others, but that these various views could still be compared and evaluated according to a "dialectic," in which some views are shown to be more developed, more inclusive, and more adequate than others.

and rather than being simply "right" or "wrong," Fichte had declared famously that "The philosophy a man chooses depends upon the kind of man that he is." Hegel goes a giant step further and provides a long series of possible conceptions of the world—or "forms of consciousness"—conceptions that are not divided into "practical" and "theoretical" but, Hegel tells us, all of which have both their practical and their theoretical aspects. (Once again Hegel rejects an age-old dichotomy.) Such views are not simply alternative options, as if we could each simply choose one or another (as Kierkegaard would argue some years later). The way we view the world is already determined by our place in history, our language, and our society. Nor is the variety of forms of consciousness a demonstration of the now-popular view that there is no "correct" way of knowing. The various forms of consciousness emerge one from another by way of improvement or by way of opposition (as, for example, scientific theories tend to follow one another), and (again, as in science) there is always the necessary sense that they are all moving toward some final end—the correct view. So, too, Hegel insists that all these different conceptions and ways of viewing the world are leading up to something—to a viewpoint that is not relative to any particular viewpoint or perspective. This is the standpoint he calls "absolute knowing."

This idea that the various forms of consciousness emerge one from another and lead us eventually to the absolute is perhaps Hegel's most exciting philosophical contribution to Western thinking. Virtually every other philosopher we have discussed, whether metaphysician or epistemologist, essentially offered us a static view of knowledge, a concept of the understanding that—except for education from childhood and the detailed knowledge gained by the sciences—did not change, did not grow, did not develop. Hegel provides philosophy (and humanity) with a historical perspective. Our knowledge is not, as many philosophers had insisted ever since ancient times, about what is apart from our knowledge of it. Truth develops, as the human mind develops. Truth is not being but becoming. Knowledge develops through conflict and confrontation, or what Hegel famously calls a **dialectic** (a term he borrowed from Kant but which goes back to the Greeks).

In an important sense, it is Hegel who discovers (or invents) the history of philosophy. Other philosophers had talked about their predecessors, of course. (Aristotle, for instance, provided us with much of what we know about the pre-Socratic philosophers.) But what Hegel suggests is that something more is to be gleaned than a mere sequence of refutations, additions, and improvements to thought; it is reality itself that is being converted. The history of philosophy, accordingly, is but one aspect of an incredible cosmic odyssey, a "phenomenology of spirit"—the development through time not only of consciousness but of reality too.

The selection that follows is from the Introduction of Hegel's 1807 masterpiece, *The Phenomenology of Spirit*. In this book, Hegel presents a dialectic of various forms of consciousness, from the most primitive sensory perception to the most sophisticated views of the Enlightenment and "Revealed Religion" (Christianity), culminating in that final stage of "Absolute Knowing." In these paragraphs, Hegel rejects the traditional metaphors of epistemology and argues that skepticism should not be taken at all seriously. He then suggests the holistic form of his overall system.

FROM *The Phenomenology of Spirit*
BY **G. W. F. Hegel**[22]

It is a natural assumption that in philosophy, before we start to deal with its proper subject-matter, *viz.* the actual cognition of what truly is, one must first of all come to an understanding about cognition, which is regarded either as the instrument to get hold of the Absolute, or as the medium through which one discovers it. A certain uneasiness seems justified, partly because there are different types of cognition, and one of them might be more appropriate than another for the attainment of this goal, so that we could make a bad choice of means; and partly because cognition is a faculty of a definite kind and scope, and thus, without a more precise definition of its nature and limits, we might grasp clouds of error instead of the heaven of truth. This feeling of uneasiness is surely bound to be transformed into the conviction that the whole project of securing for consciousness through cognition what exists in itself is absurd, and that there is a boundary between cognition and the Absolute that completely separates form. For, if cognition is the instrument for getting hold of absolute being, it is obvious that the use of an instrument on a thing certainly does not let it be what it is for itself, but rather sets out to reshape and alter it. If, on the other hand, cognition is not an instrument of our activity but a more or less passive medium through which the light of truth reaches us, then again we do not receive the truth as it is in itself, but only as it exists through and in this medium. Either way we employ a means which immediately brings about the opposite of its own end; or rather, what is really absurd is that we should make use of a means at all.

It would seem, to be sure, that this evil could be remedied through an acquaintance with the way in which the *instrument* works; for this would enable us to eliminate from the representation of the Absolute which we have gained through it whatever is due to the instrument, and thus get the truth in its purity. But this "improvement" would in fact only bring us back to where we were before. If we remove from a reshaped thing what the instrument has done to it, then the thing—here the Absolute—becomes for us exactly what it was before this (accordingly) superfluous effort. On the other hand, if the Absolute is supposed merely to be brought nearer to us through this instrument, without anything in it being altered, like a bird caught by a lime-twig, it would surely laugh our little ruse to scorn, if it were not with us, in and for itself, all along, and of its own volition. For a ruse is just what cognition would be in such a case, since it would, with its manifold exertions, be giving itself the air of doing something quite different from creating a merely immediate and therefore effortless relationship. Or, if by testing cognition, which we conceive of as a *medium*, we get to know the law of its refraction, it is again useless to subtract this from the end result. For it is not the refraction of the ray, but the ray itself whereby truth reaches us, that is cognition; and if this were removed, all that would be indicated would be a pure direction or a blank space.

Meanwhile, if the fear of falling into error sets up a mistrust of Science, which in the absence of such scruples gets on with the work itself, and actually cognizes something, it is hard to see why we should not turn round and mistrust this very mistrust. Should we not be concerned as to whether this fear of error is not just the error itself? Indeed, this fear takes something—a great deal in fact—for granted as truth, supporting its scruples and inferences on what is itself in need of prior scrutiny

---

[22] G. W. F. Hegel, *The Phenomenology of Spirit*, trans. A. V. Miller, New York: Oxford University Press, 1977.

to see if it is true. To be specific, it takes for granted certain ideas about cognition as an *instrument* and as a *medium*, and assumes that there is a *difference between ourselves and this cognition*. Above all, it presupposes that the Absolute stands on one side and cognition on the other, independent and separated from it, and yet is something real; or in other words, it presupposes that cognition which, since it is excluded from the Absolute, is surely outside of the truth as well, is nevertheless true, an assumption whereby what calls itself fear of error reveals itself rather as fear of the truth.

This conclusion stems from the fact that the Absolute alone is true, or the truth alone is absolute.

. . .

Now, because it has only phenomenal knowledge for its object, this exposition seems not to be Science, free and self-moving in its own peculiar shape; yet from this standpoint it can be regarded as the path of the natural consciousness which presses forward to true knowledge; or as the way of the Soul which journeys through the series of its own configurations as though they were the stations appointed for it by its own nature, so that it may purify itself for the life of the Spirit, and achieve finally, through a completed experience of life itself, the awareness of what it really is in itself.

Natural consciousness will show itself to be only the Notion of knowledge, or in other words, not to be real knowledge. But since it directly takes itself to be real knowledge, this path has a negative significance for it, and what is in fact the realization of the Notion, counts for it rather as the loss of its own self; for it does lose its truth on this path. The road can therefore be regarded as the pathway of *doubt*, or more precisely as the way of despair. For what happens on it is not what is ordinarily understood when the word "doubt" is used: shilly-shallying about this or that presumed truth, followed by a return to that truth again, after the doubt has been appropriately dispelled—so that at the end of the process the matter is taken to be what it was in the first place. On the contrary, this path is the conscious insight into the untruth of phenomenal knowledge, for which the supreme reality is what is in truth only the unrealized Notion. Therefore this thoroughgoing scepticism is also not the scepticism with which an earnest zeal for truth and Science fancies it has prepared and equipped itself in their service: the *resolve*, in Science, not to give oneself over to the thoughts of others, upon mere authority, but to examine everything for oneself and follow only one's conviction, or better still, to produce everything oneself, and accept only one's deed as what is true.

The series of configurations which consciousness goes through along this road is, in reality, the detailed history of the *education* of consciousness itself to the standpoint of Science. That zealous resolve represents this education simplistically as something directly over and done with in the making of the resolution; but the way of the Soul is the actual fulfillment of the resolution, in contrast to the untruth of that view. Now, following one's own conviction is, of course, more than giving oneself over to authority; but changing an opinion accepted on authority into an opinion held out of personal conviction, does not necessarily alter the content of the opinion, or replace error with truth. The only difference between being caught up in a system of opinions and prejudices based on personal conviction, and being caught up in one based on the authority of others, lies in the added conceit that is innate in the former position. The scepticism that is directed against the whole range of phenomenal consciousness, on the other hand, renders the Spirit for the first time competent to examine what truth is. For it brings about a state of despair about all the so-called

"The Absolute alone is true, or the truth alone is absolute."

– G. W. F. HEGEL

natural ideas, thoughts, and opinions, regardless of whether they are called one's own or someone else's, ideas with which the consciousness that sets about the examination (of truth) *straight away* is still filled and hampered, so that it is, in fact, incapable of carrying out what it wants to undertake.

The necessary progression and interconnection of the forms of the unreal consciousness will by itself bring to pass the *completion* of the series. To make this more intelligible, it may be remarked, in a preliminary and general way, that the exposition of the untrue consciousness in its untruth is not a merely *negative* procedure. The natural consciousness itself normally takes this one-sided view of it; and a knowledge which makes the one-sidedness its very essence is itself one of the patterns of incomplete consciousness which occurs on the road itself, and will manifest itself in due course. This is just the scepticism which only ever sees pure nothingness in its result and abstracts from the fact that this nothingness is specifically the nothingness of that *from which it results*. For it is only when it is taken as the result of that from which it emerges, that it is, in fact, the true result; in that case it is itself a *determinate* nothingness, one which has a *content*. The scepticism that ends up with the bare abstraction of nothingness or emptiness cannot get any further from there, but must wait to see whether something new comes along and what it is, in order to throw it too into the same empty abyss. But when, on the other hand, the result is conceived as it is in truth, namely, as a *determinate* negation, a new form has thereby immediately arisen, and in the negation the transition is made through which the progress through the complete series of forms comes about of itself.

· · ·

This contradiction and its removal will become more definite if we call to mind the abstract determinations of truth and knowledge as they occur in consciousness. Consciousness simultaneously *distinguishes* itself from something, and at the same time *relates* itself to it, or, as it is said, this something exists *for* consciousness; and the determinate aspect of the *relating*, or of the *being* of something for a consciousness, is *knowing*. But we distinguish the being-for-another from *being-in-itself*; whatever is related to knowledge or knowing is also distinguished from it, and posited as existing outside of this relationship; this *being-in-itself* is called *truth*. Just what might be involved in these determinations is of no further concern to us here. Since our object is phenomenal knowledge, its determinations too will at first be taken directly as they present themselves; and they do present themselves very much as we have already apprehended them.

Now, if we inquire into the truth of knowledge, it seems that we are asking what knowledge is *in itself*. Yet in this inquiry knowledge is *our* object, something that exists *for us;* and the *in-itself* that would supposedly result from it would rather be the being of knowledge *for us*. What we asserted to be its essence would be not so much its truth but rather just our knowledge of it. The essence or criterion would lie within ourselves, and that which was to be compared with it and about which a decision would be reached through this comparison would not necessarily have to recognize the validity of such a standard.

Starting from a clearly Kantian perspective, Hegel taught that we have to stop talking about "true" and "false" philosophies, and "true" and "false" religions, political systems, societies, scientific theories, and values. There are only different "forms of consciousness,"

FIG. 3.29 Picasso's *Guernica*, an arresting image of "the slaughterhouse of history." *(Erich Lessing / Art Resource, NY / Artists Rights Society (ARS), New York)*

some more sophisticated and perspicacious than others, but none wholly true (or false) to the exclusion of others. Hegel wholly endorsed the Kantian thesis that the world is nothing other than the way in which we constitute it.

Hegel's dialectic was essentially a dialectic of ideas, a series of confrontations of various forms of consciousness so that we could see how they all form an interlocking view of reality. But although philosophy and human history improve through time—eventually reaching a form of absolute knowledge and (Hegel hoped) world peace and universal freedom—the movement itself is by no means a smooth progression. It was often violent, both in the intellectual realm and in the flesh-and-blood world of human politics, which Hegel grimly referred to as "the slaughter-bench of history."

- How does Hegel address the problem of skepticism in rejecting the "correspondence metaphors" of philosophy?

One of Hegel's most enthusiastic followers, a young student in Berlin named **Karl Marx**, thought that Hegel had the dialectic of history turned upside down. It is not ideas that determine world history, Marx argued, but rather the details of history—in particular the economic details—that determine the ideas, including the ideas of philosophers. From this notion of dialectic Marx developed his powerful and influential view of history as class conflict, replacing Hegel's abstract "forms of consciousness" with the day-to-day battles of wages, jobs, exploitation, and profits.[23]

In what follows, Hegel presents an overview of his all-embracing notion of "spirit" (also called "the Idea"). Spirit, in one sense, is God, but the concept embraces all of humanity, all of history, and all of nature as well. The point of the argument is that the world itself *develops* and *changes*, and so the virtues and truths of one generation may well become inadequate to the next generation. Yet this is not relativism in the crude sense, such that a truth, for example, is only true for a particular person or people. First, truth is not, in this

---

[23] The familiar doctrine of Hegel's dialectic is often known only in terms of "thesis-antithesis-synthesis." In fact these categories are rarely used by either Hegel or Marx.

sense, subjective; it is to be found in the world and not just in the minds of individuals or groups. Second, and even more important, to say that a truth is inadequate from a later, probably more expansive, point of view is not to say that it "was true but now is false;" rather, it shows that we are slowly approaching an ever more adequate conception of the truth and knowledge, which, in the following selection, Hegel calls "Freedom." Freedom is God's purpose developing through history and humanity.

FROM *Reason in History*
BY **G. W. F. Hegel**[24]

The question of the *means* whereby Freedom develops itself into a world leads us directly to the phenomenon of history. Although Freedom as such is primarily an internal idea, the means it uses are the external phenomena which in history present themselves directly before our eyes. The first glance at history convinces us that the actions of men spring from their needs, their passions, their interests, their characters, and their talents. Indeed, it appears as if in this drama of activities these needs, passions, and interests are the sole springs of action and the main efficient cause. It is true that this drama involves also universal purposes, benevolence, or noble patriotism. But such virtues and aims are insignificant on the broad canvas of history. We may, perhaps, see the ideal of Reason actualized in those who adopt such aims and in the spheres of their influence; but their number is small in proportion to the mass of the human race and their influence accordingly limited. Passions, private aims, and the satisfaction of selfish desires are, on the contrary, tremendous springs of action. Their power lies in the fact that they respect none of the limitations which law and morality would impose on them; and that these natural impulses are closer to the core of human nature than the artificial and troublesome discipline that tends toward order, self-restraint, law, and morality.

When we contemplate this display of passions and the consequences of their violence, the unreason which is associated not only with them, but even—rather we might say *especially*—with *good* designs and righteous aims; when we see arising therefrom the evil, the vice, the ruin that has befallen the most flourishing kingdoms which the mind of man ever created, we can hardly avoid being filled with sorrow at this universal taint of corruption. And since this decay is not the work of mere nature, but of human will, our reflections may well lead us to a moral sadness, a revolt of the good will (spirit)—if indeed it has a place within us. Without rhetorical exaggeration, a simple, truthful account of the miseries that have overwhelmed the noblest of nations and polities and the finest exemplars of private virtue forms a most fearful picture and excites emotions of the profoundest and most hopeless sadness, counterbalanced by no consoling result. We can endure it and strengthen ourselves against it only by thinking that this is the way it had to be—it is fate; nothing can be done. And at last, out of the boredom with which this sorrowful reflection threatens us, we draw back into the vitality of the present, into our aims and interests of the moment; we retreat, in short, into the selfishness that stands on the quiet shore and thence enjoys in safety the distant spectacle of wreckage and confusion.

But in contemplating history as the slaughter-bench at which the happiness of peoples, the wisdom of states, and the virtue of individuals have been sacrificed, a

---

question necessarily arises: To what principle, to what final purpose, have these monstrous sacrifices been offered?

From here one usually proceeds to the starting point of our investigation: the events which make up this picture of gloomy emotion and thoughtful reflection are only the means for realizing the essential destiny, the absolute and final purpose, or, what amounts to the same thing, the true result of world history. We have all along purposely eschewed that method of reflection which ascends from this scene of particulars to general principles. Besides, it is not in the interest of such sentimental reflections really to rise above these depressing emotions and to solve the mysteries of Providence presented in such contemplations. It is rather their nature to dwell melancholically on the empty and fruitless sublimities of their negative result. For this reason we return to our original point of view. What we shall have to say about it will also answer the questions put to us by this panorama of history.

The first thing we notice—something which has been stressed more than once before but which cannot be repeated too often, for it belongs to the central point of our inquiry—is the merely general and abstract nature of what we call principle, final purpose, destiny, or the nature and concept of Spirit. A principle, a law is something implicit, which as such, however true in itself, is not completely

FIG. 3.30 Napoleon as self-styled emperor. (© iStockphoto .com/Ivan Burmistrov)

real (actual). Purposes, principles, and the like, are at first in our thoughts, our inner intention. They are not yet in reality. That which is in itself is a possibility, a faculty. It has not yet emerged out of its implicitness into existence. A second element must be added for it to become reality, namely, activity, actualization. The principle of this is the will, man's activity in general. It is only through this activity that the concept and its implicit ("being-in-themselves") determinations can be realized, actualized; for of themselves they have no immediate efficacy. The activity which puts them in operation and in existence is the need, the instinct, the inclination, and passion of man. When I have an idea I am greatly interested in transforming it into action, into actuality. In its realization through my participation I want to find my own satisfaction. A purpose for which I shall be active must in some way be my purpose; I must thereby satisfy my own desires, even though it may have ever so many aspects which do not concern me. This is the infinite right of the individual to find itself satisfied in its activity and labor. If men are to be interested in anything they must have "their heart" in it. Their feelings of self-importance must be satisfied. But here a misunderstanding must be avoided. To say that an individual "has an interest" in something is justly regarded as a reproach or blame; we imply that he seeks only his private advantage. Indeed, the blame implies not only his disregard of the common interest, but his taking advantage of it and even his sacrificing it to his own interest. Yet, he who is active for a cause is not simply "interested," but "interested *in it*." Language faithfully expresses this distinction. Nothing therefore happens, nothing is accomplished, unless those concerned with an issue find their own satisfaction in it. They are particular individuals; they have their special needs, instincts, and interests. They have their own particular desires and volitions, their own insight and conviction, or at

"Reason governs
the world and
has consequently
governed its
history."

– G. W. F. HEGEL

least their own attitude and opinion, once the aspirations to reflect, understand, and reason have been awakened. Therefore people demand that a cause for which they should be active accord with their ideas. And they expect their opinion—concerning its goodness, justice, advantage, profit—to be taken into account. This is of particular importance today when people are moved to support a cause not by faith in other people's authority, but rather on the basis of their own independent judgment and conviction.

We assert then that nothing has been accomplished without an interest on the part of those who brought it about. And if "interest" be called "passion"—because the whole individuality is concentrating all its desires and powers, with every fiber of volition, to the neglect of all other actual or possible interests and aims, on one object—we may then affirm without qualification that *nothing great in the world* has been accomplished without passion.

. . .

[O]ne may indeed question whether those manifestations of vitality on the part of individuals and peoples in which they seek and satisfy their own purposes are, at the same time, the means and tools of a higher and broader purpose of which they know nothing, which they realize unconsciously. This purpose has been questioned, and in every variety of form denied, decried, and denounced as mere dreaming and "philosophy." On this point, however, I announced my view at the very outset, and asserted our hypothesis—which eventually will appear as the result of our investigation—namely, that Reason governs the world and has consequently governed its history. In relation to this Reason, which is universal and substantial, in and for itself, all else is subordinate, subservient, and the means for its actualization. Moreover, this Reason is immanent in historical existence and reaches its own perfection in and through this existence. The union of the abstract universal, existing in and for itself, with the particular or subjective, and the fact that this union alone constitutes truth are a matter of speculative philosophy which, in this general form, is treated in logic. But in its historical development (*the subjective side, consciousness, is not yet able to know what is*) the abstract final aim of history, the idea of Spirit, for it is then itself in process and incomplete. The idea of Spirit is not yet its distant object of desire and interest. Thus desire is still unconscious of its purpose; yet it already exists in the particular purposes and realizes itself through them. The problem concerning the union of the general and the subjective may also be raised under the form of the union of freedom and necessity. We consider the immanent development of the Spirit, existing in and for itself, as necessary, while we refer to freedom the interests contained in men's conscious volitions.

- What is Hegel's dialectic, and how does it relate to truth and knowledge as he understands it? How did Marx revise this notion?

---

2. Schopenhauer

Arthur Schopenhauer claimed to be a faithful student of Kant. Indeed, he claimed to be the only faithful interpreter of what he took to be Kant's central idea, the distinction between the constituted world of our experience and an underlying reality, which could be found in the realm of the Will. But Schopenhauer, who was one of the great eccentrics in the history of philosophy, gave Kant's philosophy a dramatic twist, encouraged by his readings of Eastern philosophy. In place of Kant's confidence in the truth of the world of our experience, Schopenhauer invokes the Buddhist conception of the "veil of Maya" and declares our experience of the world to be largely illusion. Meanwhile the Will, which Kant takes to be inherently rational, becomes an irrational, impersonal, inner force for Schopenhauer, exerting itself to no particular purpose within us. The most evident manifestation of the Will, in us and in all creatures, Schopenhauer suggests, is sexual desire, the often urgent and foolish desire to reproduce ourselves, so that our offspring can reproduce themselves, and so on and so on, to no end whatever. Thus Schopenhauer, like the Buddha, stresses the futility of desire, and his whole philosophy is aimed at giving us some relief from the Will. But the Will is ultimate reality, and within its purposeless striving dwell all of the peoples and all of the creatures of nature. The following selection is from Schopenhauer's great book, *The World as Will and Representation*.

Arthur Schopenhauer (1788-1860)

A German philosopher, famous pessimist, and man of letters. His main work, *The World as Will and Representation*, was an elaboration on Kant's philosophy. Yet instead of Kant's rationality, the irrationality of the will became the centerpiece of Schopenhauer's philosophy. Schopenhauer's *magnum opus* was first published in 1819, but did not become popular and earn its author the fame he much desired until the second half of the nineteenth century.

FIG. 3.31 The pessimist philosopher Arthur Schopenhauer is widely considered to be one of Germany's greatest writers. (© iStockphoto.com/HultonArchive)

 FROM *The World as Will and Representation*
BY **Arthur Schopenhauer**[25]

The will, considered purely in itself, is devoid of knowledge, and is only a blind, irresistible cure, as we see it appear in inorganic and vegetable nature and in their laws, and also in the vegetative part of our own life. Through the addition of the world as representation, developed for its service, the will obtains knowledge of its own willing and what it wills, namely that this is nothing but this world, life, precisely as it exists. We have therefore called the phenomenal world the mirror, the objectivity, of the will; and as what the will wills is always life, just because this is nothing but the presentation of that willing for the representation, it is immaterial and a mere pleonasm if, instead of simply saying "the will," we say "the will-to-live."

As the will is the thing-in-itself, the inner content, the essence of the world, but life, the visible world, the phenomenon, is only the mirror of the will, this world will accompany the will as inseparably as a body is accompanied by its shadow; and if will exists, then life, the world, will exist. Therefore life is certain to the will-to-live, and as long as we are filled with the will-to-live we need not be apprehensive for our existence, even at the sight of death. It is true that we see the individual come into being and pass away; but the individual is only phenomenon, exists only for knowledge involved in the principle of sufficient reason, in the *principium individuationis*. Naturally, for this knowledge, the individual receives his life as a gift, rises out of nothing, and then suffers the loss of this gift through death, and returns to nothing. We, however, wish to consider life philosophically, that is to say, according to its Ideas, and

FIG. 3.32 The god Shiva. (© iStockphoto.com/Alan Smithers)

25 Arthur Schopenhauer, *The World as Will and Representation*, pp. 275, *et supra.*, trans. E. F. Payne. Copyright © 1966 by Dover Publications, Inc.

"Now man is nature herself, and indeed nature at the highest grade of her self-consciousness, but nature is only the objectified will-to-live."

– ARTHUR SCHOPENHAUER

then we shall find that neither the will, the thing-in-itself in all phenomena, nor the subject of knowing, the spectator of all phenomena, is in any way affected by birth and death. Birth and death belong only to the phenomenon of the will, and hence to life; and it is essential to this that is manifest itself in individuals that come into being and pass away, as fleeting phenomena, appearing in the form of time, of that which in itself knows no time, but must be manifested precisely in the way aforesaid in order to objectify its real nature. Birth and death belong equally to life, and hold the balance as mutual conditions of each other, or, if the expression be preferred, as poles of the whole phenomenon of life. The wisest of all mythologies, the Indian, expresses this by giving to the very god who symbolizes destruction and death (just as Brahma, the most sinful and lowest god of the Trimurti, symbolizes generation, origination, and Vishnu preservation), by giving, I say, to Shiva as an attribute not only the necklace of skulls, but also the lingam, that symbol of generation which appears as the counterpart of death. In this way it is intimated that generation and death are essential correlatives which reciprocally neutralize and eliminate each other. It was precisely the same sentiment that prompted the Greeks and Romans to adorn the costly sarcophagi, just as we still see them, with feasts, dances, marriages, hunts, fights between wild beasts, bacchanalia, that is with presentations of life's most powerful urge. This they present to us not only through such diversions and merriments, but even in sensual groups, to the point of showing us the sexual intercourse between satyrs and goats. The object was obviously to indicate with the greatest emphasis from the death of the mourned individual the immortal life of nature, and thus to intimate, although without abstract knowledge, that the whole of nature is the phenomenon, and also the fulfillment, of the will-to-live. The form of this phenomenon is time, space, and causality, and through these individuation, which requires that the individual must come into being and pass away. But this no more disturbs the will-to-live—the individual being only a particular example or specimen, so to speak, of the phenomenon of this will—than does the death of an individual injure the whole of nature. For it is not the individual that nature cares for, but only the species; and in all seriousness she urges the preservation of the species, since she provides for this so lavishly through the immense surplus of the seed and the great strength of the fructifying impulse. The individual, on the contrary, has no value for nature, and can have none, for infinite time, infinite space, and the infinite number of possible individuals therein are her kingdom. Therefore nature is always ready to let the individual fall, and the individual is accordingly not only exposed to destruction in a thousand ways from the most insignificant accidents, but is even destined for this and is led towards it by nature herself, from the moment that individual has served the maintenance of the species. In this way, nature quite openly expresses the great truth that only the Ideas, not individuals, have reality proper, in other words are a complete objectivity of the will. Now man is nature herself, and indeed nature at the highest grade of her self-consciousness, but nature is only the objectified will-to-live; the person who has grasped and retained this point of view may certainly and justly console himself for his own death and for that of his friends by looking back on the immortal life of nature, which he himself is.

> • What follows from Schopenhauer's celebration of the Will as the "thing-in-itself," the truth behind all reality?

3. Nietzsche

After Hegel, relativism became ever more sophisticated. In Marx, differences in philosophical worldviews were explained in terms of different economic and social circumstances. The question was no longer "which view of the world is true?" but rather, "what circumstances would make a person believe that?" Hegel's rival Arthur Schopenhauer defended the radical idea that what we called reality was in fact an illusion, and a few years later, following Schopenhauer, a similar view was defended by the eccentric but brilliant iconoclast, Friedrich Nietzsche. Nietzsche, too, attacked the traditional notions of truth and knowledge with a vengeance and argued that there could be as many equally "true" (or equally "false"—it doesn't matter) worldviews as there were creative people and societies. He also urged that every person adopt for himself or herself as many different worldviews as possible, at one time or another, as a matter of "experiment."

Like Schopenhauer, he considered all such views as dictated by the Will and not merely as knowledge as such, and, like Marx, he replaced the old question, "which view of the world is true?" with a question of circumstances. But Nietzsche was not interested in economic or social circumstances so much as psychological factors. So he asked, "What kind of personality would need to believe that?" Truth is no longer even an issue. In fact, even rationality is starting to feel the threat of relativism. For, with Nietzsche, not only is truth out the window, but coherence and pragmatism are forced to take second place as well. What comes first? Excitement, adventure, heroism, creativity, and what Nietzsche generally calls "the will to power." Of course, one must still act rationally if one is to achieve these things, but thinking, in Nietzsche's view, plays at most a secondary role in our lives.

Nietzsche's view of truth was, to put it mildly, startling. His basic claim was a paradox: "truth is error." This can be interpreted in many different ways, and Nietzsche himself interprets and reinterprets it from many different perspectives—which is quite in line with his view of truth itself. "There are no facts," he tells us, "only interpretations." Elsewhere he tells us that there are only "perspectives," various ways of viewing the world and no ultimately correct (or incorrect) way. The very idea of "Truth," he writes, and the curious obsession with truth enjoyed by the scholars, is a kind of pathology, or at least a real curiosity, that requires examination. Why are we so enamored with the idea of "the Truth"? How and why did philosophers ever get the idea that there is another world, more real and "better" than this one?

FIG. 3.33 A famous photograph of Friedrich Nietzsche, taken in 1887. *(Bildarchiv Preussischer Kulturbesitz / Art Resource, NY)*

 FROM **On Truth**
BY **Friedrich Nietzsche**[26]

Sense for Truth.—I welcome every skepticism to which I may answer: "Let us try it out!" But I no longer want to hear anything about things and questions that cannot be tested. This is the limit of my "sense for truth": for courage has there lost its right.

Life no Argument.—We have organized for ourselves a world to live in—by postulating bodies, lines, surfaces, causes and effects, motion and rest, form and content: without these instances of belief no one could manage to live today! But nevertheless they are yet unproven. Life is no argument; error might be among the conditions of life.

Ultimate Skepticism.—But in the end what are human truths?—They are our *irrefutable* errors.

Truth is the sort of error without which a particular species of life could not live. In the end the value for *life* is what decides the matter.

26 All Nietzsche translations are by Clancy Martin.

The criterion of truth is in the enhancement of the feeling of power.

What is truth?—Inertia; that supposition that provides ease; the smallest cost in spiritual power; etc.

There are all kinds of eyes. Even the sphinx has eyes:—and thus there are all kinds of "truths," and thus there is no truth.

For us the falseness of a judgment is not on that account an objection to a judgment . . . The question is how far is it life-promoting, life-preserving, species-preserving, perhaps even species-propagating; and our fundamental inclination is to insist that the falsest judgments (such as synthetic a priori judgments) are for us the most indispensable, that without admitting as true the fictions of logic, without measuring reality against the entirely invented world of the unconditional and self-identical, without constant falsification of the world through numbers, human beings could not live—that to renounce false judgments would be to renounce life, would be to deny life.

HOW THE "TRUE WORLD" AT LAST BECAME A FABLE: THE HISTORY OF AN ERROR

1. The true world:—attainable for the wise, the pious, the virtuous; he lives in it, *he is it*. (The oldest form of the idea, comparably sensible, simple, and compelling. . . .)

2. The true world:—unattainable for now, but promised for the wise, the pious, the virtuous ("for the sinner who repents"). (Progress of the idea: it becomes more subtle, sinister, incomprehensible: it becomes Christian.)

3. The true world:—unattainable, indemonstrable, unpromisable; but the very thought of it—a consolation, a duty, an imperative. (The old sun, really, but viewed through fog and skepticism. The idea has become elusive, pale, Nordic. Kantian.)

4. The true world:—unattainable? At least, unattained. And as unattained, also *unknown*. Thus no consolation, redemption, or obligation: how could something unknown obligate us? (Grey dawn. Reason's first yawn. . . .)

5. The "true" world:—an idea that is no longer of any use, not even for obligating— an idea that has become worthless and superfluous—*consequently*, a refuted idea: let us abolish it! (Bright day; breakfast, return of *bons sens* and cheerfulness; . . .)

6. The true world:—we have abolished. What world is left? Perhaps the apparent? But no! *With the true world we have abolished the apparent as well.* (Noon; . . . end of the longest error; high point of humanity.)

Although Nietzsche wrote in the last half of the nineteenth century, his works were ignored until the twentieth century, when they made an enormous impact (not all of it positive), first in Germany, then more widely in Europe and in the United States. Nietzsche's relativistic view of truth, while very much at home with many current thinkers, was still quite alien to the ideas of the nineteenth century, when thinkers—following Hegel or Kant or natural science—were still trying to develop a unified and "true" picture of the world. However, one of Nietzsche's German colleagues did have an impact, just at the end of the last century, and though his relativistic view of truth was not nearly so extreme as Nietzsche's, he provoked extensive activity and comment. We speak of Wilhelm Dilthey. The doctrine he promoted, which is still tremendously influential in both Europe and the United States, is called **historicism**.

Historicism is Hegel's dialectic of forms of consciousness, pinned down to precise social and historical periods. It is the thesis, simply, that truth and rationality are relative to particular peoples at particular times in history and that overall comparison of them, with the intention of finding out which is "true," is totally mistaken. It is, obviously, a very strong relativist doctrine, so strong and so influential that the absolutists in philosophy, who had had much less publicity and success than the relativists for the last century, started looking around for a champion. They found him in the "phenomenologist" **Edmund Husserl.**

- Is "historicism" a form of relativism? What is the difference between the two?

G. Phenomenology

Phenomenology is a self-consciously "scientific" and "rigorous" discipline, modeled after mathematics (as it was for Descartes and the ancient Greeks). Phenomenology is the study of the essential structures of the human mind, and because these are essential, they can be known to be true, universally and necessarily. Husserl was a new kind of rationalist, who believed that the truths of arithmetic and geometry are known—and known with certainty—by appeal to a certain kind of intuition, which he called "essential" intuition. Believing that such intuitions are adequate for arithmetic and geometry, Husserl turned his theory elsewhere, to philosophy in general. Husserl, as much as any philosopher of his time (the early twentieth century), was horrified by what he saw as rampant relativism. He saw it, in fact, not only as a crisis in philosophy but as "a crisis in European civilization." So he turned his phenomenology to attack it. Turning against Dilthey, for example, he argued:

Edmund Husserl (1859–1938)

A German-Czech philosopher and mathematician who was the founder of phenomenology, a modern form of rational intuitionism. With Gottlob Frege, Husserl fought against the empiricist view of necessary truth defended by John Stuart Mill and developed an alternative view in which matters of necessity were not matters of ordinary experience but rather of a special kind of intuition. His best-known works are *Ideas* (Vol. 1) (1913) and *Cartesian Meditations* (1931).

FIG. 3.34
Phenomenologist philosopher Edmund Husserl. *(© Bettmann/ CORBIS)*

 FROM **"Philosophy as Rigorous Science"**
BY **Edmund Husserl**[27]

Historicism takes its position in the factual sphere of the empirical life of the spirit. To the extent that it posits this latter absolutely, without exactly naturalizing it (the specific sense of nature in particular lies far from historical thinking and in any event does not influence it by determining it in general), there arises a relativism that has a close affinity to naturalistic psychologism and runs into similar sceptical difficulties.

. . .

In view of this constant change in scientific views we would actually have no right to speak of sciences as objectively valid unities instead of merely as cultural formations. It is easy to see that historicism, if consistently carried through, carries over into extreme

---

[27] Edmund Husserl, "Philosophy as Rigorous Science," in *Phenomenology and the Crisis of Philosophy*, trans. Quentin Lauer, New York: Harper & Row, 1965.

sceptical subjectivism. The ideas of truth, theory, and science would then, like all ideas, lose their absolute validity. That an idea has validity would mean that it is a factual construction of spirit which is held as valid and which in its contingent validity determines thought. There would be no unqualified validity, or validity-in-itself, which is what it is even if no one has achieved it and though no historical humanity will ever achieve it. Thus too there would then be no validity to the principle of contradiction nor to any logic, which latter is nevertheless still in full vigor in our time. The result, perhaps, will be that the logical principles of noncontradiction will be transformed into their opposites.

Using both Kant's terminology and his absolutist intentions, Husserl attacked all forms of relativism and attempted to develop a *transcendental phenomenology*, in other words, a phenomenology that discovers the basic rules of all experience (just as he had discovered them for arithmetic and geometry before). Because these rules (or "ideal laws") were discovered to be essential, they were, Husserl concluded, the only rules possible. In Husserl as in Kant, the word *transcendental* means the basic and the only rules with which we "constitute" our world. (Husserl used the notion of "constitution" also, with much the same meaning that Kant did.) But what is *phenomenology*? It is the study of human consciousness. These essential rules of experience, in other words, were to be found in consciousness, not in a mysterious Platonic "world of Being" nor simply in our language. Consciousness itself, with the objects of its own constitution, becomes our new anchor. Starting from Descartes, Husserl suggests that we go back to that "subjective" starting point—and that we look again.

 FROM **The 1929 Paris Lectures**
BY **Edmund Husserl**[28]

The splintering of contemporary philosophy and its aimless activity makes us pause. Must this situation not be traced back to the fact that the motivations from which Descartes' meditations emanate have lost their original vitality? Is it not true that the only fruitful renaissance is one which reawakens these meditations, not in order to accept them, but to reveal the profound truth in the radicalism of a return to the *ego cogito* with the eternal values that reside therein?

. . .

We thus begin, everyone for himself and in himself, with the decision to disregard all our present knowledge. We do not give up Descartes' guiding goal of an absolute foundation for knowledge. At the beginning, however, to presuppose even the possibility of that goal would be prejudice. . . . Science demands proof *by reference to the things and facts themselves, as these given in actual experience and intuition*. Thus guided, we, the beginning philosophers, make it a rule to judge only by the evidence.

. . .

Here, specifically following Descartes, we make the great shift which, when properly carried out, leads to *transcendental subjectivity*. . . . Let us consider: as radically meditating philosophers we now have neither knowledge that is valid for us nor a world that exists for us. . . . However, whatever be the veracity of the claim to being made by phenomena, whether they represent reality or appearance, phenomena in themselves

---

28 Edmund Husserl, *The 1929 Paris Lectures*, trans. Peter Koestenbaum, Hague: Nijhoff, 1975. Reprinted with kind permission from Springer Science and Business Media.

cannot be disregarded as mere "nothing." On the contrary, it is precisely the phenomena themselves which, without exception, render possible for me the very existence of both reality and appearance. This epistemological abstention is still what it is: it includes the whole stream of experienced life and all its particulars, the appearances of objects, other people, cultural situations, etc. Nothing changes, except that I no longer accept the world simply as real; I no longer judge regarding the distinction between reality and appearance. . . . This ubiquitous detachment from any point of view regarding the objective world we term the *phenomenological epoché*. It is the methodology through which I come to understand myself as that ego and life of consciousness in which and through which the entire objective world exists for me, and is for me precisely as it is. . . . Through the phenomenological *epoché* the natural human ego, specifically my own, is reduced to the transcendental ego. This is the meaning of the phenomenological reduction.

- Why does Husserl think that the method of phenomenology is a form of rationalism?
- What does Husserl mean by "transcendental subjectivity"? How is it related to Descartes' project?
- How is phenomenology supposed to defeat relativism? How might it invite relativism?

Husserl's battle, from beginning to end, was a battle against relativism, against all of those philosophies that held that there can be different equally true or equally rational worldviews. And it must be said that his phenomenology, for all of its internal struggles, was immensely successful and still attracts the attention of a great many philosophers today. But phenomenology was not the solution to relativism. Husserl thought that phenomenology could be transcendental and prove that certain rules were basic and essential to all human thinking. But just as Kant opened the door to relativism with his view that we constitute our world, Husserl opened it wider with his view that a study of consciousness was the way to do philosophy. For were there not, his followers asked, many different forms of consciousness? (Thus returning to Hegel rather than Kant.) And phenomenology as it developed in France, rather than Germany, became the source of a new relativism.

H. Hermeneutics and Pragmatism: Relativism Reconsidered

Absolutism seems to deny the obvious fact that people are different and disagree, not only in superficial ways but in terms of their most basic beliefs. Relativism, on the other hand, seems to deny the obvious similarities among people and imply that we will never be able to understand one another—or find the truth—at all. One attempt to bridge the gap between dogmatic absolutism and solipsistic relativism is **hermeneutics**.

"Hermeneutics" is an old name for "interpretation," with an eye to getting at the Truth. For many centuries, this formidable word was applied exclusively to the interpretation of the Bible, with the aim of understanding the Word of God. Today, however, the term has a much broader meaning. It is often used in literary criticism to talk about the interpretation of texts—not only the Bible, but any text. But it is now used in philosophy too to refer to the discipline of interpreting and understanding the world, which becomes, in effect, our text, and different cultures' views of the world, which may seem initially to be mutually incommensurable.

The modern father of hermeneutics is the German "historicist" Wilhelm Dilthey, whom we encountered in the previous section. Dilthey came to realize that the methods of the physical sciences were not very successful when applied to the "human sciences," in part because history played such enormous importance in human life. He also realized that there was a very real danger in the Kantian attempt to overcome traditional philosophical distinctions between appearance and reality, subjectivity, and objective truth. While his historicism lent itself to relativism, Dilthey himself was vehemently antirelativist. The problem, he argued, was to develop a method for *understanding* human differences. But he believed that all of these were ultimately superficial and thus not incommensurable at all.

Contemporary hermeneutics is just this attempt to provide a way of understanding viewpoints other than our own. It is simply dogmatic to insist—as Kant and many other philosophers have insisted—that the structures of the human mind are everywhere the same and, consequently, that we all share a common basis of knowledge. But is it simple-minded, on the other hand, to insist that we are all different and have different truths, since there is at least enough overlap for us to understand that we do disagree. For example, the medievals saw God and the earth as the spiritual and spatial centers of the universe. How can a modern-day scientist understand them? Well, not just by dismissing their views as nonsense, nor can we sensibly say, "Well, they have their opinions and we have ours." Hermeneutics is just this attempt to step into someone else's shoes (but without taking off our own shoes first).

In the twentieth century, hermeneutics was turned into a powerful style of philosophizing by the German metaphysician **Martin Heidegger**. It was Heidegger, in his monumental book *Being and Time* (1928), who suggested that life is like a text, and the purpose of our lives is to understand that text. Heidegger was a student of Husserl and was thus a phenomenologist. But in his hermeneutical phenomenology he tries to "uncover" the hidden meanings in our experience. He rejects the scientific tone of Husserl's phenomenology and prefers to talk about the structures of life itself, including our profound sense of history, which defines human life.

The most important proponent of hermeneutics, however, is a student of Heidegger, **Hans-Georg Gadamer**. In fact, Gadamer is so wary of the fact that method—and not only the scientific method—may distort our understanding that he insists that hermeneutics must resist the temptation to become another method. It is rather the attempt to overcome methods, to dispense with the overemphasis on proofs and arguments and the quest for certainty and emphasize instead the shared understandings that we already have with one another. The substance of philosophy then becomes dialogue rather than individual phenomenology or abstract proofs. Interpretation thus becomes not an abstract function of the intellect but a process that permeates our every activity.

Gadamer's hermeneutics does not reject the notion of truth, but it does give up entirely the idea that there is a Truth wholly outside of us which we need a method (rationalism, empiricism, scientific psychology) to discover. Like the coherence theorist and the pragmatist, he gives up the idea of secure *foundations* for our knowledge—such as the raw experiences or "sense data" discussed by some empiricists, or the a priori principles defended by Kant. But where both the coherence theorist and the pragmatist tend to interpret truth as a function of the present—coherence of beliefs and workability, respectively—the hermeneuticist insists that truth must be understood *historically*, in terms of a *tradition*. Thus the philosophical tradition, ironically, has tended to ignore the importance of its own tradition and look for strictly eternal truths. Gadamer's hermeneutics hold rather that it is only within a tradition, and by looking at our tradition, that philosophical truth is possible at all. Does this mean that we must accept whatever our tradition may be, even if it is wrong? But what would it be, Gadamer asks, for a tradition to be wrong? We can criticize ourselves, of course, and that is just the point of hermeneutics. But does it mean that we must also justify ourselves and what we have always believed? "Do we need to justify," he asks rhetorically, "that which has always supported us?"

Hans-Georg Gadamer (1900–2002)

The leading German promoter of twentieth-century hermeneutics, the philosophical theory of interpretation.

Does relativism mean that there can be no truth? Does relativism apply only to philosophical views, not to *real* theories? Could there be *really* different views of the world–and different worlds? But does it even make sense to talk about relative truth, that is, a truth that is only "true for" one person or group and not another?

If such a phrase even makes sense, it must mean that a statement is true for a person or group by virtue of the scheme or conceptual framework they employ; thus it is true for a certain society that the witch doctor embodies the power of the devil, but true for another society that the powers of the so-called witch doctor are nothing but the combination of natural pharmaceuticals plus the power of suggestion. But we must not fall into the radical trap of Protagoras and claim that "man is the measure of all things"–if we are to continue using the word *truth* at all. A statement or a belief cannot be true just by virtue of its being believed, in other words, if there is no possibility that a person or a group can believe what is false (or, not believe some statement that is nevertheless true). Furthermore, as in hermeneutics, it is essential that we do not close off the possibility that one truth might be understandable– perhaps in different terms–by those who believe another, apparently contradictory truth. This would be to deny the possibility of cross-cultural communication–to cut people of different cultures off from each other completely.

> • What is hermeneutics? What role does history play in hermeneutical understanding of truth?

Hermeneutics has had a recent resurgence in American philosophy, particularly in discussions of relativism and multiculturalism. In the following essay, the contemporary American philosopher, **Richard Rorty**, who claimed a profound debt to hermeneutics, defends a vision of "solidarity"–which he contrasts with the traditional notion of "objectivity" and also associates with "pragmatism." His claim is that the

> Pragmatism–the notion that the truth is slowly discovered and confirmed through experiment–was first advanced in the work of C. S. Peirce. In the nineteenth century and early twentieth century, Peirce argued that science provided a model for how philosophers should think of–and rethink–the notion of truth.

pragmatic theory of truth, which we outlined previously, is essentially the theory that truth has a moral standard–the solidarity of a community–rather than a metaphysical one–objectivity. In other words, he claims that pragmatism defines "truth" as "what it is morally best for our community to believe," and using this definition, he can claim that it is morally best for us to believe in pragmatism.

FROM **"Solidarity or Objectivity?"** BY **Richard Rorty**[29]

There are two principal ways in which reflective human beings try, by placing their lives in a larger context, to give sense to those lives. The first is by telling the story of their contribution to a community. This community may be the actual historical one in which they live, or another actual one, distant in time and place, or a quite imaginary one, consisting perhaps of a dozen heroes and heroines selected from history or fiction or both. The second way is to describe themselves as standing in immediate relation to a nonhuman reality. This relation is immediate in the sense that it does not derive from a relation between such a reality and their tribe, or their

[29] Richard Rorty, "Solidarity or Objectivity?" from *Philosophical Papers, Vol. 1: Objectivity, Relativism, and Truth*. Reprinted with the permission of Cambridge University Press.

FIG. 3.35 American pragmatist philosopher and literary theorist Richard Rorty.
(© Kathleen M. Higgins)

Richard Rorty (1931-2007)

American philosopher. Rorty was one of the most dynamic and diverse thinkers in twentieth-century American philosophy, defending his own brand of pragmatism. Rorty challenged the idea of the mind as the "mirror of nature," defending the idea that knowledge is situated in social practice and that we are in no position to know for sure that our beliefs are really true. At best we can ascertain that they meet our society's current standards for acceptance. As a consequence, philosophy amounts to an on-going, never-ending conversation.

nation, or their imagined band of comrades. I shall say that stories of the former kind exemplify the desire for solidarity, and that stories of the latter kind exemplify the desire for objectivity. Insofar as a person is seeking solidarity, he or she does not ask about the relation between the practices of the chosen community and something outside that community. Insofar as he seeks objectivity, he distances himself from the actual persons around him not by thinking of himself as a member of some other real or imaginary group, but rather by attaching himself to something which can be described without reference to any particular human beings.

. . .

Those who wish to ground solidarity in objectivity—call them "realists"—have to construe truth as correspondence to reality. So they must construct a metaphysics which has room for a special relation between beliefs and objects which will differentiate true from false beliefs. They also must argue that there are procedures of justification of belief which are natural and not merely local. So they must construct an epistemology which has room for a kind of justification which is not merely social but natural, springing from human nature itself, and made possible by a link between that part of nature and the rest of nature. On their view, the various procedures which are thought of as providing rational justification by one or another culture may or may not really *be* rational. For to be truly rational, procedures of justification *must* lead to the truth, to correspondence to reality, to the intrinsic nature of things.

By contrast, those who wish to reduce objectivity to solidarity—call them "pragmatists"—do not require either a metaphysics or an epistemology. They view truth as, in William James' phrase, what it is good for *us* to believe. So they do not need an account of a relation between beliefs and objects called "correspondence," nor an account of human cognitive abilities which ensures that our species is capable of entering into that relation. They see the gap between truth and justification not as something to be bridged by isolating a natural and transcultural sort of rationality which can be used to criticize certain cultures and praise others, but simply as the gap between the actual good and the possible better. From a pragmatist point of view, to say that what is rational for us now to believe may not be *true*, is simply to say that somebody may have come up with a better idea. It is to say that there is always room for improved belief, since new evidence, or new hypotheses, or a whole new vocabulary, may come along. For pragmatists, the desire for objectivity is not the desire to escape the limitations of one's community, but simply the desire for as much intersubjective agreement as possible, the desire to extend the reference of "us" as far as we can. Insofar as pragmatists make a distinction between topics on which such agreement is relatively easy to get and topics on which agreement is relatively hard to get.

"Relativism" is the traditional epithet applied to pragmatism by realists. Three different views are commonly referred to by this name. The first is the view that every belief is as good as every other. The second is the view that "true" is an equivocal term, having as many meanings as there are procedures of justification. The third is the view that there is nothing to be said about either truth or rationality apart from descriptions of the familiar procedures of justification which a given society—*ours*—uses in one or another area of inquiry. The pragmatist holds the ethnocentric third view. But he does not hold the self-refuting first view, nor the eccentric second view. He thinks that his views are better than the realists, but he does not think that his views correspond to the nature of things. He thinks that the very flexibility of the word "true"—the fact that it is merely an expression of commendation—insures its univocity. The term "true," on his account, means the same in all cultures, just as equally flexible terms like "here," "there," "good," "bad," "you," and "me" mean the same in all cultures. But the identity of meaning is, of course, compatible with diversity of reference, and with diversity of procedures for assigning the terms. So he feels free to use the term "true" as a general term of commendation in the same way as his realist opponent does—and in particular to use it to commend his own view.

However, it is not clear why "relativist" should be thought an appropriate term for the ethnocentric third view, the one which the pragmatist *does* hold. For the pragmatist is not holding a positive theory which says that something is relative to something else. He is, instead, making the purely *negative* point that we should drop the traditional distinction between knowledge and opinion, construed as the distinction between truth as correspondence to reality and truth as a commendatory term for well-justified beliefs. The reason that the realist calls this negative claim "relativistic" is that he cannot believe that anybody would seriously deny that truth has an intrinsic nature. So when the pragmatist says that there is nothing to be said about truth save that each of us will commend as true those beliefs which he or she finds good to believe, the realist is inclined to interpret this as one more positive theory about the nature of truth: a theory according to which truth is simply the contemporary opinion of a chosen individual or group. Such a theory would, of course, be self-refuting. But the pragmatist does not have a theory of truth, much less a relativistic one. As a partisan of solidarity, his account of the value of cooperative human inquiry has only an ethical base, not an epistemological or metaphysical one. Not having *any* epistemology, *a fortiori* he does not have a relativistic one.

· · ·

[T]he question is not about how to define words like "truth" or "rationality" or "knowledge" or "philosophy," but about what self-image our society should have of itself. The ritual invocation of the "need to avoid relativism" is most comprehensible as an expression of the need to preserve certain habits of contemporary European life. These are the habits nurtured by the Enlightenment, and justified by it in terms of an appeal of Reason, conceived as a transcultural human ability to correspond to reality, a faculty whose possession and use is demonstrated by obedience to explicit criteria. So the real question about relativism is whether these same habits of intellectual, social, and political life can be justified by a conception of rationality as criterionless muddling through, and by a pragmatist conception of truth.

I think that the answer to this question is that the pragmatist cannot justify these habits without circularity, but then neither can the realist. The pragmatists' justification of toleration, free inquiry, and the quest for undistorted communication can only take the form of a comparison between societies which exemplify these habits and those which do not, leading up to the suggestion that nobody who has experienced both would prefer the latter. It is exemplified by Winston

> "The question is not about how to define words like 'truth' or 'rationality' or 'knowledge' or 'philosophy,' but about what self-image our society should have of itself."
>
> – RICHARD RORTY

Churchill's defense of democracy as the worst form of government imaginable, except for all the others which have been tried so far.

. . .

My suggestion that the desire for objectivity is in part a disguised form of the fear of the death of our community echoes Nietzsche's charge that the philosophical tradition which stems from Plato is an attempt to avoid facing up to contingency, to escape from time and chance. Nietzsche thought that realism was to be condemned not only by arguments from its theoretical incoherence, the sort of argument we find in Putnam and Davidson, but also on practical, pragmatic grounds. Nietzsche thought that the test of human character was the ability to live with the thought that there was no convergence. He wanted us to be able to think of truth as:

a mobile army of metaphors, metonyms, and anthromorphisms—in short a sum of human relations, which have been enhanced, transposed, and embellished poetically and rhetorically and which after long use seem firm, canonical, and obligatory to a people.

Nietzsche hoped that eventually there might be human beings who could and did think of truth in this way, but who still liked themselves, who saw themselves as *good* people for whom solidarity was *enough*.

I think that pragmatism's attack on the various structure-content distinctions which buttress the realist's notion of objectivity can best be seen as an attempt to let us think of truth in this Nietzschean way, as entirely a matter of solidarity. That is why I think we need to say, despite Putnam, that "there is only the dialogue," only *us*, and to throw out the last residues of the notion of "transcultural rationality." But this should not lead us to repudiate, as Nietzsche sometimes did, the elements in our movable host which embody the ideas of Socratic conversation, Christian fellowship, and Enlightenment science. Nietzsche ran together his diagnosis of philosophical realism as an expression of fear and resentment with his own resentful idiosyncratic idealizations of silence, solitude, and violence. Post-Nietzschean thinkers like Adorno and Heidegger and Foucault have run together Nietzsche's criticisms of the metaphysical tradition on the one hand with his criticisms of bourgeois civility, of Christian love, and of the nineteenth century's hope that science would make the world a better place to live, on the other. I do not think that there is any interesting connection between these two sets of criticisms. Pragmatism seems to me, as I have said, a philosophy of solidarity rather than of despair. From this point of view, Socrates' turn away from the gods, Christianity's turn from an Omnipotent Creator to the man who suffered on the Cross, and the Baconian turn from science as contemplation of eternal truth to science as instrument of social progress, can be seen as so many preparations for the act of social faith which is suggested by a Nietzschean view of truth.

The best argument we partisans of solidarity have against the realistic partisans of objectivity is Nietzsche's argument that the traditional Western metaphysico-epistemological way of firming up our habits simply isn't working anymore. It isn't doing its job. It has become as transparent a device as the postulation of deities who turn out, by a happy coincidence, to have chosen *us* as their people. So the pragmatist suggestion that we substitute a "merely" ethical foundation for our sense of community—or, better, that we think of our sense of community as having no foundation except shared hope and the trust created by such sharing—is put forward on practical grounds. It is *not* put forward as a corollary of a metaphysical claim that the objects in the world contain no intrinsically action-guiding properties, nor of an epistemological claim that we lack a faculty of moral sense, nor of a semantic claim that truth is reducible to justification.

———

Rorty makes the point that our metaphysical theory of "truth" has political overtones. The belief that there is one, single, truth can lead to condescension and disrespect toward people who believe differently from oneself. Only, however, if the absolutist believes, in addition to his or her absolutism, that he or she or his or her culture is closer to that one truth than are others. Need the absolutist always think that the objective truth is his or her sole dominion? This seems to cut off the possibility of communication and learning between cultures.

> • What is the difference between "objectivity" and "solidarity" according to Rorty? Why does Rorty favor "solidarity"?

Is solidarity *"enough"*? In the following reading, Japanese philosopher Isamu Nagami considers the communication between individuals and cultures, which he calls "intersubjectivity," and suggests that neither "solidarity" nor "objectivity" is politically "enough." He employs hermeneutics to appreciate the complexities of not only cross-cultural but also intracultural understanding.

FROM "Cultural Gaps: Why Do We Misunderstand?" BY Isamu Nagami[30]

A well-known Japanese psychologist, Takeo Doi, expressed his frustration and puzzlement with American ways of life in his book, *The Anatomy of Dependence:*

> *From time to time I began to feel an awkwardness arising from the difference between my ways of thinking and feeling and those of my hosts (that is, Americans). For example, not long after my arrival in America I visited the house of someone to whom I had been introduced by a Japanese acquaintance, and was talking to him when he asked me, "Are you hungry? We have some ice cream if you'd like it." As I remember, I was rather hungry, but finding myself asked point-blank if I was hungry by someone whom I was visiting for the first time, I could not bring myself to admit it, and ended by denying the suggestion. I probably cherished a mild hope that he would press me again; but my host, disappointingly, said "I see" with no further ado, leaving me regretting that I had not replied more honestly. And I found myself thinking that a Japanese would almost never ask a stranger unceremoniously if he was hungry, but would produce something to give him without asking.*

Those who have lived in foreign countries have experienced more or less the sort of cultural shock Doi expressed so well. These kinds of intercultural experiences have led many thinkers to probe into the core elements of culture for comparative study. In Japan, for

Isamu Nagami (1941–)

A philosopher of religion. He has served as president of Nagoya Ryujo College in Aichi, Japan.

---

[30] Isamu Nagami, "Cultural Gaps: Why Do We Misunderstand?" from *Liberation Ethics: Essays in Religious and Social Ethics in Honor of Gibson Winter*, ed. Charles Amjad-Ali and W. Alvin Pitcher. Copyright © 1985. Reprinted by permission of the Center for the Scientific Study of Religion.

example, we find many popular writers who explain the difference between Japanese culture and that of the Western nations including the U.S.A. in terms of group orientation and individual identity. The thesis for this type of argument is that while Japanese behavior in general can be explained by orientation within the group, Americans behave on the basis of individual freedom. There is no doubt that this reveals a meaningful comparison between the two cultures to those who have journalistic interests. But if we start by inquiring into various modalities of the experiential world of daily life in culture, we find we cannot follow the above approach primarily for three reasons. (1) Those who accept the group versus individual thesis tend to explain every cultural phenomenon in terms of this and as a result they conceal many other rich possibilities which every culture may contain. (2) Certain features are common to all social worlds. In this respect every culture can share a kind of symbolic common denominator through which we can compare differences. Yet, this approach of contrast ignores the universality in human existence. (3) The very fact that people understand and describe different cultures reveals a kind of cultural ethos in which their thinking is embedded. That is to say, their ways of thinking are inescapably and necessarily cultural. This thought process is not self-critically oriented in the sense that it is not able to show its historico-cultural character and, therefore, tends to be ideological.

The most striking characteristic of these approaches is based on their inability to provide any critical perspective and at the same time on a sort of false legitimacy in our actual human life. Thus it is crucial for us to find another way to understand culture in its most sensible manners. In this respect, we would propose a method of phenomenological reflection, for phenomenology can reveal the various dimensions of human life which, I believe, symbolize culture and thereby can help us to overcome the aforementioned difficulties.

. . .

INTERSUBJECTIVITY, LANGUAGE AND TAKEN-FOR-GRANTEDNESS

When, for instance a boy and his mother see a cedar, she is most likely to call it a tree rather than a cedar. After a while if he happens to see an oak tree and asks her "What's that?" she will call it a tree. At that time he might be very confused with

FIG. 3.36 A tree is both a living thing and the source of wood. The Japanese word conveys this fact; in English, we have two different words. Does this tell us something about differences in how we think?
(© The Trustees of the British Museum / Art Resource, NY)

that term simply because there is a difference between a cedar and an oak and yet they partake of the same name, tree. But gradually he realizes that the word or sound "tree" implies a certain group of characteristics which belong to the same category. It is clear that a word "tree" signifies an abstract expression in the sense that it represents certain characteristics and ignores others such as those that belong to the category "flower." In this respect, concreteness in common sense is not concrete in reality, but rather abstract. The reason why people mistake abstract expressions for concrete reality is due to the fact that they unconsciously accept the expressions as taken-for-granted, rooted in a specific-temporal world. Hence some concrete meanings in one culture are not concrete but very enigmatic, non-concrete expressions in another. In English, people distinguish tree from parts of tree which are used for architectural and other purposes, that is "wood." But in Japanese we don't do so. We express the idea of tree and wood both with one term, *Ki*. Yet, the dictionary usually describes *Ki* as having the same meaning as tree. Languages also differ in their built-in grammatical signals, that is in semantics, syntax and phonetics. In English people are very conscious of specifying the number of people involved in what they are discussing. But in Japanese the contrary is often true. Here we can see that the very nature of language through which we comprehend the world and understand ourselves inevitably involves us in the cultural context of language. Hence languages differ immensely from one another not only in pronunciation, vocabulary and grammar, but also in the way they recognize certain things and ignore others, thereby reflecting the society and culture they serve. Experience and language are reciprocal in the sense that human beings can experience outside reality only in terms of the meanings disclosed by language. Human beings are thrown into language worlds in which they learn to identify things as well as to understand reality. In this sense it is obvious that our ways of understanding and interpreting reality are already conditioned by the socially given knowledge.

If we accept that our knowledge is socially given, it seems that we are caught in the relativistic position of suggesting that there is no such thing as objectivity. Hence, we may ask a further question: How can we affirm something as an objective entity on which everybody can agree? In this question we again need to reflect on what I will call the intersubjective world which language as well as our everyday life thinking always presupposes. Situationally we unconsciously put ourselves as the center of spatio-temporal coordinates in the world. This means that I usually see the position I occupy as "here," distinguished from "there" taken by a fellow human being. Yet we can interchange our positions freely, as if we can place ourselves in the other's situation. A saying such as "Do unto others as you would have them do unto you," implies this interchangeability. This interchangeability is possible because there is an intersubjectively acknowledged spatio-temporal world in which both s/he and I are embedded and therefore can exchange, as well as share, our positions in essentially the same fashion with essentially the same possibilities and consequences. The concept of intersubjectivity signifies this intersubjectively acknowledged spatio-temporal world. Each socio-cultural environment presupposes an intersubjective world which historically develops various conceptions of the world as symbolized in language. Those who have been living in American society share various typicalities as a horizon of familiarity and of unquestioned pre-experience. Through the use of these we can converse with one another and understand the objects of the world as the reality of the taken-for-granted. The meanings of words such as tree or flower are simply taken for granted and therefore are self-evident. In other words, we are speaking, acting and understanding within an intersubjective world in which we share our perspectives through knowledge gained by previous experience. The fact that I am able to express my thinking to a fellow human being already presupposes an intersubjective world in which both s/he and I are embedded and, therefore, s/he can share my thinking and I hers/his. This sharing is the very basis with which we can affirm objective reality for we are able to identify an entity within the same perspective. Understanding, hence, always presupposes a common social heritage of an intersubjective world with the participation of Mystery. It is in this intersubjectivity that we can understand our ways of perceiving outside reality as the objective one.

THE PROBLEM OF INTERSUBJECTIVITY

Up till this point in our discussion, intersubjectivity has not seemed to present a crucial problem to our cultural concerns. However, when we consider cases in which there are two distinctive groups responding differently according to their own intersubjective worlds, the problem of intersubjectivity can be seen. In order to reveal this problem, let me follow Alfred Schutz's notion of "in-group" and "out-group." The in-group, as defined by Schutz, are those who accept the ready-made standardized scheme of a socio-cultural environment, that is, an intersubjective world as an unquestioned and unquestionable system of knowledge. For them the system of knowledge in everyday life situation as manifested in language, tradition, habits and various social systems appears to have sufficient coherence, clarity and consistency. In contrast those who stand outside of that world are defined as the out-group. Members of the out-group sometimes feel that what is taken-for-granted by the in-group is actually an ambiguous and enigmatic reality since the out-group have not had any sharing experience with the in-group's historical traditions. Suppose, for instance, that an American who has never lived in any foreign country has to live in Japan, without first learning about the culture or studying the language, and to work at a Japanese factory in a Japanese style. Being astonished by the Japanese employee's daily singing of the company's song or quoting the company's slogan in a militaristic manner, s/he would as a result have considerable difficulty in understanding the Japanese way of life simply because s/he does not share his/her intersubjective world with that of the Japanese. The self-evidence of everyday life for the members of an in-group may not be self-evident for those of the out-group. It is this gap that creates misunderstandings.

I explained a sharing world of an in-group in distinction to that of out-groups. Actually this characterization does not really indicate the true meaning of sharing because the sharing world of an in-group eventually destroys the sharing world in the global sense. A sharing world of an in-group becomes a kind of confinement in which we tend to glorify ourselves as a sharing people, as exemplified in Germany and Japan during the Second World War. As long as we understand "sharing a world" in terms of in-group and out-group, we in a sense validate a dualism of the human condition in which in-group stands apart from out-group. This does not really signify the true meaning of sharing. To share various human concerns in the world means not to differentiate in-group from out-group, but to take part in every possible activity in the world. This participation can create a sort of "fusion of horizons" in which the differences between in-group and out-group eventually disappear, creating a new horizon of understanding which involves a broadening of the present horizon.

FUSION OF HORIZON: OPENNESS AND LISTENING

The encounter between in-group and out-group usually creates tension. How can we overcome this tension and at the same time attain a respectful understanding of each other, allowing every individual and every culture to their own dignity? Indeed this is an important question. Let us recall Gadamer's attempt to explain the encounter between text and interpreter in his *magnum opus, Truth and Method*, for his analysis is helpful in understanding the question of the encounter between in-group and out-group. He states:

> The concept of the 'horizon' suggests itself because it expresses the wide, superior vision that the person who is seeking to understand must have. To acquire a horizon means that one learns to look beyond what is close at hand—not in order to look away from it, but to see it better within a larger whole and in truer proportion.

"To acquire a horizon means that one learns to look beyond what is close at hand." What does that mean? It means that we need to learn to understand the out-group's own dignity enabling them to disclose their true nature. This requires from us an openness towards out-groups, a willingness to listen to what the members of out-groups would say. Earlier I discussed the example of the notions of tree and *Ki;* so long as we are caught up within the taken-for-grantedness of our notions in language, we will never be able to understand the real meanings of out-groups' expressions. But if we are able to admit that our understanding is historically conditioned and therefore to allow ourselves to be open to what an out-group says, then a new horizon between us may come into being in the sense that everybody will become able to realize the limitedness of both tree and *Ki* in a larger context. Openness and listening are keys to understanding other cultures as well as other human beings. It is true that an understanding of other cultures involves issues more complex than the difference between tree and *Ki.* Yet, if we lose a sense of listening and openness, there is no possibility for us to understand different cultures and people.

At present we are confronted by the nuclear crisis. This came about because we lost the attitude of listening to others, because we forgot that human beings are rooted in the common destiny of the world, because we manipulated others at our disposal, and because we lost the original meaning of the Biblical story about human beings on earth: human beings were created to bring to light and to protect the world in the context of relationships within which different people and things belong together with mutual dependency.

In the question of fusion of horizons between different cultures and people, language reveals very mysterious powers. Since every language is tied up to a particular historical setting, various languages differ from one another. Language is also the medium through which human beings are able to identify various historico-cultural phenomena in their settings. Hence, historico-cultural differences can be understood as differences among languages. In this regard, language always discloses particular characteristics of its own historico-cultural setting.

But how can we mediate these differences of language? Clearly it is also through language that differences can be fused or compared. In this respect, language discloses the universal dimension through which differences can be overcome. It is true that the English language is different from Japanese. But if English discloses totally different characteristics from Japanese, is it possible for any Japanese to understand the various meanings of English? The very fact that I can translate different English expressions into Japanese already presupposes that there are universally shared meanings between the two languages. Thus language discloses not only particular modes of being, but also the universal dimensions of our existence.

Language, furthermore, has the immanently transcending power by which I mean that language is able to overcome its own limited meaning in its historical

"Openness and listening are keys to understanding other cultures as well as other human beings."

– ISAMU NAGAMI

condition. Here, paradoxically speaking, our fateful situation is not fateful when we reflect on, and open ourselves to, the fatefulness of our existence. When I say that the tree of the English language is different from the *Ki* of Japanese, I note that the meanings of tree and *Ki* are limited. Yet, in so pointing out, language can open much larger possibilities than those of tree and *Ki*. Because any society signifies linguistically its historical heritage in which human relationality dwells, human relationships, too, disclose particular modes of being as well as universality. Human relationality contains something common to all humanity. Everywhere we find language, cultural objects, playthings for children, family life through which human beings live and celebrate such great events of life as birth, initiation, marriage and death. These are given universally. Human beings are different and yet we share various dimensions of human existence as universally shared meanings. It is in this human sharing that we can appreciate and understand different people.

We cannot escape the "taken-for-grantedness" of our world. We are fatefully thrown into that world where we must find meanings for our existence. It is impossible for us to have meaningful dialogue with others if we do not take our language for granted. For example, it is impossible for us to bring our sick baby to a doctor if we do not take some medical knowledge for granted. In this regard "taken-for-grantedness" discloses appreciative human meanings in addition to its ideological dimensions. One of the fundamental mistakes utopian theorists often make is to assume that they themselves are the vanguard as they claim *a-priori* powers to transcend the ideological power of culture. But, in so doing, they themselves become ideological in the sense that they negate the ultimate human condition: human beings are historical beings who disclose a fateful as well as a transformative mode of life and thought. It seems to me that every human being at certain points has to share in the ideological power of existence. We are, in a sense, living within original sin. However, this does not mean that we cannot transcend various modes of ideological power in our respective cultures. We are living in a constant transformative process within the horizon of encounters between different people. If we are open and responsive to other people in dialogue, then Mystery can lead humans to learn to trust and find a way of reconciling the differences of culture and existence. This awareness opens up much richer possibilities of shaping various modes of our existence in more meaningful ways. The genuine work of education, it seems to me, is to provide and teach this dialogical-critical ability to human beings so that we can create and develop meaningful societies in a global sense.

I. The Analytic Turn

At the end of the nineteenth and the beginning of the twentieth centuries, especially in England, philosophers began to suspect that many philosophical problems were the consequence of confusions and imperfections in our language. A "purely logical language" was sought (although not found) in mathematics. A new emphasis emerged, focusing on conceptual analysis: the so-called analytic turn. Increasingly philosophers in the twentieth century, especially in England and the United States, sought to make their language and arguments as clear and logically transparent as possible. One of the great founders of this movement was the British philosopher Bertrand Russell, who here argues for the "commonsense" correspondence theory of truth.

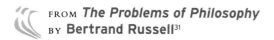

FROM *The Problems of Philosophy*
BY **Bertrand Russell**[31]

Our knowledge of truths, unlike our knowledge of things, has an opposite, namely *error*. So far as things are concerned, we may know them or not know them, but there is no positive state of mind which can be described as erroneous knowledge of things, so long, at any rate, as we confine ourselves to knowledge by acquaintance. Whatever we are acquainted with must be something: we may draw wrong inference from our acquaintance, but the acquaintance itself cannot be deceptive. Thus there is no dualism as regards acquaintance. But as regards knowledge of truths, there is a dualism. We may believe what is false as well as what is true. We know that on very many subjects different people hold different and incompatible opinions: hence some beliefs must be erroneous. Since erroneous beliefs are often held just as strongly as true beliefs, it becomes a difficult question how they are to be distinguished from true beliefs. How are we to know, in a given case, that our belief is not erroneous? That is a question of the very greatest difficulty, to which no completely satisfactory answer is possible. There is, however, a preliminary question which is rather less difficult, and that is: What do we *mean* by truth and falsehood? It is this preliminary question which is to be considered in this chapter. . . .

. . . We are not asking how we can know whether a belief is true or false: we are asking what is meant by the question whether a belief is true or false. It is to be hoped that a clear answer to this question may help us to obtain an answer to the question what beliefs are true, but for the present we ask only "What is truth?" and "What is falsehood?" not "What beliefs are true?" and "What beliefs are false?" It is very important to keep these different questions entirely separate, since any confusion between them is sure to produce an answer which is not really applicable to either.

There are three points to observe in the attempt to discover the nature of truth, three requisites which any theory must fulfill.

(1) Our theory of truth must be such as to admit of its opposite, falsehood. A good many philosophers have failed adequately to satisfy this condition: they have constructed theories according to which all our thinking ought to have been true, and have then had the greatest difficulty in finding a place for falsehood. In this respect our theory of belief must differ from our theory of acquaintance, since in the case of acquaintance it was not necessary to take account of any opposite.

(2) It seems fairly evident that if there were no beliefs there could be no falsehood, and no truth either, in the sense in which truth is correlative to falsehood. If we imagine a world of mere matter, there would be no room for falsehood in such a world, and although it would contain what may be called "facts," it would not contain any truths, in the sense in which truths are things of the same kind as falsehoods. In fact, truth and falsehood are properties of beliefs and statements: hence a world of mere matter, since it would contain no beliefs or statements, would also contain no truth or falsehood.

(3) But, as against what we have just said, it is to be observed that the truth or falsehood of a belief always depends upon something which lies outside the belief itself. If I believe that Charles I died on the scaffold, I believe truly, not because of any intrinsic

31 From Bertrand Russell, *The Problems of Philosophy* (Oxford: Oxford University Press, 1912). Reprinted by permission of Oxford University Press.

quality of my belief, which could be discovered by merely examining the belief, but because of an historical event which happened two and a half centuries ago. If I believe that Charles I died in his bed, I believe falsely: no degree of vividness in my belief, or of care in arriving at it, prevents it from being false, again because of what happened long ago, and not because of any intrinsic property of my belief. Hence, although truth and falsehood are properties of beliefs, they are properties dependent upon the relations of the beliefs to other things, not upon any internal quality of the beliefs.

The third of the above requisites leads us to adopt the view—which has on the whole been commonest among philosophers—that truth consists in some form of correspondence between belief and fact. It is, however, by no means an easy matter to discover a form of correspondence to which there are no irrefutable objections. By this partly—and partly by the feeling that, if truth consists in a correspondence of thought with something outside thought, thought can never know when truth has been attained—many philosophers have been led to try to find some definition of truth which shall not consist in relation to something wholly outside belief. The most important attempt at a definition of this sort is the theory that truth consists in *coherence*. It is said that the mark of falsehood is failure to cohere in the body of our beliefs, and that it is the essence of a truth to form part of the completely rounded system which is The Truth.

There is, however, a great difficulty in this view, or rather two great difficulties. The first is that there is no reason to suppose that only *one* coherent body of beliefs is possible. It may be that, with sufficient imagination, a novelist might invent a past for the world that would perfectly fit on to what we know, and yet be quite different from the real past. In more scientific matters, it is certain that there are often two or more hypotheses which account for all the known facts on some subject, and although, in such cases, men of science endeavor to find facts which will rule out all the hypotheses except one, there is no reason why they should always succeed.

In philosophy, again, it seems not uncommon for two rival hypotheses to be both able to account for all the facts. Thus, for example, it is possible that life is one long dream, and that the outer world has only that degree of reality that the objects of dreams have; but although such a view does not seem inconsistent with known facts, there is no reason to prefer it to the common-sense view, according to which other people and things do really exist. Thus coherence as the definition of truth fails because there is no proof that there can be only one coherent system.

The other objection to this definition of truth is that it assumes the meaning of "coherence" known, whereas, in fact, "coherence" presupposes the truth of the laws of logic. Two propositions are coherent when both may be true, and are incoherent when one at least must be false. Now in order to know whether two propositions can both be true, we must know such truths as the law of contradiction. For example, the two propositions "this tree is a beech" and "this tree is not a beech," are not coherent, because of the law of contradiction. But if the law of contradiction itself were subjected to the test of coherence, we should find that, if we choose to suppose it false, nothing will any longer be incoherent with anything else. Thus the laws of logic supply the skeleton or framework within which the test of coherence applies, and they themselves cannot be established by this test.

For the above two reasons, coherence cannot be accepted as giving the *meaning* of truth, though it is often a most important *test* of truth after a certain amount of truth has become known.

Hence we are driven back to *correspondence with fact* as constituting the nature of truth. It remains to define precisely what we mean by "fact," and what is the nature of the correspondence which must subsist between belief and fact, in order that belief may be true.

In accordance with our three requisites, we have to seek a theory of truth which (1) allows truth to have an opposite, namely falsehood, (2) makes truth a property of beliefs, but (3) makes it a property wholly dependent upon the relation of the beliefs to outside things.

The necessity of allowing for falsehood makes it impossible to regard belief as a relation of the mind to a single object, which could be said to be what is believed. If belief were so regarded, we should find that, like acquaintance, it would not admit of the opposition of truth and falsehood, but would have to be always true. This may be made clear by examples. Othello believes falsely that Desdemona loves Cassio. We cannot say that this belief consists in a relation to a single object, "Desdemona's love for Cassio," for if there were such an object, the belief would be true. There is in fact no such object, and therefore Othello cannot have any relation to such an object. Hence his belief cannot possibly consist in a relation to this object.

It might be said that his belief is a relation to a different object, namely "that Desdemona loves Cassio"; but it is almost as difficult to suppose that there is such an object as this, when Desdemona does not love Cassio, as it was to suppose that there is "Desdemona's love for Cassio." Hence it will be better to seek for a theory of belief which does not make it consist in a relation of the mind to a single object.

It is common to think of relations as though they always held between *two* terms, but in fact this is not always the case. Some relations demand three terms, some four, and so on. Take, for instance, the relation "between." So long as only two terms come in, the relation "between" is impossible: three terms are the smallest number that render it possible. York is between London and Edinburgh; but if London and Edinburgh were the only places in the world, there could be nothing which was between one place and another. Similarly *jealousy* requires three people: there can be no such relation that does not involve three at least. Such a position as "A wishes B to promote C's marriage with D" involves a relation of four terms; that is to say, A and B and C and D all come in, and the relation involved cannot be expressed otherwise than in a form involving all four. Instances might be multiplied indefinitely, but enough has been said to show that there are relations which require more than two terms before they can occur.

The relation involved in *judging* or *believing* must, if falsehood is to be duly allowed for, be taken to be a relation between several terms, not between two. When Othello believes that Desdemona loves Cassio, he must not have before his mind a single object, "Desdemona's love for Cassio," or "that Desdemona loves Cassio," for that would require that there should be objective falsehoods, which subsist independently of any minds; and this, though not logically refutable, is a theory to be avoided if possible. Thus it is easier to account for falsehood if we take judgment to be a relation in which the mind and the various objects concerned all occur severally; that is to say, Desdemona and loving and Cassio must all be terms in the relation which subsists when Othello believes that Desdemona loves Cassio. This relation, therefore, is a relation of four terms, since Othello also is one of the terms of the relation. When we say that it is a relation of four terms, we do not mean that Othello has a certain relation to Desdemona, and has the same relation to loving and also to Cassio. This may be true of some other relation than believing; but believing, plainly, is not a relation which Othello has to *each* of the three terms concerned, but to *all* of them together: there is only one example of the relation of believing involved, but this one example knits together four terms. Thus the actual occurrence, at the moment when Othello is entertaining his belief, is that the relation called "believing" is knitting together into one complex whole the four terms Othello, Desdemona, loving, and Cassio. What is called belief or judgment is nothing but this relation of believing or judging, which relates a mind to several things other than itself. An *act* of belief or of judgment is the occurrence between certain terms at some particular time, of the relation of believing or judging.

We are now in a position to understand what it is that distinguishes a true judgment from a false one. For this purpose we will adopt certain definitions. In every act of judgment there is a mind which judges, and there are terms concerning which it judges. We will call the mind the *subject* in the judgment, and the remaining terms the *objects*. Thus, when Othello judges that Desdemona loves Cassio, Othello is the subject, while the objects are Desdemona and loving and Cassio. The subject and the objects together are called the *constituents* of the judgment. It will be observed that the relation of judging has what is called a "sense" or "direction." We may say, metaphorically, that it puts its objects in a certain *order*, which we may indicate by means of the order of the words in the sentence. (In an inflected language, the same thing will be indicated by inflections, e.g., by the difference between nominative and accusative.) Othello's judgment that Cassio loves Desdemona differs from his judgment that Desdemona loves Cassio, in spite of the fact that it consists of the same constituents, because the relation of judging places the constituents in a different order in the two cases. Similarly, if Cassio judges that Desdemona loves Othello, the constituents of the judgment are still the same, but their order is different. This property of having a "sense" or "direction" is one which the relation of judging shares with all other relations. The "sense" of relations is the ultimate source of order and series and a host of mathematical concepts; but we need not concern ourselves further with this aspect.

We spoke of the relation called "judging" or "believing" as knitting together into one complex whole the subject and the objects. In this respect, judging is exactly like every other relation. Whenever a relation holds between two or more terms, it unites the terms into a complex whole. If Othello loves Desdemona, there is such a complex whole as "Othello's love for Desdemona." The terms united by the relation may be themselves complex, or may be simple, but the whole which results from their being united must be complex. Wherever there is a relation which relates certain terms, there is a complex object formed of the union of those terms; and conversely, wherever there is a complex object, there is a relation which relates its constituents. When an act of believing occurs, there is a complex, in which "believing" is the uniting relation, and subject and objects are arranged in a certain order by the "sense" of the relation of believing. Among the objects, as we saw in considering "Othello believes that Desdemona loves Cassio," one must be a relation—in this instance, the relation "loving." But this relation, as it occurs in the act of believing, is not the relation which creates the unity of the complex whole consisting of the subject and the objects. The relation "loving," as it occurs in the act of believing, is one of the objects—it is a brick in the structure, not the cement. The cement is the relation "believing." When the belief is *true*, there is another complex unity, in which the relation which was one of the objects of the belief relates the other objects. Thus, e.g., if Othello believes *truly* that Desdemona loves Cassio, then there is a complex unity, "Desdemona's love for Cassio," which is composed exclusively of the *objects* of the belief, in the same order as they had in the belief, with the relation which was one of the objects occurring now as the cement that binds together the other objects of the belief. On the other hand, when a belief is *false*, there is no such complex unity composed only of the objects of the belief. If Othello believes *falsely* that Desdemona loves Cassio, then there is no such complex unity as "Desdemona's love for Cassio."

Thus a belief is *true* when it *corresponds* to a certain associated complex, and *false* when it does not. Assuming, for the sake of definiteness, that the objects of the belief are two terms and a relation, the terms being put in a certain order by the "sense" of the believing, then if the two terms in that order are united by the relation into a complex, the belief is true; if not, it is false. This constitutes the definition of truth and falsehood that we were in search of. Judging or believing is a certain complex unity of which a mind is a constituent; if the remaining constituents, taken in the order which they have in the belief, form a complex unity, then the belief is true; if not, it is false.

Thus although truth and falsehood are properties of beliefs, yet they are in a sense extrinsic properties, for the condition of the truth of a belief is something not involving beliefs, or (in general) any mind at all, but only the *objects* of the belief. A mind, which believes, believes truly when there is a *corresponding* complex not involving the mind, but only its objects. This correspondence ensures truth, and its absence entails falsehood. Hence we account simultaneously for the two facts that beliefs (*a*) depend on mind for their *existence*, (*b*) do not depend on minds for their *truth*.

We may restate our theory as follows: If we take such a belief as "Othello believes that Desdemona loves Cassio," we will call Desdemona and Cassio the *object-terms*, and loving the *object-relation*. If there is a complex unity "Desdemona's love for Cassio," consisting of the object-terms related by the object-relation in the same order as they have in the belief, then this complex unity is called the *fact corresponding to the belief*. Thus a belief is true when there is a corresponding fact, and is false when there is no corresponding fact. . . .

. . . Minds do not *create* truth or falsehood. They create beliefs, but when once the beliefs are created, the mind cannot make them true or false, except in the special case where they concern future things which are within the power of the person believing, such as catching trains. What makes a belief true is a *fact*, and this fact does not (except in exceptional cases) in any way involve the mind of the person who has the belief.

W. V. O. Quine, one of the most influential American analytic philosophers, thought, like C. S. Peirce, that knowledge and the project of knowing were intimately tied to the sciences. Accordingly, he argued that our study of knowledge—our epistemology—should be recognized to be as "natural" as our study of the world around us. "Let us be more scientific in our epistemology!" Quine advises.

 FROM **"Epistemology Naturalized"**
BY **W. V. O. Quine**[32]

Epistemology, or something like it, simply falls into place as a chapter of psychology and hence of natural science. It studies a natural phenomenon, viz., a physical human subject. This human subject is accorded a certain experimentally controlled input—certain patterns of irradiation in assorted frequencies, for instance—and in the fullness of time the subject delivers as output a description of the three-dimensional external world and its history. The relation between the meager input and the torrential output

FIG. 3.37 American philosopher W. V. O. Quine. *(AP Photo/JULIA MALAKIE)*

is a relation that we are prompted to study for somewhat the same reasons that always prompted epistemology; namely, in order to see how evidence relates to theory, and in what ways one's theory of nature transcends any available evidence.

Such a study could still include, even, something like the old rational reconstruction, to whatever degree such reconstruction is practicable; for imaginative constructions can afford hints of actual psychological processes, in much the way that mechanical simulations can. But a conspicuous difference between old epistemology and the epistemological enterprise in this new psychological setting is that we can now make free use of empirical psychology.

The old epistemology aspired to contain, in a sense, natural science; it would construct it somehow from sense data. Epistemology in its new setting, conversely, is contained in natural science, as a chapter of psychology. But the old containment remains valid too, in its way. We are studying how the human subject of our study posits bodies and projects his physics from his data, and we appreciate that our position in the world is just like his. Our very epistemological enterprise, therefore, and the psychology wherein it is a component chapter, and the whole of natural science wherein psychology is a component book—all this is our own construction or projection from stimulations like those we were meting out to our epistemological subject. There is thus reciprocal containment, though containment in different senses: epistemology in natural science and natural science in epistemology.

This interplay is reminiscent again of the old threat of circularity, but it is all right now that we have stopped dreaming of deducing science from sense data. We are after an understanding of science as an institution or process in the world, and we do not intend that understanding to be any better than the science which is its object. . . .

One effect of seeing epistemology in a psychological setting is that it resolves a stubborn old enigma of epistemological priority. Our retinas are irradiated in two dimensions, yet we see things as three-dimensional without conscious inference. Which is to count as observation—the unconscious two-dimensional reception or the conscious three-dimensional apprehension? In the old epistemological context the conscious form had priority, for we were out to justify our knowledge of the external world by rational reconstruction, and that demands awareness. Awareness ceased to be demanded when we gave up trying to justify our knowledge of the external world by rational reconstruction. What to count as observation now can be settled in terms of the stimulation of sensory receptors, let consciousness fall where it may. . . .

Vaguely speaking, what we want of observation sentences is that they be the ones in closest causal proximity to the sensory receptors. But how is such proximity to be gauged? The idea may be rephrased this way: observation sentences are sentences which, as we learn language, are most strongly conditioned to concurrent sensory stimulation rather than to stored collateral information. Thus let us imagine a sentence queried for our verdict as to whether it is true or false, queried for our assent or dissent. Then the sentence is an observation sentence if our verdict depends only on the sensory stimulation present at the time.

But a verdict cannot depend on present stimulation to the exclusion of stored information. The very fact of our having learned the language evinces much storing of information, and of information without which we should be in no position to give verdicts on sentences however observational. Evidently then we must relax our definition of observation sentence to read thus: a sentence is an observation sentence if all verdicts on it depend on present sensory stimulation and on no stored information beyond what goes into understanding the sentence.

This formulation raises another problem: how are we to distinguish between information that goes into understanding a sentence and information that goes beyond? This is the problem of distinguishing between analytic truth, which issues from the mere meanings of words, and synthetic truth, which depends on more than meanings. Now I have long maintained that this distinction is illusory. There is one step toward such a distinction, however, which does make sense: a sentence that is true by mere meanings of words should be expected, at least if it is simple, to be subscribed to by all fluent speakers in the community. Perhaps the controversial notion of analyticity can be dispensed with, in our definition of observation sentence, in favor of this straight forward attribute of community-wide acceptance.

This attribute is of course no explication of analyticity. The community would agree that there have been black dogs, yet none who talk of analyticity would call this analytic. My rejection of the analyticity notion just means drawing no line between what goes into the mere understanding of the sentences of a language and what else the community sees eye-to-eye on. I doubt that an objective distinction can be made between meaning and such collateral information as is community-wide.

Turning back then to our task of defining observation sentences, we get this: an observation sentence is one on which all speakers of the language give the same verdict when given the same concurrent stimulation. To put the point negatively, an observation sentence is one that is not sensitive to differences in past experience within the speech community.

This formulation accords perfectly with the traditional role of the observation sentence as the court of appeal of scientific theories. For by our definition the observation sentences are the sentences on which all members of the community will agree under uniform stimulation. And what is the criterion of membership in the same community? Simply, general fluency of dialogue. This criterion admits of degrees, and indeed we may usefully take the community more narrowly for some studies than for others. What count as observation sentences for a community of specialists would not always so count for a larger community.

There is generally no subjectivity in the phrasing of observation sentences, as we are now conceiving them; they will usually be about bodies. Since the distinguishing trait of an observation sentence is intersubjective agreement under agreeing stimulation, a corporeal subject matter is likelier than not. . . .

The veteran physicist looks at some apparatus and sees an x-ray tube. The neophyte, looking at the same place, observes rather "a glass and metal instrument replete with wires, reflectors, screws, lamps, and pushbuttons." One man's observation is another man's closed book or flight of fancy. The notion of observation as the impartial and objective source of evidence for science is bankrupt. Now my answer to the x-ray example was already hinted a little while back: what counts as an observation sentence varies with the width of community considered. But we can also always get an absolute standard by taking in all speakers of the language, or most. It is ironical that philosophers, finding the old epistemology untenable as a whole, should react by repudiating a part which has only now moved into clear focus.

Clarification of the notion of observation sentence is a good thing, for the notion is fundamental in two connections. These two correspond to the duality that I remarked upon early in this essay: the duality between concept and doctrine, between knowing what a sentence means and knowing whether it is true. The observation sentence is basic to both enterprises. Its relation to doctrine, to our knowledge of what is true, is very much the traditional one: observation sentences are the repository of evidence for scientific hypotheses. Its relation to meaning is fundamental too, since observation sentences are the ones we are in a position to learn to understand first, both as children and as field linguists. For observation sentences are precisely the ones that we can correlate with observable circumstances of the occasion of utterance or assent, independently of variations in the past histories of individual informants. They afford the only entry to a language.

The observation sentence is the cornerstone of semantics. For it is, as we just saw, fundamental to the learning of meaning. Also, it is where meaning is firmest. Sentences higher up in theories have no empirical consequences they can call their own; they confront the tribunal of sensory evidence only in more or less inclusive aggregates. The observation sentence, situated at the sensory periphery of the body scientific, is the minimal verifiable aggregate; it has an empirical content all its own and wears it on its sleeve.

The predicament of the indeterminacy of translation has little bearing on observation sentences. The equating of an observation sentence of our language to an observation sentence of another language is mostly a matter of empirical generalization; it is a matter of identity between the range of stimulations that would prompt assent to the one sentence and the range of stimulations that would prompt assent to the other.

. . . Epistemology now becomes semantics. For epistemology remains centered as always on evidence, and meaning remains centered as always on verification; and evidence is verification. What is likelier to shock preconceptions is that meaning, once we get beyond observation sentences, ceases in general to have any clear applicability to single sentences; also that epistemology merges with psychology, as well as with linguistics.

This rubbing out of boundaries could contribute to progress, it seems to me, in philosophically interesting inquiries of a scientific nature. One possible area is perceptual norms. Consider, to begin with, the linguistic phenomenon of phonemes. We form the habit, in hearing the myriad variations of spoken sounds, of treating each as an approximation to one or another to a limited number of norms—around thirty altogether—constituting so to speak a spoken alphabet. All speech in our language can be treated in practice as sequences of just those thirty elements, thus rectifying small deviations. Now outside the realm of language also there is probably only a rather limited alphabet of perceptual norms altogether, toward which we tend unconsciously to rectify all perceptions. These, if experimentally identified, could be taken as epistemological building blocks, the working elements of experience. They might prove in part to be culturally variable, as phonemes are, and in part universal. . . .

J. Feminist Epistemology

In the past fifty years, feminism has grown from a worldwide social protest movement to a profound philosophical challenge to traditional theories of knowledge. It is no longer just a social-political movement striving to attain equal opportunities for women in education and in advancement in the sciences (although that is still a serious issue), but comprises a claim that women's knowledge is actually different from men's and that the pursuit of knowledge, too, is quite different for the two genders, The argument is that epistemology and knowledge, while they are presented as gender-neutral, are in fact largely male defined, that is, "patriarchal," in the now-established language of feminist discourse. In the two following selections, the idea of a feminist epistemology is presented by Australian feminist philosopher

Elizabeth Grosz and by Indian feminist philosopher **Uma Narayan**, who adds the twist of cultural diversity to the already controversial topic of gender differences.

 FROM **On Feminist Knowledge**
BY **Elizabeth Grosz**[33]

There is considerable disagreement among feminists about which approach to take in questioning philosophy's sexist, patriarchal and phallocentric assumptions. They are divided over whether to accept philosophy on its own terms, to undertake a revision of it in the light of feminist knowledges, to abandon it or actively to undermine it. Radical feminists challenge philosophy's orientation around *oneness*, unity, or identity—one truth, one method, one reality, one logic, and so on. Many have insisted that there are a plurality of perspectives and a multiplicity of models on which philosophy could base itself.

In their endorsement of plurality and multiplicity, feminists such as Le Doeuff, Irigaray, and Lloyd are not, however, committed to relativism. Relativism is the belief that there are no absolute positions of judgment or knowledge. There are many positions, each of

> **Elizabeth Grosz (1952-)**
>
> Australian philosopher and professor of women's studies and philosophy at Rutgers University, Grosz has published a number of books in feminist philosophy.

which is *equally valid*. Relativism or pluralism implies the existence of frameworks and positions which each have their own validity and standards; and the belief that none of these positions is comprehensive or all-inclusive.

Pluralism and relativism imply abandoning the right to criticize actively other positions, even those we find offensive and disturbing—phallocentric or racist statements, for example—and to accept them as having equal validity to our own positions. Radical feminists instead aim to expand and multiply the criteria for what is considered true, rational, or valid and to reject or condemn those they perceive to be discriminatory. They insist on retaining the right to judge other positions, to criticize them, and also to supersede them. Radical feminists are not absolutists nor objectivists nor relativists nor subjectivists. They advocate a *perspectivism* which acknowledges other points of view but denies them equal value.

It is at this time impossible to specify what a philosophy compatible with feminism would be like; given that it does not exist as a definite body of texts, any definition or description would be overly prescriptive. Nevertheless, some general tendencies can be briefly outlined.

Among the features a feminist philosophy may develop are the following.

(a) Instead of a commitment to truth and objectivity, it can openly accept its own status (and that of all discourses) as context-specific. It accepts its *perspectivism*, that fact that all discourses represent a point of view, have specific aims and objectives, often not coinciding with those of their authors. Rather than seeing itself as disinterested knowledge, it can openly avow its own political position: all texts speak from or represent particular positions within power relations.

(b) Instead of regarding philosophy as the unfolding of reason, a sure path of progress towards truth, a feminist philosophy can accept itself as the product of a specific socio-economic and textual-discursive history. Neither relativist nor subjectivist, it

---

[33] Elizabeth Grosz, "Philosophy" in *Feminist Knowledge: Critique and Construct*, ed. Sneja Gunew, London: Routledge, 1990.

aims to render these and other binary oppositions problematic. A feminist philosophy defies modes of conventional evaluation. This is not, however, to claim that it cannot be evaluated in any terms; simply that the criteria used must be different. A theory's validity is not judged simply according to its adoption of a fixed or pre-given form, but it may be judged according to its *intersubjective* effects, that is, its capacity to be shared, understood, and communicated by those occupying similar positions; and also by its *intertextual* effects, that is, its capacity to affirm or undermine various prevailing or subordinated discursive systems, and the effects it has on other discourses.

(c) Instead of separating the subject and object of knowledge, a feminist philosophy may instead assert a continuity or contiguity between them. The gulf necessary for objectivity is an attempt to guarantee a knowing subject free of personal, social, political, and moral interests (a Cartesian subject), unimplicated in a social context, and uninfluenced by prior ideas and knowledges. A feminist philosophy would need to reconceptualize their interrelations so that reason and knowledge include history, context, and specificity. A feminist philosophy could accept, as patriarchal discourses cannot, that subjects occupying different positions may develop different types of theory and have different investments in their relation to the object. Above all, it can accept that all knowledge is *sexualized*, that it occupies a sexually coded and structured position. However, the sexual position of the text cannot be readily identified with the sexual identity of its author; a female author, for example, does not in any way guarantee a feminine text.

(d) Instead of the dichotomous, oppositional structure, which separates subject and object, teacher and pupil, truth and falsity, etc., a feminist philosophy may regard these terms as continuities or *differences*. Distinctions or oppositions imply that two binary terms are mutually exclusive and exhaustive of the field; that one term defines the other as its negative; that this other can have a place in the binary structure; however, when terms are conceived as two among many others, they are neither contradictory nor all-inclusive. If anything, the relation of difference is based on contrariety not contradiction.

(e) Instead of aspiring to the status of truth, a feminist philosophy prefers to see itself as a form of *strategy*. Strategies are not abstractions, blueprints, or battle-plans for future action. Rather, they involve a provisional commitment to goals and ideals; a recognition of the prevailing situation, in opposition to which these ideals are erected; and an expedient relation to terms, arguments, and techniques which help transform the prevailing order into the ideal. To deny that a feminist philosophy aspires to truth is not to claim it is content with being regarded as false; rather, the opposition between truth and falsity is largely irrelevant for a strategic model.

(f) Instead of dividing theory from practice—so that practice is located chronologically before and after theory (construed as either a plan or a *post facto* reflection, respectively)—a feminist philosophy may regard theory as a form of practice, a textual, conceptual, and educational practice, one involved in struggles for theoretical ascendancy, where dominant and subordinated discourses battle with each other. Theory is not privileged by its isolation from practice and its relegation to a pure conceptual level. When it is seen as a material process, theory can be seen as a practice like any other, neither more nor less privileged in its ability to survey and assess other practices. As a material labour or practice, theory relies on concepts, words, and discursive "raw materials," processes of theoretical production (e.g. the form of argument, narrative, or linguistic structure needed to make coherent discourses) and a determined product (a text or theory). It is not hierarchically privileged over other practices, reserving the right of judgement; rather it is itself capable of being assessed by other practices.

(g) Instead of opposing reason to its others, a feminist philosophy expands the concept of reason. It has analyzed how reason as we know it is allied with masculinity and relegates feminine attributes to a repressed or subordinated status. A feminist philosophy would not reverse the relation between reason and its others, but would expand reason so that its expelled others are now included. In beginning with women's lived experiences in the production of knowledge it seeks a reason that is not separated from experience but based upon it, that is not opposed to the body but accepts it, not distinct from everyday life but cognisant of it.

(h) Instead of accepting dominant models of knowledge (with their logic, binary structure, desire for precision and clarity) a feminist philosophy can accept its status as material, textual, and institutional. As such, it can accept the provisional, not eternal, status of its postulates. It aims for the production of new methods of knowing, new forms of analysis, new modes of writing, new kinds of textual objects, new texts. No *one* method, point of view, position for subjects and objects is the norm or model for all philosophy.

> "No *one* method, point of view, position for subjects and objects is the norm or model for all philosophy."
>
> — ELIZABETH GROSZ

FROM On Feminist Epistemology
BY Uma Narayan[34]

A fundamental thesis of feminist epistemology is that our location in the world as women makes it possible for us to perceive and understand different aspects of both the world and human activities in ways that challenge the male bias of existing perspectives. Feminist epistemology is a particular manifestation of the general insight that the nature of women's experiences as individuals and as social beings, our contributions to work, culture, knowledge, and our history and political interests have been systematically ignored or misrepresented by mainstream discourses in different areas.

Women have been often excluded from prestigious areas of human activity (for example, politics or science) and this has often made these activities seem clearly "male." In areas where women were not excluded (for example, subsistence work), their contribution has been misrepresented as secondary and inferior to that of men. Feminist epistemology sees mainstream theories about various human enterprises, including mainstream theories about human knowledge, as one-dimensional and deeply flawed because of the exclusion and misrepresentation of women's contributions.

FIG. 3.38 Contemporary philosopher Uma Narayan teaches at Vassar College.
(© Uma Narayan)

Uma Narayan (1958-)

A feminist philosopher and professor at Vassar College. In addition to feminism, Narayan's work deals with post-colonial theory and the challenge it poses to assumptions in traditional Western philosophy.

---

34 Uma Narayan, "The Project of Feminist Epistemology: Perspectives from a Non-Western Feminist," in *Gender/Body/Knowledge*, ed. Alison M. Jaggar and Susan R. Bordo. Copyright © 1989 by Rutgers, The State University. Reprinted by permission of Rutgers University Press.

Feminist epistemology suggests that integrating women's contribution into the domain of science and knowledge will not constitute a mere adding of details; it will not merely widen the canvas but result in a shift of perspective enabling us to see a very different picture. The inclusion of women's perspective will not merely amount to women participating in greater numbers in the existing practice of science and knowledge, but it will change the very nature of these activities and their self-understanding.

It would be misleading to suggest that feminist epistemology is a homogenous and cohesive enterprise. Its practitioners differ both philosophically and politically in a number of significant ways (Harding 1986). But an important theme on its agenda has been to undermine the abstract, rationalistic, and universal image of the scientific enterprise by using several different strategies. It has studied, for instance, how contingent historical factors have colored both scientific theories and practices and provided the (often sexist) metaphors in which scientists have conceptualized their activity (Bordo 1986; Keller 1985; Harding and O'Barr 1987). It has tried to reintegrate values and emotions into our account of our cognitive activities, arguing for both the inevitability of their presence and the importance of the contributions they are capable of making to our knowledge. . . . It has also attacked various sets of dualisms characteristic of western philosophical thinking—reason versus emotion, culture versus nature, universal versus particular—in which the first of each set is identified with science, rationality, and the masculine and the second is relegated to the nonscientific, the nonrational, and the feminine.

. . .

At the most general level, feminist epistemology resembles the efforts of many oppressed groups to reclaim for themselves the value of their own experience. The writing of novels that focused on working-class life in England or the lives of black people in the United States shares a motivation similar to that of feminist epistemology—to depict an experience different from the norm and to assert the value of this difference.

In a similar manner, feminist epistemology also resembles attempts by third-world writers and historians to document the wealth and complexity of local economic and social structures that existed prior to colonialism. These attempts are useful for their ability to restore to colonized peoples a sense of the richness of their own history and culture. These projects also mitigate the tendency of intellectuals in former colonies who are westernized through their education to think that anything western is necessarily better and more "progressive." In some cases, such studies help to preserve the knowledge of many local arts, crafts, lore, and techniques that were part of the former way of life before they are lost not only to practice but even to memory.

These enterprises are analogous to feminist epistemology's project of restoring to women a sense of the richness of their history, to mitigate our tendency to see the stereotypically "masculine" as better or more progressive, and to preserve for posterity the contents of "feminine" areas of knowledge and expertise—medical lore, knowledge associated with the practices of childbirth and child rearing, traditionally feminine crafts, and so on. Feminist epistemology, like these other enterprises, must attempt to balance the assertion of the value of a different culture or experience against the dangers of romanticizing it to the extent that the limitations and oppressions it confers on its subjects are ignored.

. . .

I think that one of the most interesting insights of feminist epistemology is the view that oppressed groups, whether women, the poor, or racial minorities, may derive an "epistemic advantage" from having knowledge of the practices of both their own contexts and those of their oppressors. The practices of the dominant groups (for instance, men) govern a society; the dominated group (for instance, women) must acquire some fluency with these practices in order to survive in that society.

There is no similar pressure on members of the dominant group to acquire knowledge of the practices of the dominated groups. For instance, colonized people had to learn the language and culture of their colonizers. The colonizers seldom found it necessary to have more than a sketchy acquaintance with the language and culture of the "natives." Thus, the oppressed are seen as having an "epistemic advantage" because they can operate with two sets of practices and in two different contexts. This advantage is thought to lead to critical insights because each framework provides a critical perspective on the other.

I would like to balance this account with a few comments about the "dark side," the disadvantages, of being able to or of having to inhabit two mutually incompatible frameworks that provide differing perspectives on social reality. I suspect that nonwestern feminists, given the often complex and troublesome interrelationships between the contexts they must inhabit, are less likely to express unqualified enthusiasm about the benefits of straddling a multiplicity of contexts. Mere access to two different and incompatible contexts is not a guarantee that a critical stance on the part of an individual will result. There are many ways in which she may deal with the situation.

First, the person may be tempted to dichotomize her life and reserve the framework of a different context for each part. The middle class of nonwestern countries supplies numerous examples of people who are very westernized in public life but who return to a very traditional lifestyle in the realm of the family. Women may choose to live their public lives in a "male" mode, displaying characteristics of aggressiveness, competition, and so on, while continuing to play dependent and compliant roles in their private lives. The pressures of jumping between two different lifestyles may be mitigated by justifications of how each pattern of behavior is appropriate to its particular context and of how it enables them to "get the best of both worlds."

Second, the individual may try to reject the practices of her own context and try to be as much as possible like members of the dominant group. Westernized intellectuals in the nonwestern world often may almost lose knowledge of their own cultures and practices and be ashamed of the little that they do still know. Women may try both to acquire stereotypically male characteristics, like aggressiveness, and to expunge stereotypically female characteristics, like emotionality. Or the individual could try to reject entirely the framework of the dominant group and assert the virtues of her own despite the risks of being marginalized from the power structures of the society; consider, for example, women who seek a certain sort of security in traditionally defined roles.

The choice to inhabit two contexts critically is an alternative to these choices and, I would argue, a more useful one. But the presence of alternative contexts does not by itself guarantee that one of the other choices will not be made. Moreover, the decision to inhabit two contexts critically, although it may lead to an "epistemic advantage," is likely to exact a certain price. It may lead to a sense of totally lacking roots or any space where one is at home in a relaxed manner.

This sense of alienation may be minimized if the critical straddling of two contexts is part of an ongoing critical politics, due to the support of others and a

"The oppressed are seen as having an 'epistemic advantage' because they can operate with two sets of practices and in two different contexts."

– UMA NARAYAN

deeper understanding of what is going on. When it is not so rooted, it may generate ambivalence, uncertainty, despair, and even madness, rather than more positive critical emotions and attitudes. However such a person determines her locus, there may be a sense of being an outsider in both contexts and a sense of clumsiness or lack of fluency in both sets of practices. Consider this simple linguistic example: most people who learn two different languages that are associated with two very different cultures seldom acquire both with equal fluency; they may find themselves devoid of vocabulary in one language for certain contexts of life or be unable to match real objects with terms they have acquired in their vocabulary. For instance, people from my sort of background would know words in Indian languages for some spices, fruits, and vegetables that they do not know in English. Similarly, they might be unable to discuss "technical" subjects like economics or biology in their own languages because they learned about these subjects and acquired their technical vocabularies only in English.

The relation between the two contexts the individual inhabits may not be simple or straightforward. The individual subject is seldom in a position to carry out a perfect "dialectical synthesis" that preserves all the advantages of both contexts and transcends all their problems. There may be a number of different "syntheses," each of which avoids a different subset of the problems and preserves a different subset of the benefits.

No solution may be perfect or even palatable to the agent confronted with a choice. For example, some Indian feminists may find some western modes of dress (say trousers) either more comfortable or more their "style" than some local modes of dress. However, they may find that wearing the local mode of dress is less socially troublesome, alienates them less from more traditional people they want to work with, and so on. Either choice is bound to leave them partly frustrated in their desires.

Feminist theory must be temperate in the use it makes of this doctrine of "double vision"—the claim that oppressed groups have an epistemic advantage and access to greater critical conceptual space. Certain types and contexts of oppression certainly may bear out the truth of this claim. Others certainly do not seem to do so; and even if they do provide space for critical insights, they may also rule out the possibility of actions subversive of the oppressive state of affairs.

Certain kinds of oppressive contexts, such as the contexts in which women of my grandmother's background lived, rendered their subjects entirely devoid of skills required to function as independent entities in the culture. Girls were married off barely past puberty, trained for nothing beyond household tasks and the rearing of children, and passed from economic dependency on their fathers to economic dependency on their husbands to economic dependency on their sons in old age. Their criticisms of their lot were articulated, if at all, in terms that precluded a desire for any radical change. They saw themselves sometimes as personally unfortunate, but they did not locate the causes of their misery in larger social arrangements.

I conclude by stressing that the important insight incorporated in the doctrine of "double vision" should not be reified into a metaphysics that serves as a substitute for concrete social analysis. Furthermore, the alternative to "buying" into an oppressive social system need not be a celebration of exclusion and the mechanisms of marginalization. The thesis that oppression may bestow an epistemic advantage should not tempt us in the direction of idealizing or romanticizing oppression and blind us to its real material and psychic deprivations.

- How does gender supposedly make a difference in our ability to know?
- In what ways is epistemology "one-sided and deeply flawed"?
- Do you think that a feminist epistemology diminishes our ability to have universal and objective knowledge?
- Feminist philosophy claims to advocate "perspectivism," which acknowledges other points of view but denies that they have equal value. Is there anything about this view that you find problematic? How is feminist theory (as outlined by Grosz) supposed to achieve the balance between recognizing that truth is perspectival and denying all perspectives equal value?

SUMMARY AND CONCLUSION

Epistemology is the study of human knowledge—what we can know, how we can know it, and what we cannot know. In this sense, epistemology and metaphysics are complementary disciplines. Epistemology becomes the method of approach to the knowledge of the way the world really is. For some philosophers, for example, Descartes, this approach places its primary trust in reason; accordingly, they are called rationalists. For other philosophers, for example, Locke, the preferred approach is to trust the senses and experience; they are called empiricists. The problem for both the rationalists and the empiricists is to get beyond the mere appearance of things to the reality behind them. The rationalist tries to do this by appealing to intuition and certain principles from which he or she can deduce the way the world really is. The empiricist, on the other hand, appeals to his or her experiences, trying to find there evidence for the nature of reality. For both views, however, the danger is that their methods do not always seem to achieve as much as they would like. Rationalists disagree about which principles to start with and which intuitions to trust. Empiricists find that their own method of experience makes it impossible to say anything about what lies beyond experience. Thus Berkeley argues that only our ideas (including God) and the minds that have these ideas exist, and Hume concludes that we can never know anything about reality, but only about our own **associations of ideas**. Epistemologists are still working on more satisfactory answers to the questions of knowledge, and still trying to defeat or defend once and for all the skeptical conclusions so brilliantly argued by Hume. Since the writings of Immanuel Kant, the questions about knowledge have shifted from the question of how we know what the world is like to questions that presume that reality is not independent of consciousness, that we somehow "constitute" the world through our concepts. The German Idealists Fichte, Hegel, and Schopenhauer developed very different conceptions of knowledge based on the new Kantian philosophy, and Nietzsche employed it as well. Contemporary phenomenology, hermeneutics, and pragmatism put even more emphasis on culture and practicality, and, finally, attention to the differences between the sexes has further added to the complexity of our questions about knowledge. Do men and women know the world differently? How personal is knowledge—how relative to the individual and his or her cultural context and biology?

CHAPTER REVIEW QUESTIONS

1. Can you think of any way for Locke to defend his claim that substances exist, but we do not know what they are? How would Locke respond to Berkeley's conclusion that we can only know ideas?

2. Descartes reestablishes his system of beliefs because of his famous statement "I am a thing that thinks." Where is the place of the thing that thinks in Locke's system? Explain the difference between inductive and deductive reasoning and how it applies to the systems of Descartes and Locke.

3. How would you characterize skepticism? In what way have the various thinkers responded to the skeptics' challenge? How might the skeptic reply in each case?

4. Explain the difficulties associated with rationalism and empiricism.

5. What does Kant mean that we "constitute" our world? Are there other ways to "constitute" the world according to Kant?

6. How does Kant answer Hume's skeptical challenge? Does he succeed?

7. Discuss the difference between "absolutism" and "relativism" and the various problems associated with each. How do you see this debate being played out in the popular press and in the views of the public toward science, ethics, and religion?

8. What do you see as the role of language in the theories discussed in this chapter? Why would a concern with language be so central to questions about truth?

KEY TERMS

absolutism

absolutists

analytic (of a sentence or truth)

analytic philosophy

a posteriori (knowledge)

appearance

a priori (knowledge)

association of ideas

categories

causal theory of perception

causation *or* causality

cause

cogito, ergo sum

coherence theory of truth

conceptual truth

constitute

contingent (truth)

correspondence theory of truth

criterion

datum

dialectic

empirical (knowledge)

empiricism

emptiness

epistemology

explanation

generalization from experience (or induction)

hermeneutics

historicism

Hume's fork

idea

impression

induction; inductive reasoning; inductive generalization

innate ideas

intersubjectivity

intuition

justification

law of contradiction

law of the excluded middle

logical truth

masculinist

matter of fact (in Hume)

necessary (truth)

necessary and sufficient conditions

necessity

perception

phenomenology

pragmatic theory of truth

pragmatism

primary qualities

principle of induction

principle of universal causation

probable

quality

rational

rationalism

realism

reason

relations of ideas

relativism

rules of inference

secondary qualities

semantics

semantic theory of truth

sensation

sense-data

skepticism

subjective idealism

substance

synonym

synthetic (statement)

synthetic a priori knowledge

tabula rasa

tautology

transcendental

transcendental deduction

truth of reason

BIBLIOGRAPHY AND FURTHER READING

Several studies of the various problems in René Descartes' epistemology are in Willis Doney, ed., *Descartes* (New York: Doubleday, Anchor, 1967).

Gottfried W. von Leibniz's reply to John Locke is spelled out at length in Leibniz's *New Essays on Human Understanding*, trans. A. G. Langley (La Salle, IL: Open Court, 1949).

Locke's *Essay Concerning Human Understanding* is published by Dover Publications (New York, 1959).

Bishop Berkeley's *Treatise* is printed in full in T. E. Jessop, ed., *Berkeley, Philosophical Writings* (Austin, TX: University of Texas Press, 1953).

Of special interest is Berkeley's *Three Dialogues Between Hylas and Philonous* (La Salle, IL: Open Court, 1935), in which the arguments of his Treatise are worked out in entertaining dialogue form.

David Hume's *Treatise of Human Nature* is available, edited by L. A. Selby-Bigge (Oxford: Oxford University Press, 1888), but most beginners will find Hume's *Enquiry Concerning Human Understanding* (Oxford: Oxford University Press, 1902) much easier reading.

Bertrand Russell, *Problems of Philosophy* (London: Oxford University Press, 1912) is an excellent introduction to the problems of epistemology and some of the problems of metaphysics.

Some more modern epistemological studies are Ralph Baergen, *Contemporary Epistemology* (Fort Worth: Harcourt Brace College Publishers, 1995); John Greco and Ernest Sosa, *The Blackwell Guide to Epistemology* (Oxford: Blackwell, 1998); Alfred Mele and Piers Rawling, *The Oxford Handbook of Rationality* (New York: Oxford University Press, 2003); and Robert Audi, *Epistemology: A Contemporary Introduction* (New York: Routledge, 2003).

For a comprehensive anthology on epistemology, see E. Nagel and R. Brandt, eds., *Meaning and Knowledge* (New York: Harcourt Brace Jovanovich, 1965).

A modern defense of skepticism is Peter Unger, *Ignorance* (London: Oxford University Press, 1975).

On feminist theories of knowledge, see Ann Garry and Marilyn Pearsall, *Women, Knowledge and Reality* (Boston: Unwin Hyman, 1989).

William James develops his pragmatic theory in his *Pragmatism: A New Name for Some Old Ways of Thinking* (New York: Longmans Green, 1907).

Two brief but helpful introductions to Immanuel Kant's philosophy are J. Kemp, *The Philosophy of Kant* (London: Oxford University Press, 1968) and G. J. Warnock, "Kant," in *A Critical History of Western Philosophy*, ed. D. J. O'Connor (New York: Free Press, 1964).

A short introduction to German idealism is R. Solomon, *Introducing the German Idealists* (Indianapolis, IN: Hackett, 1981).

The best basic discussion of hermeneutics is David Hoy, *The Critical Circle* (Berkeley: University of California Press, 1978).

A compendium of writings by Gadamer is *Philosophical Hermeneutics*, trans. D. Linge (Berkeley: University of California Press, 1976).

Relativism is the subject of the essays collected by M. Kraucze and J. Meiland, eds. (Notre Dame, IN: University of Notre Dame Press, 1982).

A controversial discussion of the whole problem of truth and its complications is Richard Rorty, *Philosophy and the Mirror of Nature* (Princeton: Princeton University Press, 1979).

Two anthologies on necessary truth are Robert Sleigh, ed., *Necessary Truth* (Englewood Cliffs, NJ: Prentice-Hall, 1972), and L. W. Sumner and John Woods, *Necessary Truth: A Book of Readings* (New York: Random House, 1970).

A good guide to European ("continental") philosophy is Robert Solomon and David Sherman, *Blackwell Guide to Continental Philosophy* (Oxford: Blackwell, 2003).

PART II

Know Thyself

4 | Self

> *"I'm not myself today, you see,"* Alice said to the caterpillar.
> *"I don't see,"* said the caterpillar.
>
> LEWIS CARROLL

"Just be yourself!" How often have you heard that? What is it to be a "self"? And what does it mean to be a particular self? In the abstract, these questions seem obscure. But in everything that we do, we adopt some conception of our identity, both as a person and as an individual, whether we are called upon to articulate it or not. As a student, you walk into a classroom with certain conceptions of your own abilities and intelligence, your status among other students, your role vis-à-vis the professor, some haunting memories, perhaps some embarrassment or a certain vanity about your looks, your clothes, your grades, or just your new pair of shoes.

If you had to identify yourself as an individual, describe what makes you you, how would you do it? What features are essential to being a person? What are essential to being the person you are and what features distinguish you from other persons? Think for a moment of yourself in an office, applying for a job or a scholarship for professional school or just filling out one of those dozens of forms that bombard you during the year. You dutifully fill in your birthdate, where you were born, your grades in school, your service in the military if any, awards you have received, arrests and other troubles, whether you're married or not, male or female, perhaps your race and religion. This list of facts about yourself would be one way of identifying "you." But at some point, I am sure you have felt that sense of absurdity and rebellion, "this isn't me!" or "this is all irrelevant!" What may seem more relevant to your self-identity are your political views, your tastes in art and music, your favorite books and movies, your loves and hates, habits and beliefs, or just the fact, perhaps, that you think your own thoughts. These more personal, or "internal," features as well as the "cold facts," or "external" features, about yourself are important for identifying you as an individual different from other individuals.

In one sense, your **self-identity** is the way you characterize yourself as an individual. The philosophical problem of self-identity is thus concerned in part with what these characterizing qualities are. Are they just concerned with status and roles among other people? Or is there something that can truly be called "your self," your "**essence**," or maybe even your soul, without

FIG. 4.1 John Tenniel (1820-1914), *Alice Meets the Blue Caterpillar*, 1890. Does Alice's sense of self turn upside-down when she falls through the rabbit hole? *(HIP / Art Resource, NY)*

reference to anyone else? Should we think of ourselves as individuals? Or should we instead view ourselves as mere components of a larger organism—society, mankind, or perhaps the world as a whole? How should we identify ourselves?

There is another sense in which we might talk about a person's self-identity. You may know someone who has experienced a religious conversion, or who has just undergone treatment for alcoholism; or perhaps you can think of someone you see again after a long time who says, "I'm not the same person." What does this mean, and how is it possible to say you are not the same person? When someone says, "I'm not the same person I was," he or she is pointing to the fact that some significant aspects of himself or herself have changed; this person has a new self-identity. Yet, in another sense, this is still the same person; the old identity and the new identity are both identities of the same person.

So we have a second sense of "self-identity." Here your self-identity is what makes you the same person over time. Thus, the second philosophical problem, which is the one that has most concerned philosophers, is how to identify an individual as the *same* individual over time. What is it about you without which you wouldn't be you? Presumably you would still be you if you changed your religious beliefs or tastes in music. But what if you had a sex-change operation? Or what if you completely lost your memory, all recollection of your family and friends? Or what if you physically disappeared altogether, remaining only a wispy consciousness, a spirit, or a ghost without a body? Would it then make sense to say that you are still you?

There is yet a third sense in which we talk about self-identity. What is it that *allows* us to be individual people at all? Interestingly, the fact of consciousness—of having thoughts and feelings—seems the most private and individual thing a person possesses, and yet is the very thing that we tend to believe *all* people possess. Whatever our attempts to answer the problems of self-identity, they begin with a single "fact"—our own consciousness. We will see that this was the logical beginning for Descartes, who used the fact of his own consciousness as the starting point for his whole philosophy. It was true for Locke, as well, who argued that our identity is to be found in the continuity of our consciousness rather than in the continuity of our bodies. We will see that it was even used by Hume, who used his own consciousness as the basis of his denial that there is any such thing as the self!

Of course, these questions assume some metaphysical claims that can and have been questioned. Later in this chapter, we will look at some of these assumptions and some criticisms of them. Is self-identity a matter of nature? Are we born with an identity? Or is it a matter of personal choice or of environmental factors such as our upbringing or education? Must a person have only one "self," or might he or she in fact have several or many selves? Is there a "self" at all? Or is the self, as many Eastern philosophers have argued, an illusion? Should self-lessness be our ideal self-identity? Ought we even to conceive of ourselves as individuals? Or ought we instead think of ourselves as organic components of a larger community or society?

- How would you describe your "self"—that which makes you "you" and different from other people?
- How much of your self-identity is shaped by your interaction with other people, either family, friends, or strangers? To what extent do you think that your identity is self-determined?
- Do you think that there is anything that necessarily "underlies" the changes each of us undergoes as a person through the course of a lifetime?
- Are there different senses of self-identity, in your view? Or are all of them reducible to a single all-embracing sense?

In this chapter, we explore a number of different questions and conceptions about self-identity. We consider the question of what makes you *you*, both in the sense of what makes you a person, and in the sense of what makes you the particular person you are. Freud, the great nineteenth-century psychologist, once said that every man is in some ways like all other men, in some ways like some other men, and in some ways like no other man. Philosophers who investigate the problem of self-identity attempt to figure out exactly how and why this might be so. We begin with an all-important and still influential tradition in philosophy, from Descartes and Locke to Hume and Kant, which focuses on self-consciousness as the sole key to personal identity.

A. Consciousness and the Self: From Descartes to Kant

Sometimes we act out our identities without being aware of it at all. At other times, particularly when we talk about ourselves or are placed in a situation where we are forced to "look at ourselves as others see us," we are very much aware—even painfully aware—of our identities. At such times we say we are **self-conscious**. In general, most modern philosophers and psychologists would argue that you can't have a concept of who you are unless you are also sometimes (not necessarily always) self-conscious. Conversely, you can't even be self-conscious unless you have some sense of identity, no matter how crude. The two concepts, in other words, go hand in hand and cannot be separated from each other.

Many philosophers have argued that not only is self-consciousness crucial to having a concept of one's own individuality, but it is also crucial for establishing that one is an enduring self, that is, the same person over time. Descartes is an example. Remember how he characterized himself:

> But what then am I? A thing which thinks. What is a thing which thinks? It is a thing which doubts, understands, affirms, denies, wills, refuses, which also imagines and feels.

He goes on to say, I am a thing with desires, who perceives light and noise and feels heat. Clearly, Descartes' concept of "self" is of thought, or consciousness—a human essence—which each person has and with which each person identifies himself or herself. He also claims to show by his method of doubt that all of this might be so even if he were not to have a body at all. Perhaps, he argues, I am fooled about my "having" a body just as I might be fooled about all sorts of other things. Therefore, he concludes, it is not my body that provides me with an identity or with the self from which I begin my philosophy. It follows from this that the particular aspects of my self—whether I am male or female, black or white, tall or short, handsome or ugly, strong or weak—are associated with my body only and cannot be essential to my identity. My self-identity is in my mind, in my thinking, doubting, feeling, perceiving, imagining, and desiring. I am, essentially, "a thing which thinks."

 FROM **"Meditation VI"**
BY **René Descartes**[1]

Therefore, just because I know certainly that I exist, and that meanwhile I do not remark that any other thing necessarily pertains to my nature or essence, excepting that I am a thinking thing, I rightly conclude that my essence consists solely in the fact that I am a thinking thing [or a substance whose whole essence or nature is to think]. And although possibly (or rather certainly, as I shall say in a moment) I possess a body with which I am very intimately conjoined, yet because, on the one side, I have a clear and distinct idea of myself inasmuch as I am only a thinking and unextended thing, and as, on the other, I possess a distinct idea of body, inasmuch as it is only an extended and unthinking thing, it is certain that this I [that is to say, my soul by which I am what I am], is entirely and absolutely distinct from my body, and can exist without it.

It is important to appreciate the kind of step Descartes has taken here. What he is saying is that self-identity depends on consciousness. Our identity does not depend in any way on our body remaining the same, and so human identity is different from the identity of anything else in the world.

> • What is the connection between self-consciousness and self-identity? Do you think (some) animals are self-conscious? If so, do you think that they might have a self-identity?
> • What does Descartes identify as the "self"? Is this anything unique to individuals? In what sense (if any) does it individuate you as distinct from someone else?

John Locke, like Descartes, sees self-consciousness as the key to self-identity. But unlike Descartes, he argues that this identity does not depend on our remaining the same thinking substance, that is, on our having the same soul. Indeed, in the course of our life our soul might be replaced with new souls just as in the course of a tree's growth its cells are replaced with new cells. What makes the tree the same tree is the fact that the same life is present in spite of changes in its physical structure; and what makes a person the same person is that the same *consciousness* and memories are present. Thus Locke differs from Descartes in distinguishing between the soul (a substance) and consciousness. It is our consciousness that we call our "self." In *An Essay Concerning Human Understanding*, Locke argues:

---

[1] René Descartes, "Meditation VI," in *Meditations on First Philosophy*, in *The Philosophical Works of Descartes*, trans. Elizabeth S. Haldane and G. R. T. Ross, 1911. Reprinted with the permission of Cambridge University Press.

On Personal Identity
BY **John Locke**[2]

To find wherein personal identity consists, we must consider what *person* stands for;—which, I think, is a thinking intelligent being, that has reason and reflection, and can consider itself as itself, the same thinking thing, in different times and places; which it does only by that consciousness which is inseparable from thinking, and as it seems to me, essential to it: it being impossible for any one to perceive without *perceiving* that he does perceive. When we see, hear, smell, taste, feel, meditate, or will anything, we know that we do so. Thus it is always as to our present sensations and perceptions: and by this every one is to himself that which he calls *self:*—it not being considered, in this case, whether the same self be continued in the same or divers substances. For, since consciousness always accompanies thinking, and it is that which makes every one to be what he calls self, and thereby distinguishes himself from all other thinking things, in this alone consists personal identity, i.e. the sameness of a rational being: and as far as this consciousness can be extended backwards to any past action or thought, so far reaches the identity of that person; it is the same self now it was then; and it is by the same self with this present one that now reflects on it, that that action was done.

Consciousness makes personal Identity.—But it is further inquired, whether it be the same identical substance. This few[3] would think they had reason to doubt of, if these perceptions, with their consciousness, always remained present in the mind, whereby the same thinking thing would be always consciously present, and, as would be thought, evidently the same to itself. But that which seems to make the difficulty is this, that this consciousness being interrupted always by forgetfulness, there being no moment of our lives wherein we have the whole train of all our past actions before our eyes in one view, but even the best memories losing the sight of one part whilst they are viewing another; and we sometimes, and that the greatest part of our lives, not reflecting on our past selves, being intent on our present thoughts, and in sound sleep having no thoughts at all, or at least none with that consciousness which remarks our waking thoughts,—I say, in all these cases, our consciousness being interrupted, and we losing the sight of our past selves, doubts are raised whether we are the same thinking thing, i.e. the same *substance* or no. Which, however reasonable or unreasonable, concerns not *personal* identity at all. The question being what makes the same person; and not whether it be the same identical substance, which always thinks in the same person, which, in this case, matters not at all: different substances, by the same consciousness (where they do partake in it) being united into one person, as well as different bodies by the same life are united into one animal, whose identity is preserved in that change of substances by the unity of one continued life. For, it being the same consciousness that makes a man be himself to himself, personal identity depends on that only, whether it be annexed solely to one individual substance, or can be continued in a succession of several substances. For as far as any intelligent being *can* repeat the idea of any past action with the same consciousness it had of it at first, and with the same consciousness it has of any present action; so far it is the same personal self. For it is by the consciousness it

[2]John Locke, *An Essay Concerning Human Understanding*, ed. A. C. Fraser, Oxford: Clarendon Press, 1894.

[3] Locke refers here to Descartes.

has of its present thoughts and actions, that it is *self to itself* now, and so will be the same self, as far as the same consciousness can extend to actions past or to come; and would be by distance of time, or change of substance, no more two persons, than a man be two men by wearing other clothes to-day than he did yesterday, with a long or a short sleep between: the same consciousness uniting those distant actions into the same person, whatever substances contributed to their production.

Personal Identity in Change of Substance.—That this is so, we have some kind of evidence in our very bodies, all whose particles, whilst vitally united to this same thinking conscious self, so that *we feel* when they are touched, and are affected by, and conscious of good or harm that happens to them, are a part of ourselves; i.e. of our thinking conscious self. Thus, the limbs of his body are to every one a part of himself; he sympathizes and is concerned for them. Cut off a hand, and thereby separate it from that consciousness he had of its heat, cold, and other affections, and it is then no longer a part of that which is himself, any more than the remotest part of matter. Thus, we see the *substance* whereof personal self consisted at one time may be varied at another, without the change of personal identity; there being no question about the same person, though the limbs which but now were a part of it, be cut off.

. . .

If the same consciousness (which, as has been shown, is quite a different thing from the same numerical figure or motion in body) can be transferred from one thinking substance to another, it will be possible that two thinking substances may make but one person. For the same consciousness being preserved, whether in the same or different substances, the personal identity is preserved. Whether the same immaterial being, being conscious of the action of its past duration, may be wholly stripped of all the consciousness of its past existence, and lose it beyond the power of ever retrieving it again: and so as it were beginning a new account from a new period, have a consciousness that *cannot* reach beyond this new state. All those who hold pre-existence are evidently of this mind; since they allow the soul to have no remaining consciousness of what it did in the pre-existing state, either wholly separate from body, or informing any other body; and if they should not, it is plain experience would be against them. So that personal identity, reaching no further than consciousness reaches, a pre-existent spirit not having continued so many ages in a state of silence, must needs make different persons. Suppose a Christian Platonist or a Pythagorean should, upon God's having ended all his works of creation the seventh day, think his soul hath existed ever since; and should imagine it has revolved in several human bodies; as I once met with one, who was persuaded his had been the *soul* of Socrates (how reasonably I will not dispute; this I know, that in the post he filled, which was no inconsiderable one, he passed for a very rational man, and the press has shown that he wanted not parts of learning;)—would any one say, that he, being not conscious of any of Socrates' actions or thoughts, could be the same *person* with Socrates? Let any one reflect upon himself, and conclude that he has

FIG. 4.2 Frida Kahlo, *The Two Fridas* (1939). Would the real Frida Kahlo please stand up? *(Schalkwijk / Art Resource, NY /Artists Rights Society (ARS), New York)*

in himself an immaterial spirit, which is that which thinks in him, and, in the constant change of his body keeps him the same: and is that which he calls *himself*.

The body, as well as the soul, goes to the making of a Man.—And thus may we be able, without any difficulty, to conceive the same person at the resurrection, though in a body not exactly in make or parts the same which he had here,—the same consciousness going along with the soul that inhabits it. But yet the soul alone, in the change of bodies, would scarce to any one but to him that makes the soul the man, be enough to make the same man. For should the soul of a prince, carrying with it the consciousness of the prince's past life, enter and inform the body of a cobbler, as soon as deserted by his own soul, every one sees he would be the same *person* with the prince, accountable only for the prince's actions: but who would say it was the same *man?* The body too goes to the making the man, and would, I guess, to everybody determine the man in this case, wherein the soul, with all its princely thoughts about it, would not make another man: but he would be the same cobbler to every one besides himself. I know that, in the ordinary way of speaking, the same person, and the same man, stand for one and the same thing.

Consciousness alone unites actions into the same Person.—But though the same immaterial substance or soul does not alone, wherever it be, and in whatsoever state, make the same *man;* yet it is plain, consciousness, as far as ever it can be extended—should it be to ages past—unites existences and actions very remote in time into the same *person,* as well as it does the existences and actions of the immediately preceding moment: so that whatever has the consciousness of present and past actions, is the same person to whom they both belong. Had I the same consciousness that I saw the ark and Noah's flood, as that I saw an overflowing of the Thames last winter, or as that I write now, I could no more doubt that I who write this now, that saw the Thames overflowed last winter, and that viewed the flood at the general deluge, was the same *self,*—place that self in what *substance* you please—than that I who write this am the same *myself* now whilst I write (whether I consist of all the same substance, material or immaterial, or no) that I was yesterday. For as to this point of being the same self, it matters not whether this present self be made up of the same or other substances—I being as much concerned, and as justly accountable for any action that was done a thousand years since, appropriated to me now by this self-consciousness, as I am for what I did the last moment.

Self depends on Consciousness, not on Substance.—*Self* is that conscious thinking thing,—whatever substance made up of, (whether spiritual or material, simple or compounded, it matters not)—which is sensible or conscious of pleasure and pain, capable of happiness or misery, and so is concerned for itself, as far as that consciousness extends. Thus every one finds that, whilst comprehended under that consciousness, the little finger is as much a part of himself as what is most so. Upon separation of this little finger, should this consciousness go along with the little finger, and leave the rest of the body, it is evident the little finger would be the person, the same person; and self then would have nothing to do with the rest of the body. As in this case it is the consciousness that goes along with the substance, when one part is separate from another, which makes the same person, and constitutes this inseparable self: so it is in reference to the substances remote in time. That with which the consciousness of this present thinking thing *can* join itself, makes the same person, and is one self with it, and with nothing else; and so attributes to itself, and owns all the actions of that thing, as its own, as far as that consciousness reaches, and no further.

> "*Self* is that conscious thinking thing . . . which is sensible or conscious of pleasure and pain, capable of happiness or misery, and so is concerned for itself, as far as that consciousness extends."
>
> – JOHN LOCKE

FIG. 4.3 The author, Robert C. Solomon, age five. *(photo by Charles Solomon, 1948; used by permission of H. Andrew Solomon, Jon Solomon, and Kathleen M. Higgins)*

The main thesis of Locke's argument is this: Personal self-identity is based upon self-consciousness, in particular, upon memories about one's former experiences. In this, he argues, man is different from animals, whose identity (that is, "the same dog" or "the same horse") is based on the continuity of the body, just as you would say that you have had "the same car" for ten years even if almost every part except the chassis has been replaced during that time. The identity of a "person," that is, "personal" identity, depends on self-consciousness.

Locke's idea that memory is what constitutes a self-identity is inspired by the distinctly Cartesian notion that a person's relationship to his or her own thoughts is unique. You cannot think my thoughts and I cannot think yours. Since memory is a species of thought, it follows that you cannot remember my experiences, nor I yours. For example, you may remember your first day of school. Because *you* are remembering that experience as one that happened to *you*, you are self-identical to the person who had the earlier experience. According to Locke, then, memory provides an infallible link between what we might call different "stages" of a person. Memory seems to guarantee the identity of the person who is now remembering with the person who was then having the experience.

While Locke's theory has the advantage over Descartes' of allowing us to understand self-identity in terms of consciousness without requiring that we posit the existence of a persisting immaterial soul, it is not without its own difficulties. First, much of what we experience, we later forget. Do you remember everything that has ever happened to you? Undoubtedly, the answer is no. Even a person who has a very good memory does not remember being born, learning to walk, or what he had for breakfast on June 3, 2008. Probably you have completely forgotten some fairly long stretches of your past. What are we to make of these forgotten periods, with regard to our personal identity? How mistaken can we be in our memories and beliefs about ourselves? At what point of remembering would we want to say that "those memories cannot be our memories at all?"

Second, our memories are not always accurate. Sometimes we remember things that never happened. For example, you might remember very clearly lending your copy of *Introducing Philosophy* to a friend, only to find later that you had, in fact, been using it as a doorstop. Even more disturbing, though fortunately less frequent, cases of inaccurate memory occur when a person sincerely remembers experiences which, in fact, happened, but didn't happen to him. There are people who now remember delivering the Gettysburg Address, discovering radium, or singing "I wanna hold your hand" with George, John, Paul, and Ringo at Carnegie Hall. What are we to say of the memories of the deluded and the deranged? They are not *genuine* memories, but are only *apparent* memories. Clearly, Locke did not intend merely apparent memories to count among those which guarantee identity. We must, then, find a way to distinguish between those cases in which a memory is genuine and those in which it is not. But to do this, it seems that we would have to say that the memories are in fact the correct memories *of that person.* If this is so, it would appear that the Memory Theory is circular.

FIG. 4.4 Which is the "true" Robert C. Solomon: the five-year-old boy or the fifty-seven-year-old man? They are so different: how can they be identical? *(© Kathleen M. Higgins)*

A genuine memory, as opposed to a merely apparent one, is, of course, a memory of an experience the rememberer actually had. The person who is having the memory must be the one who had the experience. Now you can see that in distinguishing genuine from apparent memory, we have presupposed the existence of a persisting, self-identical person. That would be all very well were it not for the fact that the concept of self-identity is precisely what we are trying to explain. We cannot use the concept of memory to explain self-identity and then use the concept of self-identity to explain memory. Moreover, once we reflect on the nature of genuine memory, we can see that Locke was, indeed, putting the cart before the horse. When a person says, "I remember when I learned to ride my bike," the truth of his statement presupposes, rather than establishes, that he is self-identical to the little boy with the scabby knees.

Nevertheless, modern theories of personal identity have by and large appealed to some notion of memory, self-consciousness, or psychological continuity. It is worth mentioning that ancient philosophers, Aristotle for example, did not believe this and probably would not even have understood much of what Descartes and Locke were arguing about. For Aristotle, self-identity was essentially bodily identity, without any particular reference to self-consciousness. But neither must it be thought that the modern thesis has been without its critics, in fact, its devastating critics.

> - How does the role of consciousness differ in the accounts of self-identity of Locke and Descartes?
> - Can you think of a time when you were "unaware" of your self, i.e., contrary to Locke, you were not aware of your awareness and you did not perceive that you were perceiving? Describe this situation.
> - What is the difference between individual substance and personal identity for Locke? What constitutes individual substance? What constitutes personal identity?
> - Does Locke think that the preexistence of the soul entails the preexistence of one's self?
> - What is the difference between "the person" and "the man" for Locke? What is required for each?

Hume completely undercuts Descartes' and Locke's view of self-identity. Relying on his belief that any idea must be derived from an impression, Hume argues that when we are self-conscious we are only aware of fleeting thoughts, feelings, and perceptions; we do not have an impression of the self or a thinking substance. He concludes that the idea of the self is simply a fiction. Moreover, since we are never aware of any enduring self, we are never justified in claiming we are the same person we were a year or a minute ago.

 On "There Is No Self" BY David Hume[4]

There are some philosophers, who imagine we are every moment intimately conscious of what we call our SELF, that we feel its existence and its continuance in existence and are certain, beyond the evidence of a demonstration, both of its perfect identity and simplicity. The strongest sensation, the most violent passion, say they, instead of distracting us from this view, only fix it the more intensely, and make us consider their influence on *self* either by their pain or pleasure. To attempt a farther

---

4David Hume, *A Treatise of Human Nature*, ed. L. A. Selby-Bigge, Oxford: Oxford University Press, 1888.

proof of this were to weaken its evidence; since no proof can be deriv'd from any fact, of which we are so intimately conscious; nor is there any thing of which we can be certain, if we doubt of this.

Unluckily all these positive assertions are contrary to that very experience, which is pleaded for them, nor have we any idea of *self*, after the manner it is here explain'd. For from what impression cou'd this idea be deriv'd? This question 'tis impossible to answer without a manifest contradiction, and absurdity; and yet 'tis a question, which must necessarily be answer'd, if we wou'd have the idea of self pass for clear and intelligible. It must be some one impression, that gives rise to every real idea. But self or person is not any one impression, but that to which our several impressions and ideas are suppos'd to have a reference. If any impression gives rise to the idea of self, that impression must continue invariably the same, thro' the whole course of our lives; since self is suppos'd to exist after that manner. But there is no impression constant and invariable. Pain and pleasure, grief and joy, passions and sensations succeed each other, and never all exist at the same time. It cannot, therefore, be from any of these impressions, or from any other, that the idea of self is deriv'd; and consequently there is no such idea.

But farther, what must become of all our particular perceptions upon this hypothesis? All these are different, and distinguishable, and separable from each other and may be separately consider'd, and may exist separately, and have no need of any thing to support their existence. After what manner, therefore, do they belong to self and how are they connected with it? For my part, when I enter most intimately into what I call *myself*, I always stumble on some particular perception or other, of heat or cold, light or shade, love or hatred, pain or pleasure. I never can catch *myself* at any time without a perception, and never can observe any thing but the perception. When my perceptions are remov'd for any time, as by sound sleep; so long am I insensible of myself, and may truly be said not to exist. And were all my perceptions remov'd by death, and cou'd I neither think, nor feel, nor see, nor love, nor hate after the dissolution of my body, I shou'd be entirely annihilated, nor do I conceive what is further requisite to make me a perfect nonentity. If any one upon serious and unprejudiced reflexion, thinks he has a different notion of *himself*, I must confess I can reason no longer with him. All I can allow him is, that he may be in the right as well

FIG. 4.5 *(© iStockphoto.com/Robert Churchill)*

as I, and that we are essentially different in this particular. He may, perhaps, perceive something simple and continu'd, which he calls *himself;* tho' I am certain there is no such principle in me.

But setting aside some metaphysicians of this kind, I may venture to affirm of the rest of mankind, that they are nothing but a bundle or collection of different perceptions, which succeed each other with an inconceivable rapidity, and are in a perpetual flux and movement. Our eyes cannot turn in their sockets without varying our perceptions. Our thought is still more variable than our sight; and all our other senses and faculties contribute to this change; nor is there any single power of the soul, which remains unalterably the same, perhaps for one moment. The mind is a kind of theatre, where several perceptions successively make their appearance; pass, repass, glide away, and mingle in an infinite variety of postures and situations. There is properly no *simplicity* in it at one time, nor *identity* in different; whatever natural propension we may have to imagine that simplicity and identity. The comparison of the theatre must not mislead us. They are the successive perceptions only, that constitute the mind: nor have we the most distant notion of the place, where these scenes are represented, or of the materials, of which it is compos'd.

What then gives us so great a propension to ascribe an identity to these successive perceptions, and to suppose ourselves possest of any invariable and uninterrupted existence thro' the whole course of our lives?

To answer this question, Hume draws an analogy between the fictitious identity we ascribe to persons and the equally fictitious identity we ascribe to things. Just as we can never find an impression of the self that will explain human identity, so we can never find an impression of an object or substance to explain the identity of plants, animals, and things. According to Hume, then, we are never justified in claiming that, for example, a tree we see now is the same tree we saw five years ago or even five minutes ago. The cells and parts of the tree are continuously being replaced so that at no time is it ever literally the same tree. But Hume's argument goes further than this; even if that were not so, we would still have no way of justifying our belief that this tree is the same one we saw some time ago, rather than another, reasonably similar to it, but yet different. How do we know, for example, that someone has not come along and replaced it with another?

The temptation to ascribe identity to things and persons, Hume thinks, arises in part from the spatiotemporal continuity of the thing; the tree is in the same place at different times. People, however, have the troublesome habit of moving around, going to Europe for the summer or college for the semester; we still see the continuity of his or her movement, receive postcards from the appropriate places at the appropriate times, and so we conclude that it is the same person. In addition to spatiotemporal continuity, we ordinarily rely on **resemblance** as a **criterion** of identity. We tolerate small changes, a haircut or a new scar, perhaps even a lost leg or a bit of plastic surgery. As long as there is a strong resemblance between two individuals, for example before and after a haircut, we think of them as the same. Only when there is a great change, as from Dr. Jekyll to Mr. Hyde, do we question the identity of the two individuals.

Hume, however, argues that spatiotemporal continuity and resemblance do not in fact guarantee identity:

The identity, which we ascribe to the mind of man, is only a fictitious one, and of a like kind with that which we ascribe to vegetables and animal bodies. It cannot, therefore, have a different origin, but must proceed from a like operation of the imagination upon his objects.

"I may venture to affirm of the rest of mankind, that they are nothing but a bundle or collection of different perceptions, which succeed each other with an inconceivable rapidity, and are in a perpetual flux and movement."

– DAVID HUME

We have a distinct idea of an object, that remains invariable and uninterrupted thro' a suppos'd variation of time; and this idea we call that of *identity* or *sameness*. We have also a distinct idea of several different objects existing in succession, and connected together by a close relation; and this to an accurate view affords as perfect a notion of *diversity*, as if there was no manner of relation among the objects. But tho' these two ideas of identity, and a succession of related objects be in themselves perfectly distinct, and even contrary, yet 'tis certain, that in our common way of thinking they are generally confounded with each other. That action of the imagination, by which we consider the uninterrupted and invariable object, and that by which we reflect on the succession of related objects, are almost the same to the feeling, nor is there much more effort to thought requir'd in the latter case than in the former. The relation facilitates the transition of the mind from one object to another, and renders its passage as smooth as if it contemplated one continu'd object. This resemblance is the cause of the confusion and mistake, and makes us substitute the notion of identity, instead of that of related objects.

Our last resource is to . . . boldly assert that these different related objects are in effect the same, however interrupted and variable. In order to justify to ourselves this absurdity, we often feign some new and unintelligible principle, that connects the objects together, and prevents their interruption or variation. Thus we feign the continu'd existence of the perceptions of our senses, to remove the interruption; and run into the notion of a *soul*, and *self*, and *substance*, to disguise the variation. But we may farther observe, that where we do not give rise to such a fiction, our propension to confound identity with relation is so great, that we are apt to imagine something unknown and mysterious connecting the parts, beside their relation; and this I take to be the case with regard to the identity we ascribe to plants and vegetables. And even when this does not take place, we still feel a propensity to confound these ideas, tho' we are not able fully to satisfy ourselves in that particular, nor find any thing invariable and uninterrupted to justify our notion of identity.

· · ·

Suppose any mass of matter, of which the parts are contiguous and connected, to be plac'd before us; 'tis plain we must attribute a perfect identity to this mass, provided all the parts continue uninterruptedly and invariably the same, whatever motion or change of place we may observe either in the whole or in any of the parts. But supposing some very *small* or *inconsiderable* part to be added to the mass, or subtracted from it; tho' this absolutely destroys the identity of the whole, strictly speaking; yet as we seldom think so accurately, we scruple not to pronounce a mass of matter the same, where we find so trivial an alteration. The passage of the thought from the object before the change to the object after it, is so smooth and easy, that we scarce perceive the transition, and are apt to imagine, that 'tis nothing but a continu'd survey, of the same object.

• How do you understand Hume's claim that the self is nothing but a bundle of perceptions? Where, then, do we get our idea of identity, according to Hume?

Hume's argument is familiar to us from our discussion of empiricism in Chapter 3. All we perceive, he says, is a sequence of impressions, and nowhere do we encounter an impression either of a substance (an enduring object) or of the self. What right do we have, therefore, to identify the object of this impression with the object of another? What right do we have to identify the person we are now with someone in the past?

But Hume's argument that "I never can catch myself" suffers from a peculiar but obvious form of self-contradiction. He can't even deny that there is a self without in some sense pointing to himself in order to do it. This point was not missed by Kant. Kant agrees with Hume that the enduring self is not to be found in self-consciousness. The enduring self is not an object of experience—Hume was right on this point and both Descartes and Locke were mistaken. In Kant's words, the enduring self is not empirical. It is transcendental.

By "transcendental" Kant means what is a necessary condition for the possibility of *any* experience. Kant saw that if there were a different self at each moment of consciousness, we would not be able to perceive anything. In order to experience an object, we must be able to combine our various impressions of it in a unified consciousness. Thus, if we do in fact experience objects, we must assume that we have a unified consciousness that combines these impressions into the perception of an object. Or, to take a different example, Hume talks of different sorts of relations of impressions, for example, succession. In order for an individual to perceive two impressions as successive, these impressions must have been perceived by the *same* consciousness.

The self of "I" for Kant, then, is the necessary logical subject of any thought, perception, feeling, and so on. It is not an object of experience but transcends and is presupposed by all experience.

Hume's error, as in other matters, was in confusing the supposed experience of self-consciousness with the transcendental rules with which we tie these various experiences together. Accordingly, Kant argues, Descartes and Locke are both correct in equating self-identity and self-consciousness, but it must not be thought that the self is therefore a "thing" (as Descartes said) that we find in experience.

According to Kant, the self is the activity of consciousness, in particular the activity of organizing our various experiences. Kant borrows Hume's argument, but he turns it toward the opposite conclusion: True, I never find a self "in" my experiences, but I can always find myself in that "I" that has the experience. Kant's "self," in other words, is the act of having experiences rather than anything that we experience itself. But for Kant this self is not merely the passive recipient of experiences, and here is where the notion of self as activity becomes all-important. The self is the activity of applying the rules by which we organize our experience. Moreover, Kant argues that one of the most basic rules of this activity is that the self organize its experience as its own experience. The rule is that we must always "synthesize" our various experiences into a unity, for we could not come to have any knowledge whatever of a scattering of various impressions and sensations without this synthesis. (Think, for example, of the slightly painful and generally meaningless sensations you have when someone sets off a camera flashbulb in your eyes.) This basic rule of synthesis allows Kant to say that not only is the self the activity that applies the various rules to experience but its existence as a unified self with a unified synthesis of experiences is itself a rule.

Kant gives this curious idea of the self as a rule a formidable name, "the transcendental unity of apperception." What is important in this concept is that the self for Kant is indeed essential to self-consciousness, but it is not "in" self-consciousness. Metaphorically, it is often said that it is "behind" self-consciousness, that is, it is the activity of bringing our various experiences together in accordance with the basic rules of our experience. Accordingly, Kant refers to this self as the **transcendental ego**, "transcendental" because it is basic and necessary for all possible human experience. The difference between Hume and Kant is sometimes illustrated in this way: Hume looks for the self among our experiences and doesn't find it; Kant agrees with Hume but argues that he looked in the wrong place. The self, Kant says, is the thread that ties together our various experiences. Accordingly, the self is not in the bundle of our experiences; it is rather the "transcendental" thread that holds them all together and is as real as any experience.

Kant returns to Descartes and challenges his main theses, even while agreeing with parts of them. First, while Descartes thought that we had to be self-conscious all the time, Kant insists that it is only necessary for "the 'I think' to be able to accompany all experiences." It is not necessary to be always conscious of our selves but only to be, at any point in our experience, capable of becoming self-conscious; we can turn our attention when we want to from whatever we are doing and watch ourselves doing what we are doing. This is an important point: Our concern with self-consciousness is given impetus just because we are often not self-conscious. In fact, several philosophers (and many mystics) have argued that self-consciousness is bad, a useless thing, and should be avoided as much as possible. According to Descartes, this is not possible, for to exist at all as a human being is to exist self-consciously. According to Kant, on the other hand, to exist as a human being is "to be able" to be self-conscious.

Second, Kant objects to Descartes' belief that the thinking self is a thinking thing. He objects to this, first of all, because of his insistence (as a result of Hume's argument) that the self (or "transcendental ego") is not in our experience but rather "behind" it and responsible for it. More literally, he says that the self must be thought of as an activity. You can see what a radical move this is when you recall the traditional doctrine of the soul in Plato, in Christianity, and in much of modern thought. The soul, quite simply, is the self conceived of as a thing, an enduring thing that can survive the death of the body. By saying that the self is an activity, Kant undermines (as Hume had intended to undermine) the traditional concept of soul.[5]

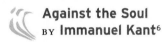

Against the Soul
BY Immanuel Kant[6]

Pure reason requires us to seek for every predicate of a thing its own subject, and for this subject, which is itself necessarily nothing but a predicate, its subject, and so on indefinitely (or as far as we can reach). But hence it follows that we must not hold anything at which we can arrive to be an ultimate subject.

Now we appear to have this substance in the consciousness of ourselves (in the thinking subject), and indeed in an immediate intuition; for all the predicates of an internal sense refer to the *ego*, as a subject, and I cannot conceive myself as the predicate of any other subject. Hence completeness in the reference of the given concepts as predicates to a subject—not merely an Idea, but an object—that is, the absolute subject itself, seems to be given in experience. But this expectation is disappointed. For the ego is not a concept, but only the indication of the object of the inner sense, so far as we know it by no further predicate. Consequently it cannot indeed be itself a predicate of any other thing; but just as little can it be a definite concept of an absolute subject, but is, as in all other cases, only the reference of the inner phenomena to their unknown subject. Yet this idea (which serves very well as a regulative principle totally to destroy all materialistic explanations of the internal phenomena of the soul) occasions by a very natural misunderstanding a very specious argument, which infers its nature from this supposed knowledge of the substance of our thinking being. This is specious so far as the knowledge of it falls quite without the complex of experience.

---

[5] It is worth mentioning that Kant held onto the Christian concept of soul; to do so, he defended it as a "postulate of practical reason," in other words, as a strictly moral claim, much as he had defended his belief in God. Later philosophers borrowed Kant's arguments to get rid of the concept of the soul altogether.

[6] Immanuel Kant, *Prolegomena to Any Future Metaphysics*, trans. Lewis White Beck. Copyright © 1959. Reprinted by permission of Pearson Education, Inc., Upper Saddle River, NJ.

But though we may call this thinking self (the soul) "substance," as being the ultimate subject of thinking which cannot be further represented as the predicate of another thing, it remains quite empty and without significance if permanence—the quality which renders the concept of substances in experience fruitful—cannot be proved of it.

But permanence can never be proved of the concept of a substance as a thing in itself, but for the purposes of experience only.

If, therefore, from the concept of the soul as a substance we would infer its permanence, this can hold good as regards possible experience only, not of the soul as a thing in itself and beyond all possible experience. Life is the subjective condition of all our possible experience; consequently we can only infer the permanence of the soul in life, for the death of a man is the end of all experience which concerns the soul as an object of experience, except the contrary be proved—which is the very question in hand. The permanence of the soul can therefore only be proved (and no one cares to do that) during the life of man, but not, as we desire to do, after death. The reason for this is that the concept of substance, so far as it is to be considered necessarily with the concept of permanence, can be so combined only according to the principles of possible experience, and therefore for the purposes of experience only.

> "Life is the subjective condition of all our possible experience; consequently we can only infer the permanence of the soul in life, for the death of a man is the end of all experience."
>
> – IMMANUEL KANT

Third, Kant argued that we need two very different conceptions of self. He saw that this conception of self as self-consciousness was not sufficient to do the whole job that philosophers had wanted it to do. One part of Descartes' enterprise was to find out what was essential to his existence, what could not be doubted and so could serve as a first premise for his *Meditations*. So too Locke and Hume had tried to find (though Locke did and Hume didn't) that self that defined us through our various changes, which identified Jekyll and Hyde and identifies us from year to year, day to day, and mood to mood. But the function of the self was also to serve as a way of identifying ourselves in distinction from other people and other things. Thus Descartes' concept of the self as a thinking thing was not sufficient to tell us what made one person different from another, and he found it necessary to supplement his concept of self with an account of how a person was composed of a self and a body in some special way.

> - How does Kant answer Hume's challenge that there is no enduring self of which we are aware?
> - Why is the transcendental self lacking as an explanation for self-identity? What does Kant introduce into his theory that would account for the differences we observe among persons?

Similarly, Locke distinguishes between personal identity and identity as a man (that is, as a biological example of the species *Homo sapiens*) and tells us that both are necessary for us to understand how one particular person is different from another particular person. We can now clearly see that the question of self-identity divides into two questions: (1) What is essential to being a self? and (2) What is essential to being a particular self? Kant's conception of self as that which has experiences, the transcendental self, only answers the first question. Nothing in the notion of transcendental self allows us to distinguish between different people and tell them apart. Accordingly, he identifies another "self" that he calls the **empirical ego**, which includes all of those particular things about us that make us different people. Differences in our bodies, our looks, our size, our strength would be such differences. So too would our different personalities, our different thoughts and memories. It is the empirical self that identifies us as individual persons. The transcendental self makes possible human consciousness.[7]

These have been the traditional answers to the philosophical problem of self-identity. What is it that makes one "the same person" from moment to moment and year to year? The spatiotemporal **continuity** of the body would seem to be a part of the answer. But philosophers since (and before) Descartes have seen quite clearly that this is never enough, that it is also self-consciousness that provides the key to self-identity. But even this has not solved the problem. To see this, consider these bizarre but illuminating examples:

Jones has an emergency brain operation. His own brain is removed and replaced by the brain of Brown (who is recently deceased). "Jones" still looks like Jones, still carries the same driver's license and lives in the same house, but all of his memories and personality traits are those of Brown. Is he still Jones? Or is he Brown in Jones's body? Suppose you had been (or are) Brown, could you claim to be still alive in Jones's body?

Or, suppose Smith undergoes a personality split of the most radical kind imaginable. Like the one-celled animal, the amoeba, Smith splits, head to toe, each half of him forming an exact duplicate of the original—same memories and personality, same habits, knowledge, likes and dislikes, skills, and so on. Which of the two is Smith? Does it make any sense to say that both are? Suppose that you are one of the two resultant Smiths. Would you—could you—intelligibly say that the other Smith is also you? But, given your common origins and exact similarities, could you say that the other Smith was merely someone else?

In the movie *All of Me*, the soul of a woman who has recently died (played by Lily Tomlin) winds up occupying the body of a male lawyer (played by Steve Martin). The resulting character, played by Martin, still looks, acts, and thinks like the Steve Martin character, but now also possesses the memories and personality traits of Lily Tomlin's original character. Who is this dual character?

To consider the bizarre complications, here is Massachusetts philosopher **Meredith Michaels**, who has written extensively on the problem of personal identity:

On "Personal Identity"
BY **Meredith Michaels**[8]

While they are illuminating, particularly in relation to one another, these traditional answers to the philosophical problem of self–identity raise as many questions as they answer. To see this, let us travel to a not very distant make-believe world.

One night, after a serious bout with the library, you and your best friend Wanda Bagg (or Walter, if you prefer) decide to indulge yourselves at the College Haven. Before you can stop her, Wanda steps out in front of a steamroller that happens to be moving down Main Street. Wanda is crushed. Witnessing the horror of the accident, you have a stroke. Fortunately, Dr. Hagendaas, the famous neurosurgeon who has

---

[7]Ludwig Wittgenstein, for example, used a Kantian thesis to deny the existence of the subject altogether. In his *Tractatus Logico-Philosophicus*, he tells us: "The thinking, presenting subject–there is no such thing. *In an important sense* there is no subject. The subject does not belong to the world, but is a limit of the world. There is [therefore] really a sense in which in philosophy we can talk nonpsychologically of the I. The I occurs in philosophy through the fact that the 'world is my world.' The philosophical I is not the man, not the human body, or the human soul of which psychology treats, but the metaphysical subject, the limit–not a part of the world."

[8]Meredith Michaels, "Personal Identity," in Robert C. Solomon, *Introducing Philosophy: A Text with Readings*, 3rd ed. (San Diego: Harcourt Brace Jovanovich, 1977). Reprinted with permission.

been visiting the campus, is also on the way to the College Haven. Taking charge, he rushes you and Wanda to the Health Center, where he performs a "body transplant." He takes Wanda's brain, which miraculously escaped the impact of the steamroller, and puts it in the place of yours, which was, of course, severely damaged by the stroke. After several days, the following battle ensues: Wanda's parents claim that they are under no obligation to continue paying tuition. After all, Wanda was killed by a steamroller. Your parents claim that they are under no obligation to continue paying tuition. After all, you died of a stroke. It is clear, then, that a basic question is in need of an answer: who is the person lying in bed in the Health Center? Is it Wanda? Is it you? Is it someone else altogether? For the sake of discussion, let us call the person lying in the bed Schwanda. What reasons do we have for believing that Schwanda is Wanda? Given that one's self-consciousness, one's thoughts, beliefs and feelings are all mental phenomena, we might naturally conclude that a person goes wherever her brain goes (on the assumption that our mental characteristics are more likely "located" in the brain than in, say, our smallest left toe). Schwanda will remember having set off for the College Haven with you; she will remember receiving the college acceptance letter addressed: "Dear Wanda, We are happy to inform you that . . ."; she'll remember being hugged by Wanda's mother on the afternoon of her first day of school. That is, Schwanda will *believe* that she's Wanda.

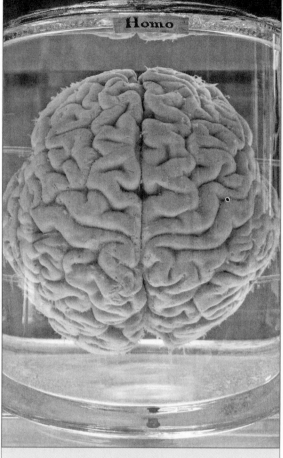

FIG. 4.6 Is the brain the self? (© iStockphoto.com/Baloncici)

Nevertheless, the fact that Schwanda believes herself to be Wanda does not in itself guarantee that she is. Do we have any basis for insisting that Schwanda is Wanda and not someone who is *deluded* into thinking that she's Wanda? How can we determine whether Schwanda's Wanda memories are genuine and not merely apparent? As we came to realize in our discussion of Locke's Memory Theory, it is not legitimate at this point to appeal to the self-identity of Schwanda and Wanda, since that is precisely what we're trying to determine. In other words, in attempting to establish that Schwanda's Wanda memories are genuine memories, we cannot argue that they are genuine on the grounds that Schwanda *is* Wanda.

Perhaps it is possible to stop short of circularity. Why couldn't we say that Schwanda's Wanda memories are genuine because the *brain* that is remembering is the same as the brain that had the original experiences. Thus, the experiences are preserved in the very organ that underwent them. Though there is an initial plausibility to this response, it fails to solve our problem. Suppose that Schwanda is Wanda—remembering the experience of learning to ride a bicycle. Though the brain in question is indeed the same, it is nonetheless clear to all of us that brains alone do not learn to ride bicycles. Nor, indeed, do brains alone remember having done so. *People* learn to ride bicycles and *people* remember having done so. And the question we are trying to answer is whether Schwanda (who is remembering) is the same person as Wanda (who did the bicycling). The appeal to the fact that the same brain is involved in each event does not provide us with a way out of the Lockean circle.

It is at this point that philosophers begin to reconsider the Aristotelian position, mentioned earlier, that self-identity is essentially *bodily* identity. If the Body Theory of Personal Identity is true, then the person lying in bed at the Health Center is you, deluded into believing that you are Wanda. That is, Schwanda is self-identical to you.

You might wonder, at this point, whether there are any positive reasons for endorsing the Body Theory, or whether it is simply a place to which one retreats only in defeat? The following case is designed to persuade you that there is at least *some* plausibility to the Body Theory. Suppose that an evil scientist, Dr. Nefarious, has selected you as his prime subject for a horrible experiment. You are dragged into his office. He says, "Tomorrow at 5:00, you will be subjected to the most terrible tortures. Your nails will be pulled out one by one. Rats will be caged around your head. Burning oil will drip slowly on your back. The remainder I leave as a surprise."

Are you worried about what will happen to you at 5:00 tomorrow? If you have any sense, you are. You think of the excruciating pain and suffering you will undergo and would surely do just about anything to avoid it.

But now, Dr. Nefarious says, "Tomorrow at 4:55, I will use my Dememorizer to erase your memory of this conversation." Are you still anxious about what is going to happen to you tomorrow at 5:00? Surely you are. After all the fact that you won't, between 4:55 and 5:00, be anticipating your torture doesn't entail that the torture itself will be any less painful. When you forget that your Calculus professor told the class there would be a test on Friday, you aren't thereby spared the experience of taking the test (in fact, in that case the experience is made worse by your not having had the opportunity to anticipate it).

Now, Dr. Nefarious says, "Tomorrow at 4:57, I will use my Dememorizer to erase *all* of your memories." Are you still anxious about what will happen tomorrow at 5:00? Isn't it natural to describe the situation as one in which you will undergo horrible torture, though you won't know who you are or why this is happening to you? *You* will still experience *your* fingernails being pulled out, *your* back being burned, *your* face being eaten up by rats. Surely, those experiences are ones you would like to avoid.

Finally, Dr. Nefarious says to you, "Tomorrow at 4:58, I am going to use my Rememorizer to implant in your brain all of Ronald Reagan's memories." Though this may not please you for personal or political reasons, the relevant question remains this: are you still worried about what is going to happen tomorrow at 5:00? Isn't it again perfectly natural to describe the situation as one in which you will undergo horrible torture, all the while believing that you are Ronald Reagan. Do you not *now* remain concerned that you are Ronald Reagan? Do you not *now* remain concerned that you will experience excruciating pain and intolerable suffering? Look at your fingernails while you consider your answer to this question.

What this story demonstrates is not the conclusive superiority of the Body Theory over the Memory (or Brain) Theory, but rather the importance of our bodies to our self-identity. This is something that tends to get lost in the traditional conceptions of personal identity. Furthermore, returning to the case of Schwanda, we can now see that it is not altogether preposterous to argue that Schwanda is indeed you, deluded into believing that she is Wanda. In other words, anyone who wishes to dismiss the possibility must also dismiss the possibility that the person who undergoes the torture is indeed you, deluded into believing that you are Ronald Reagan.

While it is true that we tend to identify ourselves with and by our thoughts, beliefs, inclinations and feelings, our discussion of the Body Theory should remind us that there are reasons for believing that our bodies are, at the very least, important to who we are. Some philosophers would argue that our bodies *are* who we are, that self-identity *is* bodily identity.

In considering these admittedly fanciful problem cases, we have seen that we lack a concept of self-identity that allows us to predict when we would or wouldn't persist through time. This might suggest to us that our concept of self-identity is not an all-or-nothing one, that, in fact, our concept is one which admits of degrees. If so, we are no longer talking about identity per se, which is an all-or-nothing concept, but rather about some other relation of psychological and physical connectedness. Nevertheless, we can now see first, that the answer to the question "Who ought to pay Schwanda's tuition?" will depend upon which theory of personal identity we are inclined to endorse and second, that the answer may not be as clear and unequivocal as we would like it to be.

> "We lack a concept of self-identity that allows us to predict when we would or wouldn't persist through time."
> – MEREDITH MICHAELS

B. Existentialism: Self-Identity and the Responsibility of Choice

The idea of a multiple, or nonself introduced a very important alternative to Western, essentially Judeo-Christian conceptions. In addition to the concern for survival in Heaven or Hell, this Western conception is typically concerned with striving and ambition, status and planning for the future, "making something of yourself." **Existentialism** is one form of this conception. The American dream and the Protestant and capitalist ethics in general are another. But from the conception of nonself comes a very different picture—of unqualified acceptance of things as they are rather than struggling to change them, which involves a rejection of such notions as "status" and "making something of yourself."

Once again we must not confuse this rejection of traditional Western conceptions of the self with a rejection of the philosophical question of self-identity. "Who am I?" is as important a question for the mystic as it is for the Western philosopher. It is just that the mystic's answer to the question is radically different. Does it make sense to say that the one is more "correct" than the other? This too is part of the question of self-identity. Must there be a single "correct" answer for everyone? There is nothing necessary about this, or even desirable. The problem of self-identity, both in each individual case and as a general problem, is the problem of deciding which of the many possible characteristics (not necessarily one) should be chosen as our own standards for self-identity, and that choice is not just one that philosophers make, but one which each person makes at some point or points during his or her life.

A self-identity isn't simply a label you throw on yourself in the casual discussion of a philosophy class. It is a mask and a role that you wear in every social encounter (though perhaps slightly different masks and roles for significantly different encounters). It is the way you think of yourself and the standards by which you judge yourself in every moment of reflection and self-evaluation. It is the self-image you follow in every action, when you decide that one thing is "worth doing" more than another or when you decide how to act in a given circumstance. Because of it, you feel proud, guilty, ashamed, or delighted after you have done something. The problem of self-identity is not just a problem for philosophers; it is a problem we all face, either explicitly or implicitly, every self-conscious minute of our lives.

But, you might say, why make it sound as if there is any single notion or goal of a correct self-identity? The way in which a contemporary Chinese farmer thinks of himself and judges himself is very different from that of a contemporary American college student. And a very handsome but stupendously dumb bully will surely have a very different conception of self-identity than an extremely intelligent and talented college mathematics major. This may not stop the medieval scholastic, who will immediately declare all of that irrelevant and insist that "before God" all of us are the same and our identities are to be judged accordingly. And most of us, despite the glib relativism we usually defend, would insist on a category that transcends all such individual considerations; we call it "being a good person." Ultimately we would judge the dumb bully and the budding young artist according to the same criterion, and, in doing so, we would think that they should share the criterion "being a good person." Even where cultural differences would seem to demand entirely different conceptions of self-identity, we might still insist on applying the same criterion. For example, a South Sea Islander might well think of himself or herself in terms that would be wholly unacceptable to us, but we can always reduce any variance from our norms to mere "accidental differences," insisting that we are essentially the same. Of course people are different and think differently of themselves; but it does not follow that those differences are essential, nor does it follow that relativism is true. Ultimately when you say that all people are "essentially the same," then you believe that there are, indeed, universal criteria for self-identity and that the differences between people, though we need not deny them, are merely superficial.

One of the most powerful schools of contemporary thought, however, has been dedicated to the idea that self-identity, in every case, is a matter of individual choice. This school, which we have briefly met before, is existentialism. Its most powerful advocate is the French philosopher **Jean-Paul Sartre**. According to Sartre, there are no set standards for self-identity, either for individuals or for people in general. There is, he argues, no such thing as "human nature," and what we are—and what it means to be a human being—are always matters of decision. There is no correct choice; there are only choices, he claims. In a well-known essay from the late 1940s, he argues:

On Existentialism
BY Jean-Paul Sartre[9]

What existentialists have in common is simply the fact that they believe that *existence* comes before *essence*—or, if you will, that we must begin from the subjective. What exactly do we mean by that?

If one considers an article of manufacture—as, for example, a book or paper-knife—one sees that it has been made by an artisan who had a conception of it; and he has paid attention, equally, to the conception of a paper-knife and to the pre-existent technique of production which is a part of that conception and is, at bottom, a formula. Thus the paper-knife is at the same time an article producible in a certain manner and one which, on the other hand, serves a definite purpose, for one cannot suppose that a man would produce a paper-knife without knowing what it was for. Let us say, then, of the paper-knife that its essence—that is to say the sum of the formulae and the qualities which made its production and its definition possible—precedes its existence. The presence of such-and-such a paper-knife or book is thus determined before my eyes. Here, then, we are viewing the world from a technical standpoint, and we say that production precedes existence.

When we think of God as the creator, we are thinking of him, most of the time, as a supernal artisan. Whatever doctrine we may be considering, whether it

9 Jean-Paul Sartre, *Existentialism as a Humanism*, trans. Phillip Mairet, New York: Philosophical Library of New York, 1949.

be a doctrine like that of Descartes, or of Leibniz himself, we always imply that the will follows, more or less, from the understanding or at least accompanies it, so that when God creates he knows precisely what he is creating. Thus, the conception of man in the mind of God is comparable to that of the paper-knife in the mind of the artisan: God makes man according to a procedure and a conception, exactly as the artisan manufactures a paper-knife, following a definition and a formula. Thus each individual man is the realisation of a certain conception which dwells in the divine understanding. In the philosophic atheism of the eighteenth century, the notion of God is suppressed, but not, for all that, the idea that essence is prior to existence; something of that idea we still find everywhere, in Diderot, in Voltaire and even in Kant. Man possesses a human nature; that "human nature," which is the conception of human being, is found in every man; which means that each man is a particular example of an universal conception, the conception of Man. In Kant, this universality goes so far that the wild man of the woods, man in the state of nature and the bourgeois are all contained in the same definition and have the same fundamental qualities. Here again, the essence of man precedes that historic existence which we confront in experience.

. . .

What do we mean by saying that existence precedes essence? We mean that man first of all exists, encounters himself, surges up in the world—and defines himself afterwards. If man as the existentialist sees him is not definable, it is because to begin with he is nothing. He will not be anything until later, and then he will be what he makes of himself. Thus, there is no human nature, because there is no God to have a conception of it. Man simply is. Not that he is simply what he conceives himself to be, but he is what he wills, and as he conceives himself after already existing—as he wills to be after that leap towards existence. Man is nothing else but that which he makes of himself. That is the first principle of existentialism. And this is what people call its "subjectivity," using the word as a reproach against us. But what do we mean to say by this, but that man is of a greater dignity than a stone or a table? For we mean to say that man primarily exists—that man is, before all else, something which propels itself towards a future and is aware that it is doing so. Man is, indeed, a project which possesses a subjective life, instead of being a kind of moss, or a fungus or a cauliflower. Before that projection of the self nothing exists; not even in the heaven of intelligence: man will only attain existence when he is what he purposes to be. Not, however, what he may wish to be. For what we usually understand by wishing or willing is a conscious decision taken—much more often than not—after we have made ourselves what we are. I may wish to join a party, to write a book or to marry—but in such a case what is usually called my will is probably a manifestation of a prior and more spontaneous decision. If, however, it is true that existence is prior to essence, man is responsible for what he is. Thus, the first effect of existentialism is that it puts every man in possession of himself as he is, and places the entire responsibility for his existence squarely upon his own shoulders. And, when we say that man is responsible for himself, we do not mean that he is responsible only for his own individuality, but that he is responsible for all men.

When we say that man chooses himself, we do mean that every one of us must choose himself; but by that we also mean that in choosing for himself he chooses for all men. For in effect, of all the actions a man may take in order to create himself as he wills to be, there is not one which is not creative, at the same time, of an image of man such as he believes he ought to be.

"When we say that man is responsible for himself, we do not mean that he is responsible only for his own individuality, but that he is responsible for all men."

– JEAN-PAUL SARTRE

- To what extent is self-identity a matter of choice?
- In what way do we choose for everyone when we choose for ourselves, as Sartre sees it?

But this existentialist doctrine of choice doesn't make the problem of self-identity any easier. In fact, it complicates it enormously. Earlier in this section, we began by asking whether the facts about a person are sufficient to determine his or her identity. We said surely not all of them are necessary; some are more essential than others. But this isn't yet an answer to the question, for it may be that all the essential facts are still not sufficient to determine a person's identity.

According to the existentialist, this is made even more complex by the fact that a person chooses which facts are to be considered as essential. Are the facts alone ever sufficient to determine our identity? Sartre's answer, which he adapted from German existentialist Martin Heidegger, is "never!" The facts that are true of a person are always, at least so long as a person is alive, only indicative of what a person has been and done so far. In judging a person's identity, we must always consider more than the facts that are true of him or her (which Sartre and Heidegger collectively name, somewhat technically, a person's **facticity**); we must also consider their projections into the future, their ambitions, plans, intentions, hopes, and fantasies. (Sartre calls these considerations a person's **transcendence**. Notice that this is the third different way in which "transcendence" has been used, so be careful.) This way of viewing the person makes the question of self-identity impossibly complex, in fact, irresolvable. For example, consider Sartre's example of what he calls "bad faith" in one of his most important works, *Being and Nothingness* (1943).

Bad faith, quite simply, is refusing to accept yourself.[10] This can happen in two different ways. Either you can refuse to accept the facts and actions as relevant to your self-identity (for example, denying that your repeated cowardly behavior establishes your identity as a coward). Or you can go too far in the opposite direction, believing that your actions conclusively and unalterably establish your self-identity (for example, denying that you could ever alter your cowardly self-identity through an act of heroism).

On Bad Faith
BY **Jean-Paul Sartre**[11]

Let us take an example: A homosexual frequently has an intolerable feeling of guilt, and his whole existence is determined in relation to this feeling. One will readily foresee that he is in bad faith. In fact it frequently happens that this man, while recognizing his homosexual inclination, while avowing each and every particular misdeed which he has committed, refuses with all his strength to consider himself "*a homosexual.*" His case is always "different," peculiar; there enters into it something of a game, of chance, of bad luck; the mistakes are all in the past; they are explained by a certain conception of the beautiful which women cannot satisfy; we should see in them the results of a restless search, rather than the manifestations of a deeply rooted tendency, etc., etc. Here is assuredly a man in bad faith who borders on the comic

---

[10] This is, however, the main concept of *Being and Nothingness* and takes well over seven hundred pages to analyze correctly.

[11] Jean-Paul Sartre, *Being and Nothingness*, trans. Hazel E. Barnes, New York: Philosophical Library of New York, 1956.

since, acknowledging all the facts which are imputed to him, he refuses to draw from them the conclusion which they impose. His friend, who is his most severe critic, becomes irritated with this duplicity. The critic asks only one thing—and perhaps then he will show himself indulgent: that the guilty one recognize himself as guilty, that the homosexual declare frankly—whether humbly or boastfully matters little— "I am a homosexual." We ask here: Who is in bad faith? The homosexual or the champion of sincerity?

The homosexual recognizes his faults, but he struggles with all his strength against the crushing view that his mistakes constitute for him a *destiny*. He does not wish to let himself be considered as a thing. He has an obscure but strong feeling that a homosexual is not a homosexual as this table is a table or as this red-haired man is red-haired. It seems to him that he has escaped from each mistake as soon as he has posited it and recognized it; he even feels that the psychic duration by itself cleanses him from each misdeed, constitutes for him an undetermined future, causes him to be born anew. Is he wrong? Does he not recognize in himself the peculiar, irreducible character of human reality? His attitude includes then an undeniable comprehension of truth. But at the same time he needs this perpetual rebirth, this constant escape in order to live; he must constantly put himself beyond reach in order to avoid the terrible judgment of collectivity. Thus he plays on the word *being*. He would be right actually if he understood the phrase, "I am not a homosexual" in the sense of "I am not what I am." That is, if he declared to himself, "To the extent that a pattern of conduct is defined as the conduct of a paederast and to the extent that I have adopted this conduct, I am a homosexual. But to the extent that human reality cannot be finally defined by patterns of conduct, I am not one." But instead he slides surreptitiously toward a different connotation of the word "being." He understands "not being" in the sense of "not-being-in-itself." He lays claim to "not being a homosexual" in the sense in which this table *is not* an inkwell. He is in bad faith.

- What is the difference between "facticity" and "transcendence"? How does Sartre employ these concepts to claim that there is no self-identity?
- What is "bad faith"? Describe a time when you acted in bad faith.

Of course, one can be gay without being in bad faith—and there are real pressures that keep gay people "in the closet." Sartre's point is not about whether or not a particular person is gay, but about how we define ourselves and how we "own" or "own up to" our self-characterizations.

For Sartre, bad faith points to the most important single fact about personal self-identity—there isn't any. In somewhat paradoxical terminology, Sartre tells us, "one is what one is not, and one is not what one is." In other words, whatever the facts about you, you are always something more than those facts. The homosexual in Sartre's example *is* a homosexual to the extent that all his past actions and desires are those of a homosexual. He falls into bad faith by refusing to see that his past actions point to his having a self-identity as a homosexual. Yet at the same time, there is a genuine sense in which he is *not* a homosexual: In the future, he may radically alter his lifestyle. It would, then, also be bad faith were he to totally accept his self-identity as a homosexual, denying that he could be anything else. As long as a person is alive, he or she is identified by intentions, plans, dreams, and hopes as much as by what is already true by virtue of the facts. Given this complexity, the problem of deciding "who I am" takes on dramatic and extravagant complications. Consider the following scene from Sartre's famous play, *No Exit*, in which one of the characters (now dead and "living" in hell) tries to justify his image of himself as a hero, despite the facts of his life, which would indicate that he was a coward.

FROM *No Exit*
BY **Jean-Paul Sartre**[12]

GARCIN: They shot me.

ESTELLE: I know. Because you refused to fight. Well, why shouldn't you?

GARCIN: I—I didn't exactly refuse. [*In a far-away voice*] I must say he talks well, he makes out a good case against me, but he never says what I should have done instead. Should I have gone to the general and said: "General I decline to fight"? A mug's game; they'd have promptly locked me up. But I wanted to show my colors, my true colors, do you understand? I wasn't going to be silenced. [*To* ESTELLE] So I—I took the train. . . . They caught me at the frontier.

ESTELLE: Where were you trying to go?

GARCIN: To Mexico. I meant to launch a pacifist newspaper down there. [*A short silence.*] Well, why don't you speak?

ESTELLE: What could I say? You acted quite rightly, as you didn't want to fight. [GARCIN *makes a fretful gesture.*] But, darling, how on earth can I guess what you want me to answer?

INEZ: Can't you guess? Well, *I* can. He wants you to tell him that he bolted like a lion. For "bolt" he did, and that's what's biting him.

GARCIN: "Bolted," "went away"—we won't quarrel over words.

ESTELLE: But you *had* to run away. If you'd stayed they'd have sent you to jail, wouldn't they?

GARCIN: Of course. [*A pause.*] Well, Estelle, am I a coward?

ESTELLE: How can I say? Don't be so unreasonable, darling. I can't put myself in your skin. You must decide that for yourself.

GARCIN: [*wearily*]: I can't decide.

ESTELLE: Anyhow, you must remember. You must have had reasons for acting as you did.

GARCIN: I had.

ESTELLE: Well?

GARCIN: But were they the real reasons?

ESTELLE: You've a twisted mind, that's your trouble. Plaguing yourself over such trifles!

GARCIN: I'd thought it all out, and I wanted to make a stand. But was that my real motive?

FIG. 4.7 Existentialist philosopher Jean-Paul Sartre. *(AP Photo)*

12 From *No Exit and The Flies* by Jean-Paul Sartre, trans. Stuart Gilbert. Copyright © 1946 by Stuart Gilbert, renewed 1974, 1975 by Maris Agnes Mathilde Gilbert. Reprinted by permission of Alfred A. Knopf, a Division of Random House, Inc., and Editions Gallimard, Paris.

INEZ: Exactly. That's the question. Was that your real motive? No doubt you argued it out with yourself, you weighed the pros and cons, you found good reasons for what you did. But fear and hatred and all the dirty little instincts one keeps dark—they're motives too. So carry on, Mr. Garcin, and try to be honest with yourself—for once.

GARCIN: Do I need you to tell me that? Day and night I paced my cell, from the window to the door, from the door to the window. I pried into my heart, I sleuthed myself like a detective. By the end of it I felt as if I'd given my whole life to introspection. But always I harked back to the one thing certain—that I had acted as I did, I'd taken that train to the frontier. But why? Why? Finally I thought: My death will settle it. If I face death courageously, I'll prove I am no coward.

FIG. 4.8 Garcin bolted . . . but like a lion? *(Image © 2011. Used under license from Shutterstock.com)*

INEZ: And how did you face death?

GARCIN: Miserably. Rottenly. [INEZ *laughs*.] Oh, it was only a physical lapse—that might happen to anyone; I'm not ashamed of it. Only everything's been left in suspense, forever. [*To* ESTELLE] Come here, Estelle. Look at me. I want to feel someone looking at me while they're talking about me on earth. . . . I like green eyes.

INEZ: Green eyes! Just hark to him! And you, Estelle, do you like cowards?

ESTELLE: If you knew how little I care! Coward or hero, it's all one—provided he kisses well.

GARCIN: There they are, slumped in their chairs, sucking at their cigars. Bored they look. Half-asleep. They're thinking: "Garcin's a coward." But only vaguely, dreamily. One's got to think of something. "That chap Garcin was a coward." That's what they've decided, those dear friends of mine. In six months' time they'll be saying: "Cowardly as that skunk Garcin." You're lucky, you two; no one on earth is giving you another thought. But I—I'm long in dying.

GARCIN: [*putting his hands on* (INEZ*'s*) *shoulders*]: Listen! Each man has an aim in life, a leading motive; that's so, isn't it? Well, I didn't give a damn for wealth, or for love. I aimed at being a real man. A tough, as they say. I staked everything on the same horse. . . . Can one possibly be a coward when one's deliberately courted danger at every turn? And can one judge a life by a single action?

INEZ: Why not? For thirty years you dreamt you were a hero, and condoned a thousand petty lapses—because a hero, of course, can do no wrong. An easy method obviously. Then a day came when you were up against it, the red light of real danger—and you took the train to Mexico.

GARCIN: I "dreamt," you say. It was no dream. When I chose that hardest path, I made my choice deliberately. A man is what he wills himself to be.

INEZ: Prove it. Prove it was no dream. It's what one does, and nothing else, that shows the stuff one's made of.

> "It's what one does, and nothing else, that shows the stuff one's made of."
>
> – JEAN-PAUL SARTRE

GARCIN: I died too soon. I wasn't allowed time to—to do my deeds.

INEZ: One always dies too soon—or too late. And yet one's whole life is complete at that moment, with a line drawn neatly under it, ready for the summing up. You are—your life, and nothing else.

C. The Individual and the Community

So far, both our defenses and criticisms of the Cartesian model have focused on the individual. We have considered the individual and individual consciousness, asking whether or not it conforms to the Cartesian picture of the self. There is a wholly different alternative, however, which we haven't discussed yet (although Sartre's *No Exit* does touch upon it).

Even within discussions of the individual self, it becomes evident that the individual self is largely, if not entirely, a social product and a self defined by society. We have all had the experience of finding ourselves in company in which we "could not be ourselves" or, even worse, in which we acted according to an identity that was wholly imposed upon us by other people. When going to school, for example, we played the role of "student," ingratiating and oppressed, long before we started to recognize that it is a role, and not a very pleasant one at that. Now we see it as a role that has been formulated solely for the advantage of other people—teachers, administrators, parents—so that we could be forced to "behave." Have you started to wonder how many other aspects of your identity have been similarly imposed upon you, not chosen at all, much less created by you? How much of your behavior has been "programmed" or "conditioned" by parents, society, television, movies, friends, and schoolmates? The suspicion deepens, and soon you start to see a split developing in your thinking about yourself: First, there is your conception of your own identity; second, there is the identity that has been imposed upon you. The two drift apart like boat and dock, and you find yourself falling between.

No wonder, then, that one of the leading psychiatrists of our times, R. D. Laing, has looked at this problem not only as the basis of much of our everyday unhappiness but as the cause of some of our most serious psychological breakdowns as well. Laing describes what he calls "ontological insecurity" as just this split between your awareness of yourself by yourself and the awareness that is imposed upon yourself as an object of other people's attention. Guilt is an example of this split; in excess (as Freud often argued) such emotions tend to be pathological. One definition of guilt is that it is a kind of self-consciousness that is caught between the need for approval and recognition by others and the feeling that you must be "yourself." Thus we tend to get the idea of a "true self" that lies concealed behind the masks that we present in public, even to our closest friends. We get the sense that our real selves are known only to ourselves, but at the same time we do not really exist except with other people.

But this is an extremely negative view of a tension that is in fact central to our whole Western notion of self, the tension between individual-

R. D. Laing (1927-1989)

A Scottish psychiatrist and philosopher who wrote extensively about selfhood and personality.

FIG. 4.9 Philosopher and psychiatrist R. D. Laing, photographed here by the poet Allen Ginsberg.
(© Allen Ginsberg/CORBIS)

ity and social self-identity. In most societies, Plato and Aristotle's Greece, for example, a person would always see his or her own identity in terms of the society of which one was a member. The idea of a self that was antagonistic to society would have been completely foreign to them (Consider, for instance, Socrates' speech in *The Crito*, in our Introduction, in which he says, in effect, that he cannot serve his own interests against the state without betraying himself.) Yet our own idea of self-identity has become so individualistic that the very idea that self-identity is really social-identity flies in the face of that whole Cartesian tradition—and much of Western thinking—that begins with the autonomy of the self and self-consciousness.

An attempt at individual rebellion was launched by Kierkegaard, the Christian philosopher who has often been claimed as the father of existentialism. Kierkegaard deplores what he sarcastically calls "the public" and urges an end to collective identity and social roles in favor of renewed respect for the individual.

On "The Public"
BY **Søren Kierkegaard**[13]

Despite all his work, the subjective thinker obtains only a modest return. The more the collective idea comes to dominate even the ordinary perspective, the more forbidding seems the transition to becoming an individual existing human being instead of losing oneself in the race and saying "we," "our age," "the nineteenth century." That it is a very little thing [to be an existing human being] is not to be denied; thus it takes a great deal of resignation not to disparage it. For what is an individual existing human being? Our age knows all too well how little it is, but just here is the particular immorality of our age. Every age has its own particular immorality: the immorality of our age is perhaps not lust, pleasure and sensuality, but rather a degenerate and pantheistic contempt for the individual. In the midst of all our elation over our age and the nineteenth century there sounds a note of hidden contempt for the individual; in the midst of the self-importance of the generation there is a despair over being human. Everything must be joined to everything else; people strive to deceive themselves in the totality of things, in world history; no one wants to be an individual human being.

FIG. 4.10 *(© iStockphoto.com/Linda Steward)*

In fact, so adamant is Kierkegaard on this issue that he argues that a person who "follows the crowd" and does not choose his or her own identity and live passionately as an individual cannot even be said to really exist.

---

[13] Søren Kierkegaard, *Concluding Unscientific Postscript*, trans. Clancy Martin.

 On Self and Passion
BY **Søren Kierkegaard**[14]

It is impossible to exist without passion, unless existing means just any sort of so-called existence. For this reason every Greek thinker was essentially a passionate thinker. I have often wondered how one might bring a man to passion. So I have thought I might seat him on a horse and frighten the horse into a wild gallop, or still better, in order to bring out the passion properly, I might take a man who wants to go somewhere as quickly as possible (and so was already in a sort of passion) and seat him on a horse that can barely walk. But this is just how existence is, if one becomes conscious of it. Or if someone hitched a carriage with Pegasus and an old nag, and told the driver, who was not usually inclined to passion, "Now, drive": I think that would succeed. And this is just how existence is, if one becomes conscious of it. Eternity is the winged horse, infinitely quick, and time is the old nag, and the existing individual is the driver; that is to say, he is the driver when his existence is not merely a so-called existence, for then he is no driver, but a drunken peasant who sleeps in the wagon and lets the horses fend for themselves. True, he also drives, he is a driver, and so there are perhaps many who—also exist.

And, borrowing from both Kierkegaard and Nietzsche, the German existentialist Martin Heidegger has argued against collective social identity in terms of what he (also ironically) calls *das Man*, an extremely useful German expression that roughly translates as "they" in *"they say that garlic cures colds."* Who are "they"? No one at all, Heidegger says, just an anonymous no one. In dense philosophical prose,[15] he presents the following argument:

 On "Dasein" and the "They"
BY **Martin Heidegger**[16]

Dasein, as everyday Being-with-one-another, stands in *subjection* to Others. It itself *is* not; its Being has been taken away by the Others. Dasein's everyday possibilities of Being are for the Others to dispose of as they please. These Others, moreover, are not *definite* Others. On the contrary, any Other can represent them. What is decisive is just that inconspicuous domination by Others which has already been taken over unawares from Dasein as Being-with. One belongs to the Others oneself and enhances their power. "The Others" whom one thus designates in order to cover up the fact of one's belonging to them essentially oneself, are those who proximally and for the most part *"are there"* in everyday Being-with-one-another. The "who" is not this one, not that one, not oneself, not some people, and not the sum of them all. The "who" is the neuter, the *"they"* [*das Man*].

. . .

Everyone is the other, and no one is himself. The *"they,"* which supplies the answer to the question of the "who" of everyday Dasein, is the *"nobody"* to whom every Dasein has already surrendered itself in Being-among-one-another.

> "Everyone is the other, and no one is himself."
>
> – MARTIN HEIDEGGER

---

[14] Søren Kierkegaard, *Concluding Unscientific Postscript*, trans. Clancy Martin.

[15] For "Dasein," read "individual human being"; for "Being-with," read "being around other people."

[16] Martin Heidegger, *Being and Time*, trans. J. MacQuarrie and E. Robinson, New York: Harper & Row, 1962.

Against this "surrender," Heidegger urges us to "take hold of ourselves" as individuals and find our "authentic" selves.

> The Self of everyday Dasein is the *they-self*, which we distinguish from the *authentic Self*—that is, from the Self which has been taken hold of in its own way.

This individualist movement is not unique to existentialism; it is in the mainstream of Western thinking, from ancient Socrates through Reformation Christianity to contemporary capitalism. Socrates' rebellion was, in a very important way, an existential rebellion. He stood up for his principles against the opinions of the age. Luther's Reformation was, among other things, very much a reassertion of the individual (individual conscience, individual actions) against the all-embracing spirit of the Catholic Church. Today, virtually every American would agree that every individual deserves at least some individual rights and respect. But individualism has always had its doubters. Individualism arises largely as a reaction against the awareness of how socially conditioned we really are. As an instrument of personal growth and as a defense against excessive socialization, individualism is extremely valuable. But when individualism becomes so powerful that personal interests eclipse the interests of everyone else and individual values begin to destroy the community, then it may be time to bring the limits of individualism into question as well. Furthermore, an excessive emphasis on individuality may lead us to forget that there are other human ways of living that are not individualistic at all. There are limits to the degree to which we can challenge the values and customs of our upbringing. Some rebellion is required for growth and change of the society as well as of the individual. But too much rebellion can be self-destructive as well as destructive to the community. For our self-identities, no matter how hard we try to think of ourselves as total individuals, are inextricably tied to the communities and values in which we were raised.

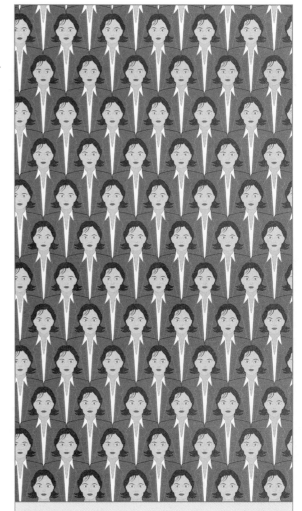

FIG. 4.11 das Man, or, "the They." *(Image © John Rawsterne, 2011. Used under license from Shutterstock.com)*

- In what ways is your self-identity socially constituted? Do you think that who you are is entirely determined by your social relations? What is left after you subtract the entirety of those relations that seem to define you?

The American sociologist David Reisman looks again at individualism in the light of these considerations and defends it as follows:

On Individualism
by **David Reisman**[17]

Social science has helped us become more aware of the extent to which individuals, great and little, are the creatures of their cultural conditioning; and so we neither blame the little nor exalt the great. But the same wisdom has sometimes led us to the fallacy that, since all men have their being in culture and as the result of the culture, they owe a debt to that culture which even a lifetime of altruism could not repay. (One might as well argue, and in fact many societies in effect do, that since we are born of parents, we must feel guilt whenever we transcend their limitations!) Sometimes the point is pushed to the virtual denial of individuality: since we arise in society, it is assumed with a ferocious determinism that we can never transcend it. All such concepts are useful correctives of an earlier solipsism. But if they are extended to hold that conformity with society is not only a necessity but also a duty, they destroy that margin of freedom which gives life its savor and its endless possibility for advance.

David Reisman (1909–2002)

A Harvard sociologist who focused on the American middle class, life in the modern urban environment, higher education, and American foreign relations, especially in connection with the nuclear arms race.

1. Voices of Protest

In contemporary times, the question of how individuals are defined by or in society is a deeply political issue. It is tied to questions of how we categorize our society ethnically, sexually, and racially. In our pluralist American society, we tend to believe that individual freedoms play more of a role in defining us within society than do, say, our family lineage or professional organizations. We are particularly sensitive, then, to racial or sexual stereotyping and to strict enforcement of social roles, because we feel that our identities are thereby taken out of our own control and our individuality is overlooked. This concern is similar to the concern that **dualists** have about materialism. We worry that if we "are" just our bodies—or similarly if we "are" just what our society makes us—then we are not the free, rational creatures we would like to be.

In the passage that follows, the Black Nationalist leader **Malcolm X** argues the extent to which African-Americans' self-identities are defined for them by American society in which whites are a majority.

On Being "African"
by **Malcolm X**[18]

Right now, in this country, if you and I, 22 million African-Americans—that's what we are—Africans who are in America. You're nothing but Africans. Nothing but Africans. In fact, you'd get farther calling yourself African instead of Negro. Africans don't catch hell. You're the only one catching hell. They don't have to pass civil-rights bills for Africans. An African can go anywhere he wants right now. All you've got to do is tie your head up. That's right, go anywhere you want. Just stop being a Negro.

[17] David Reisman, *Individualism Reconsidered*, New York: Doubleday, 1954.

[18] Malcolm X, "The Ballot or the Bullet" from *Malcolm X Speaks*. Copyright © 1965, 1989 by Betty Shabazz and Pathfinder Press.

Change your name to Hoogagagooba. That'll show you how silly the white man is. You're dealing with a silly man. A friend of mine who's very dark put a turban on his head and went into a restaurant in Atlanta before they called themselves desegregated. He went into a white restaurant, he sat down, they served him, and he said, "What would happen if a Negro came in here?" And there he's sitting, black as night, but because he had his head wrapped up the waitress looked back at him and says, "Why, there wouldn't no nigger dare come in here."

Malcolm X (1925-1965)
An outspoken leader of the black nationalist movement in this country. He was assassinated in 1965, upon his return from a trip to the Middle East.

Malcolm X explains the moral of the story in another famous speech:

FROM **"At the Audubon"** BY **Malcolm X**[19]

One of the best ways to safeguard yourself from being deceived is always to form the habit of looking at things for yourself, listening to things for yourself, thinking for yourself, before you try and come to any judgment. Never base your impression of someone on what someone else has said. Or upon what someone else has written. Or upon what you read about someone that somebody else wrote. Never base your judgment on things like that. Especially in this kind of country and in this kind of society which has mastered the art of very deceitfully painting people whom they don't like in an image that they know you won't like. So you end up hating your friends and loving their enemies.

- Have you ever felt a conflict between your conception of yourself and the ways in which others view you? Describe such a situation and how it made you feel.
- Do you think that it is possible for us to "rebel" against our socialized selves and create ourselves as unique, independent, "authentic" individuals? What problems or limitations do you foresee in such an enterprise?

Obviously, social roles have been binding to the "free individuality" of other groups, too, like women. Many contemporary feminists have analyzed how sex roles, perhaps more than anything else, falsely define us and undermine our individuality. In a now-famous article, **Sherry Ortner** considers the way society identifies women.

[19] Malcolm X, "At the Audubon" from *Malcolm X Speaks*. Copyright © 1965, 1989 by Betty Shabazz and Pathfinder Press.

FROM "Is Female to Male as Nature is to Culture?" BY Sherry Ortner[20]

Much of the creativity of anthropology derives from the tension between two sets of demands: that we explain human universals, and that we explain cultural particulars. By this canon, woman provides us with one of the more challenging problems to be dealt with. The secondary status of woman in society is one of the true universals, a pan-cultural fact. Yet within that universal fact, the specific cultural conceptions and symbolizations of woman are extraordinarily diverse and even mutually contradictory. Further, the actual treatment of women and their relative power and contribution vary enormously from culture to culture, and over different periods in the history of particular cultural traditions. Both of these points—the universal fact and the cultural variation—constitute problems to be explained.

My interest in the problem is of course more than academic: I wish to see genuine change come about, the emergence of a social and cultural order in which as much of the range of human potential is open to women as is open to men. The universality of female subordination, the fact that it exists within every type of social and economic arrangement and in societies of every degree of complexity, indicates to me that we are up against something very profound, very stubborn, something we cannot rout out simply by rearranging a few tasks and roles in the social system, or even by reordering the whole economic structure. In this paper I try to expose the underlying logic of cultural thinking that assumes the inferiority of women; I try to show the highly persuasive nature of the logic, for if it were not so persuasive, people would not keep subscribing to it. But I also try to show the social and cultural sources of that logic, to indicate wherein lies the potential for change.

Sherry Ortner (1941–)

An American anthropologist, best known for her work in cross-cultural gender distinctions.

FIG. 4.12 Sherry Ortner
(Used by permission of Sherry Ortner)

THE UNIVERSALITY OF FEMALE SUBORDINATION

What do I mean when I say that everywhere, in every known culture, women are considered in some degree inferior to men? First of all, I must stress that I am talking about *cultural* evaluations; I am saying that each culture, in its own way and on its own terms, makes this evaluation. But what would constitute evidence that a particular culture considers women inferior?

Three types of data would suffice: (1) elements of cultural ideology and informants' statements that *explicitly* devalue women, according them their roles, their tasks, their products, and their social milieux less prestige than are accorded men and the male correlates; (2) symbolic devices, such as the attribution of defilement, which may be interpreted as *implicitly* making a statement of interior valuation; and (3) social-structural arrangements that exclude women from participation in or contact with some realm in which the highest powers of the society are felt to reside. These three types of data may all of course be interrelated in any particular system, though they need not necessarily be. Further, any one of them will usually be sufficient to make the point of female inferiority in a given culture. Certainly, female exclusion from the most sacred rite or the highest political council is sufficient evidence. Certainly, explicit cultural ideology devaluing women (and their tasks, roles, products, etc.) is sufficient evidence. Symbolic indicators such as defilement are usually sufficient, although in a few cases in which, say, men and women are equally polluting to one another, a further indicator is required—and is, as far as my investigations have ascertained, always available.

On any or all of these counts, then, I would flatly assert that we find women subordinated to men in every known society.

· · ·

NATURE AND CULTURE

How are we to explain the universal devaluation of women? We could of course rest the case on biological determinism. There is something genetically inherent in the male of the species, so the biological determinists would argue, that makes them the naturally dominant sex; that "something" is lacking in females, and as a result women are not only naturally subordinate but in general quite satisfied with their position, since it affords them protection and the opportunity to maximize maternal pleasures, which to them are the most satisfying experiences of life. Without going into a detailed refutation of this position, I think it fair to say that it has failed to be established to the satisfaction of almost anyone in academic anthropology. This is to say, not that biological facts are irrelevant, or that men and women are not different, but that these facts and differences only take on significance of superior/inferior within the framework of culturally defined value systems.

If we are unwilling to rest the case on genetic determinism, it seems to me that we have only one way to proceed. We must attempt to interpret female subordination in light of other universals, factors built into the structure of the most generalized situation in which all human beings, in whatever culture, find themselves. For example, every human being has a physical body and a sense of nonphysical mind, is part of a society of other individuals and an inheritor of a cultural tradition, and must engage in some relationship, however mediated, with "nature," or the nonhuman realm, in order to survive. Every human being is born (to a mother) and ultimately dies, all are assumed to have an interest in personal survival, and society/culture has its own interest in (or at least momentum toward) continuity and survival, which transcends the lives and deaths of particular individuals. And so forth. It is in the realm of such universals of the human condition that we must seek an explanation for the universal fact of female devaluation.

I translate the problem, in other words, into the following simple question. What could there be in the generalized structure and conditions of existence, common to every culture, that would lead every culture to place a lower value upon women? Specifically, my thesis is that woman is being identified with—or, if you will, seems to be a symbol of—something that every culture devalues, something that every culture defines as being of a lower order of existence than itself. Now it seems that there is only one thing that would fit that description, and that is "nature" in the most generalized sense. Every culture, or, generically, "culture," is

"Even if women are not equated with nature, they are nonetheless seen as representing a lower order of being, as being less transcendental of nature than men are."

– SHERRY ORTNER

engaged in the process of generating and sustaining systems of meaningful forms (symbols, artifacts, etc.) by means of which humanity transcends the givens of natural existence, bends them to its purposes, controls them in its interest. We may thus broadly equate culture with the notion of human consciousness, or with the products of human consciousness (i.e., systems of thought and technology), by means of which humanity attempts to assert control over nature.

. . .

Returning now to the issue of women, their pan-cultural second-class status could be accounted for, quite simply, by postulating that women are being identified or symbolically associated with nature, as opposed to men, who are identified with culture. Since it is always culture's project to subsume and transcend nature, if women were considered part of nature, then culture would find it "natural" to subordinate, not to say oppress, them. Yet although this argument can be shown to have considerable force, it seems to oversimplify the case. The formulation I would like to defend and elaborate on in the following section, then, is that women are seen "merely" as being *closer* to nature than men. That is, culture (still equated relatively unambiguously with men) recognizes that women are active participants in its special processes, but at the same time sees them as being more rooted in, or having more direct affinity with, nature.

The revision may seem minor or even trivial, but I think it is a more accurate rendering of cultural assumptions. Further, the argument cast in these terms has several analytic advantages over the simpler formulation; I shall discuss these later. It might simply be stressed here that the revised argument would still account for the pan-cultural devaluation of women, for even if women are not equated with nature, they are nonetheless seen as representing a lower order of being, as being less transcendental of nature than men are.

. . .

In short, the postulate that woman is viewed as closer to nature than man has several implications for further analysis, and can be interpreted in several different ways. If it is viewed simply as a *middle* position on a scale from culture down to nature, then it is still seen as lower than culture and thus accounts for the pan-cultural assumption that woman is lower than man in the order of things. If it is read as a *mediating* element in the culture-nature relationship, then it may account in part for the cultural tendency not merely to devalue woman but to circumscribe and restrict her functions, since culture must maintain control over its (pragmatic and symbolic) mechanisms for the conversion of nature into culture. And if it is read as an *ambiguous* status between culture and nature, it may help account for the fact that, in specific cultural ideologies and symbolizations, woman can occasionally be aligned with culture, and in any event is often assigned polarized and contradictory meanings within a single symbolic system. Middle status, mediating functions, ambiguous meaning—all are different readings, for different contextual purposes, of woman's being seen as intermediate between nature and culture.

FIG 4.13 Boy or girl? (He's a boy.) *(Image © Hugo Maes, 2011. Used under license from Shutterstock.com)*

> • How does your own culture define women as inferior to men? How do you explain
> this? Do you find Ortner's argument convincing? Are there ways you would argue that
> women are superior to men? Or do you think that very idea of a "superior" sex/gender
> is somehow absurd?

How would a society *without* clear social and sexual roles function? Is it even possible
that we could interact with each other as entirely free individuals? Some feminists, like Ann
Ferguson, believe so. She believes, however, that in order to achieve such an ideal, we must
all embrace an "androgynous" sexuality.

On Androgyny
BY Ann Ferguson[21]

There is good evidence that human babies are bisexual, and only *learn* a specific male
or female identity by imitating and identifying with adult models. This evidence
comes from the discovery that all human beings possess both male and female hor-
mones (androgen and estrogen respectively), and also from concepts first developed
at length by Freud. Freud argued that heterosexual identity is not achieved until the
third stage of the child's sexual development. Sex identity is developed through the
resolution of the Oedipus complex, in which the child has to give up a primary attachment to the mother and learn either to identify with, or love, the father. But
Shulamith Firestone suggests that this process is not an inevitable one, as Freud presents it to be. Rather, it is due to the power dynamics of the patriarchal nuclear family.
Note that, on this analysis, if the sexual division of labor were destroyed, the mechanism that trains boys and girls to develop heterosexual sexual identities would also
be destroyed. If fathers and mothers played equal nurturant roles in child-rearing and
had equal social, economic, and political power outside the home, there would be
no reason for the boy to have to reject his emotional side in order to gain the power
associated with the male role. Neither would
the girl have to assume a female role in rejecting her assertive, independent side in order to
attain power indirectly through manipulation
of males. As a sexual identity, bisexuality would
then be the norm rather than the exception.

> **Ann Ferguson (1938-)**
>
> An emerita professor of philosophy and women's studies at the Univer-
> sity of Massachusetts.

In the twentieth century, under the mixed influences of existentialism, especially as espoused by the German Martin Heidegger, and of German Idealism, especially Hegel and Marx,
a new philosophical school became very popular. It is called "**deconstruction**," a name coined
by its founder, the Frenchman **Jacques Derrida**. Deconstruction is the attempt to offer a social
analysis and criticism which recognizes its own identification with the culture it criticizes. To
"deconstruct" a theory or a belief or a tradition, then, is neither to destroy it nor to rebuild it, but
rather to "reread" it, and thereby change it, see into it, add to it, *make* it our own, perhaps more
plural, more disperse, action. In his early work, Derrida argues that the school of deconstruction

---

[21] Ann Ferguson, "Androgyny as a Progressive Ideal for Human Development," in *Feminism and Philosophy*, ed. Mary
Vetterling-Braggin, Frederick A. Elliston, and Jane English, Lanham, MD: Littlefield, Adams, 1977.

Jacques Derrida (1930-2004)

A French philosopher and founder of the school of "deconstruction." He taught at the Ecole Normal Superior in France, but was occasionally a visiting lecturer at American universities. He taught at Yale, Cornell, and the University of California at Irvine.

FIG. 4.14
French philosopher Jacques Derrida.
(AP Photo/ALEXIS DUCLOS)

itself—of rereading, criticizing, and dispersing our cultural institutions and the philosophers who come from them—is itself an epitomal product of our cultural institutions. His claim is that the "unified self" is just a product of Western culture, and that it is now dying at the hands of its own creator. If there is "self," he suggests, "it must be *plural*."[22]

Some contemporary political thinkers—especially feminist and African-American philosophers—have found deconstruction attractive. Some of the contemporary philosophical debate about individual freedoms has evolved into criticisms and defenses of the "Western philosophy" Derrida describes. If only "Western philosophy" were so univocally definable, then perhaps all its mistakes and cruelties could be identified and avoided. As we've seen, however, and as Derrida admits, these very modern criticisms form an integral part of the complex, culturally interwoven philosophical debate around the world.

It is important to emphasize that none of these philosophers actually denies the individual, or individual respect, or individual rights. They are, however, insisting that an individual derives his or her rights only insofar as he or she is a member of a community. This does not mean that a person cannot be eccentric, like the weirdo artist or the spaced-out rock musician, but it does mean that even their eccentricity, as well as their talents, must be viewed as social contributions. What they are denying, in other words, is what has sometimes been called "vulgar individualism," that form of self-identity that denies all social relevance and social obligations.

Hermann Hesse (1877-1962)

A Swiss philosopher, novelist, poet, and painter. He won the Nobel Prize for literature in 1946.

FIG. 4.15 Novelist, philosopher, and Nobel laureate Hermann Hesse.
(© Estate of Fred Stein / Art Resource, NY / Artists Rights Society (ARS), New York)

D. One Self? Any Self? Questioning the Concept of Personal "Essence"

So far, we have talked as if self-identity is something singular, a unified set of ideals and characteristics according to which one identifies himself or herself. But need we think of the "self" in this way?

In his novel *Steppenwolf*, Hermann Hesse presents a character whose "self" is something quite different. Hesse's Harry Haller is a *multiple* or *pluralistic* self, a collection of "selves," with no one of them "real" or "essential." Like many of us, he lives with the myth of "two selves," one human, rational, and well behaved, the other beastly, wild, and wolflike. He is torn between the two. But, Hesse tells

---

[22]Jacques Derrida, "The Ends of Man," trans. Alan Bass in *Margins of Philosophy*, Chicago: University of Chicago Press, 1982.

us, Harry's unhappiness is not, as he thinks, a result of his "war between the selves" at all but rather the result of an oversimplified notion of self. "The Steppenwolf is a fiction," writes Hesse, a "mythological simplification." The idea of two selves, one wolf, one man, is as old as the mind-body distinction, as the Christian division between the body and the soul—even older, in fact, dating back to Pythagoras and Plato. Hesse's argument is that this simple self is a strictly "bourgeois convention," a middle-class argument for the simplicity and unity of the self; indeed, Harry is unhappy because of the tension and complexity of only two selves: the "human" who has culture and cultivated thoughts and feelings and the "wolf" who is savage and cruel, the dark world of Freud's **unconscious** instincts and raw, untamed nature. He argues the following:

FROM *Steppenwolf*
BY **Hermann Hesse**[23]

Suppose that Harry tried to ascertain in any single moment of his life, any single act, what part the man had in it and what part the wolf, he would find himself at once in a dilemma, and his whole beautiful wolf theory would go to pieces. For there is not a single human being . . . not even the idiot, who is so conveniently simple that his being can be explained as the sum of two or three principal elements; and to explain so complex a man as Harry by the artless division into wolf and man is a hopelessly childish attempt. Harry consists of a hundred or a thousand selves, not of two. His life oscillates, as everyone's does, not merely between two poles, such as the body and the spirit, the saint and the sinner, but between thousand and thousands.

Why is it, Hesse asks, that we all seem to have this need to think of ourselves in such deceptive terms and regard the self as a single unit? Because, he suggests, we are deluded by an analogy; since each of us has but one body, it is assumed that each of us has a single soul too. From this analogy we assume that there must be one self within each body. But it is here that Hesse contrasts our view with the views of ancient India and notes with admiration that there is no trace of such a notion in the poems of the ancient Asiatics. He then offers us his own analogy:

FIG. 4.16 *(Image © Memo Angeles, 2011. Used under license from Shutterstock.com)*

Man is an onion made up of a hundred integuments, a texture made up of many threads. The ancient Asiatics knew this well enough, and in the Buddhist Yoga an exact technique was devised for unmasking the illusion of the personality. The human merry-go-round sees many changes: The illusion that cost India the efforts of thousands of years to unmask is the same illusion that the West has labored just as hard to maintain and strengthen.

· What would it mean to have a pluralistic self or selves? Do you find this view plausible? Have you ever felt as though you were somehow a multiplicity of selves or identities? (We're not talking craziness here.) Describe such an experience.

Hesse refers to Buddhist concepts of the self with praise. Although he remains entrenched in Western ideas as well, Hesse is already more than halfway to one of the ancient Eastern conceptions of self, which is essentially a denial of the self as we think of it. As we've

---

[23] Hermann Hesse, *Steppenwolf*, trans. Basil Creighton and Rev. Joseph Mileck, New York: Holt, Rinehart and Winston, 1929.

Luce Irigaray (1930-)

A French feminist philosopher. Her work incorporates literary criticism, feminism, and philosophy. Her best-known works are *Speculum of the Other Woman* and *This Sex Which Is Not One*.

seen in Chapter 1, the Buddhist says, "give up your self-identity," "give up your self-consciousness," and finally, "give up your self." This is a familiar refrain among many Eastern mystics. It may also be an ideal secular aspiration, however. For instance, the contemporary French philosopher and feminist **Luce Irigaray** claims that the unified, "essential" self is a limiting and oppressive notion, particularly when applied to women. In her book *This Sex Which Is Not One* she claims that the genuine and free identity of a woman is a multiplicity or plurality of characters. Note the deliberate play on words in her title: "this sex which is not one." With it, she implies a multiplicity of meanings: The female sex is not singular and unified; women are not unified together; the female is not *a* sex at all. With this last reading, we see that Irigaray is not only claiming that a woman has multiple selves instead of a single body and a single soul, but also that all human beings, men included, may have multiple sexualities, multiple identities—that there may not be any natural masculinity or femininity at all in the plural "self" from which we sort them out. Thus, Irigaray is making a feminist criticism of all our social and sexual roles at the same time as she offers a theory of self-identity.

FROM *This Sex Which Is Not One*
BY **Luce Irigaray**[24]

. . . not knowing what she wants, ready for anything, even asking for more, so long as he will "take" her as his "object" when he seeks his own pleasure. Thus she will not say what she herself wants; moreover, she does not know, or no longer knows, what she wants. As Freud admits, the beginnings of the sexual life of a girl child are so "obscure," so "faded with time," that one would have to dig down very deep indeed to discover beneath the traces of this civilization, of this history, the vestiges of a more archaic civilization that might give some clue to woman's sexuality. That extremely ancient civilization would undoubtedly have a different alphabet, a different language. . . . Woman's desire would not be expected to speak the same language as man's; woman's desire has doubtless been submerged by the logic that has dominated the West since the time of the Greeks.

. . .

"She" is indefinitely other in herself. This is doubtless why she is said to be whimsical, incomprehensible, agitated, capricious . . . not to mention her language, in which "she" sets off in all directions leaving "him" unable to discern the coherence of any meaning. Hers are contradictory words, somewhat mad from the standpoint of reason, inaudible for whoever listens to them with ready-made grids, with a fully elaborated code in hand. For in what she says, too, at least when she dares, woman is constantly touching herself. She steps ever so slightly aside from herself with a murmur, an exclamation, a whisper, a sentence left unfinished. . . . When she returns, it is to set off again from elsewhere. From another point of pleasure, or of pain. One would have to listen with another ear, as if hearing *an "other meaning" always in the process of weaving itself, of embracing itself with words, but also of getting rid of words in order not to become fixed, congealed in them.* For if "she" says something, it is not, it is already no longer, identical with what she means. What she says is never identical with any-

---

thing, moreover; rather, it is contiguous. *It touches (upon).* And when it strays too far from that proximity, she breaks off and starts over at "zero," her body-sex.

It is useless, then, to trap women in the exact definition of what they mean, to make them repeat (themselves) so that it will be clear; they are already elsewhere in that discursive machinery where you expected to surprise them. They have returned within themselves. Which must not be understood in the same way as within yourself. They do not have the interiority that you have, the one *you* perhaps suppose they have. Within themselves means *within the intimacy of that silent, multiple, diffuse touch.* And if you ask them insistently what they are thinking about, they can only reply: Nothing. Everything.

Thus what they desire is precisely nothing, and at the same time everything. Always something more and something else besides that *one*—sexual organ, for example—that you give them, attribute to them. Their desire is often interpreted, and feared, as a sort of insatiable hunger, a voracity that will swallow you whole. Whereas it really involves a different economy more than anything else, one that upsets the linearity of a project, undermines the goal-object of a desire, diffuses the polarization toward a single pleasure, disconcerts fidelity to a single discourse.

. . .

Must this multiplicity of female desire and female language be understood as shards, scattered remnants of a violated sexuality? A sexuality denied? The question has no simple answer. The rejection, the exclusion of a female imaginary certainly puts woman in the position of experiencing herself only fragmentarily, in the little-structured margins of a dominant ideology, as waste, or excess, what is left of a mirror invested by the (masculine) "subject" to reflect himself, to copy himself. Moreover, the role of "femininity" is prescribed by this masculine specularization and corresponds scarcely at all to woman's desire, which may be recovered only in secret, in hiding, with anxiety and guilt.

But if the female imaginary were to deploy itself, if it could bring itself into play otherwise than as scraps, uncollected debris, would it represent itself, even so, in the form of *one* universe? Would it even be volume instead of surface? No.

. . .

(Re-)discovering herself, for a woman, thus could only signify the possibility of sacrificing no one of her pleasures to another, of identifying herself with none of them in particular, *of never being simply one.* A sort of expanding universe to which no limits could be fixed and which would not be incoherence . . . nonetheless—nor that polymorphous perversion of the child in which the erogenous zones would lie waiting to be regrouped under the primacy of the phallus.

Woman always remains several, but she is kept from dispersion because the other is already within her and is autoerotically familiar to her. Which is not to say that she appropriates the other for herself, that she reduces it to her own property. Ownership and property are doubtless quite foreign to the feminine. At least sexually. But not *nearness.* Nearness so pronounced that it makes all discrimination of identity, and thus all forms of property, impossible.

> "The role of 'femininity' is prescribed by this masculine specularization and corresponds scarcely at all to woman's desire, which may be recovered only in secret, in hiding, with anxiety and guilt."
>
> – LUCE IRIGARAY

Irigaray is not the only feminist philosopher to criticize the notion of "self" that was assumed by Descartes and adopted by many of his successors. Many feminists are critical of the Cartesian notion "self" particularly because of the way the mind-body distinction is related

Genevieve Lloyd (1941–)

Australian feminist philosopher. She is professor emerita at the University of New South Wales in Australia.

to stereotypes of gender. Because our society has come to accept the "masculinity" of the mind and the "femininity" of the body, these feminists claim, the philosophical notion of the "self" as consciousness or mind incorporates sexism right into our notions of human nature.

In the following passage, **Genevieve Lloyd**, a contemporary feminist and philosopher, criticizes the mind-body distinction over its whole history from a feminist perspective.

FROM "The Man of Reason" BY **Genevieve Lloyd**[25]

By the Man of Reason I mean the ideal of rationality associated with the rationalist philosophies of the seventeenth century. And, secondly, something more nebulous—the residue of that ideal in our contemporary consciousness, our inheritance from seventeenth century rationalism. This is, I think, a substantial component in what reason has come to be. But it is not, of course, the only component. In focusing on it to the exclusion of any other developments in the notion of reason since the seventeenth century, this paper inevitably presents an incomplete picture of reason, but one that does highlight, I think, some aspects of reason that are of considerable relevance to philosophical aspects of feminism.

The main feature of the Man of Reason that I am concerned to bring into focus is his maleness. This in itself, I think, is a matter of philosophical interest. More is involved here than the supposedly "neutral" sense of "man" to include women. We are all familiar with the fact that linguistic usage commonly fails to recognize that humanity comprises two sexes. But there is something deeper to the maleness of the Man of Reason; something more deeply engrained in consciousness. He is after all a creation of reflective consciousness. When the Man of Reason is extolled, philosophers are not talking about idealizations of human beings. They are talking about ideals of manhood.

What I want to do in this paper is to bring this undoubted maleness of the Man of Reason into clearer focus. There are, I think, reasons that belong in the history of philosophy for the association between reason and masculinity. Some parts of the history of philosophy can throw light here on a very confused and tension-ridden area of human experience. Past philosophical reflection has after all helped form our present thought structures. And the creature I am calling the Man of Reason embodies some of the fundamental ideals of our culture. Let us try then to bring him into sharper focus.

THE ASSOCIATION OF "MALE" WITH "RATIONAL"

The associations between "male" and "rational" and between "female" and "non-rational" have, of course, a very long history. The idea that the rational is somehow specially associated with masculinity goes back to the Greek founding fathers of rationality as we know it. Aristotle thought that woman was "as it were an impotent male, for it is through a certain incapacity that the female is female." This intrinsic female incapacity was a lack in the "principle of soul" and hence associated with an

[25]Genevieve Lloyd, "The Man of Reason," first published in *Metaphilosophy* 10, 1 (January 1979): 18–37; reprinted in *Women, Knowledge, and Reality: Explorations in Feminist Philosophy*, ed. Ann Garry and Marilyn Pearsall, Boston: Unwin, Hyman. Reprinted with permission.

incapacity in respect of rationality. The claim is not of course that women do not have rationality, but they have it in an inferior, fainter way. They have rationality; they are distinguished from the animals by being rational. Yet they are not equal to men. They are somehow *lesser* men, lesser in respect of the all-important thing; rationality.

· · ·

REASON IN THE SEVENTEENTH CENTURY

One of the most striking things that happens to reason in the seventeenth century is the attempt to encapsulate it in a systematic method for attaining certainty. The paradigm of this approach to reason is Descartes' *Regulae*, the *Rules for the Direction of the Mind*, written in 1628. Here there emerges a new conception of what is involved in knowledge. The acquisition of knowledge is a matter of the systematic pursuit of an orderly method. The essence of the method is to break down all the complex operations involved in reasoning into their most basic constituents and to render the mind adept in performing these simple operations—intuition and deduction. Intuition is the undoubting conception of an unclouded and attentive mind which comes from the light of reason alone. This is the basis for Descartes' later influential doctrine of clear and distinct ideas. Deduction is the process by which we extend knowledge beyond intuitions by connecting them in series. These are the only mental operations Descartes will admit into his method; but the proper understanding and use of them will, he thinks, yield all that lies within the province of knowledge. Anything else is in fact an impediment to knowledge:

> nothing can be added to the pure light of reason which does not in some way obscure it.

The method is universally applicable, regardless of any difference in subject matter:

> we must not fancy that one kind of knowledge is more obscure than another, since all knowledge is of the same nature throughout, and consists solely in combining what is self evident.

This universality of Cartesian method is emphasized in the *Discourse on Method*, published in 1637:

> provided only that we abstain from receiving anything as true which is not so, and always retain the order which is necessary in order to deduce the one conclusion from the other, there can be nothing so remote that we cannot reach to it, nor so recondite that we cannot discover it.

For Descartes, then, all knowledge consists in self-evident intuition and necessary deduction. We are to break down the complex and obscure into what is simple and self-evident, then combine the resultant units in an orderly manner. In order to know we must isolate the "simple natures," the objects of intuition, and "scrutinise them separately with steadfast mental gaze." We then combine them in chains of deductions. The whole of human knowledge consists in a distinct perception of the way in which these simple natures combine in order to build up other objects.

There is a deeper, metaphysical, dimension to the Cartesian treatment of reason. In the course of elaborating a method for attaining certain knowledge Descartes thinks he is uncovering the unity of all the sciences, the unity of knowledge. For him this is identical with the order of thought itself, with the very structure of the knowing mind. And this order of thought is taken as transparently reflecting the order of things. In the *Regulae* there is no gap between intuitions and the simple natures that are their objective correlates. In the later *Meditations* (1641) the possibility of radical doubt opens a gap between ideas and the material world, between the structure of the mind and the structure of the reality it attempts to know. But this gap is then closed by the existence of a veracious God. Introspection of the nature of thought in an individual mind ultimately yields access to universal reason, God given and God guaranteed, and hence to the structure of reality itself, conceived by Cartesian rationalism to be identical with that of the mind.

This isomorphism, between reason and reality, founded on a veracious God, gives reason a quasi-divine character. Reason is God imbued, the divine spark in man. This is the seventeenth century version of the treatment of man's rational faculty as reflecting the godhead, as that in virtue of which man is made in God's image.

Another feature of Descartes' treatment of reason that is crucial here is its connection with his antithesis between mind and matter. The basic units of Cartesian method are discrete, sharp edged and self-contained mental items. This becomes even more pronounced in his later works. The vehicles of knowledge are clear, precisely bordered mental states, sharply separated from one another:

> The distinct is that which is so precise and different from all other objects that it contains within itself nothing but what is clear.

And this discrete, delineated character of the units of knowledge is grounded in Descartes's distinction between mind and matter. The absolute certainty that accompanies clear and distinct ideas derives from their purely mental character. Intuition, as Descartes puts it, is free of the "fluctuating testimony of the senses" and the "blundering constructions of imagination." Cartesian method is essentially a matter of forming the "habit of distinguishing intellectual from corporeal matters." It is a matter of shedding the sensuous from thought.

The search for the "clear and distinct," the separating out of the emotional, the sensuous, the imaginative, now makes possible polarizations of previously existing contrasts—intellect versus the emotions; reason versus imagination; mind versus matter. We have seen that the claim that women are somehow lacking in respect of rationality, that they are more impulsive, more emotional, than men is by no means a seventeenth century innovation. But these contrasts were previously contrasts *within* the rational. What ought to be dominated by reason had not previously been so sharply delineated from the intellectual. The conjunction of Cartesian down-grading of the sensuous with the use of the mind-matter distinction to establish the discrete character of Cartesian ideas introduces possibilities of polarization that were not there before.

Another relevant factor here is that shedding the non-intellectual from our mental states is something that demands training. In earlier centuries too, of course, it was thought appropriate to give the education of women a different character from that of men. And it was possible to present this as justified by their being different in respect of rationality. But with the seventeenth century there is a new dimension. Women can now be excluded from training *in* reason, that is, from the acquisition of method. And since this training is explicitly a matter of learning to leave one's emotions, imagination, etc., out of account, there now emerges a new dimension to the idea that women are more emotional or more impulsive, etc., than men. If they are excluded from training in rationality, women are perforce *left* emotional, impulsive, fancy ridden. They are not trained out of the "blundering constructions of the imagination" to enter the rarified air of reason. So thought styles, that are in the seventeenth century sense pre-rational, can survive in women. This *makes* it true, in a way it need not have been before, that women are less rational than men.

Also, it now becomes possible, as it was not before, to have a reasoned basis for assigning the emotions, the imagination, the sensuous in general, to women as their special area of responsibility. The training of a Man of Reason does after all involve getting him to shed many of his normal characteristics. It can now be seen as woman's role to preserve for him the areas of warmth and sensuousness that training in reason demands that he himself transcend. A great deal happens of course between the time of Descartes and that of Rousseau. But we can see this theme, elaborated almost to the point of parody, in Rousseau's views on the education of women in *Emile*, which so outraged Mary Wollstonecraft in the *Vindication of the Rights of Women*:

> To be pleasing in his sight, to win his respect and love, to train him in childhood, to tend him in manhood, to counsel and console, to make his life pleasant and happy, these are the duties of woman for all time, and this is what she should be taught while she is young.

The contrast involved in the idea that man was made in God's image and woman was made to be a companion for man thus takes on a new dimension in the seventeenth century. We now have a separation of functions backed by a theory of mind. Given an already existing situation of sexual inequality, reason—the godlike, the spark of the divine in man—is assigned to the male. The emotions, the imagination, the sensuous are assigned to women. They are to provide comfort, relief, entertainment and solace for the austerity that being a Man of Reason demands.

FIG. 4.17 Auguste Rodin (1840-1917), *The Thinker* (1902). The man of reason? (© iStockphoto.com/Vladimir Liverts)

Something like this had of course been the case before. Different training was given to men and women to fit them for different life styles. But now the transcending of the sensuous can be seen as an end in itself. It is not in order to fit him for the heroic that the Man of Reason is to be trained out of his soft emotions and his sensuousness, but because that is precisely what it is to be rational. The division between reason and the non-rational can now be seen as reflexing and as being reenacted in the division between the sexes—in a way it was not before.

The stage is now set for the emergence of the Man of Reason as a male character ideal.

- Do you agree that the "Man of Reason" is necessarily male? In what ways (if any) is rationality or reflective consciousness distinctly masculine?

Although these feminist criticisms are contemporary, there has long been criticism of the notion of the unified "self" in the Eastern religions, as Hesse noted. Around the world, in fact, mystic sects of all faiths have tended toward a different conception of self-identity from that which has been dominant in Western philosophy. Of course, even these mystics admit that people have "personalities" and "egos" in some sense; most people most of

"Given an already existing situation of sexual inequality, reason—the godlike, the spark of the divine in man—is assigned to the male. The emotions, the imagination, the sensuous are assigned to women."

– GENEVIEVE LLOYD

FIG. 4.18 The Buddha. *(Image © 2011. Used under license from Shutterstock.com)*

the time think of "themselves." Some Eastern religions claim, however, that this vision of "ourselves" is a false image. It is just an illusion that one accepts out of ignorance. In Buddhism, for example, existence of the the non-self is an ideal understanding, which can be fully achieved only with enlightenment.

An early Buddhist work, for instance, *The Dhammapada* (ca. 250 B.C.E.), contains several passages about this ideal.

 FROM *The Dhammapada*[26]

CHAPTER XII SELF

Let each man first direct himself to what is proper, then let him teach others; thus a wise man will not suffer.

If a man make himself as he teaches others to be, then, being himself well-subdued, he may subdue others; for one's own self is difficult to subdue.

Self is the lord of self, who else could be the lord? With self well-subdued, a man finds a lord such as few can find.

The evil done by one's self, born of one's self, begotten by one's self, crushes the foolish, as a diamond breaks even a precious stone.

. . .

---

[26] From *The Dhammapada*, parts reprinted in *The Teachings of the Compassionate Buddha: Early Discourses, the Dhammapada, and Later Basic Writings*, ed. E. A. Burtt, New York: New American Library, 1955. Reprinted by permission of W. B. Brinster.

The foolish man who scorns the instruction of the saintly, of the elect [ariya], of the virtuous, and follows a false doctrine—he bears fruit to his own destruction, like the fruits of the *Katthaka* reed.

By one's self the evil is done, by one's self one suffers; by one's self evil is left undone; by one's self one is purified. The pure and the impure stand and fall by themselves; no one can purify another.

Let no one forget his own duty for the sake of another's, however great; let a man after he has discerned his own duty, be faithful to his duty.

All forms are unreal—he who knows and sees this is at peace though in a world of pain; this is the way that leads to purity.

· · ·

Through zeal knowledge is gained, through lack of zeal knowledge is lost; let a man who knows this two-fold path of gain and loss thus place himself that knowledge may grow.

Cut down the whole forest of desires, not a tree only! Danger comes out of the forest of desires. When you have cut down both the forest of desires and its undergrowth, then, *bhikshus*, you will be rid of the forest and of desires!

· · ·

Cut out the love of self, like an autumn lotus with your hand! Cherish the road to peace. Nirvana has been shown by the Blessed One.

The thirteenth poem of the *Dao De Jing* touches on the same theme:

FROM ***Dao De Jing***
BY **Laozi**[27]

13

Success is as dangerous as failure,
and we are often our own worst enemy.

What does it mean that success is as dangerous as failure?
He who is superior is also someone's subordinate.
Receiving favor and losing it both cause alarm.
That is what is meant by success is as dangerous as failure.
What does it mean that we are often our own worst enemy?
The reason I have an enemy is because I have "self."
If I no longer had a "self," I would no longer have an enemy.

Love the whole world as if it were your self;
then you will truly care for all things.

22

If you want to become whole,
first let yourself become broken.

> "The reason I have an enemy is because I have 'self.' If I no longer had a 'self,' I would no longer have an enemy."
>
> – LAOZI

27 From Lao-Tzu, *Tao Te Ching*, trans. J. H. McDonald, 1996 (for the public domain).

FIG. 4.19 A Chinese Taoist scroll painting of Laozi. *(Foto Marburg / Art Resource, NY)*

If you want to become straight,
first let yourself become twisted.
If you want to become full,
first let yourself become empty.
If you want to become new,
first let yourself become old.

For this reason the Master embraces the Tao,
as an example for the world to follow.
Because she isn't self centered,
people can see the light in her.
Because she does not boast of herself,
she becomes a shining example.
Because she does not glorify herself,
she becomes a person of merit.
Because she wants nothing from the world,
the world can not overcome her.

When the ancient Masters said,
"If you want to become whole,
then first let yourself be broken,"
they weren't using empty words.
All who do this will be made complete.

These Eastern examples are certainly not the only alternatives to the early modern European notion of the self accepted by Descartes. There have always been challenges to the notion of a unified self, by Islamic, Christian, and Jewish mystics in the West, among others.

SUMMARY AND CONCLUSION

Self-identity is a question of essential properties: What is it about you that makes you a particular person and the same person over time? In this chapter we have reviewed a series of different answers to this question. The tradition from Descartes and Locke to Kant stresses the importance of consciousness in our conception of ourselves, that is, the importance of our minds over our bodies. (Even Hume, who denies that there is a self, is part of this tradition.) Then there is the general question, how much is the self something that we can choose, and how much is it something that is determined for us? Does each person have just one self, one set of essential properties, or might a single "person" be several people, with several selves? Or might there really be no self at all? And how much should we conceive of ourselves as individuals, and how much as organic components of a larger community? None of these questions has any firmly agreed-upon answers, but all of us adopt one view or another, even if just for a short time, every time we attempt to define ourselves or just "be ourselves."

CHAPTER REVIEW QUESTIONS

1. In Kant's view of the self, what is the difference between the transcendental ego and the empirical ego? Why does Kant need both notions?

2. How does Sartre's conception of the self complicate the idea of an individual self? How does he explain the paradox that he creates between the self "being what it is and being what it is not"? Why does he believe this?

3. Nietzsche and Kierkegaard both believe that the "enemy" is social identity and conformity to "the herd." Explain why. Are there ways in which you find yourself identifying socially and "going along" in ways that seem untrue to yourself? What does this feel like? What are the negative consequences that can arise from too much conformity? From too much individuality?

4. What role, if any, does the body play in self-identity or identity of personhood? Or do you agree that consciousness, memory, or some mental aspect is sufficient to establish personal identity? Could you conceive of your consciousness and memory states inhabiting some other body? What would make that person you?

KEY TERMS

bad faith	empirical ego	resemblance
continuity (spatiotemporal continuity)	essence	self-consciousness
criterion	existentialism	self-identity
deconstruction	facticity	transcendence
dualism	immediate	transcendental ego
	incorrigibility	unconscious

BIBLIOGRAPHY AND FURTHER READING

Two anthologies on the question of self-identity are John Perry, ed., *Personal Identity* (New York: Lieber-Atherton, 1975) and Owen J. Flanagan and Amélie O. Rorty, eds., *Identity, Character, and Morality: Essays in Moral Psychology* (Cambridge: MIT Press, 1993).

An extended study of this traditional problem is Sidney Shoemaker, *Self-Knowledge and Self-Identity* (Ithaca, NY: Cornell University Press, 1963).

Jean-Paul Sartre's existentialist view of the self is developed in his essay *Transcendence of the Ego* (New York: Noonday, 1957).

Hermann Hesse's complex theory of the self is best developed in *Steppenwolf*, rev. ed., trans. Basil Creighton (New York: Holt, Rinehart and Winston, 1970), but it is most simply portrayed in *Siddhartha*, trans. H. Rosner (New York: New Directions, 1951).

Further reading in Eastern conceptions of the self may begin with D. Suzuki, *Zen Buddhism*, ed. W. Barrett (New York: Doubleday, 1956) or C. Moore, ed., *The Individual in East and West* (Honolulu: East-West Center Press, 1967).

A good introduction of G. W. F. Hegel's very difficult philosophy is the introduction to his lectures on the philosophy of history in his *Reason in History*, trans. R. Hartman (New York: Bobbs-Merrill, 1953).

An exceptionally rich but difficult study of the history of self is Charles Taylor, *Sources of the Self* (Cambridge: Harvard University Press, 1994).

Two other studies worth recommending are Quassim Cassam, *Self-Knowledge* (New York: Oxford University Press, 1994), and Richard Ashmore and Lee Jussim, *Self and Identity* (New York: Oxford University Press, 1997).

5 | Mind and Body

It is certain that I (that is, my mind, by which I am what I am) is entirely and truly distinct from my body, and may exist without it.

RENÉ DESCARTES

Whatever our attempts to answer the problems of self-identity, they begin with a single "fact," our own consciousness. This was the logical beginning for Descartes, who used the fact of his own consciousness as the starting point for his whole philosophy. It was true for Locke, who argued that our identity is to be found in the continuity of our consciousness rather than in the continuity of our bodies. It was even used by Hume, who used his own consciousness as the basis of his denial that there was any such thing as the self. It was the starting point of Kant's philosophy; his transcendental ego, like Descartes' "I think," gave him the basis for the rest of his philosophy. Even those philosophers who have not been interested in these logical arguments—Buddhists, Marxists, and existentialists—have begun with at least one of a variety of considerations of consciousness; the fact of our own self-consciousness, the facts of consciousness, or just the fact that only people seem capable of or interested in asking the question "Who am I?" But now what is this "consciousness"? As soon as we ask the question, we find ourselves once again up to our eyeballs in the labyrinth of traditional metaphysics.

A. What Is Consciousness?

We can begin to appreciate the problems of consciousness by returning to the attempts of the eighteenth-century rationalist metaphysicians to be clear about their notion of "substance." Descartes said that there were two different kinds of substances; mind, or mental substance, and body, or physical substance. Accordingly, he is usually called a *dualist* and the position, in general, that mind and body are different substances is called Cartesian **dualism**.[1] You remember that Descartes insisted that his identity was as a "thinking thing," in other words, a mental substance. But now, what of his body? We have seen that he believed that he could intelligibly

---

[1] Named after Descartes. As a matter of fact, Descartes believed that there were three kinds of substances, the third being God. But we need not worry about that third substance at this point. For our purposes, Descartes is simply a dualist.

doubt the existence of his body but not of his mind. But what is so special about this body that, unlike other bodies (the chair in front of him, the body of the king), was so intimately connected to his mind? It moved when he willed it to move, it walked when he decided to walk, it wrote what he wanted to write. In the last of his six *Meditations*, he returns to this problem.

FROM "Meditation VI"
BY René Descartes[2]

Firstly, then, I perceived that I had a head, hands, feet, and other members composing that body which I considered as part, or perhaps even as the whole, of myself. I perceived further, that that body was placed among many others, by which it was capable of being affected in diverse ways, both beneficial and hurtful; and what was beneficial I remarked by a certain sensation of pleasure, and what was hurtful by a sensation of pain. And, besides this pleasure and pain, I was likewise conscious of hunger, thirst, and other appetites, as well as certain corporeal inclinations towards joy, sadness, anger, and similar passions.

. . .

Nor was I altogether wrong in likewise believing that that body which, by a special right, I called my own, pertained to me more properly and strictly than any of the others; for in truth, I could never be separated from it as from other bodies: I felt in it and on account of it all my appetites and affections, and in fine I was affected in its parts by pain and the titillation of pleasure, and not in the parts of the other bodies that were separated from it. But when I inquired into the reason why, from this I know not what sensation of pain, sadness of mind should follow, and why from the sensation of pleasure joy should arise, or why this indescribable twitching of the stomach, which I call hunger, should put me in mind of taking food, and the parchedness of the throat of drink, and so in other cases, I was unable to give any explanation, unless that I was so taught by nature; for there is assuredly no affinity, at least none that I am able to comprehend, between this irritation of the stomach and the desire of food, any more than between the perception of an object that causes pain and the consciousness of sadness which springs from the perception. And in the same way it seems to me that all the other judgments I had formed regarding the objects of sense, were dictates of nature; because I remarked that those judgments were formed in me, before I had leisure to weigh and consider the reasons that might constrain me to form them.

But, afterwards, a wide experience by degrees sapped the faith I had reposed in my senses; for I frequently observed

FIG. 5.1 How is the mind joined to the body? Do they often feel at odds with one another? *(© iStockphoto.com/ © Drazen Vukelic)*

2 René Descartes, "Meditation VI," in *Meditations on First Philosophy*, in *The Philosophical Works of Descartes*, trans. Elizabeth S. Haldane and G. R. T. Ross, 1911. Reprinted with the permission of Cambridge University Press.

"Because, on the one hand, I have a clear and distinct idea of myself . . . as . . . only a thinking and unextended thing, and as, on the other hand, I possess a distinct idea of body . . . only an extended and unthinking thing, it is certain that I am entirely and truly distinct from my body, and may exist without it."

– RENÉ DESCARTES

that towers, which at a distance seemed round, appeared square when more closely viewed, and that colossal figures, raised on the summits of these towers, looked like small statues, when viewed from the bottom of them; and, in other instances without number, I also discovered error in judgments founded on the external senses; and not only in those founded on the external, but even in those that rested on the internal senses; for is there aught more internal than pain? and yet I have sometimes been informed by parties whose arm or leg had been amputated, that they still occasionally seemed to feel pain in that part of the body which they had lost,—a circumstance that led me to think that I could not be quite certain even that any one of my members were affected when I felt pain in it. And to these grounds of doubt I shortly afterwards also added two others of very wide generality: the first of them was that I believed I never perceived anything when awake which I could not occasionally think I also perceived when asleep, and as I do not believe that the ideas I seem to perceive in my sleep proceed from objects external to me, I did not any more observe any ground for believing this of such as I seem to perceive when awake; the second was that since I was as yet ignorant of the author of my being, or at least supposed myself to be so, I saw nothing to prevent my having been so constituted by nature as that I should be deceived even in matters that appeared to me to possess the greatest truth.

. . .

But now that I begin to know myself better, and to discover more clearly the author of my being, I do not, indeed, think that I ought rashly to admit all which the senses seem to teach, nor, on the other hand, is it my conviction that I ought to doubt in general of their teachings.

And, firstly, because I know that all which I clearly and distinctly conceive can be produced by God exactly as I conceive it, it is sufficient that I am able clearly and distinctly to conceive one thing apart from another, in order to be certain that the one is different from the other, seeing they may at least be made to exist separately, by the omnipotence of God; and it matters not by what power this separation is made, in order to be compelled to judge them different; and, therefore, merely because I know with certitude that I exist, and because, in the meantime, I do not observe that aught necessarily belongs to my nature or essence beyond my being a thinking thing, I rightly conclude that my essence consists only in my being a thinking thing [or a substance whose whole essence or nature is merely thinking]. And although I may, or rather, as I will shortly say, although I certainly do possess a body with which I am very closely conjoined; nevertheless, because, on the one hand, I have a clear and distinct idea of myself, in as far as I am only a thinking and unextended thing, and as, on the other hand, I possess a distinct idea of body, in as far as it is only an extended and unthinking thing, it is certain that I [that is, my mind, by which I am what I am] am entirely and truly distinct from my body, and may exist without it.

Then comes Descartes' proof that, in general, he could not be fooled about the existence of bodies "outside" of him.

But there is nothing which that nature teaches me more expressly [or more sensibly] than that I have a body which is ill affected when I feel pain, and stands in need of food and drink when I experience the sensations of hunger and thirst, etc. And therefore I ought not to doubt but that there is some truth in these informations.

Nature likewise teaches me by these sensations of pain, hunger, thirst, etc., that I am not only lodged in my body as a pilot in a vessel, but that I am besides so intimately conjoined, and as it were intermixed with it, that my mind and body compose a certain unity. For if this were not the case, I should not feel pain when my body is hurt, seeing I am merely a thinking thing, but should perceive the wound by the understanding alone, just as a pilot perceives by sight when any part of his vessel is damaged; and when my body has need of food or drink, I should have a clear knowledge of this, and not be made aware of it by the confused sensations of hunger and thirst: for, in truth, all these sensations of hunger, thirst, pain, etc., are nothing more than certain confused modes of thinking, arising from the union and apparent fusion of mind and body.

Besides this, nature teaches me that my own body is surrounded by many other bodies . . . some are agreeable, and others disagreeable, there can be no doubt that my body, or rather my entire self, in as far as I am composed of body and mind, may be variously affected, both beneficially and hurtfully, by surrounding bodies.

But how can two different substances, particularly two such different kinds of substances, interact? We know what it is for two bodies to interact, but how can a body make contact with a mind, which seems so intangible and "ghostly"? Descartes never answers this problem to his or to his critics' satisfaction. Spinoza, seeing Descartes' troubles, insists that there is only one substance and that body and mind are but different "attributes" of that one substance. That avoids the metaphysical question, for there is no trouble about interaction within a substance. But it still leaves a sizable problem, namely, how these two attributes are coordinated. That is a question Spinoza never answers; and Leibniz, attacking the same problem, finds it preferable to deny the reality of physical substance altogether. There are only mental substances, monads, each locked into its own experience. The extravagance of these two solutions should give you some idea of the difficulty of the problem.

We can get a more specific clue to the mysterious quality of "consciousness" if we consider the following. Descartes, Spinoza, and Leibniz, you recall, define mind as "unextended," that is, unextended in space. (Bodies, on the other hand, are defined as extended in space.) In other words, it is essential that minds, unlike bodies, cannot be said to be "this large" or to be located in such and such a place. But despite this definition, notice how much of our talk about consciousness consists of metaphors of spatial form; we talk about something being "in" our minds. We talk about something "slipping (out of) our minds." Philosophers often talk about the "contents" of consciousness, and a popular phrase from William James is the "stream of consciousness." Now we might say, "those are just metaphors"; but why are such metaphors necessary?

How would you answer the question "What is it to be conscious?" You might say something about "awareness" or "feelings," but that only restates the problem with different words. When we try to describe an image we do so in terms appropriate to physical things (namely, what it is an image *of*). We try to describe a pain and come out with metaphors ("it's as if a vice were closing on my head") or comparisons ("it feels the same as when . . ."). The retreat to spatial metaphors reflects this difficulty. We talk about our experiences as if we were describing other things but then qualify our descriptions by saying that they are "in" consciousness rather than in the world.

How can we describe consciousness itself? There is a further difficulty: If I can talk about my mind only with difficulty, how can I talk about your mind at all? I can experience only what is "in" my mind, I can't feel your pain. Even if I feel "sympathy pains" with you, it is my pain I feel. So I can't describe your mind at all, and evidently I have difficulty describing my mind as well. Therefore, how can we talk about "mind" at all? Not surprisingly, many psychologists and philosophers have rejected the idea of "mind" altogether, preferring to talk only about what is mutually observable and "extended" in physical space (for example, neurology and overt behavior).

We shall later consider some of these attempts to reject the idea of "mind" altogether. But what should seem fairly obvious to you is that this idea can be rejected only with reference to other people, not with reference to ourselves. *Why? Because of Descartes' first premise, to put it bluntly*. The same logic that allows him to assert with certainty "I am thinking" and "I exist as a thinking thing" now forces us to admit that "I am not thinking" and "I am not a thinking thing" are utterly absurd and unintelligible statements. They are self-refuting in exactly the same sense that "I am thinking" is self-confirming. (This isn't to say that you are thinking clearly, or well, or enjoying it; only that, in some minimal sense, you are thinking.) Therefore, you must have a mind. In one's own case, the fact that a person is conscious is the last thing one could ever deny.

> • What does Descartes mean when he says that the mind's awareness of bodily sensations and interactions demonstrates a connection between mind and body? Can you think of counterexamples to this claim (i.e., a time when your mind was unaware of something occurring within the body or something occurring within the mind with no bodily manifestations)? Do these counterexamples prove Descartes wrong? Or are they impossible in some way? What might be another explanation for the perceived intimacy between physical and mental states?
>
> • Is the existence of your consciousness irrefutable? The existence of particular conscious states (moods, ideas, sensations, emotions)? How can you be certain of your knowledge of them?

It is important to appreciate the fact that Descartes did not defend the idea of a radical difference between mind and body only as a metaphysical or scientific thesis. There is much in "common sense" that supports it, and the separation of mind or soul from physical body obviously serves a long-standing religious concern as well. It makes sense of the thesis that the soul might survive the body after death, and it safely separates the realms of religion and science. It even provides an argument for the necessity of God's existence. Descartes points out (in "Meditation III") that his various fleeting thoughts could not be unified into a coherent, enduring self without the intervention of a higher power.

 FROM **"Meditation III"**
BY **René Descartes**[3]

But though I assume that perhaps I have always existed just as I am at present, neither can I escape the force of this reasoning, and imagine that the conclusion to be drawn from this is, that I need not seek for any author of my existence. For all the course of my life may be divided into an infinite number of parts, none of which is in any way dependent on the other; and thus from the fact that I was in existence a short time ago it does not follow that I must be in existence now, unless some cause at this instant, so to speak, produces me anew, that is to say, conserves me. It is as a matter of fact perfectly clear and evident to all those who consider with attention the nature of time, that, in order to be conserved in each moment in which it endures, a

---

3 René Descartes, "Letter of Dedication to the Dean and Doctors of the Faculty of Sacred Theology of Paris," in *Meditations on First Philosophy*, in *The Philosophical Works of Descartes*, trans. Elizabeth S. Haldane and G. R. T. Ross, 1911. Reprinted with the permission of Cambridge University Press.

substance has need of the same power and action as would be necessary to produce and create it anew, supposing it did not yet exist, so that the light of nature shows us clearly that the distinction between creation and conservation is solely a distinction of the reason.

And in the dedication of the same work, he writes,

And as regards the soul, although many have considered that it is not easy to know its nature, and some have even dared to say that human reasons have convinced us that it would perish with the body, and that faith alone could believe the contrary, nevertheless, inasmuch as the Lateran Council held under Leo X (in the eighth session) condemns these tenets, and as Leo expressly ordains Christian philosophers to refute their arguments and to employ all their powers in making known the truth, I have ventured in this treatise to undertake the same task.

B. The Problem of Dualism

How is consciousness connected to your body? You decide to raise your hand, and your hand goes up. You formulate an answer to your friend's question, and it comes out of your mouth. How does what takes place "in your mind" determine what happens with your body? A familiar image, borrowed from untold numbers of cartoons, is the little man (or woman) in your head, operating your body as a construction worker operates a giant steam shovel. But this is no answer at all. First, there is no little man. But even if there were, the same problem would then focus on him (or her). How does he or she move a body by making certain mental decisions? The same problem arises in the other direction, from body to mind. A friend steps on your toe—your physiology teacher can explain to you what happens: nerves are pinched and signals are sent through your central nervous system into that huge complex of fat cells called your brain. But then, at some point, there is something else, the feeling, the pain. How does this happen? How does a feeling emerge from that complex and still unknown network of neurological reactions going on in your body?

You can see that this problem of mind-body interaction is no longer just a technical metaphysical problem having to do with the special notion of substance. The problem of "interaction" is the same for Spinoza and his one substance as it is for Descartes and his dualism. Even if you don't want to talk of substances at all, there is still the problem of explaining how your mind affects your body and how your body affects your mind. For whether or not you accept the special problems of the eighteenth-century metaphysicians, you have to admit that your mind is very different from your body, and that is the source of the trickiest of all modern philosophy problems—the mind-body problem. How are mind and body related?

The human body, like any other physical body, can be described in terms of its size, weight, chemical composition, and movements in space. The workings of the human nervous system, although very complex and not yet adequately understood, can be described just like any other biological reaction, in terms of the changes in cell membranes and

FIG. 5.2 The discipline of yoga seems to find and cultivate unity between the mind and the body. (© iStockphoto.com/Lev Dolgatshjov)

chemical reactions, the procession of chemoelectric nerve "impulses," and the computer-like network of different nerve components that are stimulated at any given time. The human brain can be seen as a complex machine, like a gooey computer. The human mind, however, is not to be characterized in any such spatial or chemical terms. The mind is not the same as the brain. It has no shape, no weight, and has the awkward property of being observable—in any particular case—by one and only one person. (Anyone can see my brain if they can get inside my skull.) We can understand how a body might interact with another body, even when the "forces" involved are hard to picture (for example, the gravitational attraction between two distant planets). But how does a body interact with something that has none of the crucial characteristics of a body? You might think of "energy" here, for energy would seem to have at least some of the intangible and "unextended" features of mind. It too, in a very limited sense, "has no size or weight." But energy is a function of physical bodies, force is a function of mass and acceleration. They are not, like our experiences, "private": a lightning bolt is observable to anyone who looks. And no one has ever claimed that descriptions of energy states, like descriptions of our ideas, are incorrigible. While it has often been demonstrated (by Einstein) that energy and mass are interconvertible, any such "interconvertibility" of mind and matter is still at the highly speculative stage, limited to freak performances by a few isolated and not wholly dependable "psychics" and such. We may well talk about "mental energy," but it is far from clear what we mean.

How can something so different as ideas and sensations interact with nervous systems and brain cells? Philosophers have proposed a number of solutions, all of them controversial and none of them yet satisfactory. But even before we look at some of them, it is important to stress the following point: The "mind-body problem" is not simply a matter of how little we still know about the human nervous system. No matter how our knowledge develops, we will still be faced with that mysterious gap between the last known neurological occurrence and the experience. Right now we can trace our neural impulses only so far, and the "last known neurological occurrence" is not very far along. But even when we have complete "brain maps" and can say for every mental occurrence what is going on in the brain at the same time, the problem will still remain: How are the two related?[4]

The classic attempt to resolve the problem of dualism is by Descartes. The following selection is from his essay "The Passions of the Soul."

 ### FROM "The Passions of the Soul" ### BY René Descartes[5]

But in order to understand all these things more perfectly, we must know that the soul is really joined to the whole body, and that we cannot, properly speaking, say that it exists in any one of its parts to the exclusion of the others, because it is one and in some manner indivisible, owing to the disposition of its organs, which are so related to one another that when any one of them is removed, that renders the whole body defective; and because it is of a nature which has no relation to extension, nor dimensions, nor other properties of the matter of which the body is composed, but only to the whole conglomerate of its organs, as appears from the fact

> "The soul is really joined to the whole body, and . . . we cannot, properly speaking, say that it exists in any one of its parts to the exclusion of the others."
>
> – RENÉ DESCARTES

---

4 It is logically possible, although it is extremely unlikely, that scientific research could show that the brain and our mind have very little to do with each other, that the presumed coordination between the two does not exist. It once was thought, for example, that the heart had to do with emotions (Aristotle and Descartes, for example). Science has proved them wrong. But science cannot do more than lay the groundwork for the problem.

5 René Descartes, "The Passions of the Soul," in *The Philosophical Works of Descartes*, trans. Elizabeth S. Haldane and G. R. T. Ross, 1911. Reprinted with the permission of Cambridge University Press.

that we could not in any way conceive of the half or the third of a soul, nor of the space it occupies, and because it does not become smaller owing to the cutting off of some portion of the body, but separates itself from it entirely when the union of its assembled organs is dissolved.

It is likewise necessary to know that although the soul is joined to the whole body, there is yet in that a certain part in which it exercises its functions more particularly than in all the others; and it is usually believed that this part is the brain, or possibly the heart: the brain, because it is with it that the organs of sense are connected, and the heart because it is apparently in it that we experience the passions. But, in examining the matter with care, it seems as though I had clearly ascertained that the part of the body in which the soul exercises its functions immediately is in nowise the heart, nor the whole of the brain, but merely the most inward of all its parts, to wit, a certain very small gland which is situated in the middle of its substance and so suspended above the duct whereby the animal spirits in its anterior cavities have communication with those in the posterior, that the slightest movements which take place in it may alter very greatly the course of these spirits; and reciprocally that the smallest changes which occur in the course of the spirits may do much to change the movements of this gland.[6]

. . .

Let us then conceive here that the soul has its principal seat in the little gland that exists in the middle of the brain, from whence it radiates forth through all the remainder of the body by means of the animal spirits, nerves, and even the blood, which, participating in the impressions of the spirits, can carry them by the arteries into all the members. Recollecting what has been said above about the machine of our body, that is, that the little filaments of our nerves are so distributed in all its parts, that on the occasion of the diverse movements which are there excited by sensible objects, they open in diverse ways the pores of the brain, which causes the animal spirits contained in these cavities to enter in diverse ways into the muscles, by which means they are capable of being moved; and also that all the other causes which are capable of moving the spirits in diverse ways suffice to conduct them into diverse muscles; let us here add that the small gland which is the main seat of the soul is so suspended between the cavities which contain the spirits that it can be moved by them in as many different ways as there are sensible diversities in the object, but that it may also be moved in diverse ways by the soul, whose nature is such that it receives in itself as many diverse impressions, that is to say, that it possesses as many diverse perceptions as there are diverse moments in this gland. Reciprocally, likewise, the machine of the body is so formed that from the simple fact that this gland is diversely moved by the soul, or by such other cause, whatever it is, it thrusts the spirits which surround it towards the pores of the brain, which conduct them by the nerves into the muscles, by which means it causes them to move the limbs.

The technical name given to this theory is **causal interactionism**, in other words, mental changes cause bodily changes, and vice versa. Unlike his followers, Descartes did not seriously take the problem of separate substances or radically different changes causally affecting one

---

6 The gland Descartes is referring to is what is now called the pineal gland, a small endocrine gland at the base of the brain. It had only recently been discovered in Descartes' time, and its functions are still not adequately understood. It is currently hypothesized that it controls mating cycles in higher animals and possibly any number of other activity cycles.

another. He apparently felt satisfied if not exactly comfortable, with such a causal account. He was vigorously attacked in this by most of his immediate followers, including Spinoza, Leibniz, and many of the empiricists. "Different substances cannot interact," they insisted. Or, in more modern dress, they argued that only physical bodies can causally interact, not anything so different as physical bodies and minds. Yet one thing remains obvious, and that is that the familiar coordination of our mental activities and the movements of our bodies must be accounted for. To do so, without bringing in causal interaction, required considerable ingenuity on the part of Descartes' critics.

We have already seen the two metaphysical alternatives that immediately followed Descartes. The first was formulated by Leibniz as part of his overall theory of monads. He insisted that there could be no causal interaction between monads, and specifically, there could be no sense made out of the claim that mental substances interacted with anything that we call "physical bodies." So what could he suggest as an alternative? His answer to the problem was that God, who had created monads in the first place, had also "programmed" them in such a way that our mental activities and what we call our bodily activities are exactly coordinated. Leaving aside the rest of Leibniz's theory and looking just at the mind-body problem, we can restate his solution as a form of what is called **parallelism**. His "**preestablished harmony**" between monads can now be viewed as the somewhat strange theory that our mental lives and the movements of our bodies are exactly coordinated (so that I feel pain when you step on my toe and so that my hand goes up just when I "decide" that it should). Yet there is no causal interaction between them whatsoever. It is like the sound and visual tracks of a movie film, moving along exactly parallel but never in fact interacting. (That is, the character who appears to be talking in the movie does not cause the sounds that you hear as if he or she were producing them. The sounds are actually produced separately and would continue even if the projector bulb burned out and the figure on the screen disappeared altogether.) Of course, to accept this theory you must also accept the considerable metaphysical and theological supports that it requires. If you don't believe in a God who could set up this complex system, there is absolutely no way of explaining the remarkable coordination of mind and body. Even if you do believe in God, you may well think that the mind-body problem requires some more plausible and secular solution.

Spinoza's theory need not be kept in the "one substance" metaphysics that he used to present it. In fact, much the same theory was defended only a few years ago by Bertrand Russell, without reference to the metaphysical notion of substance at all. Russell said, as Spinoza had said centuries before, that mind and body, mental events and physical changes, were different aspects of one and the same "something." For Spinoza, the "something" was "the one substance" and the aspects were what he called "attributes." Russell claimed only that our experiences and ideas were one aspect of some events or activities of which the various chemical reactions of the brain were another aspect. Accordingly, the theory has often been called the **dual aspect theory**, whether or not it is specifically addressed to the problem of substances and their attributes. Since we are now talking about two "aspects" of the same thing rather than two different things, the problem of interaction doesn't arise. But, as we complained before, this only hides the problem rather than solves it. What is this mysterious "something" of which mind and body are merely "aspects"? It is neither brain nor mind, so what could it be? By the nature of the case, we can't find out, which leaves us with the equally embarrassing question, "How could one and the same thing have such different aspects?" You might say, "Well, a hot coal has both 'aspects' of being heavy and being hot." But that we can explain. What are we to say of a "something" that is neither brain nor mind, but both?

- Outline the various solutions to the mind-body problem (e.g., causal interactionism, parallelism, dual aspect theory).

C. The Rejection of Dualism

If the problem is dualism, then perhaps the answer is the rejection of dualism. Of course, we still have to account for the obvious facts of the case: that we feel something when certain things happen to our bodies, that we do something when we mentally decide to. But philosophers of recent years—and nearly all psychologists—have taken a dim view toward dualism in all the foregoing forms.

A first, still timid step toward eliminating dualism consists of minimizing, though not rejecting, the mental side of dualism. This theory is usually called **epiphenomenalism**, and William James was one of its best-known defenders. Epiphenomenalism allows for causal interaction, but only in one direction. Bodies and changes in bodies cause mental events. You might think of a boiler system or automobile engine equipped with various gauges to tell us how the machine is functioning at any given time. The machine works on, registering certain results on the attached gauges. But notice that the gauge is relatively unimportant to the working of the machine. In fact, the gauge can break and the machine can function for years. What is the significance of such a theory? Many philosophers and psychologists are interested primarily in the continuity of physical and physiological laws without the problematic disruption of mysterious "mental causes." For them, such a theory allows them to concentrate wholly on the physical side of the matter and ignore "the mind" completely. If an objection is raised, one can always insist: "Oh, I'm not denying that you feel something, too." But this is an unimportant detail, a side-product, an epiphenomenon, that need not be taken all that seriously.

- Does epiphenomenalism solve the problem of dualism? Why or why not?

1. Radical Behaviorism

Epiphenomenalism is a timid rejection of dualism. It doesn't actually reject dualism, but it minimizes one half the duality. Other forms of attack are not so timid. In psychology, many authors have long accepted that all talk of "the mental" is a hopeless tangle of confusions that, by the nature of the case, cannot be resolved through any experiment whatsoever. (That is, only one person could observe the results of the experiment in any given case, and the very nature of a scientific experiment is that it must be observable by anyone.) Accordingly, many psychologists practice what they call **behaviorism**.

The best-known behaviorist is the late psychologist **B. F. Skinner**.[7] Behaviorism, as a form of science, refuses to even consider any events that cannot be publicly witnessed. That immediately and logically excludes mental events. Behaviorism is primarily a scientific method and need not deny the existence of mental events. Most behaviorists, however, have gone beyond the method—which only says that they will not scientifically study such events—and have done a bit of metaphysics as well; they also deny that there

---

[7] Selections by B. F. Skinner can be found in Chapter 6 on pages 426-429.

FIG. 5.3 The psychologist and philosopher B. F. Skinner was the founder of behaviorism.
(© Bettmann/CORBIS)

can be any mental events. Watson, for example, goes so far as to suggest that belief in consciousness goes back to the ancient days of superstition and magic. He insists that any good behaviorist can catch the average undergraduate student in a mess of tongue-tied contradictions but concludes from this not that our concept of consciousness is complicated and confused but rather that there could not possibly be any such thing. His argument is self-consciously "scientific," the alternative to which is being a mere "savage and still believing in magic." His test is simply whether the soul (philosophers and psychologists often shift too easily between "soul" and "consciousness") can be experienced; "no one has ever touched a soul, or seen one in a test tube, or has in any other way come into relationship with it as he has with the other objects of his daily experience."[8] Thus Watson shifts from his view as a scientist, able to write about only what he can measure and observe, to a view as a metaphysician, insisting that there cannot be any such thing as consciousness and that no rational person should believe that there is.

- In denying the legitimacy of anything that cannot be "publicly witnessed," how does behaviorism reject dualism?
- Do you think behaviorism is a sensible scientific program?

2. Logical Behaviorism

Philosophers have also turned to behaviorism as a way of escaping the problems of Cartesian dualism. Oxford philosopher **Gilbert Ryle**, following some suggestions by Ludwig Wittgenstein, established a new form of behaviorism—*logical* behaviorism—in his book *The Concept of Mind* (1949). Its first chapter is appropriately called "Descartes' Myth." First, Ryle describes what he calls "the official doctrine":

FROM *The Concept of Mind* BY **Gilbert Ryle**[9]

There is a doctrine about the nature and place of minds which is so prevalent among theorists and even among laymen that it deserves to be described as the official theory. Most philosophers, psychologists and religious teachers subscribe, with minor reservations, to its main articles and, although they admit certain theoretical difficulties in it, they tend to assume that these can be overcome without serious modifications being made to the architecture of the theory. It will be argued here that the central

---

8 John Watson, *Behaviorism*, New York: Norton, 1930.

9 Gilbert Ryle, *The Concept of Mind*, London: Hutchinson, 1949. Reprinted with permission of Taylor and Francis Books UK, with the permission of the Principal, Fellows, and Scholars of Hertford College in the University of Oxford.

principles of the doctrine are unsound and conflict with the whole body of what we know about minds when we are not speculating about them.

The official doctrine, which hails chiefly from Descartes, is something like this. With the doubtful exceptions of idiots and infants in arms every human being has both a body and a mind. Some would prefer to say that every human being has both a body and a mind. His body and his mind are ordinarily harnessed together, but after the death of the body his mind may continue to exist and function.

Human bodies are in space and are subject to the mechanical laws which govern all other bodies in space. Bodily processes and states can be inspected by external observers. So a man's bodily life is as much a public affair as are the lives of animals and reptiles and even as the careers of trees, crystals and plants.

But minds are not in space, nor are their operations subject to mechanical laws. The workings of one mind are not witnessable by other observers; its career is private. Only I can take direct cognisance of the states and processes of my own mind. A person therefore lives through two collateral histories, one consisting of what happens in and to his body, the other consisting of what happens in and to his mind. The first is public, the second private. The events in the first history are events in the physical world, those in the second are events in the mental world.

It has been disputed whether a person does or can directly monitor all or only some of the episodes of his own private history; but, according to the official doctrine, of at least some of these episodes he has direct and unchallengeable cognisance. In consciousness, self-consciousness and introspection he is directly and authentically apprised of the present states and operations of his mind. He may have great or small uncertainties about concurrent and adjacent episodes in the physical world, but he can have none about at least part of what is momentarily occupying his mind.

It is customary to express this bifurcation of his two lives and of his two worlds by saying that the things and events which belong to the physical world, including his own body, are external, while the workings of his own mind are internal. This antithesis of outer and inner is of course meant to be construed as a metaphor, since minds, not being in space, could not be described as being spatially inside anything else, or as having things going on spatially inside themselves. But relapses from this good intention are common and theorists are found speculating how stimuli, the physical sources of which are yards or miles outside a person's skin, can generate mental responses inside his skull, or how decisions framed inside his cranium can set going movements of his extremities.

Even when "inner" and "outer" are construed as metaphors, the problem of how a person's mind and body influence one another is notoriously charged with theoretical difficulties. What the mind wills, the legs, arms and the tongue execute; what affects the ear and the eye has something to do with what the mind perceives; grimaces and smiles betray the mind's moods and bodily castigations lead, it is hoped, to moral improvement. But the actual transactions between the episodes of the private history and those of the public history remain mysterious, since by definition they can belong to neither series. They could not be reported among the happenings described in a person's autobiography of his inner life, but nor could they be reported among those described in someone else's biography of that person's overt career. They can be inspected neither by introspection nor by laboratory experiment. They are theoretical shuttlecocks which are forever being bandied from the physiologist back to the psychologist and from the psychologist back to the physiologist.

Underlying this partly metaphorical representation of the bifurcation of a person's two lives there is a seemingly more profound and philosophical assumption. It is assumed that there are two different kinds of existence or status. What exists or happens may have the status of physical existence, or it may have the status of mental existence. Somewhat as the faces of coins are either heads or tails, or somewhat as living creatures are either male or female, so, it is supposed, some existing is physical existing, other existing is mental existing. It is a necessary feature of what has physical existence that it is in space and time; it is a necessary feature of what has mental existence that it is in time but not in space. What has physical existence is composed of matter, or else is a function of matter; what has mental existence consists of consciousness, or else is a function of consciousness.

. . .

What sort of knowledge can be secured of the workings of a mind? On the one side, according to the official theory, a person has direct knowledge of the best imaginable kind of the workings of his own mind. Mental states and processes are (or are normally) conscious states and processes, and the consciousness which irradiates them can engender no illusions and leaves the door open for no doubts. A person's present thinkings, feelings and willings, his perceivings, rememberings and imaginings are intrinsically "phosphorescent"; their existence and their nature are inevitably betrayed to their owner. The inner life is a stream of consciousness of such a sort that it would be absurd to suggest that the mind whose life is that stream might be unaware of what is passing down it.

. . .

On the other side, one person has no direct access of any sort to the events of the inner life of another. He cannot do better than make problematic inferences from the observed behaviour of the other person's body to the states of mind which, by analogy from his own conduct, he supposes to be signalized by that behaviour. Direct access to the workings of a mind is the privilege of that mind itself; in default of such privileged access, the workings of one mind are inevitably occult to everyone else. For the supposed arguments from bodily movements similar to their own to mental workings similar to their own would lack any possibility of observational corroboration. Not unnaturally, therefore, an adherent of the official theory finds it difficult to resist this consequence of his premises, that he has no good reason to believe that there do exist minds other than his own. Even if he prefers to believe that to other human bodies there are harnessed minds not unlike his own, he cannot claim to be able to discover their individual characteristics, or the particular things that they undergo and do. Absolute solitude is on this showing the ineluctable destiny of the soul. Only our bodies can meet.

Then, in section 2, Ryle argues that the "official doctrine" is "absurd" and is based upon what he calls "a category mistake":

FIG. 5.4 Philosopher Gilbert Ryle (© Hulton-Deutsch Collection/CORBIS)

Gilbert Ryle (1900–1978)

The Oxford "ordinary-language" philosopher whose book *The Concept of Mind* (1949) set the stage for several decades of debate over his quasi-behavioristic resolution of the mind-body problem. His main thesis is that the distinction between mind and body rests on what he calls a "category mistake," that is, wrongly believing something to be one kind of thing when it is really another. In particular, it has been thought that mental events were events on a par with, but wholly different from, bodily events. Instead, Ryle argues, to talk about mind is to talk about behavioral dispositions and abilities. (To say that a person *wants* to do something is to say that he *would* do it if given the opportunity.)

Such in outline is the official theory. I shall often speak of it with deliberate abusiveness, as "the dogma of the Ghost in the Machine." I hope to prove that it is entirely false, and false not in detail but in principle. It is not merely an assemblage of particular mistakes. It is one big mistake and a mistake of a special kind. It is, namely, a category-mistake. It represents the facts of mental life as if they belonged to one logical type of category (or range of types or categories), when they actually belong to another. The dogma is therefore a philosopher's myth. In attempting to explode the myth I shall probably be taken to be denying well-known facts about the mental life of human beings, and my plea that I aim to do nothing more than rectify the logic of mental-conduct concepts will probably be disallowed as mere subterfuge.

I must first indicate what is meant by the phrase "Category-mistake." This I do in a series of illustrations.

A foreigner visiting Oxford or Cambridge for the first time is shown a number of colleges, libraries, playing fields, museums, scientific departments and administrative offices. He then asks "But where is the university? I have seen where the members of the Colleges live, where the Registrar works, where the scientists experiment and the rest. But I have not yet seen the University in which reside and work the members of your University." It has then to be explained to him that the University is not another collateral institution, some ulterior counterpart to the colleges, laboratories and offices which he has seen. The University is just the way in which all that he has already seen is organized. When they are seen and when their coordination is understood, the University has been seen. His mistake lay in his innocent assumption that it was correct to speak of Christ Church, the Bodleian Library, the Ashmolean Museum *and* the University, to speak, that is, as if "the University" stood for an extra member of the class of which these other units are members. He was mistakenly allocating the University to the same category as that to which the other institutions belong.

. . .

One more illustration. A foreigner watching his first game of cricket learns what are the functions of the bowlers, the batsmen, the fielders, the umpires and the scorers. He then says "But there is no one left on the field to contribute the famous element of team-spirit. I see who does the bowling, the batting and the wicket-keeping; but I do not see whose role it is to exercise esprit de corps." Once more, it would have to be explained that he was looking for the wrong type of thing. Team-spirit is not another cricketing-operation supplementary to all of the other special tasks. It is, roughly, the keenness with which each of the special tasks is performed, and performing a task keenly is not performing two tasks. Certainly exhibiting team-spirit is not the same thing as bowling or catching, but nor is it a third thing such that we can say that the bowler first bowls *and* then exhibits team-spirit or that a fielder is at a given moment *either* catching *or* displaying esprit de corps.

These illustrations of category-mistakes have a common feature which must be noticed. The mistakes were made by people who did

FIG. 5.5 I see the batter and the bowler, but who's in charge of team spirit? If no one is the "team spirit" player, how could it exist? *(Image © Lance Bellers, 2011. Used under license from Shutterstock.com)*

not know how to wield the concepts *University* . . . and *team-spirit*. Their puzzles arose from inability to use certain items in the English vocabulary.

A category mistake, in general, is mistaking one *type* of thing for another. For example, it would be a category mistake to ask, "what color is the number 3?" The philosophically interesting mistakes, of course, are neither so obvious nor so silly as that example. They are mistakes made when we try to think abstractly. Most important are the category mistakes that philosophers make when they talk about "the mind":

> My destructive purpose is to show that a family of radical category-mistakes is the source of the double-life theory. The representation of a person as a ghost mysteriously ensconced in a machine derives from this argument. Because, as is true, a person's thinking, feeling and purposive doing cannot be described solely in the idioms of physics, chemistry and physiology, therefore they must be described in counterpart idioms. As the human body is a complex organised unit, so the human mind must be another complex organized unit, though one made of a different sort of stuff and with a different sort of structure. Or, again, as the human body, like any other parcel of matter, is a field of causes and effects, so the mind must be another field of causes and effects, though not (Heaven be praised) mechanical causes and effects.

This unfortunate category mistake, which Ryle attributes primarily to Descartes, is thinking that "the mind" and its events are some strange and mysteriously private sort of *thing* behind our behavior, when, in fact, mind is the *pattern* of our behavior and not "behind" behavior at all.

> When two terms belong to the same category, it is proper to construct conjunctive propositions embodying them. Thus a purchaser may say that he bought a left-hand glove and a right-hand glove, but not that he bought a left-hand glove, a right-hand glove and a pair of gloves. "She came home in a flood of tears and a sedan-chair" is a well-known joke based on the absurdity of conjoining terms of different types. It would have been equally ridiculous to construct the disjunction "She came home either in a flood of tears or else in a sedan-chair." Now the dogma of the Ghost in the Machine does just this. It maintains that there exist both bodies and minds; that there occur physical processes and mental processes; that there are mechanical causes of corporeal movements and mental causes of corporeal movements. I shall argue that these and other analogous conjunctions are absurd; but, it must be noticed, the argument will not show that either of the illegitimately conjoined propositions is absurd in itself. I am not, for example, denying that there occur mental processes. Doing long division is a mental process and so is making a joke. But I am saying that the phrase "there occur mental processes" does not mean the same sort of thing as "there occur physical processes," and, therefore, that it makes no sense to conjoin or disjoin the two.

The key to Ryle's analysis is what he calls a disposition. A disposition is a tendency for something to happen given certain conditions. For example, we say that "if the lever is disturbed, the mousetrap will snap closed." The key is the *"if . . . then"* (or "hypothetical") form of the statement. Ryle explains this in the following way:

> There are at least two quite different senses in which an occurrence is said to be "explained"; and there are correspondingly at least two quite different senses in which we ask "why" it occurred and two quite different senses in which we say that it happened "because" so and so was the case. The first sense is the causal sense. To ask

"The phrase 'there occur mental processes' does not mean the same sort of thing as 'there occur physical processes,' and, therefore . . . it makes no sense to conjoin or disjoin the two."

– GILBERT RYLE

why the glass broke is to ask what caused it to break, and we explain, in this sense, the fracture of the glass when we report that a stone hit it. The "because" clause in the explanation reports an event, namely the event which stood to the fracture of the glass as cause to effect.

But very frequently we look for and get explanations of occurrences in another sense of "explanation." We ask why the glass shivered when struck by the stone and we get the answer that it was because the glass was brittle. Now "brittle" is a dispositional adjective; that is to say, to describe the glass as brittle is to assert a general hypothetical proposition about the glass. So when we say that the glass broke when struck because it was brittle, the "because" clause does not report a happening or a cause; it states a law-like proposition. People commonly say of explanations of this second kind that they give the "reason" for the glass breaking when struck.

How does the law-like general hypothetical proposition work? It says, roughly, that the glass, *if* sharply struck or twisted, etc. *would* not dissolve or stretch or evaporate but fly into fragments. The matter of fact that the glass did at a particular moment fly into fragments, when struck by a particular stone, is explained, in this sense of "explain," when the first happening, namely the impact of the stone, satisfies the protasis of the general hypothetical proposition, and when the second happening, namely the fragmentation of the glass, satisfies its apodosis.

He then applies this concept of disposition to his analysis of "mind." (This occupies him for most of his book.) The main idea is this: Everything "mental" is really a disposition to behave in certain ways. Consider, for example, his brief analysis of acting from vanity:

The statement "he boasted from vanity" ought, on one view, to be construed as saying that "he boasted and the cause of his boasting was the occurrence in him of a particular feeling or impulse of vanity." On the other view, it is to be construed as saying "he boasted on meeting the stranger and his doing so satisfies the law-like proposition that whenever he finds a chance of securing the admiration and envy of others, he does whatever he thinks will produce this admiration and envy."

Then the general argument:

To say that a person knows something, or aspires to be something, is not to say that he is at a particular moment in process of doing or undergoing anything, but that he is able to do certain things, when the need arises, or that he is prone to do and feel certain things in situations of certain sorts. . . .

Abandonment of the two-worlds legend involves the abandonment of the idea that there is a locked door and a still to be discovered key. Those human actions and reactions, those spoken and unspoken utterances, those tones of voice, facial expressions and gestures, which have always been the data of all the other students of men, have, after all, been the right and the only manifestations to study. They and they alone have merited, but fortunately not received, the grandiose title "mental phenomena."

Ryle's (and Wittgenstein's) logical behaviorism differs from the radical behaviorism of the psychologists in that it is not a theory about behavior and its causes so much as it is a theory about the language of mind, about the meaning of "mentalistic" terms such as "wants," "believes," "hurts," "loves," "feels," and "thinks." Ryle's basic thesis, stripped of his polemic against "the ghost in the machine," is that applying a mental term—attributing a

FIG. 5.6 Could a robot perfectly imitate a human being? Suppose one could: what would that mean for behaviorism? (© iStockphoto.com/Simon Oxley)

mental property to a person—is logically equivalent to saying that the person will act in a certain way. The advantage of this is that it eliminates all mysterious things mental by translating the mental terminology into statements about behavior, not "inner events." Instead of thinking of love as "a feeling deep inside," for example, the logical behaviorist would say, unromantically perhaps, that "John loves Mary" means that John will be with Mary every chance he gets, he will buy her flowers if flowers are available, he will take her to the movies if she utters the stimulating words, "Let's go to the movies!" As you can see from this example, the number of acts and possible acts involved in the translation of a mentalistic term can be indefinitely large, since, in various circumstances and with various opportunities, a person in love might do almost anything. (The case is not so complicated, usually, with such mental predicates as "is thirsty" and "has an itch.") But however complicated the translation from mental language to behavioral disposition, the problem of dualism does not arise. The causal interaction between mind and body has been reformulated as the causal connection between a physical state—a disposition to behave in certain ways—and the actual consequent behavior. Saying "he will marry her because he loves her" is therefore no more metaphysically problematic than saying "the glass will break because it is brittle."

There is a problem with all forms of behaviorism—both radical and logical. However tempting such a theory might be when we are studying other people at a distance, it seems utterly absurd when we try to think behavioristically while talking to a friend or listening to someone talk to us. And behaviorism becomes pure nonsense in one's own case, when we are trying to understand and talk about our own mental states. My pain is not the same as my behavior, and no matter how easy it may be for you to infer from my behavior that I am in pain, that is certainly not how *I* know that I am in pain, and it is not what I mean by my report, "I am in pain." Indeed, when I tell you "I am in pain," I am not predicting my behavior. I am telling you what I *feel*, quite apart from anything I might *do*. Whatever the logic of mental language, that undeniable feeling seems to remind us that behaviorism, however therapeutic in psychology and however powerful as an antidote to Cartesianism, cannot be the whole story. Watson's behaviorism helped correct an absurd amount of mentalistic theorizing about the behavior of animals ("the rat is trying to figure out how to get the door open"). So too, Ryle's behaviorism is a vital challenge to the too-easy supposition that our "minds" are ghostly containers filled with equally ghostly entities and processes. But as an alternative account of the mind, behaviorism inevitably bangs up against that ultimate mark of the mental, Descartes' "I think." There is no way you can think consistently that you never think or think that your thinking is nothing but your tendency to behave. As one of Watson's early critics commented, "What behaviorism shows is that psychologists do not always think very well, not that they don't think at all."

The rejection of dualism need not be a rejection of the mental side of the duality, although that is the obvious preference of most scientists. We have seen at least one philosopher, however, who escapes the problems of Cartesian dualism by rejecting the physical side of the problem. That is Bishop Berkeley, who quite clearly, in attacking Locke and defending his own "subjective idealism," provides a radical solution to the mind-body problem as well. His theory is that there are only minds and their ideas, no physical bodies. Therefore, there is no problem of interaction. He too (like Leibniz), however, needs God to hold his system together. But idealism has not been as rare an answer to the mind-body problem as you might think, although we see little of it nowadays. The religious idealists of the past century, in the

United States as well as in England and Europe, were so powerful that they virtually ruled philosophy for a number of decades.

> • How has dualism committed a "category mistake," according to Ryle? Do you think our use of "mind" is akin to our use of "university"?
> • Can the mind be described in dispositional terms? How does doing so avoid interpreting the mind as a substance?

3. The Identity Theory

The most powerful and most plausible rejection of dualism, however, consists neither of denying consciousness nor of denying physical bodies. To deny dualism by denying mind or body strikes us as a bit simple-minded. There is a better way. Why not say that there are not two things at all, as there appear to be, but only one. In other words, mind and body, or more accurately, mental events and certain bodily events (presumably brain events) are identical. This theory, accordingly, is called the **identity theory**, and it once was one of the hottest controversies in American philosophy. You can see that it was anticipated, in a sense, by Spinoza and Russell with their dual aspect theory. But the identity theory, unlike the others, tries to tie itself as closely as possible with current scientific research, and although it is not a scientific theory itself, it will allow no such mysterious "something" such as we found in Spinoza and Russell. Accordingly, it is usually considered a form of materialism (although it does not deny the existence—only the ontological independence—of mental events).

The identity theory says that there are mental events, but they are identical to—the same thing as—certain physical events, that is, processes in the brain. Unlike behaviorism (radical or logical), the identity theory does not deny that mentalistic terms refer to something. The identity theory rather denies dualism by insisting that what mentalistic terms such as "wants," "believes," and "loves" refer to is not only some further unspecifiable mental state; it is also a neurological process that scientists, someday, will be able to specify precisely. Dualism is eliminated because there are no longer two things to interact; there is just a single event, a mental-neurological event, which can be described in either of two ways, in either of two quite different languages. One can (truthfully) say, "I have a headache" or, if one knows an extensive amount of neurology, one could just as well say, "such and such (the details are not for a philosophy book) is going on in my brain."

The following essay is one of the classic statements of the identity theory by Australian philosopher **J. J. C. Smart**.

 FROM **"Sensations and Brain Processes"**
BY **J. J. C. Smart**[10]

It seems to me that science is increasingly giving us a viewpoint whereby organisms are able to be seen as physico-chemical mechanisms: it seems that even the behavior of man himself will one day be explicable in mechanistic terms. There does seem to be, so far as science is concerned, nothing in the world but increasingly complex arrangements of physical constituents. All except for one place: in consciousness. That is, for a full description of what is going on in a man you would have to mention not

---

[10] J. J. C. Smart, "Sensations and Brain Processes," in *Philosophical Review* 68 (1959): 141-56. Copyright © 1959 by Cornell University. Reprinted by permission of the publisher.

only the physical processes in his tissue, glands, nervous system, and so forth, but also his states of consciousness: his visual, auditory, and tactual sensations, his aches and pains. That these should be *correlated* with brain processes does not help, for to say that they are *correlated* is to say that they are something "over and above." You cannot correlate something with itself. You correlate footprints with burglars, but not Bill Sikes the burglar with Bill Sikes the burglar. So sensations, states of consciousness, do seem to be the one sort of thing left outside the physicalist picture, and for various reasons I just cannot believe that this can be so. That everything should be explicable in terms of physics (together of course with descriptions of the ways in which the parts are put together—roughly, biology is to physics as radio-engineering is to electromagnetism) except the occurrence of sensations seems to me to be frankly unbelievable. Such sensations would be "nomological danglers," to use Feigl's expression. It is not often realized how odd would be the laws whereby these nomological danglers would dangle. It is sometimes asked, "Why can't there be psycho-physical laws which are of a novel sort, just as the laws of electricity and magnetism were novelties from the standpoint of Newtonian mechanics?" Certainly we are pretty sure in the future to come across new ultimate laws of a novel type, but I expect them to relate simple constituents: for example, whatever ultimate particles are then in vogue. I cannot believe that ultimate laws of nature could relate simple constituents to configurations consisting of perhaps billions of neurons (and goodness knows how many billion billions of ultimate particles) all put together for all the world as though their main purpose in life was to be a negative feedback mechanism of a complicated sort. Such ultimate laws would be like nothing so far known in science. They have a queer "smell" to them. I am just unable to believe in the nomological danglers themselves, or in the laws whereby they would dangle. If any philosophical arguments seemed to compel us to believe in such things, I would suspect a catch in the argument. In any case it is the object of this paper to show that there are no philosophical arguments which compel us to be dualists.

. . .

Why should sensations just be brain processes of a certain sort? There are, of course, well-known (as well as lesser-known) philosophical objections to the view that reports of sensations are reports of brain-processes, but I shall try to argue that these arguments are by no means as cogent as is commonly thought to be the case.

Let me first try to state more accurately the thesis that sensations are brain processes. It is not the thesis that, for example, "after-image" or "ache" means the

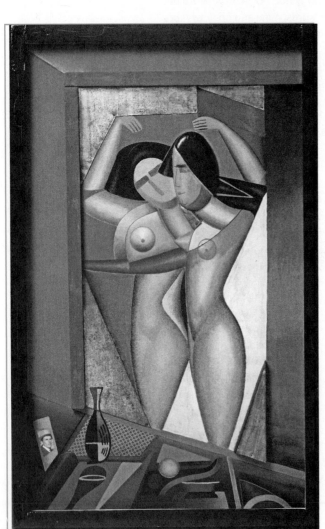

FIG. 5.7 Alexander Archipenko, *In the Boudoir (Before the Mirror)* (1915). Imagining the many dimensions of identity. *(The Philadelphia Museum of Art / Art Resource, NY / Artists Rights Society (ARS), New York)*

same as "brain process of sort X" (where "X" is replaced by a description of a certain sort of brain process). It is that, in so far as "after-image" or "ache" is a report of a process, it is a report of a process that *happens to be* a brain process. It follows that the thesis does not claim that sensation statements can be *translated* into statements about brain processes. Nor does it claim that the logic of a sensation statement is the same as that of a brain-process statement. All it claims is that in so far as a sensation statement is a report of something, that something is in fact a brain process. Sensations are nothing over and above brain processes. Nations are nothing "over and above" citizens, but this does not prevent the logic of nation statements being very different from the logic of citizen statements, nor does it insure the translatability of nation statements into citizen statements. (I do not, however, wish to assert that the relation of sensation statements to brain-process statements is very like that of nation statements to citizen statements. Nations do not just *happen to be* nothing over and above citizens, for example. I bring in the "nations" example merely to make a negative point: that the fact that the logic of A-statements is different from that of B-statements does not insure that A's are anything over and above B's.)

Remarks on identity (When I say that a sensation is a brain process or that lightning is an electric discharge, I am using "is" in the sense of strict identity. Just as in the—in this case necessary—proposition "7 is identical with the smallest prime number greater than 5.") When I say that a sensation is a brain process or that lightning is an electric discharge I do not mean just that the sensation is somehow spatially or temporally continuous with the brain process or that the lightning is just spatially or temporally continuous with the discharge. When on the other hand I say that the successful general is the same person as the small boy who stole the apples I mean only that the successful general I see before me is a time slice of the same four-dimensional object of which the small boy stealing apples is an earlier time slice. However, the four-dimensional object which has the general-I-see-before-me for its late time slice is identical in the strict sense with the four-dimensional object which has the small-boy-stealing-apples for an early time slice. I distinguish these two senses of "is identical with" because I wish to make it clear that the brain-process doctrine asserts identity in the *strict* sense.

> "Sensations are nothing over and above brain processes."
> – J. J. C. SMART

As compatible as the identity theory may seem with contemporary science and as plausible as it may seem as a way of rejecting dualism without rejecting the obvious facts about feelings and thinking, the identity theory too runs up against its share of paradoxes. The idea that one thing (a brain event = a mental event) can be referred to and described in two different languages sounds plausible and impressive. But, in this case, the two languages are so very different that there is very good reason to suppose that the thing(s) they refer to is/are very different as well. To pursue this line of criticism, here is a reevaluation of the identity theory by the American philosopher **Jerome Shaffer**.

Jerome Shaffer (1929-)

An American philosopher, presently teaching at the University of Connecticut. He is one of the best-known critics of the now influential "identity theory" of mind and body.

Against the Identity Theory
BY **Jerome Shaffer**[11]

The sense of "identity" relevant here is that in which we say, for example, that the morning star is "identical" with the evening star. It is not that the expression "morning star" means the same as the expression "evening star"; on the contrary, these expressions mean something different. But the object referred to by the two expressions is one and the same; there is just one heavenly body, namely, Venus, which when seen in the morning is called the morning star and when seen in the evening is called the evening star. The morning star is identical with the evening star; they are one and the same object.[12]

Of course, the identity of the mental with the physical is not exactly of this sort, since it is held to be simultaneous identity rather than the identity of a thing at one time with the same thing at a later time. To take a closer example, one can say that lightning is a particularly massive electrical discharge from one cloud to another or to the earth. Not that the word "lightning" *means* "a particularly massive electrical discharge . . ."; when Benjamin Franklin discovered that lightning was electrical, he did not make a discovery about the meaning of words. Nor when it was discovered that water was H_2O was a discovery made about the meanings of words; yet water is identical with H_2O.

In a similar fashion, the identity theorist can hold that thoughts, feelings, wishes, and the like are identical with physical states. Not "identical" in the sense that mentalistic terms are synonymous in meaning with physicalistic terms but "identical" in the sense that the actual events picked out by mentalistic terms are one and the same events as those picked out by physicalistic terms.

. . .

What are the advantages of the identity theory? As a form of materialism, it does not have to cope with a world which has in it both mental phenomena and physical phenomena, and it does not have to ponder how they might be related. There exist only the physical phenomena, although there do exist two different ways of talking about such phenomena: physicalistic terminology and, in at least some situations, mentalistic terminology. We have here a dualism of language, but not a dualism of entities, events or properties.

But do we have merely a dualism of languages and no other sort of dualism? In the case of Venus, we do indeed have only one object, but the expression "morning star" picks out one phase of that object's history, where it is in the mornings, and the expression "evening star" picks out another phase of the object's history, where it is in the evenings. If that object did not have these two distinct aspects, it would not have been a *discovery* that the morning star and the evening star were indeed one and the same body, and, further, there would be no point to the different ways of referring to it.

Now it would be admitted by identity theorists that physicalistic and mentalistic terms do not refer to different phases in the history of one and the same object. What sort of identity is intended? Let us turn to an allegedly closer analogy, that of the identity of lightning and a particular sort of electrical phenomenon. Yet here again

---

[11] Jerome Shaffer, *Philosophy of Mind.* Copyright © 1994. Reprinted with permission of the author.

[12] Both refer to the planet Venus, one as seen in the morning, the other as seen at night. But it took many years for this identity to be discovered.

we have two distinguishable aspects, the appearance to the naked eye on the one hand and the physical composition on the other. And this is also not the kind of identity which is plausible for mental and physical events. The appearance *to the naked eye* of a neurological event is utterly different from the experience of having a thought or a pain.

It is sometimes suggested that the physical aspect results from looking at a particular event "from the outside," whereas the mental results from looking at the same event "from the inside." When the brain surgeon observes my brain he is looking at it from the outside, whereas when I experience a mental event I am "looking" at my brain "from the inside."

Such an account gives us only a misleading analogy, rather than an accurate characterization of the relationship between the mental and the physical. The analogy suggests the difference between a man who knows his own house from the inside, in that he is free to move about within, seeing objects from different perspectives, touching them, etc., but can never get outside to see how it looks from there, and a man who cannot get inside and therefore knows

FIG. 5.8 What is the relationship between your thoughts and your brain? Is thought in any way independent of the brain? *(Image © jumpingsack, 2011. Used under license from Shutterstock.com)*

only the outside appearance of the house, and perhaps what he can glimpse through the windows. But what does this have to do with the brain? Am I free to roam about inside my brain, observing what the brain surgeon may never see? Is not the "inner" aspect of my brain far more accessible to the brain surgeon than to me? He has the X rays, probes, electrodes, scalpels, and scissors for getting at the inside of my brain. If it is replied that this is only an analogy, not to be taken literally, then the question still remains how the mental and the physical are related.

· · ·

One of the leading identity theorists, J. J. C. Smart, holds that mentalistic discourse is simply a vaguer, more indefinite way of talking about what could be talked about more precisely by using physiological terms. If I report a red after-image, I mean (roughly) that something is going on which is like what goes on when I really see a red patch. I do not actually *mean* that a particular sort of brain process is occurring, but when I say something is going on I refer (very vaguely, to be sure) to just that brain process. Thus the thing referred to in my report of an afterimage is a brain process. Hence there is no need to bring in any nonphysical features. Thus even the taint of dualism is avoided.

Does this ingenious attempt to evade dualistic implications stand up under philosophical scrutiny? I am inclined to think it will not. Let us return to the man reporting the red afterimage. He was aware of the occurrence of something or other, of some feature or other. Now it seems to me obvious that he was not necessarily aware of the state of his brain at that time (I doubt that most of us are ever aware of the state of our brain) nor, in general, necessarily aware of any physical features of his body at that time. He might, of course, have been incidentally aware of some physical feature but not insofar as he was aware of the red afterimage as such. Yet he was definitely aware of something, or else how could he have made that report? So he must have been aware of some non-physical feature. That is the only way of explaining how he was aware of anything at all.

Of course, the thing that our reporter of the afterimage was aware of might well have had further features which he was *not* aware of, particularly, in this connection, physical features. I may be aware of certain features of an object without being aware of others. So it is not ruled out that the event our reporter is aware of might be an event with predominantly physical features—he just does not notice those. But he must be aware of some of its features, or else it would not be proper to say he was aware of *that* event. And if he is not aware of any physical features, he must be aware of something else. And that shows that we cannot get rid of those nonphysical features in the way that Smart suggests.

. . .

If by X-rays or some other means we were able to see every event which occurred in the brain, we would never get a glimpse of a thought. If, to resort to fantasy, we could so enlarge a brain or so shrink ourselves that we could wander freely through the brain, we would still never observe a thought. All we could ever observe in the brain would be the *physical* events which occur in it. If mental events had location in the brain, there should be some means of detecting them there. But of course there is none. The very idea of it is senseless.

- Is the identity theory of mind a form of materialism? If not, how do the two differ? How does it differ from epiphenomenalism?
- How could psychophysics describe your experience of pain or of seeing red? Do you think that psychophysics could fully capture what it is like to have these experiences? Does the identity theorist claim to capture your experience of pain when he describes it in terms of physical laws?
- What does Smart mean when he claims, "sensations are nothing over and above brain processes"? What does he mean by "strict identity"?
- How are mental properties different from physical properties? Does this show that they cannot be identical?

Shaffer disagrees with the identity theory, but both his presentation and his criticism of it are central to the ongoing debate. In defending the identity theory, it is most important to stress that the identity of brain processes and thoughts is an empirical identity, that is, an identity that must be discovered through experiment and experience. It is not a logical identity, as if the two terms "brain process" and "thought" are synonymous. The latter suggestion is obviously false, and modern defenders of the identity theory are always emphasizing that future neurophysiological research will prove them right. Shaffer's criticism, however, is based on a principle that must be distinguished from the all-too-easy attack on the logical identity suggestion. The principle is that if two things are identical, then they must have all the same properties. But, Shaffer argues, no amount of research could possibly show that brain processes and thought have the same properties. Most importantly, brain processes take place in the brain and can be traced like any other physical processes; thoughts, on the other hand, have no spatial location, and there is nothing that research can "discover" that will show that they do. Of course, research can and has shown that certain thoughts are correlated with certain brain processes, but correlation is not yet identity.

4. *Eliminative Materialism*

To most materialists, the identity theory seemed promising, even if its arguments proved inadequate. The real question was whether there might be some other version of the thesis—that mental states were "nothing but" brain states—that did not claim the kind of "one-to-one match" required by the identity theory. One suggestion (still popular in many quarters) is the thesis called **eliminative materialism**, which proposes to defend materialism without claiming an identity between what we call "mental states" and the workings of the brain. Rather, the argument goes, our increasing knowledge of the workings of the brain will make outmoded our "folk-psychology" talk about the mind and we will all learn to talk the language of neurology instead.

In the following excerpt, **Paul M. Churchland** defends the opposition (rather than the complementarity) of neurological explanations of human behavior and the familiar mentalistic accounts. With increased knowledge of neurology, our ordinary language will be replaced or, at least, seriously revised.

> **Paul Churchland (1942–)**
>
> An American philosopher at the University of California, San Diego. He is a specialist in cognitive science and the interplay among philosophy, computer science, and neurology.

On Eliminative Materialism
BY **Paul M. Churchland**[13]

The identity theory was called into doubt not because the prospects for a materialist account of our mental capacities were thought to be poor, but because it seemed unlikely that the arrival of an adequate materialist theory would bring with it the nice one-to-one match-ups, between the concepts of folk psychology and the concepts of theoretical neuroscience, that intertheoretic reduction requires. The reason for that doubt was the great variety of quite different physical systems that could instantiate the required functional organization. *Eliminative materialism* also doubts that the correct neuroscientific account of human capacities will produce a neat reduction of our common-sense framework, but here the doubts arise from a quite different source.

As the eliminative materialists see it, the one-to-one match-ups will not be found, and our common-sense psychological framework will not enjoy an intertheoretic reduction, *because our commonsense psychological framework is a false and radically misleading conception of the causes of human behavior and the nature of cognitive activity.* On this view, folk psychology is not just an incomplete representation of our inner natures; it is an outright *mis*-representation of our internal states and activities. Consequently, we cannot expect a truly adequate neuroscientific account of our inner lives to provide theoretical categories that match up nicely with the categories of our common-sense framework. Accordingly, we must expect that the older framework will simply be eliminated, rather than be reduced, by a matured neuroscience.

HISTORICAL PARALLELS

As the identity theorist can point to historical cases of successful intertheoretic reduction, so the eliminative materialist can point to historical cases of the outright elimination of the ontology of an older theory in favor of the ontology of a new and superior theory.

. . .

---

[13] Paul M. Churchland, *Matter and Consciousness: A Contemporary Introduction to the Philosophy of Mind*, Cambridge, MA: MIT Press, 1988, pp. 43–49.

FIG. 5.9 (© iStockphoto.com/higyou)

It used to be thought that when a piece of wood burns, or a piece of metal rusts, a spiritlike substance called "phlogiston" was being released: briskly, in the former case, slowly in the latter. Once gone, that "noble" substance left only a base pile of ash or rust. It later came to be appreciated that both processes involve, not the loss of something, but the *gaining* of a substance taken from the atmosphere: oxygen. Phlogiston emerged, not as an incomplete description of what was going on, but as a radical misdescription. Phlogiston was therefore not suitable for reduction to or identification with some notion from within the new oxygen chemistry, and it was simply eliminated from science.

. . .

The concepts of folk psychology—belief, desire, fear, sensation, pain, joy, and so on—await a similar fate, according to the view at issue. And when neuroscience has matured to the point where the poverty of our current conceptions is apparent to everyone, the superiority of the new framework is established, we shall then be able to set about *re*conceiving our internal states and activities, within a truly adequate conceptual framework at last. Our explanations of one another's behavior will appeal to such things as our neuropharmacological states, the neural activity in specialized anatomical areas, and whatever other states are deemed relevant by the new theory. Our private introspection will also be transformed, and may be profoundly enhanced by reason of the more accurate and penetrating framework it will have to work with—just as the astronomer's perception of the night sky is much enhanced by the detailed knowledge of modern astronomical theory that he or she possesses.

The magnitude of the conceptual revolution here suggested should not be minimized: it would be enormous. And the benefits to humanity might be equally great. If each of us possessed an accurate neuroscientific understanding of (what we now conceive dimly as) the varieties and causes of mental illness, the factors involved in learning, the neural basis of emotions, intelligence, and socialization, then the sum total of human misery might be much reduced. The simple increase in mutual understanding that the new framework made possible could contribute substantially toward a more peaceful and humane society. Of course, there would be dangers as well: increased knowledge means increased power, and power can always be misused.

ARGUMENTS FOR ELIMINATIVE MATERIALISM

The arguments for eliminative materialism are diffuse and less than decisive, but they are stronger than is widely supposed. The distinguishing feature of this position is its denial that a smooth intertheoretic reduction is to be expected—even a species-specific reduction—of the framework of folk psychology to the framework of a matured neuroscience. The reason for this denial is the eliminative materialist's conviction that folk psychology is a hopelessly primitive and deeply confused conception of our internal activities. But why this low opinion of our common-sense conceptions?

There are at least three reasons. First, the eliminative materialist will point to the widespread explanatory, predictive, and manipulative failures of folk psychology. So much of what is central and familiar to us remains a complete mystery from within folk psychology. We do not know what *sleep* is, or why we have to have it, despite spending a full third of our lives in that condition. (The answer, "For rest," is mistaken. Even if people are allowed to rest continuously, their need for sleep is undiminished. Apparently, sleep serves some deeper functions, but we do not yet know what they are.) We do not understand how *learning* transforms each of us from a gaping infant to a cunning adult, or how differences in *intelligence* are grounded. We have not the slightest idea how *memory* works, or how we manage to retrieve relevant bits of information instantly from the awesome mass we have stored. We do not know what *mental illness* is, nor how to cure it.

In sum, the most central things about us remain almost entirely mysterious from within folk psychology.

. . .

This argument from explanatory poverty has a further aspect. So long as one sticks to normal brains, the poverty of folk psychology is perhaps not strikingly evident. But as soon as one examines the many perplexing behavioral and cognitive deficits suffered by people with *damaged* brains, one's descriptive and explanatory resources start to claw the air. . . . As with other humble theories asked to operate successfully in unexplored extensions of their old domain (for example, Newtonian mechanics in the domain of velocities close to the velocity of light, and the classical gas law in the domain of high pressures or temperatures), the descriptive and explanatory inadequacies of folk psychology become starkly evident.

The second argument tries to draw an inductive lesson from our conceptual history. Our early folk theories of motion were profoundly confused, and were eventually displaced entirely by more sophisticated theories. Our early folk theories of the structure and activity of the heavens were wildly off the mark, and survive only as historical lessons in how wrong we can be. Our folk theories of the nature of fire, and the nature of life, were similarly cockeyed. And one could go on, since the vast majority of our past folk conceptions have been similarly exploded. All except folk psychology, which survives to this day and has only recently begun to feel pressure. But the phenomenon of conscious intelligence is surely a more complex and difficult phenomenon than any of those just listed. So far as accurate understanding is concerned, it would be a *miracle* if we had got *that* one right the very first time, when we fell down so badly on all the others. Folk psychology has survived for so very long, presumably, not because it is basically correct in its representations, but because the phenomena addressed are so surpassingly difficult that any useful handle on them, no matter how feeble, is unlikely to be displaced in a hurry.

. . .

ARGUMENTS AGAINST ELIMINATIVE MATERIALISM

The initial plausibility of this rather radical view is low for almost everyone, since it denies deeply entrenched assumptions. That is at best a question-begging complaint, of course, since those assumptions are precisely what is at issue. But the following line of thought does attempt to mount a real argument.

Eliminative materialism is false, runs the argument, because one's introspection reveals directly the existence of pains, beliefs, desires, fears, and so forth. Their existence is as obvious as anything could be.

> "The most central things about us remain almost entirely mysterious from within folk psychology."
> – PAUL M. CHURCHLAND

The eliminative materialist will reply that this argument makes the same mistake that an ancient or medieval person would be making if he insisted that he could just see with his own eyes that the heavens form a turning sphere, or that witches exist. The fact is, all observation occurs within some system of concepts, and our observation judgments are only as good as the conceptual framework in which they are expressed. In all three cases—the starry sphere, witches, and the familiar mental states—precisely what is challenged is the integrity of the background conceptual frameworks in which the observation judgments are expressed. To insist on the validity of one's experiences, *traditionally interpreted*, is therefore to beg the very question at issue. For in all three cases, the question is whether we should *reconceive* the nature of some familiar observational domain.

. . .

A final criticism draws a much weaker conclusion, but makes a rather stronger case. Eliminative materialism, it has been said, is making mountains out of molehills. It exaggerates the defects in folk psychology, and underplays its real successes. Perhaps the arrival of a matured neuroscience will require the elimination of the occasional folk-psychological concept, continues the criticism, and a minor adjustment in certain folk-psychological principles may have to be endured. But the large-scale elimination forecast by the eliminative materialist is just an alarmist worry or a romantic enthusiasm.

Perhaps this complaint is correct. And perhaps it is merely complacent. Whichever, it does bring out the important point that we do not confront two simple and mutually exclusive possibilities here: pure reduction versus pure elimination. Rather, these are the end points of a smooth spectrum of possible outcomes, between which there are mixed cases of partial elimination and partial reduction. Only empirical research . . . can tell us where on that spectrum our own case will fall. Perhaps we should speak here, more liberally, of "revisionary materialism," instead of concentrating on the more radical possibility of an across-the-board elimination.

Churchland's primary aim in this final section of argument is to present as at least intelligible his position that "our collective conceptual destiny lies substantially toward the revolutionary end of the spectrum."

- In what sense do the eliminative materialists (such as Churchland) agree with those who reject the identity theory (such as Shaffer)? In what important ways do they differ?
- What is "folk psychology"? Can you give an example of a folk psychological explanation for falling in love, being sad, embarrassment followed by anger, hunger dissipating after a few days of fasting, and the need for sleep?

5. Functionalism: The Mind and the Computer

Despite the claims of Cartesians that "minds are nonphysical," at least in the obvious sense, Churchland and other materialists based their notion of the "self" on what they felt to be scientific fact, the physical basis of minds—the brain and the central nervous system. It is the brain that makes minds possible.

On the one hand, this was a rather remarkable discovery in the history of biology. It is by no means obvious, looking at the gooey cauliflower-shaped stuff inside the skull, that in that space is packed billions of tiny neural networks that control our every experience, our every action, including the inner actions of our bodies of which we may not even be aware (control of metabolism and blood flow, for example). But since the introduction of computers, scientific criticisms of dualism have taken another line. Is it so obvious that minds could *only* be the product of brains? Could mental processes be based on physical processes that are not brain processes? Could, for example, mental processes be based upon a network of electronic signals in a properly designed complex of transistors and circuit boards? In other words, could mental processes be the product of a computer? Could the brain be nothing but an organic computer? Could computers—the kind that we make out of metal and minerals—have minds?

It is no coincidence that the past decade or so of computer breakthroughs has produced a revolution in the way some philosophers think about selves and minds. The philosophical position is called **functionalism**, and its basic insight is that minds are produced not so much by particular kinds of materials (for example, brains) but rather by the *relations* between parts. In another few decades, it may in fact be possible, according to the most optimistic functionalists, to build a human mind out of computer parts. But whether or not computer scientists achieve such a (frightening) miracle, less optimistic functionalists hold that the mind is, in effect, a *function* of the patterns of neurological activity in the brain.

In computer technology (now at least in part included in our everyday language), there is a crucial distinction between "hardware" and "software." Hardware is the actual computer with its circuits. In the case of human minds, the hardware would be the brain and its neurological circuits. Software is the program that gives the computer specific instructions. (Sometimes, specific instructions can be "hardwired," as in the case of instinct, but these are not the exciting cases that inspire most functionalists and computer scientists.) The view of the functionalists is that the mind is nothing other than an elaborate program of sorts, which is the product of a spectacularly complicated pattern embodied in the physical workings of the brain.

In the following selection, **David Braddon-Mitchell** and **Frank Jackson** give a brief defense of functionalism.

FROM *Philosophy of Mind and Cognition*
BY **David Braddon-Mitchell** AND **Frank Jackson**[14]

The world is full of states, devices, stations in life, objects, processes, properties and events that are defined wholly or partly by their functional roles. Thermostats are defined by how they control temperature by switching machines on and off; burglar alarms are defined by how they function to produce loud noises on being disturbed in various ways (only sometimes by burglars, unfortunately); the office of vice-chancellor is defined by its function in a university; filtration is defined as a process that takes as input solids in liquid suspension and delivers as separate outputs the solid and the liquid; a graduation ceremony is an event in part defined by its role of producing graduates; a dangerous corner is the kind that tends to take approaching cars and deliver accidents; and so on and so forth. In all these cases there is a distinction to be drawn between the functional role and what occupies or fills it. Some thermostats are bimetallic strips; some are more complex electronic devices. Either way, they count as thermostats provided they do the required regulating of temperature. Many different people might be vice-chancellor of the university. Burglar alarms come in many shapes and sizes. There are many ways a corner can be dangerous.

---

[14] David Braddon-Mitchell and Frank Jackson, *Philosophy of Mind and Cognition*, London: Blackwell, 1996.

David Braddon-Mitchell (1959–)

A professor of philosophy at the University of Sydney in Australia.

Frank Jackson (1943–)

An Australian philosopher and professor at Australian National University.

In the same way functionalists about the mind distinguish the functional roles specified by the input, output and internal role clauses from what occupies them, and insist that what matters for being in one or another mental state are the roles that are occupied, not what occupies them. Provided the right roles are occupied, it does not matter what occupies them. Sometimes it is claimed that as a matter of empirical fact what occupies the relevant roles most likely varies. It is claimed that what plays the belief-that-there-is-food-nearby role in dogs is most likely different from what plays that role in cats; or perhaps the occupant of the role varies from one kind of dog to another; or perhaps it is different in left-handed people as opposed to right-handed people. Sometimes the claim is simply that it is abstractly possible that what plays or realizes the role associated with a given mental state varies. What is agreed though is that what matters for being in a given mental state are the roles occupied, not what occupies them. This is the famous multiple realizability thesis distinctive of functionalist theories of mind. Multiple realizability is appealing for a number of reasons:

1. We ascribe mental states on the basis of behaviour in circumstances and without much regard to what realizes the various functional roles. Indeed, we do not know in any detail what realizes the roles, and until relatively recently we did not know even in broad outline.

2. We have all read science fiction stories about creatures—traditionally called "Martians" in philosophical discussions—whose chemistry is, say, silicon-based, in-

FIG. 5.10 Is the brain like a computer's central processing unit? (If a computer had a brain, wouldn't it be the CPU?) (© iStockphoto.com/Amy Walters)

stead of carbon-based like ours, and who interact with the environment much as we do, plan our defeat, fall in love with some of us, admire characteristics that we abhor, shame us with their compassion and understanding, are vastly more intelligent than we are, or whatever. These stories strike us as perfectly coherent, despite the fact that it is part of the story that the states that realize the relevant functional roles in them are quite different from those that realize the roles in us. As the conclusion from these science fiction considerations is often put, we should not be chauvinists about the mind.

3. There is considerable evidence that our brains start out in a relatively plastic state, and that as we grow and the environment impacts on us, states come to occupy new functional roles, those subserving language, for instance. The usual explanation as to why language cannot be learnt past a certain age appeals to this point. Past a certain age it is too late for the right changes in brain function to occur. This opens up the possibility that the way your brain changed to subserve the functional roles needed for language was different from the way my brain did. But, provided the job gets done, it does not seem to matter.

4. An important part of making a good recovery from a stroke is getting an undamaged part of the brain to do something previously done by the part damaged by the stroke. Stroke victims do not worry about whether the new part of the brain counts as a different realizer of the old role. What they worry about is whether the job will be well done, and that seems exactly the right attitude to take.

5. Prosthetic surgery for the brain seems no more problematic *in principle* than does prosthetic surgery in general. We can imagine that, as they degenerate, parts of someone's brain are progressively replaced by silicon implants. Provided the implants fill the same functional roles, surely the surgery would count as successful. But then it must be the case that mental life is preserved despite the radical change in what realizes the various functional roles.

Multiple realizability, then, in addition to being common ground among functionalists, is a point in favour of their theory. It is widely accepted that any theory of mind should accommodate multiple realizability, and it is very much a point in functionalism's favour that it does this so naturally. What is not common ground is the question of which functional roles are essential to which mental states and the more general question of where functionalism should stand on how we might answer this question.

One response is to leave the question to someone else. Some functionalists hold that the question of which functional roles mental states occupy should be left to empirical psychology and neuroscience. We can distinguish very many functional roles played by mental states, and the study of the mind is the study of these many functional roles. But it is no part of functionalism, on this view, to argue for one or another answer to conceptual issues concerning how to analyse what it is to be in pain, believe that it will rain soon, or whatever. But if the key to the mind lies in functional roles, it seems fair to ask for some sort of guide as to which functional roles matter. A burglar alarm may play many functional roles. Perhaps it plays the role of being a drain on your bank balance, being a conversation piece at dinner parties, and making a loud noise when burglars are near. We know which role matters for its being a burglar alarm. The last role is the one that matters. That is why if it stops breaking down—and so stops being a drain on your bank balance—and if it stops being unusual in the neighbourhood—and so stops being a conversation piece—it will still be a burglar alarm. Among the various functional roles it has, we discriminate between those that matter for its counting as a burglar alarm and those that do not matter. The same is true for all the examples we gave earlier. Any particular vice-chancellor, thermostat or dangerous corner will play many roles, but only some will matter for being a vice-chancellor, a thermostat or a dangerous corner. Why, then, should it be impossible to make the same kind of discrimination in the case of mental states? We know that not all the roles which various mental states fill matter equally for its being the mental state that it is—for instance, pain's playing the role of being the example most often chosen for discussion by philosophers is irrelevant to its being pain; it wouldn't hurt any less if philosophers instead began to discuss itching—so surely it is fair to ask the functionalist for some guide as to which functional roles of a mental state matter for its being the mental state that it is.

The best answer, in our view, to the question of which functional roles matter is the answer given by common-sense functionalism. Common-sense functionalism aims to give an analysis of what it is to be in one or another mental state in broadly functional terms, in the same general way that we can give an analysis of being a burglar alarm in broadly functional terms.

FIG. 5.11 What does it mean for human "thought" when a computer can play chess more nimbly (more intelligently?) than we can? (© iStockphoto.com/Konstantin Inozemtsev)

The idea that the computer will someday provide a single model of mental states and information processes has been called into question recently. It is not at all clear that the mind works like a computer, or whether instead it works on different parallel levels in a manner substantially more complicated and considerably faster than any known computer.

Nevertheless, like any bold new hypothesis, the functionalist-analogy analysis of the mind as a computer has crashed head-on into some of the most entrenched ideas and experiences of common sense. In defense of common sense, **John R. Searle**—one of the leading analysts of ordinary human language and the special features of human communication—attacks the notion that computers are sufficiently intelligent to threaten or to challenge human intelligence anytime soon. He suggests a powerful counterexample to the widespread claim that "the conclusive proof of the presence of mental states and capacities [in a computer system or elsewhere] is the ability to convince a competent expert, for example, if a machine could converse with a native Chinese speaker in such a way as to convince the speaker that it understood Chinese."[15]

---

[15] This is the so-called Turing test, named after logician/computer scientist Alan Turing (1912-1954).

FROM **"The Myth of the Computer"**
BY **John R. Searle**[16]

The details of how the brain works are immensely complicated and largely unknown, but some of the general principles of the relations between brain functioning and computer programs can be stated quite simply. First, we know that brain processes cause mental phenomena. Mental states are caused by and realized in the structure of the brain. From this it follows that any system that produced mental states would have to have powers equivalent to those of the brain. Such a system might use a different chemistry, but whatever its chemistry it would have to be able to cause what the brain causes. We know from the [previous] argument digital computer programs by themselves are never sufficient to produce mental states. Now since brains do produce minds, and since programs by themselves can't produce minds, it follows that the way the brain does it can't be by simply instantiating a computer program. (Everything, by the way, instantiates some program or other, and brains are no exception. So in that trivial sense brains, like everything else, are digital computers.) And it also follows that if you wanted to build a machine to produce mental states, a thinking machine, you couldn't do it solely in virtue of the fact that your machine ran a certain kind of computer program. The thinking machine couldn't work solely in virtue of being a digital computer but would have to duplicate the specific causal powers of the brain.

> "Since brains do produce minds, and since programs by themselves can't produce minds, it follows that the way the brain does it can't be by simply instantiating a computer program."
> – JOHN R. SEARLE

John Searle (1932–)

An American philosopher at the University of California, Berkeley; the best-known proponent of "speech-act theory" in the philosophy of language and the author of many controversial books and articles, including a series of attacks on the ambitions of cognitive science and computer models of the mind.

A lot of the nonsense talked about computers nowadays stems from their relative rarity and hence mystery. As computers and robots become more common, as common as telephones, washing machines, and forklift trucks, it seems likely that this aura will disappear and people will take computers for what they are, namely useful machines.

- How is the mind similar to a computer? In what ways does it differ? How does a functionalist view of mind argue that they are the same?

 FROM *Minds, Brains, and Science*
BY **John R. Searle**[17]

Imagine that a bunch of computer programmers have written a program that will enable a computer to simulate the understanding of Chinese. So, for example, if the computer is given a question in Chinese, it will match the question against its memory, or data base, and produce appropriate answers to the questions in Chinese. . . . Does the computer, on the basis of this, understand Chinese, does it literally understand Chinese, in the way that Chinese speakers understand Chinese? Well, imagine that you are locked in a room, and in this room are several baskets full of Chinese symbols.

---

[16] John R. Searle, "The Myth of the Computer," in the *New York Review of Books*. Reprinted with permission from *The New York Review of Books*. Copyright © 1982 by NYREV, Inc.

[17] John R. Searle, *Minds, Brains, and Science*, Cambridge: Harvard University Press, 1984.

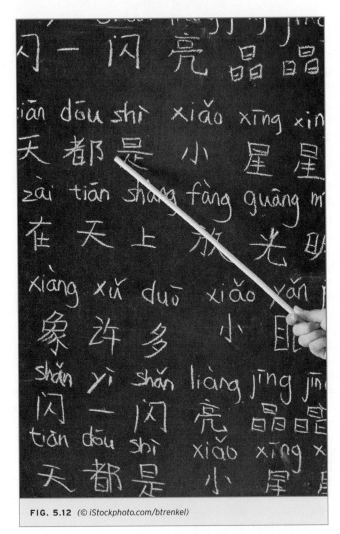

FIG. 5.12 (© iStockphoto.com/btrenkel)

Imagine that you (like me) do not understand a word of Chinese, but that you are given a rule book in English for manipulating these Chinese symbols. The rules specify the manipulations of the symbols purely formally, in terms of their syntax, not their semantics. So the rule might say: "Take a squiggle-squiggle sign out of basket number one and put it next to a squoggle-squoggle sign from basket number two." Now suppose that some other Chinese symbols are passed into the room, and that you are given further rules for passing back Chinese symbols out of the room. Suppose that unknown to you the symbols passed into the room are called "questions" by the people outside the room, and the symbols you pass back out of the room are called "answers to the questions." Suppose, furthermore, that the programmers are so good at designing the programs and that you are so good at manipulating the symbols, that very soon your answers are indistinguishable from those of a native Chinese speaker. There you are locked in your room shuffling your Chinese symbols and passing out Chinese symbols in response to incoming Chinese symbols. On the basis of the situation as I have described it, there is no way you could learn any Chinese simply by manipulating these formal symbols.

Now the point of the story is simply this: by virtue of implementing a formal computer program from the point of view of an outside observer, you behave exactly as if you understood Chinese, but all the same you don't understand a word of Chinese. But if going through the appropriate computer program for understanding Chinese is not enough to give *you* an understanding of Chinese, then it is not enough to give *any other digital computer* an understanding of Chinese. . . . All that the computer has, as you have, is a formal program for manipulating uninterpreted Chinese symbols.

• How would you answer Searle and his "Chinese room" thought experiment? Does it prove what he wants it to prove?

6. Connectionism

Not all criticisms of functionalism are nonmaterialist. Recently, objections have been raised against functionalism from neurophysiologists who claim that functionalism is just too simplistic in its vision of the brain and of computers. Connectionists complain that functionalism is a "top-down," "software" approach, which can never be accurate in its representation of the "hardware" of either the brain or the computer. In other words, say the connectionists, a functionalist starts with behavior—either human behavior or computer behavior—and claims that understanding human consciousness is just a matter of finding the "program" for that behavior. The functionalist claims that to understand the "program" is to understand the behavior, regardless of the mechanical and physical interactions which make the program run. The connectionist, on the other hand, claims that the mechanical and physical interactions that occur in the brain determine the kinds of behavior—which kinds of software—that computers are capable of processing. Connectionists therefore advocate a "bottom-up" approach to understanding the mind. Connectionists are still materialists, but not in the simple, reductionist, way of their predecessors. They believe that consciousness—in its full color and quality—is a result of the complicated "connections" that really do go on in the brain. There is no one-to-one correspondence between neurons and thoughts or perceptions; rather, they claim, the "hardware" of the brain is an immensely complex mechanism to which the functionalists do not do justice.

- What are the similarities and differences between functionalists and connectionists?

D. The Problem of Consciousness

Descartes claimed he knew what was going on in his mind with an **immediate** certainty that he could never have about what was going on in the world "outside" him. In his first "Meditation," he talks about his seeming to be sitting in front of the fire and the fact that he might be wrong (if he were in bed asleep at the time). But what he could not be wrong about is his seeming to be sitting in front of the fire. Similarly, you think you see a friend walking across the street. You are wrong, for your friend is in fact in Alaska this week. But you can still be certain that you thought that you saw him, even if you didn't. Philosophers often refer to this special kind of "immediate" certainty in the case of our own conscious experiences as **incorrigibility**. You might make a mistake in any factual claim about the world, for you might be hallucinating, or dreaming, or simply fooled by circumstances. But nothing could lead you to suspect that you might be mistaken about your own experiences. Given enough evidence against you, you might be willing to change from "but I know that I saw it" to "well, I thought I saw it." But nothing could convince you that you were wrong in thinking that you saw whatever it was. That claim, the claim about your experience, is incorrigible. Your claim about what you saw, however, is always open to further questioning.

For many years, this notion of incorrigibility served as part of the definition of "mind" and therefore, as Churchland implies, also a defense against materialism. Whatever was mental could be described incorrigibly, and this is very different than is the case with physical things. But doubts have begun to creep in recently. Part of the problem was Sigmund Freud's introduction of the notion of the **unconscious**. According to Freud's famous "psychoanalytic" theory, not everything mental is knowable, and therefore surely not everything "in the mind" can be described incorrigibly. In a famous passage from his "Introductory Lectures," Freud says the following:

On the "Unconscious"
BY Sigmund Freud[18]

There is no need to discuss what is to be called conscious: it is removed from all doubt. The oldest and best meaning of the word "unconscious" is the descriptive one; we call a psychical process unconscious whose existence we are obliged to assume—for some such reason as that we infer it from its effects—, but of which we know nothing. In that case we have the same relation to it as we have to a physical process in another person, except that it is in fact one of our own. If we want to be still more correct, we shall modify our assertion by saying that we call a process unconscious if we are obliged to assume that it is being activated *at the moment* though *at the moment* we know nothing about it.

Notice that Freud starts from a Cartesian position, the idea that "conscious is removed from all doubt." But then he suggests what no Cartesian can tolerate, the idea that there are ideas (experiences, intentions) in our minds that we do not and sometimes cannot know, much less know with certainty. And if we accept this notion of "the unconscious" (or even the weaker notion of "preconscious"), the traditional notion of the "incorrigibility" of the mental is seriously challenged.

The argument, however, cuts both ways. Many philosophers have rejected Freud just because his notion of "the unconscious" goes against the notion of incorrigibility. "If it isn't knowable incorrigibly," these philosophers have said, "then it can't be mental at all." Even Freud himself was forced to admit that his theory flew in the face of our normal "manner of speaking." The debate continues. Can you be wrong about what is going on in your own mind? For a long time, it was generally agreed that you could not be. Now we aren't so sure. You are certain that you are over an old love affair, but, without too much difficulty, a friend or a psychologist convinces you that you have been thinking about it constantly. You are certain that you are angry, but on closer examination, and in retrospect, you decide that you really felt guilty. You thought that you were thinking about your professor, when suddenly you realize that in fact it was the face of your father!

Is there anything about which we could not be mistaken? What of those basic bits of data that the empiricists talked about—sensations or impressions? Could we possibly be wrong in our confidence that "right now, I am experiencing a cold feeling in my hand"? The empiricists assumed that one could not be wrong about this, for it was on the basis of such certainties that we were able to construct, through inductive reasoning, our theories about the world. Could we be wrong even about our own sensations? Consider this example (it comes from Bishop Berkeley): A mischievous friend tells you that he is going to touch your hand with a very hot spoon. When you aren't looking, he touches you with a piece of ice. You scream and claim, with seeming certainty, that he has given you an uncomfortable sensation of heat. But you're wrong. What you felt was cold. What you seemed to feel was heat. But even your "seeming," in this case, was mistaken.

Philosophers have also pointed out that what is unique to mind as opposed to body is the fact that one and only one person can (and must) experience what is going on. I can (and must) feel only my pains, I can't experience your pains. Philosophers have referred to this as **privileged access**, sometimes as the **privacy** of mental events. The "privilege" is the fact

---

[18] Sigmund Freud, *New Introductory Lectures on Psychoanalysis*, ed. and trans. James Strachey, New York: Norton, 1964.

that, whatever is going on in your mind, you are not only the first but the only one to know of it directly. The "privacy" refers to the fact that if you decide not to tell anyone or betray yourself (through your facial expressions or your behavior), no one else need ever know. If you have a wart on your thigh, you can keep it contingently "private" by choosing suitable clothing. But if you have a "dirty little secret" in your mind, you have a logical guarantee of its privacy—it is private necessarily.

"Incorrigible" means "beyond correction"; "privileged access" means "known in a special way." (These concepts must be kept separate.) Because of privileged access and the "privacy" of consciousness, our states of mind have the very peculiar status of being always knowable to ourselves (though whether or not we want to say "knowable with certainty" depends on our views about incorrigibility) and yet possibly unknowable to anyone else. That is why, as you learned in grade school, you could always fake a headache to stay home for the day but you couldn't fake a fever or a sore. As long as it was purely mental, it was also purely private. Your success depended wholly upon how good (or bad) an actor you were. But when it comes to your body, you were in no privileged position. It was the thermometer, not your opinions, that told whether you had a fever or not. And it was the doctor, not you, who decided how serious your sore really was. But when it came to your own consciousness, you were in a truly privileged and irrefutable position.

- What does it mean to say that your own mental experiences are "incorrigible"? How does this notion resist materialism? How does Freud undermine the claim to incorrigibility?

This peculiarity of the first-person position, of our relationship to our own consciousness, is one of the things that makes the notion of "self" so difficult and that makes the problem so seemingly unresolvable. It makes the way that we establish our own identity seem categorically different from how others know it. Against all forms of reductionism and materialism, philosopher **Thomas Nagel** has argued in an ingenious fashion that it is consciousness, or what he calls "subjectivity," that makes the problem so "intractable." If "subjectivity" can be loosely defined as "what it's like" to be something, Nagel introduces his concern about the mind-body problem with the intriguing question: "What is it like to be a bat?"

 FROM *Mortal Questions*
BY **Thomas Nagel**[19]

Conscious experience is a widespread phenomenon. It occurs at many levels of animal life, though we cannot be sure of its presence in the simpler organisms, and it is very difficult to say in general what provides evidence of it. (Some extremists have been prepared to deny it even of mammals other than man.) No doubt it occurs in countless forms totally unimaginable to us, on other planets in other solar systems throughout the universe. But no matter how the form may vary, the fact that an organism has conscious experience *at all* means, basically, that there is something it is like to *be* that organism. There may be further implications about the form of the experience; there may even (though I doubt it) be implications about the behavior of the organism. But fundamentally an organism has conscious mental states if and only if there is something that it is like to *be* that organism—something it is like *for* the organism.

"Fundamentally an organism has conscious mental states if and only if there is something that it is like to *be* that organism— something it is like *for* the organism."

– THOMAS NAGEL

Thomas Nagel (1937-)
An American philosopher at New York University and a broad-ranging thinker who has written on a spectrum of topics from sex and death to political philosophy and racism in South Africa. He is the author of *Mortal Questions* and *The View from Nowhere*.

FIG. 5.13 The philosopher Thomas Nagel teaches at New York University. *(AP Photo / GREGORIO BORGIA)*

We may call this the subjective character of experience. It is not captured by any of the familiar, recently devised reductive analyses of the mental, for all of them are logically compatible with its absence. It is not analyzable in terms of any explanatory system of functional states, or intentional states, since these could be ascribed to robots or automata that behaved like people though they experienced nothing. It is not analyzable in terms of the causal role of experiences in relation to typical human behavior—for similar reasons. I do not deny that conscious mental states and events cause behavior, nor that they may be given functional characterizations. I deny only that this kind of thing exhausts their analysis. Any reductionist program has to be based on an analysis of what is to be reduced. If the analysis leaves something out, the problem will be falsely posed. It is useless to base the defense of materialism on any analysis of mental phenomena that fails to deal explicitly with their subjective character.

. . .

I assume we all believe that bats have experience. After all, they are mammals, and there is no more doubt that they have experience than that mice or pigeons or whales have experience. I have chosen bats instead of wasps or flounders because if one travels too far down the phylogenetic tree, people gradually shed their faith that there is experience there at all. Bats, although more closely related to us than those other species, nevertheless present a range of activity and a sensory apparatus so different from ours that the problem I want to pose is exceptionally vivid (though it certainly could be raised with other species). Even without the benefit of philosophical reflection, anyone who has spent some time in an enclosed space with an excited bat knows what it is to encounter a fundamentally *alien* form of life.

I have said that the essence of the belief that bats have experience is that there is something that it is like to be a bat. Now we know that most bats (the microchiroptera, to be precise) perceive the external world primarily by sonar, or echolocation, detecting the reflections, from objects within range, of their own rapid, subtly modulated, high-frequency shrieks. Their brains are designed to correlate the outgoing impulses with the subsequent echoes, and the information thus acquired enables bats to make precise discriminations of distance, size, shape, motion, and texture comparable to those we make by vision. But bat sonar, though clearly a form of perception, is not similar in its operation to any sense that we possess, and there is no reason to suppose that it is subjectively like anything we can experience or imagine. This appears to create difficulties for the notion of what it is like to be a bat. We must consider whether any method will permit us to extrapolate to the inner life of the bat from our own case, and if not, what alternative methods there may be for understanding the notion.

Our own experience provides the basic material for our imagination, whose range is therefore limited. It will not help to try to imagine that one has webbing on one's arms, which enables one to fly around at dusk and dawn catching insects in one's mouth; that one has very poor vision, and perceives the surrounding world by a system of reflected high-frequency sound signals; and that one spends the day hanging upside down by one's feet in an attic. Insofar as I can imagine this (which is not very far), it tells me only what it would be like for *me* to behave as a bat behaves. But that is not the question. I want to know what it is like for a *bat* to be a bat. Yet if I try to imagine this, I am restricted to the resources of my own mind, and those resources are inadequate to the task. I cannot perform it either by imagining additions to my present experience, or by imagining segments gradually subtracted from it, or by imagining some combination of additions, subtractions, and modifications.

FIG. 5.14 *(© iStockphoto.com/Alexei Zaycev)*

To the extent that I could look and behave like a wasp or a bat without changing my fundamental structure, my experiences would not be anything like the experiences of those animals. On the other hand, it is doubtful that any meaning can be attached to the supposition that I should possess the internal neurophysiological constitution of a bat. Even if I could by gradual degrees be transformed into a bat, nothing in my present constitution enables me to imagine what the experiences of such a future stage of myself thus metamorphosed would be like. The best evidence would come from the experiences of bats, if we only knew what they were like.

> • Explain "privileged access." How is it distinct from incorrigibility? How does "privileged access" pose the problem of knowing what it is like to be a bat? (What would it be like to be a bat?)

Taking this argument one step farther, **Colin McGinn** insists that consciousness is a "mystery" that neither philosophy nor science can resolve. He introduces the important notion of **intentionality**, the "aboutness" of consciousness, its relation to the world. The question is whether a "naturalistic" (materialistic) theory of the mind can account for this essential feature of mind.

On "The Mystery of Consciousness" BY Colin McGinn[20]

Naturalism in the philosophy of mind is the thesis that every property of mind can be explained in broadly physical terms. Nothing mental is physically mysterious. There are two main problems confronting a naturalistically inclined philosopher of mind. There is, first, the problem of explaining consciousness in broadly physical terms: in virtue of what does a physical organism come to have conscious states? And, second, there is the problem of explaining representational content—intentionality—in broadly physical terms: in virtue of what does a physical organism come to be intentionally directed toward the world? We want to know how consciousness depends

---

20 Colin McGinn, "Consciousness and Content," *Proceedings of the British Academy* 74 (1988): 219-39.

upon the physical world; and we want to know, in natural physical terms, how it is that thoughts and experiences get to be *about* states of affairs. We want a naturalistic account of subjectivity and mental representation. Only then will the naturalist happily accept that there are such things as consciousness and content.

. . .

[I]ntentionality is a property precisely of conscious states, and arguably only of conscious states (at least originally). Moreover, the content of an experience (say) and its subjective features are, on the face of it, inseparable from each other. How then can we pretend that the two problems can be pursued quite independently? In particular, how can we prevent justified pessimism about consciousness spreading to the problem of content? If we cannot say, in physical terms, what makes it the case that an experience is *like* something for its possessor, then how can we hope to say, in such terms, what makes it the case that the experience is *of* something in the world—since what the experience is like and what it is of are not, prima facie, independent properties of the experience? That is the question I shall be addressing.

. . .

This question is especially pressing for me, since I have come to hold that it is literally impossible for us to explain how consciousness depends upon the brain, even though it does so depend. Yet I also believe (or would like to believe) that it is possible for us to give illuminating accounts of content. Let me briefly explain my reasons for holding that consciousness systematically eludes our understanding. Noam Chomsky distinguishes between what he calls "problems" and "mysteries" that confront the student of mind. Call that hopeful student *S*, and suppose *S* to be a normal intelligent human being. Chomsky argues that *S*'s cognitive faculties may be apt for the solution of some kinds of problem but radically inadequate when it comes to others. The world need not in all of its aspects be susceptible of understanding by *S*, though another sort of mind might succeed where *S* constitutionally fails. *S* may exhibit, as I like to say, *cognitive closure* with respect to certain kinds of phenomena: her intellectual powers do not extend to comprehending these phenomena, and this as a matter of principle. When that is so Chomsky says that the phenomena in question will be a perpetual mystery for *S*. He suspects that the nature of free choice is just such a mystery for us, given the way our intellects operate. That problem need not, however, be intrinsically harder or more complex than other problems we can solve; it is just that our cognitive faculties are skewed away from solving it. The structure of a knowing mind determines the scope *and limits* of its cognitive powers. Being adept at solving one kind of problem does not guarantee explanatory omniscience. Human beings seem remarkably good (surprisingly so) at understanding the workings or the physical world—matter in motion, causal agents in space—but they do far less well when it comes to fathoming their own minds. And why, in evolutionary terms, should they be intellectually equipped to grasp how their minds ultimately operate?

Now I have come to the view that the nature of the dependence of consciousness on the physical world, specifically on the brain, falls into the category of mysteries for us human beings, and possibly for all minds that form their concepts in ways constrained by perception and introspection. Let me just summarize why I think this; a longer treatment would be needed to make the position plausible. Our concepts of the empirical world are fundamentally

Colin McGinn (1950–)

A British philosopher specializing in philosophy of mind, who currently teaches at the University of Miami.

controlled by the character of our perceptual experience and by the introspective access we enjoy to our own minds. We can, it is true, extend our concepts some distance beyond these starting-points, but we cannot prescind from them entirely (this is the germ of truth Kant recognized in classical empiricism). Thus our concepts of consciousness are constrained by the specific form of our own consciousness, so that, we cannot form concepts for quite alien forms of consciousness possessed by other actual and possible creatures. Similarly, our concepts of the body, including the brain, are constrained by the way we perceive these physical objects; we have, in particular, to conceive of them as spatial entities essentially similar to other physical objects in space, however inappropriate this manner of conception may be for understanding how consciousness arises from the brain. But now these two forms of conceptual closure operate to prevent us from arriving at concepts for the property or relation that intelligibly links consciousness to the brain. For, first, we cannot grasp other forms of consciousness, and so we cannot grasp the theory that explains these other forms: that theory must be general, but *we* must always be parochial in our conception of consciousness. It is as if we were trying for a general theory of light but could only grasp the visible part of the spectrum. And, second, it is precisely the perceptually controlled conception of the brain that we have which is so hopeless in making consciousness an intelligible result of brain activity. No property we can ascribe to the brain on the basis of how it strikes us perceptually, however inferential the ascription, seems capable of rendering perspicuous how it is that damp gray tissue can be the crucible from which subjective consciousness emerges fully formed. That is why the feeling is so strong in us that there has to be something *magical* about the mind-brain relation. There must *be* some property of the brain that accounts non-magically for consciousness, since nothing in nature happens by magic, but no form of inference from what we perceive of the brain seems capable of leading us to the property in question. We must therefore be getting a partial view of things. It is as if we were trying to extract psychological properties themselves from our awareness of mere physical objects; or again, trying to get normative concepts from descriptive ones. The problem is not that the brain lacks the right explanatory property; the problem is that this property does not lie along any road we can travel in forming our concepts of the brain. Perception takes us in the wrong direction here. We feel the tug of the occult because our methods of empirical concept formation are geared toward properties of kinds that cannot in principle solve the problem of how consciousness depends upon the brain. The situation is analogous to the following possibility: that the ultimate nature of matter is so different from anything we can encounter by observing the material world that we simply cannot ever come to grasp it. Human sense organs are tuned to certain kinds of properties the world may instantiate, but it may be that the theoretically basic properties are not ones that can be reached by starting from perception and working outward; the starting point may point us in exactly the wrong direction. Human reason is not able to travel unaided in just any theoretical direction, irrespective of its basic input. I think that honest reflection strongly suggests that nothing *we* could ever empirically discover about the brain *could* provide a fully satisfying account of consciousness. We shall either find that the properties we encounter are altogether on the wrong track or we shall illicitly project traits of mind into the physical basis. In particular, the essentially spatial conception we have, so suitable for making sense of the nonmental properties of the brain, is inherently incapable of removing the sense of magic we have about the fact that consciousness depends upon the brain. We need something radically different from this but, given the way we form our concepts, we cannot free ourselves of the conceptions that make the problem look insoluble. Not only, then, is it *possible* that the question of how consciousness arises from the physical world cannot be answered by minds constructed as ours are, but there is also strong positive reason for supposing that this is actually the case. The centuries of failure and bafflement have a deep source: the very nature of our concept-forming capacities. The mind-body problem is a "mystery" and not merely a "problem."

1. Changing Our Minds: Holism and Consciousness

When Aristotle wrote about "the soul," he meant nothing other than "the form of the body":

 FROM *De Anima*
BY **Aristotle**[21]

One can no more ask if the body and the soul are one than if the wax and the impression it receives are one, or speaking generally the matter of each thing and the form of which it is the matter; for admitting that the terms unity and existence are used in many senses, the paramount sense is that of actuality. We have, then, given a general definition of what the soul is: it is substance expressed as form. It is this which makes a body what it is.

This is not behaviorism. Aristotle is not denying the existence of anything that we normally believe in. Yet it is clearly not a dualism of the Cartesian variety, and this raises the following question: Are there ways of conceiving of ourselves without falling into the Cartesian trap of talking about minds and bodies?

We can only suggest a few possibilities here. The first, perhaps, was advanced by **Ludwig Wittgenstein** in his *Philosophical Investigations*. Although he is usually considered to be an unconfessed behaviorist, a more recent and perhaps more plausible interpretation is that Wittgenstein wanted to deny the very idea that human beings are a curious combination of two very different substances or kinds of entities or events. Rather, there are just people, not minds plus bodies.

A very different kind of answer comes to us from Husserl's phenomenology. Although Husserl was not particularly concerned with the mind-body problem as such, he was obviously very interested in the nature of consciousness, since consciousness provides the subject matter of his entire life's work.

Ludwig Wittgenstein (1889-1951)

An Austrian-born philosopher who became the single most powerful influence on twentieth-century "analytic" philosophy. He entered philosophy as an engineer, studied with Bertrand Russell, and wrote the book *Tractatus Logico-Philosophicus* (1922), which inspired logical positivism. Giving up philosophy for a number of years and changing his mind about his arguments in the *Tractatus*, he returned to philosophy at Cambridge and developed that "therapeutic" brand of philosophy that became known as "ordinary-language" philosophy. In his later works, culminating in his *Philosophical Investigations* (1953, published posthumously), Wittgenstein initiated a devastating attack on Cartesian dualism and the problems it carried with it. His so-called private language argument, culled from a series of aphorisms, argues that even if there were such "private" occurrences as mental events, we should have no way of talking about them and no way of knowing about them, even in our own case. But although he is often described as a "behaviorist," Wittgenstein is better described as one of those philosophers who was groping for an entirely new conception of a "person" or, at least, attempting to reject all the old ones.

---

[21] Reprinted by permission of the publishers and the Loeb Classical Library from *Aristotle: Minor Works, Volume XIV*, trans. W. S. Hett, Cambridge, MA: Harvard University Press, 1936.

What Husserl argued began with a violent attack on the spatial metaphors we use in talking about consciousness. At the beginning of the chapter, we mentioned these, suggesting that they were "just metaphors," symptoms of a problem but not a problem themselves. Well, Husserl shows that they are a problem, that philosophers have not used them merely as metaphors, and that it is because of their taking these metaphors literally that our problems about consciousness arise in the first place.

What Husserl attacks is the very idea of consciousness as a mysterious container, "in" which one finds ideas, thoughts, feelings, desires, and so on. The same objection holds of such metaphors as "the stream of consciousness," with emotions, thoughts, and feelings floating by like so much flotsam and jetsam. Consciousness must rather be viewed in two parts (though Husserl insists these must not be thought of as a separate "dualism"): There are acts of consciousness, and there are the objects of those acts.

Simply stated, a phenomenologist would analyze my seeing a tree into (1) my act of seeing and (2) the tree as seen. So far, this looks innocent enough. But its consequences are not so innocent. First, just in passing, notice what this does to Berkeley's idealism. Berkeley's whole argument rested on his thesis that all we can experience are ideas. But this is a confusion, Husserl insists, of our act of experiencing with the objects experienced. The object experienced (the tree) is not merely my idea. Accordingly, Husserl concludes that Berkeley's idealism is "absurd." And in general, Husserl's phenomenological theory insists that philosophers have been neglectful of this crucial distinction. Many attributes of the act of experiencing do not hold of the object; for example, the object, unlike the act, is not "private." One and only one person, namely, myself, can perform my act of seeing. But any number of people can see the object of my seeing, the tree. Moreover, there can be no such thing, Husserl argues, as a conscious act without an object. You can see how this might provide a powerful argument against many traditional forms of skepticism.

Our concern here is Husserl's conception of consciousness, which depends (as in McGinn) on intentionality. (Accordingly, the act is often called the "intentional act," and the object is called the "intentional object.") To say that consciousness is intentional means (among other things, which are irrelevant to this chapter) that our conscious acts are always directed toward objects and that we should not, therefore, talk about conscious acts as self-contained "contents" that are mysteriously coordinated with the movements of our bodies. Rather, we can simply say that among our various acts as persons are intentional conscious acts as well as physical actions. We can look at a tree and we can kick a tree. But there is no problem of "coordination" or interaction.

This theory was never actually developed by Husserl himself, but it was worked out in great detail by one of his "existential" followers in France, **Maurice Merleau-Ponty** (a close friend and student of Sartre). Coming from a very different starting point, Merleau-Ponty arrives at a position surprisingly close to that of Wittgenstein. It must not be called "behaviorist," but like Wittgenstein, Merleau-Ponty does reject the traditional way of dividing up mind and body and thereby suggests a very different conception of persons in which such problematic distinctions are not allowed to arise.

Merleau-Ponty attacks dualism from the side that has so far seemed least controversial—the idea that the human body is just another "bit of matter." He introduces the notion of a "dialectic" between mind and body, by which he means that there is no ultimate distinction between them. From one point of view, he argues, it is possible to see the body as

Maurice Merleau-Ponty (1908-1961)

A French "existentialist," the most serious of the existential phenomenologists who followed Husserl in France. His most important work is his *Phenomenology of Perception* (1945). He is also well known for his political writings and his art criticism. In his early *Structure of Behavior* (1942), he argued that the human body cannot be considered merely another "fragment of matter," in other words, merely a body, but must be viewed as the center of our experience.

"the cause of the structure of consciousness," for example, as a physiologist interested in the workings of the brain and the sense organs. From another point of view, it is possible to see the body as a mere "object of knowledge," for example, when a medical student dissects a body in his anatomy class. But it is a mistake, Merleau-Ponty argues, to confuse either of these viewpoints with the "correct" view of the body, either as a cause of consciousness or as something wholly distinct from it. Only the *living* body can count as *my* body, except in a very special and not everyday sense, namely, the sense in which I can talk about what will happen to my body after I die.

"The body is not a self-enclosed mechanism" he argues, nor does it makes sense to treat "the soul" or consciousness as a distinct entity with some mysterious relationship with the body. "There is not a duality of substances," he writes, but only "the dialectic of living being in its biological milieu." Merleau-Ponty sometimes says that consciousness is nothing but "the meaning of one's body," all of which is to say, in extremely difficult prose, that mind and body are nothing other than a single entity, and the distinctions we make between them are always special cases. "I live my body," he says; there is no enigma of "my body" to be explained.[22]

In his difficult "dialectical" language, Merleau-Ponty defends a thesis that is strikingly similar to that defended by Wittgenstein: One cannot treat a person as an uneasy conglomerate of mental parts and body parts but must begin with the whole person. But where Wittgenstein proceeds by attacking the mental side of Cartesian dualism, Merleau-Ponty attacks anyone who would treat the human as "just another body." The body itself is not only alive but, in an important sense, conscious. This does not mean, as in Descartes, that it is connected with a consciousness. It is itself aware, as we often notice when we talk of "bodily awareness" or "feeling our way." The difference between the body of a living person and a corpse is not just a difference in physiology, nor is it the difference between an "inhabited" body and an "uninhabited" body. My body and myself are essentially one, and to try to separate them, as Descartes had done, is to make the relationship between "me and my body" into an unnecessary mystery.

A similar view has been defended by analytic philosopher Galen Strawson, following Husserl and Merleau-Ponty, but objecting to a standard analysis of consciousness by analytic philosophy. According to that analysis, consciousness consists of two elements, sensations and intentionality (Hume's "impressions and ideas"). Strawson objects that there is a more holistic concept that is essential, what he calls "cognitive experience."

On "Cognitive Experience"
BY Galen Strawson[23]

Consider (experience) the difference, for you, between my saying: "I'm reading *War and Peace*" and my saying "barath abalori trafalon." In both cases you experience sounds, but in the first case you experience something more: you have understanding-experience, cognitive experience.

Why isn't this point universally acknowledged? *Have you had only sensory experience for the last two minutes?* One problem is that there has been a terminological lock-in. When analytic philosophers talk generally about what I call "EQ content"—when they talk generally of the "subjective character" of experience, or "what-it's-likeness," or "qualitative character," or "phenomenology" in the current deviant use of the term (It is incorrect first because "phenomenology" is the study of experience,

---

22 Maurice Merleau-Ponty, *The Structure of Behavior*, trans. Alden L. Fisher, Boston: Beacon Press, 1963.

23 From *Phenomenology and the Philosophy of Mind*, eds. David Woodruff Smith and Amie L. Thomasson. New York: Oxford University Press, 2005.

not experience itself, second because when it is used to mean experience itself it is used too narrowly to mean only sensory content.)—they standardly have only *sensory* EQ content, in mind, and the mistake has already been made. For this terminological habit simply forbids expression of the idea that there may be non-sensory or *cognitive* EQ content.

One doesn't have to be Husserl to be astounded by this terminological folly, and the metaphysical folly that it entrains—the denial of the existence of cognitive experience—as one negotiates the unceasing richness of every-

Galen Strawson (1919-2006)

A contemporary Oxford philosopher whose book *Individuals* (1959) was responsible for reintroducing systematic metaphysics into current British philosophy. He called his metaphysics "descriptive," however, by which he meant to insist that it was to be construed only as an analysis and description of "our conceptual framework," not of "reality-in-itself." In the third chapter of *Individuals*, Strawson argues the thesis that the distinction between mind and body can be made only after we have recognized the primary category of "persons." Persons are not conglomerates of minds and bodies, and we can talk of minds and bodies only because we first have a way of specifying the different attributes of a person.

day experience. It beggars belief. It amounts to an outright denial of the existence of almost all our actual experience, or rather of fundamental features of almost all (perhaps all) our experience. And yet it is terminological orthodoxy in present-day analytic philosophy of mind.

How did this happen? It was, perhaps, an unfortunate by-blow of the correct but excessively violent rejection, in the twentieth century, of the "image theory of thinking" or "picture theory of thinking" seemingly favoured, in various degrees, by the British empiricists and others. But rejecting the picture theory of thinking didn't require denying the existence of cognitive experience. On the contrary. Liberation from the picture-theory idea that cognitive experience centrally and constitutively involves sensory experience, and is indeed (somehow or other) a kind of internal sensory experience, is a necessary first step towards a decent account of what cognitive experience is. Schopenhauer certainly didn't reject the existence of cognitive experience when he refuted the picture theory of thinking in 1819 in terms that no one has improved on:

> *While another person is speaking, do we at once translate his speech into pictures of the imagination that instantaneously flash upon us and are arranged, linked, formed, and coloured according to the words that stream forth, and to their grammatical inflexions? What a tumult there would be in our heads while we listened to a speech or read a book! This is not what happens at all. The meaning of the speech is immediately grasped, accurately and clearly apprehended, without as a rule any conceptions of fancy being mixed up with it.*

When it comes to EQ content, then, when it comes to *the strictly qualitative character of experience*, which is wholly what it is considered entirely independently of its causes there is *cognitive* EQ content as well as sensory or non-cognitive EQ content. There is cognitive experience. Its existence is obvious to unprejudiced reflection, but some philosophers have denied it fiercely and, it must be said, rather scornfully.

It can seem difficult to get a decent theoretical grip on it. It is, for one thing, hard to pin down the contribution to the character of your current experience that is being made now by the content of this very sentence in such a way as to be able to take it as the object of reflective thought. (It is far easier to do this in the case of the phenomenological character of an experience of yellow, let the "transparent-ists" say what they will.) In fact, when it comes to the attempt to figure to oneself the phenomenological character of understanding a sentence like "Consider your hearing and understanding of this very sentence and the next" it seems that all one can really do is rethink the sentence as a whole, comprehendingly; and the trouble

FIG. 5.15 It is hard not to see emotional intelligence in this baby's expression. *(Image © 2011. Used under license from Shutterstock.com)*

with doing this is that it seems to leave one with no mental room to stand back in such a way as to be able to take the phenomenological character of one's understanding of the sentence, redelivered to one by this rethinking, as the principal object of one's attention: one's mind is taken up with the sense of the thought in such a way that it is very hard to think about the experience of having the thought.

This is, as it were, a merely practical difficulty. It is I think a further point that there is in any case something fundamentally insubstantial, intangible, unpindownable, about the character of much cognitive experience, and that this is so even though cognitive experience can also and simultaneously have a character of great determinacy. Consider, for example, your experience of understanding this very sentence, uneventful as it is. Or the sentence "This sentence has five words." Determinate but insubstantial.

I use quiet sentences to make the point, rather than sentences like "A thousand bonobos hurtled past on bright green bicycles," simply because it helps to still the imagistic or emotional accompaniments of thought or understanding as far as possible. It is then easier to see that what is left is something completely different, something that is equally real and definite and rich although it can seem troublesomely intangible when one tries to reflect on it: the experience that is standardly involved in the mere comprehending of words, read, thought, or heard—right now—, where this comprehending is (once again) considered quite independently of any imagistic or emotional accompaniments. Cognitive experience, we may say, is a matter of whatever EQ content is involved in such episodes after one has subtracted any non-cognitive EQ content trappings or accompaniments that such episodes may have.

I think we have no choice but to grant that our capacity for cognitive experience is a distinct naturally evolved *experiential modality* that is, whatever its origins, fundamentally different from all the sensory experiential modalities (at least as we currently understand them). This is a radical claim in the current context of discussion of experience or consciousness, especially given all the input from psychology and neuropsychology, which very strongly constrains people to think that all experience *must* be somehow sensory.

We also have to think through very dearly the initially difficult fact that cognitive EQ content is, in itself, purely a matter of experiential qualitative character, wholly what it is considered entirely independently of its causes. We may have to dwell on the point, work on it, especially if we have been trained up as analytic philosophers at any time in the last fifty years. Try now to imagine life without cognitive experience being part of the (experiential) qualitative character of experience. Consider yourself reading this now and try to convince yourself that all that is going on is sensory experience (accompanied by non-experiential changes in your dispositional set).

Finally, a view that is strikingly similar to the phenomenological theory was defended in the United States by William James. But instead of giving consciousness the attention it receives in Husserl, he argues that there is no such thing as consciousness as an entity, only different functions of experience:

FROM "Does Consciousness Exist?" BY William James[24]

"Thoughts" and "things" are names for two sorts of objects, which common sense will always find contrasted and will always practically oppose to each other. Philosophy, reflecting on the contrast, has varied in the past in her explanations of it, and may be expected to vary in the future. At first, "spirit and matter," "soul and body," stood for a pair of equipollent substances quite on a par in weight and interest. But one day Kant undermined the soul and brought in the transcendental ego, and ever since then the bipolar relation has been very much off its balance. The transcendental ego seems nowadays in rationalist quarters to stand for everything, in empiricist quarters for almost nothing. In the hands of . . . writers . . . the spiritual principle attenuates itself to a thoroughly ghostly condition, being only a name for the fact that the "content" of experience is *known*. It loses personal form and activity—these passing over to the content—and becomes a bare [consciousness], of which in its own right absolutely nothing can be said.

I believe that "consciousness," when once it has evaporated to this estate . . . is on the point of disappearing altogether. It is the name of a nonentity, and has no right to a place among first principles. Those who still cling to it are clinging to a mere echo, the faint rumor left behind by the disappearing "soul" upon the air of philosophy. During the past year, I have read a number of articles whose authors seemed just on the point of abandoning the notion of consciousness, and substituting for it that of an absolute experience not due to two factors. But they were not quite radical enough, not quite daring enough in their negations. For twenty years past I have mistrusted "consciousness" as an entity; for seven or eight years past I have suggested its non-existence to my students, and tried to give them its pragmatic-equivalent in realities of experience. It seems to me that the hour is ripe for it to be openly and universally discarded.

To deny plumply that "consciousness" exists seems so absurd on the face of it—for undeniably "thoughts" do exist—that I fear some readers will follow me no farther. Let me then immediately explain that I mean only to deny that the word stands for an entity, but to insist most emphatically that it does stand for a function. There

FIG. 5.16 (© iStockphoto.com/Anton Brand)

---

[24] William James, "Does Consciousness Exist?" in *Journal of Philosophy, Psychology and Scientific Methods*, September 1, 1904.

"Consciousness . . .
is fictitious, while
thoughts in the
concrete are fully real.
But thoughts in the
concrete are made
of the same stuff
as things are."

– WILLIAM JAMES

is, I mean, no aboriginal stuff or quality of being, contrasted with that of which material objects are made, out of which our thoughts of them are made; but there is a function in experience which thoughts perform, and for the performance of which this quality of being is invoked. That function is *knowing*. "Consciousness" is supposed necessary to explain the fact that things not only are, but get reported, are known. Whoever blots out the notion of consciousness from his list of first principles must still provide in some way for that function's being carried on.

. . .

My thesis is that if we start with the supposition that there is only one primal stuff or material in the world, a stuff of which everything is composed, and if we call that stuff "pure experience," then knowing can easily be explained as a particular sort of relation towards one another into which portions of pure experience may enter. The relation itself is a part of pure experience; one of its "terms" becomes the subject or bearer of the knowledge, the knower, the other becomes the object known.

. . .

I am as confident as I am of anything that, in myself, the stream of thinking (which I recognize emphatically as a phenomenon) is only a careless name for what, when scrutinized, reveals itself to consist chiefly of the stream of my breathing. The "I think" which Kant said must be able to accompany all my objects, is the "I breathe" which actually does accompany them. There are other internal facts besides breathing (intracephalic muscular adjustments, etc., of which I have said a word in my larger Psychology), and these increase the assets of "consciousness," so far as the latter is subject to immediate perception; but breath, which was ever the original of "spirit," breath moving outwards, between the glottis and the nostrils, is, I am persuaded, the essence out of which philosophers have constructed the entity known to them as consciousness. *That entity is fictitious, while thoughts in the concrete are fully real. But thoughts in the concrete are made of the same stuff as things are.*

- What does James mean when he claims "I mean only to deny that the word [*consciousness*] stands for an entity, but to insist most emphatically that it does stand for a function"? Is James simply a functionalist?

Finally, Friedrich Nietzsche suggests that consciousness, far from being the most immediate, self-evident thing, is ultimately dispensable:

On the "Genius of the Species"
BY **Friedrich Nietzsche**[25]

The problem of consciousness (more precisely, of becoming conscious of something) confronts us only when we start to understand how we might dispense with it; and now physiology and animal history put us at the beginning of such understanding (it took them two centuries to catch up with *Leibniz's* suspicion that soared ahead). For we could think, feel, will, and remember, and we could also "act" in all senses of the word, and yet none of any of it would have to "enter our consciousness" (as one

---

25 Translated from *The Gay Science* by Clancy Martin.

metaphorically says). The whole of life would be possible without its, so to speak, seeing itself in the mirror. Indeed by far the largest part of our life even now in fact takes place without this mirroring; and that is true even of our thinking, feeling, and willing life, however offensive this may sound to older philosophers. So *what purpose* has any consciousness at all when it is generally *superfluous*?

SUMMARY AND CONCLUSION

Since Descartes' discussion of mind and body as two separate and different substances, philosophers have struggled with a number of theories to explain how mind and body worked together to constitute a complete human being. Certain properties of mind—its lack of "extension" and seeming "privileged access," and the "incorrigibility" of mental claims—made the connection between mind and body extremely problematic. Therefore, philosophers suggested that mental events and bodily events are different aspects of some other event (dual aspect theory), or that they occur in parallel, like the sound and visual tracks on a film (parallelism or pre-established harmony), or that bodily events cause mental events but not the other way around (epiphenomenalism), or that mental events and bodily events are in fact identical (identity theory). Many philosophers and psychologists embraced behaviorism, arguing that "mental event" is in fact only shorthand for a complex description of patterns of behavior. More recently, many philosophers have come to reject the distinction between mind and body altogether, insisting on the primacy and indivisibility of the concept of a person. Other philosophers have come to embrace functionalism, which holds that the brain is in fact an extremely sophisticated computer, and the mind is causally but not logically dependent on the brain. But other philosophers dismiss all such theories as essentially hopeless, insisting on the intractibility of the mind-body problem.

CHAPTER REVIEW QUESTIONS

1. What is the identity theory? What problem is it called on to answer? In what ways is the dual aspect theory a version of the identity theory? In what ways is it similar to Merleau-Ponty's notion of a unified body? What are the differences and similarities in these views?

2. The argument for functionalism is ultimately concerned with the relations between elements of the brain. Mental acts occur as a "function" of elements. Logical behaviorism claims that mind is only the "pattern" of our behavior. What is different about these two accounts? What is similar about them? In what ways are they using the same ideas to provide different accounts of the mind?

3. Recall that Ryle rejects dualism because, according to him, Descartes committed a category mistake. In what sense do phenomenologists, like Husserl and Merleau-Ponty, agree with Ryle? How might their accounts differ? In what respect does William James's theory resemble Ryle's? What are the differences?

4. Discuss how Nagel's question, "What is it like to be a bat?" confronts the challenge of the eliminative materialists. Can you think of how an eliminative materialist might respond? How might some of the other theorists who reject dualism respond to the claim that "subjectivity" is essential to our concept of ourselves?

KEY TERMS

behaviorism
causal interactionism
dual aspect theory
dualism
eliminative materialism
epiphenomenalism

functionalism
identity theory
immediate
incorrigibility
inference-ticket
intentionality

parallelism
preestablished harmony
privacy
private language argument
privileged access
unconscious

BIBLIOGRAPHY AND FURTHER READING

Many excellent collections and studies of the mind-body problem fall under the rubric of "cognitive science" these days. Particularly recommended are Stephen Stich, *Blackwell Guide to Philosophy of Mind* (Oxford: Blackwell, 2003); David Rosenthal, *The Nature of Mind* (New York: Oxford University Press, 1997); and David Chalmers, *Philosophy of Mind: Classical and Contemporary Readings* (New York: Oxford University Press, 2002).

Two collections on the "identity theory" are David Rosenthal, ed., *Materialism and the Mind-Body Problem* (Englewood Cliffs, NJ: Prentice-Hall, 1971) and C. V. Borst, ed., *The Mind-Brain Identity Theory* (New York: St. Martin's Press, 1970).

Two delightful presentations of the functionalist position are the collection of essays by Dan Dennett, *Brainstorms* (Newton Center, MA: Bradford Books, 1979) and his *Consciousness Explained* (Boston: Little Brown, 1991).

See also J. Margolis, *The Philosophy of Psychology* (Englewood Cliffs, NJ: Prentice-Hall, 1983), Jay L. Garfield, *Foundations of Cognitive Science* (New York: Paragon House, 1990), and David Chalmers, *The Conscious Mind* (New York: Oxford University Press, 1996).

6 | Freedom

"Two plus two equals four"—*as if freedom means that!*

FYODOR DOSTOYEVSKY

"The murderer had been raised in a slum. His father abandoned him when he was seven months old; he was beaten by his older siblings and constantly abused by his mother. He never had the chance to attend school; he never could get or hold a job. By the time he robbed the store, he was near starvation, addicted to hard drugs, without friends, and without help of any kind. His sister said, 'I've known since he was a child that he would do this some day.' His mother complained, 'I don't understand!' The prosecutor called it a 'cold-blooded, premeditated act.' The defense accused the whole of society, claiming that it had, through its neglect as well as its negative conditioning, made this man an inevitable killer." We know the rest of the arguments; what we do not know is their resolution. Should a man be held responsible for an act for which he has been conditioned his whole life? Or must we not hold out that no matter what the circumstances, he could have resisted; that he could have decided not to commit the crime; and therefore that he must be held responsible?

Of all the abstract problems of philosophy, the problem of **freedom** has the most obvious practical consequences. If we believe that a person is free to choose his or her actions and destiny, we tend to load the person with moral **responsibility**, praise or blame; if we believe a person is simply a victim of the fates, a cog in a mechanical universe, or a pawn in the abstract hands of society, then our attitude toward his or her actions can be no different than our attitudes toward the movement of glaciers and the growth of flowers. "It happens that way," that's all.

A. Fatalism and Karma

Are we cogs in the universe? Are we pawns of the fates? People have often thought so. In the West, our tendency to believe in fate goes back to the ancient Greeks. Most of the ancient Greeks believed that our destinies were already decided for us; no matter what our actions, the outcome was settled. Today, many people believe that our actions and character are the causal result of our genes and our upbringing, and perhaps also the result of unconscious fears and desires that we may never even recognize. Then, too, astrology and other theories

FIG. 6.1 Eugene Delacroix's *Liberty Leading the People* (1830) personifies political freedom as a woman who is leading people from various social classes. *(Réunion des Musées Nationaux / Art Resource, NY)*

of external determination have always been popular. (For instance, *"Virgo:* It's going to be a bad day: don't get out of bed and don't talk to anyone.") And we can see why they would be. The more our actions are the results of other forces and not our own doing, the less we need feel responsible for them, and the less we need worry about deciding what to do. It is already decided, and not by us.

Consider for example, the following news article, a modified version of one that appeared throughout the United States in April 1980:

> *The way lawyer John Badger*[1] *saw it, he was giving the judge a chance to "follow the flow into the brotherhood of man" by entertaining the notion that his client's life of crime was ordained by the stars.*
>
> *But Circuit Judge Ruben Costa, who said he was "inclined to believe there is a certain verity" to astrology, threw out the proposed defense at a pretrial hearing Monday for 23-year-old John Matthew Gopel, who is charged with rape, robbery and assault.*
>
> *Badger had planned to argue Gopel was insane by virtue of his astrological destiny.*
>
> *Badger said his client, born at 8:14 p.m. on Aug. 8, 1956, was literally "a born loser."*

---

[1] All names in this article have been invented to protect the individuals involved.

"There is a force in the life of this young man that forced him to go on transmission fluid, sniff gasoline, cocaine, anything he could get his hands on," he said.

Badger said he intended to present testimony from astrologers, scientists and mental health experts, as well as a bartender who would describe the effects of the full moon on human behavior.

The list of defense evidence included the song "When You Wish Upon A Star," Spiderman *comic books and the plays* King Lear *and* Hamlet.

The ancient Greek tragedies, like *Oedipus the King*, presuppose **fatalism**, the view that whatever a person's actions and circumstances, however free they may seem, his or her predetermined end is inevitable. The story of Oedipus most famously recounted in the tragedy by Sophocles is perhaps the most stirring picture of Greek determinism. Oedipus and his wife, Iocasta, both scoffed at the prophets and made efforts to avoid their prophesied destinies.

 FROM *Oedipus the King*
BY **Sophocles**[2]

OEDIPUS: I went to Delphi. Phoebus . . . declared
A thing most horrible: he foretold that I
Should mate with my own mother, and beget
A brood that men would shudder to behold,
And that I was to be the murderer
Of my own father.-
Therefore, back to Corinth
I never went—the stars alone have told me
Where Corinth lies—that I might never see
Cruel fulfillment of that oracle.

IOCASTA: Listen to me
And you will hear the prophetic art
Touches our human fortunes not at all.
I soon can give you proof.—An oracle
Once came to [my husband] . . .
His fate it was, that he should have a son
By me, that son would take his father's life.
But he was killed—or so they said—by
Strangers.
By brigands, at a place where three ways meet.
As for the child, it was not three days old
When [my husband] fastened both its feet together
And had it cast off a precipice.
Therefore Apollo failed . . .
So much for what prophetic voices have uttered.

---

[2] Sophocles, *Three Tragedies: Antigone, Oedipus the King, Electra*, trans. H. D. F. Kitto, Oxford University Press, 1962. Reprinted with permission.

Sophocles (c. 496 B.C.E.-406 B.C.E.)

One of the great tragic playwrights of ancient Athens. Among the seven of his plays that survive are *Oedipus the King* and *Antigone*, enduring masterpieces that have been influential in Western philosophy and culture in general.

Unbeknown to either of them, of course, the "brigand" who killed Iocasta's husband was Oedipus himself, Iocasta's son, saved as a baby from the precipice and adopted by the man he had thought was his father, from whom he had fled. Thus, both their destinies had been fulfilled. Neither had any control over—nor even knowledge of—what happened to them, and so neither acted freely at all. Thus, the Chorus of observers declares:

> I pray that I might pass my life in reverent holiness of word and deed
> For there are laws enthroned above,
> Heaven created them,
> Olympus was their father,
> And mortal men had no part in their birth.

How should we deal with our fate? Should we try to know our fate? Iocasta advocates that "ignorance is bliss" and tries hard throughout the play not to acknowledge her growing suspicions. If we cannot do anything about our fate, she reasons, then we should not even think about it. But Oedipus insists on finding out the truth, and, as a whole, the play seems to advocate facing the fact of our destinies.

> IOCASTA: Why should we fear, seeing that man is ruled
> By chance, and there is room for no clear forethought?
> No: live at random, live as best one can....
> Whoever thinks
> The least of this, he lives most comfortably.
>
> OEDIPUS: Alas! you generations of men!
> Even while you live you are next to nothing!
> Has any man won for himself
> More than the shadow of happiness? . . .
> Time sees all, and Time, in your despite
> Disclosed and punished your unnatural marriage
>
> CREON [OEDIPUS' UNCLE/BROTHER-IN-LAW]:
> Seek not to have your way in all things.
> Where you had your way before,
> Your mastery broke before the end.

The anthropomorphic Greek gods were integral to the ancient Greek notion of fate. Human choices were considered impotent to change one's fate because human beings were thought to be at the mercy of the gods' whims. But another conception of fate, the Buddhist conception, sees human choices as tremendously important—not because they are free, but precisely the opposite. In Buddhism, all human choices are gestures of *attachment* to the physical world, each one binding its maker more and more to a difficult fate. The effects of one's choices, as we have seen in Chapter 1, are called his or her *karma*, which one can only escape by living out the consequences that one's actions have set in motion. Buddhism does have a concept of freedom, a state called *nirvana*, but it is not a freedom of the self or the individual. In fact, it is a freedom *from* the self and the individual, achieved only when there is no longer a self at all. It is our foolish attachment to this world, the Buddhist claims, that fosters the illusion that we are individuals at all. In a sense, then, our fate is entirely determined; yet ironically, if we submit ourselves to fate and accept its authority, if we can stop making choices that further delude us into believing we are free, then and only then, can we ultimately become really free.

Consider the following excerpt from a contemporary Japanese philosopher, Keiji Nishitani, who has written extensively on the Buddhist concept of "nothingness" and the Western concept of "nihilism," which he says has now infected Japan.

On Fate
BY **Keiji Nishitani**[3]

From that viewpoint [the standpoint of nothingness] the world of karma is a world where each individual is determined by its ties and causal kinship within an endless world nexus, and yet each instance of individual existence and behavior, as well as each moment of their time, arises as something totally new, possessed of freedom and creativity.

Although the ebb and flow of the total nexus "since time past without beginning" is conceived as an infinite chain of causal necessity, its having no beginning implies, conversely, a *before* previous to any and all conceivable pasts. For such time to have no end means that it has an *after* that is future even to the most remote of possible futures. Any such before and after (beyond any definite before and after) lies in the present of every man and makes the present into free and creative activity.

FIG. 6.2 Fate was personified by the ancient Greeks as three sewing women, the Fates, who measured and cut the thread that determined the length of each person's life. (*Victoria & Albert Museum, London / Art Resource, NY*)

. . .

The karmic deeds that make manifest this restless, incessant becoming always return thereby at the same time to the home-ground of karma, to the home-ground of the present. In other words, doing opens itself up on each occasion to the openness of nihility and thus preserves the dimension of ecstatic transcendence.

This means that the self is at all times itself. Even as in my karma I constantly constitute my existence as a becoming *qua* being, in the home-ground of that karma I am ever in my own homeground: I am always myself. This is why restless, incessant becoming within time is at all times *my* existence. Karma is at all times *my* karma. And this means that it is free karma, that it implies an ecstatic transcendence to nihility.

[3] Keiji Nishitani, *Religion and Nothingness*, ed. and trans. Jan Van Bragt. Copyright © 1982 by Keiji Nishitani. Published by the University of California Press.

Of course, although we call it freedom or creativity, it is not at this point true freedom or creativity. Freedom here is one with an inner necessity compelling us constantly to be doing something. It is in unison with that infinite drive and that infinite drive in turn is in unison with freedom. To be within the limitless world-nexus ceaselessly relating to something or other, and to be conditioned and determined in these relations by the world-nexus, is, seen from the other side, a self-determination. While the present karma is here the free work of the self, it appears at the same time to be possessed of the character of fate. Fate arises to awareness in unison with that freedom. Here the present karma reaches awareness under its form of infinity as infinite drive, in its "willful" essence.

The self's relation with something, seen as a self-determination, is the self's exercise of free will. Of its own accord, the self accepts a thing as good or rejects it as bad. But insofar as it is determined through causal kinship within the total nexus, this free will is a fate, a causal necessity, without thereby ceasing to be free will. To accept or reject something implies a simultaneous "attachment" to it. The karma that relates to something by lusting after it is at once voluntary and compulsory. The being of the self that comes about in that karma is at once a freedom and a burden. Here spontaneity becomes a burden and a debt.

. . .

All of this indicates how deeply rooted self-centeredness is. So deeply underground do the roots of the self extend that no karmic activity can ever reach them. The karma of the self at all times returns to its own home-ground, namely, to the self itself, but it cannot get back to the home-ground of the self as such. Karma can do no more than go back to its own home-ground in the self and there reinstate its debt-laden existence. In karma, the self is constantly oriented inward to the home-ground of the self; and yet the only thing it achieves by this is the constant reconstitution of being *qua* becoming in a time without beginning or end. To transit endlessly through time in search of the home-ground of the self is the true form of our karma, that is, of our being in time, our life.

The karma of "time past without beginning" is the true form of our life. It implies a sense of essential "despair." Karma is what Kierkegaard calls the "sickness unto death." Its despair rises to awareness from directly underfoot of the work of our present deed, word, and thought, from the fountainhead of time without beginning or end, and of being within that time, in short from our self-centeredness. We can see an awareness of that despair also underlying the confession of the Buddhist *Verse of Repentance*, which suggests that every sort of karma stemming from the body, mouth, and mind of the self is grounded in a greed, anger, and folly without beginning.

. . .

Karma here comes to bear the marks of guilt and sin. In a certain sense, it takes on the character of original sin, namely, sin that is as equally elemental as the free work and existence of man. Karma is freedom determined by causal necessity within the whole infinite nexus, a freedom of spontaneity in "attachment" and, therefore, a freedom totally *bound* by fate. At the same time, having reduced the whole causal nexus to its own center, it is a freedom altogether *unbound*. In karma these two aspects of freedom and causal necessity become one. Consequently, as a freedom that derives entirely from the determining force of causal necessity, as a freedom chased out and driven away from necessity, karma binds itself in attachment to the other, while at the same time it remains an altogether unbound freedom, gathering every other into the center of the self. This freedom is in the mode of an original sin.

"Karma is freedom determined by causal necessity within the whole infinite nexus, a freedom of spontaneity in 'attachment' and, therefore, a freedom totally bound by fate."

– KEIJI NISHITANI

- Do you agree with Nishitani that the doctrine of karma is compatible with freedom? Why or why not?
- What are the similarities and differences between the notion of fate and the notion of karma? How is the notion of luck different from both of them?
- Do you believe that fate dictates the basic plot of one's life and death?

B. Predestination

Fatalism, in its Greek or Buddhist sense, is the claim that our future is determined by a play of forces beyond our understanding. But what if these forces are understood and, in fact, *created* by one superhuman, being? **Predestination** has been the view of many theologians, who hold that our every action (and every event in the universe) is known, if not also caused in advance, by God. Predestination, like fatalism, does not depend upon any particular antecedent conditions unless we want to say that God is an antecedent condition.

All the Western theologians have had to ponder the problem of predestination and freedom, since all the Western religions' scriptures claim that God created, or caused, everything. As we saw in Chapter 1, this is of particular concern when considering evil. In that chapter, the "problem of evil" was described as the question of how evil could be caused by a good God. We now can see that the crux of the "problem of evil" is the question of freedom. It would be easy to explain much of the world's evil if human beings were free. In that case, we, not an all-good God, would be the **cause** of evil. But if, as is stated in scripture, God created and caused everything, then surely, God creates our human actions, too. Humans sin—so it seems that we are back to the drawing board. How can an all-good God cause us or let us be free to sin?

The following lines from St. Augustine summarize the problem of freedom and one Christian solution to it. God made human beings free because He is all good, and free actions are better than unfree ones. However, since freedom allows us to sin, we are responsible for bringing evil into the world.

 FROM *On Free Choice of the Will*
BY **St. Augustine**[4]

1. WHY DID GOD GIVE FREEDOM OF THE WILL TO MEN, SINCE IT IS BY THIS THAT MEN SIN?

EVODIUS: Now, if possible, explain to me why God gave man free choice of the will since if he had not received it he would not be able to sin.

AUGUSTINE: Are you perfectly sure that God gave to man what you think ought not to have been given?

EVODIUS: As far as I seem to understand the discussion in the first book, we have freedom of will, and could not sin if we were without it.

AUGUSTINE: I, too, remember that this was made clear to us. But I just asked you whether you know that it was God who gave us that which we possess, through which it is clear that we commit sin.

---

[4] St. Augustine, *On Free Choice of the Will*, trans. Anna S. Benjamin and L. H. Hackstaff. Copyright © 1964. Reprinted by permission of Prentice-Hall, Inc., Upper Saddle River, NJ.

EVODIUS: No one else. For we are from Him, and whether we sin or whether we do right, we earn reward or punishment from Him.

AUGUSTINE: I want to ask, as well: do you know this clearly, or do you believe it willingly without really knowing it, because you are prompted by authority?

EVODIUS: I admit that at first I trusted authority on this point. But what can be more true than that all good proceeds from God, that everything just is good, and that it is just to punish sinners and to reward those who do right? From this it follows that through God sinners are afflicted with unhappiness, and those who do right endowed with happiness.

AUGUSTINE: I do not object, but let me ask another question: how do you know that we are from God? You did not answer that; instead, you explained that we merit punishment and reward from God.

EVODIUS: The answer to *that* question, too, is clear, if for no other reason than the fact that, as we have already agreed, God punished sins. All justice is from God, and it is not the role of justice to punish foreigners, although it is the role of goodness to bestow benefits on them. Thus it is clear that we belong to God, since He is not only most generous in bestowing benefits upon us, but also most just in punishing us. Also, we can understand that man is from God through the fact, which I proposed and you conceded, that every good is from God. For man himself, insofar as he is a man, is a good, because he can live rightly when he so wills.

AUGUSTINE: If this is so, the question that you proposed is clearly answered. If man is a good, and cannot act rightly unless he wills to do so, then he must have free will, without which he cannot act rightly. We must not believe that God gave us free will so that we might sin, just because sin is committed through free will. It is sufficient for our question, why free will should have been given to man, to know that without it man cannot live rightly. That it was given for this reason can be understood from the following: if anyone uses free will for sinning, he incurs divine punishment. This would be unjust if free will had been given not only that man might live rightly, but also that he might sin. For how could a man justly incur punishment who used free will to do the thing for which it was given? When God punishes a sinner, does He not seem to say, "Why have you not used free will for the purpose for which I gave it to you, to act rightly?" Then too, if man did not have free choice of will, how could there exist the good according to which it is just to condemn evildoers and reward those who act rightly? What was not done by will would be neither evildoing nor right action. But punishment and reward would be unjust if man did not have free will. Moreover, there must needs be justice both in punishment and in reward, since justice is one of the goods that are from God. Therefore, God must needs have given free will to man.

One's opinion on the question of freedom was a crucial determinant of one's sectarian alliance in early Islam. Islam is sometimes understood in the West as a "fatalist" religion; in other words, it is thought that all Muslims believe that human beings are not free. However, the Mu'tazilites, one of the first Islamic sects, claimed that the human will is free, despite passages in scripture that would lead one to believe the contrary, such as the following:

No misfortune befalls except by Allah's [God's] will. He guides the hearts of those who believe in him. Allah has knowledge of all things. (64:11)

. . .

Every misfortune that befalls the earth or your own persons, is ordained before we bring it into being. (57:22-23)

Thus, Islam provides an interesting breadth of argument on the question of freedom. The Mu'tazilites claimed that human freedom is consistent with God's power by distinguishing between two types of action, or causality. God's actions are "necessary," or lawlike. They *must* happen. Human actions, however, are "intentional"; they are contingent upon God's actions, which are their necessary conditions and consequences. Thus, a person is free, for instance, to hit a billiard ball with his or her pool cue. But he or she is *not* free to hit the ball and have it stay still or to hit it in one direction and have it go in another. Only God is "free" to make necessary physical laws. For the Mu'tazilites, human freedom amounts to *directing* God's actions along various possible paths. We are responsible for how we direct God's creations, and so we are rightly rewarded or punished by God for our choices.

Another important Islamic school, the Ash'arites, reacted against the Mu'tazilites in favor of a more liberal interpretation of scriptural passages like the ones just quoted. The Ash'arites, however, wound up making a distinction with regard to the question of freedom that was similar to that of the Mu'tazilites. The Ash'arites claimed that only God is free and that all human actions are determined by God. God's "predestination" here, however, is more like an offer of a gift. God offers us various actions, which we can accept, or "acquire." Only God, therefore, can create an action, according to the Ash'arites. Human beings merely acquire them, "secondhand" so to speak. When we acquire good actions, we deserve our reward. When we acquire bad ones, we deserve our punishment.

Although one may conclude that overall, then, Islamic tradition does seem to believe more in God's predestination than does Christianity, the Islamic stance on the question of freedom is really a complex one. The debate within Islam about freedom continues to this day. Here is an example from an important twentieth-century Islamic theologian, Sir Muhammad Iqbal.

 FROM *The Reconstruction of Religious Thought in Islam* BY **Muhammad Iqbal**[5]

Does the ego then determine its own activity? If so, how is the self-determination of the ego related to the determination of the spatio-temporal order? Is personal causality a special kind of causality, or only a disguised form of the mechanism of Nature? It is claimed that the two kinds of determinism are not mutually exclusive and that the scientific method is equally applicable to human action. The human act of deliberation is understood to be a conflict of motives which are conceived, not as the ego's own present or inherited tendencies of action or inaction, but as so many external forces fighting one another, gladiator-like, on the arena of the mind. Yet the final choice is regarded as a fact determined by the *strongest* force, and not by the resultant of contending motives, like a purely physical effect. I am, however, firmly of the opinion that the controversy between the advocates of Mechanism and Freedom arises from a wrong view of intelligent action which modern psychology, unmindful of its own independence as a science, possessing a special set of facts to observe, was bound to take on account of its slavish imitation of physical sciences.

. . .

[5] Muhammad Iqbal, *The Reconstruction of Religious Thought in Islam*, London: Oxford University Press, 1934.

FIG. 6.3 Islamic scholars have defended various interpretations of human freedom as being compatible with the Qur'an. (© iStockphoto.com/Ahmed Refaat)

Muhammad Iqbal (1877-1938)

An Indian philosopher, politician, and poet. A leader in the All India Muslim League, Iqbal encouraged an Islamic spiritual revival and called for the development of cooperative ties among Muslims regardless of nationality. He was among the first to propose a separate Muslim state in British-controlled India, a vision that was realized after his death with the creation of Pakistan.

"[Fatalism] is life and boundless power which recognizes no obstruction, and can make a man calmly offer his prayers when bullets are showering around him."

— MUHAMMAD IQBAL

Thus the element of guidance and directive control in the ego's activity clearly shows that the ego is a free personal causality. He shares in the life and freedom of the Ultimate Ego who, by permitting the emergence of a finite ego, capable of private initiative, has limited this freedom of His own free will. This freedom of conscious behaviour follows from the view of ego–activity which the Quran takes. There are verses which are unmistakably clear on this point:

"And say: The truth is from your Lord: Let him, then, who will, believe: and let him who will, be an unbeliever." (18:28)

"If ye do well to your own behoof will ye do well: and if ye do evil against yourselves will ye do it." (17:7)

Indeed Islam recognizes a very important fact of human psychology, i.e., the rise and fall of the power to act freely, and is anxious to retain the power to act freely as a constant and undiminished factor in the life of the ego. The timing of the daily prayer, which according to the Quran restores "self-possession" to the ego by bringing it into closer touch with the ultimate source of life and freedom, is intended to save the ego from the mechanizing effects of sleep and business. Prayer in Islam is the ego's escape from mechanism to freedom.

The fatalism implied in this attitude is not negation of the ego . . . it is life and boundless power which recognizes no obstruction, and can make a man calmly offer his prayers when bullets are showering around him.

A different example of determinism comes from the African Yoruba nation. In the Yoruba version, there is a place for human freedom within a larger determinist context. Here it is described by philosopher Jacqueline Trimier:

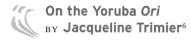

On the Yoruba *Ori*
BY **Jacqueline Trimier**[6]

In Yoruba philosophy, the *ori* [or "inner head"] determines one's fate, and, contrary to most alternative cultural accounts of the soul, the Yoruba actually chooses his *ori*. In the creation myth *Ajala*, the "potter of heads," provides each body with a head. But before a person arrives on earth, he or she must go to the house of *Ajala* to choose a head. To make matters more complicated, *Ajala* has a reputation for being irresponsible and careless. As a result, *Ajala* molds many bad heads; he sometimes forgets to fire some, misshapes others, and overburns still others. Because it is said that he owes money to many people, *Ajala* commonly hides in the ceiling to avoid creditors and neglects some of the heads he put on the fire, leaving them to burn. But beneath this earthy and all-too-human depiction of the deity, certain classic concepts of fate and freedom are evident. People choose their destinies, but it is a choice that is fraught with dangers and uncertainties. *Ajala* molds many bad heads and only a few good ones. When a person gets to *Ajala*'s storehouse of heads, he or she does not know which heads are bad or good—all people choose heads in ignorance. If a person picks a bad head, he or she is doomed to failure in life. Moreover, before a person reaches earth with a body, head, and soul, rain can erode an imperfectly made head. On earth, hard work would be useless to affect one's fortune because all of one's energy would have been used for repairing the damaged, useless head. Yet, if a person picks a really good head, the person is destined to have a good, prosperous life. With hard work, he or she will surely be successful, since little or no energy need be expended in costly head repairs.

The concept of the *ori* or inner head carries with it a profound belief in predestination. The life one leads depends upon the head one chooses. One myth from *Ifa* literary corpus tells about three friends *Oriseeku*, *Orileemere*, and *Afuwape* who needed heads to travel from heaven to earth. They went to find the house of *Ajala* to choose their heads. Before leaving heaven, they were told not to stop at any place along the way. However, *Afuwape* did not listen; he visited his father, and his two friends left him behind. When the latter reached *Ajala*'s house, they did not find him because, as usual, he was hiding in the rafters from creditors. Instead of waiting for *Ajala* to appear, the two friends picked their heads without knowing which ones were properly made; and as they descended

Jacqueline Trimier (1968-)

A philosopher at the College of Lake County, Grayslake, Illinois.

FIG 6.4 Jacqueline Trimier *(Used by permission of Jacqueline Trimier)*

6 Jacqueline Trimier, "African Philosophy," from *World Philosophy*, ed. R. C. Solomon and K. Higgins, New York: McGraw-Hill, 1994. Reprinted by permission of the author.

to earth, rain wore out their heads. Consequently, they lived unsuccessful lives on earth.

Afuwape got to the home of his father, *Orunmila* (god of wisdom), who was consulting his *Ifa* (divination texts). When *Afuwape* told his father of his plan to see *Ajala*, the *Ifa* priests consulted for *Afuwape* and said *Orunmila* should offer money and salt as a sacrifice and that *Afuwape* should carry part of these offerings on his journey. *Afuwape* left his father's home and, along the way, asked a gatekeeper for the way to *Ajala's* house. The gatekeeper had never used salt before and was cooking his soup over a flame and salting it with ashes. *Afuwape* offered the gatekeeper some salt which he liked. To return the kindness, the gatekeeper took *Afuwape* to the house of *Ajala*.

When *Afuwape* found *Ajala's* house, *Ajala* was not at home but one of the creditors was waiting for him. The gatekeeper had advised *Afuwape* to help *Ajala* pay part of his debt so that *Ajala* would help him choose the best head possible. *Afuwape* paid the debt, and the creditor left. When *Ajala* came home, he was so grateful that he took *Afuwape* to his storehouse and helped him choose the best head. Consequently, *Afuwape's* head withstood the hazards of a journey to earth, and he had a good life on earth.

To Americans, the most familiar version of belief in predestination comes from that school of Protestant Christianity called Calvinism. In the following passage, the famous American Calvinist theologian, **Jonathan Edwards** (1703–1758), gives a defense of his belief in predestination.

FROM "Freedom of the Will" BY Jonathan Edwards[7]

Wherein it is considered whether there is or can be any such sort of freedom of will, as that wherein Arminians[8] place the essence of the liberty of all moral agents; and whether any such thing ever was or can be conceived of.

. . .

First, I am to prove, that God has an absolute and certain foreknowledge of the free actions of moral agents.

One would think, it should be wholly needless to enter on such an argument with any that profess themselves Christians: but so it is; God's certain foreknowledge

---

7 Jonathan Edwards, "Freedom of the Will," from *The Works of President Edwards, In Four Volumes*, Vol. 2, New York: Leavitt and Allen, 1856.

8 Jacobus Arminius (1560–1609) was a Dutch theologian who claimed that although God has foreknowledge of our actions, human beings nonetheless act freely. Edwards aims his arguments against Arminius' followers throughout.

of the free acts of moral agents, is denied by some that pretend to believe the Scriptures to be the word of God; and especially of late. I therefore shall consider the evidence of such a prescience in the Most High, as fully as the designed limits of this essay will admit of; supposing myself herein to have to do with such as own the truth of the Bible.

Arg I. My first argument shall be taken from God's *prediction* of such events. Here I would, in the first place, lay down these two things as axioms.

(1) If God does not foreknow, he cannot foretell such events; that is, he cannot peremptorily and certainly foretell them. If God has no more than an uncertain guess concerning events of this kind, then he can declare no more than an uncertain guess. Positively to foretell, is to profess to foreknow, or to declare positive foreknowledge.

(2) If God does not certainly foreknow the future volitions of moral agents, then neither can he certainly foreknow those events which are consequent and dependent on these volitions. The existence of the one depending on the existence of the other; the knowledge of the existence of the one depends on the knowledge of the existence of the other; and the one cannot be more certain than the other.

Therefore, how many, how great and how extensive soever the consequences of the volitions of moral agents may be; though they should extend to an alteration of the slate of things through the universe, and should be continued in a series of successive events to all eternity, and should in the progress of things branch forth into an infinite number of series, each of them going on in an endless line or chain of events; God must be as ignorant of all these consequences, as he is of the volitions whence they take their rise: all these events, and the whole slate of things depending on them, how important, extensive and vast soever, must be hid from him.

John Calvin (1509-1564)

A French theologian and a major leader in the Protestant Reformation. He was the author of a magnum opus on theology, the *Institutes of the Christian Religion*. In that work, he defends the doctrine of predestination, which holds that God has predetermined who will be eternally saved and who will not be.

FIG. 6.6 John Calvin preached that God had predestined certain people, the Elect, to be saved from eternal damnation. *(© iStockphoto .com/Georgios Kollidas)*

SECTION XII.

God's certain Foreknowledge of the future Volitions of moral Agents, inconsistent with such a Contingence of those Volitions as is without all Necessity.

Having proved that God has a certain and infallible prescience of the act of the Will of moral agents, I come now, in the *second* place, to show the consequence; to show how it follows from hence, that these events are *necessary*, with a Necessity of connection or consequence.

The chief Arminian divines, so far as I have opportunity to observe, deny this consequence; and affirm, that if such Foreknowledge be allowed, it is no evidence of any Necessity of the event foreknown. Now I desire, that this matter may be particularly and thoroughly inquired into. I cannot but think that, on particular and full consideration, it may be perfectly determined, whether it be indeed so or not.

"If there be any
such thing
as a divine
Foreknowledge
of the volitions of
free agents, that
Foreknowledge . . .
is a thing which
already has, and
long ago had,
existence; and so,
now its existence is
necessary; it is now
utterly impossible
to be otherwise
than that this
Foreknowledge
should be, or
should have been."

– JONATHAN EDWARDS

In order to a proper consideration of this matter, I would observe the following things.

I. It is very evident, with regard to a thing whose existence is infallibly and indissolubly connected with something which already hath or has had existence, the existence of that thing is necessary. Here may be noted:

1. I observed before, in explaining the nature of Necessity, that in things which are past, their existence is now necessary: having already made sure of existence, it is too late for any possibility of alteration in that respect: it is now impossible that it should be otherwise than true, that that thing has existed.

2. If there be any such thing as a divine Foreknowledge of the volitions of free agents, that Foreknowledge, by the supposition, is a thing which already has, and long ago had, existence; and so, now its existence is necessary; it is now utterly impossible to be otherwise than that this Foreknowledge should be, or should have been.

3. It is also very manifest, that those things which are indissolubly connected with other things that are necessary, are themselves necessary. As that proposition whose truth is necessarily connected with another proposition, which is necessarily true, is itself necessarily true. To say otherwise, would be a contradiction: it would be in effect to say, that the connection was indissoluble, and yet was not so, but might be broken. If that, whose existence is indissolubly connected with something whose existence is now necessary, is itself not necessary, then it may possibly not exist, notwithstanding that indissoluble connection of its existence.—Whether that absurdity be not glaring, let the reader judge.

4. It is no less evident, that if there be a full, certain, and infallible Foreknowledge of the future existence of the volitions of moral agents, then there is a certain infallible and indissoluble connection between those events and that Foreknowledge; and that therefore, by the preceding observations, those events are necessary events; being infallibly and indissolubly connected with that whose existence already is, and so is now necessary, and cannot but have been.

To say the Foreknowledge is certain and infallible, and yet the connection of the event with that Foreknowledge is not indissoluble, but dissoluble and fallible, is very absurd. To affirm it, would be the same thing as to affirm that there is no necessary connection between a proposition's being infallibly known to be true, and its being true indeed. So that it is perfectly demonstrable, that if there be any infallible knowledge of future volitions, the event is necessary; or, in other words, that it is impossible but the event should come to pass. For if it be not impossible but that it may be otherwise, then it is not impossible but true. But how absurd is that, on the supposition that there is now an infallible knowledge (i.e. knowledge which it is impossible should fail) that it is true. There is this absurdity in it, that it is not impossible but that there now should be no truth in that proposition which is now infallibly known to be true.

II. That no future event can be certainly foreknown, whose existence is contingent, and without all necessity, may be proved thus; it is impossible for a thing to be certainly known to any intellect without evidence. To suppose otherwise, implies a contradiction: because, for a thing to be certainly known to any understanding, is for it to be evident to that understanding: and for a thing to be evident to any understanding, is the same thing as for that understanding to see evidence of it: but no understanding, created or uncreated, can see evidence where there is none: for is the same thing as to see that to be which is not. And therefore, if there be any truth which is absolutely without evidence, that truth is absolutely unknowable, insomuch that it implies a contradiction to suppose that it is known. . . .

III. To suppose the future volitions of moral agents not to be necessary events; or, which is the same thing, events which it is not impossible but that they may not come to pass; and yet to suppose that God certainly foreknows them, and knows all things, is to suppose God's knowledge to be inconsistent with itself. For to say, that God certainly, and without all conjecture, knows that a thing will infallibly be, which at the same time he knows to be so contingent that it may possibly not be, is to suppose his knowledge inconsistent with itself; or that one thing that he knows, is utterly inconsistent with another thing that he knows.

Jonathan Edwards
(1703-1758)

American philosopher and Calvinist theologian. At the time of his death, he was president of what is now Princeton University.

FIG. 6.7 Jonathan Edwards, a Calvinist, defended predestination on the ground that God has foreknowledge of everything we do. *(© Stock Montage / SuperStock)*

- How do predestination and fatalism differ? In what respects are they similar? Is predestination a version of fatalism?
- How is predestination related to the problem of evil? What account does St. Augustine offer to tie them together? How, then, does his account allow room for free will?
- What are the differences between the Mu'tazilites' and Ash'arites' conceptions of human freedom and predestination?
- How do the Yoruba and the Calvinist views of predestination compare?

C. Determinism

As we have seen, the problem of freedom occurs in different contexts, from pagan fatalism to Christian predestination. The problem occurs in connection with the most abstract thesis that the universe as a whole is a single great machine or "substance" (as in Newton or Spinoza) and in localized theories about the psychology of the human personality. At all levels, however, the problem has usually been identified with a single claim, defended as the position called **determinism**. We briefly introduced determinism in Chapter 2: Spinoza defended it in his metaphysical system; Newton gave it a convincing scientific interpretation with his physical theories. In a phrase, determinism can be characterized by a principle that is already familiar to you from Chapter 3, the "principle of universal causation." "Every event has its cause(s)." Determinism is the thesis that everything that happens in the universe is determined according to the *laws of nature*. The problem is that human actions, whatever else they may be, are also events in the physical universe. But if human action is just another law-determined natural occurrence, can it also be free? It is as if we were to start praising people (or blaming them) for obeying the law of gravity. What else could they possibly do?

Determinism, as we have defined it, is related to, but different from, fatalism and predestination. According to fatalism, despite what happens, the end is inevitable. In predestination, God's will has power over *both* human choices and natural law. According to determinism, however, an event will necessarily happen if its antecedent conditions are fulfilled. Determinism need not say that any event is inevitable; it insists only that *if* certain conditions exist, *then* a certain kind of event will take place. (For example, if a pot of water is heated sufficiently, then it will boil, or if a person is forced to choose between losing his or her life and killing an insect, then the person will take the life of the insect.) This "if . . . then" structure is essential to determinism. (There need be no such "ifs" or "thens" in fatalism or predestination.)

Determinism is the theory that every event in the universe, including every human action, has its natural causes; given certain **antecedent conditions**, an event will take place necessarily, according to the laws of nature. But we must fill out the determinist's premise by at least one more step. It is not enough to say "every event has its natural cause(s)," since this would leave open the possibility that although every event requires certain antecedent conditions to take place, the event may still be a matter of chance, at least to some extent, or a matter of human choice. We must say that "every event has its sufficient natural cause(s)." A **sufficient cause** is capable of bringing the event about by itself. Then there is no room for chance and no room for choice. This view, which we call "hard" determinism ("hard" as in "hardhearted," as well as a "hard" conclusion to accept), clearly leaves no room for human freedom. Without choice, there can be no freedom, and without freedom, there is no reason to hold a person responsible for his or her action, no matter how virtuous or how vicious it may be. According to the hard determinist thesis, we can barely be said to be "acting" at all, for our "actions" are nothing but the result of antecedent conditions and laws of nature that leave no room for our "doing something" at all.

1. Hard Determinism

The hard determinist premise received its greatest impetus from Isaac Newton's physics and his picture of the universe as "matter in motion," determined according to the laws of motion and gravitation that he so elegantly formulated. But his followers applied these laws not only to the movements of the planets and the stars or to the ball rolling down an inclined plane. According to them, we, too, are "matter in motion," physical bodies that are subject to all the laws of nature. What we "do" is just as determined by these laws as any other event in nature.

This "hardheaded" determinism has maintained a powerful hold on philosophers ever since Newton published his theories in the seventeenth century. The philosopher Pierre Simon La Place had such confidence in the Newtonian system that he claimed that if he knew the location and motion of every object in the universe, he could predict the location and motion of every object in the universe at any time in the future. (He could also **retrodict**, or look back to, every past state of the universe.) La Place's statement means that if he had a proper map of the universe, including the material parts of our own bodies, he could predict everything that would ever happen and everything that we would ever do. If he could do so, what possible sense could we make of our vain claims to have choices of actions, to decide what to do, or to hold ourselves and others responsible for what we have done?

La Place's confidence in the hard determinist thesis was common among the immediate successors and enthusiasts of Newton. For example, one of the philosophers of the French Enlightenment, **Baron Paul Henri d'Holbach**, defended the hard determinist viewpoint so uncompromisingly that he shocked even his colleagues as well as many traditionalists.

FROM *System of Nature*
BY **Baron Paul Henri d'Holbach**[9]

In whatever manner man is considered, he is connected to universal nature, and submitted to the necessary and immutable laws that she interposes on all beings she contains, according to their peculiar essences or to the respective properties with which, without consulting them, she endows each particular species. Man's life is a line that nature commands him to describe upon the surface of the earth, without his ever being able to swerve from it, even for an instant. He is born without his own consent; his organization does in nowise depend upon himself; his ideas come to him involuntarily; his habits are in the power of those who cause him to contract them; he is unceasingly modified by causes, whether visible or concealed, over which he has no control, which necessarily regulate his mode or existence, give the hue to his way of thinking, and determine his manner of acting. He is good or bad, happy or miserable, wise or foolish, reasonable or irrational, without his will being for anything in these various states. Nevertheless, in spite of the shackles by which he is bound, it is pretended he is a free agent, or that independent of the causes by which he is moved, he determines his own will, and regulates his own condition.

However slender the foundation of his opinion, of which everything ought to point out to him the error, it is current at this day and passes for an incontestable truth with a great number of people, otherwise extremely enlightened; it is the basis of religion, which supposing relations between man and the unknown being she has placed above nature, has been incapable of imagining how man could merit reward or deserve punishment from this being, if he was not a free agent. Society has been believed interested in his system; because an idea has gone abroad, that if all the actions of man were to be contemplated as necessary, the right of punishing those who injure their associates would no longer exist. At length human vanity accommodated itself to a hypothesis which, unquestionably, appears to distinguish man from all other physical beings, by assigning to him the special privilege of a total independence of all other causes, but of which a very little reflection would have shown him the impossibility.

The will, as we have elsewhere said, is a modification of the brain, by which it is disposed to action, or prepared to give play to the organs. This will be necessarily determined by the qualities, good or bad, agreeable or painful, of the object or the motive that acts upon his sense, or of which the idea

Baron Paul Henri d'Holbach (1723-1789)

A French philosopher and one of the leaders of the Enlightenment. An ardent materialist and atheist, he represented the most radical fringe of the brilliant freethinkers of prerevolutionary France.

FIG. 6.8 Baron Paul Henri d'Holbach, depicted by Luis Carrogis Carmontelle, denied human freedom, claiming that our actions are as much the outcome of necessary causal laws as any physical event. *(Réunion des Musées Nationaux / Art Resource, NY)*

9 Baron Paul Henri d'Holbach, *System of Nature*, London: Kearsley, 1797.

"In short, the actions of man are never free; they are always the necessary consequence of his temperament, of the received ideas, and of the notions, either true or false, which he has formed to himself of happiness; of his opinions, strengthened by example, by education, and by daily experience."

– BARON PAUL HENRI D'HOLBACH

remains with him, and is resuscitated by his memory. In consequence, he acts necessarily, his action is the result of the impulse he receives either from the motive, from the object, or from the idea which has modified his brain, or disposed his will. When he does not act according to his impulse, it is because there comes some new cause, some new motive, some new idea, which modified his brain in a different manner, gives him a new impulse, determines his will in another way, by which the action of the former impulse is suspended: thus, the sight of an agreeable object, or its idea, determines his will to set him in action to procure it; but if a new object or a new idea more powerfully attracts him, it gives a new direction to his will, annihilates the effect of the former, and prevents the action by which it was to be procured. This is the mode in which reflection, experience, reason, necessarily arrests or suspends the action of man's will: without this he would of necessity have followed the anterior impulse which carried him toward a then desirable object. In all this he always acts according to necessary laws from which he has no means of emancipating himself.

. . .

In short, the actions of man are never free; they are always the necessary consequence of his temperament, of the received ideas, and of the notions, either true or false, which he has formed to himself of happiness; of his opinions, strengthened by example, by education, and by daily experience. So many crimes are witnessed on the earth only because every thing conspires to render man vicious and criminal; the religion he has adopted, his government, his education, the examples set before him, irresistibly drive him on to evil: under these circumstances, morality preaches virtue to him in vain. In those societies where vice is esteemed, where crime is crowned, where venality is constantly recompensed, where the most dreadful disorders are punished only in those who are too weak to enjoy the privilege of committing them with impunity, the practice of virtue is considered nothing more than a painful sacrifice of happiness. Such societies chastise, in the lower orders, those excesses which they respect in the higher ranks; and frequently have the injustice to condemn those in the penalty of death, whom public prejudices, maintained by constant example, have rendered criminal.

Man, then, is not a free agent in any one instant of life; he is necessarily guided in each step by those advantages, whether real or fictitious, that he attaches to the objects by which his passions are roused: these passions themselves are necessary in a being who unceasingly tends towards his own happiness; their energy is necessary, since that depends on his temperament; his temperament is necessary, because it depends on the physical elements which enter into his composition; the modification of his temperament is necessary, as it is the infallible and inevitable consequence of the impulse he receives from the incessant action of moral and physical beings.

Given the scientific paradigm that is still widespread in philosophy, determinism is still an influential thesis, despite the shifts in science that make d'Holbach's conception of nature quite outdated. But not everyone today finds determinism a convincing thesis. **Daniel Dennett**, argues that determinism is dismissed, in part, because of popular images that associate it with particular "bogeyman" images that he thinks are absurd.

FROM *Elbow Room*
BY **Daniel Dennett**[10]

1. THE PERENNIAL GRIPPING PROBLEM

The idea of Fate is older than philosophy itself, and since the dawn of the discipline philosophers have been trying to show what is wrong with the idea that our fates are sealed before we are born. It has seemed very important to demonstrate that we are not just acting out our destinies but somehow choosing our own courses, making decisions—not just having "decisions" occur in us.

Ideas about causation were at the focus of attention in the early days of Greek philosophy, and it occurred to some to wonder whether all physical events are caused or determined by the sum total of all prior events. If they are—if, as we say, *determinism* is true—then our actions, as physical events, must themselves be determined. If determinism is true, then our every deed and decision is the inexorable outcome, it seems, of the sum of physical forces acting at the moment, which in turn is the inexorable outcome of the forces acting an instant before, and so on, to the beginning of time.

. . .

Why do people find the free will problem gripping? In part, surely, because it touches deep and central questions about our situation in the universe, about "the human condition," as one portentously says. But also, I will argue, because philosophers have conjured up a host of truly frightening bugbears and then subliminally suggested, quite illicitly, that the question of free will is whether any of these bugbears actually exist.

. . .

[T]here are a host of analogies to be found in the literature: not having free will would be somewhat like being in prison, or being hypnotized, or being paralyzed, or being a puppet, or . . . (the list continues).

I do not think these analogies are merely useful illustrations, merely graphic expository devices. I think they are at the very foundation of the problem. Without them to anchor the philosophical discussions, the free will problem would float away, at best a curious issue to bemuse metaphysicians and puzzlemongers.

2. THE BOGEYMEN

The first of the bugbears are quite literally bogey*men*—bogey*persons* if you insist—for they are all conceived as *agents* who vie with us for control of our bodies, who compete against us, who have interests antithetical to or at least independent of our own. These fearsome fellows are often used by philosophers as reverse cheerleaders (gloomleaders, you might call them) ushered onto the stage whenever anxiety flags, whenever the urgency of the topic under discussion becomes doubtful. As intricacy piles on intricacy, the reader begins to yawn and fidget, but is quickly regalvanized by a nudging analogy: "But that would be like finding yourself in the clutches of . . ."

The Invisible Jailer: Prisons are dreadful. Prisons are to be shunned. Anyone who fails to understand this is not one of *us*. Well, if prison is bad, what does it contrast

---

[10] Daniel Dennett, *Elbow Room*, Cambridge, MA: MIT Press, 1984.

Daniel Dennett (1942-)

An American philosopher and cognitive scientist who teaches at Tufts University.

with? If one is not in prison, one is free (in one important sense), and each of us can reflect gratefully on how glad we are not to be in prison. "Aha!" says the fearmonger. "What makes you so sure you're not in prison?" Sometimes it's obvious when one is in prison, but sometimes it isn't. A sly jailer may conceal the steel bars in the window mullions, and install dummy doors in the walls (if you opened one, you would see a brick wall behind it). It might be some time before a prisoner realized he was in prison.

Are you *sure* you're not in some sort of prison? Here one is invited to consider a chain of transformations, taking us from obvious prisons to unobvious (but still dreadful) prisons, to utterly invisible and undetectable (but still dreadful?) prisons. Consider a deer in Magdalen College park. Is it imprisoned? Yes, but not much. The enclosure is quite large. Suppose we moved the deer to a larger enclosure—the New Forest with a fence around it. Would the deer still be imprisoned? In the State of Maine, I am told, deer almost never travel more than five miles from their birthplace during their lives. If an enclosure were located outside the normal unimpeded limits of a deer's lifetime wanderings would the deer enclosed be imprisoned? Perhaps, but note that it makes a difference to our intuitions whether some*one* installs the enclosure. Do you feel imprisoned on Planet Earth—the way Napoleon was stuck on Elba? It is one thing to be born and live on Elba, and another to be put and kept on Elba by *someone*. A jail without a jailer is not a jail. Whether or not it is an undesirable abode depends on other features; it depends on just how (if at all) it cramps the style of its inhabitants.

The Nefarious Neurosurgeon: How would you like to have someone strap you down and insert electrodes in your brain, and then control your every thought and deed by pushing buttons on the "master" console? Consider, for instance, the entirely typical invocation of this chap by Fischer:[11] the ominous Dr. Black, who arranges things in poor Jones' brain so that Black can "control Jones' activities. Jones, meanwhile, knows nothing of this." First, we may ask—as we always should—why is this other, rival *agent* introduced? Why bring Dr. Black into it? Couldn't the example get off the ground just as well, for instance, if Jones had a brain tumor that produced odd results? What makes Fischer's version more dreadful is that Jones' *control* of his own activities has been usurped by another controller, Dr. Black. A tumor might cause this or that in someone's brain, and it would be terrible indeed to have a debilitating brain tumor, but it would take an awfully smart tumor to control someone's brain.

Variations on the Nefarious Neurosurgeon are the Hideous Hypnotist and the Peremptory Puppeteer. We all know about stage hypnotists (we think we do, in any case) and what is particularly chilling about them is that unlike the Nefarious Neurosurgeons, they may leave no physical trace of their influence.

. . .

The Malevolent Mindreader: This agent is essentially an opponent, but he does not cause or control your moves; he just foresees them and stymies them. Playing "rock, paper, or scissors" against this fellow is hopeless, for since he knows exactly what rut you're in, what policy you're following, he can see in advance which move you intend to make and always counters successfully.[12] If only you could shield your mind

[11] J. Fischer, *Journal of Philosophy* 79, January 1982, pp. 24-40.

[12] D. Hofstadter, *Scientific American* 247, August 1982, pp. 16-24.

from him! If only you could find a strategy of unpredictability that would be proof against his calculations! Then you wouldn't be so impotent, so vulnerable in the game of Life. Predictions matter in a special way when one has a stake in them, when they are not merely future tense statements but rather wagers which one might want to *make* come true and an opponent might want to make come false. In real life one often comes into competition with other people, and even with other organisms (outwitting the rat or mosquito, for instance), but in the cosmic game of Life against whom is one wagering?

I cannot prove that none of the bogeymen in this rogues' gallery really exist, any more than I can prove that the Devil, or Santa Claus, doesn't exist. But I am prepared to put on a sober face and assure anyone who needs assur-

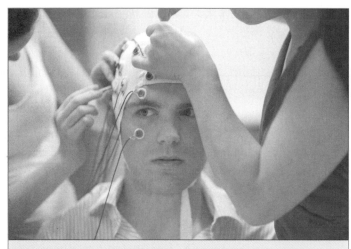

FIG. 6.9 Daniel Dennett thinks that resistance to determinism is encouraged by various bogeymen in the popular imagination, such as the "Nefarious Neurosurgeon," who would use brain science to control another person's actions. (© *iStockphoto.com/annedde*)

ing that there is absolutely no evidence to suggest that any of these horrible agents exists. But of course if any of them did, woe on us! A closet with a ghost in it is a terrible thing, but a closet that is just like a closet with a ghost in it (except for lacking the ghost) is nothing to fear, so we arrive at what may turn out to be a useful rule of thumb: whenever you spy a bogey *man* in a philosophical example, check to see if this scary agent, who is surely fictitious, is really doing all the work.

Dennett urges us to reconsider determinism after dissociating it from these far-fetched figments of imagination. He presents an account of the instinctive behavior of wasps and asks whether our behavior could be analogous. Might we, too, be at the mercy of "brute causation"?

3. SPHEXISHNESS AND OTHER WORRIES

There are other fears fueling the free will problem that do not have personified objects. It often seems to people that if determinism were true, there would have to be something "mechanical" about our processes of deliberation that we would regret. We could not be free agents, but only *automata*, insectlike in our behavior. Consider the digger wasp, *Sphex ichneumoneus*:

When the time comes for egg laying, the wasp Sphex builds a burrow for the purpose and seeks out a cricket which she stings in such a way as to paralyze but not kill it. She drags the cricket into the burrow, lays her eggs alongside, closes the burrow, then flies away, never to return. In due course, the eggs hatch and the wasp grubs feed off the paralyzed cricket, which has not decayed, having been kept in the wasp equivalent of deep freeze. To the human mind, such an elaborately organized and seemingly purposeful routine conveys a convincing flavor of logic and thoughtfulness—until more details are examined. For example, the Wasp's routine is to bring the paralyzed cricket to the burrow, leave it on the threshold, go inside to see that all is well, emerge, and then drag the cricket in. If the cricket is moved a few inches away while the wasp is inside making her preliminary inspection, the wasp, on emerging from the burrow, will bring the cricket back to the threshold, but not inside, and will then repeat the preparatory procedure of entering the burrow to see that everything is all right. If again the cricket is removed a few inches while the wasp is inside, once again she will move the cricket up to the threshold and re-enter the burrow for a final check. The wasp never thinks of pulling the cricket straight in. On one occasion this procedure was repeated forty times, always with the same result.[13]

- What does "hard determinism" mean, as opposed to "determinism" without this modifier? Why is hard determinism incompatible with the possibility of human freedom?
- What are the implications of giving up the determinists' premise that every event has a sufficient natural cause? Would abandoning this claim solve the problem of freedom?
- Does the determinist thesis necessarily entail that our actions are compelled? How might we say that our acts are still free, even if they are determined?
- Can you think of an instance in which one of Dennett's "bogeymen" is involved in an argument about human freedom (in the popular press, on television, in politics)?

2. Determinism versus Indeterminism

Should we accept the determinist's premise? Without it, determinism cannot get to first base. Well, we have already seen the arguments traditionally advanced in earlier chapters, even by philosophers who are not themselves hard determinists. The most general argument in favor of determinism is that only by assuming from the outset that every event has its (sufficient natural) cause(s) can we ever understand anything. Otherwise, we should have auto mechanics always giving us back our cars (with their bills) and making the unhelpful statement that "there's no cause for your troubles." We could expect the same from doctors whenever a diagnosis gave them the least bit of trouble, and we would use it ourselves every time a problem began to get difficult.

A much stronger argument was made by Kant, who said that the basic rule of determinism, the principle of universal causation, is one of the rules by which we must interpret every experience. Even Hume, who denied that this principle can be justified either through reason or through experience, insisted that it is a "natural habit" or custom that is indispensable to us and that we could not give up even if we wanted to. The consensus, then, has been that the principle itself is inescapable. And Leibniz, who rejected the idea of causation altogether, insisted on his "Principle of Sufficient Reason," which came to the similar conclusion that "every event has its sufficient reason."

The agreement of so many philosophers indicates the strength of the hard determinist position. Without the assumption that "every event has its sufficient natural cause(s)," human knowledge would seem to be without one of its most vital presuppositions. Not only scientific research, but even our most ordinary, everyday beliefs would be forced to an intolerable skeptical standstill. Our every experience would be unintelligible, and our universe would appear to be nothing but a disconnected stream of incoherent happenings from which nothing could be **predicted** and nothing understood. So the answer to the question, "Why should we accept the determinist's premise?" seems to be, "We cannot give it up; how could we possibly do without it?" For no matter how it is rephrased or philosophically altered (for example, by Leibniz, who eliminated the concept of "cause" from it), the assumption that every event in the universe, including our own actions, can be explained and understood if only one knows enough about it and its antecedent conditions is a presupposition of all human thinking that we cannot imagine doing without.

---

[13] D. Wooldridge, *The Machinery of the Brain*, New York: McGraw-Hill, 1963, p. 82.

Even if the hard determinist's premise seems undeniable, it is not yet clear how we are to understand that premise. The older determinists of the Newtonian period (La Place, d'Holbach) understood the idea of a cause as a literal push or compulsion, as if one were given a shove down the stairs. On this model, our actions are no different, except in complexity, from the "actions" of billiard balls on a felt-covered table, the motion of each wholly determining the motion of the next. The exact movements of every ball, of course, are not always evident. In the opening break, for example, even the most expert player cannot predict with accuracy where each ball will go. But we can be sure that each one is absolutely determined by the movements of the other balls that make contact with it, just as with the simple predictable case of a single ball hitting another straight on.

If we view human beings as nothing more than physical bodies—bones, muscles, nerve cells, and the like—then this mechanical billiard ball model may make some sense. But a much weaker interpretation of the hard determinist premise does not require us so radically to reduce people to mere bodies. Instead of talking about actual physical pushes and compulsions, we can interpret the determinist premise in the following way: To say that every event has its cause(s) is to say that if certain antecedent conditions are satisfied, then we can predict that such and such will occur. On the stronger mechanistic determinist interpretation, causes are actual pushes and, with such an interpretation, the notion of freedom is clearly impossible. But the weaker interpretation of determinism as predictability may yet offer room for us to talk about freedom of action. For example, we may be able to predict our friend's decision, but that does not seem to mean that he was forced to make it. We may be able to predict his action, but only because, knowing him, we know what he will probably do. On the second interpretation, perhaps we can have determinism and freedom.

Many philosophers defend determinism only as predictability on the basis of probability. We may easily be wrong. To say that every event is determined, in this view, means only that it is predictable if we know enough about antecedent conditions. But it has been objected, against the determinist, that the fact of such predictability is not sufficient to defend determinism in anything like the "hard" sense. It is one thing to say that all events, including human actions, are actually caused or compelled by physical forces. It is something quite different to say that all events, including human actions, are predictable. Events may be predictable, for example, only on the basis of certain statistical probabilities. "Most people in this circumstance would do that." "The odds are for it," in other words. Or, in the case of human actions, the predictability may still be due to human choices; we can predict each other's actions because we know how we would probably choose in the same circumstances. But there is no need here to talk about "causes" or compulsions. Nor, it has been argued, should we even talk any longer about "determinism," if this is all that we mean.

In contrast, the antideterminist thesis, called **indeterminism**, rejects both versions of determinism. Indeterminism claims that not every event has its sufficient natural cause(s). This theory at least appears to leave room for **free will**, for as soon as we allow that there are some events that are uncaused, human actions may be among them. Thus it would seem that we can be held properly responsible for our actions. But is the indeterminist thesis plausible?

The indeterminist argument has recently received a boost from physics, the very science that gave rise to the determinist threat in the first place. It was Newtonian physics that gave determinism its strongest claims. Remember La Place boasting that if he knew the location and motion of every particle in the universe, he could predict every future state of the universe at any time. But it has been shown in recent physics that such knowledge is impossible. One of the most important discoveries of modern physics is the **Heisenberg uncertainty principle** (named after its discoverer, Werner Heisenberg), which says that we cannot know both the location and the momentum of a subatomic particle. In coming to know the one, we make it impossible for us to know the other at the same time.

From this principle, the British physicist-philosopher Sir Arthur Eddington advanced the indeterminist argument that determinism is false on physical grounds. Not every event in the universe is predictable. Furthermore, many scientists now agree, on the basis of such considerations, that the concept of "cause" does not apply to certain subatomic particles either. The determinist premise that "every event in the universe has its sufficient natural cause" is false. Some events, namely, those involving some subatomic particles, are not caused, not predictable, and therefore not determined, on any interpretation. But if not all events are determined, then perhaps human actions are not determined but free; if they are predictable, it is not because they are caused.

The object of indeterminism is to deny the determinist position in order to make room for human freedom. But there are, unfortunately, two serious objections to this indeterminist argument. First, even if we suppose that the conclusions of modern physical ("quantum") theory are correct (a matter still in dispute among physicists), it is clear that determinism is of importance to us primarily as a theory of macroscopic bodies (that is, objects of visible size—people, trees, cars), not subatomic particles. No one has ever concluded that quantum theory and modern physics actually refute Newton's theories. Rather, quantum theory supplements them, puts them in their place, and qualifies them in ways that would have been unthinkable in the eighteenth century. But as for the determinism of the gravitation of the planets or the rolling of a ball down an inclined plane, the spectacular discoveries of modern particle physics do not affect them in the least.

Werner Heisenberg
(1901-1976)

A German physicist who revolutionized the field of quantum mechanics.

FIG. 6.10 German physicist Werner Heisenberg provided support for the opponents of determinism by establishing that we cannot know both the momentum and the position of a subatomic particle and that therefore we cannot make accurate predictions of its behavior. (© *Estate of Fred Stein / Art Resource, NY / Artists Rights Society (ARS), New York*)

Physical determinism with regard to our own bodies, also remains as before. It may be true that it is impossible to predict what a subatomic particle in our bodies may do. But it does not follow that it is impossible to predict what our bodies will do. Falling out of a plane, we still fall at exactly the same speed as a sack of potatoes, which is all that determinists need to continue their attack on our concept of freedom.

Second, even if there should be subatomic indeterminism, indeterminism is not the same as freedom. Suppose there should be a "gap" in the causal determination of our decisions by the various neurological processes of our brains; that would mean, at most, that what we do is not determined at all—or is determined only randomly. Suppose all of a sudden your legs started moving and you found yourself kicking a fire hydrant; surely, this is not what we mean by a "free action." Freedom means, at least, that we are free to choose what we shall do and that our decisions are effective. Indeterminism robs us of our freedom, therefore, just as much as determinism. And the argument against determinism, in any case, is not yet sufficiently persuasive to allow the indeterminists their conclusions. Here, presenting this argument, is philosopher **Robert Kane**.

On Indeterminism
BY **Robert Kane**[14]

Yet such thoughts only lead to a further problem that has haunted free will debates for centuries: if this deeper freedom is not compatible with determinism, it does not seem to be compatible with *indeterminism* either. An event which is undermined might occur or might not occur, given the entire past. (A determined event *must* occur, given the entire past.) Thus, whether or not an undetermined event actually occurs, given its past, is a matter of chance. But chance events occur spontaneously and are not under the control of anything, hence not under the control of agents. How then could they be free actions? If, for example, a choice occurred by virtue of a quantum jump or other undetermined event in one's brain, it would seem a fluke or accident rather than a responsible choice.

Undetermined events in the brain or body it seems would inhibit or interfere with our freedom, occurring spontaneously and not under our control. They would turn out to be a nuisance—or perhaps a curse, like epilepsy—rather than an enhancement of our freedom.

Or look at the problem in another way that goes a little deeper. If my choice is really undetermined, that means I could have made a different choice *given exactly the same past* right up to the moment when I did choose. That is what indeterminism and the denial of determinism mean: exactly the same past, different outcomes. Imagine, for example, that I had been deliberating about where to spend my vacation, in Hawaii or Colorado, and after much thought and deliberation had decided I preferred Hawaii and chose it. If the choice

Robert Kane (1938-)

A professor of philosophy at the University of Texas at Austin. He is the author of *Through the Moral Maze*, *The Importance of Free Will*, and other books and many articles.

FIG. 6.11 Philosopher Robert Kane *(Used by permission of Robert Kane)*

was undetermined, then exactly the same deliberation, the same thought processes, the same beliefs, desires and other motives—not a sliver of difference—that led up to my favoring and choosing Hawaii over Colorado, might by chance have issued in my choosing Colorado instead. That is very strange. If such a thing happened it would seem a fluke or accident, like that quantum jump in the brain just mentioned, not a rational choice. Since I had come to favor Hawaii and was about to choose it, when by chance I chose Colorado, I would wonder what went wrong and perhaps consult a neurologist. For reasons such as these, people have argued that undetermined free choices would be "arbitrary," "capricious," "random," "irrational," "uncontrolled," and "inexplicable," not really free and responsible choices at all. If free will is not compatible with determinism, it does not seem to be compatible with indeterminism either.

- What implications do recent developments in physics (the Heisenberg uncertainty principle, quantum mechanics) have for the determinist thesis?
- What are the objections to indeterminism? Is indeterminism compatible with freedom?

---

[14] Courtesy of Robert Kane.

3. The Role of Consciousness

Hard determinism is true of us as physical bodies. But, you may insist, we are not just physical bodies, we are also conscious. We can make decisions. We have wills of our own. The problem of freedom is often called "the free will problem." But we shall not use this terminology here.

The question of whether we are free or not is intimately joined to the question of who "we" are, as was discussed in Chapter 5. Are we the meeting place of a body *and* a mind, or is our consciousness "just" brain processes? Whatever we are besides physical bodies, our physical bodies are still subject to all the laws of Newtonian physics. You can see the problem. If our bodies are just cogs in the universe, what does it matter whether we are conscious or not? If you fall out of an airplane, you fall and accelerate at exactly the same rate as a sack of potatoes. The fact that you, unlike the potatoes, are aware of your falling, scared out of your mind, and wishing or praying like crazy that some miracle will save you makes not a bit of difference. But perhaps this is so with all our actions as well. Our bodies are composed of bits of matter, various molecules undergoing chemical interactions and acted upon by the various laws of physics. No one can deny that they are subject to all the laws of physical nature. But once all the parts are determined in their various movements and activities, what is left for consciousness to do?

Suppose one insists that consciousness, unlike our physical bodies, is not part of the scheme of determinism. Consciousness, unlike our bodies, is free—free to make decisions, free to choose what to do. But if our bodies are determined in their movements, then what can consciousness do even if it is "free"? Whatever consciousness decides, it cannot have any possible effect on the movements of our bodies; in other words, it cannot affect our actions. Our "decisions," then, would be mere vanities, like fancy switches on a machine that do not do anything at all. Consciousness, in this view, is nothing but a sideshow, for whatever it "decides," what we will do and what will happen are already determined by other antecedent conditions that have nothing to do with the "decision." In crude form, this was Spinoza's ethical position, as well as that of some of the early **Stoic** philosophers. Everything is determined by the laws of nature; it is absurd to fight against nature. All we can do is to accept the necessity of whatever happens and recognize our consciousness and our apparent freedom as a luxurious vanity. Every human action has its sufficient natural causes apart from consciousness, so consciousness can make no difference whatsoever.

Most hard determinists, however, would probably not agree with the idea that any event, even a nonphysical event such as an act of consciousness, could be "outside" the determinism of nature. Most hard determinists would argue that our thoughts and feelings, even our decisions, are caused by the states of our brains and nervous systems. Our "decisions" are nothing but the conscious effects of complex causal antecedents—most of which we still do not understand—but are definitely part of the deterministic scheme of things. How consciousness enters this deterministic scheme is open to all the questions that we asked in the previous chapter—whether, for example, there can be causal connections between consciousness and our bodies, whether consciousness is merely an "epiphenomenon" of our brain states or identical to them, or whether we should no longer speak of "consciousness" at all. But, however these disputes are resolved, the hard determinist will insist that consciousness cannot be an exception to determinism.

If consciousness is part of the deterministic scheme of things, could we not say that what happens in consciousness, particularly our decisions, thereby causes movements of our bodies, and therefore controls our actions? This attractive compromise faces an overwhelming problem, however. If one accepts the determinist's premise, then our decisions cannot cause our actions unless it is also true that our decisions, as part of the deterministic scheme, are caused in turn. Our decisions, therefore, are also determined, and no matter that it may seem as if we have a choice of actions, what we decide has already been determined by those antecedent conditions that determine our decision.

Suppose, for example, you are deciding whether or not to go to the movies. Whether or not you go depends upon your decision. But your decision, in turn, depends upon its causal antecedents. Now suppose that we knew enough about your upbringing and tastes, your character, and the workings of your brain that we could see that your decision—let's say to go to the movies—is nothing more than the result of all these conditions. What sense would it make, then, to say that you decided to go? Of course, it is true that you went through all the motions of "making a decision." But the outcome of that decision, even if it was the causal result of the decision, was nevertheless nothing more than the result of conditions that preceded and had nothing to do with the decision. It is as if I gave you a choice of two alternatives, only one of which was possible anyway. That is hardly a choice. Therefore, if a decision enters into our actions, it may be a decision whose outcome is already determined in advance. The hard determinist thus wins in either case. If consciousness is not part of the deterministic scheme, it can have no possible effects on our actions. If it is part of the deterministic scheme of things, then it cannot be free. In either case, hard determinism is undeniable, and freedom turns out to be an illusion.

- How does the problem of mind-body dualism affect or complicate the issue of freedom and determinism?
- Do you think that consciousness is part of the deterministic scheme of things? Can you think of any alternative possibilities?

4. Soft Determinism

The philosophers of the Newtonian tradition, those hard determinists who believe that determinism precludes the possibility of freedom of choice and action, have always had a powerful and simple argument on their side. But because of the urgency of our demand that we hold ourselves and each other responsible for our actions, most philosophers have not accepted hard determinism, even though they have accepted the determinist argument. Accordingly, many philosophers have espoused what has been called **soft determinism**. (The name was coined by William James.) Soft determinists, unlike the uncompromising hard determinists, believe that human freedom and determinism are compatible positions. On the one hand, they accept the determinist's argument, but, on the other, they refuse to give up the all-important demand for human freedom and responsibility. (Accordingly, they are often called *compatibilists*, and their position, **compatibilism**.)

The key to the soft determinist position is that an action or a decision, although fully determined, is free if it "flows from the agent's character." **John Stuart Mill**, for example, defends such a position in the following way:

On Causation and Necessity
BY **John Stuart Mill**[15]

The question, whether the law of causality appears in the same strict sense to human actions as to other phenomena, is the celebrated controversy concerning the freedom of the will; which, from at least as far back as the time of Pelagius, has divided both the philosophical and the religious world. The affirmative opinion is commonly called the doctrine of Necessity, as asserting human volitions and actions to be *necessary* and inevitable. The negative maintains that the will is not determined, like other phenomena, by antecedents, but determines itself; that our volitions are not, properly speaking, the effects of causes, or at least no causes which they uniformly and implicitly obey.

I have already made it sufficiently apparent that the former of these opinions is that which I consider the true one; but the misleading terms in which it is often expressed, and in the indistinct manner in which it is usually apprehended, have both obstructed its reception, and perverted its influence when received. The metaphysical theory of free-will, as held by philosophers (for the practical feeling of it, common in a great or less degree to all mankind, is in no way inconsistent with the contrary theory), was invented because the supposed alternative of admitting human actions to be necessary was deemed inconsistent with every one's instinctive consciousness, as well as humiliating to the pride and even degrading to the moral nature of man. Nor do I deny that the doctrine, as sometimes held, is open to these imputations; for the misapprehension in which I shall be able to show that they originate, unfortunately is not confined to the opponents of the doctrine, but is participated in by many, perhaps we might say by most, of its supporters.

Correctly conceived, the doctrine called Philosophical Necessity is simply this: that, given the motives which are present to an individual's mind, and given likewise the character and disposition of the individual, the manner in which he will act might be unerringly inferred; that if we knew the person thoroughly, and knew all the inducements which are acting upon him, we could foretell his conduct with as much certainty as we can predict any physical event. This proposition I take to be a mere interpretation of universal experience, a statement in words of what every one is internally convinced of. No one who believed that he knew thoroughly the circumstances of any case, and the characters of the different persons concerned, would hesitate to foretell how all of them would act. Whatever degree of doubt he may in fact feel, arises from the uncertainty whether he really knows the circumstances, or

PUNCH, OR THE LONDON CHARIVARI.—March 30, 1867.

VOTE

MILL'S LOGIC; OR, FRANCHISE FOR FEMALES.
"PRAY CLEAR THE WAY, THERE, FOR THESE—A—PERSONS."

FIG. 6.12 Other people's ability to predict our behavior correctly does not, according to John Stuart Mill, establish that our behavior is not free. Mill was also a prominent advocate of practical freedom for women for which he is lampooned in this cartoon. *(HIP / Art Resource, NY)*

John Stuart Mill (1806-1873)

Son of James Mill, also a philosopher, and one of the documented geniuses of modern history. His intellectual feats by the age of ten would have been to the credit of most scholars at the age of sixty. Mill pushed himself so hard, however, that he suffered a nervous breakdown in 1826, at the age of twenty, and turned his attention from the "hard" sciences to poetry and political reform. He is best known for his moral and political writings, particularly *On Liberty* (1859) and *Utilitarianism* (1861). His logic and epistemology are the best to be found in the British empiricist tradition of the nineteenth century. His views on mathematics, for example, became one of those positions that every writer on the subject had either to accept or to fight forcefully.

[15] John Stuart Mill, *A System of Logic*, 8th ed., New York: Harper & Row, 1874.

the character of some one or other of the persons, with the degree of accuracy required; but by no means from thinking that if he did know these things, there could be any uncertainty what the conduct would be. Nor does this full assurance conflict in the smallest degree with what is called our feeling of freedom. We do not feel ourselves the less free, because those to whom we are intimately known are well assured how we shall will to act in a particular case. We often, on the contrary, regard the doubt what our conduct will be, as a mark of ignorance of our character, and sometimes even resent it as an imputation. The religious metaphysicians who have asserted the freedom of the will, have always maintained it to be consistent with divine foreknowledge of our actions: and if with divine, then with any other foreknowledge. We may be free, and yet another may have reason to be perfectly certain what use we shall make of our freedom. It is not, therefore, the doctrine that our volitions and actions are invariable consequents of our antecedent states of mind, that is either contradicted by our consciousness, or felt to be degrading.

But the doctrine of causation, when considered as obtaining between our volitions and their antecedents, is almost universally conceived as involving more than this. Many do not believe, and very few practically feel, that there is nothing in causation but invariable, certain, and unconditional sequence. There are few to whom mere constancy of succession appears a sufficient stringent bond of union for so peculiar a relation as that of cause and effect. Even if the reason repudiates, the imagination retains, the feeling of some more intimate connection, of some peculiar tie, or mysterious constraint exercised by the antecedent over the consequent. Now this it is which, considered as applying to the human will, conflicts with our consciousness, and revolts our feelings. We are certain that, in the case of our volitions, there is not this mysterious constraint. We know that we are not compelled, as by a magical spell, to obey any particular motive. We feel, that if we wished to prove that we have the power of resisting the motive, we could do so (that wish being, it needs scarcely be observed, a *new antecedent*); and it would be humiliating to our pride, and (what is of more importance) paralyzing to our desire of excellence, if we thought otherwise. But neither is any such mysterious compulsion now supposed, by the best philosophical authorities, to be exercised by any other cause over its effect. Those who think that causes draw their effects after them by a mystical tie, are right in believing that the relation between volitions and their antecedents is of another nature. But they should go farther, and admit that this is also true of all other effects and their antecedents. If such a tie is considered to be involved in the word Necessity, the doctrine is not true of human actions; but neither is it then true of inanimate objects. It would be more correct to say that matter is not bound by necessity, than that mind is so.

. . .

A fatalist believes, or half believes (for nobody is a consistent fatalist), not only that whatever is about to happen will be the infallible result of the causes which produce it (which is the true necessitarian doctrine), but moreover that there is no use in struggling against it; that it will happen however we may strive to prevent it. Now, a necessitarian, believing that our actions follow from our characters, and that our characters follow from our organization, our education, and our circumstances, is apt to be, with more or less of consciousness on his part, a fatalist as to his own actions, and to believe that his nature is such, or that his education and circumstances have so moulded his character, that nothing can now prevent him from feeling and acting in a particular way, or at least that no effort of his own can hinder it. In the words of the sect which in our own day has most perseveringly inculcated and most

"Given the motives which are present to an individual's mind, and given likewise the character and disposition of the individual, the manner in which he will act might be unerringly inferred."

– JOHN STUART MILL

perversely misunderstood this great doctrine, his character is formed *for* him, and not *by* him; therefore his wishing that it had been formed differently is of no use; he has no power to alter it. But this is a grand error. He has, to a certain extent, a power to alter his character. Its being, in the ultimate resort, formed for him, is not inconsistent with its being, in part formed *by* him as one of the intermediate agents. His character is formed by his circumstances (including among these his particular organization); but his own desire to mould it in a particular way, is one of those circumstances, and by no means one of the least influential. We can not, indeed, directly will to be different from what we are. But neither did those who are supposed to have formed our characters directly will that we should be what we are. Their will had no direct power except over their own actions. They made us what they did make us, by willing, not the end, but the requisite means; and we, when our habits are not too inveterate, can, by similarly willing the requisite means, make ourselves different. If they could place us under the influence of certain circumstances, we, in like manner, can place ourselves under the influence of other circumstances. We are exactly as capable of making our own character, *if we will*, as others are of making it for us.

Yes (answers the Owenite[16]), but these words, "if we will," surrender the whole point: since the will to alter our own character is given us, not by any efforts of ours, but by circumstances which we can not help, it comes to us either from external causes, or not at all. Most true: if the Owenite stops here, he is in a position from which nothing can expel him. Our character is formed by us as well as for us; but the wish which induces us to attempt to form it is formed for us; and how? Not, in general, by our organization, nor wholly by our education, but by our experience; experience of the painful consequences of the character we previously had; or by some strong feeling of admiration or aspiration, accidentally aroused. But to think that we have no power of altering our character, and to think that we shall not use our power unless we desire to use it, are very different things, and have a very different effect on the mind. A person who does not wish to alter his character, can not be the person who is supposed to feel discouraged or paralyzed by thinking himself unable to do it. The depressing effect of the fatalist doctrine can only be felt where there *is* a wish to do what that doctrine represents as impossible. It is of no consequence what we think forms our character, when we have no desire of our own about forming it; but it is of great consequence that we should not be prevented from forming such a desire by thinking the attainment impracticable, and that if we have the desire, we should know that the work is not so irrevocably done as to be incapable of being altered.

And indeed, if we examine closely, we shall find that this feeling, of our being able to modify our own character *if we wish*, is itself the feeling of moral freedom which we are conscious of. A person feels morally free who feels that his habits or

Robert Owen (1771–1858)

A Welsh social reformer and a leader in the socialist movement that was budding in his era. He denied free will, contending that people are not responsible for their actions. Rather, Owen contended, actions are guided by people's characters, which external influences had shaped. Owen defended educational and labor reform, hoping to improve the environment that played such an important role in shaping people's lives.

FIG. 6.13 Robert Owen believed that education led people to have the characters they do, so they are not ultimately responsible for actions that flow from their characters. *(HIP / Art Resource, NY)*

his temptations are not his masters, but he theirs; who, even in yielding to them, knows that he could resist; that were he desirous of altogether throwing them off, there would not be required for the purpose a stronger desire than he knows himself to be capable of feeling. It is of course necessary, to render our consciousness of freedom complete, that we should have succeeded in making our character all we have hitherto attempted to make it; for if we have wished and not attained, we have, to that extent, not power over our own character; we are not free. Or at least, we must feel that our wish, if not strong enough to alter our character, is strong enough to conquer our character when the two are brought into conflict in any particular case of conduct. And hence it is said with truth, that none but a person of confirmed virtue is completely free.

In this section, Mill glides between the harsh alternatives of hard determinism and indeterminism. He begins by accepting determinism and the idea that all human actions are "necessary and inevitable," given their causes. But he then goes on to say that these causes are themselves within human control, that we can alter the causes of events and even, by taking certain steps, alter our own characters. But this is not in the least to deny determinism; nor does it deny that we are in control and have "free will" in an important sense. Human actions, following from their various causes (including "character" or personality), are as predictable as any other events. But predictability is not incompatible with freedom, for freedom means, according to Mill, nothing other than acting in accordance with one's own character, desires, and wishes. Since these are the causes of our actions, that means that Mill can defend both determinism and freedom at the same time.

David Hume is also a soft determinist, and he, too, argues that the reconciliation of "liberty and necessity" is to be found in the fact that a person's actions "flow from one's character or disposition." In defending soft determinism, Hume contends that we cannot mean by a free action one that is uncaused, a matter of chance, for this flies in the face of our common assumption that every event must have a cause. Such a view of freedom is also incoherent: The free-will advocate wants to ensure that we can hold people responsible for their actions; but if people's actions were merely a matter of chance, over which they have no control, we surely would not hold them responsible. On the contrary, actions that we praise or blame are precisely those determined by the person's character.

Although Hume defends a soft determinist position, there is a sense in which he is not a determinist at all. Recall from Chapter 3 that Hume thinks that causality is a fiction and our penchant for seeking out causes merely a habit. Thus he can argue that just as we are never rationally justified in claiming that a particular event has a cause, so we are never fully justified in claiming that human actions have causes.

On Causation and Character
BY David Hume[17]

But to proceed in this reconciling project with regard to the question of liberty and necessity; the most contentious question of metaphysics, the most contentious science; it will not require many words to prove, that all mankind have ever agreed in the doctrine of liberty as well as in that of necessity, and that the whole dispute, in this respect also, has been hitherto merely verbal. For what is meant by liberty, when applied to voluntary actions? We cannot surely mean that actions have so little connexion with

---

[17] David Hume, *An Enquiry Concerning Human Understanding*, 2nd ed., ed. L. A. Selby-Bigge, Oxford, U.K.: Oxford University Press, 1902.

"By liberty, . . . we can only mean a power of acting or not acting according to the determinations of the will."

– DAVID HUME

motives, inclinations, and circumstances, that one does not follow with a certain degree of uniformity from the other, and that one affords no inference by which we can conclude the existence of the other. For these are plain and acknowledged matters of fact. By liberty, then, we can only mean *a power of acting or not acting according to the determinations of the will;* that is, if we choose to remain at rest, we may; if we choose to move, we also may. Now this hypothetical liberty is universally allowed to belong to everyone who is not a prisoner and in chains. Here then is no subject of dispute.

Whatever definition we may give of liberty, we should be careful to observe two requisite circumstances: *first*, that it be consistent with plain matter of fact; *secondly*, that it be consistent with itself. If we observe these circumstances and render our definition intelligible, I am persuaded that all mankind will be found of one opinion with regard to it.

It is universally allowed that nothing exists without a cause of its existence, and that chance, when strictly examined, is a mere negative word and means not any real power which has anywhere a being in nature. But it is pretended that some causes are necessary, some not necessary. Here then is the advantage of definitions. Let anyone *define* a cause without comprehending it, as part of the definition, a *necessary connexion* with its effect, and let him show distinctly the origin of the idea expressed by the definition, and I shall readily give up the whole controversy. But if the foregoing explication of the matter be received, this must be absolutely impracticable. Had not objects a regular conjunction with each other, we should never have entertained any notion of cause and effect; and this regular conjunction produces that inference of the understanding which is the only connexion that we can have any comprehension of. Whoever attempts a definition of cause exclusive of these circumstances will be obliged either to employ unintelligible terms or such as are synonymous to the term which he endeavours to define. And if the definition above mentioned be admitted, liberty, when opposed to necessity, not to constraint, is the same thing with chance, which is universally allowed to have no existence. . . . All laws being founded on rewards and punishments, it is supposed as a fundamental principle, that these motives have a regular and uniform influence on the mind, and both produce the good and prevent the evil actions. We may give to this influence what name we please; but, as it is usually conjoined with the action, it must be esteemed a *cause*, and be looked upon as an instance of that necessity, which we would here establish.

The only proper object of hatred or vengeance is a person or creature, endowed with thought and consciousness; and when any criminal or injurious actions excite that passion, it is only by their relation to the person, or connexion with him. Actions are, by their very nature, temporary and perishing; and where they proceed not from some *cause* in the character and disposition of the person who performed them, they can neither redound to his honour, if good; nor infamy, if evil. The actions themselves may be blameable; they may be contrary to all the rules of morality and religion: But the person is not answerable for them; and as they proceeded from nothing in him that is durable and constant, and leave nothing of that nature behind them, it is impossible he can, upon their account, become the object of punishment or vengeance. According to the principle, therefore,

FIG. 6.14 Rembrandt, *Self-Portrait* (1664). Much of the debate over determinism focuses on whether we are responsible for our own characters and the acts that flow from them. *(Scala / Art Resource, NY)*

which denies necessity, and consequently causes, a man is as pure and untainted, after having committed the most horrid crime, as at the first moment of his birth, nor is his character anywise concerned in his actions, since they are not derived from it, and the wickedness of the one can never be used as a proof of the depravity of the other.

Men are not blamed for such actions as they perform ignorantly and casually, whatever may be the consequences. Why? but because the principles of these actions are only momentary, and terminate in them alone. Men are less blamed for such actions as they perform hastily and unpremeditatedly than for such as proceed from deliberation. For what reason? but because a hasty temper, though a constant cause or principle in the mind, operates only by intervals, and infects not the whole character. Again, repentance wipes off every crime, if attended with a reformation of life and manners. How is this to be accounted for? but by asserting that actions render a person criminal merely as they are proofs of criminal principles in the mind; and when, by an alteration of these principles, they cease to be just proofs, they likewise cease to be criminal. But, except upon the doctrine of necessity, they never were just proofs, and consequently never were criminal.

It will be equally easy to prove, and from the same arguments, that *liberty*, according to that definition above mentioned, in which all men agree, is also essential to morality, and that no human actions, where it is wanting, are susceptible of any moral qualities, or can be the objects either of approbation or dislike. For as actions are objects of our moral sentiment, so far only as they are indications of the internal character, passions, and affections; it is impossible that they can give rise either to praise or blame, where they proceed not from these principles, but are derived altogether from external violence.

In other words, Hume too suggests that not only is freedom of choice and action possible within the framework of determinism, but determinism is even necessary if we are to make sense out of the notion of freedom of choice and responsibility. His language is convoluted, but his point is plain: We can make sense of the notion of voluntary action only because there is a uniform ("necessary") connection between our motives, inclinations, circumstances, and characters and what we do. But "soft determinism" raises the same old questions yet again. Can we be said to be responsible even for those acts that are caused by our character? Can we choose our character, as Mill suggests? Could we have done other than what we did, even if we had wanted to? Consider the following argument from Robert Kane.

On "Wiggle Room"
BY Robert Kane[18]

Frequently in everyday life we act from our existing motives without having to think or deliberate about what to do. At such times, we may very well be determined by our existing characters and motives. Yet we may also be acting "of our own free wills" to the extent that we formed our present characters and motives (our wills) by earlier choices or actions that were not themselves determined. Let us call these earlier choices or actions "self-forming" choices or actions.

Now I believe that such undetermined self-forming choices or actions occur at those difficult times of life when we are torn between competing visions of what we should do or become; and they are more frequent than we think. Perhaps we are

18 Courtesy of Robert Kane.

torn between doing the moral thing or acting from ambition, or between powerful present desires and long term goals, or we are faced with difficult tasks for which we have aversions. In all such cases, we are faced with competing motivations and have to make an effort to overcome temptation to do something else we also strongly want. There is tension and uncertainty in our minds about what to do at such times that, I suggest, is reflected in appropriate regions of our brains by movement away from thermodynamic equilibrium—in short, a kind of stirring up of chaos in the brain that makes it sensitive to micro-indeterminacies at the neuronal level. The uncertainty and inner tension we feel at such soul-searching moments of self-formation *would* thus be reflected in the indeterminacy of our neural processes themselves. What is experienced personally as uncertainty would correspond physically to the opening of a window of opportunity that temporarily screens off complete determination by influences of the past. (By contrast, when we act from predominant motives or settled dispositions, the uncertainty or indeterminacy is muted. If it did play a role in such cases, it would be a mere nuisance or fluke.)

When we do decide under such conditions of uncertainty, the outcome is not determined because of the preceding indeterminacy—and yet it can be willed (and hence rational and voluntary) either way owing to the fact that in such self-formation, the agents' prior wills are divided by conflicting motives. Consider a businesswoman who faces a conflict of this kind. She is on the way to a business meeting important to her career when she observes an assault taking place in an alley. An inner struggle ensues between her moral conscience, to stop and call for help, and her career ambitions which tell her she cannot miss this meeting. She has to make an effort of will to overcome the temptation to go on to her meeting. If she overcomes this temptation, it will be the result of her effort, but if she fails, it will be because she did not *allow* her effort to succeed. And this is due to the fact that, while she wanted to overcome temptation, she also wanted to fail, for quite different and incommensurable reasons. When we, like the businesswoman, decide in such circumstances, and the indeterminate efforts we are making become determinate choices, we *make* one set of competing reasons or motives prevail over the others at that moment *by deciding*.

How do we "make" a set of competing reasons or motives prevail? One classic response to this question was introduced by Princeton philosopher **Harry Frankfurt** about forty years ago, when he redefined the concept of free will in his essay "Freedom of the Will and the Concept of a Person."

FROM "Freedom of the Will and the Concept of a Person" BY **Harry Frankfurt**[19]

It is my view that one essential difference between persons and other creatures is to be found in the structure of a person's will. Human beings are not alone in having desires and motives, or in making choices. They share these things with the members of certain other species, some of whom even appear to engage in deliberation and to make decisions based upon prior thought. It seems to be peculiarly characteristic of humans, however, that they are able to form what I shall call "second-order desires" or "desires of the second order."

[19] Harry Frankfurt, "Freedom of the Will and the Concept of a Person," in *Journal of Philosophy* 68, no. 1 (January 14, 1971): 5-20.

Besides wanting and choosing and being moved *to do* this or that, men may also want to have (or not to have) certain desires and motives. They are capable of wanting to be different, in their preferences and purposes, from what they are. Many animals appear to have the capacity for what I shall call "first-order desires" or "desires of the first order," which are simply desires to do or not to do one thing or another. No animal other than man, however, appears to have the capacity for reflective self-evaluation that is manifested in the formation of second-order desires.

Harry Frankfurt (1929–)
An American moral philosopher, currently teaching at Princeton University.

FIG. 6.15 Philosopher Harry Frankfurt *(Used by permission of Harry Frankfurt)*

. . .

Someone has a desire of the second order either when he wants simply to have a certain desire or when he wants a certain desire to be his will. In situations of the latter kind, I shall call his second-order desires "second-order volitions" or "volitions of the second order." Now it is having second-order volitions, and not having second-order desires generally, that I regard as essential to being a person. It is logically possible, however unlikely, that there should be an agent with second-order desires but with no volitions of the second order. Such a creature, in my view, would not be a person. I shall use the term "wanton" to refer to agents who have first-order desires but who are not persons because, whether or not they have desires of the second order, they have no second-order volitions.

The essential characteristic of a wanton is that he does not care about his will. His desires move him to do certain things, without its being true of him either that he wants to be moved by those desires or that he prefers to be moved by other desires. The class of wantons includes all nonhuman animals that have desires and all very young children. Perhaps it also includes some adult human beings as well. In any case, adult humans may be more or less wanton; they may act wantonly, in response to first-order desires concerning which they have no volitions of the second order, more or less frequently.

The fact that a wanton has no second-order volitions does not mean that each of his first-order desires is translated heedlessly and at once into action. He may have no opportunity to act in accordance with some of his desires. Moreover, the translation of his desires into action may be delayed or precluded either by conflicting desires of the first order or by the intervention of deliberation. For a wanton may possess and employ rational faculties of a high order. Nothing in the concept of a wanton implies that he cannot reason or that he cannot deliberate concerning how to do what he wants to do. What distinguishes the rational wanton from other rational agents is that he is not concerned with the desirability of his desires themselves. He ignores the question of what his will is to be. Not only does he pursue whatever course of action he is most strongly inclined to pursue, but he does not care which of his inclinations is the strongest.

Thus a rational creature, who reflects upon the suitability to his desires of one course of action or another, may nonetheless be a wanton. In maintaining that the essence of being a person lies not in reason but in will, I am far from suggesting that a creature without reason may be a person. For it is only in virtue of his rational capacities that a person is capable of becoming critically aware of his own will and of forming volitions of the second order. The structure of a person's will presupposes, accordingly, that he is a rational being.

The distinction between a person and a wanton may be illustrated by the difference between two narcotics addicts. Let us suppose that the physiological condition accounting for the addiction is the same in both men, and that both succumb inevitably to their periodic desires for the drug to which they are addicted. One of the addicts hates his addiction and always struggles desperately, although to no avail, against its thrust. He tries everything that he thinks might enable him to overcome his desires for the drug. But these desires are too powerful for him to withstand, and invariably, in the end, they conquer him. He is an unwilling addict, helplessly violated by his own desires.

The unwilling addict has conflicting first-order desires: he wants to take the drug, and he also wants to refrain from taking it. In addition to these first-order desires, however, he has a volition of the second order. He is not a neutral with regard to the conflict between his desire to take the drug and his desire to refrain from taking it. It is the latter desire, and not the former, that he wants to constitute his will; it is the latter desire, rather than the former, that he wants to be effective and to provide the purpose that he will seek to realize in what he actually does.

The other addict is a wanton. His actions reflect the economy of his first-order desires, without his being concerned whether the desires that move him to act are desires by which he wants to be moved to act. If he encounters problems in obtaining the drug or in administering it to himself, his responses to his urges to take it may involve deliberation. But it never occurs to him to consider whether he wants the relations among his desires to result in his having the will he has. The wanton addict may be an animal, and thus incapable of being concerned about his will. In any event he is, in respect of his wanton lack of concern, no different from an animal.

The second of these addicts may suffer a first-order conflict similar to the first-order conflict suffered by the first. Whether he is human or not, the wanton may (perhaps due to conditioning) both want to take the drug and want to refrain from taking it. Unlike the unwilling addict, however, he does not prefer that one of his conflicting desires should be paramount over the other; he does not prefer that one first-order desire rather than the other should constitute his will. It would be misleading to say that he is neutral as to the conflict between his desires, since this would suggest that he regards them as equally acceptable. Since he has no identity apart from his first-order desires, it is true neither that he prefers one to the other nor that he prefers not to take sides.

It makes a difference to the unwilling addict, who is a person, which of his conflicting first-order desires wins out. Both desires are his, to be sure; and whether he finally takes the drug or finally succeeds in refraining from taking it, he acts to satisfy what is in a literal sense his own desire. In either case he does something he himself wants to do, and he does it not because of some external influence whose aim happens to coincide with his own but because of his desire to do it. The unwilling addict identifies himself, however, through the formation of a second-order volition, with one rather than with the other of his conflicting first-order desires. He makes one of them more truly his own and, in so doing, he withdraws himself from the other. It is in virtue of this identification and withdrawal, accomplished through the formation of a second-order volition, that the unwilling addict may meaningfully make the analytically puzzling statements that the force moving him to take the drug is a force other than his own, and that it is not of his own free will but rather against his will that this force moves him to take it.

. . .

There is a very close relationship between the capacity for forming second-order volitions and another capacity that is essential to persons—one that has often been considered a distinguishing mark of the human condition. It is only because a person has volitions of the second order that he is capable both of enjoying and of lacking freedom of the will. The concept of a person is not only, then, the concept of a type of entity that has both first-order desires and volitions of the second order. It can also be construed as the concept of a type of entity for whom the freedom of its will may be a problem. This concept excludes all wantons, both infrahuman and human, since they fail to satisfy an essential condition for the enjoyment of freedom of the will. And it excludes those suprahuman beings, if any, whose wills are necessarily free.

Just what kind of freedom is the freedom of the will?

. . .

According to one familiar philosophical tradition, being free is fundamentally a matter of doing what one wants to do. Now the notion of an agent who does what he wants to do is by no means an altogether clear one: both the doing and the wanting, and the appropriate relation between them as well, require elucidation. But although its focus needs to be sharpened and its formulation refined, I believe that this notion does capture at least part of what is implicit in the idea of an agent who *acts* freely. It misses entirely, however, the peculiar content of the quite different idea of an agent whose *will* is free.

A particularly interesting example of first- versus second-order desires is presented in Albert Camus's widely read novel *The Stranger*. The central character ("antihero") Meursault displays a "strange" disconnect between first-order desires and the second-order desires through which most of us regulate (or try to regulate) our lives. It is not as if, as it is so often argued, Meursault is a man without feelings. What makes Meursault so strange is the absence of second-order desires, despite his having quite strong impulses and first-order desires throughout the book. But it is not as if he is some sort of automaton and devoid of self-awareness. The contemporary philosopher **David Zimmerman** spells out the oddity this way:

> It is a different story with Camus's Meursault. Wantons need not be (virtually) blank slates. In fact, one of the truly unnerving things about Meursault is that he is at one-and-the-same-time extraordinarily observant about his environment (he is, after all, the first-person narrator of the novel), but also completely indifferent to anything but the purely sensuous

Albert Camus (1913–1960)

A philosopher, novelist, playwright, and journalist. He won the Nobel Prize for literature in 1957. Perhaps his most famous work was his first novel, *The Stranger*.

FIG. 6.16 Albert Camus's novel *The Stranger* features a character who is deficient in the ability to make judgments about his first-order desires. He is, in Harry Frankfurt's term, a wanton. *(Adoc-photos / Art Resource, NY)*

David Zimmerman (1942–)

Am American philosopher who is a professor of philosophy at Simon Fraser University. He has written extensively on ethics and the free will/determinism issue.

and very occasionally sensual aspects of it. He is not a pure spectator, because he does have many first-order desires: to swim in the warm sea, to drink wine to the point of muzziness, to kiss Marie. Meursault is also much affected by his physical surroundings: the waxing of the sun frequently makes him drowsy; he is finely attuned to the shifts and changes of light playing across the Algerian landscape. (The sun is, in fact, a major character in the novel, arguably more responsible for the pivotal murder than Meursault himself. But more of that later.)

Meursault also manages to register things that go on in the social environment. It would be too much to say that he is actually sensitive to what people say and think and feel. However, he does take note of these things, sometimes even to the point of avowing that he can see someone else's point of view. But seeing never triggers real sympathy. He closely observes the people around him—the mourners at his mother's funeral, the old man and his scrofulous dog, the pimp Raymond, Marie—but they do not touch his feelings, not in the way the sun, the sea, the air touch his sensations. Meursault may well be a kind of psychopath or sociopath, but he lacks one crucial characteristic of this pathology, viz. any urge for self-interested calculation, a lack which in the end is his undoing.

A baffling case, then, a man with acute cognitive faculties of awareness and even self-awareness, with a range of first-order desires, with the capacity to entertain higher-order beliefs about his own first-order beliefs and desires, as well as about other people's beliefs, desires, emotions, with the capacity to feel even the occasional self-referential emotion like embarrassment, but with no other-directed emotions and certainly no higher-order desires much less volitions. If not an existentialist hero, then a cognitively and conceptually sophisticated wanton.[20]

- "Compatibilists" hold that freedom and determinism are compatible. Do you think that they are? (Just because you are unwilling to give up either one of them does not mean that they are compatible.)
- Have you ever been a "wanton," in Frankfurt's terms? If so, describe your experience.
- What is an example of a second-order desire regarding a first-order desire?
- One "commonsense" objection to determinism is that it conflicts with our experience of freedom. How does Mill address this objection? How does he distinguish between different ideas of causation?
- Hume suggests that determinism is necessary for us to make sense of action and responsibility. Is acting from character sufficient for freedom?

D. Compulsion and Ignorance

The basis of compatibilism or soft determinism is that we somehow carve a space within determinism for those actions that we insist on calling "free" and for which we hold ourselves and other people responsible. But this means that "free actions" must also be actions that are determined by antecedent conditions and causes. Free as well as unfree acts (like falling

---

20 David Zimmerman, *Doing and Time: Autonomous Agency in the Natural Order.* Reprinted with the permission of the author.

down the stairs) are caused, according to the determinist argument. The distinction, therefore, as we saw in both Mill and Hume, depends upon whether the determining factors are within or "outside" the agent. If they are outside the person, we say that the act was not free but *compelled* or "done under **compulsion**." This distinction, of course, has important moral implications. We often say of a person who is *not morally responsible* for an action that he or she is *not free not* to do it. This distinction is not a new one. Aristotle, for example, many centuries ago defined a voluntary action as one that was (1) not done under compulsion and (2) not done from ignorance.

On Voluntary Action
BY Aristotle [21]

It is only voluntary feelings and actions for which praise and blame are given; those that are involuntary are condoned, and sometimes even pitied. Hence it seems to be necessary for the student of ethics to define the difference between the Voluntary and the Involuntary; and this will also be of service to the legislator in assigning rewards and punishments.

It is then generally held that actions are involuntary when done (a) under compulsion or (b) through ignorance, and that (a) an act is compulsory when its origin is from without, being of such a nature that the agent, or person compelled, contributes nothing to it: for example, when a ship's captain is carried somewhere by stress of weather, or by people who have him in their power. But there is some doubt about actions done through fear of a worse alternative, or for some noble object—as for instance if a tyrant having a man's parents and children in his power commands him to do something base, when if he complies their lives will be spared but if he refuses they will be put to death. It is open to question whether such actions are voluntary or involuntary. A somewhat similar case is when cargo is jettisoned in a storm; apart from circumstances, no one voluntarily throws away his property, but to save his own life and that of his shipmates any sane man would do so. Acts of this kind, then, are "mixed" or composite; but they approximate rather to the voluntary class. For at the actual time when they are done they are chosen or willed; and the end or motive of an act varies with the occasion, so that the terms "voluntary" and "involuntary" should be used with reference to the time of action; now the actual deed in the cases in question is done voluntarily, for the origin of the movement of the parts of the body instrumental to the act lies in the agent; and when the origin of an action is in oneself, it is in one's own power to do it or not. Such acts therefore are voluntary, though perhaps involuntary apart from circumstances—for no one would choose to do any such action in and for itself.

. . .

What kind of actions then are to be called "compulsory"? Used without qualification, perhaps this term applies to any case where the cause of the action lies in things outside the agent, and when the agent contributes nothing. But when actions intrinsically involuntary are yet in given circumstances deliberately chosen in preference to a given alternative, and when their origin lies in the agent, these actions are to

[21] Reprinted by permission of the publishers and the Trustees of the Loeb Classical Library from *Aristotle: Minor Works, Volume XIX*, Vol. 73, trans. H. Rackham, Cambridge, MA: Harvard University Press. Copyright © 1926 by the President and Fellows of Harvard College. The Loeb Classical Library® is a registered trademark of the President and Fellows of Harvard College.

FIG. 6.17 Aristotle considered the life of contemplation the best life for human beings, in part because a contemplative life is a quintessentially free life. Rembrandt portrayed Aristotle himself as engaging in contemplation while observing a bust of Homer. *(Image copyright © The Metropolitan Museum of Art / Art Resource, NY)*

be pronounced intrinsically involuntary but voluntary in the circumstances, and in preference to the alternative. They approximate however rather to the voluntary class, since conduct consists of particular things done, and the particular things done in the cases in question are voluntary. But it is not easy to lay down rules for deciding which of two alternatives is to be chosen, for particular cases differ widely.

To apply the term "compulsory" to acts done for the sake of pleasure or for noble objects, on the plea that these exercise constraint on us from without, is to make every action compulsory. For (1) pleasure and nobility between them supply the motives of all actions whatsoever. Also (2) to act under compulsion and involuntarily is painful, but actions aiming at something pleasant or noble are pleasant. And (3) it is absurd to blame external things, instead of blaming ourselves for falling an easy prey to their attractions; or to take the credit of our noble deeds to ourselves, while putting the blame for our disgraceful ones upon the temptations of pleasure. It appears therefore that an act is compulsory when its origin is from outside, the person compelled contributing nothing to it.

Everything that is done by reason of ignorance is *not* voluntary; it is only what produces pain and repentance that is *in*voluntary. For the man who has done something owing to ignorance, and feels not the least vexation at his action, has not acted voluntarily, since he did not know what he was doing, nor yet involuntarily, since he is not pained. Of people, then, who act by reason of ignorance he who repents is thought an involuntary agent, and the man who does not repent may, since he is different, be called a not voluntary agent; for, since he differs from the other, it is better that he should have a name of his own.

Acting by reason of ignorance seems also to be different from acting *in* ignorance; for the man who is drunk or in a rage is thought to act as a result not of ignorance but of one of the causes mentioned, yet not knowingly but in ignorance.

Now every wicked man is ignorant of what he ought to do and what he ought to abstain from, and it is by reason of error of this kind that men become unjust and in general bad; but the term "involuntary" tends to be used not if a man is ignorant of what is to his advantage—for it is not mistaken purpose that causes involuntary action (it leads rather to wickedness), nor ignorance of the universal (for *that* men are *blamed*), but ignorance of particulars, i.e., of the circumstances of the action and the objects with which it is concerned. For it is on these that both pity and pardon depend, since the person who is ignorant of any of these acts involuntarily.

"Now every wicked man is ignorant of what he ought to do and what he ought to abstain from, and it is by reason of error of this kind that men become unjust and in general bad."

– ARISTOTLE

What is compulsion? According to Aristotle, an act is compulsory "when its origin is without" such that the person who acts "contributes nothing to it." Thus a person who is literally pushed into doing something is compelled rather than free. But what are we to say, for example, of the person who is neurotic, who acts compulsively or "irrationally" because of mental illness? It might once have been said that such a person was "possessed," as if something "external" (a demon or an evil spirit) had "taken over" and compelled certain actions.

This, in a sense, is what Aristotle means by "ignorance." Factors unknown to the agent influence his or her choice. But, also, what you do not know seriously does restrict your freedom. Think of college students back in 1950, whose knowledge of sex, even the most rudimentary information about pregnancy and sexual well-being, was all but nonexistent. To say that such ignorance limited their freedom would have been an understatement, to put it mildly. (At the same time, of course, those who were leery of teenage sexual activity were more than happy to restrict freedom through such ignorance.) What follows is a 2005 review of the movie, *Kinsey*, about the life of the sex researcher who lifted the veil on much of that ignorance.

FIG 6.17 A Titian, *Tarquinius and Lucrecia*. Coercion interferes with freedom to the point that a person is compelled to perform a specific action.
(Erich Lessing / Art Resource, NY)

"Sex, Ignorance, and Freedom"
BY **Judith Orr** [22]

Alfred Kinsey got into the study of human sexual behavior (after years of research into the evolution of gall wasps) when he experienced the impact of ignorance about sex first hand—both he and his wife were virgins when they married. He started a "marriage course" at Indiana University. It was a sensation. The movie shows that as word spread that his lectures were frank, informative and open, young people crammed into the lecture theatre, some pretending to be engaged, desperate for the most basic information about sex. One student tells him she thought that women gave birth through their belly button, so when Kinsey spelt out the biology of women's sexual pleasure it was a revelation to the 18 year olds in the room!

His wider research flowed from these lectures as he realized so little was known about people's sexual habits. He is portrayed as a man with a mission, embarking on a mass study with his unique method of interviewing with codes to keep the histories confidential. His staff were trained to draw people out, to use words they were comfortable with, to control their reactions to people's intimate revelations so that they were seen as non-judgmental and unshockable. These interviews filmed full face to camera are powerful

Judith Orr

A leader in the British Socialist Workers Party and editor of *Socialist Review*.

---

22 Judith Orr, "Intimate Truths." *The Socialist Review*, March 2005. Reprinted by permission.

Alfred Charles Kinsey (1894–1956)

An American biologist whose pioneering work on human sexuality had a great impact on sociology, philosophy, and many other disciplines.

FIG. 6.18 Alfred Kinsey's mission was to make people more aware of—and thus freer with respect to—the facts of sexuality through his studies of human sexual behavior. *(AP Photo / JWB)*

and give a feel of just how much Kinsey and his team were breaking new ground.

The results of the studies—they did 18,000 in the end—were explosive. Kinsey published the instantly famous statistic that 10 percent of the population were gay. He also announced that "37 percent of all men had had a homosexual experience, nearly 50 percent of women were engaged in premarital sex, 62 percent of women masturbated, 49 percent of men had had oral sex within marriage," and so it went on. In fact Kinsey wouldn't put people in "boxes" according to their sexuality. Instead his approach was revolutionary for its time—he described sexuality as a continuum with someone who was totally gay or straight on either end, with many people, including himself, falling somewhere in between.

It is hard to overestimate the impact of an analysis which denied there was such a thing as "normal" sexual behavior. Kinsey said there was only "common" or "rare" behavior. The liberating effect of the whole experience is reflected in the look and color of the movie as the black and white and gloom of the early days is gradually lightened and colored. But although many say that Kinsey laid the foundations for the sexual revolution of the 1960s, and indeed Kinsey and his team practiced a form of "free love" and sexual experimentation in their own relationships, the 1950s were still characterized by sexual repression and taboo. The establishment saw his writing as a challenge to their authority and Kinsey is shown being hauled in front of the Un-American Activities Committee, accused of Communist-inspired plots to weaken American values (but only after he refused Hoover's request to "root out homosexuals" in the State Department).

The movie gives you a real sense of the personal anguish caused by enforced ignorance about sex. The revival of campaigns encouraging abstinence in teenagers in the U.S. today is an attempt to put the clock back to such days and is being funded by the Bush administration, which has pledged $170 million this year. Today only 14 out of 50 states require that the issue of contraception be covered in schools at all, and abstinence educators can only discuss contraception in order to emphasize its limitations.

Today we talk about "compulsions" and "denial" of the facts as conditions within the person, not as "external" influences. In fact, psychologists would say that the neurotic always contributes to the neurosis as well as suffers from it, and thus, according to Aristotle's criterion, such acts are not really compelled at all, but voluntary, like the acts of a drunkard.

To take a much more difficult kind of case, what are we to say of those celebrated cases of "brain-washing" (as the Chinese did to UN prisoners of war during the Korean War) in which a person seemingly performs an action voluntarily, but only after he or she has been "conditioned" in a dramatic and sometimes brutal way? Sometimes even the person's "character" itself is changed. Should we hold a person responsible for such actions? (This question has been an issue in some war-crimes cases, for example.) Similarly, should we go against Aristotle and hold a person responsible for actions performed under great stress or as the result of a violent emotion (rage or infatuation, for example)? Should we hold a person responsible for actions performed under the influence of drugs or alcohol (assuming that we may well hold them responsible for taking the drugs or drinking in the first place)? You can see that the distinction between "free" actions and acts that are "compelled" is not nearly as clear as it first seemed. We can easily distinguish between a person who breaks into a store and a person who is pushed through the front window. But in many cases in which freedom is most in question, in cases of neurosis, brainwashing, great passion, and chemical "influences," the distinction between what is "external" to the person and what is within his or her character is not clear at all.

There are more serious problems with the notion of compulsion, however. Even if we admit that some problematic examples of actions are not clearly either "free" or "compelled" (neurosis and brainwashing, great passion and drugs), we would want to insist that at least some actions are clearly free and not compelled. For example, you write a check to the American Cancer Society just because you believe that it is an important organization and you want to make a contribution. No one solicited you, no one encouraged you to do it, and no one need know that you did it. Can even this act, so seemingly performed "of your own free will," be counted as a "free action"? The soft determinist would say that this action is "free" because it flows from your generous character. But what has gone into *making* your character? Your education and upbringing? Your social class? What about your national origin or your gender? Perhaps even your height and weight affect your choices.

Even in our "freest" acts, it can be argued that the desires and decisions, in short, our "personality" is wholly determined by forces outside us and beyond our control. Consider the following argument, for example, by Professor **John Hospers**, who uses Freud and psychoanalysis as the basis for his claim that all our acts are compelled and not free, insofar as all our acts are brought about by a set of psychological determinants over which we have no control.

FROM "What Means This Freedom?" BY John Hospers[23]

[Are we] in the final analysis, *responsible for any of our actions at all* [?] The issue may be put this way: How can anyone be responsible for his actions, since they grow out of his character, which is shaped and molded and made what it is by influences— some hereditary, but most of them stemming from early parental environment—that were not of his own making or choosing? This question, I believe, still troubles many people who would agree to all the distinctions we have just made but still have the feeling that "this isn't all." They have the uneasy suspicion that there is a more ultimate sense, a "deeper" sense, in which we are *not* responsible for our actions, since we are not responsible for the character out of which those actions spring.

. . .

Let us take as an example a criminal who, let us say, strangled several persons and is himself now condemned to die in the electric chair. Jury and public alike hold him fully responsible (at least they utter the words "he is responsible"), for the murders were planned

John Hospers (1918–2003)

A former professor of philosophy at the University of Southern California, an articulate follower of Ayn Rand, and a onetime Libertarian candidate for president of the United States.

23 John Hospers, "What Means This Freedom?" in *Determinism and Freedom in the Age of Modern Science*, ed. Sidney Hook, New York: New York University Press, 1958. Reprinted by permission of Ernest B. Hook, M.D.

down to the minutest detail, and the defendant tells the jury exactly how he planned them. But now we find out how it all came about; we learn of parents who rejected him from babyhood, of the childhood spent in one foster home after another, where it was always plain to him that he was not wanted; of the constantly frustrated early desire for affection, the hard shell of nonchalance and bitterness that he assumed to cover the painful and humiliating fact of being unwanted, and his subsequent attempts to heal those wounds to his shattered ego through defensive aggression. . . . The poor victim is not conscious of the inner forces that exact from him this ghastly toll; he battles, he schemes, he revels in pseudo-aggression, he is miserable, but he does not know what works within him to produce these catastrophic acts of crime. His aggressive actions are the wriggling of a worm on a fisherman's hook. And if this is so, it seems difficult to say any longer, "He is responsible." Rather, we shall put him behind bars for the protection of society, but we shall no longer flatter our feeling of moral superiority by calling him personally responsible for what he did.

Let us suppose it were established that a man commits murder only if sometime during the previous week, he has eaten a certain combination of foods—say, tuna fish salad at a meal also including peas, mushroom soup, and blueberry pie. What if we were to track down the factors common to all murders committed in this country during the last twenty years and found this factor present in all of them, and only in them? The example is of course empirically absurd; but may it not be that there is *some* combination of factors that regularly leads to homicide, factors such as are described in general terms in the above quotation? (Indeed the situation in the quotation is less fortunate than in our hypothetical example, for it is easy to avoid certain foods once we have been warned about them, but the situation of the infant is thrust on him; something has already happened to him once and for all, before he knows it has happened.) When such specific factors are discovered, won't they make it clear that it is foolish and pointless, as well as immoral, to hold human beings responsible for crimes? Or, if one prefers biological to psychological factors, suppose a neurologist is called in to testify at a murder trial and produces X-ray pictures of the brain of the criminal; anyone can see, he argues, that the *cella turcica* was already calcified at the age of nineteen; it should be a flexible bone, growing, enabling the gland to grow. All the defendant's disorders might have resulted from this early calcification. Now, this particular explanation may be empirically false; but who can say that no such factors, far more complex, to be sure, exist?

When we know such things as these, we no longer feel as much tempted to say that the criminal is responsible for his crime; and we tend also (do we not?) to excuse him—not legally (we still confine him to prison) but morally; we no longer call him a monster or hold him personally responsible for what he did. Moreover, we do this in general, not merely in the case of crime: "You must excuse Grandmother for being irritable; she's really quite ill and is suffering some pain all the time." Or: "The dog always bites children after she's had a litter of pups; you can't blame her for it: she's not feeling well, and besides she naturally wants to defend them." Or: "She's nervous and jumpy, but do excuse her: she has a severe glandular disturbance."

. . .

But one may still object that so far we have talked only about neurotic behavior. Isn't nonneurotic or normal or not unconsciously motivated (or whatever you want to call it) behavior still within the area of responsibility? There are reasons for answering "No" even here, for the normal person no more than neurotic one has caused his own character, which makes him what he is. Granted that neurotics are not responsible for their behavior (that part of it which we call neurotic) because it stems from undigested infantile conflicts that they had no part in bringing about, and that are external to them just as surely as if their behavior had been forced on them by a malevolent deity (which is indeed one theory on the subject); but the so-called normal person is equally the product of causes in which his volition took no part. And if, unlike the neurotic's, his behavior is changeable by rational considerations, and if he has the will power to overcome the effects of an unfortunate early environment, this again is no credit to him; he is just lucky. If energy is available to him in a form in which it can be mobilized for constructive purposes, this is no credit to him, for this too is part of his psychic legacy. Those of us who can discipline ourselves and develop habits of concentration of purpose tend to blame those who cannot, and call them lazy and weak-willed; but what we fail to see is that they literally cannot do what we expect; if their psyches were structured like ours, they could, but as they are burdened with a tyrannical super-ego (to use psychoanalytic jargon for the moment), and a weak defenseless ego whose energies are constantly consumed in fighting endless charges of the super-ego, they simply cannot do it, and it is irrational to expect it of them. We cannot with justification blame them for

FIG. 6.19 The death penalty presupposes that people are responsible for their actions, but John Hospers challenged this idea. *(AP Photo / Bill Chaplis)*

their inability, any more than we can congratulate ourselves for our ability. This lesson is hard to learn, for we constantly and naïvely assume that other people are constructed as we ourselves are.

· · ·

The position, then, is this: if we *can* overcome the effects of early environment, the ability to do so is itself a product of the early environment. We did not give ourselves this ability; and if we lack it we cannot be blamed for not having it. Sometimes, to be sure, moral exhortation brings out an ability that is there but not being used, and in this lies its *occasional* utility; but very often its use is pointless, because the ability is not there. The only thing that can overcome a desire, as Spinoza said, is a stronger contrary desire; and many times there simply is no wherewithal for producing a stronger contrary desire. Those of us who do have the wherewithal are lucky.

While Hospers's example of eating a tuna sandwich as a kind of physiological compulsion may seem exaggerated, we may more easily accept many physical factors as having a decisive influence on our character. Many have argued, for instance, that a person's sex or race is an inescapable physical factor that compels him or her to make certain decisions. Determinist arguments of this sort have been made even among members of oppressed groups who are seeking tolerance. In a well-publicized example, a lawyer defended her client against

> "If we can overcome the effects of early environment, the ability to do so is itself a product of the early environment."
>
> – JOHN HOSPERS

charges of assault by claiming that her client's actions were determined by her overwhelming case of premenstrual syndrome![24]

If we believe that most of our actions are physiologically compelled, then no matter how we try to wriggle free of total determinism, it seems as if we keep finding ourselves enmeshed back in hard determinism. We suggested that perhaps an act is free if one of its causes is a decision, but if the decision itself is caused in turn, ours is not really a decision at all. We suggested that an action is free if it "flows from a person's character," but then we saw that it can be argued that an act that "flows from a person's character" is no more within his or her control and no more his or her responsibility than any other act. We may want to say that a person's act is free if, in this case, he or she could have done otherwise, but what does this mean, given the previous arguments, except that the act would have been different if the circumstances had been different or if the person had been, in effect, another person?

For example, it is true that you could have changed the course of World War II—but *if what?* If you had been born Winston Churchill, perhaps. But that is a nonsensical "if." Does it make any more sense, however, to say that "you could have been a professional football player?" If what? If circumstances had been different? If you had been born with a different body or raised in a different environment? But isn't this to say, for each of these "ifs," that you would be (slightly but significantly) a different person than you are? It looks as if we are trapped by the tautology that each of us is whoever he or she is. It is true of the geranium that if it had been planted in better soil, it would be larger; if a ball had been dropped from a greater height, it would have landed harder; and if you were raised differently, placed in different circumstances, then you might have acted other than you did. But does this have anything to do with "freedom"? Are your actions any more free than the growth of the plant or the falling of the ball? Of course, there is a difference: You think that you have made some decision. But why should what you think change the way things are determined? You may pretend to be flying after you have fallen out of the plane. But you are still falling, and whatever you think or do does not slow you down at all.

Not everyone views determinism with horror. The eminent American psychologist **B. F. Skinner**, for example, applauds the determinist's argument as a means of controlling human behavior and changing it for the better. In his best-seller *Beyond Freedom and Dignity*, Skinner argues that we have made a fetish of freedom and that we should replace it with an acceptance of determinism. Behavioral scientists, he contends, can and should be given the power to "engineer" human behavior in accordance with an agreed-upon set of ideals (social harmony, individual happiness, and productivity).

Beyond Freedom
BY B. F. Skinner[25]

Perhaps the most crucial part of our democratic philosophy to be reconsidered is our attitude toward freedom—or its reciprocal, the control of human behavior. We do not oppose all forms of control because it is "human nature" to do so. The reaction is not characteristic of all men under all conditions of life. It is an attitude which has been carefully engineered, in large part by what we call the "literature" of democracy. With respect to some methods of control (for example,

---

[24] David Bird, "Defense Linked to Menstruation Dropped in Case," *New York Times*, November 4, 1982. Copyright © 1982 by New York Times, Inc.

[25] B. F. Skinner, "Freedom and the Control of Men," in *The American Scholar*, 1955–56. Courtesy of the B. F. Skinner Foundation.

the threat of force), very little engineering is needed, for the techniques or their immediate consequences are objectionable. Society has suppressed these methods by branding them "wrong," "illegal," or "sinful." But to encourage these attitudes toward objectionable forms of control, it has been necessary to disguise the real nature of certain indispensable techniques, the commonest examples of which are education, moral discourse, and persuasion. The actual procedures appear harmless enough. They consist of supplying information, presenting opportunities for action, pointing out logical relationships, appealing to reason or "enlightened understanding," and so on. Through a masterful piece of misrepresentation, the illusion is fostered that these procedures do not involve the control of behavior; at most, they are simply ways of "getting someone to change his mind." But analysis not only reveals the presence of well-defined behavioral processes, it demonstrates a kind of control no less inexorable, though in some ways more acceptable, than the bully's threat of force.

Ivan Pavlov (1848-1936)

A Russian physician, physiologist, and psychologist whose work on conditioning behavior had an enormous impact on psychology and philosophy. He won the Nobel Prize for medicine in 1904.

FIG. 6.20 Ivan Petrovich Pavlov (1849-1936) did famous experiments on dogs, demonstrating that they could be conditioned to salivate on cue. *(Image © rook76, 2011. Used under license from Shutterstock.com)*

Let us suppose that someone in whom we are interested is acting unwisely—he is careless in the way he deals with his friends, he drives too fast, or he holds his golf club the wrong way. We could probably help him by issuing a series of commands: don't nag, don't drive over sixty, don't hold your club that way. Much less objectionable would be "an appeal to reason." We could show him how people are affected by his treatment of them, how accident rates rise sharply at higher speeds, how a particular grip on the club alters the way the ball is struck and corrects a slice. In doing so we resort to verbal mediating devices which emphasize and support certain "contingencies of reinforcement"—that is, certain relations between behavior and its consequences—which strengthen the behavior we wish to set up. The same consequences would possibly set up the behavior without our help, and they eventually take control no matter which form of help we give. The appeal to reason has certain advantages over the authoritative command. A threat of punishment, no matter how subtle, generates emotional reactions and tendencies to escape or revolt. Perhaps the controllee merely "feels resentment" at being made to act in a given way, but even that is to be avoided. When we "appeal to reason," he "feels freer to do as he pleases." The fact is that we have exerted *less* control than in using a threat; since other conditions may contribute to the result, the effect may be delayed or, possibly in a given instance, lacking. But if we have worked a change in his behavior at all, it is because we have altered relevant environmental conditions, and the processes we have set in motion are just as real and just as inexorable, if not as comprehensive, as in the most authoritative coercion.

"Arranging an opportunity for action" is another example of disguised control. The power of the negative form has already been exposed in the analysis of censorship. Restriction of opportunity is recognized as far from harmless. As Ralph Barton Perry said in an article which appeared in the Spring, 1953, *Pacific Spectator,*

"Whoever determines what alternatives shall be made known to man controls what that man shall choose *from*. He is deprived of freedom in proportion as he is denied access to *any* ideas, or is confined to any range of ideas short of totality of relevant possibilities." But there is a positive side as well. When we present a relevant state of affairs, we increase the likelihood that a given form of behavior will be emitted. To the extent that the probability of action has changed, we have made a definite contribution. The teacher of history controls a student's behavior (or, if the reader prefers, "deprives him of freedom") just as much in *presenting* historical facts as in suppressing them. Other conditions will no doubt affect the student, but the contribution made to his behavior by the presentation of material is fixed and, within its range, irresistible.

The methods of education, moral discourse, and persuasion are acceptable not because they recognize the freedom of the individual or his right to dissent, but because they make only *partial* contributions to the control of his behavior. The freedom they recognize is freedom from a more coercive form of control. The dissent which they tolerate is the possible effect of other determiners of action. Since these sanctioned methods are frequently ineffective, we have been able to convince ourselves that they do not represent control at all. When they show too much strength to permit disguise, we give them other names and suppress them as energetically as we suppress the use of force. Education grown too powerful is rejected as propaganda or "brain-washing," while really effective persuasion is decried as "undue influence," "demagoguery," "seduction," and so on.

If we are not to rely solely upon accident for the innovations which give rise to cultural evolution, we must accept the fact that some kind of control of human behavior is inevitable. We cannot use good sense in human affairs unless someone engages in the design and construction of environmental conditions which affect the behavior of men. Environmental changes have always been the condition for the improvement of cultural patterns, and we can hardly use the more effective methods of science without making changes on a grander scale. We are all controlled by the world in which we live, and part of the world has been and will be constructed by men. The question is this: Are we to be controlled by accident, by tyrants, or by ourselves in effective cultural design?

The danger of the misuse of power is possibly greater than ever. It is not allayed by disguising the facts. We cannot make wise decisions if we continue to pretend that human behavior is not controlled, or if we refuse to engage in control when valuable results might be forthcoming. Such measures weaken only ourselves, leaving the strength of science to others. The first step in a defense against tyranny is the fullest possible exposure of controlling techniques. A second step has already been taken successfully in restricting the use of physical force. Slowly, and as yet imperfectly, we have worked out an ethical and governmental design in which the strong man is not allowed to use the power deriving from his strength to control his fellow men. He is restrained by a superior force created for that purpose—the ethical pressure of the group, or more explicit religious and governmental measures. We tend to distrust superior forces, as we currently hesitate to relinquish sovereignty in order to set up an international police force. But it is only through such counter-control that we have achieved what we call peace—a condition in which men are not permitted to control each other through force. In other words, control itself must be controlled.

"We are all controlled by the world in which we live, and part of the world has been and will be constructed by men. The question is this: Are we to be controlled by accident, by tyrants, or by ourselves in effective cultural design?"

– B. F. SKINNER

Science has turned up dangerous processes and materials before. To use the facts and techniques of a science of man to the fullest extent without making some monstrous mistake will be difficult and obviously perilous. It is no time for self-deception, emotional indulgence, or the assumption of attitudes which are no longer useful. Man is facing a difficult test. He must keep his head now, or he must start again—a long way back.

In his novel *Walden Two*, Skinner gives us a prototype for his deterministic utopia.

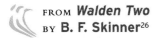

FROM *Walden Two*
BY **B. F. Skinner**[26]

"When a particular emotion is no longer a useful part of a behavioral repertoire, we proceed to eliminate it."

"Yes, but how?"

"It's simply a matter of behavioral engineering," said Frazier.

"Behavioral engineering?"

"Each of us," Frazier began, "is engaged in a pitched battle with the rest of mankind."

"A curious premise for a Utopia," said Castle. "Even a pessimist like myself takes a more hopeful view than that."

"You do, you do," said Frazier. "But let's be realistic. Each of us has interests which conflict with the interests of everybody else. That's our original sin, and it can't be helped. Now, 'everybody else' we call 'society.' It's a powerful opponent, and it always wins. Oh, here and there an individual prevails for a while and gets what he wants. Sometimes he storms the culture of a society and changes it slightly to his own advantage. But society wins in the long run, for it has the advantage of numbers and of age. Many prevail against one, and men against a baby. Society attacks early, when the individual is helpless. It enslaves him almost before he has tasted freedom. The 'ologies' will tell you how it's done. Theology calls it building a conscience or developing a spirit of selflessness. Psychology calls it the growth of the super-ego.

"Considering how long society has been at it, you'd expect a better job. But the campaigns have been badly planned and the victory has never been secure. The behavior of the individual has been shaped according to revelations of 'good conduct,' never as the result of experimental study. But why not experiment? The questions are simple enough. What's the best behavior for the individual so far as the group is concerned? And how can the individual be induced to behave in that way? Why not explore these questions in a scientific spirit?"

Philosopher Robert Kane thinks about Skinner this way:

Beyond Skinner
BY **Robert Kane**[27]

The problem is brought out in a striking way by twentieth-century utopian novels, like Aldous Huxley's *Brave New World* and B. F. Skinner's *Walden Two*. In the fictional societies described in these famous works, people can have and do what they will or choose, but only to the extent that they have been conditioned by behavioral engineers or neurochemists to will or choose what they can have and do. In *Brave New World*, the lower-echelon workers are under the influence of powerful drugs so that they do not dream of things they cannot have. They are quite content to play miniature golf all weekend. They can do what they want, though their wants are meager and controlled by drugs.

The citizens of *Walden Two* have a richer existence than the workers of *Brave New World*. Yet their desires and purposes are also covertly controlled, in this case by behavioral engineers. Walden Two-ers live collectively in a kind of rural commune; and because they share duties of farming and raising children, they have plenty of leisure. They pursue arts, sciences, crafts, engage in musical performances and enjoy what appears to be a pleasant existence. The fictional founder of Walden Two, a fellow named Frazier, forthrightly says that their pleasant existence is brought about by the fact that, in his community, persons can do whatever they want or choose because they have been behaviorally conditioned since childhood to want and choose only what they can have and do. In other words, they have maximal *surface freedom* of action and choice (they can choose or do anything they want), but they lack a *deeper freedom* of the will because their desires and purposes are created by their behavioral conditioners or controllers. Their wills are not of "their own" making. Indeed, what happens in Walden Two is their surface freedom to act and choose *as* they will is maximized by minimizing the deeper freedom to have the ultimate say in what they will.

Thus Frazier can say that Walden Two "is the freest place on earth," since he has surface freedoms in mind. For there is no *coercion* in Walden Two and no *punishment* because no one has to be forced to do anything against his or her will. The citizens can have anything they want because they have been conditioned not to want anything they cannot have. As for the deeper freedom, or free will, it does not exist in Walden Two, as Frazier himself admits. But this is no loss, according to Frazier. Echoing *Walden Two*'s author, B. F. Skinner (a foremost defender of behaviorism in psychology), Frazier thinks the deeper freedom of the will is an illusion in the first place. We do not have it anyway, inside or outside Walden Two. In our ordinary lives, he argues, we are just as much the products of upbringing and social conditioning as the citizens of Walden Two, though we may delude ourselves into thinking otherwise. In our case, the conditioners are parents, teachers, coaches, schoolmates, peers, makers of TV programs, films, videos and other creators of the cultures and societies in which we live. The difference is that, unlike Walden Two, such everyday conditioning is often haphazard, incompetent and harmful.

Why then, Skinner asks, reject the maximal surface freedom and happiness of Walden Two for a deeper freedom of the will that is something we do not and cannot have anyway? Along with many other scientists, he thinks the idea that we could be *ultimate* determiners of our own ends or purposes (which is what the deeper freedom of the will would require) is an impossible ideal that cannot fit into the modern scientific picture of the world. To have such freedom, we would have to have been

---

[27] Courtesy of Robert Kane.

the original creators of our own wills—of ourselves. But if we trace the psychological springs of action back further and further to childhood, we find that we were less free back then, not more, and more subject to conditioning. We thus delude ourselves into thinking that we have sacrificed some real (deeper) freedom for the happiness of Walden Two. Rather we have gained a maximum amount of the only kind of freedom we really can have (surface freedom), while giving up an illusion (free will).

Seductive as these arguments may be, there are many people who continue to believe that something important is missing in Walden Two and that the deeper freedom is not a mere illusion. Such persons want to be the ultimate designers of their own lives as Frazier was for the lives of Walden Two. They want to be the creators, as he was, not the pawns—at least for their own lives. What they long for is what was traditionally meant by "free will."

Not every visionary has looked upon determinism with delight. More often determinism has appeared in novels as a nightmare, as the philosophical basis of societies that are more oppressive and authoritarian than any we have ever seen. The most famous examples are George Orwell's *1984* and Aldous Huxley's *Brave New World*. In both novels, psychology and drugs are used to manipulate the inhabitants of entire societies and force them to conform to a single set of behavioral standards, concerning which they have no choice whatsoever. In a somewhat more recent novel, *A Clockwork Orange*, Anthony Burgess presents a nightmarish fantasy in which a young hoodlum named Alex is "reconditioned" to be "good" through a series of experiments in which his viewing of violent movies is accompanied by a drug that makes him violently ill. It works (after a fashion), but the prison chaplain summarizes the philosophical difficulties this treatment raises:

 FROM ***A Clockwork Orange***
BY **Anthony Burgess**[28]

"You are to be made into a good boy, 6655321. Never again will you have the desire to commit acts of violence or to offend in any way whatsoever against the State's Peace. I hope you take all that in. I hope you are absolutely clear in your own mind about that." I said:

"Oh, it will be nice to be good, sir." But I had a real horrorshow smeck at that inside, brothers. He said:

"It may not be nice to be good, little 6655321. It may be horrible to be good. And when I say that to you I realize how self-contradictory that sounds. I know I shall have many sleepless nights about this. What does God want? Does God want goodness or the choice of goodness? Is a man who chooses the bad perhaps in some way better than a man who has the good imposed upon him? Deep and hard questions, little 6655321. But all I want to say to you now is this: if at any time in the future you look back to these times and remember me, the lowest and humblest of all God's servitors, do not, I pray, think evil of me in your heart, thinking me in any way involved in what is

John Burgess Wilson (1917-1993)

An English novelist, playwright, linguist, composer, and critic. He published under the pen name Anthony Burgess.

FIG. 6.21 Alex, the main character in Stanley Kubrick's *A Clockwork Orange* (based on the novel by Anthony Burgess), is conditioned to have an aversion to classical music that he had formerly loved. *(© Bettmann/CORBIS)*

now about to happen to you. And now, talking of praying, I realize sadly that there will be little point in praying for you. You are passing now to a region where you will be beyond the reach of the power of prayer. A terrible terrible thing to consider. And yet, in a sense, in choosing to be deprived of the ability to make an ethical choice, you have in a sense really chosen the good. So I shall like to think. So, God help us all, 6655321, I shall like to think." And he began to cry.

The claims of behavioral scientists like Skinner have provoked among contemporary ethicists similar responses to those that have provoked religious determinists. The repercussions are frightening. What if, for instance, instead of associating violent movies with illness and repulsion, the scientists in *A Clockwork Orange* were to associate them with pleasure? Well, that is exactly what our society does, claims **Catharine MacKinnon**, an American feminist philosopher. MacKinnon claims that advertisers, moviemakers, pornographers, and others in the media in our society *make* men's treatment of women fundamentally violent.

On Coercion of Women's Sexuality
BY Catharine MacKinnon[29]

"Representation of the world," de Beauvoir writes, "like the world itself, is the work of men; they describe it from their own point of view, which they confuse with the absolute truth." The parallel between representation and construction should be sustained: men *create* the world from their own point of view, which then *becomes* the truth to be described. This is a closed system, not anyone's confusion. *Power to create the world from one's point of view is power in its male form.* The male epistemological

---

[29] Catharine MacKinnon, "Feminism, Marxism, Method, and the State: An Agenda for Theory," from *The Signs Reader*, ed. Elizabeth Abel and Emily K. Abel. Copyright © 1982 by The University of Chicago Press. Reprinted by permission of the publisher.

stance, which corresponds to the world it creates, is objectivity: the ostensibly noninvolved
stance, the view from a distance and from no
particular perspective, apparently transparent
to its reality. It does not comprehend its own
perspectivity, does not recognize what it sees as

Catherine MacKinnon (1946-)

An American professor of law at the University of Michigan Law School,
known particularly for her writings on philosophy of law and feminism.

subject like itself, or that the way it apprehends its world is a form of its subjugation
and presupposes it. The objectively knowable is object. Woman through male eyes is
sex object, that by which man knows himself at once as man and as subject. What
is objectively known corresponds to the world and can be verified by pointing to it
(as science does) because the world itself is controlled from the same point of view.
Combining, like any form of power, legitimation with force, male power extends
beneath the representation of reality to its construction: it makes women (as it were)
and so verifies (makes true) who women "are" in its view, simultaneously confirming
its way of being and its vision of truth. The eroticism that corresponds to this is "the
use of things to experience self." As a coerced pornography model put it, "You do it,
you do it, and you do it; then you become it." The fetish speaks feminism.

Objectification makes sexuality a material reality of women's lives, not just a psychological, attitudinal, or ideological one. It obliterates the mind/matter distinction
that such a division is premised upon. Like the value of a commodity, women's sexual
desirability is fetishized: it is made to appear a quality of the object itself, spontaneous and inherent, independent of the social relation which creates it, uncontrolled by
the force that requires it. It helps if the object cooperates: hence, the vaginal orgasm;
hence, faked orgasms altogether. Women's sexualness, like male prowess, is no less
real for being mythic. It is embodied. Commodities do have value, but only because

FIG. 6.22 Alfred Hitchcock's *Rear Window* (1954). Catharine MacKinnon argued that the media promotes
violence against women by subjecting women to sexual objectification. *(© Sunset Boulevard/Corbis)*

value is a social property arising from the totality of the same social relations which, unconscious of their determination, fetishize it. Women's bodies possess no less real desirability—or, probably, desire. Sartre exemplifies the problem on the epistemological level: "But if I desire a house, or a glass of water, or a woman's body, how could this body, this glass, this piece of property reside in my desire and how can my desire be anything but the consciousness of these objects as desirable?" Indeed. Objectivity is the methodological stance of which objectification is the social process. Sexual objectification is the primary process of the subjection of women. It unites act with word, construction with expression, perception with enforcement, myth with reality. Man [*expletive deleted*] woman; subject verb object.

Note that MacKinnon's argument, despite its opposition to the media conditioning of sexual oppression, is thoroughly determinist. She believes that our traditions and media *cause* violence and oppression. This seems like a slippery slope: If any of our actions can really be compelled through psychological conditioning, then why not all our actions? And if our actions, good or bad, are compelled, then it does not seem to make sense to hold anyone responsible for his or her actions (even the people doing the conditioning). If Skinner is right, then moral education and political activity can be reduced to the results of multiple conditions and reinforcements. If MacKinnon is right, we are all the victims of our pervasive social-sexual conditioning.

- Assess Aristotle's criteria for an involuntary action. Can you think of any modifications that should be added? How would you characterize those actions that Aristotle considers hard to classify as involuntary or voluntary (such as actions motivated by fear or extortion)?
- Do you agree with Hospers that we are no more justified in holding a "normal" person responsible for her actions than in holding a "neurotic" person responsible, given that neither is the "cause" of her character? If not, what considerations would justify discriminating between the two cases?
- Do you think that there is any moral distinction between acts that are "compelled" from "outside" the agent and those acts that are "compelled" from within the agent (when the agent's actions are determined by antecedent psychological or neurological conditions)?
- Ironically, Skinner suggests that we are enslaved by our notion of freedom and that we should engage in a form of behavior control. Do you find his proposal at all plausible?
- Are those who are dissatisfied with Skinner's vision and resist the idea that we do not possess "deeper freedom" or free will (as Kane suggests) engaging in anything more than wishful thinking, or do you think that there is something to this objection?
- Do you agree with MacKinnon that images that objectify result in violence toward women? Do you think that such images amount to a form of conditioning that limits freedom?

E. Freedom in Practice: Kant's Solution

As many of the foregoing arguments have shown, it is not enough just to answer the metaphysical question about the causes of human action. The demand for freedom and responsibility is not going to be satisfied by different variations of determinism, no matter how "soft" they pretend to be. If we are to understand the role of freedom in our daily lives, what we need is a breach in determinism, a conception of our actions, or at least our decisions, as truly free and not determined in any of the ways discussed previously.

The classic statement of this claim to freedom and responsibility is to be found in the philosophy of Immanuel Kant. (No doubt, you now appreciate how truly monumental Kant's philosophy is. We present more of him in the next chapter as well.) We have already noted that Kant gave an unqualified endorsement of determinism, arguing that the principle (of universal causation) upon which it is based is nothing less than a necessary rule of all human experience, including human actions:

> Actions of men are determined in conformity with the order of Nature, by their empirical character and other causes; if we could exhaust all the appearances, there would not be found a single human action which would not be predicted with certainty.[30]

This is surely a statement of the hardest of "hard" determinism. But Kant also appreciated, as much as any philosopher ever has, the importance of unqualified freedom for human responsibility. (He called freedom, as he had called God, a "postulate" [or presupposition] of practical reason.) But how could he defend both universal determinism and human freedom? Determinism is true of every possible event and object of human knowledge, Kant says, but it does not follow that it is also applicable to human acts of will or decisions to act. Action is a wholly different matter than knowledge. The metaphysics with which Kant defends this view is far too complicated even to summarize here. But the basic principle is simple enough: Kant says that we adopt two different standpoints toward the world, one theoretical, one practical. Insofar as we want to know something, we adopt the standpoint of science and determinism. Within that standpoint, every event, including human actions, is determined, brought about by sufficient natural causes (including the states of our brains and various psychological factors). But when we are ready to do something, we switch to the practical standpoint. The main point is this: Insofar as we are acting or deciding to act, we *must* consider our own acts of will and decisions as the sufficient causes of our actions, and we cannot continue the causal chain backward to consider whether those acts of will are themselves caused. When we act, in other words, we cannot think of ourselves except as acting freely.

Suppose that you are about to make a decision: You are finally going to give up smoking. A friend offers you a cigarette on the second day. Yes or no? Do you smoke it? Now it may very well be that given your personality, your weakness for past habits, and any number of other psychological factors, you are clearly determined to accept and thus break your resolution. Your friend, who knows you quite well, may even know this. But you cannot think of yourself in this deterministic way, for insofar as you have to make a decision, you cannot simply "find out" what you will do. In other words, you cannot simply predict your own behavior, no matter how much you know about the various causes and factors that allow your friend to predict your behavior. If you were to predict, "I'm going to start smoking again anyway," you would not be simply predicting; you would be, in that very act, breaking your resolution, that is, deciding to break it. So, when your own acts and decisions are concerned, you have to act as if you were totally free. This, in a way, denies determinism. It says that since you are the one who has to make the decision, determinism is not relevant. (Kant says, "and to have to think yourself free is to *be* free.")

Kant defends both freedom and determinism, and so he undermines the distinction that philosophers had drawn between them. Kant implies that a careful reconsideration of human

---

30 Immanuel Kant, *The Critique of Pure Reason*, trans. Norman Kemp Smith, New York: St. Martin's Press, 1933.

action from the point of view of practice may put the metaphysicians' insistence on freedom as a type of causation in a new light and may allow us to think of freedom in a new way. For Kant, freedom is a certain *type of experience*, not an "internal cause."

- Do you really have to think yourself free, as Kant claims? Is thinking yourself free the same as being free?
- Would being a determinist resolve all the difficulties you face when you have to make a decision? Why or why not?

F. Radical Freedom: Existentialism

Kant's suggestion has been taken up in a different way in European philosophy, particularly by the existentialists. Like Kant, the existentialists accept (or at least do not bother to reject) determinism in science. But they insist that even if determinism is true, one must always view *himself* or *herself as agent* as necessarily free. When you have to decide what to do, all the knowledge of the possible factors determining your decision is not sufficient to cause you to decide. For you cannot predict your own decision without at the same time making it.

Jean-Paul Sartre, the French existentialist, took the Kantian claim for human freedom as far as it could possibly be defended. In his mammoth book *Being and Nothingness*, he argues that we are, always, absolutely free. By this Sartre means, as Kant had insisted, that insofar as we act (and Sartre says that we are always acting), our decisions and actions cannot be viewed as having any causes whatsoever. As beings who possess consciousness (who are "for-itself," in Sartre's terminology), we must make decisions, and no amount of information and no number of causal circumstances can ever replace our need to make them. We can, of course, refuse to make decisions, acting as if they were made for us, as if circumstances already determined them, as if the fates had already established the outcome. But even in these cases, we are making decisions, "choosing not to choose," as Sartre classically puts it. We are "condemned to be free," Sartre says, in a phrase that has since become famous. Again, desires may enter into consideration, but only as "considerations." We can always act against a desire, any desire, no matter how strong, if only we have sufficiently decided that we shall do so. A starving man may refuse food if, for example, he is taking part in a hunger strike for a political cause to which he is dedicated. A mother may refuse to save her own life if it would be at the expense of her children. A student may miss his favorite television show if he has resolved to study for tomorrow's test. Whether trivial or grandiose, our every act is a decision, and our every decision is free. Even if we fail to live up to our decisions or find that we "cannot" make them, we are responsible nevertheless. There is no escape from freedom or responsibility.

FIG. 6.23 Although Jean-Paul Sartre claimed that we are radically free, he acknowledged that we are limited by the facts of our situation, including the constraints of physical laws. *(Photothèque R. Magritte-ADAGP / Art Resource, NY / Artists Rights Society (ARS), New York)*

On "Absolute Freedom"
BY Jean-Paul Sartre[31]

Although the considerations which are about to follow are of interest primarily to the ethicist, it may nevertheless be worthwhile after these descriptions and arguments to return to the freedom of the for-itself and try to understand what the fact of this freedom represents for human destiny.

The essential consequence of our earlier remarks is that man being condemned to be free carries the weight of the whole world on his shoulders; he is responsible for the world and for himself as a way of being. We are taking the word "responsibility" in its ordinary sense as "consciousness (of) being the incontestable author of an event or of an object." In this sense the responsibility of the for-itself is overwhelming since he is the one by whom it happens that *there is* a world; since he is also the one who makes himself be, then whatever may be the situation in which he finds himself, the for-itself must wholly assume this situation with its peculiar coefficient of adversity, even though it be insupportable. He must assume the situation with the proud consciousness of being the author of it, for the very worst disadvantages or the worst threats which can endanger my person have meaning only in and through my project; and it is on the ground of the engagement which I am that they appear. It is therefore senseless to think of complaining since nothing foreign has decided what we feel, what we live, or what we are.

Furthermore this absolute responsibility is not resignation; it is simply the logical requirement of the consequences of our freedom. What happens to me happens through me, and I can neither affect myself with it nor revolt against it nor resign myself to it. Moreover everything which happens to me is *mine*. By this we must understand first of all that I am always equal to what happens to me *qua* man, for what happens to a man through other men and through himself can be only human. The most terrible situations of war, the worst tortures do not create a non-human state of things; there is no non-human situation. It is only through fear, flight, and recourse to magical types of conduct that I shall decide on the non-human, but this decision is human, and I shall carry the entire responsibility for it. But in addition the situation is *mine* because it is the image of my free choice of myself, and everything which it presents to me is *mine* in that this represents me and symbolizes me. Is it not I who decide the coefficient of adversity in things and even their unpredictability by deciding myself?

Thus there are no *accidents* in life; a community event which suddenly burst forth and involves me in it does not come from the outside. If I am mobilized in a war, this war is *my* war; it is in my image and I deserve it. I deserve it first because I could always get out of it by suicide or by desertion; these ultimate possibles are those which must always be present for us when there is a question of envisaging a situation. For lack of getting out of it, I have *chosen* it. This can be due to inertia, to cowardice in the face of public opinion, or because I prefer certain other values to the value of the refusal to join in the war (the good opinion of my relatives, the honor of my family, etc.). Any way you look at it, it is a matter of choice. This choice will be repeated later on again and again without a break until the end of the war. Therefore we must agree with the statement by J. Romains, "In war there are no innocent victims." If

31 Jean-Paul Sartre, *Being and Nothingness*, trans. Hazel E. Barnes. Copyright © 1956. Reprinted by permission of the Philosophical Library of New York.

FIG. 6.24 Although few of us are in a position to declare war, Sartre claimed that we each have the war we deserve. *(Image © Alexander Smulskiy, 2011. Used under license from Shutterstock.com)*

therefore I have preferred war to death or to dishonor, everything takes place as if I bore the entire responsibility for this war. Of course others have declared it, and one might be tempted perhaps to consider me as a simple accomplice. But this notion of complicity has only a juridical sense, and it does not hold here. For it depended on me that for me and by me this war should not exist, and I have decided that it does exist. There was no compulsion here, for the compulsion could have got no hold on a freedom. I did not have any excuse; . . . the peculiar character of human-reality is that it is without excuse. Therefore it remains for me only to lay claim to this war.

But in addition the war is *mine* because by the sole fact that it arises in a situation which I cause to be and that I can discover it there only by engaging myself for or against it, I can no longer distinguish at present the choice which I make of myself from the choice which I make of the war. To live this war is to choose myself through it and to choose it through my choice of myself. There can be no question of considering it as "four years of vacation" or as "reprieve," as a "recess," the essential part of my responsibilities being elsewhere in my married, family, or professional life. In this war which I have chosen I choose myself from day to day, and I make it mine by making myself. If it is going to be four empty years, then it is I who bear the responsibility for this.

Finally, . . . each person is an absolute choice of self from the standpoint of a world of knowledges and of techniques which this choice both assumes and illumines; each person is an absolute upsurge at an absolute date and is perfectly unthinkable at another date. It is therefore a waste of time to ask what I should have been if this war had not broken out, for I have chosen myself as one of the possible meanings of the epoch which imperceptibly led to war. I am not distinct from this same epoch; I could not be transported to another epoch without contradiction. Thus *I am* this war which restricts and limits and makes comprehensible the period which preceded it. In this sense we may define more precisely, the responsibility of the for-itself if to the earlier quoted statement, "There are no innocent victims," we added the words, "We have the war we deserve." Thus, totally free, undistinguishable from the period for which I have chosen to be the meaning, as profoundly responsible for the war as if I had myself declared it, unable to live without integrating it in *my* situation, engaging myself in it wholly and stamping it with my seal, I must be without remorse or regrets as I am without excuse; for from the instant of my upsurge into being, I carry the weight of the world by myself alone without anything or any person being able to lighten it.

Yet this responsibility is of a very particular type. Someone will say, "I did not ask to be born." This is a naïve way of throwing greater emphasis on our facticity. I am responsible for everything, in fact, except for my very responsibility, for I am not the foundation of my being. Therefore everything takes place as if I were compelled to be responsible. I am *abandoned* in the world, not in the sense that I might remain abandoned and passive in a hostile universe like a board floating on the water, but rather in the sense that I find myself suddenly alone and without help,

"From the instant of my upsurge into being, I carry the weight of the world by myself alone without anything or any person being able to lighten it."

— JEAN-PAUL SARTRE

engaged in a world for which I bear the whole responsibility without being able, whatever I do, to tear myself away from this responsibility for an instant. For I am responsible for my very desire of fleeing responsibilities. To make myself passive in the world, to refuse to act upon things and upon Others is still to *choose* myself, and suicide is one mode among others of being-in-the-world. Yet I find an absolute responsibility for the fact that my facticity (here the fact of my birth) is directly inapprehensible and even inconceivable, for this fact of my birth never appears as a brute fact but always across a projective reconstruction of my for-itself. I am ashamed of being born or I am astonished at it or I rejoice over it, or in attempting to get rid of my life I affirm that I live and I assume this life as bad. Thus in a certain sense I choose being born. This choice itself is integrally affected with facticity since I am not able not to choose, but this facticity in turn will appear only in so far as I surpass it toward my ends. Thus facticity is everywhere but inapprehensible; I never encounter anything except my responsibility. That is *why* I can not ask, "Why was I born?" or curse the day of my birth or declare that I did not ask to be born, for these various attitudes toward my birth—i.e., toward the *fact* that I realize a presence in the world—are absolutely nothing else but ways of assuming this birth in full responsibility and of making it *mine*. Here again I encounter only myself and my projects so that finally my abandonment—i.e., my facticity—consists simply in the fact that I am condemned to be wholly responsible for myself. I am the being which *is* in such a way that in its being its being is in question. And this "is" of my being *is* as present and inapprehensible.

Under these conditions since every event in the world can be revealed to me only as an *opportunity* (an opportunity made use of, lacked, neglected, etc.) or better yet since everything which happens to us can be considered as a *chance* (i.e., can appear to us only as a way of realizing this being which is in question in our being) and since others as transcendences-transcended are themselves only *opportunities* and *chances*, the responsibility of the for-itself extends to the entire world as a peopled-world. It is precisely thus that the for-itself apprehends itself in anguish; that is, as a *being* which is neither the foundation of its own being nor of the Other's being nor of the in-itselfs which form the world, but a being which is compelled to decide the meaning of being—within it and everywhere outside of it. The one who realizes in anguish his condition as being thrown into a responsibility which extends to his very abandonment has no longer either remorse or regret or excuse; he is no longer anything but a freedom which perfectly reveals itself and whose being resides in this very revelation. But as we pointed out . . . , most of the time we flee anguish in bad faith.

Sartre's position is the culmination of a full century of existentialist thought, beginning with Søren Kierkegaard in the 1840s. Kierkegaard, too, argued that one is responsible for whatever one is and that self-conscious choice and commitment are the factors that make a person most human. Sartre's strong sense of responsibility goes even so far as to ascribe an act of choice to those situations in which we seem clearly to be only victims, for example, in war. "There are no accidents in life," he argues. Each of us always chooses a way to act in and deal with a situation. One can always complain, "I didn't ask to be born," Sartre says, but this is only one of many ways we have of trying to avoid responsibility. Given the fact that we have been born, raised in certain conditions, and so forth, it is now entirely up to us as to what we shall make of all this. Instead of looking at the events of the world as problems and intrusions,

Sartre ultimately says, we should learn to look at everything as an opportunity. Here is the optimistic note to his strong defense of human freedom.

What all these arguments demand is the following: In one's own case, in making your decision, there can be no appeal to determinism even if determinism is true. Whatever may be theoretically determined, in practice, you must choose. Since freedom is the key to our self-esteem and our pride in ourselves, some people will demand it at any cost.

The most brilliant, if bizarre, example of this existentialist demand is formulated by the strange character in Dostoyevsky's short novel *Notes from the Underground*. The argument is simple. Any prediction can be thwarted as long as you know about it. If they say, "you'll do *x*," do *y*. Now, suppose that determinism is true. In particular, suppose that psychological determinism is true and that its basic law is this: "people always act to their own advantage." Now, what does this have to do with the predictability of a person's actions? Absolutely nothing if you are sufficiently determined not to be predictable. Accordingly, the character in this novel is, more than anything else, spiteful. His main concern is not being predictable, in proving his freedom even if it means making himself miserable. Now you might say that his spite itself is the determinant of his behavior, and, of course, it is. But the very point of the argument is that causes and explanations of any kind are simply beside the point. Let the underground man know what you expect him to do, and he will do precisely the opposite. If you predict that he will act spiteful, he will be as agreeable as can be—just out of spite!

 FROM **"The Most Advantageous Advantage"**
BY **Fyodor Dostoyevsky**[32]

I am a sick man . . . I am a spiteful man. I am an unpleasant man. I think my liver is diseased. However, I don't know beans about my disease, and I am not sure what is bothering me. I don't treat it and never have, though I respect medicine and doctors. Besides, I am extremely superstitious, let's say sufficiently so to respect medicine. (I am educated enough not to be superstitious, but I am.) No, I refuse to treat it out of spite. You probably will not understand that. Well, but *I* understand it.

· · ·

Why, in the first place, when in all these thousands of years has there ever been a time when man has acted only for his own advantage? What is to be done with the millions of facts that bear witness that men, *knowingly*, that is, fully understanding their real advantages, have left them in the background and have rushed headlong on another path, to risk, to chance, compelled to this course by nobody and by nothing, but, as it were, precisely because they did not want the beaten track, and stubbornly, wilfully, went off on another difficult, absurd way seeking it almost in the darkness. After all, it means that this stubbornness and wilfulness were more pleasant to them than any advantage. Advantage! What is advantage? And will you take it upon yourself to define with perfect accuracy in exactly what the advantage of man consists of? And what if it so happens that a man's advantage *sometimes* not only may, but even must, consist exactly in his desiring under certain conditions what is harmful to himself and not what is advantageous. And if so, if there can be such a condition then the whole principle becomes worthless.

· · ·

32 Fyodor Dostoyevsky, *Notes from the Underground*, in *Notes from the Underground and The Grand Inquisitor*, trans. Ralph Matlaw, New York: E. P. Dutton, 1960.

The fact is, gentlemen, it seems that something that is dearer to almost every man than his greatest advantages must really exist, or (not to be illogical) there is one most advantageous advantage (the very one omitted of which we spoke just now) which is more important and more advantageous than all other advantages, for which, if necessary, a man is ready to act in opposition to all laws, that is, in opposition to reason, honor, peace, prosperity— in short, in opposition to all those wonderful and useful things if only he can attain that fundamental, most advantageous advantage which is dearer to him than all.

What is that "advantageous advantage?" Nothing other than

One's own free unfettered choice, one's own fancy, however wild it may be, one's own fancy worked up at times to frenzy. That is the "most advantageous advantage," which is always overlooked.

FIG. 6.25 Dostoyevsky's narrator in *Notes from the Underground* uses his freedom spitefully to defy others' expectations. *(© iStockphoto.com/Iconogenic)*

Freedom, in other words, is itself what we most demand, whatever the cost, whatever the difficulties, and whatever the arguments against it. Whatever else may be true, we will refuse to see ourselves as anything but free. For it is freedom that makes us human. Dostoyevsky's picture of this radical, desperate freedom is perhaps not an uplifting one. A similar sentiment, however, can give a joyous image of freedom. Here is a sample from **Thich Nhat Hanh**, a Vietnamese Buddhist monk. It is a prayer to say when turning on the television:

 FROM **"Turning on the Television"** BY **Thich Nhat Hanh**[33]

> The mind is a television
> with thousands of channels.
> I choose a world that is tranquil and calm
> so that my joy will always be fresh.

Mind is consciousness. Consciousness includes the subject which knows and the object which is known. The two aspects, subject and object, depend on each other in order to exist. As the Vietnamese meditation master, Huong Hai, said, "In seeing matter, you are at the same time seeing mind. Without the arising of the object, the subject does not arise." When our mind is conscious of something, we *are* that thing. When we contemplate a snow-covered mountain, we are that mountain. When we watch a noisy film, we are that noisy film.

Our mind is like a television set with thousands of channels, and the channel we switch on is the channel we are at that moment. When we turn on anger, we are

> "Our mind is like a television set with thousands of channels, and the channel we switch on is the channel we are at that moment."
>
> – THICH NHAT HANH

33 Thich Nhat Hanh, "Turning on the Television," from *Present Moment, Wonderful Moment.* Copyright © 1990 by Parallax Press. Reprinted by permission of the publisher.

Thich Nhat Hanh (1926–)
A Vietnamese Buddhist monk, peace activist, and writer. He currently lives in France and occasionally teaches in the United States.

FIG. 6.26 Thich Nhat Hanh argues that we should beware of becoming victims of our televisions. *(AP Photo / RICHARD VOGEL)*

anger. When we turn on peace and joy, we are peace and joy. We have the ability to select the channel. *We are what we choose to be.* We can select any channel of the mind. Buddha is a channel, Mara is a channel, remembering is a channel, forgetting is a channel, calm is a channel, agitation is a channel. Changing from one state of being to another is as simple as the change from a channel showing a film to a channel playing music.

There are people who cannot tolerate peace and quiet, who are afraid of facing themselves, so they turn on the television in order to be preoccupied with it for a whole evening. In contemporary culture, people rarely like to be with themselves, and they frequently seek forgetfulness—downtown at the theater or other places of amusement. People rarely like to look deeply and compassionately at themselves. Young people in America watch television more than five hours per day, and they also have all sorts of electronic games to occupy them. Where will a culture in which people do not have the chance to face themselves or form real relationships with others lead us?

There are many interesting, instructive programs on television, and we can use the TV guide to select programs which encourage mindfulness. We should decide to watch only the programs we have selected and avoid becoming a victim of the television.

- How is Sartre's view of freedom similar to Kant's? Is thinking that you are free proof that in some important sense you are free?
- Explain what Sartre means by in "choosing not to choose, we are condemned to be free."
- Do you agree with Sartre that we are always responsible insofar as everything in our life is, in effect, a free choice (including war—in war, "there are no innocent victims")?
- To what extent is it possible to choose otherwise or "to negate" certain facts about yourself? Could you choose to be taller, better looking, or more intelligent? How would Sartre or Dostoyevsky reply?
- To what extent are we free to choose our states of consciousness?

SUMMARY AND CONCLUSION

To say that a person's act is free is to be able to ascribe responsibility. The defense of freedom therefore becomes extremely important to us. Our confidence in the universality of scientific explanations, however, seems to imply the thesis of determinism, which holds that every event has its sufficient natural cause. Human actions, as events, thus seem to be determined and thus not free. In this chapter, we have explored the various ways in which philosophers have attempted to reconcile these two vital beliefs—that at least some human acts are free and that science can ultimately (at least in principle) explain everything.

Some philosophers have defended determinism ("hard determinism") to the exclusion of freedom. Others ("indeterminists") have defended freedom to the exclusion of determinism. Most philosophers, however, have tried to defend both theses (and so are often called "compatibilists"). They ("soft determinists") have argued that determinism does not preclude freedom if an act flows from a person's decision or character; that we can be more and less susceptible to determinists; or that even if determinism is true, we cannot help but think of ourselves as free.

CHAPTER REVIEW QUESTIONS

1. Compare and contrast hard determinism, soft determinism, and indeterminism. Explain why indeterminism is just as problematic as hard determinism.

2. Compare and contrast the ideas of a universe ruled by chance, divine predestination, fatalism, and karma. Which view do you find most appealing?

3. What is the Islamic conception of predestination? How does it compare with other religious views you have studied?

4. Defenders of free will argue that there is a notion of freedom that is undetermined. Do you find this view problematic? How would you defend this view against the determinists' objections?

5. Discuss the relationship between moral responsibility and freedom. What similarities and differences can you discern among Aristotle, Skinner, and Sartre? What would the others say to Sartre's claim that in war there are no innocent victims?

KEY TERMS

antecedent conditions	freedom	prediction
cause	free will	responsibility
compatibilism	Heisenberg uncertainty	retrodict
compulsion	principle	soft determinism
determinism	indeterminism	sufficient cause
fatalism	predestination	

BIBLIOGRAPHY AND FURTHER READING

Three good collections of essays on the free will problem are Gary Watson, ed., *Free Will* (New York: Oxford University Press, 2003); Robert Kane, ed., *Free Will* (Oxford, U.K.: Blackwell, 2002); and Robert Kane, ed., *The Oxford Handbook of Free Will* (New York: Oxford University Press, 2002).

Also recommended are Alfred Mele, ed., *The Philosophy of Action* (New York: Oxford University Press, 1997); Robert Kane, *The Significance of Free Will* (New York: Oxford University Press, 1996); and Daniel C. Dennett, *Elbow Room: The Varieties of Free Will Worth Wanting* (Cambridge, MA: MIT Press, 1984).

PART III

The Good and the Right

7 | Ethics

"From now on I'm thinking only of me."
Major Danby replied indulgently with a superior smile,
"But Yossarian, suppose everyone felt that way?"
"Then I'd certainly be a—fool to feel any other way, wouldn't I?"

JOSEPH HELLER, *CATCH-22*

What should we do, and what should we not do? Which acts should we praise? Which acts should we condemn and blame? These are questions of **ethics**, the concern for which Socrates was willing to give up his life. A core concern of ethics is **morality**. Morality is a set of fundamental rules that guide our actions; for example, they may forbid us to kill each other, encourage us to help each other, tell us not to lie, and command us to keep our promises.

Most of the moral rules we accept and follow are ones that we have learned and adopted from our parents, friends, teachers, and society. At times, though, others may challenge our moral rules, demanding that we defend them. Why should we help each other? Why shouldn't we ever cheat? What reasons can we give to defend one sexual ethic rather than another? New social and technological developments may also force us to reevaluate our morality. Since minorities and women have participated more and more in public debates on moral issues, we have become more aware of the injustices of discrimination on the basis of race or sex. The development of sophisticated life-sustaining devices has forced both physicians and philosophers to question whether it is always a moral duty to preserve life whenever possible.

Whenever we try to defend or criticize a moral belief we enter the realm of ethics. Ethics is not restricted to specifying moral rules, but instead is concerned with the foundation of morality and with providing general principles that will both help us evaluate the validity of a moral rule and choose among different moralities (different sets of moral rules). For example, some ethical theorists, called **utilitarians**, hold that any good moral rule should promote the greatest **happiness** for the greatest number. Other theorists, for example, Aristotle and Kant, have argued that a good moral rule helps us act in the most rational way possible.

Ethics is also concerned with whether or not to take into account others' or our own interests and desires when deciding what we ought to do. For some ethicists, morality is tied to self-interest at least in an abstract way, and they argue that morality is the best way of satisfying everyone's interests. Other philosophers retain the rigid distinction between morality

447

and self-interest and insist that obedience to morality is good for its own sake, equivalent to being rational, or simply required in order to make us human. Finally some authors have argued that morality is only one among many sets of principles, which we may but need not choose to obey.

In this chapter, we begin by raising some of the perennial problems of ethics, including the nature of morality and the problem of moral relativism. Then, we address the familiar claim that the basis of all human behavior—moral behavior included—is selfishness, or **egoism**. Finally we examine several different ethical theories, different ways of conceiving of morals and (or) justifying moral beliefs:

- The ethics of Aristotle, who based his view of morality on the concept of "virtue" and his idea that man is by nature a social and rational animal. Aristotle argues that being virtuous—controlling our feelings and acting rationally—enables us to become fully human. In this discussion, we have the opportunity to examine a moral system that is significantly different from our own, but still sufficiently similar for us to understand it.

- The view that morality is essentially a matter of feeling; David Hume and Jean-Jacques Rousseau are its representatives.

- The monumental ethical theory of Immanuel Kant, who insisted that morality is strictly a matter of practical reason, divorced from our personal interests and desires and based solely on universal principles or **laws**. Thus, according to Kant, we cannot justify the morality of our actions simply by appealing to the good consequences of our actions for others or ourselves. We also consider subsequent efforts to support or criticize Kant's view.

- The ethical theories of the utilitarians, who argued (in contrast to Kant) that moral rules are merely rules of thumb for achieving the greatest good for the greatest number of people, and who thereby tried to reconcile the interests of each individual with the interests of everyone else.

- The radical theories of Nietzsche and the **existentialists**, who insist that, in an important sense, we choose our moralities and that this choice cannot be justified in any of the ways argued by other modern philosophers. For Nietzsche, at least, this view also included a retrospective appreciation of the morality of the ancient Greeks, and he argued that we should inject some of their conceptions into our own. We also look at subsequent efforts to support the idea that morality is conventional—a matter of custom within specific societies.

- Recent feminist theories, which argue that the moral tradition has overemphasized principles and procedures and neglected the moral importance of interpersonal roles and relationships.

A. Morality

Morality gives us the rules by which we live with other people. It sets limits to our desires and our actions. It tells us what is permitted and what is not. It gives us guiding principles for making decisions. It tells us what we ought and ought not to do. But what is this "morality" that sounds so impersonal and "above" us? It is important to begin with an appreciation for the metaphor, which so well characterizes moral rules. Nietzsche describes it this way: "A tablet of virtues hangs over every people."

The "tablet of virtues" is morality. The prototype of morality, in this view, is those ancient codes, carved in stone, with commands that are eternal and absolute, such as the two tablets inscribed by God in front of Moses that we call the Ten *Commandments*. And they are indeed commandments. They all say "Thou shalt" or "Thou shalt not." This is the essence of morality. It consists of commands. These commands do not appeal to individual pleasures or desires. They do not make different demands on different individuals or societies. Quite to the contrary, they are absolute rules that tell us what we must or must not do, no matter who we are, no matter what we want, and regardless of whether or not our interests will be served by the command. "Thou shalt not kill" means that even if you want to, even if you have the power to, and even if you can escape all punishment, you are absolutely forbidden to kill.

The image of morality as coming "from above" is appropriate. First, because moral laws are often said, and not only in our society, to come from God. Second, because we learn these laws from our parents, who literally "stand over us" and indoctrinate us with them through their shouts, commands, examples, threats, and gestures. Finally, and most important, morality itself is "above" any given individual or individuals, whether it is canonized in the laws of society or not. Morality is not just another aid in getting us what we want; it is entirely concerned with right and wrong. And these considerations are "above" tampering by any individual, no matter how powerful, as if they have a life of their own.

This characteristic of morality as independent of individual desires and ambitions has led many people to characterize morality simply in terms of some absolute and independent agency. Most often, this absolute and independent agency is God. St. Thomas Aquinas, for example, refers to God as the source of moral law: "Therefore by divine law precepts had to be given, so that each man would give his neighbor his due and would abstain from doing injuries to him."[1] And in the Bible we read, "When thou shalt harken–to the voice of the Lord thy God, to keep all his commandments, which I command thee this day, to do that which is right in the eyes of the Lord thy God."[2]

But whether or not one believes in God, it is clear that something further is needed to help us define morality. Even assuming that there is a God, we need a way of determining what His moral commands must be. One may say that He has given these commands to various individuals, but the fact is that different people seem to have very different ideas about the morality that God has given them. Some, for example, would say that it explicitly rules out abortion and infanticide. Others would argue that God does not rule these out but makes it clear that they are, like other forms of killing (a "holy war," for example), justifiable only in certain circumstances. In view of such disagreements, we cannot simply appeal to God but must, for reasons that we can formulate and defend, define our morality for ourselves. There is the further question, which has often been debated, but was raised originally by Plato, in his dialogue, *Euthyphro*. Should we follow God's laws just because they are His or rather, because His laws are good? If the latter, then we have to decide what is good in order to know that God is good. If the former, then one has to decide whether or not to believe in God precisely on the basis of whether we can accept those laws. Either way, we have to decide for ourselves what laws of morality we are willing to accept.

Similar considerations hold true for that familiar appeal to conscience in determining what we ought or ought not do. Even if one believes that conscience is God-given, the same problems emerge again. Should we follow our consciences just because our "conscience tells us to"? Or do we follow our conscience just because we know that what our conscience commands is good? How does one decide whether a nagging thought is or is not the prompting of God? Probably on the basis of whether what it demands is good or not. (Thus one readily attributes to conscience the nagging reminder that one should not have cheated an unsuspecting child,

---

[1] St. Thomas Aquinas, *Summa Contra Gentiles*, Bk. III (New York: Doubleday, 1955).

[2] Deuteronomy 13:18.

but one does not attribute to conscience the nagging thought that one could have gotten away with shoplifting if only one had had the daring to do it.) If one believes that conscience is simply the internalization of the moral teachings of one's parents and society, then the question takes an extra dimension: Should we accept or reject what we have been taught? Since our consciences often disagree, we must still decide whose conscience and which rules of conscience we ought to obey. Identifying morality with the promptings of one's conscience is both plausible and valuable, but philosophically it only moves the question one step back: How do we know what is, and what is not, the prompting of conscience? And is it always right to follow one's conscience? But these two questions are, in fact, just another way of asking what is moral. What should I do?

Morality is not just obedience—whether obedience to a king, a pope, the law, or one's conscience. Morality is doing what is *right*, whether or not it is commanded by any person or law and whether or not one "feels" it in one's conscience. One way of putting it—defended later by Immanuel Kant—is to say that morality involves **autonomy**, that is, the ability to think for oneself and decide, for oneself, what is right and what is wrong, whom to obey and whom to ignore, what to do and what not to do. The danger is that this conception of morality as autonomy seems to leave us without a place to learn morality in the first place. How do we learn to judge right and wrong but from our parents, our friends, our teachers, and our society and its models? But if we try to tie morality too closely to our upbringing and our society, then it looks as if there is no room for autonomy, no way in which we could disagree with our family or society, no way to criticize the way in which we have been raised. Furthermore, tying morality to particular societies raises an additional question: whether morality (or mora*lities*) may not be relative to particular societies and cultures.

- In your opinion, which is the more appropriate interpretation of the view that morality coincides with what God commands: (1) the moral law is right because God commands it? or (2) God commands the moral law because it is right? What are the advantages and disadvantages of each view?
- Why does it make you uncomfortable when you ignore your conscience? Does it help if others tell you that ignoring it is right?

B. Is Morality Relative?

Moralities, like lifestyles, vary from culture to culture and even from person to person. But while there is nothing surprising about the fact that lifestyles vary, there is a problem in the variation of moralities. Morality, by its very nature, is supposed to be a set of universal principles—principles that do not distinguish between cultures or peoples or lifestyles. If it is morally reprehensible to kill for fun, then it is morally reprehensible in every society, in every culture, for every lifestyle, and for every person, no matter who he or she is. It will be true even if the society or person in question does not agree with that moral principle.

Aristotle, for example, discusses at length what he calls "the wicked man," who does evil because he believes in immoral principles and therefore acts without regret, unlike the person who acts badly from momentary weakness, force of circumstances, desperation, or misinformation. But on what grounds can one society or person claim that another society's or person's principles are immoral? How could European Christians, for example, be justified in criticizing the sexual morality of Polynesians in the South Pacific? The Polynesians they encountered were a separate society, with their own mores and principles that worked quite well for them, possibly even better in certain ways than the European customs worked in

Europe. Yet European missionaries felt no hesitation in condemning their sexual practices as "immoral." Similarly but more seriously, what gives us the right to criticize a culture across the world that believes in genocide as a legitimate aim of war or in torture as a way of keeping civil order? We surely feel that we have the right to speak up in such cases, but then we are asserting the universality of our morality, extending it even to people who may explicitly reject our principles. How can we do so? What justifies such an extension?

The problem of **relativism** has been extremely controversial since the nineteenth century, when anthropologists began telling us in the West of exotic societies with moralities that were quite different from ours. In a sense, relativism has always been a threat to established morality, for even the Greeks came into contact with societies that were much different from theirs. (They tended immediately to label anything non-Greek "barbarian," so they did not have to consider the possibility of relativism.) Kant was the most vigorous opponent of relativism, for his conception of morality was such that if a human being was to count as rational at all, he or she had to agree to at least the basic principles of a universal morality. There were people and societies that did not, but that, according to Kant, only proved that they were less than rational (and implicitly less than human as well). Today we tend to be more liberal in our acceptance of different styles of life, but few people would deny that at least some moral principles hold for every society. The principle that unnecessary cruelty is wrong, for example, would be such a principle, although people may well disagree about what is "cruel" and what is "unnecessary."

Philosophers generally distinguish two theses. First, there is the factual claim that different societies have different moralities. This thesis is called **cultural relativism**. The difficult question is whether these different moralities are only different superficially or whether they are fundamentally different. For example, in earlier times, certain indigenous Arctic tribes sometimes thinned their numbers in response to famine by letting elderly members die of exposure. We consider that act grossly immoral (we send most of our elders to frigid "old-age homes" instead). But the question of cultural relativity is whether this difference is merely the reflection of different interpretations of some basic moral principle (such as, do not kill anyone unless it is absolutely necessary for the survival of the rest) or whether it really is a wholly different morality. This is among the most controversial anthropological questions of our time. But philosophers are interested in a somewhat different question: Assuming that two moralities really are fundamentally different, is it possible that each is as correct as the other? The philosopher who says yes is an **ethical relativist**, and ethical relativism is what occupies us here.

In the following selection, **Gilbert Harman** presents a contemporary defense of the relativist position.

 FROM **"Moral Relativism Defended"**
BY **Gilbert Harman**[3]

My thesis is that morality arises when a group of people reach an implicit agreement or come to a tacit understanding about their relations with one another. Part of what I mean by this is that moral judgments—or, rather, an important class of them—make sense only in relation to and with reference to one or another such agreement or understanding. This is vague, and I shall try to make it more precise in what follows. But it should be clear that I intend to argue for a version of what has been called moral relativism.

---

[3] Gilbert Harman, "Moral Relativism Defended," in *Philosophical Review* 75 (1975): 3-22.

Gilbert Harman (1938-)

An American philosopher who specializes in ethics, epistemology, and cognition science. He teaches at Princeton University.

FIG. 7.1 Princeton Professor Gilbert Harman argues that morality is a matter of group agreement and that groups can legitimately have different moralities.
(Used by permission of Gilbert Harman)

In doing so, I am taking sides in an ancient controversy. Many people have supposed that the sort of view which I am going to defend is obviously correct—indeed, that it is the only sort of account that could make sense of the phenomenon of morality. At the same time there have also been many who have supposed that moral relativism is confused, incoherent, and even immoral, at the very least obviously wrong.

Most arguments against relativism make use of a strategy of dissuasive definition; they define moral relativism as an inconsistent thesis. For example, they define it as the assertion that (*a*) there are no universal moral principles and (*b*) one ought to act in accordance with the principles of one's own group, where this latter principle, (*b*), *is* supposed to be a universal moral principle. It is easy enough to show that this version of moral relativism will not do, but that is no reason to think that a defender of moral relativism cannot find a better definition.

My moral relativism is a soberly logical thesis—a thesis about logical form, if you like. Just as the judgment that something is large makes sense only in relation to one or another comparison class, so too, I will argue, the judgment that it is wrong of someone to do something makes sense only in relation to an agreement or understanding. A dog may be large in relation to chihuahuas but not large in relation to dogs in general. Similarly, I will argue, an action may be wrong in relation to one agreement but not in relation to another. Just as it makes no sense to ask whether a dog is large, period, apart from any relation to a comparison class, so too, I will argue, it makes no sense to ask whether an action is wrong, period, apart from any relation to an agreement.

There is an agreement, in the relevant sense, if each of a number of people intends to adhere to some schedule, plan, or set of principles, intending to do this on the understanding that the others similarly intend. The agreement or understanding need not be conscious or explicit; and I will not here try to say what distinguishes moral agreements from, for example, conventions of the road or conventions of etiquette, since these distinctions will not be important as regards the purely logical thesis that I will be defending.

Although I want to say that certain moral judgments are made in relation to an agreement, I do not want to say this about all moral judgments. Perhaps it is true that all moral judgments are made in relation to an agreement; nevertheless, that is not what I will be arguing. For I want to say that there is a way in which certain moral judgments are relative to an agreement but other moral judgments are not. My relativism is a thesis only about what I will call "inner judgments," such as the judgment that someone ought or ought not to have acted in a certain way or the judgment that it was right or wrong of him to have done so. My relativism is not meant to apply, for example, to the judgment that someone is evil or the judgment that a given institution is unjust.

In particular, I am not denying (nor am I asserting) that some moralities are "objectively" better than others or that there are objective standards for assessing moralities. My thesis is a soberly logical thesis about logical form.

I. INNER JUDGMENTS

We make inner judgments about a person only if we suppose that he is capable of being motivated by the relevant moral considerations. We make other sorts of judgment about those who we suppose are not susceptible of such motivation. Inner judgments include judgments in which we say that someone should or ought to have done something or that someone was right or wrong to have done something. Inner judgments do not include judgments in which we call someone (literally) a savage or say that someone is (literally) inhuman, evil, a betrayer, a traitor, or an enemy.

Consider this example. Intelligent beings from outer space land on Earth, beings without the slightest concern for human life and happiness. That a certain course of action on their part might injure one of us means nothing to them; that fact by itself gives them no reason to avoid the action. In such a case it would be odd to say that nevertheless the beings ought to avoid injuring us or that it would be wrong for them to attack us. Of course we will want to resist them if they do such things and we will make negative judgments about them; but we will judge that they are dreadful enemies to be repelled and even destroyed, not that they should not act as they do.

Similarly, if we learn that a band of cannibals has captured and eaten the sole survivor of a shipwreck, we will speak of the primitive morality of the cannibals and may call them savages, but we will not say that they ought not to have eaten their captive.

Again, suppose that a contented employee of Murder, Incorporated was raised as a child to honor and respect members of the "family" but to have nothing but contempt for the rest of society. His current assignment, let us suppose, is to kill a certain bank manager, Bernard J. Ortcutt. Since Ortcutt is not a member of the "family," the employee in question has no compunction about carrying out his assignment. In particular, if we were to try to convince him that he should not kill Ortcutt, our argument would merely amuse him. We would not provide him with the slightest reason to desist unless we were to point to practical difficulties, such as the likelihood of his getting caught. Now, in this case it would be a misuse of language to say of him that he ought not to kill Ortcutt or that it would be wrong of him to do so, since that would imply that our own moral considerations carry some weight with him, which they do not. Instead we can only judge that he is a criminal, someone to be hunted down by the police, an enemy of peace-loving citizens, and so forth.

. . .

Of course, I do not want to deny that for various reasons a speaker might pretend that an agent is or is not susceptible to certain moral considerations. For example, a speaker may for rhetorical or political reasons wish to suggest that someone is beyond the pale, that he should not be listened to, that he can be treated as an enemy. On the other hand, a speaker may pretend that someone is susceptible to certain moral considerations in an effort to make that person or others susceptible to those considerations. Inner judgments about one's children sometimes have this function. So do inner judgments made in political speeches that aim at restoring a lapsed sense of morality in government.

II. THE LOGICAL FORM OF INNER JUDGMENTS

Inner judgments have two important characteristics. First, they imply that the agent has reasons to do something. Second, the speaker in some sense endorses these reasons and supposes that the audience also endorses them. Other moral judgments about an agent, on the other hand, do not have such implications; they do not imply that the agent has reasons for acting that are endorsed by the speaker.

. . .

Now we need not suppose that the agreement or understanding in question is explicit. It is enough if various members of society knowingly reach an agreement in intentions—each intending to act in certain ways on the understanding that the others have similar intentions. Such an implicit agreement is reached through a process of mutual adjustment and implicit *bargaining*.

Indeed, it is essential to the proposed explanation of this aspect of our moral views to suppose that the relevant moral understanding is thus the result of bargaining. It is necessary to suppose that, in order to further our interests, we form certain conditional intentions, hoping that others will do the same. The others, who have different interests, will form somewhat different conditional intentions. After implicit bargaining, some sort of compromise is reached.

Seeing morality in this way as a compromise based on implicit bargaining helps to explain why our morality takes it to be worse to harm someone than to refuse to help someone. The explanation requires that we view our morality as an implicit agreement about what to do. This sort of explanation could not be given if we were to suppose, say, that our morality represented an agreement only about the facts (naturalism). Nor is it enough simply to suppose that our morality represents an agreement in attitude, if we forget that such agreement can be reached, not only by way of such principles as are mentioned, . . . but also through bargaining.

Although contemporary awareness of what is happening around the globe makes us mindful of the diversity of cultural views, the issue of ethical relativism has been around for centuries. In the thirteenth century, St. Thomas Aquinas took up the question of ethical relativism and concluded that it was false. He answered the question that Plato raised in the *Euthyphro* by claiming that it is right to follow God's laws because they are good. They are good, in fact, because they conform to nature, and most often they will result in what is best for us. **Natural law** is the term for the moral law as it inheres in nature. Aquinas noted, "It is apparent that things prescribed by divine law are right, not only because they are put forth by law, but also because they are in accord with nature."[4] God gave each thing in creation a nature that directs it toward what is good for it. In the case of human beings, this nature involves free will, the pursuit of what is good for us is subject to our free choice. But we are given guidance by using our reason and objectively attending to our nature as human beings to ascertain what actions are consistent with providing for our various needs in a harmonious way. Every human being is in a position to know the general prescriptions of moral law.

When asked how natural law can be universal if cultures vary in their moral views, Aquinas distinguishes between the fundamental principles of natural law and the practices that apply these principles. Knowledge of the former is present in every society. However, as circum-

---

4 Thomas Aquinas, *Summa Contra Gentiles*, Bk. III (New York Doubleday, 1955).

stances vary, so do the applications of these principles. In other words, Aquinas acknowledges the factual claim of cultural relativism but concludes that it offers no evidence for the truth of ethical relativism. One can recognize the diversity of moral practices and still hold that in essence, the same moral law holds for everyone.

 FROM **The *Summa Theologica*** BY **St. Thomas Aquinas**[5]

THE NATURAL LAW

. . . to the natural law belongs those things to which a man is inclined naturally: and among these it is proper to man to be inclined to act according to reason. Now the process of reason is from the common to the proper, as stated in *Phys.* i. The speculative reason, however, is differently situated in this matter, from the practical reason. For, since the speculative reason is busied chiefly with necessary things, which cannot be otherwise than they are, its proper conclusions, like the universal principles, contain the truth without fail. The practical reason, on the other hand, is busied with contingent matters, about which human actions are concerned: and consequently, although there is necessity in the general principles, the more we descend to matters of detail, the more frequently we encounter defects. Accordingly then in speculative matters truth is the same in all men, both as to principles and as to conclusions: although the truth is not known to all as regards the conclusions, but only as regards the principles which are called common notions. But in matters of action, truth or practical rectitude is not the same for all, as to matters of detail, but only as to the general principles: and where there is the same rectitude in matters of detail, it is not equally known to all.

It is therefore evident that, as regards the general principles whether of speculative or of practical reason, truth or rectitude is the same for all, and is equally known by all. As to the proper conclusions of the speculative reason, the truth is the same for all, but is not equally known to all: thus it is true for all that the three angles of a triangle are together equal to two right angles, although it is not known to all. But as to the proper conclusions of the practical reason, neither is the truth or rectitude the same for all, nor, where it is the same, is it equally known by all. Thus it is right and true for all to act according to reason: and from this principle it follows as a proper conclusion, that goods entrusted to another should be restored to their owner. Now this is true for the majority of cases: but it may happen in a particular case that it would be injurious, and therefore unreasonable, to restore goods held in trust; for instance if they are claimed for the purpose of fighting against one's country. And this principle will be found to fail the more, according as we descend further into detail, *e.g.*, if one were to say that goods held in trust should be restored with such and such a guarantee, or in such and such a way; because the greater the number of conditions added, the greater the number of ways in which the principle may fail, so that it be not right to restore or not to restore.

Consequently we must say that the natural law, as to general principles, is the same for all, both as to rectitude and as to knowledge. But as to certain matters of detail, which are conclusions, as it were, of those general principles, it is the same for all in the majority of cases, both as to rectitude and as to knowledge; and yet in some few cases it may fail, both as to rectitude, by reason of certain obstacles (just as natures

5 Thomas Aquinas, *Summa Contra Gentiles*, Bk. III (New York Doubleday, 1955).

subject to generation and corruption fail in some few cases on account of some obstacle), and as to knowledge, since in some the reason is perverted by passion, or evil habit, or an evil disposition of nature . . .

Aquinas's argument that every human being has access to the basic precepts of moral law depends on the idea that we can recognize actions as being consistent with or contrary to nature. The same assumption is at work in contemporary arguments that certain behaviors (often sexual practices) are unnatural and should therefore be condemned. Sexual practices, in particular, have been the focus of such assertions. Philosopher **John Corvino** challenges this line of reasoning when applied to homosexuality. He argues that *unnatural* is a vague term with various meanings, but that on any construal the charge that homosexuality is unnatural would not establish that it is immoral.

FROM *Same Sex: Debating the Ethics, Science, and Culture of Homosexuality*
BY **John Corvino**[6]

HOMOSEXUAL SEX IS "UNNATURAL"

Many contend that homosexual sex is "unnatural." But what does that mean? Many things that people value—clothing, houses, medicine, and government, for example—are unnatural in some sense. On the other hand, many things that people detest—disease, suffering, and death, for example—are "natural" in the sense that they occur "in nature." If the unnaturalness charge is to be more than empty rhetorical flourish, those who levy it must specify what they mean. Borrowing from Burton Leiser, I will examine several possible meanings of "unnatural."

WHAT IS UNUSUAL OR ABNORMAL IS UNNATURAL

One meaning of "unnatural" refers to that which deviates from the norm, that is, from what most people do. Obviously, most people engage in heterosexual relationships. But does it follow that it is wrong to engage in homosexual relationships? Relatively few people read Sanskrit, pilot ships, play the mandolin, breed goats, or write with both hands, yet none of these activities is immoral simply because it is unusual. As the Ramsey Colloquium, a group of Jewish and Christian scholars who oppose homosexuality, writes, "The statistical frequency of an act does not determine its moral status." So while homosexuality might be unnatural in the sense of being unusual, that fact is morally irrelevant.

FIG. 7.2 Philosopher John Corvino *(© Cybelle Codish. Used by permission of J. Corvino)*

John Corvino (1969–)

An associate professor of philosophy at Wayne State University in Detroit and the author of *Same Sex*.

6 John Corvino, *Same Sex: Debating the Ethics, Science, and Culture of Homosexuality*, (Lanham, MA: Rowman & Littlefield, 1997), pp. 4–7. Reprinted with permission.

WHAT IS NOT PRACTICED BY OTHER ANIMALS IS UNNATURAL

Some people argue, "Even animals know better than to behave homosexually; homosexuality must be wrong." This argument is doubly flawed. First, it rests on a false premise. Numerous studies—including Anne Perkins's study of "gay" sheep and George and Molly Hunt's study of "lesbian" seagulls—have shown that some animals do form homosexual pair-bonds. Second, even if animals did not behave homosexually, that fact would not prove that homosexuality is immoral. After all, animals don't cook their food, brush their teeth, participate in religious worship, or attend college; human beings do all of these without moral censure. Indeed, the idea that animals could provide us with our standards—especially our sexual standards—is simply amusing.

FIG. 7.2-A One person's view of what is natural need not be another's. (© iStockphoto.com/Kjell Westergren)

WHAT DOES NOT PROCEED FROM INNATE DESIRES IS UNNATURAL

Recent studies suggesting a biological basis for homosexuality have resulted in two popular positions. One side proposes that homosexual people are "born that way" and that it is therefore natural (and thus good) for them to form homosexual relationships. The other side maintains that homosexuality is a lifestyle choice, which is therefore unnatural (and thus wrong). Both sides assume a connection between the origin of homosexual orientation, on the one hand, and the moral value of homosexual activity, on the other. And insofar as they share that assumption, both sides are wrong.

Consider first the pro-homosexual side: "They are born that way; therefore it's natural and good." This inference assumes that all innate desires are good ones (i.e., that they should be acted upon). But that assumption is clearly false. Research suggests that some people are born with a predisposition toward violence, but such people have no more right to strangle their neighbors than anyone else. So while people like Tommy and Jim may be born with homosexual tendencies, it doesn't follow that they ought to act on them. Nor does it follow that they ought *not* to act on them, even if the tendencies are not innate. I probably do not have any innate tendency to write with my left hand (since I, like everyone else in my family, have always been right-handed), but it doesn't follow that it would be immoral for me to do so. So simply asserting that homosexuality is a lifestyle choice will not show that it is an immoral lifestyle choice.

Do people "choose" to be homosexual? People certainly don't seem to choose their *sexual feelings*, at least not in any direct or obvious way. (Do you? Think about it.) Rather, they find certain people attractive and certain activities arousing, whether they "decide" to or not. Indeed, most people at some point in their lives wish that they could control their feelings more—for example, in situations of unrequited love—and find it frustrating that they cannot. What they *can* control to a considerable degree is how and when they act upon those feelings. In that sense, both homosexuality and heterosexuality involve lifestyle choices. But in either case, determining the origin of the feelings will not determine whether it is moral to act on them.

WHAT VIOLATES AN ORGAN'S PRINCIPAL PURPOSE IS UNNATURAL

Perhaps when people claim that homosexual sex is unnatural they mean that it cannot result in procreation. The idea behind the argument is that human organs have various natural purposes: eyes are for seeing, ears are for hearing, genitals are for procreating. According to this argument, it is immoral to use an organ in a way that violates its particular purpose.

Many of our organs, however, have multiple purposes. Tommy can use his mouth for talking, eating, breathing, licking stamps, chewing gum, kissing women, or kissing Jim; and it seems rather arbitrary to claim that all but the last use are "natural." (And if we say that some of the other uses are "unnatural, but not immoral," we have failed to specify a morally relevant sense of the term "natural.")

Just because people can and do use their sexual organs to procreate, it does not follow that they should not use them for other purposes. Sexual organs seem very well suited for expressing love, for giving and receiving pleasure, and for celebrating, replenishing, and enhancing a relationship—even when procreation is not a factor. Unless opponents of homosexuality are prepared to condemn heterosexual couples who use contraception or individuals who masturbate, they must abandon this version of the unnaturalness argument. Indeed, even the Roman Catholic Church, which forbids contraception and masturbation, approves of sex for sterile couples and of sex during pregnancy, neither of which can lead to procreation. The Church concedes here that intimacy and pleasure are morally legitimate purposes for sex, even in cases where procreation is impossible. But since homosexual sex can achieve these purposes as well, it is inconsistent for the Church to condemn it on the grounds that it is not procreative.

One might object that sterile heterosexual couples do not *intentionally* turn away from procreation, whereas homosexual couples do. But this distinction doesn't hold. It is no more possible for Tommy to procreate with a woman whose uterus has been removed than it is for him to procreate with Jim. By having sex with either one, he is intentionally engaging in a nonprocreative sexual act.

Yet one might press the objection further and insist that Tommy and the woman *could* produce children if the woman were fertile: whereas homosexual relationships are essentially infertile, heterosexual relationships are only incidentally so. But what does that prove? Granted, it might require less of a miracle for a woman without a uterus to become pregnant than for Jim to become pregnant, but it would require a miracle nonetheless. Thus it seems that the real difference here is not that one couple is fertile and the other not, nor that one couple "could" be fertile (with the help of a miracle) and the other not, but rather that one couple is male-female and the other male-male. In other words, sex between Tommy and Jim is wrong because it's male-male—i.e., because it's homosexual. But that, of course, is no argument at all.

WHAT IS DISGUSTING OR OFFENSIVE IS UNNATURAL

It often seems that when people call homosexuality "unnatural" they really just mean that it's disgusting. But plenty of morally neutral activities—handling snakes, eating snails, performing autopsies, cleaning toilets, and so on—disgust people.

"It often seems that when people call homosexuality 'unnatural' they really just mean that it's disgusting. But plenty of morally neutral activities— handling snakes, eating snails, performing autopsies, cleaning toilets, and so on— disgust people."

– JOHN CORVINO

Indeed, for centuries, most people found interracial relationships disgusting, yet that feeling—which has by no means disappeared—hardly proves that such relationships are wrong. In sum, the charge that homosexuality is unnatural, at least in its most common forms, is longer on rhetorical flourish than on philosophical cogency. At best it expresses an aesthetic judgment, not a moral judgment.

One need not rely on natural law to challenge moral relativism. However, the idea that nature is a guide to morality is a theme that appears in various theories that we will consider. It is most noticeable in Aristotle's moral theory, but implicit in some of Kant's arguments as well. We will also return to the issue of moral relativism when we consider recent critics of the Western moral tradition in the last few sections of this chapter.

- What is ethical relativism? Does it undermine morality's claim to authority?
- Can you think of a way in which one might account for the variety of moral principles (cultural relativism) without adopting ethical relativism? Do you think Aquinas succeeds in demonstrating that this is possible?
- What is ethical absolutism? Does it capture how you think of morality? What problems do you see with it?
- Why does Harman insist that he is giving "only the logical form" of relativism? What does this mean? What is he not claiming?
- Harman supposes that the foundation for morality is an implicit social agreement? Do you agree?
- Are you convinced by Aquinas's argument that cultures all recognize the same basic moral principles and that their disagreements have to do with applications of these basic principles?
- Do you agree with Corvino that we cannot base what is moral on what is natural and what is immoral on what is unnatural? How might Aquinas reply?

C. Egoism and Altruism

Most moral rules enjoin us to take into account the interests, feelings, or welfare of other people. The commands not to lie, not to kill, and not to steal, as well as the commands to keep our promises, treat others fairly, and be generous, are all commands that concern our relationships to other persons. (There can, of course, be moral rules that require us to take into account our own interests; for example, the prohibition of suicide or, as Kant thought, the **obligation** to develop our talents.)

One of the important assumptions of any morality, then, is that it is possible for us to act in the interests of other people. In addition, morality assumes that it is possible for us to do so *because* we are concerned about others' welfare or because we recognize that we ought to be. Someone who refrains from cheating, for example, simply because he or she is afraid of being caught acts purely self-interestedly; we would not think this person is morally praiseworthy. Again, a person who visits a dying relative in the hospital because he or she wants to ensure a substantial inheritance is not acting morally. Only if actions are motivated by a concern for others' interests do we call them truly moral actions.

One important theory, though, denies that we can be motivated simply by a concern for others. This is **psychological egoism**. Psychological egoism is the thesis that everyone, in fact, acts for his or her own advantage, and the only reason why people act respectfully or kindly toward each other is that that too, for one reason or another, is to their advantage. It might be fear of punishment that makes them act "correctly." Some have "ulterior motives"; that is, they expect other things later on, perhaps a favor in return or a reward in heaven after they die, or they are trying to avoid guilt or want a feeling of self-satisfaction. In popular language, the egoist position is often called **selfishness**.

One should be careful, though, to distinguish psychological egoism from ethical egoism. Psychological egoism asserts that our psychology is such that we cannot help but act in our own interests. In contrast, **ethical egoism** claims that even though we can act in others' interests because we are concerned for others, we *ought* always to act in our own interest. One of the most widely read contemporary ethical egoists was the late Ayn Rand, who wrote of "the virtue of selfishness."

It is psychological, not ethical, egoism that challenges the very possibility of any morality. One of Socrates' opponents in *The Republic* states the psychological egoist's view with brutal clarity:

 FROM **The *Republic***
BY **Plato**[7]

They say that to do wrong is naturally good, to be wronged is bad, but the suffering of injury so far exceeds in badness the good of inflicting it that when men have done wrong to each other and suffered it, and have had a taste of both, those who are unable to avoid the latter and practise the former decide that it is profitable to come to an agreement with each other neither to inflict injury nor to suffer it. As a result they begin to make laws and covenants, and the law's command they call lawful and just. This, they say, is the origin and essence of justice; it stands between the best and the worst, the best being to do wrong without paying the penalty and the worst to be wronged without the power of revenge. The just then is a mean between two extremes; it is welcomed and honoured because of men's lack of the power to do wrong. The man who has that power, the real man, would not make a compact with anyone not to inflict injury or suffer it. For him that would be madness. This then, Socrates, is, according to their argument, the nature and origin of justice.

Even those who practise justice do so against their will because they lack the power to do wrong. This we could realize very clearly if we imagined ourselves granting to both the just and the unjust the freedom to do whatever they liked. We could then follow both of them and observe where their desires led them, and we would catch the just man redhanded travelling the same road as the unjust. The reason is the desire for undue gain which every organism by nature pursues as a good, but the law forcibly sidetracks him to honour equality. The freedom I just mentioned would most easily occur if these men had the power which they say the ancestor of the Lydian Gyges possessed. The story is that he was a shepherd in the service of the ruler of Lydia. There was a violent rainstorm and an earthquake which broke open the ground and created a chasm at the place where he was tending sheep. Seeing this and marvelling, he went down into it. He saw, besides many other wonders of which we are told, a hollow bronze horse. There were window–like openings in it; he climbed through them and caught sight of a corpse which seemed of more than human stature, wearing nothing but a ring of gold on its finger. This ring the

---

shepherd put on and came out. He arrived at the usual monthly meeting which reported to the king on the state of the flocks, wearing the ring. As he was sitting among the others he happened to twist the hoop of the ring towards himself, to the inside of his hand, and as he did this he became invisible to those sitting near him and they went on talking as if he had gone. He marvelled at this and, fingering the ring, he turned the hoop outward again and became visible. Perceiving this he tested whether the ring had this power and so it happened: if he turned the hoop inwards he became invisible, but was visible when he turned it outwards. When he realized this, he at once arranged to become one of the messengers to the king. He went, committed adultery with the king's wife, attacked the king with her help, killed him, and took over the kingdom.

Now if there were two such rings, one worn by the just man, the other by the unjust, no one, as these people think, would be so incorruptible that he would stay on the path of justice or bring himself to keep away from other people's property and not touch it, when he could with impunity take whatever he wanted from the market, go into houses and have sexual relations with anyone he wanted, kill anyone, free all those he wished from prison, and do the other things which would make him like a god among

FIG. 7.3 Plato's character Glaucon suggests that we would all behave immorally if we were confident that we would not get caught. *(© iStockphoto.com/parema)*

men. His actions would be in no way different from those of the other and they would both follow the same path. This, some would say, is a great proof that no one is just willingly but under compulsion, so that justice is not one's private good, since wherever either thought he could do wrong with impunity he would do so. Every man believes that injustice is much more profitable to himself than justice, and any exponent of this argument will say that he is right. The man who did not wish to do wrong with that opportunity, and did not touch other people's property, would be thought by those who knew it to be very foolish and miserable. They would praise him in public, thus deceiving one another, for fear of being wronged. So much for my second topic.

Both egoist positions are contrasted with what is usually called **altruism**, that is, acting for the sake of other people's interests. There are degrees of altruism. One may be altruistic because one acts morally because one recognizes an obligation to other people. Or one may be altruistic in actually taking another person's interests (such as those of one's lover or brother or sister) as important or even more important than one's own. Altruism can also be divided into two distinct theses, although these are not so often distinguished. Psychological altruism says that people "naturally" act for each other's sakes. (This thesis is defended by several important philosophers in later sections.) It has rarely been argued, however, that people are compelled to act altruistically. Thus psychological egoism is usually defended for all cases; *psychological altruism*, in contrast, is defended only for some cases. *Ethical altruism*, on the other hand, says that people ought to act with each other's interests in mind. This is, of course, a basic statement of morality, best summarized in the so-called **Golden Rule:** "Do unto others as you would have them do unto you." (We shall see a modern version of this ancient teaching in the philosophy of Kant.)

The most familiar and most difficult question is about psychological egoism: Is it true that people act only for their own self-interest? A famous story about Abraham Lincoln is an apt illustration of the thesis. As Lincoln was arguing the psychological egoist position with a friend, his coach was passing a mud slide where a mother pig was squealing as her piglets were drowning. Lincoln stopped the coach, saved the piglets, then moved on. His friend asked him whether that wasn't a clear case of altruism. Lincoln replied: "Why that was the very essence of selfishness. I should have had no peace of mind all day had I gone on and left that suffering old sow worrying over those piglets. I did it to get peace of mind, don't you see?"[8]

Many actions are based upon self-interest and are "selfish" without any question. The question is, are there any actions that are not based on self-interest? Lincoln's response is an excellent example because it would seem as if his action is not for selfish reasons at all. Yet, according to him, there was a selfish reason behind his actions—his own sense of satisfaction and "peace of mind." Could this be true of all our actions?

Consider the following debate between two famous ancient Chinese philosophers.

D. Are We Naturally Selfish? A Debate

At the bottom of the ongoing debates about justice, government, and the role of society in constituting and enforcing justice, a deeper debate about human nature is always just under the surface. In the Western tradition, we know this debate by way of two thousand years of arguments about so-called original sin, that is, the idea that people are essentially flawed just by virtue of the fact that they are human. If this is so, if people are, for instance, naturally selfish, then that fact would seem to dictate corrective governmental or cultural sanctions. Thomas Hobbes's view of man in the state of nature makes this point quite clear. On the other hand, if one has a more benign view of human nature, as, for example, in the philosophy of Jean-Jacques Rousseau, then the sanctions of the state should be more modest, perhaps even minimal. (These views of Hobbes and Rousseau will be considered later in this chapter.) But here we look at a different version of that debate in the philosophies of ancient China. On the one hand, there is the philosophy of **Mencius**, a disciple of the great Chinese philosopher Confucius. Mencius argues that humanity is basically benevolent, that every person has within him or her a sense of compassion for others. Against this view, the later Confucian philosopher **Xunzi** argues that people are naturally selfish and that cultivation is necessary to correct their evil dispositions.

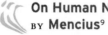 **On Human Nature: Man Is Good**
BY Mencius[9]

6. Mencius said, "No man is devoid of a heart sensitive to the suffering of others. Such a sensitive heart was possessed by the Former Kings and this manifested itself in compassionate government. With such a sensitive heart behind compassionate government, it was as easy to rule the Empire as rolling it on your palm.

"My reason for saying that no man is devoid of a heart sensitive to the suffering of others is this. Suppose a man were, all of a sudden, to see a young child on

8 Quoted in F. Sharp, *Ethics* (New York: Appleton-Century-Crofts, 1928).

9 Mencius, *Human Nature*, trans. D. C. Lau, (New York: Penguin Classics, 1970), pp. 82–83. Copyright © 1970 by D. C. Lau. Reprinted by permission of Penguin Books, Ltd.

the verge of falling into a well. He would certainly be moved to compassion, not because he wanted to get in the good graces of the parents, nor because he wished to win the praise of his fellow villagers or friends, nor yet because he disliked the cry of the child. From this it can be seen that whoever is devoid of the heart of compassion is not human, whoever is devoid of the heart of shame is not human, whoever is devoid of the heart of courtesy and modesty is not human, and whoever is devoid of the heart of right and wrong is not human. The heart of compassion is the germ of benevolence; the heart of shame, of dutifulness; the heart of courtesy and modesty, of observance of the rites; the heart of right and wrong, of wisdom. Man has these four germs just as he has four limbs. For a man possessing these four germs to deny his own potentialities is for him to cripple himself; for him to deny the potentialities of his prince is for him to cripple his prince. If a man is able to develop all these four germs that he possesses, it will be like a fire starting up or a spring coming through. When these are fully developed, he can take under his protection the whole realm within the Four Seas, but if he fails to develop them, he will not be able to serve his parents."

7. Mencius said, "Is the maker of arrows really more unfeeling than the maker of armour? He is afraid lest he should fail to harm people, whereas the maker of armour is afraid lest he should fail to protect them. The case is similar with the sorcerer-doctor and the coffin-maker. For this reason one cannot be too careful in the choice of one's calling.

FIG. 7.4 Mencius believed that we would all feel compelled to stop a young child from harming himself or herself. (© iStockphoto.com/Anyka)

"Confucius said, 'The best neighbourhood is where benevolence is to be found. Not to live in such a neighbourhood when one has the choice cannot by any means be considered wise.' Benevolence is the high honour bestowed by Heaven and the peaceful abode of man. Not to be benevolent when nothing stands in the way is to show a lack of wisdom. A man neither benevolent nor wise, devoid of courtesy and dutifulness, is a slave. A slave ashamed of serving is like a maker of bows ashamed of making bows, or a maker of arrows ashamed of making arrows. If one is ashamed, there is no better remedy than to practise benevolence. Benevolence is like archery: an archer makes sure his stance is correct before letting fly the arrow, and if he fails to hit the mark, he does not hold it against his victor. He simply seeks the cause within himself."

Mencius (372-289 B.C.E.)
A Confucian philosopher who emphasized our natural compassion and virtue.

"Crooked wood
needs to undergo
steaming and
bending by the
carpenter's tools;
then only is it
straight. Blunt
metal needs to
undergo grinding
and whetting;
then only is it
sharp. Now the
original nature
of man is evil, so
he must submit
himself to teachers
and laws before he
can be just."

– XUNZI

FROM "Human Nature Is Evil"
BY Xunzi[10]

The nature of man is evil; his goodness is acquired.

His nature being what it is, man is born, first, with a desire for gain. If this desire is followed, strife will result and courtesy will disappear. Second, man is born with envy and hate. If these tendencies are followed, injury and cruelty will abound and loyalty and faithfulness will disappear. Third, man is born with passions of the ear and eye as well as the love of sound and beauty. If these passions are followed, excesses and disorderliness will spring up and decorum and righteousness will disappear. Hence to give rein to man's original nature and to yield to man's emotions will assuredly lead to strife and disorderliness, and he will revert to a state of barbarism. Therefore it is only under the influence of teachers and laws and the guidance of the rules of decorum and righteousness that courtesy will be observed, etiquette respected, and order restored. From all this it is evident that the nature of man is evil and that his goodness is acquired.

Crooked wood needs to undergo steaming and bending by the carpenter's tools; then only is it straight. Blunt metal needs to undergo grinding and whetting; then only is it sharp. Now the original nature of man is evil, so he must submit himself to teachers and laws before he can be just; he must submit himself to the rules of decorum and righteousness before he can be orderly. On the other hand, without teachers and laws, men are biased and unjust; without decorum and righteousness, men are rebellious and disorderly. In ancient times the sage-kings knew that man's nature was evil and therefore biased and unjust, rebellious and disorderly. Thereupon they created the codes of decorum and righteousness and established laws and ordinances in order to bend the nature of man and set it right, and in order to transform his nature and guide it. All men are thus made to conduct themselves in a manner that is orderly and in accordance with the Way. At present, those men who are influenced by teachers and laws, who have accumulated culture and learning, and who are following the paths of decorum and righteousness, are the gentlemen. On the other hand those who give rein to their nature, who indulge in their willfulness, and who disregard decorum and righteousness, are the inferior men. From all this it is evident that the nature of man is evil and that his goodness is acquired.

Mencius says: "The reason man is ready to learn is that his nature is originally good." I reply: This is not so. This is due to a lack of knowledge about the original nature of man and of understanding of the distinction between what is natural and what is acquired. Original nature is a heavenly endowment; it cannot be learned, and it cannot be striven after. As to rules of decorum and righteousness, they have been brought forth by the sages, they can be attained by learning, and they can be achieved by striving. That which cannot be learned and cannot be striven after and rests with Heaven is what I call original nature. That which can be attained by learning and achieved by striving and

Xunzi (298-230 B.C.E.)

A Confucian philosopher who emphasized the importance of culture in replacing man's natural selfishness with virtue.

FIG. 7.5 William Blake's *The body of Abel found by Adam and Eve*. The story of Cain and Abel suggests that evil behavior has been part of the human world (virtually) since the beginning. *(Tate, London / Art Resource, NY)*

rests with man is what I call acquired character. This is the distinction between original nature and acquired character. Now by the nature of man, the eye has the faculty of seeing and the ear has the faculty of hearing. But the keenness of the faculty of sight is inseparable from the eye, and the keenness of the faculty of hearing is inseparable from the ear. It is evident that keenness of sight and keenness of hearing cannot be learned.

Mencius says: "The original nature of man is good; but because men all ruin it and lose it, it becomes evil." I reply: In this he is gravely mistaken. Regarding the nature of man, as soon as he is born, he tends to depart from its original state and depart from its natural disposition, and he is bent on ruining it and losing it. From all this, it is evident that the nature of man is evil and that his goodness is acquired.

To say that man's original nature is good means that it can become beautiful without leaving its original state and it can become beneficial without leaving its natural disposition. This is to maintain that beauty pertains to the original state and disposition and goodness pertains to the heart and mind in the same way as the keenness of the faculty of sight is inseparable from the eye and the keenness of the faculty of hearing is inseparable from the ear, just as we say that the eye is keen in seeing or the ear is keen in hearing. Now as to the nature of man, when he is hungry he desires to be filled, when he is cold he desires warmth, when he is tired he desires rest. This is man's natural disposition. But now a man may be hungry and yet in the presence of elders he dare not be the first to eat. This is because he

FIG. 7.6 Are we naturally selfish? *(© iStockphoto.com/Dzianis Davydau)*

has to yield precedence to someone. He may be tired and yet he dare not take a rest. This is because he has to labor in the place of someone. For a son to yield to his father and a younger brother to yield to his older brother, for a son to labor in the place of his father and a younger brother to labor in the place of his older brother—both of these kinds of actions are opposed to man's original nature and contrary to man's feeling. Yet they are the way of the filial son and in accordance with the rules of decorum and righteousness. It appears if a person follows his natural disposition he will show no courtesy, and if he shows courtesy he is acting contrary to his natural disposition. From all this it is evident that the nature of man is evil and that his goodness is acquired.

It may be asked: "If man's original nature is evil, whence do the rules of decorum and righteousness arise?" I reply: All rules of decorum and righteousness are the products of the acquired virtue of the sage and not the products of the nature of man. Thus, the potter presses the clay and makes the vessel—but the vessel is the product of the potter's acquired skill and not the product of his original nature. Or again, the craftsman hews pieces of wood and makes utensils—but utensils are the product of the carpenter's acquired skills and not the product of his original nature. The sage gathers many ideas and thoughts and becomes well versed in human affairs, in order to bring forth the rules of decorum and righteousness and establish laws and institutions. So then the rules of decorum and righteousness and laws and institutions are similarly the products of the acquired virtue of the sage and not the products of his original nature.

. . .

Man wishes to be good because his nature is evil. If a person is unimportant he wishes to be important, if he is ugly he wishes to be beautiful, if he is confined he wishes to be at large, if he is poor he wishes to be rich, if he is lowly he wishes to be honored—whatever a person does not have within himself, he seeks from without. But the rich do not wish for wealth and the honorable do not wish for position, for whatever a person has within himself he does not seek from without. From this it may be seen that man wishes to be good because his nature is evil. Now the original nature of man is really without decorum and righteousness, hence he strives to learn and seeks to obtain them.

The arguments that are still considered to be the most powerful and definitive against psychological egoism were formulated as sermons by an English bishop, **Joseph Butler**. Bishop Butler argues that such reasoning as Lincoln's turns on a number of fallacies. Butler begins by accepting the distinction between "private good and a person's own preservation and happiness" and "respect to society and the promotion of public good and the happiness of society." But then he insists that these are not, as the egoists argue, always in conflict and fighting against each other. To the contrary, they are almost always in perfect harmony.

Against Egoism
BY **Joseph Butler**[11]

From this review and comparison of the nature of man as respecting self and as respecting society, it will plainly appear that there are as real and the same kind of indications in human nature that we were made for society and to do good to our fellow creatures, as that we were intended to take care of our own life and health and private good; and that the same objections lie against one of these assertions as against the other.

First, there is a natural principle of *benevolence* in man, which is in some degree to *society* what *self-love* is to the *individual*. And if there be in mankind any disposition to friendship; if there be any such thing as compassion, for compassion is momentary love; if there be any such thing as the paternal or filial affections; if there be any affection in human nature the object and end of which is the good of another—this is itself benevolence or the love of another. Be it ever so short, be it in ever so low a degree, or ever so unhappily confined, it proves the assertion and points out what we were designed for, as really as though it were in a higher degree and more extensive. I must however remind you that though benevolence and self-love are different, though the former tends most directly to public good, and the latter to private, yet they are so perfectly coincident that the greatest satisfactions to ourselves depend upon our having benevolence in a due degree, and that self-love is one chief security of our right behavior toward society. It may be added that their mutual coinciding, so that we can scarce promote one without the other, is equally a proof that we were made for both.

Secondly, this will further appear, from observing that the *several passions and affections*, which are distinct both from benevolence and self-love, do in general contribute and lead us to *public* good as really as to *private*. It might be thought too minute and particular, and would carry us too great a length, to distinguish between and compare together the several passions or appetites distinct from benevolence, whose primary use and intention is the security and good of society; and the passions distinct from self-love, whose primary intention and design is the security and good of the individual. It is enough to the present argument that desire of esteem from others, contempt and esteem of them, love of society as distinct from affection to the good of it, indignation against successful vice—that these are public affections or passions, have an immediate respect to others, naturally lead us to regulate our behavior in such a manner as will be of service to our fellow creatures. If any or all of these may be considered likewise as private affections, as tending to private good, this does not hinder them from being public affections, too, or destroy the good influence of them upon society, and their tendency to public good. It may be added that as persons without any conviction from reason of the desirableness of life would yet of course preserve it merely from the appetite of hunger, so by acting merely from regard (suppose) to reputation, without any consideration of the good of others, men

Bishop Joseph Butler (1692–1752)

A powerful English clergyman who formulated what are still recognized as the standard arguments against psychological egoism in his *Fifteen Sermons* (1726).

---

[11] Joseph Butler, *Sermons* (Boston: Hillard, Gray, Little, and Wilkins, 1827).

FIG. 7.7 Butler argues that we have a natural tendency toward benevolence toward others, and that we can hardly promote our own well-being without promoting that of others (and vice versa).
(© iStockphoto.com/Elena Elisseeva)

often contribute to public good. In both these instances they are plainly instruments in the hands of another, in the hands of Providence, to carry on ends, the preservation of the individual and good of society, which they themselves have not in their view or intention. The sum is, men have various appetites, passions, and particular affections, quite distinct both from self-love and from benevolence—all of these have a tendency to promote both public and private good, and may be considered as respecting others and ourselves equally and in common; but some of them seem most immediately to respect others, or tend to public good, others of them most immediately to respect self, or tend to private good; as the former are not benevolence, so the latter are not self-love; neither sort are instances of our love either to ourselves or others, but only instances of our Maker's care and love both of the individual and the species, and proofs that He intended we should be instruments of good to each other, as well as that we should be so to ourselves.

Thirdly, there is a principle of reflection in men by which they distinguish between, approve and disapprove, their own actions. We are plainly constituted such sort of creatures as to reflect upon our own nature. The mind can take a view of what passes within itself, its propensions, aversions, passions, affections, as respecting such objects and in such degrees, and of the several actions consequent thereupon. In this survey it approves of one, disapproves of another, and toward a third is affected in neither of these ways, but is quite indifferent. This principle in man by which he approves or disapproves his heart, temper, and actions, is conscience. . . . That this faculty tends to restrain men from doing mischief to each other, and leads them to do good, is too manifest to need being insisted upon. Thus a parent has the affection of love to his children; this leads him to take care of, to educate, to make due provision for them; the natural affection leads to this, but the reflection that it is his proper business, what belongs to him, that it is right and commendable so to do—this added to the affection becomes a much more settled principle and carries him on through more labor and difficulties for the sake of his children than he would undergo from that affection alone, if he thought it, and the course of action it led to, either indifferent or criminal. This indeed is impossible, to do that which is good and not to approve of it; for which reason they are frequently not considered as distinct, though they really are, for men often approve of the actions of others which they will not imitate, and likewise do that which they approve not. It cannot possibly be denied that there is this principle of reflection or conscience in human nature. Suppose a man to relieve an innocent person in great distress, suppose the same man afterwards, in the fury of anger, to do the greatest mischief to a person who had given no just cause of offense; to aggravate the injury, add the circumstances of former friendship and obligation from the injured person, let the man who is supposed to have done these two different actions coolly reflect upon them afterwards, without regard to their consequences to himself; to assert that any common man would be affected in the same way toward these different actions, that he would make no distinction between them, but approve or disapprove them equally, is too glaring a falsity to need being confuted. There is therefore this principle of reflection or conscience in mankind.

. . .

If it be said that there are persons in the world who are in great measure without the natural affections toward their fellow creatures, there are likewise instances of persons without the common natural affections to themselves; but the nature of man is not to be judged of by either of these, but by what appears in the common world, in the bulk of mankind.

———————

In short, Butler argues that merely acting on one's own desires does not make an action selfish, for all actions are, in some sense, based on our desires, but at least some of those desires are desires to serve someone else's interests. Thus the "object" of desire is what makes an act selfish or unselfish, not merely the fact that one's own desire is acted upon. Nor can simply acting with some benefit to oneself make an action selfish, for even if we agreed that an act gives us some benefit (for example, peace of mind), it may still be the case that most of the benefit is for someone else. Even if peace of mind typically follows virtuous actions, that does not show that our motivation is selfish. The satisfaction that accompanies good acts is itself not the motivation of the act. Here is the answer to Lincoln. His act was, despite his philosophical claims, an altruistic one; his satisfaction was not the motive of the act but only its consequence.

- How are psychological egoism and ethical egoism distinguished? Do you agree with either? Are you convinced by the story of the magical ring of Gyges, a story that suggests that a person who could do wrong with impunity would do so?
- Mencius argues that human beings "by nature" have sympathy for one another. Why do you think, then, that some people display utter callousness toward others, and we all find it difficult to sympathize with some people?
- What do you think Mencius means when he quotes Confucius as saying, "A man neither benevolent nor wise, devoid of courtesy and dutifulness, is a slave"?
- Xunzi argues that people are by nature evil and unjust and that they require teachers and laws to become good and just. If so, then how can we be sure that our teachings and laws are just and good, since they are made and taught by human beings whose nature is evil? Wouldn't good teachings and laws require some kernel of natural goodness? Does Xunzi offer a solution to this problem?
- Are ethical altruism and psychological egoism compatible? How does Bishop Butler reconcile the two?
- How is it that our private good is so bound up with the public good?

E. Morality as Virtue: Aristotle

Aristotle's *Ethics* (properly called *The Nicomachean Ethics*) is the best systematic guide to ancient Greek moral and ethical thinking. The significant feature of Greek ethics is its stress on being virtuous as opposed to merely following moral rules. Aristotle's concept of virtue is based on a very special conception of man as a rational being. **Virtue**, accordingly, is rational activity, activity in accordance with a rational principle. Having defined virtue in this way,

"If it be said that there are persons in the world who are in great measure without the natural affections toward their fellow creatures, there are likewise instances of persons without the common natural affections to themselves; but the nature of man is not to be judged of by either of these, but by what appears in the common world, in the bulk of mankind."

– JOSEPH BUTLER

Aristotle can then defend, for example, courage as a virtue by showing that the courageous man is more rational than the coward.

Aristotle arrives at his conception of man as an essentially rational being by asking what "the natural good for man" is. This, he argues, will be discovered by finding what all men desire "for its own sake" and not "for the sake of anything else."

FROM *The Nicomachean Ethics*
BY Aristotle[12]

Every art and every kind of inquiry, and likewise every act and purpose, seems to aim at some good; and so it has been well said that the good is that at which everything aims. But a difference is observable among these aims or ends. What is aimed at is sometimes the exercise of a faculty, sometimes a certain result beyond that exercise. And where there is an end beyond that act, there the result is better than the exercise of the faculty. Now since there are many kinds of actions and many arts and sciences, it follows that there are many ends also; *e.g.* health is the end of medicine, ships of shipbuilding, victory of the art of war, and wealth of economy. But when several of these are subordinated to some one art or science,—as the making of bridles and other trappings to the art of horsemanship, and this in turn, along with all else that the soldier does, to the art of war, and so on,—then the end of the master art is always more desired than the end of the subordinate arts, since these are pursued for its sake. And this is equally true whether the end in view be the mere exercise of a faculty or something beyond that, as in the above instances.

If then in what we do there be some end which we wish for on its own account, choosing all the others as means to this, but not every end without exception as a means to something else (for so we should go on *ad infinitum*, and desire would be left void and objectless),—this evidently will be the good or the best of all things.

FIG. 7.8 Raphael contrasts Aristotle's down-to-earth approach with Plato's theory of transcendent Forms. *(Scala / Art Resource, NY)*

We see here the same logical strategy that Aristotle used in Chapter 2—the idea that every act is for the sake of something else (we want to earn a dollar to buy ourselves some food, and we want that food to satisfy our hunger). But since there can be no "infinite regress," there must be some ultimate end. Aristotle examines two popular conceptions of this ultimate end that is the natural good for man: pleasure and success. He rejects both because neither pleasure nor success is desired for its own sake. Rather, happiness is what all men desire for its own sake, and it is therefore the natural good for man.

It seems that men not unreasonably take their notions of the good or happiness from the lives actually led, and that the masses who are the least refined suppose it to be pleasure, which is the reason why they aim at

---

12 Aristotle, *The Nicomachean Ethics*, 8th ed., trans. by F. H. Peters (London: K. Paul, Trench, Tubner & Co., Ltd., 1888).

nothing higher than the life of enjoyment. For the most conspicuous kinds of life are three: this life of enjoyment, the life of the statesman, and, thirdly, the contemplative life. The mass of men show themselves utterly slavish in their preference for the life of brute beasts, but their views receive consideration because many of those in high places have the tastes of Sardanapalus. Men of refinement with a practical turn prefer honour; for I suppose we may say that honour is the aim of the statesman's life. But this seems too superficial to be the good we are seeking: for it appears to depend upon those who give rather than upon those who receive it; while we have a pre-sentiment that the good is something that is peculiarly a man's own and can scarce be taken away from him. Moreover, these men seem to pursue honour in order that they may be assured of their own excellence,—at least, they wish to be honoured by men of sense, and by those who know them, and on the ground of their virtue or excel-lence. It is plain, then, that in their view, at any rate, virtue or excellence is better than honour; and perhaps we should take this to be the end of the statesman's life, rather than honour. But virtue or excellence also appears too incomplete to be what we want; for it seems that a man might have virtue and yet be asleep or be inactive all his life, and, moreover, might meet with the greatest disasters and misfortunes; and no one would maintain that such a man is happy, except for argument's sake. But we will not dwell on these matters now, for they are sufficiently discussed in the popular treatises. The third kind of life is the life of contemplation: we will treat of it further on. As for the money-making life, it is something quite contrary to nature; and wealth evidently is not the good of which we are in search, for it is merely useful as a means to some-thing else. So we might rather take pleasure and virtue or excellence to be ends than wealth; for they are chosen on their own account. But it seems that not even they are the end, though much breath has been wasted in attempts to show that they are.

· · ·

Let us return once more to the question, what this good can be of which we are in search. It seems to be different in different kinds of action and in different arts,—one thing in medicine and another in war, and so on. What then is the good in each of these cases? Surely that for the sake of which all else is done. And that in medicine is health, in war is victory, in building is a house,—a different thing in each different case, but always, in whatever we do and in whatever we choose, the end. For it is always for the sake of the end that all else is done. If then there be one end of all that man does, this end will be the realizable good,—or these ends, if there be more than one.

By this generalization our argument is brought to the same point as before. This point we must try to explain more clearly. We see that there are many ends. But some of these are chosen only as means, as wealth, flutes, and the whole class of instru-ments. And so it is plain that not all ends are final. But the best of all things must, we conceive, be something final. If then there be only one final end, this will be what we are seeking—or if there be more than one, then the most final of them. Now that which is pursued as an end in itself is more final than that which is pursued as means to something else, and that which is never chosen as means than that which is chosen both as an end in itself and as means, and that is strictly final which is always chosen as an end in itself and never as means.

Happiness seems more than anything else to answer to this description: for we always choose it for itself, and never for the sake of something else; while honour and pleasure and reason, and all virtue or excellence, we choose partly indeed for them-selves (for, apart from any result, we should choose each of them), but partly also for the sake of happiness, supposing that they will help to make us happy. But no one chooses happiness for the sake of these things, or as a means to anything else at all. We seem to be led to the same conclusion when we start from the notion of self-sufficiency. The final good is thought to be self-sufficing [or all-sufficing]. In applying this term we do not regard a man as an individual leading a solitary life, but we also take account of parents, children, wife, and, in short, friends and fellow-citizens generally, since man is naturally a social being. Some limit must indeed be set to this; for if you go on to parents and descendants and friends of friends, you will never come to a stop. But this we will consider further on: for the present we will take self-sufficing to mean what by itself makes life desirable and in want of nothing. And happiness is believed to answer to this description. And further, happiness is believed to be the most desirable thing in the world, and that not merely as one among other good things: if it were merely one among other good things [so that other things could be added to it], it is plain that the addition of the least of other goods must make it more desirable; for the addition becomes a surplus of good, and of two goods the greater is always more desirable. Thus it seems that happiness is something final and self-sufficing, and is the end of all that man does.

We need some idea of what happiness is, and Aristotle here gives us his idea: Happiness is living according to **rationality**, thereby exercising our most vital human faculty.

But perhaps the reader thinks that though no one will dispute the statement that happiness is the best thing in the world, yet a still more precise definition of it is needed. This will best be gained, I think, by asking, What is the function of man? For as the goodness and the excellence of a piper or a sculptor, or the practiser of any art, and generally of those who have any function or business to do, lies in that function, so man's good would seem to lie in his function, if he has one. But can we suppose that, while a carpenter [or] a cobbler has a function and a business of his own, man has no business and no function assigned him by nature? Nay, surely as his several members, eye and hand and foot, plainly have each his own function, so we must suppose that man also has some function over and above all these.

What then is it? Life evidently he has in common even with the plants, but we want that which is peculiar to him. We must exclude, therefore, the life of mere nutrition and growth. Next to this comes the life of sense; but this too he plainly shares with horses and cattle and all kinds of animals. There remains then the life whereby he acts—the life of his rational nature, with its two sides or divisions, one rational as obeying reason, the other rational as having and exercising reason. But as this expression is ambiguous, we must be understood

FIG. 7.9 The Nike, the Greek goddess of Victory, rewarded those who showed excellence in battle. A virtue, according to Aristotle, is a particular excellence that has become habitual.

(Image © Slimewoo, 2011. Used under license from Shutterstock.com)

to mean thereby the life that consists in the exercise [not the mere possession] of the faculties; for this seems to be more properly entitled to the name.

The function of man, then, is exercise of his vital faculties [or soul] on one side in obedience to reason, and on the other side with reason. But what is called the function of a man of any profession and the function of a man who is good in that profession are, generically the same, e.g., of a harper and of a good harper; and this holds in all cases without exception, only that in the case of the latter his superior excellence at his work is added; for we say a harper's function is to harp, and a good harper's to harp well. Man's function then being, as we say, a kind of life—that is to say, exercise of his faculties and action of various kinds with reason—the good man's function is to do this well and beautifully [or nobly]. But the function of anything is done well when it is done in accordance with the proper excellence of that thing. If this be so the result is that the good of man is exercise of his faculties in accordance with excellence or virtue, or, if there be more than one, in accordance with the best and most complete virtue. But there must also be a full term of years for this exercise; for one swallow or one fine day does not make a spring, nor does one day or any small space of time make a blessed or happy man.

It is important to notice the structure of Aristotle's argument here, for you will see it emerge often in philosophy as well as in your own thoughts. The argument is an argument on the basis of what is "natural" to man. (We have already shown that Aquinas used this reasoning, an approach that he credited to Aristotle.) The good for man is that which is "natural" to him, and that means, according to Aristotle, what is special or unique to him as well. Thus mere "nutrition and growth," that is, eating and keeping physically healthy, cannot in themselves be happiness (although they are necessary for happiness) because even plants, Aristotle says, have this "goal." Nor can happiness lie in simple experience, even exciting experiences, since even a cow has this as the "end" of its life. What is unique to man, Aristotle concludes, is his rationality, his ability to act on rational principles. But action according to rational principles, is, as we shall see, precisely what Aristotle thinks virtue is. Thus happiness turns out to be an "activity of the soul in accordance with perfect virtue." (This is the key phrase of his work.) This "perfect virtue" is also called "excellence," and Aristotle's ethics is often called an ethics of self-realization, the goal of which is to make each individual as perfect as possible in all ways:

Indeed, in addition to what we have said, a man is not good at all unless he takes pleasure in noble deeds. No one would call a man just who did not take pleasure in doing justice, nor generous who took no pleasure in acts of generosity, and so on. If this be so, the manifestations of excellence will be pleasant in themselves. But they are also both good and noble, and that in the highest degree—at least, if the good man's judgment about them is right, for this is his judgment. Happiness, then, is at once the best and noblest and pleasantest thing in the world.

So far, however, it seems as if virtue and happiness are strictly individual matters. But this is not the case. Aristotle's well-known belief that man is a social animal is as important as these other principles. Thus, the principles of reason and rationality that enter into his *Ethics* will have the interests of society as well as the individual built into them. (Aristotle even says that there is no real distinction between ethics and politics and that the proper end of ethics is politics.) Virtue, accordingly, is also a social conception, and most of the virtues that Aristotle discusses have much to do with one's role in society. (Courage, for example, is particularly applicable to soldiers.) Happiness in general, therefore, has its social dimensions.

"The good of man is exercise of his faculties in accordance with excellence or virtue, or, if there be more than one, in accordance with the best and most complete virtue."

– ARISTOTLE

For example, Aristotle argues that both respect and honor are ingredients in the good life. For Aristotle, the happy person, the virtuous person, is mainly a good citizen. It is necessary to add, however, that the only people who could qualify for Aristotle's good life were Greek citizens, which meant that women, children, slaves, and anyone who did not have the good fortune to be born Greek did not even have a chance at being happy, in Aristotle's sense.[13]

Not only does happiness have a social dimension and not only are the virtues socially defined, but the good life, according to Aristotle, must be taught us by society. Accordingly, Aristotle talks a great deal about the need for a "good education," and he goes so far as to say that if a person has not been brought up "properly," then no amount of philosophy will be able to make him either virtuous or happy. He also says that young people, because they are "inexperienced in the actions of life" and are "so ruled by their passions," should not try to learn moral philosophy, which depends upon maturity and rationality. On this point, however, we will ignore Aristotle's warnings. For growing older and more "mature" is certainly no guarantee of wisdom, and the passions of youth are sometimes more geared toward virtue than the "rationality" of established maturity.

We have already seen Aristotle's starting point: Every act has its goal (or "good"), and ultimately there is a goal (or "chief good") toward which all human acts aim, and it is generally called happiness (**eudaimonia**). But, Aristotle adds, this is not much help, for people give very different accounts of what they take to be the ingredients in happiness. Some say that it is pleasure, others say it is wealth or honor. We have seen Aristotle's arguments against these views and his conclusion that happiness must be "activity in accordance with rational principle," which means, virtuous activity. The key to Aristotle's ethics, then, lies in his concept of virtue.

Aristotle distinguishes two kinds of virtues, the practical or moral virtues (courage, generosity, and so on) and the intellectual virtues (skill in mathematics and philosophy). Although Aristotle thinks the highest virtue is the intellectual virtue of philosophical **contemplation**, most of his discussion of virtue centers on the moral virtues. We now take a closer look at how moral virtues are acquired, what Aristotle means by a moral virtue, and what the moral virtues are.

> Excellence, then, being of these two kinds, intellectual and moral, intellectual excellence owes its birth and growth mainly to instruction, and so requires time and experience, while moral excellence is the result of habit or custom and has accordingly in our language received a name formed by a slight change from the word for custom. From this it is plain that none of the moral excellences or virtues is implanted in us by nature; for that which is by nature cannot be altered by training. For instance, a stone naturally tends to fall downwards, and you could not train it to rise upwards, though you tried to do so by throwing it up ten thousand times, nor could you train fire to move downwards, nor accustom anything which naturally behaves in one way to behave in any other way. The virtues, then, come neither by nature nor against nature, but nature gives the capacity for acquiring them, and this is developed by training.
>
> Again, where we do things by nature we get the power first, and put this power forth in act afterwards: as we plainly see in the case of the senses; for it is not by

---

[13] It is necessary to say something about Aristotle's special notion of *happiness*, which is not at all like our conception of "feeling happy." Aristotle's term (*eudaimonia*) means more like "living well," and it includes such matters as one's status in society and virtuous acts as well as good feelings. No matter how good you feel about yourself—even if you are in a state of ecstasy all the time—you would not be happy in Aristotle's sense unless you had these other advantages and acted virtuously as well.

constantly seeing and hearing that we acquire those faculties, but, on the contrary, we had the power first and then used it, instead of acquiring the power by the use. But the virtues we acquire by doing the acts, as is the case with the arts too. We learn an art by doing that which we wish to do when we have learned it; we become builders by building, and harpers by harping. And so by doing just acts we become just, and by doing acts of temperance and courage we become temperate and courageous.

. . .

Again, both the moral virtues and the corresponding vices result from and are formed by the same acts; and this is the case with the arts also. It is by harping that good harpers and bad harpers alike are produced: and so with builders and the rest; by building well they will become good builders, and bad builders by building badly. Indeed, if it were not so, they would not want anybody to teach them, but would all be born either good or bad at their trades. And it is just the same with the virtues also. It is by our conduct in our intercourse with other men that we become just or unjust, and by acting in circumstances of danger, and training ourselves to feel fear or confidence, that we become courageous or cowardly. So, too, with our animal appetites and the passion of anger; for by behaving in this way or in that on the occasions with which these passions are concerned, some become temperate and gentle,

FIG. 7.10 The sculpture of Thomas Jefferson in the Jefferson Monument portrays him as a man of contemplation in Aristotle's sense. He appears full of life and vitality and interested in the world around him. *(Image © 2011. Used under license from Shutterstock.com)*

and others profligate and ill-tempered. In a word, acts of any kind produce habits or characters of the same kind. Hence we ought to make sure that our acts be of a certain kind; for the resulting character varies as they vary. It makes no small difference, therefore, whether a man be trained from his youth up in this way or in that, but a great difference, or rather all the difference.

Aristotle's point here is not just that the virtues are acquired by practice; he is also arguing that virtue is a state of character. The virtuous person wants to do virtuous acts, and he does them "naturally." We sometimes think that we are moral just because we believe in moral principles. But believing is not enough—virtuous action is required. But not even virtuous action by itself is enough to make us virtuous. We sometimes think a person is virtuous because he "forces himself" to do what he is supposed to. Not according to Aristotle. The virtuous person is one who does what he is supposed to do because he wants to because it is built into his very character. It is even essential, according to Aristotle, that the virtuous man enjoys being virtuous:

And, further, the life of these men is in itself pleasant. For pleasure is an affection of the soul, and each man takes pleasure in that which he is said to love,—he who loves horses in horses, he who loves sight-seeing in sight-seeing, and in the same way he who loves justice in acts of justice, and generally the lover of excellence or virtue in virtuous acts or the manifestation of excellence. And while with most men there

FIG. 7.11 Practice is typically necessary to develop skill in choosing the mean between extremes. *(© iStockphoto.com/Juanmonino)*

is a perpetual conflict between the several things in which they find pleasure, since these are not naturally pleasant, those who love what is noble take pleasure in that which is naturally pleasant. For the manifestations of excellence are naturally pleasant, so that they are both pleasant to them and pleasant in themselves. Their life, then, does not need pleasure to be added to it as an appendage, but contains pleasure in itself.

Here Aristotle gives us perhaps his most famous doctrine, the idea that virtues are "**means between the extremes.**" This phrase is often misinterpreted, however, to read, "everything in moderation." What Aristotle teaches is quite different; he tells us that we cannot do too much of a good thing, that is, if it is a virtue. One cannot be too courageous (as opposed to being rash or cowardly) or too just. What he intends by "the means between the extremes" is this:

By the absolute mean, or mean relatively to the thing itself, I understand that which is equidistant from both extremes, and this is one and the same for all. By the mean relatively to us I understand that which is neither too much nor too little for us; and this is not one and the same for all. For instance, if ten be too large and two too small, six is the mean relatively to the thing itself: for it exceeds one extreme by the same amount by which it is exceeded by the other extreme: and this is the mean in arithmetical proportion. But the mean relatively to us cannot be found in this way. If ten pounds of food is too much for a given man to eat, and two pounds too little, it does not follow that the trainer will order him six pounds: for that also may perhaps be too much for the man in question, or too little; too little for Milo, too much for the beginner. The same holds true in running and wrestling. And so we may say generally that a master in any art avoids what is too much and what is too little, and seeks for the mean and chooses it—not the absolute but the relative mean.

If, then, every art or science perfects its work in this way, looking to the mean and bringing its work up to this standard (so that people are wont to say of a good work that nothing could be taken from it or added to it, implying that excellence is destroyed by excess or deficiency, but secured by observing the mean; and good artists, as we say, do in fact keep their eyes fixed on this in all that they do), and if virtue, like nature, is more exact and better than any art, it follows that virtue also must aim at the mean—virtue of course meaning moral virtue or excellence; for it has to do with passions and actions, and it is these that admit of excess and deficiency and the mean. For instance, it is possible to feel fear, confidence, desire, anger, pity, and generally to be affected pleasantly and painfully, either too much or too little, in either case wrongly; but to be thus affected at the right times, and on the right occasions, and towards the right persons, and with the right object, and in the right fashion, is the mean course and the best course, and these are characteristics of virtue. And in the same way our outward acts also admit of excess and deficiency, and the mean or due amount. Virtue, then, has to deal with feelings or passions and with outward acts, in which excess is wrong and deficiency also is blamed, but the mean amount is praised, and is right—both of which are characteristics of virtue. Virtue, then, is a kind of moderation inasmuch as it aims at the mean.

"Virtue, then, has to deal with feelings or passions and with outward acts, in which excess is wrong and deficiency also is blamed, but the mean amount is praised, and is right—both of which are characteristics of virtue. Virtue, then, is a kind of moderation inasmuch as it aims at the mean."

– ARISTOTLE

Again, there are many ways of going wrong (for evil is infinite in nature, to use a Pythagorean figure, while good is finite), but only one way of going right; so that the one is easy and the other hard—easy to miss the mark and hard to hit. On this account also, then, excess and deficiency are characteristic of vice, hitting the mean is characteristic of virtue.

. . .

Virtue, then, is a habit or trained faculty of choice, the characteristic of which lies in moderation or observance of the mean relatively to the persons concerned, as determined by reason, i.e. by the reason by which the prudent man would determine it. And it is a moderation, firstly, inasmuch as it comes in the middle or mean between two vices, one on the side of excess, the other on the side of defect; and, secondly, inasmuch as, while these vices fall short of or exceed the due measure in feeling and in action, it finds and chooses the mean, middling, or moderate amount. Regarded in its essence, therefore, or according to the definition of its nature, virtue is a moderation or middle state, but viewed in its relation to what is best and right it is the extreme of perfection.

But it is not all actions nor all passions that admit of moderation; there are some whose very names imply badness, or malevolence, shamelessness, envy, and, among acts, adultery, theft, murder. These and all other like things are blamed as being bad in themselves, and not merely in their excess or deficiency. It is impossible therefore to go right in them; they are always wrong: rightness and wrongness in such things (e.g. in adultery) does not depend upon whether it is the right person and occasion and manner, but the mere doing of any one of them is wrong. It would be equally absurd to look for moderation or excess or deficiency in unjust cowardly or profligate conduct; for then there would be moderation in excess or deficiency, and excess in excess, and deficiency in deficiency. The fact is that just as there can be no excess or deficiency in temperance or courage because the mean or moderate amount is, in a sense, an extreme, so in these kinds of conduct also there can be no moderation or excess or deficiency, but the acts are wrong however they be done. For, to put it generally, there cannot be moderation in excess or deficiency, nor excess or deficiency in moderation.

We see that Aristotle defines "moral virtue" as a mean both in feeling and action. Thus courage is a virtue because the courageous man feels neither too little nor too much fear. His fear is appropriate to the dangerousness of his situation. Because the courageous person feels the right amount of fear, he acts in the right way, neither plunging rashly into danger nor fleeing from it in terror. Now, finally, Aristotle gives us his examples of virtue:

Moderation in the feelings of fear and confidence is courage: of those that exceed, he that exceeds in fearlessness has no name (as often happens), but he that exceeds in confidence is foolhardy, while he that exceeds in fear, but is deficient in confidence, is cowardly. Moderation in respect of certain pleasures and also (though to a less extent) certain pains is temperance, while excess is profligacy. But defectiveness in the matter of these pleasures is hardly ever found, and so this sort of people also have as yet received no name: let us put them down as "void of sensibility." In the matter of giving and taking money, moderation is liberality, excess and deficiency are prodigality and illiberality. But both vices exceed and fall short in giving and taking in contrary ways: the prodigal exceeds in spending, but falls short in taking; while the illiberal man exceeds in taking, but falls short in spending. . . . But, besides these, there are other dispositions in the matter of money: there is a moderation which is called magnificence (for the magnificent is not the same as the liberal man: the former deals with large sums, the latter with small), and an excess which is called bad taste or vulgarity, and a deficiency which is called meanness. . . . With respect to honour and disgrace, there is a moderation which is pride, an excess which may be called vanity, and a deficiency which is humility.

But just as we said that liberality is related to magnificence, differing only in that it deals with small sums, so here there is a virtue related to high-mindedness, and differing only in that it is concerned with small instead of great honours. A man may have a due desire for honour, and also more or less than a due desire: he that carries this desire to excess is called ambitious, he that has not enough of it is called unambitious, but he that has the due amount has no name. . . . In the matter of anger also we find excess and deficiency and moderation. The characters themselves hardly have recognized names, but as the moderate man is here called gentle, we will call his character gentleness; of those who go into extremes, we may take the term wrathful for him who exceeds, with wrathfulness for the vice, and wrathless for him who is deficient, with wrathlessness for his character.

. . .

In the matter of truth, then, let us call him who observes the mean a true [or truthful] person, and observance of the mean truth [or truthfulness]: pretence, when it exaggerates, may be called boasting, and the person a boaster; when it understates, let the names be irony and ironical. With regard to pleasantness in amusement, he who observes the mean may be called witty, and his character wittiness; excess may be called buffoonery, and the man a buffoon; while boorish may stand for the person who is deficient, and boorishness for his character. With regard to pleasantness in the other affairs of life, he who makes himself properly pleasant may be called friendly, and his moderation friendliness; he that exceeds may be called obsequious if he have no ulterior motive, but a flatterer if he has an eye to his own advantage; he that is deficient in this respect, and always makes himself disagreeable, may be called a quarrelsome or peevish fellow.

Moreover, in mere emotions and in our conduct with regard to them, there are ways of observing the mean; for instance, shame is not a virtue, but yet the modest man is praised. For in these matters also we speak of this man as observing the mean, of that man as going beyond it (as the shamefaced man whom the least thing makes shy), while he who is deficient in the feeling, or lacks it altogether, is called shameless; but the term modest is applied to him who observes the mean. Righteous indignation, again, hits the mean between envy and malevolence. These have to do with feelings of pleasure and pain at what happens to our neighbours. A man is called righteously indignant when he feels pain at the sight of undeserved prosperity, but your envious man

FIG. 7.12 Jan Steen's paintings (such as this one, *The Merry Company*) frequently depict lives of immoderation, precisely the opposite of what Aristotle extols as the good life. *(Scala / Art Resource, NY)*

goes beyond him and is pained by the sight of any one in prosperity, while the malevolent man is so far from being pained that he actually exults in the misfortunes of his neighbours.

It is worth making a short list of Aristotle's moral virtues. Many of them we would cite as virtues also, but some of them are far more appropriate to an aristocratic, warrior society than they are to our own. To illustrate Aristotle's idea that virtues are the means between the extremes, we have included "the extremes" in parentheses for contrast:

Courage, particularly courage in battle (extremes: cowardice, rashness). What motivates courage, Aristotle tells us, is a sense of honor, not fear of punishment nor desire for reward, nor merely a sense of duty. The courageous man is afraid, he adds, because without fear there would be no courage. The man who feels no fear in the face of danger is rather rash.

Temperance, particularly concerning bodily pleasures, such as sex, food, and drinking (extremes: self-indulgence or piggishness, insensitivity). Notice that Aristotle does not say, along with many modern moralists, that pleasures are either "bad" or unimportant; in fact, he attacks the man who does not enjoy sex, food, and drinking as much as he attacks the man who overindulges himself. He considers such people "not even human."

Liberality, we would say, charity (extremes: prodigality or waste, meanness or stinginess). It is worth noting that Aristotle would ridicule the man who gives more than he can afford to charity as much as he would chastize the man who did not give at all.

Magnificence, in other words, how extravagantly you live (extremes: vulgarity, miserliness). Aristotle says that one ought to live "like an artist" and spend lavishly. (There is little of the ascetic in Aristotle.)

Pride (extremes: humility, vanity). It is worth noting that pride is one of the seven deadly sins in Christian morality while humility is a virtue. In Aristotle's ethics, this is reversed.

Good temper (extremes: irascibility or bad temper, being too easygoing). It is important to get angry, according to Aristotle, about the right things, but not too much (which "makes a person impossible to live with").

Friendliness (extremes: obsequiousness, churlishness). Friendship, for Aristotle, is one of the most important ingredients in the good life, and being friendly, therefore, is an extremely important virtue. But Aristotle does not say that we should be friendly to everyone; the person who is indiscriminately friendly toward everyone is not worth being a friend with at all.

Truthfulness (extremes: lying, boasting), especially telling the truth about oneself.

Wittiness (extremes: buffoonery, boorishness). We think of wittiness as a personal asset, but rarely as a virtue. Aristotle thinks that people who are incapable of telling a joke or who tell bad jokes are actually inferior. Fun is an important ingredient in Greek virtuousness.

Shame. Aristotle calls this a "quasi-virtue" (extreme: shamelessness). We all make mistakes, and it is a sign of virtue, according to Aristotle, that the good man feels shame when he makes them. Shamelessness is a sign of wickedness. Aristotle does not even talk of the other extreme, which he did not consider a problem. (We certainly would. We call it excessive guilt.)

Justice, the cardinal virtue of the Greeks. The need for lawful and fair (which does not mean equal) treatment of other men. (The sense in which justice is a mean between extremes is too complex to discuss here. Aristotle spends a full chapter explaining it. We consider his view of justice in the following chapter.)

Finally, Aristotle gives us his view of the good life for humankind; it is the life of activity in accordance with virtue, but it is also, ideally, a life of intellectual activity, or what he calls "the life of contemplation." In other words, the happiest person is the philosopher:

We said that happiness is not a habit or trained faculty. If it were, it would be within the reach of a man who slept all his days and lived the life of a vegetable, or of a man who met with the greatest misfortunes. As we cannot accept this conclusion, we must place happiness in some exercise of faculty, as we said before. But as the exercises of faculty are sometimes necessary (i.e. desirable for the sake of something else), sometimes desirable in themselves, it is evident that happiness must be placed among those that are desirable in themselves, and not among those that are desirable for the sake of something else: for happiness lacks nothing; it is sufficient in itself.

Now, the exercise of faculty is desirable in itself when nothing is expected from it beyond itself. Of this nature are held to be (1) the manifestations of excellence; for to do what is noble and excellent must be counted desirable for itself: and (2) those amusements which please are more apt to be injured than to be benefited by them, through neglect of their health and fortunes. Now, most of those whom men call happy have recourse to pastimes of this sort. And on this account those who show a ready wit in such pastimes find favour with tyrants; for they make themselves pleasant in that which the tyrant wants, and what he wants is pastime. These amusements, then, are generally thought to be elements of happiness, because princes employ their leisure in them. But such persons, we may venture to say, are no criterion. For princely rank does not imply the possession of virtue or of reason, which are the sources of all excellent exercise of faculty. And if these men, never having tasted pure and refined pleasure, have recourse to the pleasures of the body, we should not on that account think these more desirable; for children also fancy that the things which they value are better than anything else. It is only natural, then, that as children differ from men in their estimate of what is valuable, so bad men should differ from good.

As we have often said, therefore, that is truly valuable and pleasant which is so to the perfect man. Now, the exercise of those trained faculties which are proper to him is what each man finds most desirable; what the perfect man finds most desirable, therefore, is the exercise of virtue. Happiness, therefore, does not consist in amusement; and indeed it is absurd to suppose that the end is amusement, and that we toil and moil all our life long for the sake of amusing ourselves. We may say that we choose everything for the sake of something else, excepting only happiness; for it is the end. But to be serious and to labour for the sake of amusement seems silly and utterly childish; while to amuse ourselves in order that we may be serious, as Anacharsis says, seems to be right; for amusement is a sort of recreation, and we need recreation because we are unable to work continuously. Recreation then, cannot be the end; for it is taken as a means to the exercise of our faculties.

Again, the happy life is thought to be that which exhibits virtue; and such a life must be serious and cannot consist in amusement. Again, it is held that things of serious importance are better than laughable and amusing things, and that the better the organ or the man, the most important is the function; but we have already said that the function or exercise of that which is better is higher and more conducive to happiness. Again, the enjoyment of bodily pleasures is within the reach of anybody, of a slave no less than the best of men; but no one supposes that a slave can participate in happiness, seeing that he cannot participate in the proper life of man. For indeed happiness does not consist in pastimes of this sort, but in the exercise of virtue, as we have already said.

But if happiness be the exercise of virtue, it is reasonable to suppose that it will be the exercise of the highest virtue; and that will be the virtue or excellence of the best part of us. Now, that part or faculty—call it reason or what you will—which seems naturally to rule and take the lead, and to apprehend things noble and divine—whether it be itself divine, or only the divinest part of us—is the faculty the exercise of which, in its proper excellence, will be perfect happiness. . . . this consists in speculation or theorizing.

This conclusion would seem to agree both with what we have said above, and with known truths. This exercise of faculty must be the highest possible; for the reason is the highest of our faculties and of all knowable things those that reason deals with are the highest. Again, it is the most continuous; for speculation can be carried on more continuously than any kind of action whatsoever. We think too that pleasure ought to be one of the ingredients of happiness; but of all virtuous exercises it is allowed that the pleasantest is the exercise of wisdom. At least philosophy is thought to have pleasures that are admirable in purity and steadfastness; and it is reasonable to suppose that the time passes more pleasantly with those who possess, than with those who are seeking knowledge. Again, what is called self-sufficiency will be most of all found in the speculative life. The necessaries of life, indeed, are needed by the wise man as well as by the just man and the rest; but, when these have been provided in due quantity, the just man further needs persons towards whom, and along with whom, he may act justly; and so does the temperate and the courageous man and the rest; while the wise man is able to speculate even by himself, and the wiser he is the more is he able to do this. He could speculate better, we may confess, if he had others to help him, but nevertheless he is more self-sufficient than anybody else. Again, it would seem that this life alone is desired solely for its own sake; for it yields no result beyond the contemplation, but from the practical activities we get something more or less besides action.

. . .

[It] follows that the exercise of reason will be the complete happiness of man, i.e. when a complete term of days is added; for nothing incomplete can be admitted into our idea of happiness. But a life which realized this idea would be something more than human; for it would not be the expression of man's nature, but of some divine element in that nature—the exercise of which is as far superior to the exercise of the other kind of virtue, as this divine element is superior to our compound human nature. If then reason be divine as compared with man, the life which consists in the exercise of reason will also be divine in comparison with human life. Nevertheless, instead of listening to those who advise us as men and mortals not to lift our thoughts above what is human and mortal, we ought rather, as far as possible, to put off our mortality and make every effort to live in the exercise of the highest of our faculties; for though it be but a small part of us, yet in power and value it far surpasses all the rest. And indeed this part would even seem to constitute our true self, since it is the sovereign and the better part. It would be strange, then, if a man were to prefer the life of something else to the life of his true self. Again, we may apply here what we said above—for every being that is best and pleasantest which is naturally proper to it. Since, then, it is the reason that in the truest sense is the man, the life that consists in the exercise of the reason is the best and pleasantest for man—and therefore the happiest.

Still, it must not be thought that Aristotle's ideal philosopher does nothing but contemplate. He may also enjoy pleasure, wealth, honor, success, and power. As a man among men, he is also virtuous and chooses to act virtuously like all good men. But in addition, he has an understanding and an appreciation of reason that makes him "dearest to the Gods and presumably the happiest among men." This is surely a flattering portrait of the place of the philosopher! If we ignore this final self-congratulation, however, we can see in Aristotle a powerful conception of morality, with its emphasis on virtue, excellence, and a kind of heroism (whether intellectual or moral), that is in some ways very different from our own conception of morality and the good life.

- What does Aristotle mean by happiness? How does this conception differ from the way in which we usually think of happiness?
- What role does society or the community play in Aristotle's ethics?
- How does Aristotle define virtue? What does he mean by the mean between extremes? What are some examples of the virtues? In what sense are they the mean between the extreme? Can you identify any virtues that do not seem to have a corresponding extreme (whether excess or deficiency)?
- How does Aristotle characterize human excellence? How does this characterization differ from your own conception of the good life?

F. Morality and Sentiment: Hume and Rousseau

Morality for Aristotle depended upon rules embedded and learned in a particular society, an elite society of the privileged males of the Greek aristocracy. Modern conceptions of morality, on the other hand, are usually thought to be universal, that is, not restricted to a particular society or a particular elite. They apply to women, men, poor people, rich people, adults, and children, even if they are only a few years old. At the same time, however, most modern conceptions of morality minimize Aristotle's emphasis on society and upbringing, preferring to place morals on some individual basis. In Kant's moral philosophy, the key to morality is *individual autonomy*, the idea that every person can find for himself or herself, just through the use of reason, what acts are moral and what acts are not. Before Kant, the ruling conception of morality was based upon a conception of personal feelings of a special moral kind, a "natural desire" to help one's fellow man. (As in Aristotle, this philosophy insisted that morality had to be viewed as a part of nature.)

It should be clear how this conception of morality has a distinct advantage in reconciling personal interests and moral principles. Since strong moral feelings are a kind of personal interest, one can satisfy one's personal feelings and the demands of morality at the same time. (Again, this notion lies at the heart of Bishop Butler's arguments.) Of course, other personal feelings—jealousy, greed, and envy—can act against these moral feelings. But at least some of our feelings are satisfied by moral action. And according to philosophers who argue this position, such moral feelings can be found in virtually all of us.

The two most famous of these philosophers are David Hume and the French-Swiss philosopher **Jean-Jacques Rousseau**. The key to both of their philosophies is the notion of **sentiment** ("feeling") and the notion of **sympathy** ("fellow feeling" or feeling pity for other people and taking their interests into account as well as our own). Hume says:

> *The hypothesis which we embrace is plain. It maintains that morality is determined by sentiment. It defines virtue to be whatever mental action or quality gives to a spectator the pleasing sentiment of approbation; and vice the contrary.*[14]

The central concern in Hume's moral philosophy distinguishes those who defend morality as a function of reason from those who say that it is rather a matter of sentiment and passion. Elsewhere Hume gives us his strong opinion that "reason is, and ought to be, the slave of the passions." Here is his argument:

On "Reason as Slave of the Passions"
BY David Hume[15]

There has been a controversy started of late, much better worth examination, concerning the general foundation of *morals;* whether they be derived from *reason* or from *sentiment;* whether we attain the knowledge of them by a chain of argument and induction or by an immediate feeling and finer internal sense; whether, like all sound judgment of truth and falsehood, they should be the same to every rational, intelligent being, or whether, like the perception of beauty and deformity, they be founded entirely on the particular fabric and constitution of the human species.

The ancient philosophers, though they often affirm that virtue is nothing but conformity to reason, yet, in general, seem to consider morals as deriving their existence from taste and sentiment. On the other hand, our modern inquirers, though they also talk much of the beauty of virtue and deformity of vice, yet have commonly endeavored to account for these distinctions by metaphysical reasonings and by deductions from the most abstract principles of the understanding. Such confusion reigned in these subjects that an opposition of the greatest consequence could prevail between one system and another, and even in the parts of almost each individual system, and yet nobody, till very lately, was ever sensible of it.

. . .

It must be acknowledged that both sides of the question are susceptible of specious arguments. Moral distinctions, it may be said, are discernible by pure *reason;* else, whence the many disputes that reign in common life, as well as in philosophy with regard to this subject, the long chain of proofs often produced on both sides, the examples cited, the authorities appealed to, the analogies employed, the fallacies detected, the inferences drawn, and the several conclusions adjusted to their proper principles? Truth is disputable, not taste: what exists in the nature of things is the standard of our judgment: what each man feels within himself is the standard of sentiment. Propositions in geometry may be proved, systems in physics may be controverted, but the harmony of verse, the tenderness of passion, the brilliancy of wit must give immediate pleasure. No man reasons concerning another's beauty, but frequently concerning the justice or injustice of his actions. In every criminal trial,

---

[14] David Hume, *Enquiry Concerning the Principles of Morals* (La Salle, IL: Open Court Press, 1912).

[15] Ibid.

the first object of the prisoner is to disprove the facts alleged and deny the actions imputed to him; the second, to prove that, even if these actions were real, they might be justified as innocent and lawful. It is confessedly by deductions of the understanding that the first point is ascertained; how can we suppose a different faculty of the mind is employed in fixing the other?

On the other hand, those who would resolve all moral determinations into *sentiments* may endeavor to show that it is impossible for reason ever to draw conclusions of this nature. To virtue, say they, it belongs to be *amiable* and vice *odious*. This forms their very nature or essence. But can reason or argumentation distribute these different epithets to any subjects and pronounce beforehand that this must produce love and that hatred? Or what other reason can we ever assign for these affections but the original fabric and formation of the human mind, which is naturally adapted to receive them?

The end of all moral speculations is to teach us our duty, and, by proper representations of the deformity of vice and beauty of virtue, beget correspondent habits and engage us to avoid the one and embrace the other. But is this ever to be expected from inferences and conclusions of the understanding, which of themselves have no hold of the affections or set in motion the active powers of men? They discover truths. But where the truths which they discover are indifferent and beget no desire or aversion, they can have no influence on conduct and behavior. What is honorable, what is fair, what is becoming, what is noble, what is generous takes possession of the heart and animates us to embrace and maintain it. What is intelligible, what is evident, what is probable, what is true procures only the cool assent of the understanding and, gratifying a speculative curiosity, puts an end to our researches.

. . .

Extinguish all the warm feelings and prepossessions in favor of virtue, and all disgust or aversion to vice; render men totally indifferent toward these distinctions, and morality is no longer a practical study nor has any tendency to regulate our lives and actions.

These arguments on each side (and many more might be produced) are so plausible that I am apt to suspect they may, the one as well as the other, be solid and satisfactory and that *reason* and *sentiment* concur in almost all moral determinations and conclusions. The final sentence, it is probable, which pronounces characters and actions amiable or odious, praiseworthy or blamable; that which stamps on them the mark of honor or infamy, approbation or censure; that which renders morality an active principle and constitutes virtue our happiness, and vice our misery—it is probable, I say, that this final sentence depends on some internal sense of feeling which nature has made universal in the whole species.

It is worth noting here that Hume's moral philosophy, like his philosophy of knowledge, is strictly empiricist:

Men are now cured of their passion for hypotheses and systems in natural philosophy and will hearken to no arguments but those which are derived from experience. It is full time they should attempt a like reformation in all moral disquisitions and reject every system of ethics, however subtle or ingenious, which is not founded on fact and observation.

Reason, Hume argues, may be of use in deciding how we can get what we want, but it is incapable of ever telling us what we ultimately want. Notice the familiar argument against an infinite regress; notice also Hume's sharp distinction between reason (which is concerned with knowledge, truth, and falsehood) and taste or sentiment (which judges values, which, in turn, ultimately depend upon pleasure and pain):

It appears evident that the ultimate ends of human actions can never, in any case, be accounted for by *reason*, but recommend themselves entirely to the sentiments and affections of mankind without any dependence on the intellectual faculties. Ask a man *why he uses exercise;* he will answer, *because he desires to keep his health.* If you then inquire *why he desires health,* he will readily reply, *because sickness is painful.* If you push your inquiries further and desire a reason *why he hates pain,* it is impossible he can ever give any. This is an ultimate end and is never referred to any other object.

Perhaps to your second question, *why he desires health,* he may also reply that *it is necessary for the exercise of his calling.* If you ask *why he is anxious on that head,* he will answer, *because he desires to get money.* If you demand, *why? It is the instrument of pleasure,* says he. And beyond this, it is an absurdity to ask for a reason. It is impossible there can be a progress *in infinitum* and that one thing can always be a reason why another is desired. Something must be desirable on its own account and because of its immediate accord or agreement with human sentiment and affection.

Now, as virtue is an end and is desirable on its own account, without fee or reward, merely for the immediate satisfaction which it conveys, it is requisite that there should be some sentiment which it touches—some internal taste or feeling, or whatever you please to call it, which distinguishes moral good and evil and which embraces the one and rejects the other.

Thus, the distinct boundaries and offices of *reason* and of *taste* are easily ascertained. The former conveys the knowledge of truth and falsehood; the latter gives the sentiment of beauty and deformity, vice and virtue. The one discovers objects as they really stand in nature, without addition or diminution; the other has a productive faculty; and gliding or straining all natural objects with the colors borrowed from internal sentiment, raises, in a manner, a new creation. Reason, being cool and disengaged, is no motive to action and directs only the impulse received from appetite or inclination by showing us the means of attaining happiness or avoiding misery. Taste, as it gives pleasure or pain, and thereby constitutes happiness or misery, becomes a motive to action and is the first spring or impulse to desire and volition. From circumstances and relations, known or supposed, the former leads us to the discovery of the concealed and unknown. After all circumstances and relations are laid before us, the latter makes us feel from the whole a new sentiment of blame or approbation.

Elsewhere Hume argues a razor-sharp distinction between facts and values. He argues with characteristic conciseness that "it is impossible to derive an 'ought' from an 'is,'" that is, any notions of value or what we *ought to do* cannot be derived from any statements of fact. One can know, as a matter of fact, that pushing this button will kill a thousand innocent children, but from this fact

"[T]he distinct boundaries and offices of *reason* and of *taste* are easily ascertained. The former conveys the knowledge of truth and falsehood; the latter gives the sentiment of beauty and deformity, vice and virtue."

– DAVID HUME

FIG. 7.13 Hume argues that moral discrimination, like artistic taste, is a matter of sentiment. *(Snark / Art Resource, NY)*

alone, it does not follow that I ought not push the button. What I ought to do—or ought not to do—depends on something that is not a matter of fact or reason at all, my moral feelings or sentiments. Without these sentiments, no action is either moral or immoral, praiseworthy or blameworthy, or of any value whatever. Accordingly, in one of his most shocking statements, Hume says that it would not be irrational for him to prefer the death of half the world to the pricking of his little finger. This is not to say that he would prefer it, but there is *nothing in reason* to forbid it. Values are a matter of sentiment, not of reason.

A similar theory of sentiment is defended by Jean-Jacques Rousseau. Although Rousseau is often characterized as the first great "Romantic," it is worth noting that he is not nearly so antagonistic to reason as his reputation suggests. Sentiment, according to his theory, is tied to a kind of "natural reason." The key to his theory, therefore, is the concept of **conscience**, a powerful type of moral feeling that has its own kind of divine reason. Like Hume, Rousseau argues that detached reason offers us no guidance. Notice that he too reconciles "self-love" and "moral goodness" as ultimately having the same goals:

FROM *Émile*
BY **Jean-Jacques Rousseau**[16]

Let us lay it down as an incontrovertible rule that the first impulses of nature are always right; there is no original sin in the human heart, the how and why of the entrance of every vice can be traced. The only natural passion is self-love or selfishness taken in a wider sense. This selfishness is good in itself and in relation to ourselves; and as the child has no necessary relations to other people he is naturally indifferent to them; his self-love only becomes good or bad by the use made of it and the relations established by its means. Until the time is ripe for the appearance of reason, that guide of selfishness, the main thing is that the child shall do nothing because you are watching him or listening to him; in a word, nothing because of other people, but only what nature asks of him; then he will never do wrong.

I do not mean to say that he will never do any mischief, never hurt himself, never break a costly ornament if you leave it within his reach. He might do much damage without doing wrong, since wrong-doing depends on the harmful intention which will never be his. If once he meant to do harm, his whole education would be ruined; he would be almost hopelessly bad.

. . .

The morality of our actions consists entirely in the judgments we ourselves form with regard to them. If good is good, it must be good in the depth of our heart as well as in our actions; and the first reward of justice is the consciousness that we are acting justly. If moral goodness is in accordance with our nature, man can only be healthy in mind and body when he is good. If it is not so,

Jean-Jacques Rousseau (1712-1778)

A stormy Enlightenment philosopher who fought with most of his peers (including David Hume) and developed a dramatic conception of "natural morality," which he contrasted to what he saw as the fraud and hypocrisy of contemporary civilized man. Rousseau formulated a picture of man in "the state of nature," before civilization, in which man's "natural goodness" was not yet "corrupted" by society. The key to this idea was his conception of moral sentiment, which was innate in all people and not learned from society. His writings were condemned, and he spent much of his life running from the police. Rousseau died in poverty, but only a few years after his death, his political ideas became the central ideology of the French Revolution.

FIG. 7.14 Jean-Jacques Rousseau (© iStockphoto.com/Georgios Kollidas)

16 Jean-Jacques Rousseau, *Émile*, trans. Barbara Foxley (New York: E. P. Dutton, 1968). Reprinted by permission of Everyman's Library, an imprint of Alfred A. Knopf.

and if man is by nature evil, he cannot cease to be evil without corrupting his nature, and goodness in him is a crime against nature. If he is made to do harm to his fellow-creatures, as the wolf is made to devour his prey, a humane man would be as depraved a creature as a pitiful wolf; and virtue alone would cause remorse.

My young friend, let us look within, let us set aside all personal prejudices and see whither our inclinations lead us. Do we take more pleasure in the sight of the sufferings of others or their joys? Is it pleasanter to do a kind action or an unkind action, and which leaves the more delightful memory behind it? Why do you enjoy the theatre? Do you delight in the crimes you behold? Do you weep over the punishment which overtakes the criminal? They say we are indifferent to everything but self-interest; yet we find our consolation in our sufferings in the charms of friendship and humanity, and even in our pleasures we should be too lonely and miserable if we had no one to share them with us. If there is no such thing as morality in man's heart, what is the source of his rapturous admiration of noble deeds, his passionate devotion to great men? What connection is there between self-interest and this enthusiasm for virtue?

· · ·

Take from our hearts this love of what is noble and you rob us of the joy of life. The mean-spirited man in whom these delicious feelings have been stifled among vile passions, who by thinking of no one but himself comes at last to love no one but himself, this man feels no raptures, his cold heart no longer throbs with joy, and his eyes no longer fill with the sweet tears of sympathy, he delights in nothing; the wretch has neither life nor feeling, he is already dead.

There are many bad men in this world, but there are few of these dead souls, alive only to self-interest, and insensible to all that is right and good. We only delight in injustice so long as it is to our own advantage; in every other case we wish the innocent to be protected. If we see some act of violence or injustice in town or country, our hearts are at once stirred to their depths by an instinctive anger and wrath, which bids us go to the help of the oppressed; but we are restrained by a stronger duty, and the law deprives us of our right to protect the innocent. On the other hand, if some deed of mercy or generosity meets our eye, what reverence and love does it inspire! Do we not say to ourselves, "I should like to have done that myself"? What does it matter to us that two thousand years ago a man was just or unjust? and yet we take the same interest in ancient history as if it happened yesterday. What are the crimes of Cataline to me? I shall not be his victim. Why then have I the same horror of his crimes as if he were living now? We do not hate the wicked merely because of the harm they do to ourselves, but because they are wicked. Not only do we wish to be happy ourselves, we wish others to be happy too, and if this happiness does not interfere with our own happiness, it increases it. In conclusion, whether we will or not, we pity the unfortunate; when we see their suffering we suffer too. Even the most depraved are not wholly without this instinct, and it often leads them to self-contradiction. The highwayman who robs the traveller, clothes the nakedness of the poor; the fiercest murderer supports a fainting man.

Men speak of the voice of remorse, the secret punishment of hidden crimes, by which such are often brought to light. Alas! who does not know its unwelcome voice? We speak from experience and we would gladly stifle this imperious feeling which causes us such agony. Let us obey the call of nature; we shall see that her yoke is easy and that when we give heed to her voice we find a joy in the answer of a

> "To know good is not to love it; this knowledge is not innate in man; but as soon as his reason leads him to perceive it, his conscience impels him to love it; it is this feeling which is innate."
>
> – JEAN-JACQUES ROUSSEAU

good conscience. The wicked fears and flees from her; he delights to escape from himself; his anxious eyes look around him for some object of diversion; without bitter satire and rude mockery he would always be sorrowful; the scornful laugh is his one pleasure. Not so the just man, who finds his peace within himself; there is joy not malice in his laughter, a joy which springs from his own heart; he is as cheerful alone as in company, his satisfaction does not depend on those who approach him; it includes them.

. . .

It is no part of my scheme to enter at present into metaphysical discussions which neither you nor I can understand, discussions which really lead nowhere. I have told you already that I do not wish to philosophise with you, but to help you to consult your own heart. If all the philosophers in the world should prove that I am wrong, and you feel that I am right, that is all I ask.

For this purpose it is enough to lead you to distinguish between our acquired ideas and our natural feelings; for feeling precedes knowledge; and since we do not learn to seek what is good for us and avoid what is bad for us, but get this desire from nature, in the same way the love of good and the hatred of evil are as natural to us as our self-love. The decrees of conscience are not judgments but feelings. Although all our ideas come from without, the feelings by which they are weighed are within us, and it is by these feelings alone that we perceive fitness or unfitness of things in relation to ourselves, which leads us to seek or shun these things.

To exist is to feel; our feeling is undoubtedly earlier than our intelligence, and we had feelings before we had ideas. Whatever may be the cause of our being, it has provided for our preservation by giving us feelings suited to our nature; and no one can deny that these at least are innate. These feelings, so far as the individual is concerned, are self-love, fear, pain, the dread of death, the desire for comfort. Again, if, as it is impossible to doubt, man is by nature sociable, or at least fitted to become sociable, he can only be so by means of other innate feelings, relative to his kind; for if only physical well-being were considered, men would certainly be scattered rather than brought together. But the motive power of conscience is derived from the moral system formed through this twofold relation to himself and to his fellow-men. To know good is not to love it; this knowledge is not innate in man; but as soon as his reason leads him to perceive it, his conscience impels him to love it; it is this feeling which is innate.

So I do not think, my young friend, that it is impossible to explain the immediate force of conscience as a result of our own nature, independent of reason itself. And even should it be impossible, it is necessary; for those who deny this principle, admitted and received by everybody else in the world, do not prove that there is no such thing; they are content to affirm, and when we affirm its existence we have quite as good grounds as they, while we have moreover the witness within us, the voice of conscience, which speaks on its own behalf. If the first beams of judgment dazzle us and confuse the objects we behold, let us wait till our feeble sight

FIG. 7.15 Rousseau argues that conscience conjoins the demands of emotion and reason. (© iStockphoto.com/ auke herrema)

grows clear and strong, and in the light of reason we shall soon behold these very objects as nature has already showed them to us. Or rather let us be simpler and less pretentious; let us be content with the first feelings we experience in ourselves, since science always brings us back to these, unless it has led us astray.

Conscience! Conscience! Divine instinct, immortal voice from heaven; sure guide for a creature ignorant and finite indeed; yet intelligent and free; infallible judge of good and evil, making man like to God! In these consists the excellence of man's nature and the morality of his actions; apart from thee, I find nothing in myself to raise me above the beasts—nothing but the sad privilege of wandering from one error to another, by the help of an unbridled understanding and a reason which knows no principle.

As we pointed out before, there is a problem with this notion of conscience and with all appeals of morality to personal feeling. What if different people disagree? Whose conscience or whose feelings should we accept? And even if we find ourselves in agreement, how do we know that our consciences or feelings are right? It is with these questions in mind that we turn to the moral philosophy of Kant.

- Can morality be based on natural, human sentiment? Does this view seem too "subjective"? How might it be made less so?
- Why is morality usually thought to be based on reason, according to Hume? What argument does Hume give to support the claim that morality is based on sentiment? How does Hume envision the relationship between reason and the passions, or sentiments? Do you agree?
- What does Rousseau mean when he claims that a child will never do wrong if left to act according to his nature? How could this bold claim be defended?
- Why is Rousseau convinced that our capacity for morality is a natural response?

G. Morality and Practical Reason: Kant

Aristotle, Hume, and Rousseau all give feeling an important place in their conceptions of morality. For Aristotle, the virtuous man wants to act virtuously and enjoys doing so. For Hume and Rousseau, sentiment defines morality. On all such accounts, our concept of *duty*–what we ought to do–is derivative, at least in part, from such feelings and from our upbringing. But what if feelings disagree? What if people are brought up to value different things? What are we to say of a person who is brought up by criminals to value what is wicked and to enjoy cruelty? And what are we to say, most important of all, in those familiar cases in which a person's feelings all draw him or her toward personal interests but duty calls in the opposite direction? This is the problem that Kant considered, and because of it, he rejected all attempts to base morality on feelings of any kind. Morality, he argued, must be based solely on reason and reason alone. Its central concept is the concept of **duty**, and so morality is a matter of **deontology** (from the Greek word *dein*, or "duty").

Hume restricted the notion of reason to concern with knowledge, truth, and falsity. Kant replies that reason also has a practical side, one that is capable of telling us what to do as well as how to do it. Rousseau said that morality must be universal, common to all men, even in a presocietal "state of nature." Kant (who very much admired Rousseau) agrees but says that the nature of this universality cannot lie in people's feelings, which may vary from person

FIG. 7.16 According to Immanuel Kant, a good will is good in itself.

to person and society to society, but only in reason, which, by its very nature, must be universal. Aristotle insisted that morality must be taught within society and that morals are very much a matter of public opinion and practices. Kant, however, insisted on the independence of morality from society. What is most important, he argues, is that morality should be autonomous, a function of individual reason, such that every rational person is capable of finding out what is right and what is wrong for himself or herself. Where Hume and Rousseau had looked for morality in individual feeling, Kant again insists that it must be found through an examination of reason, nothing else. This is the key to Kant's moral philosophy: Morality consists solely of *rational* principles.

Since morality is based on reason, according to Kant, it does not depend on particular societies or particular circumstances. Nor does it depend on individual feelings or desires. (Kant categorizes all such personal feelings, desires, ambitions, impulses, and emotions as **inclinations**.) The purpose of moral philosophy is to examine our ability to reason practically and to determine from this examination the fundamental principles that lie at the basis of every morality, for every person, and in every society. In direct contrast to Aristotle, Kant begins by saying that the benefits and virtues that make up happiness are not ultimately good. Instead, the only thing in this world that is intrinsically good is a good will. A good will, in turn, is the will that exercises pure practical reason.

 FROM *Fundamental Principles of the Metaphysics of Morals*
BY **Immanuel Kant**[17]

Nothing can possibly be conceived in the world, or even out of it, which can be called good without qualification, except a *good will*. Intelligence, wit, judgment, and other *talents* of the mind, however they may be named, or courage, resolution, perseverance, as qualities of temperament, are undoubtedly good and desirable in many respects; but these gifts of nature may also become extremely bad and mischievous if the will which is to make use of them, and which, therefore, constitutes what is called *character*, is not good. It is the same with the *gifts of fortune*. Power, riches, honor, even health, and the general well being and contentment with one's condition which is called *happiness*, inspire pride and often presumption, if there is not a good will to correct the influence of these on the mind, and with this also to rectify the whole principle of acting, and adapt it to its end. The sight of a being who is not adorned with a single feature of a pure and good will, enjoying unbroken prosperity, can never give pleasure to an impartial rational spectator. Thus a good will appears to constitute the indispensable condition even of being worthy of happiness.

The argument behind this opening move is this: It makes no sense to blame or praise a person for his or her character or abilities or the consequences of his or her actions. Many factors contribute to a person's circumstances. Whether or not a person is wealthy, intelligent, courageous, witty, and so on—whether the person possesses Aristotle's virtues—is often due to his or her upbringing and heredity, rather than to any personal choice. But what we *will*, that is, what we try to do, is wholly within our control. Therefore it is the only thing that is ultimately worth moral consideration. Notice that Kant is concerned with questions of mo-

17 Immanuel Kant, *Fundamental Principles of the Metaphysics of Morals*, trans. T. K. Abbott (New York: Longmans, Green, 1898).

rality, not questions of the good life in general. What makes us happy is not particularly his concern. He is concerned only with what makes a person morally *worthy* of being happy.

A good will is good not because of what it performs or effects, not by its aptness for the attainment of some proposed end, but simply by virtue of the volition—that is, it is good in itself, and considered by itself is to be esteemed much higher than all that can be brought about by it in favor of any inclination, nay, even of the sum-total of all inclinations. Even if it should happen that, owing to special disfavor of fortune, or the niggardly provision of a step-motherly nature, this will should wholly lack power to accomplish its purpose, if with its greatest efforts it should yet achieve nothing, and there should remain only the good will (not, to be sure, a mere wish, but the sum-moning of all means in our power), then, like a jewel, it would still shine by its own light, as a thing which has its whole value in itself. Its usefulness or fruitlessness can neither add to nor take away anything from this value. It would be, as it were, only the setting to enable us to handle it the more conveniently in common commerce, or to attract it to the attention of those who are not yet connoisseurs, but not to recom-mend it to true connoisseurs, or to determine its value.

There is, however, something so strange in this idea of the absolute value of the mere will, in which no account is taken of its utility, that notwithstanding the thor-ough assent of even common reason to the idea, yet a suspicion must arise that it may perhaps really be the product of mere high-flown fancy, and that we may have misunderstood the purpose of nature in assigning reason as the governor of our will. Therefore we will examine this idea from this point of view.

Kant's argument here is surprisingly similar to Aristotle's argument in his *Ethics*. There Aristotle argues that the good for man must be found in man's nature, in that which is unique to him. The assumption is that since man is singularly endowed with reason, reason must have a special significance in human life. Kant's argument also begins with the observation that man, unlike other creatures, is capable of reasoning. But why should he have such a ca-pacity? Not in order to make him happy, Kant argues, because any number of instincts would have served that end more effectively. (Remember that Kant is presupposing God as Creator here, so he believes, like Leibniz, that everything exists for some sufficient reason.)

[Our] existence has a different and far nobler end, for which and not for happiness, reason is properly intended, and which must, therefore, be regarded as the supreme condition to which the private ends of man must, for the most part, be postponed.

This "far nobler end" and "supreme condition" is what Kant calls *duty*. "The notion of duty," he tells us, "includes that of a good will," but a good will that subjects itself to rational prin-ciples. These rational principles are moral laws, and it is action in accordance with such laws that alone makes a man good.

It is important, however, to make a distinction that Aristotle also makes: It is one thing to do what duty requires for some personal interest, and it is something else to do one's duty just because it is one's duty. For example, a grocer may refuse to cheat his customers (which is his duty) because it would be bad for business; then he is not acting for the sake of duty, but for personal interests. But he may refuse to cheat his customers just because he knows that he ought not to. This does count as doing his duty and thereby makes him morally worthy.

I omit here all actions which are already recognized as inconsistent with duty, al-though they may be useful for this or that purpose, for with these the question whether they are done *from duty* cannot arise at all, since they even conflict with it. I also set aside those actions which really conform to duty, but to which men have *no* direct *inclination*, performing them because they are impelled thereto by some other inclination. For in this case we can readily distinguish whether the action which agrees with duty is done *from duty* or from a selfish view. It is much harder to make this distinction when the action accords with duty, and the subject has besides a *direct* inclination to it. For example, it is always a matter of duty that a dealer should not overcharge an inexperienced purchaser; and wherever there is much commerce the prudent tradesman does not overcharge, but keeps a fixed price for everyone, so that a child buys of him as well as any other. Men are thus *honestly* served; but this is not enough to make us believe that the tradesman has so acted from duty and from principles of honesty; his own advantage required it; it is out of the question in this case to suppose that he might besides have a direct inclination in favor of the buyers, so that, as it were, from love he should give no advantage to one over another. Accordingly the action was done neither from duty nor from direct inclination, but merely with a selfish view.

On the other hand, it is a duty to maintain one's life; and, in addition, everyone has also a direct inclination to do so. But on this account the often anxious care which most men take for it has no intrinsic worth, and their maximum has no moral import. They preserve their life *as duty requires*, no doubt, but not *because duty requires*. On the other hand, if adversity and hopeless sorrow have completely taken away the relish for life, if the unfortunate one, strong in mind, indignant at his fate rather than desponding or dejected, wishes for death, and yet preserves his life without loving it—not from inclination or fear, but from duty—then his maxim has a moral worth.

To be beneficent when we can is a duty; and besides this, there are many minds so sympathetically constituted that, without any other motive of vanity or self-interest, they find a pleasure in spreading joy around them, and can take delight in the satisfaction of others so far as it is their own work. But I maintain that in such a case an action of this kind, however proper, however amiable it may be, has nevertheless no true moral worth, but is on a level with other inclinations, for example, the inclination to honor, which, if it is happily directed to that which is in fact of public utility and accordant with duty, and consequently honorable, deserves praise and encouragement, but not esteem. For the maxim lacks the moral import, namely, that such actions be done *from duty*, not from inclination. Put the case that the mind of that philanthropist was clouded by sorrow of his own extinguishing all sympathy with the lot of others, and that while he still has the power to benefit others in distress he is not touched by their trouble because he is absorbed with his own; and now suppose that he tears himself out of this dread insensibility and performs the action without any inclination to it, but simply from duty, then first has his action its genuine moral worth. Further still, if nature has put little sympathy in the heart of this or that man, if he, supposed to be an upright man, is by temperament cold and indifferent to the sufferings of others, perhaps because in respect of his own he is provided with the special gift of patience and fortitude and supposes, or even requires, that others should have the same—and such a man would certainly not be the meanest product of nature—but if nature had not specially framed him for a philanthropist, would he not still find in himself a source from whence to give himself a far higher worth than that of a good-natured temperament could be? Unquestionably. It is just in this that the moral worth of the character is brought out which is incomparably the highest of all, namely, that he is beneficent, not from inclination, but from duty.

In a curious two short paragraphs, Kant tells us that we have a duty to make ourselves happy, not because we want to be happy (wants are never duties), but because it is necessary for us to do our other duties. Then, with reference to the Bible, Kant makes a famous (or in-famous) distinction between two kinds of love: practical love, which is commanded as a duty, and pathological love, in other words, what we would call the *emotion* of love.

To secure one's own happiness is a duty, at least indirectly; for discontent with one's condition, under a pressure of many anxieties and amidst unsatisfied wants, might easily become a great *temptation to transgression of duty*. But here again, without look-ing to duty, all men have already the strongest and most intimate inclination to hap-piness, because it is just in this idea that all inclinations are combined in one total. But the precept of happiness is often of such a sort that it greatly interferes with some inclinations, and yet a man cannot form any definite and certain conception of the sum of satisfaction of all of them which is called happiness. It is not then to be wondered at that a single inclination, definite both as to what it promises and as to the time within which it can be gratified, is often able to overcome such a fluctuating idea, and that a gouty patient, for instance, can choose to enjoy what he likes, and to suffer what he may, since, according to his calculation, on this occasion at least, he has [only] not sacrificed the enjoyment of the present moment to a possibly mistaken expectation of a happiness which is supposed to be found in health. But even in this case, if the general desire for happiness did not influence his will, and supposing that in his particular case health was not a necessary element in this calculation, there yet remains in this, as in all other cases, this law—namely, that he should promote his happiness not from inclination but from duty, and by this would his conduct first acquire true moral worth.

It is in this manner, undoubtedly, that we are to understand those passages of Scripture also in which we are commanded to love our neighbor, even our enemy. For love, as an affection, cannot be commanded, but beneficence for duty's sake may, even though we are not impelled to it by any inclination—nay, are even repelled by a natural and unconquerable aversion. This is *practical* love, and not *pathological*—a love which is seated in the will, and not in the propensions of sense—in principles of ac-tion and not of tender sympathy; and it is this love alone which can be commanded.

Having thus defended his primary proposition—that what is ultimately good is a good will acting in accordance with practical reason, in other words, from duty—Kant moves on to two corollary propositions:

The second proposition is: That an action done from duty derives its moral worth, *not from the purpose* which is to be attained by it, but from the maxim by which it is determined, and therefore does not depend on the realization of the object of the action, but merely on the *principle of volition* by which the action has taken place, without regard to any object of desire. It is clear from what precedes that the pur-poses which we may have in view in our actions, or their effects regarded as ends and springs of the will cannot give to actions any unconditional or moral worth. In what, then, can their worth lie if it is not to consist in the will and in reference to its expected effect? It cannot lie anywhere but in the *principle of the will* without regard to the ends which can be attained by the action. For the will stands between its a priori principle, which is formal, and its a posteriori spring which is material, as between two roads, and as it must be determined by something, it follows that it must be determined by the formal principle of volition when an action is done from duty, in which case every material principle has been withdrawn from it.

The third proposition, which is a consequence of the two preceding, I would express thus: *Duty is the necessity of acting from respect for the law.* I may have *inclination*

> "[A]n action done from duty must wholly exclude the influence of inclination, and with it every object of the will."
>
> – IMMANUEL KANT

for an object as the effect of my proposed action, but I cannot have *respect* for it just for this reason that it is an effect and not an energy of will. Similarly, I cannot have respect for inclination, whether my own or another's; I can at most, if my own, approve it; if another's, sometimes even love it, that is, look on it as favorable to my own interest. It is only what is connected with my will as a principle, by no means as an effect—what does not subserve my inclination, but overpowers it, or at least in case of choice excludes it from its calculation—in other words, simply the law of itself, which can be an object of respect, and hence a command. Now an action done from duty must wholly exclude the influence of inclination, and with it every object of the will, so that nothing remains which can determine the will except objectively the *law*, and subjectively *pure respect* for this practical law, and consequently the maxim that I should follow this law even to the thwarting of all my inclinations.

Thus the moral worth of an action does not lie in the effect expected from it, nor in any principle of action which requires to borrow its motive from this expected effect. For all these effects—agreeableness of one's condition, and even the promotion of the happiness of others—could have been also brought about by other causes, so that for this there would have been no need of the will of a rational being; whereas it is in this alone that the supreme and unconditional good can be found. The pre-eminent good which we call moral can therefore consist in nothing else than *the conception of law* in itself, *which certainly is only possible in a rational being*, in so far as this conception, and not the expected effect, determines the will. This is a good which is already preset in the person who acts accordingly, and we have not to wait for it to appear first in the result.

By what sort of law can that be the conception of which must determine the will, even without paying any regard to the effect expected from it, in order that this will may be called good absolutely and without qualification? As I have deprived the will of every impulse which could arise to it from obedience to any law, there remains nothing but the universal conformity of its actions to law in general, which alone is to serve the will as a principle.

FIG. 7.17 Morality has nothing to do with our satisfaction, according to Kant; it is concerned solely with doing our duty. *(© iStockphoto.com/Magdalena Tworkowska)*

The conception of "universal conformity to law" is Kant's central notion of duty. He defines it, as we shall see, as a generalized version of the Golden Rule: "Do unto others as you would have them do unto you." The point is, decide what you ought to do by asking yourself the question, "What if everyone were to do that?" The rule, as he states it, is as follows:

I am never to act otherwise than so, *that I could also will that my maxim should become* a universal law. Here, now, it is the simple conformity to law in general, without assuming any particular law applicable to certain actions, that serves the will as its principle, and must so serve it if duty is not to be a vain delusion and a chimerical notion. The common reason of men in its practical judgments perfectly coincides with this, and always has in view the principle here suggested. Let the question be, for example: May I when in distress make a promise with the intention not to keep it? I readily distinguish here between the two significations which the question may have: whether it is prudent or whether it is right to make a false promise? The former may undoubtedly often be the case. I see clearly indeed that it is not enough to extricate myself from a present difficulty by means of this subterfuge, but it must be well considered whether there may not hereafter spring from this lie much greater inconvenience than that from which I now free myself, and as, with all my supposed *cunning*, the consequences cannot be so easily foreseen but that credit once lost may be much more injurious to me than any mischief which I seek to avoid at present, it should be considered whether it would not be more *prudent* to act herein according to a universal maxim, and to make it a habit to promise nothing except with the intention of keeping it. But it is soon clear to me that such a maxim will still only be based on the fear of consequences. Now it is a wholly different thing to be truthful from duty, and to be so from apprehension of injurious consequences. In the first case, the very notion of the action implies a law for me; in the second case, I must first look about elsewhere to see what results may be combined with it which would affect myself. For to deviate from the principle of duty is beyond all doubt wicked; but to be unfaithful to my maxim of prudence may often be very advantageous to me, although to abide by it is certainly safer. The shortest way, however, and an unerring one, to discover the answer to this question whether a lying promise is consistent with duty, is to ask myself, Should I be content that my maxim (to extricate myself from difficulty by a false promise) should hold good as a universal law, for myself as well as for others; and should I be able to say to myself, "Every one may make a deceitful promise when he finds himself in a difficulty from which he cannot otherwise extricate himself"? Then I presently become aware that, while I can will the lie, I can by no means will that lying should be a universal law. For with such a law there would be no promises at all, since it would be in vain to allege my intention in regard to my future actions to those who would not believe this allegation, or if they over-hastily did so, would pay me back in my own coin. Hence my maxim, as soon as it should be made a universal law, would necessarily destroy itself.

The impressive name Kant gives to this general formulation of his notion of duty is the **categorical imperative**. An **imperative** is just what we called a command in our preliminary discussion of morality. It is of the form "do this!" or "don't do this!" Some imperatives tell us to "do this!" but only to get or do something else. Kant calls these "**hypothetical impera-tives.**" For example, "go to law school" (if you want to be a lawyer) or "don't eat very hot curry" (unless you don't mind risking an ulcer). But imperatives with a moral *ought* in them are not tied to any such "if" or "in order to" conditions. They are simply "do this" or "don't do this," whatever the circumstances, whatever you would like or enjoy personally—for example, "don't lie" (no matter what). This is what Kant means by "categorical."

Now all *imperatives* command either *hypothetically* or *categorically*. The former represent the practical necessity of a possible action as means to something else that is willed (or at least which one might possibly will). The categorical imperative would be that which represented an action as necessary of itself without reference to another end, that is, as objectively necessary.

Since every practical law represents a possible action as good, and on this account, for a subject who is practically determinable by reason as necessary, all imperatives are formulae determining an action which is necessary according to the principle of a will good in some respects. If now the action is good only as a means *to something else*, then the imperative is *hypothetical;* if it is conceived as good *in itself* and consequently as being necessarily the principle of a will which of itself conforms to reason, then it is *categorical*.

With hypothetical imperatives, what is commanded depends upon particular circumstances. With moral or categorical imperatives, there are universal laws that tell us what to do in every circumstance. (A **maxim**, according to Kant, is a "subjective principle of action," or what we would call an *intention*, formulated as a general principle. It is distinguished from an "objective principle," that is, a universal law of reason.)

There is therefore but one categorical imperative, namely, this: *Act only on that maxim whereby thou canst at the same time will that it should become a universal law.*

Now if all imperatives of duty can be deduced from this one imperative as from their principle, then, although it should remain undecided whether what is called duty is not merely a vain notion, yet at least we shall be able to show what we understand by it and what this notion means.

Since the universality of the law according to which effects are produced constitutes what is properly called *nature* in the most general sense (as to form)—that is, the existence of things so far as it is determined by general laws—the imperative of duty may be expressed thus: *Act as if the maxim of thy action were to become by thy will a universal law of nature.*

FIG. 7.18 Kant's categorical imperative applies to all human beings everywhere at all times. (© iStockphoto.com/Amanda Rohde)

We will now enumerate a few duties, adopting the usual division of them into duties to ourselves and to others, and into perfect and imperfect duties.

1. A man reduced to despair by a series of misfortunes feels wearied of life, but is still so far in possession of his reason that he can ask himself whether it would not be contrary to his duty to himself to take his own life. Now he inquires whether the maxim of his action could become a universal law of nature. His maxim is: From self-love I adopt it as a principle to shorten my life when its longer duration is likely to bring more evil than satisfaction. It is asked then simply whether this principle founded on self-love can become a universal law of nature. Now we see at once that a system of nature of which it should be law to destroy life by means of the very feeling whose special nature it is to impel to the improvement of life would contradict itself, and therefore could not exist as a system of nature; hence that maxim cannot possibly exist as a universal law of nature, and consequently would be wholly inconsistent with the supreme principle of all duty.

2. Another finds himself forced by necessity to borrow money. He knows that he will not be able to repay it, but sees also that nothing will be lent to him unless he promises stoutly to repay it in a definite time. He desires to make this promise, but he has still so much conscience as to ask himself: Is it not unlawful and inconsistent with duty to get out of a difficulty in this way? Suppose, however, that he resolves to do so, then the maxim of his action would be expressed thus: When I think myself in want of money, I will borrow money and promise to repay it, although I know that I

never can do so. Now this principle of self-love or of one's own advantage may per-haps be consistent with my whole future welfare; but the question now is, Is it right? I change then the suggestion of self-love into a universal law, and state the question thus: How would it be if my maxim were a universal law? Then I see at once that it could never hold as a universal law of nature, but would necessarily contradict itself. For supposing it to be a universal law that everyone when he thinks himself in a difficulty should be able to promise whatever he pleases, with the purpose of not keeping his promise, the promise itself would become impossible, as well as the end that one might have in view in it, since no one would consider that anything was promised to him, but would ridicule all such statements as vain pretenses.

3. A third finds in himself a talent which with the help of some culture might make him a useful man in many respects. But he finds himself in comfortable cir-cumstances and prefers to indulge in pleasure rather than to take pains in enlarging and improving his happy natural capacities. He asks, however, whether his maxim of neglect of his natural gifts, besides agreeing with his inclination to indulgence, agrees also with what is called duty. He sees then that a system of nature could indeed subsist with such a universal law, although men (like the South Sea island-ers) should let their talents rest and resolve to devote their lives merely to idleness, amusement, and propagation of their species—in a word, to enjoyment; but he cannot possibly *will* that this should be a universal law of nature, or be implanted in us as such by a natural instinct. For, as a rational being, he necessarily wills that his faculties be developed, since they serve him, and have been given him, for all sorts of possible purposes.

4. A fourth, who is in prosperity, while he sees that others have to contend with great wretchedness and that he could help them, thinks: What concern is it of mine? Let everyone be as happy as Heaven pleases, or as he can make himself; I will take nothing from him nor even envy him, only I do not wish to contribute anything to his welfare or to his assistance in distress! Now no doubt, if such a mode of thinking were a universal law, the human race might very well subsist, and doubtless even bet-ter than in a state in which everyone talks of sympathy and good-will, or even takes care occasionally to put it into practice, but, on the other side, also cheats when he can, betrays the rights of men, or otherwise violates them. But although it is possible that a universal law of nature might exist in accordance with that maxim, it is impos-sible to *will* that such a principle should have the universal validity of a law of nature. For a will which resolved this would contradict itself, inasmuch as many cases might occur in which one would have need of the love and sympathy of others, and in which, by such a law of nature, sprung from his own will, he would deprive himself of all hope of the aid he desires.

These are a few of the many actual duties, or at least what we regard as such, which obviously fall into two classes on the one principle that we have laid down. We must be *able to will* that a maxim of our action should be a universal law. This is the canon of the moral appreciation of the action generally. Some actions are of such a character that their maxim cannot without contradiction be even *conceived* as a universal law of nature, far from it being possible that we should *will* that it *should* be so. In others, this intrinsic impossibility is not found, but still it is impossible to *will* that their maxim should be raised to the universality of a law of nature, since such a will would contradict itself. It is easily seen that the former violate strict or rigorous (inflexible) duty; the latter only laxer (meritorious) duty. Thus it has been completely shown by these examples how all duties depend as regards the nature of the obligation (not the object of the action) on the same principle.

Another way of describing the categorical imperative, using a term from Kant that we have already encountered, is to say that it is an **a priori** principle, independent of any particular circumstances. Moral principles are necessary for the same reason that certain principles of knowledge are necessary, according to Kant: they are essential to our nature. It is important, therefore, for Kant to insist that moral principles, as a priori principles of reason, hold for every human being. In fact, Kant claims that they hold "for every rational creature." (There is an extremely important point hidden in this phrase. Traditionally, morality has been defended on the basis of God's will. That is, the traditional view has been that we ought to be moral because God gave us the moral laws. According to Kant, however, God does not give the laws, but as a rational creature, He is bound by them just as we are. Thus, in answer to the question, Are the laws of morality good because God is good, or is God good because he obeys the laws of morality? Kant would claim the latter.)

Kant's discussion of the categorical imperative is made confusing because after he has told us that "there is but one categorical imperative," he then goes on to give us others. He calls these "alternative formulations of the categorical imperative," but their effect on most readers is to confuse them unnecessarily. In actuality, for Kant there are a great many categorical imperatives. The first one Kant gave us is merely the most general. More specific examples are "don't lie!" and "keep your promises!" Another general categorical imperative is "never use people!" We should recognize that there is a sense in which "using people" may be perfectly innocent. For example, you "use" another person in order to play tennis, since you could not play alone. In such a case, the other person derives as much benefit from your "using" him or her as you do, and we could say that the person is "using you" as well. But there are cases in which we are tempted to "use" people for our own benefit without any regard to their interests. This is what this categorical imperative forbids.

Now I say: man and generally any rational being *exists* as an end in himself, *not merely as a means* to be arbitrarily used by this or that will, but in all his actions, whether they concern himself or other rational beings, must be always regarded at the same time as an end. All objects of the inclinations have only a conditional worth; for if the inclinations and the wants founded on them did not exist, then their object would be without value. But the inclinations themselves, being sources of want, are so far from having an absolute worth for which they should be desired that, on the contrary, it must be the universal wish of every rational being to be wholly free from them. Thus the worth of any object which is *to be acquired* by our action is always conditional. Beings whose existence depends not on our will but on nature's, have nevertheless, if they are not rational beings, only a relative value as means, and are therefore called *things;* rational beings, on the contrary, are called *persons,* because their very nature points them out as ends in themselves, that is, as something which must not be used merely as means, and so far therefore restricts freedom of ac-

FIG. 7.19 Hypothetical imperatives, which apply only to some, depending on their goals, are familiar in everyday life.
(Image © Radu Razvan, 2011. Used under license from Shutterstock.com)

tion (and is an object of respect). These, therefore, are not merely subjective ends whose existence has a worth *for us* as an effect of our action, but *objective ends*, that is, things whose existence is an end in itself—an end, moreover, for which no other can be substituted, which they should subserve *merely* as means, for otherwise nothing whatever would possess *absolute worth;* but if all worth were conditioned and therefore contingent, then there would be no supreme practical principle of reason whatever.

If then there is a supreme practical principle or, in respect of the human will, a categorical imperative, it must be one which, being drawn from the conception of that which is necessarily an end for everyone because it is *an end in itself*, constitutes an *objective* principle of will, and can therefore serve as a universal practical law. The foundation of this principle is: *rational nature exists as an end in itself.* Man necessarily conceives his own existence as being so; so far then this is a subjective principle of human actions. But every other rational being regards its existence similarly, just on the same rational principle that holds for me; so that it is at the same time an objective principle from which as a supreme practical law all laws of the will must be capable of being deduced. Accordingly the practical imperative will be as follows: *So act as to treat humanity, whether in thine own person or in that of any other in every case as an end withal, never as means only.* We will now inquire whether this can be practically carried out.

To abide by the previous examples:

First, under the head of necessary duty to oneself: He who contemplates suicide should ask himself whether his action can be consistent with the idea of humanity *as an end in itself.* If he destroys himself in order to escape from painful circumstances, he uses a person merely as *a mean* to maintain a tolerable condition up to the end of life. But a man is not a thing, that is to say, something which can be used merely as means, but must in all his actions be always considered as an end in himself. I cannot, therefore, dispose in any way of a man in my own person so as to mutilate him, to damage or kill him. (It belongs to ethics proper to define this principle more precisely, so as to avoid all misunderstanding, for example, as to the amputation of the limbs in order to preserve myself; as to exposing my life to danger with a view to preserve it, etc. This question is therefore omitted here.)

Secondly, as regards necessary duties, or those of strict obligation, towards others: He who is thinking of making a lying promise to others will see at once that he would be using another man *merely as a mean*, without the latter containing at the same time the end in himself. For he whom I propose by such a promise to use for my own purpose cannot possibly assent to my mode of acting towards him, and therefore cannot himself contain the end of this action. This violation of the principle of humanity in other men is more obvious if we take in examples of attacks on the freedom and property of others. For then it is clear that he who transgresses the rights of men intends to use the person of others merely as means, without considering that as rational beings they ought always to be esteemed also as ends, that is, as beings who must be capable of containing in themselves the end of the very same action.

Thirdly, as regards contingent (meritorious) duties to oneself: It is not enough that the action does not violate humanity in our own person as an end in itself, it must also *harmonize with it.* Now there are in humanity capacities of greater perfection which belong to the end that nature has in view in regard to humanity in ourselves as the subject; to neglect these might perhaps be consistent with the *maintenance of* humanity as an end in itself, but not with the *advancement* of this end.

> "[R]ational beings, on the contrary, are called persons, because their very nature points them out as ends in themselves, that is, as something which must not be used merely as means."
>
> – IMMANUEL KANT

FIG. 7.20 Helping others in distress is a duty that can never be completely fulfilled. It is an ongoing obligation. *(Image © sababa66, 2011. Used under license from Shutterstock.com)*

Fourthly, as regards meritorious duties towards others: The natural end which all men have is their own happiness. Now humanity might indeed subsist although no one should contribute anything to the happiness of others, provided he did not intentionally withdraw anything from it; but after all, this would only harmonize negatively, not positively, with *humanity as an end in itself*, if everyone does not also endeavor, as far as in him lies, to forward the ends of others. For the ends of any subject which is an end in himself ought as far as possible to be *my* ends also, if that conception is to have its *full* effect with me.

This principle that humanity and generally every rational nature is *an end in itself* (which is the supreme limiting condition of every man's freedom of action), is not borrowed from experience, *first*, because it is universal, applying as it does to all rational beings whatever, and experience is not capable of determining anything about them; *secondly*, because it does not present humanity as an end to men (subjectively), that is, as an object which men do of themselves actually adopt as an end; but as an objective end which must as a law constitute the supreme limiting condition of all our subjective ends, let them be what we will; it must therefore spring from pure reason.

In Kant's own terms, every human will is a will that is capable of acting according to universal laws of morality, not based upon any personal inclinations or interests but simply in obedience to rational principles that are categorical. Using this as a definition of morality, Kant then looks back at his predecessors:

Looking back now on all previous attempts to discover the principle of morality, we need not wonder why they all failed. It was seen that man was bound to laws by duty, but it was not observed that the laws to which he is subject are *only those of his own giving*, though at the same time they are *universal*, and that he is only bound to act in conformity with his own will—a will, however, which is designed by nature to give universal laws. For when one has conceived man only as subject to a law (no matter what), then this law required some interest, either by way of attraction or constraint, since it did not originate as a law from *his own will*, but this will was according to a law obliged by *something else* to act in a certain manner. Now by this necessary consequence all the labor spent in finding a supreme principle of *duty* was irrevocably lost. For men never elicited duty, but only a necessity of acting from a certain interest.

Any morality worthy of the name, in other words, must be a product of a person's own autonomous reason yet universal at the same time, as a product of rational will and independent of personal feeling or interest. All previous philosophies, however, have insisted upon appealing to such personal feelings and interests. They thus ended up with principles that were in every case hypothetical and not, according to Kant, categorical or morally obligatory.

For example, morality for Aristotle depended upon a person's being a male Greek citizen. For Kant, morality and duty are completely set apart from such personal circumstances and concerns. Morality and duty have no qualifications, and, ultimately, they need have nothing to do with the good life or with happiness. In a perfect world, perhaps, doing our duty may also bring us happiness. But this is not such a world, Kant observes. Happiness and morality are two separate concerns, with the second always to be considered the most important. (It is at this point, however, that Kant introduces his "Postulates of Practical Reason," and God in particular, to give us some assurance that, at least in the [very] long run, doing our duty will bring us some reward.)

Kant's conception of morality is so strict that it is hard for most people to accept. What is most difficult to accept is the idea that morality and duty have nothing to do with our personal desires, ambitions, and feelings, which Kant called our inclinations. We can agree that at least sometimes our duties and our inclinations are in conflict. But many philosophers have thought that Kant went much too far the other way in separating them entirely.

Furthermore, Kant's emphasis on the categorical imperative systematically rules out all reference to particular situations and circumstances. In response to Kant, one may ask: Isn't the right thing to do often determined only within the particular context or situation? (A relatively recent moral philosophy called "situation ethics" has insisted upon this idea.) Don't we have to know the particular problems and persons involved? What is right in one situation may very well be wrong in another, just because of different personalities, for example. Some people may be extremely hurt if we tell them the "truth" about themselves. On the other hand, a little "white" lie will make them feel much better. Other people are offended by any lie, however, and prefer even hurtful truths to the "ignorant bliss" of not knowing. Must not all moral rules be tempered to the particular situation?

The Kantian response to this objection would be that there are many ways to avoid hurting people other than telling lies. One can say, "no comment." One can cough conveniently or drop the platter in one's hand. The fact that certain deceptions are institutionalized in our society (such as "regrets" for not attending a dinner party) does not mean that a Kantian should defend them. The question, then, becomes how one formulates an accurate description of the options in such cases. Is it ever the case that one has only two alternatives—hurt someone or tell a lie?

In a more general way, some have objected that Kant's unqualified concept of morality is much too general to help us decide what to do in any particular situation. As an example, take the categorical imperative "do not steal!" Although the imperative itself, as a categorical one, must be unqualified, in order to apply it at all, we have to understand the kinds of circumstances to which it applies. Can't we have a right to steal in certain circumstances? Or, to put the same point differently, aren't there some circumstances in which "stealing" isn't really stealing at all? What, then, of the situation in which a starving man steals a loaf of bread from an extremely wealthy baker. Surely he is stealing, but wouldn't we say that under the circumstances he is justified in doing so? The Kantian reply here is to distinguish between the question of whether that person is *wrong* in stealing and the question of whether (or how) he should be punished. In this case, we can presume, Kant would insist that the man did wrong, but nevertheless agree that he should not be punished.

How do we decide "under which circumstances" a moral law is to be applied? Kant's formulation of the categorical imperative tells us only that we must act in such a way that anyone in similar circumstances would act the same way. What defines these "similar" circumstances? Suppose a person were to tailor a maxim so that it is unlikely to apply to anyone else—for example, "anyone in these circumstances, namely, being five-foot-seven and born in Detroit in 1942, having blond hair and blue eyes, and being a graduate of C. High School, may steal." How can we avoid such trickery? Not by any considerations within the categorical imperative itself, for by its very nature (being designed to apply across the board), it is incapable of telling us under what circumstances a moral law applies.

Another way of making the same objection is to complain that there is no way of deciding how detailed the imperative must be. For example, should we simply say, "do not steal!" or rather "do not steal unless you are starving and the other person is not!" or else, "do not steal unless you are blond and blue-eyed!" and so on? Kant's reply, to prevent such abuses, is quite clearly to leave out all mention of particular circumstances in the formulation of principles. Nevertheless we have to decide in what circumstances to apply what principles, for example, in what cases it is relevant to consider the principle, "Do not steal." And here the question comes up once again. Which circumstances are relevant to the formulation of a categorical imperative? Surely it would not be right to say that *none* is relevant. At least we must know enough to know whether or not a particular act is an instance of stealing.

There have been other objections to Kant's severe philosophy. For example, if moral principles are categorical, then what do we do when two different moral principles conflict? The rule that tells us "do not lie!" is categorical; so is the rule that tells us "keep your promises!" Suppose that I promise not to tell anyone where you will be this weekend. Then some people who want to kill you force me to tell them where you are. I have to say something. Either I break the promise or I lie. Kant gives us no adequate way of choosing between the promise and the lie. He has ruled out any appeal to the consequences of our actions. In Kant's argument, even if your enemies are trying to kill you, this is not morally relevant. Most important, Kant has ruled out any appeal to what will make people happy, and this applies not only to the person who must either lie or break a promise but to everyone else who is involved as well. Kant would reply, presumably, that such cases of apparent conflict are due to a misrepresentation of the case. For example, one could respond to the intruders by playing dumb, or refusing to say anything, or trying to make them go away with force.

The question of moral conflict thus becomes critical for Kant's moral philosophy. If moral principles conflict, we need a way of choosing between them. If Kant is right that they do not conflict, then we need a way of accounting for apparent conflicts and resolving them. It is not clear that the Kantian theory gives us either a satisfactory criterion for getting out of moral quandaries or for explaining away some of the very painful moral conflicts in which we occasionally find ourselves.

- What role does reason play in Kant's morality? Kant claims to be indebted to Rousseau—how is he like Rousseau? How does he differ from Rousseau?
- What does Kant mean by a "good will"? What makes a will good, according to Kant?
- What makes an act "morally worthy," according to Kant?
- What is a categorical imperative? How does it differ from a hypothetical imperative? What is a maxim? How does Kant first formulate the categorical imperative in terms of maxims? How does he use this formulation to show that lying is wrong?
- What does it mean to say that we are "ends"? How do you treat someone as an end? What does Kant mean when he tells us not to treat others as a means only? What would be an example of treating another person as a means only? Are there any circumstances under which it may be permissible to do so?
- Do you find Kant's view that moral worth has nothing to do with our own personal inclinations, passions, and feelings convincing? Why is he so concerned with separating morality from inclinations?

H. Utilitarianism

Partially in response to the austere Kantian view of morality, with its neglect of happiness and the good life, a number of British philosophers, chiefly **Jeremy Bentham**, James Mill, and his son **John Stuart Mill**, developed a conception of morality that is called utilitarianism. Utilitarianism was an attempt to bring back personal inclinations and interests into moral considerations. Utilitarians wanted to reconsider the consequences as well as the intentions of an action and to consider particular circumstances in an attempt to determine what is morally right. Most important, utilitarianism was an attempt to return morality to the search for the personally satisfying life, which Kant had neglected.

FIG. 7.21 Jeremy Bentham
(© Stock Montage / SuperStock)

**Jeremy Bentham
(1748-1832)**

A leader in the legal reform movement in England and the founding father of that ethical position called utilitarianism. His *principle of utility*, which says that one should act to produce the greatest good for the greatest number of people, was the central theme of utilitarianism and slowly worked its way into the confusion of rules and statutes that constituted the English legal system of his day. Bentham's best-known work is his *Introduction to the Principles of Morals and Legislation* (1789).

The basis of utilitarianism is a form of **hedonism**, a conception of the good life that says that the ultimate good is pleasure and that we want and ought to want pleasure. But whereas traditional hedonism is concerned only with one's personal pleasure, utilitarianism is concerned with pleasure in general—both one's own pleasure and the pleasure of other people. In many utilitarian writings, the notions of pleasure and happiness are used interchangeably. From our earlier discussions (especially our discussion of Aristotle), you know that we must be cautious of such an exchange. Many short-lived pleasures do not make us happy, and happiness is much more than mere pleasure. The utilitarians are concerned with acknowledging this point, however. Their whole theory revolves around a single aim, to make the most people as happy as possible, sometimes sacrificing short-term pleasures for enduring ones. Their central principle is often summarized as "the greatest good for the greatest number."

Jeremy Bentham was motivated to formulate his utilitarian theories not so much by the strict moralism of Kant's philosophy as by the absurd complexity of the British legal system. Just as Kant sought a single principle that would simplify all morality, Bentham looked for a single principle that would simplify the law. Bentham began with the fact that people seek pleasure and avoid pain and developed the **"principle of utility,"** to be applied to policy decisions as well as to personal ones.

 FROM *An Introduction to the Principles of Morals and Legislation*
BY **Jeremy Bentham**[18]

I. Nature has placed mankind under the governance of two sovereign masters, pain and pleasure. It is for them alone to point out what we ought to do, as well as to determine what we shall do. On the one hand the standard of right and wrong, on the other the chain of causes and effects, are fastened to their throne. They govern us in all we do, in all we say, in all we think; every effort we can make to throw off our subjection, will serve but to demonstrate and confirm it. In words a man may pretend to abjure their empire; but in reality he will remain subject to it all the while. The principle of utility recognizes the subjection, and assumes it for the foundation of that system, the object of which is to tear the fabric of felicity by the hands of reason

---

18 Jeremy Bentham, *An Introduction to the Principles of Morals and Legislation* (Oxford, U.K.: Clarendon Press, 1879).

and of law. Systems which attempt to question it, deal in sounds instead of sense, in caprice instead of reason, the darkness instead of light.

But enough of metaphor and declamation: it is not by such means that moral science is to be improved.

II. The principle of utility is the foundation of the present work; it will be proper therefore at the outset to give an explicit and determinate account of what is meant by it. By the principle of utility is meant that principle which approves or disapproves of every action whatsoever, according to the tendency which it appears to have to augment or diminish the happiness of the party whose interest is in question; or, what is the same thing in other words, to promote or to oppose that happiness. I say of every action whatsoever; and therefore not only of every action of a private individual, but of every measure of government.

III. By utility is meant that property in any object, whereby it tends to produce benefit, advantage, pleasure, good, or happiness, (all this in the present case comes to the same thing) or (what comes again to the same thing) to prevent the happening of mischief, pain, evil, or unhappiness to the party whose interest is considered: if that party be the community in general, then the happiness of the community: if a particular individual, then the happiness of that individual.

IV. The interest of the community is one of the most general expressions that can occur in the phraseology of morals: no wonder that the meaning of it is often lost. When it has a meaning, it is this. The community is a fictitious body, composed of the individual persons who are considered as constituting as it were its members. The interest of the community then is, what?—the sum of the interests of the several members who compose it.

V. It is in vain to talk of the interest of the community, without understanding what is the interest of the individual. A thing is said to promote the interest, or to be for the interest, of an individual, when it tends to add to the sum total of his pleasures: or, what comes to the same thing, to diminish the sum total of his pains.

VI. An action then may be said to be conformable to the principle of utility, or, for shortness' sake, to utility, (meaning with respect to the community at large) when the tendency it has to augment the happiness of the community is greater than any it has to diminish it.

VII. A measure of government (which is but a particular kind of action, performed by a particular person or persons) may be said to be conformable to or dictated by the principle of utility, when in like manner the tendency which it has to augment the happiness of the community is greater than any which it has to diminish it.

Morality, according to Bentham's principle of utility, demands nothing other than action that tends to increase the amount of pleasure rather than diminish it.

X. Of an action that is conformable to the principle of utility, one may always say either that it is one that ought to be done, or at least that it is not one that ought not to be done. One may say also, that it is right it should be done; at least that it is not wrong it should be done: that it is a right action; at least that it is not a wrong action. When thus interpreted, the words ought, and right and wrong, and others of that stamp, have a meaning: when otherwise, they have none.

How does one defend this principle of utility? One cannot, Bentham tells us. To try to prove the principle is "as impossible as it is needless." People quite "naturally," whether they admit

> "An action . . .
> may be said to be
> conformable . . .
> to utility . . . when
> the tendency it
> has to augment
> the happiness of
> the community is
> greater than any it
> has to diminish it."
>
> – JEREMY BENTHAM

to it or not, act on the basis of it. This is not to say that they always act on it, but when they do not, it is only because they do not always know what is best for them. The reason for articulating the principle is to enable them to figure it out.

The heart of Bentham's theory is the formulation of a procedure for deciding, in every possible case, the value of alternative courses of action. The procedure simply involves the determination of alternative amounts of pleasures and pain, according to what has appropriately been called the **happiness calculus**.

I. Pleasures then, and the avoidance of pains, are the *ends* which the legislator has in view; it behoves him therefore to understand their *value*. Pleasures and pains are the *instruments* he has to work with: it behoves him therefore to understand their force, which is gain, in other words, their value.

II. To a person considered by *himself*, the value of a pleasure or pain considered *by itself*, will be greater or less, according to the four following circumstances.
1. Its *intensity*.
2. Its *duration*.
3. Its *certainty* or *uncertainty*.
4. Its *propinquity* or *remoteness*.

III. These are the circumstances which are to be considered in estimating a pleasure or a pain considered each of them by itself. But when the value of any pleasure or pain is considered for the purpose of estimating the tendency of any *act* by which it is produced, there are two other circumstances to be taken into the account; these are,
5. Its *fecundity*, or the chance it has of being followed by sensations of the *same* kind: that is, pleasures, if it be a pleasure: pains, if it be a pain.
6. Its *purity*, or the chance it has of *not* being followed by sensations of the *opposite* kind: that is, pains, if it be a pleasure: pleasures, if it be a pain.

Bentham proceeds to the test itself:

V. To take an exact account then of the general tendency of any act by which the interests of a community are affected, proceed as follows. Begin with any one person of those whose interests seem most immediately to be affected by it; and take an account,
1. Of the value of each distinguishable *pleasure* which appears to be produced by it in the *first* instance.
2. Of the value of each *pain* which appears to be produced by it in the *first* instance.
3. Of the value of each pleasure which appears to be produced by it *after* the first. This constitutes the *fecundity* of the first *pleasure* and the *impurity* of the first *pain*.
4. Of the value of each *pain* which appears to be produced by it after the first. This constitutes the *fecundity* of the first *pain*, and the *impurity* of the first pleasure.
5. Sum up all the values of all the *pleasures* on the one side, and those of all the pains on the other. The balance, if it be on the side of pleasure, will give the *good* tendency of the act upon the whole, with respect to the interests of that *individual* person; if on the side of pain, the *bad* tendency of it upon the whole.
6. Take an account of the *number* of persons whose interests appear to be concerned; and repeat the above process with respect to each. *Sum up* the numbers expressive of the degrees of *good* tendency, which the act has, with respect to

each individual, in regard to whom the tendency of it is *good* upon the whole: do this again with respect to each individual, in regard to whom the tendency of it is *bad* upon the whole. Take the balance; which, if on the side of *pleasure*, will give the general *good tendency* of the act, with respect to the total number of community of individuals concerned; if on the side of pain the general *evil tendency*, with respect to the same community.

Let us provide an example. Bentham discusses the problem of lust (Prop. XXX), which he says is always bad. Why? "Because if the effects of the motive are not bad, then we do not call it lust." Lust, in other words, is sexual desire that is so excessive that it brings about more pain than pleasure. Suppose you are sexually attracted to another person. How do you decide (assuming that there is already mutual agreement) whether to follow through or not?

Here is Bentham's proposal: First, you estimate the amount of pleasure each person will gain. An important question is whether the pleasure of only these two people should be estimated or the pleasure of others besides. If it is a question of adultery, then the interests of at least a third person should be considered. Even assuming that no such direct complications are involved, the indirect interests of the rest of society must be considered. (If you and your potential lover are sufficiently young, should the happiness of your parents enter into your decision?)

Then, after you have considered the initial pleasure that will result, estimate the initial pain. (In this case, we may presume it will be slight.) Then ask about the longer-term pleasures and pains for each person involved. If a sexual relationship will leave you feeling happy about yourself and the other person, then the subsequent pleasure will be considerable. If either person will feel regrets, or degraded, or embarrassed; if sex will spoil a good friendship; or if a sexual relationship will set up expectations that one or both of you is unwilling to fulfill, the amount of subsequent pain may be overwhelming.

After pursuing all these considerations, add up the pleasures and pains for each person (and for others who may be affected); match the total amount of pleasure against the total pain; and if the balance is positive, go ahead. If the balance is negative, don't do it. Suppose, for example, that you each expect a great deal of initial pleasure, and one of you expects nothing but good feelings afterward while the other expects only mild regrets. No one else need even know, so the balance is clearly very positive. But suppose neither of you expects to enjoy it all that much, and the subsequent hassles will be a prolonged and troublesome bother, then, very likely the balance will be negative.

We do not often make this kind of decision in this way. We simply do what we want to do at the time. And this is precisely what Bentham says we should not do. Bentham argues that it is because we so often act on the basis of impulses without rational calculations that we end up unhappy. In other words, the fact that we are usually irrational is not an argument against Bentham's principles. Their purpose is precisely to make us rational, to help us get what we really want.

There are problems with Bentham's theory. All that is considered, according to his "happiness calculus," is the amount of pleasure and pain. But some of you, in response to our preceding example, may well say, "It doesn't matter how much pleasure and how little pain two people will gain if they get into a sexual relationship. Under certain circumstances (if it is adultery or simply if they are not married) such behavior is wrong! Mere pleasure is not enough!" Here we see the beginning of a swing back toward Kant. Regardless of your reaction to the previous example, such a move is necessary. To see why, let us examine the following objection to Bentham.

Suppose a great many people would get a great deal of pleasure out of seeing some innocent person tortured and slaughtered like a beast. Of course, the victim would suffer a great deal of pain, but by increasing the size of the crowd, we could eventually obtain an amount of pleasure for everyone else that more than balanced the suffering of the victim. Bentham's calculus has no way of rejecting such a gruesome outcome. A less horrible example is this: If a person gets great pleasure from some activity and no pain, there are no other considerations that apply to him or her (assuming that his or her actions do not affect others). Are we then to say that a life of sloth and self-indulgence, if it satisfies everyone and gives them a lot of pleasure and no pain, is to be preferred to any other life of any kind? Does Bentham give us any reason to try for anything "better" than being happy pigs? This was the problem that bothered Bentham's godson, John Stuart Mill.

Mill's version of utilitarianism added an important qualification to Bentham's purely quantitative calculus. Mill said that it is not only the quantity of pleasure that counts, but the quality as well. Needless to say, this makes the calculations much more complicated. In fact, it makes them impossible, for there cannot be precise calculations of quality, even though there can be precise calculations of quantity. Mill's now-famous example is the following: If a pig can live a completely satisfied life, while a morally concerned and thoughtful individual like Socrates cannot ever be so satisfied, is the life of the pig therefore preferable? Mill's answer is this:

> It is better to be a human being dissatisfied than a pig satisfied; better to be Socrates dissatisfied than a fool satisfied.

On what grounds can he say this? Aren't the pig and the fool happier?

> If the fool, or the pig, are of a different opinion, it is because they only know their own side of the question. The other party [Socrates] knows both sides.[19]

Some problems emerge from this theory. How are we to evaluate different "qualities" of pleasure, even if we have tried them all? First let us look to Mill's revision of utilitarianism, as summarized in his popular pamphlet, appropriately called *Utilitarianism*. (It was Mill, not Bentham, who invented this term.) It begins with a general consideration of morality and of Kant's moral philosophy in particular.

 FROM *Utilitarianism*
BY **John Stuart Mill**[20]

Our moral faculty, according to all those of its interpreters who are entitled to the name of thinkers, supplies us only with the general principles of moral judgments; it is a branch of our reason, not of our sensitive faculty; and must be looked to for the abstract doctrines of morality, not for perception of it in the concrete. The intuitive, no less than what may be termed the inductive, school of ethics, insists on the necessity of general laws. They both agree that the morality of an individual action is not a question of direct perception, but of the application of a law to an individual case. They recognise also, to a great extent, the same moral laws; but differ as to their evidence, and the source from which they derive their authority. According to the one opinion, the principles of morals are evident a priori, requiring nothing to command assent, except that the meaning of the terms be understood. According to the

---

[19] John Stuart Mill, *Utilitarianism* (London: J. M. Dent, 1910).

[20] Ibid.

FIG. 7.22 A nineteenth-century engraving of John Stuart Mill *(The New York Public Library / Art Resource, NY)*

other doctrine, right and wrong, as well as truth and falsehood, are questions of observation and experience. But both hold equally that morality must be deduced from principles; and the intuitive school affirm as strongly as the inductive, that there is a science of morals. Yet they seldom attempt to make out a list of the a priori principles which are to serve as the premises of the science; still more rarely do they make any effort to reduce those various principles to one first principle, or common ground of obligation. They either assume the ordinary precepts of morals as of a priori authority, or they lay down as the common groundwork of those maxims, some generality much less obviously authoritative than the maxims themselves, and which has never succeeded in gaining popular acceptance. Yet to support their pretensions there ought either to be some one fundamental principle or law, at the root of all morality, or if there be several, there should be a determinate order of precedence among them; and the one principle, or the rule for deciding between the various principles when they conflict, ought to be self-evident.

To inquire how far the bad effects of this deficiency have been mitigated in practice, or to what extent the moral beliefs of mankind have been vitiated or made uncertain by the absence of any distinct recognition of an ultimate standard, would imply a complete survey and criticism of past and present ethical doctrine. It would, however, be easy to show that whatever steadiness or consistency these moral beliefs have attained, has been mainly due to the tacit influence of a standard not recognised. Although the non-existence of an acknowledged first principle has made ethics not so much a guide as a consecration of men's actual sentiments, still, as men's sentiments, both of favour and of aversion, are greatly influenced by what they suppose to be the effects of things upon their happiness, the principle of utility, or as Bentham latterly called it, the greatest happiness principle, has had a large share in forming the moral doctrines even of those who most scornfully reject its authority. Nor is there any school of thought which refuses to admit that the influence of actions on happiness is a most material and even predominant consideration in many of the details of morals, however unwilling to acknowledge it as the fundamental principle of morality, and the source of moral obligation. I might go much further, and say that to all those a priori moralists who deem it necessary to argue at all, utilitarian arguments are indispensable. It is not my present purpose to criticise these thinkers; but I cannot help referring, for illustration, to a systematic treatise by one of the most illustrious of them, the *Metaphysics of Ethics*, by Kant. This remarkable man, whose system of thought will long remain one of the landmarks in the history of philosophical speculation, does, in the treatise in question, lay down a universal first principle as the origin and ground of moral obligation; it is this:—"So act, that the rule on which thou actest would admit of being adopted as a law by all rational beings." But when he begins to deduce from this precept any of the actual duties of morality, he fails, almost grotesquely, to show that there would be any contradiction, any logical (not to say physical) impossibility, in the adoption by all rational beings of the most outrageously immoral rules of conduct. All he shows is that the *consequences* of their universal adoption would be such as no one would choose to incur.

Mill next gets down to the business of redefining utilitarianism. Like Bentham, he insists that the principle of utility cannot be proved as such, for it is the ultimate end in terms of which everything else is justified. But there is, Mill tells us, a "larger sense of the word 'proof'":

> On the present occasion, I shall, without further discussion of the other theories, attempt to contribute something towards the understanding and appreciation of the Utilitarian or Happiness theory, and towards such proof as it is susceptible of. It is evident that this cannot be proof in the ordinary and popular meaning of the term. Questions of ultimate ends are not amenable to direct proof. Whatever can be proved to be good must be so by being shown to be a means to something admitted to be good without proof. The medical art is proved to be good by its conducing to health; but how is it possible to prove that health is good? The art of music is good, for the reason, among others, that it produces pleasure; but what proof is it possible to give that pleasure is good? If, then, it is asserted that there is a comprehensive formula, including all things which are in themselves good, and that whatever else is good, is not so as an end, but as a mean, the formula may be accepted or rejected, but is not a subject of what is commonly understood by proof. We are not, however, to infer that its acceptance or rejection must depend on blind impulse, or arbitrary choice. There is a larger meaning of the word proof, in which this question is as amenable to it as any other of the disputed questions of philosophy. The subject is within the cognisance of the rational faculty; and neither does that faculty deal with it solely in the way of intuition. Considerations may be presented capable of determining the intellect either to give or withhold its assent to the doctrine; and this is equivalent to proof.

Mill concerns himself with dispelling a popular misconception, which views the principle of utility as advocating "usefulness" in opposition to pleasure. Here he points out that, by utility, proponents of the theory have always meant "not something to be contradistinguished from pleasure, but pleasure itself, together with exemption from pain." The greatest happiness principle, in turn, holds that actions are right to the extent that they promote happiness and are wrong to the extent that they diminish happiness. By "happiness," of course, Mill means pleasure and the absence of pain. Pleasure or happiness, according to Mill, is the only thing desirable as an end (it is therefore an *intrinsic good*), and all other desirable things are desired for the pleasure that they produce. These other goods are simply means toward pleasure (and are therefore *instrumental goods*).

A passing remark is all that needs be given to the ignorant blunder of supposing that those who stand up for utility as the test of right and wrong, use the term in that restricted and merely colloquial sense in which utility is opposed to pleasure. An apology is due to the philosophical opponents of utilitarianism, for even the momentary appearance of confounding them with any one capable of so absurd a misconception; which is the more extraordinary, inasmuch as the contrary accusation, of referring everything to pleasure, and that too in its grossest form, is another of the common charges against utilitarianism: and, as has been pointedly remarked by an able writer, the same sort of persons, and often the very same persons, denounce the theory "as impracticably dry when the word utility precedes the word pleasure, and as too practicably voluptuous when the word pleasure precedes the word utility." Those who know anything about the matter are aware that every writer, from Epicurus to Bentham, who maintained the theory of utility, meant by it, not something to be contradistinguished from pleasure, but pleasure itself, together with exemption from pain; and instead of opposing the useful to the agreeable or the ornamental,

"Questions of ultimate ends are not amenable to direct proof. Whatever can be proved to be good must be so by being shown to be a means to something admitted to be good without proof."

– JOHN STUART MILL

have always declared that the useful means these, among other things. Yet the common herd, including the herd of writers, not only in newspapers and periodicals, but in books of weight and pretension, are perpetually falling, into this shallow mistake. Having caught up the word utilitarian, while knowing nothing whatever about it but its sound, they habitually express by it the rejection, or the neglect, of pleasure in some of its forms; of beauty, of ornament, or of amusement. Nor is the term thus ignorantly misapplied solely in disparagement, but occasionally in compliment; as though it implied superiority to frivolity and the mere pleasures of the moment. And this perverted use is the only one in which the word is popularly known, and the one from which the new generation are acquiring their sole notion of its meaning. Those who introduced the word, but who had for many years discontinued it as a distinctive appellation, may well feel themselves called upon to resume it, if by doing so they can hope to contribute anything towards rescuing it from this utter degradation.

The creed which accepts as the foundation of morals, Utility or the Greatest Happiness Principle, holds that actions are right in proportion as they tend to promote happiness, wrong as they tend to produce the reverse of happiness. By happiness is intended pleasure, and the absence of pain; by unhappiness, pain, and the privation of pleasure. To give a clear view of the moral standard set up by the theory, much more requires to be said; in particular, what things it includes in the ideas of pain and pleasure; and to what extent this is left an open question. But these supplementary explanations do not affect the theory of life on which this theory of morality is grounded—namely, that pleasure, and freedom from pain, are the only things desirable as ends; and that all desirable things (which are as numerous in the utilitarian as in any other scheme) are desirable either for the pleasure inherent in themselves, or as means to the promotion of pleasure and the prevention of pain.

After defining the principle of utility, Mill turns his attention to the objection (one often levied against the Epicureans) that to claim that pleasure is the highest good for human beings is to degrade human life to the level of pigs. Mill responds that it is not the advocates of pleasure who degrade human life, but their critics, since they assume that humans are capable only of the same types of pleasures as swine. Mill distinguishes between higher and lower pleasures and says that humans, unlike pigs, are capable of both because we possess higher cognitive faculties. Hence, when Mill says that the highest good is pleasure, he is referring primarily to the higher types of pleasures.

How do we know which pleasures are higher or what makes one pleasure higher than another? Mill's answer is simple: If we are considering two pleasures, then the higher pleasure will be the one that is preferred by those who have experienced both. Human beings will prefer to satisfy their higher faculties over satisfying their lower ones, even though the higher faculties are much more difficult to satisfy. Few among us would consent to exchange our life with the life of a satisfied pig, even if we seem to be less satisfied than a pig. We hardly think that the life of a satisfied pig is a dignified one. Thus, Mill

FIG. 7.23 Mill claims that no human being, no matter how miserable, would willingly exchange places with a satisfied pig. *(© iStockphoto.com/ Ekspansio)*

reaches his conclusion: "it is better to be a human being dissatisfied than a pig satisfied; better to be Socrates dissatisfied than a fool satisfied."

Now, such a theory of life excites in many minds, and among them in some of the most estimable in feeling and purpose, inveterate dislike. To suppose that life has (as they express it) no higher end than pleasure—no better and nobler object of desire and pursuit—they designate as utterly mean and grovelling; as a doctrine worthy only of swine, to whom the followers of Epicurus were, at a very early period, contemptuously likened; and modern holders of the doctrine are occasionally made the subject of equally polite comparisons by its German, French, and English assailants.

When thus attacked, the Epicureans have always answered, that it is not they, but their accusers, who represent human nature in a degrading light; since the accusation supposes human beings to be capable of no pleasures except those of which swine are capable. If this supposition were true, the charge could not be gainsaid, but would then be no longer an imputation; for if the sources of pleasure were precisely the same to human beings and to swine, the rule of life which is good enough for the one would be good enough for the other. The comparison of the Epicurean life to that of beasts is felt as degrading, precisely because a beast's pleasures do not satisfy a human being's conceptions of happiness. Human beings have faculties more elevated than the animal appetites, and when once made conscious of them, do not regard anything as happiness which does not include their gratification. I do not, indeed, consider the Epicureans to have been by any means faultless in drawing out their scheme of consequences from the utilitarian principle. To do this in any sufficient manner, many Stoic, as well as Christian elements require to be included. But there is no known Epicurean theory of life which does not assign to the pleasures of the intellect, of the feelings and imagination, and of the moral sentiments, a much higher value as pleasures than to those of mere sensation. It must be admitted, however, that utilitarian writers in general have placed the superiority of mental over bodily pleasures chiefly in the greater permanency, safety, uncostliness, etc., of the former—that is, in their circumstantial advantages rather than in their intrinsic nature. And on all these points utilitarians have fully proved their case; but they might have taken the other, and, as it may be called, higher ground, with entire consistency. It is quite compatible with the principle of utility to recognise the fact, that some *kinds* of pleasure are more desirable and more valuable than others. It would be absurd that while, in estimating all other things, quality is considered as well as quantity, the estimation of pleasures should be supposed to depend on quantity alone.

If I am asked, what I mean by difference of quality in pleasures, or what makes one pleasure more valuable than another, merely as a pleasure, except its being greater in amount, there is but one possible answer. Of two pleasures, if there be one to which all or almost all who have experience of both give a decided preference, irrespective of a feeling of moral obligation to prefer it, that is the more desirable pleasure. If one of the two is, by those who are competently acquainted with both, placed so far above the other that they prefer it, even though knowing it to be attended with a greater amount of discontent, and would not resign it for any quantity of the other pleasure which their nature is capable of, we are justified in ascribing to the preferred enjoyment a superiority in quality, so far outweighing quantity as to render it, in comparison, of small account.

Now it is an unquestionable fact that those who are equally acquainted with, and equally capable of appreciating and enjoying, both, do give a most marked preference

"Of two pleasures, if there be one to which all or almost all who have experience of both give a decided preference, irrespective of a feeling of moral obligation to prefer it, that is the more desirable pleasure."

– JOHN STUART MILL

to the manner of existence which employs their higher faculties. Few human creatures would consent to be changed into any of the lower animals, for a promise of the fullest allowance of a beast's pleasures; no intelligent human being would consent to be a fool, no instructed person would be an ignoramus, no person of feeling and conscience would be selfish and base, even though they should be persuaded that the fool, the dunce, or the rascal is better satisfied with his lot than they are with theirs. They would not resign what they possess more than he for the most complete satisfaction of all the desires which they have in common with him. If they ever fancy they would, it is only in cases of unhappiness so extreme, that to escape from it they would exchange their lot for almost any other, however undesirable in their own eyes. A being of higher faculties requires more to make him happy, is capable probably of more acute suffering, and certainly accessible to it at more points, than one of an inferior type; but in spite of these liabilities, he can never really wish to sink into what he feels to be a lower grade of existence. We may give what explanation we please of this unwillingness; we may attribute it to pride, a name which is given indiscriminately to some of the most and to some of the least estimable feelings of which mankind are capable: we may refer it to the love of liberty and personal independence, an appeal to which was with the Stoics one of the most effective means for the inculcation of it; to the love of power, or to the love of excitement, both of which do really enter into and contribute to it: but its most appropriate appellation is a sense of dignity, which all human beings possess in one form or other, and in some, though by no means in exact, proportion to their higher faculties, and which is so essential a part of the happiness of those in whom it is strong, that nothing which conflicts with it could be, otherwise than momentarily, an object of desire to them. Whoever supposes that this preference takes place at a sacrifice of happiness—that the superior being, in anything like equal circumstances, is not happier than the inferior— confounds the two very different ideas, of happiness, and content. It is indisputable that the being whose capacities of enjoyment are low, has the greatest chance of having them fully satisfied; and a highly endowed being will always feel that any happiness which he can look for, as the world is constituted, is imperfect. But he can learn to bear its imperfections, if they are at all bearable; and they will not make him envy the being who is indeed unconscious of the imperfections, but only because he feels not at all the good which those imperfections qualify. It is better to be a human being dissatisfied than a pig satisfied; better to be Socrates dissatisfied than a fool satisfied. And if the fool, or the pig, are of a different opinion, it is because they only know their own side of the question. The other party to the comparison knows both sides.

Mill does recognize that cultivating the higher faculties is a difficult thing to do. We know many among us who do not pursue the higher pleasures, but seem constantly to seek bodily satisfaction. Mill explains the behavior of these types of people in a number of ways. They may be lazy, they may have had little opportunity to cultivate their higher faculties in the past and are now incapable of them, they may be ignorant, or they may have what is referred to as "weakness of will." Weakness of will is that familiar experience of knowing what is the right thing to do, yet choosing, giving into temptation and failing to do it.

Mill thinks that the cultivation of noble character is necessary for the utilitarian. Not only will noble or virtuous people be more receptive to cultivating their higher faculties and therefore more apt to pursue higher pleasures, they tend to make others happy. Since the goal of utilitarianism is to increase not just the agent's happiness, but the greatest total amount of happiness of everyone, the utilitarian is obligated to cultivate the virtues in himself and others.

It may be objected, that many who are capable of the higher pleasures, occasionally, under the influence of temptation, postpone them to the lower. But this is quite compatible with a full appreciation of the intrinsic superiority of the higher. Men often, from infirmity of character, make their election for the nearer good, though they know it to be the less valuable; and this no less when the choice is between two bodily pleasures, than when it is between bodily and mental. They pursue sensual indulgences to the injury of health, though perfectly aware that health is the greater good. It may be further objected, that many who begin with youthful enthusiasm for everything noble, as they advance in years sink into indolence and selfishness. But I do not believe that those who undergo this very common change, voluntarily choose the lower description of pleasures in preference to the higher. I believe that before they devote themselves exclusively to the one, they have already become incapable of the other. Capacity for the nobler feelings is in most natures a very tender plant, easily killed, not only by hostile influences, but by mere want of sustenance; and in the majority of young persons it speedily dies away if the occupations to which their position in life has devoted them, and the society into which it has thrown them, are not favourable to keeping that higher capacity in exercise. Men lose their high aspirations as they lose their intellectual tastes, because they have not time or opportunity for indulging them; and they addict themselves to inferior pleasures, not because they deliberately prefer them, but because they are either the only ones to which they have access, or the only ones which they are any longer capable of enjoying. It may be questioned whether any one who has remained equally susceptible to both classes of pleasures, ever knowingly and calmly preferred the lower; though many, in all ages, have broken down in an ineffectual attempt to combine both.

From this verdict of the only competent judges, I apprehend there can be no appeal. On a question which is the best worth having of two pleasures, or which of two modes of existence is the most grateful to the feelings, apart from its moral attributes and from its consequences, the judgment of those who are qualified by knowledge of both, or, if they differ, that of the majority among them, must be admitted as final. And there needs be the less hesitation to accept this judgment respecting the quality of pleasures, since there is no other tribunal to be referred to even on the question of quantity. What means are there of determining which is the acutest of two pains, or the intensest of two pleasurable sensations, except the general suffrage of those who are familiar with both? Neither pains nor pleasures are homogeneous, and pain is always heterogeneous with pleasure. What is there to decide whether a particular pleasure is worth purchasing at the cost of a particular pain, except the feelings and judgment of the experienced? When, therefore, those feelings and judgment declare the

FIG. 7.24 Shakespearean plays, such as *King John*, are among the higher pleasures that Mill considers qualitatively superior to bodily gratification. (© iStockphoto.com/Eduardo Jose Bernardino)

pleasures derived from the higher faculties to be preferable *in kind*, apart from the question of intensity, to those of which the animal nature, disjoined from the higher faculties, is susceptible, they are entitled on this subject to the same regard.

I have dwelt on this point, as being a necessary part of a perfectly just conception of Utility or Happiness, considered as the directive rule of human conduct. But it is by no means an indispensable condition to the acceptance of the utilitarian standard; for that standard is not the agent's own greatest happiness, but the greatest amount of happiness altogether; and if it may possibly be doubted whether a noble character is always the happier for its nobleness, there can be no doubt that it makes other people happier, and that the world in general is immensely a gainer by it. Utilitarianism, therefore, could only attain its end by the general cultivation of nobleness of character, even if each individual were only benefited by the nobleness of others, and his own, so far as happiness is concerned, were a sheer deduction from the benefit. But the bare enunciation of such an absurdity as this last, renders refutation superfluous.

According to the Greatest Happiness Principle, as above explained, the ultimate end, with reference to and for the sake of which all other things are desirable (whether we are considering our own good or that of other people), is an existence exempt as far as possible from pain, and as rich as possible in enjoyments, both in point of quantity and quality; the test of quality, and the rule for measuring it against quantity, being the preference felt by those who in their opportunities of experience, to which must be added their habits of self-consciousness and self-observation, are best furnished with the means of comparison. This, being, according to the utilitarian opinion, the end of human action, is necessarily also the standard of morality; which may accordingly be defined, the rules and precepts for human conduct, by the observance of which an existence such as has been described might be, to the greatest extent possible, secured to all mankind; and not to them only, but, so far as the nature of things admits, to the whole sentient creation.

- What is the principle of utility? Is pleasure quantifiable? How does Bentham suggest that we calculate utility? Consider two courses of action and compare them according to the Benthamite calculus.
- Why is Mill's modification of Bentham's view so significant? Can you provide examples of higher pleasures? (Lower pleasures are pretty obvious.) Mill recognizes that humans do not always seek higher pleasures. Do you find his explanations for this convincing?
- What is hedonism? Is Mill a hedonist? How does hedonism differ from Aristotle's view of the good life? In what ways does Mill's notion of higher pleasure seem closer to Aristotle's conception of *eudaimonia* than Bentham's idea of pleasure?
- Do you see any problems with trying to base a morality on considerations of pain and pleasure?

I. The Creation of Morality: Nietzsche and Existentialism

The single term *morality* must not mislead us. We have been discussing not simply different theories of the nature of morality, but different *conceptions* of morality—different moralities, in other words, even if they should have many principles in common. The problem of relativism is not confined to the comparison of exotically different cultures. It faces us in a far more urgent form in our own conceptions of morality. We may agree that killing without extreme provocation is wrong. But why do we believe that it is wrong? One person claims that it is wrong because the Ten Commandments (orders from God) forbid it. Another says it is wrong because it is a mark of insensitivity that demonstrates a flaw in character. Another says it is wrong because it violates people's rights, while still another says it increases the amount of pain in the world without equally adding to happiness. They all agree that killing is wrong, but the different reasons point to different circumstances in which each would kill: the first, if God commanded him or her to; the second, if the killing could be seen as a sign of strength and heroism; the third, if he or she found another right that overrode the right to live; the fourth, if the death of one person was more than balanced by the increased welfare of the others (as in a criminal execution).

From the three great moral philosophies we have presented, four such conceptions emerge. They all agree on many principles, but the reasons differ widely, and some of the principles do as well. Most dramatic is the difference between Aristotle's ancient Greek morality and Kant's modern morality of duty. Kant's morality may be taken as a fair representation of the modern Judeo-Christian morality in its strictest form: the emphasis on moral principle and laws, the emphasis on reason and individual autonomy, and the emphasis on good intentions ("a good will") and on doing one's duty. There are small differences that we have already pointed out: the Greek emphasis on pride as a virtue in contrast to the Christian condemnation of pride as a "deadly sin" (or, at least, a personality flaw) and its emphasis on humility. One of Aristotle's first virtues was courage in battle, while most modern moralities consider courage as a special case, not as a matter of being an everyday "good person" at all. This difference may well be attributed to the different political climates of the two societies. But that is not enough. As we shall see, the differences are much deeper than that.

There are crucial differences between ancient and modern moral perspectives. The most striking is the difference in the scope of their applicability. In Aristotle's moral philosophy, only a small elite is thought to be capable of true happiness (*eudaimonia*) through virtuous action and contemplation. Other people (women, slaves, and noncitizens) may live comfortably enough and do their duties and chores efficiently, but they cannot be called "happy." The elite, however, are characterized by their excellence; by their individual achievements, including wealth, power, honor, intelligence, and wit; and by all those rewards that come with an aristocratic upbringing—the best education and a life in which basic comforts are guaranteed from birth.

In Kant's conception of morality, by contrast, all people who are rational (that is, everyone except the severely retarded, young children, and popular musicians) are to be judged by the same moral standards—the standards of duty. There are no elites. And since the judgments of moral worth are made solely on the basis of good intentions, no "external" advantages are relevant to a person's goodness or badness. In fact, it is possible that a perfectly "good" person would, with only the best intentions, cause chaos and unhappiness around him wherever he goes. And the harder he tries to make amends, the more he fouls them up. Dostoyevsky wrote one of his greatest novels, *The Idiot*, about just this—a perfectly good man, with all the right intentions, causes suffering and even death every time he tries to do good. Yet (and this is Dostoyevsky's point) he is, by this modern conception, still the perfectly good man. Aristotle would find this laughable. How could we call a man virtuous just because of his intentions? How can a perfect failure be an example of ideal goodness?

In Aristotle's morality, the only people who operate on the basis of duty are those who are incapable of being truly good and truly happy. Duty is a morality for women and servants. For the elite, it is rather a question of personal excellence—in battle, in games, in business, in love, in debate, and in all things, especially philosophy. And where Kant's morality consists mostly (like the Ten Commandments) of "thou shalt not . . ." Aristotle's morality appropriately emphasizes personal desires and ambitions, not commands to achieve, and certainly not negative commands. The key element of Kant's philosophy, duty, is treated minimally in Aristotle, where the emphasis is on personal growth and achievement. On the other side, the image of the well-rounded, successful man, excellent in all things and the envy of his

516 | CHAPTER 7 · ETHICS

fellow men, plays only a secondary role in Kant's philosophy (for example, in his *Doctrine of Virtue*, the second part of the *Fundamental Principles of the Metaphysics of Morals*). For Kant, what is important is the person who does what he or she is supposed to do. For Aristotle, the ideal is to strive for personal excellence, and doing what a person is supposed to do is simply taken for granted along the way.

Now notice that both moralities have many of the same results. Aristotle's morality praises many and condemns most of the same acts as Kant's morality: Killing needlessly and stealing are wrong; telling the truth and keeping promises are right. But their conceptions of morality and, consequently, their conceptions of people are distinctively different. If we appreciate the nature of this difference, we will be in a position to understand one of the most dramatic moral revolutions of modern times, initiated by Friedrich Nietzsche. Nietzsche called himself an **immoralist**, and he attacked morality as viciously as he attacked Christianity. But though he has often been interpreted as saying that we should give up morality and feel free to kill, steal, and commit crimes of all kinds, his moral philosophy does not in fact say any such thing. What Nietzsche did was to attack modern morality, as summarized by Kant and Christianity, and to urge us to return to ancient Greek morality, as summarized by Aristotle. Nietzsche also attacked utilitarianism, which he considered "vulgar."

Like a great many philosophers of the nineteenth century (particularly German philosophers: Fichte, Hegel, and Marx), Nietzsche saw in the ancient Greeks a sense of personal harmony and a sense of excellence that had been lost in the modern world. Nietzsche, like Aristotle, viewed the concept of duty as fit for servants and slaves, but thought that such a morality was wholly inadequate to motivate us to personal excellence and achievement. And Nietzsche, like Aristotle, was an unabashed elitist. Only a few people were capable of this "higher" morality. For the rest, the "**slave morality**" of duty would have to suffice. But for the elite, nothing was more important than to give up the "thou shalt not . . ." of Judeo-Christian morality and to seek one's own virtues and abilities. This does not mean that such a person need ever violate the laws of morality, although it must be said that Nietzsche's belligerent style and often warlike terminology certainly suggests that his **master morality** would include a good amount of cruelty and immorality. But it is clear that Nietzsche does not consider obedience to laws as the most important thing in life. Nor does this mean that Nietzsche is (as he is often thought to be) an ethical egoist. To say that a person should develop his or her own virtues and become excellent in as many ways as possible is not to say that one must act only in one's own interests. As in Aristotle, the excellence of the individual is part of and contributes to the excellence of mankind as a whole.

Nietzsche takes his central project as a philosopher to be what he calls "the creation of values." In this he is rightly listed among the existentialist philosophers or, at least, as one of their most important predecessors. The phrase *creation of values* is perhaps misleading, however. What Nietzsche is doing is not inventing new values so much as reasserting ancient ones. Furthermore, Nietzsche, like Aristotle, takes ethics to be based solely upon human nature, so it is not a question of "creating values" as much as finding them in oneself. But where such a philosophy for Aristotle was in agreement with most of the thinking of his times, Nietzsche's thought was a radical disruption of the usual Kantian style of thinking of the modern period, and so it takes on the tone of violent destructiveness rather than—as in Aristotle—the self-satisfied tones of a gentleman. Since Nietzsche, unlike Aristotle, did not believe that every human "nature" was the same, moreover, he taught that different individuals would most assuredly find and follow different values, different conceptions of excellence, and thus have different moralities. For this reason, students who read Nietzsche looking for concrete moral advice, a set of principles to act on, are always disappointed. Nietzsche's central teaching is rather "follow yourself, don't follow me." Consequently, Nietzsche can't—and won't—try to tell

FIG. 7.25 According to Nietzsche, morality for most people is like the behavior of herd animals, a matter of conformity in which one person follows another. *(© iStockphoto.com/muha04)*

you how to live. But he does tell you to live fully and to give up the servile views of ourselves that we in the West have held for many centuries.

Nietzsche's moral philosophy is largely critical, and most of his efforts have gone into the rejection of the Kantian approach to morality in order to make room for individual self-achieving as found in Aristotle. His argument, however, is not a refutation in the usual sense. Instead, he undermines morality by showing that the motivation behind it is decrepit and weak. The categories in his philosophy are strength and weakness, and Nietzsche considers the Greek tradition of personal excellence a source of strength and the modern conception of morality a facade for weakness. Accordingly, he calls the first a "master morality" and the second, a "slave morality" or, with reference to modern mass movements, a "herd instinct." The excerpts that follow illustrate Nietzsche's general attack on morality. But never forget that his purpose is not merely destructive but, in his eyes, creative. The point is to get us to look to ourselves for values and to excel, each in our own ways. (The phrase **"will to power"** refers to just this effort to excel as individuals.)

On "Morality as Herd-Instinct" by **Friedrich Nietzsche**[21]

Wherever we meet with a morality we find a valuation and order of rank of the human impulses and activities. These valuations and orders of rank are always the expression of the needs of a community or herd: that which is in the first place to *its* advantage—and in the second place and third place—is also the authoritative standard for the worth of every individual. By morality the individual is taught to become a function of the herd, and to ascribe to himself value only as a function. As

> "By morality the individual is taught to become a function of the herd, and to ascribe to himself value only as a function."
>
> – FRIEDRICH NIETZSCHE

---

[21] Friedrich Nietzsche, *The Gay Science*, trans. Walter Kaufmann (New York: Random House, 1974).

the conditions for the maintenance of one community have been very different from those of another community, there have been very different moralities; and in respect to the future essential transformations of herd and communities, states and societies, one can prophesy that there will still be very divergent moralities. Morality is the herd-instinct in the individual.

On "Master and Slave Morality"
BY **Friedrich Nietzsche**[22]

Apart from the value of claims like "there is a categorical imperative in us," the question remains: what does this sort of claim tell us about the ones who make it? There are moralities that are meant to justify their creator in the eyes of others, and other moralities that are meant to calm him and help him to be content with himself; still others allow him to crucify and humiliate himself. With others he wants to take revenge, with others to hide, with others to transfigure himself and remove himself to the heights. There are moralities that help their creators to forget, and others that allow him—or something about him—to be forgotten. Many moralists want to exercise their power and creative whims on humanity, some others, perhaps even Kant himself, suggest with their morality: "What deserves respect in me is that I can obey—and you *ought* not to be different than me!"—in short, morality is merely a *sign language of the passions!*

. . .

On a journey through the many finer and coarser moralities that have so far ruled or still rule on earth I found that certain properties recurred regularly together and were closely related: until at last I found two fundamental types and one fundamental difference. There are *master morality* and *slave morality*—I add immediately that in all the higher and mixed cultures there also appear attempts at a blending of both moralities, and still more often the interpenetration and mutual misunderstanding of both, indeed at times they are hard against one another—even in the same human being, within a *single* soul. The moral discrimination of values has originated either in a ruling group whose understanding of its difference from the ruled was felt with well-being—or among the ruled, the slaves and dependents of every grade. In the first case, when it is the rulers who determine what is "good," the lofty proud states of soul are experienced as conferring distinction and determining the order of rank. The noble human distances from himself those in whom the contrary of such lofty proud states finds expression: he despises them. One should immediately note that in this first kind of morality the opposition of "good" and "bad" means about the same as "noble" and "contemptible." The opposition of "good" and "evil" has a different origin. Despised are the cowardly, the anxious, the petty, those who think about narrow utility; even so the suspicious with their constrained glances, those who humble themselves, the dog-kind of humans who allow themselves to be maltreated, the fawning flatterers, above all the liars. It is a fundamental belief of all aristocrats that the common people lie. "We truthful ones" thus the nobility of ancient Greece named itself. It is obvious that moral designations were everywhere first applied to humans and only derivatively and late to actions: which is why it is a serious error

---

22 Friedrich Nietzsche, *Beyond Good and Evil*, trans. Clancy Martin.

when historians of morality begin with questions like "why was the pitying act praised?" The noble kind of human feels itself as establishing values, it has no need for approval, it judges "what is harmful to me is harmful in itself," it knows itself to be that which first grants things their honor, it is value-creating. It honors everything that it knows as part of itself: such a morality is self-glorification.

It is different with the second type of morality, slave morality. Suppose the raped, oppressed, suffering, bound, timorous and exhausted moralize: what will their moral valuations have in common? Probably a pessimistic suspicion about the whole human condition will make itself known, perhaps a condemnation of humankind along with its condition. The glance of the slave is adverse to the virtues of the powerful: he has skepticism and

FIG. 7.26 Differences in relative rank and power result in different moral outlooks, according to Nietzsche (Nietzsche, it should be added, did not endorse slavery). *(Photo Ann Ronan/Heritage Images/Scala, Florence)*

mistrust, he has subtle mistrust of all the "good" that is honored there, he would like to persuade himself that even their happiness is not real. Conversely, those qualities are brought forth and brightly illuminated that serve to lighten existence for the suffering: here pity, the obliging helpful hand, the warm heart, patience, industry, humility, and friendliness come to be honored, for here these are the most useful qualities and nearly the sole means for enduring the stress of existence. Slave morality is essentially a morality of utility. Here is the place for the source of that famous opposition between good and "evil": into evil were projected power and dangerousness, a certain fearfulness, subtlety and strength, that does not permit contempt to arise. For slave morality the "evil" therefore inspire fear; for master morality it is precisely the "good" that inspire and want to inspire fear, while the "bad" are felt to be contemptible. The opposition comes to a peak when, as a direct consequence of slave morality, a touch of scorn comes along with the "good" of this morality. This may be slight and benevolent because the good must be harmless in the slave's way of thinking: he is good-natured, easy to deceive, a bit stupid perhaps, *un bonhomme* ["a nice person"]. In general, where slave morality becomes predominant, language tends to bring the words "good" and "stupid" closer together.

Nietzsche's ethics is not all criticism, however. Nietzsche also vigorously argues for an alternative morality, a heroic morality, not unlike that of the ancient Greeks. In his book, a long quasi-biblical epic called *Thus Spoke Zarathustra*, he introduces his famous idea of the *Übermensch*, the superman who is more than human and superior in his virtues. Our virtues, in turn, should be aimed at making such a supervirtuous person possible (for example, by defending our own idealism and by educating future generations to be better than we are).

Man is a rope stretched between the animal and the Übermensch, a rope over an abyss.

A dangerous crossing, a dangerous on-the-way, a dangerous looking-back, a dangerous trembling and halting.

> *What is great in man is that he is a bridge and not a goal: what is lovable in man is that he is an over-going and a going under.*
>
> *I love those that do not know how to live except by going under, for they are those who go over.*
>
> *I love the great despisers, because they are the great adorers and arrows of longing for the other shore.*
>
> *I love those who do not first seek a reason beyond the stars for going under and being sacrifices, but sacrifice themselves to the earth, that the earth may some day belong to the Übermensch.*
>
> *I love him who lives in order to know, and seeks to know in order that the Übermensch may live some day. And thus he wants to go under.*
>
> *I love him who loves his virtue: for virtue is the will to going under, and an arrow of longing.*
>
> *I love him who reserves not one drop of spirit for himself, but wants to be wholly the spirit of his virtue: thus he strides as spirit over the bridge.*
>
> *I love him who makes his virtue his addiction and his catastrophe: thus, for the sake of his virtue, he wants to live on and to live no more . . .*
>
> *I love him whose soul is so overfull that he forgets himself, and all things are in him: thus all things become his going under.*
>
> *I love him who has a free spirit and a free heart: thus his head is only the guts of his heart; his heart, however, causes his going under.*
>
> *Behold, I am a herald of the lightning, and a heavy drop out of the cloud: the lightning, however, is the Übermensch.*[23]

And

> *True philosophers . . . are commanders and legislators: they say, "thus it shall be!" First they determine the "where to" and the "what for" of humankind, and thus they have at hand the preliminary work of all philosophical laborers, of everyone who has overcome the past. With a creative hand they reach for the future, and all that is and has been becomes a means for them, a tool, a hammer. Their "knowing" is creating, their creating is a legislating, their will to truth is—will to power.—Are there such philosophers today? Have there been such philosophers yet? Must there not be such philosophers?*[24]

Nietzsche is often viewed as the most extreme of the antimoralists, those who attack the traditional duty-bound Kantian-Christian conception of morality. In fact, he is but one among many philosophers who have rejected that morality in exchange for a more personal and individual set of principles. Given his emphasis on human "nature," we can say that even Nietzsche is much more traditional than is usually supposed (although the tradition he holds to is the Aristotelian, not the Kantian one). In the past several decades, however, morality has become far more personalized than even Nietzsche suggested. For some Anglo-American philosophers, largely in the wake of logical positivism, ethics has been reduced to a matter of emotions, prescriptions, and attitudes, rather than of principles and rational laws. (Ironically, Nietzsche has always been in extreme disfavor among such philosophers, while Kant has been considered with extreme favor.)

The attack on the idea of absolute moral principles of reason, which are the same for everyone, has been one of the most vigorous philosophical movements of the twentieth cen-

---

[23] Friedrich Nietzsche, *Thus Spoke Zarathustra*, trans. Clancy Martin (New York: Barnes & Noble, 2005).

[24] Friedrich Nietzsche, from *Beyond Good and Evil*, trans. Clancy Martin.

tury, so much so that many philosophers, religious leaders, and moralists have become alarmed at the destruction of uniform moral codes and have attempted to reassert the old moral laws in new ways. The problem is relativism. Is there a single moral code? Or are there possibly as many moralities as there are people? There are intermediary suggestions, such as relativizing morals to particular groups or societies, but the question remains the same: "Is there ultimately any way of defending one moral code against any other?"

The most extreme relativist position has emerged from Nietzsche's existentialist successors, particularly Jean-Paul Sartre. In Sartre's philosophy, not only the idea of a uniform morality but the idea of a human nature upon which this morality may be based is completely rejected. It is rejected not because different people may have different "natures," as in Nietzsche, but because for Sartre our values are literally a question of creation, of personal **commitment**. In answer to any question about morality, the only ultimate answer is "because I choose to accept these values." What is most fascinating about Sartre's conception of morality as choice is that he does not therefore abandon general principles as Nietzsche does. Quite the contrary, he makes the almost Kantian assertion that

FIG. 7.27 Nietzsche claims that human beings and animals are motivated by the same basic drive: the will to power. *(Image © Ludmila Yilmaz, 2011. Used under license from Shutterstock.com)*

each of us needs to choose principles for all mankind, not just for oneself. The difference is that Sartre, unlike Kant, makes no claims about the singular correctness of these principles. All he can say is "this is what I choose mankind to be." Thus Sartre's moral philosophy is a curious mixture of the most radical relativism and the most traditional moralizing.

 FROM *Existentialism as a Humanism*
BY **Jean-Paul Sartre**[25]

Man is nothing else but that which he makes of himself. That is the first principle of existentialism. And this is what people call its "subjectivity," using the word as a reproach against us. But what do we mean to say by this, but that man is of a greater dignity than a stone or a table? For we mean to say that man primarily exists—that man is, before all else, something which propels itself towards a future and is aware that it is doing so. Man is, indeed, a project which possesses a subjective life, instead of being a kind of moss, or a fungus or a cauliflower. Before that projection of the self nothing exists; not even in the heaven of intelligence; man will only attain existence when he is what he purposes to be. Not, however, what he may wish to be. For what we usually understand by wishing or willing is a conscious decision taken—much more often than not—after we have made ourselves what we are. I may wish to join a party, to write a book or to marry—but in such a case what is usually called my will is probably a manifestation of a prior and more spontaneous decision. If, however, it

25 Jean-Paul Sartre, *Existentialism as a Humanism*, trans. Philip Mairet (New York: Philosophical Library of New York, 1949). Reprinted by permission.

> "When we say that man is responsible for himself, we do not mean that he is responsible only for his own individuality, but that he is responsible for all men."
>
> – JEAN-PAUL SARTRE

is true that existence is prior to essence, man is responsible for what he is. Thus, the first effect of existentialism is that it puts every man in possession of himself as he is, and places the entire responsibility for his existence squarely upon his own shoulders. And, when we say that man is responsible for himself, we do not mean that he is responsible only for his own individuality, but that he is responsible for all men. The word "subjectivism" is to be understood in two senses, and our adversaries play upon only one of them. Subjectivism means, on the one hand, the freedom of the individual subject and, on the other, that man cannot pass beyond human subjectivity. It is the latter which is the deeper meaning of existentialism. When we say that man chooses himself, we do mean that every one of us must choose himself; but by that we also mean that in choosing for himself he chooses for all men. For in effect, of all the actions a man may take in order to create himself as he wills to be, there is not one which is not creative, at the same time, of an image of man such as he believes he ought to be. To choose between this or that is at the same time to affirm the value of that which is chosen; for we are unable ever to choose the worse. What we choose is always the better and nothing can be better for us unless it is better for all. If, moreover, existence precedes essence and we will to exist at the same time as we fashion our image, that image is valid for all and for the entire epoch in which we find ourselves. Our responsibility is thus much greater than we had supposed, for it concerns mankind as a whole. If I am a worker, for instance, I may choose to join a Christian rather than a Communist trade union. And if, by that membership, I choose to signify that resignation is, after all, the attitude that best becomes a man, that man's kingdom is not upon this earth, I do not commit myself alone to that view. Resignation is my will for everyone, and my action is, in consequence, a commitment on behalf of all mankind. Or if, to take a more personal case, I decide to marry and to have

FIG. 7.28 "To choose between this or that is at the same time to affirm the value of that which is chosen."–Jean-Paul Sartre *(Image © Greg Epperson, 2011. Used under license from Shutterstock.com)*

children, even though this decision proceeds simply from my situation, from my passion or my desire, I am thereby committing not only myself, but humanity as a whole, to the practice of monogamy. I am thus responsible for myself and for all men, and I am creating a certain image of man as I would have him to be. In fashioning myself I fashion man.

. . .

Who can prove that I am the proper person to impose, by my own choice, my conception of man upon mankind? I shall never find any proof whatever; there will be no sign to convince me of it.

. . .

If I regard a certain course of action as good, it is only I who choose to say that it is good and not bad. . . . nevertheless I also am obliged at every instant to perform actions which are examples. Everything happens to every man as though the whole human race had its eyes fixed upon what he is doing and regulated its conduct accordingly.

. . .

As an example by which you may the better understand this state of abandonment, I will refer to the case of a pupil of mine, who sought me out in the following circumstances. His father was quarrelling with his mother and was also inclined to be a "collaborator"; his elder brother had been killed in the German offensive of 1940 and this young man, with a sentiment somewhat primitive but generous, burned to avenge him. His mother was living alone with him, deeply afflicted by the semi-treason of his father and by the death of her eldest son, and her only consolation was in this young man. But he, at this moment, had the choice between going to England to join the Free French Forces or of staying near his mother, and helping her to live. He fully realized that this woman lived only for him and that his disappearance—or perhaps his death—would plunge her into despair. He also realized that, concretely and in fact, every action he performed on his mother's behalf would be sure of effect in the sense of aiding her to live, whereas anything he did in order to go and fight would be an ambiguous action which might vanish like water into sand and serve no purpose. For instance, to set out for England he would have to wait indefinitely in a Spanish camp on the way through Spain; or, on arriving in England or in Algiers he might be put into an office to fill up forms. Consequently, he found himself confronted by two very different modes of action; the one concrete, immediate, but directed towards only one individual; and the other an action addressed to an end infinitely greater, a national collectivity, but for that very reason ambiguous—and it might be frustrated on the way. At the same time, he was hesitating between two kinds of morality; on the one side the morality of sympathy, of personal devotion and, on the other side, a morality of wider scope but of more debatable validity. He had to choose between those two. What could help him to choose? Could the Christian doctrine? No. Christian doctrine says: Act with charity, love your neighbour, deny yourself for others, choose the way which is hardest, and so forth. But which is the harder road? To whom does one owe the more brotherly love, the patriot or the mother? Which is the more useful aim, the general one of fighting in and for the whole community, or the precise aim of helping one particular person to live? Who can give an answer to that a priori? No one. Nor is it given in any ethical scripture. The Kantian ethic says, Never regard another as a means, but always as an end. Very well; if I remain with my mother, I shall be regarding her as the end

FIG. 7.29 When we make a decision, we show what our values really are. *(© iStockphoto.com/Kemter)*

and not as a means: but by the same token I am in danger of treating as means those who are fighting on my behalf; and the converse is also true, that if I go to the aid of the combatants I shall be treating them as the end at the risk of treating my mother as a means.

If values are uncertain, if they are still too abstract to determine the particular, concrete case under consideration, nothing remains but to trust in our instincts. That is what this young man tried to do; and when I saw him he said, "In the end, it is feeling that counts; the direction in which it is really pushing me is the one I ought to choose. If I feel that I love my mother enough to sacrifice everything else for her—my will to be avenged, all my longings for action and adventure—then I stay with her. If, on the contrary, I feel that my love for her is not enough, I go." But how does one estimate the strength of a feeling? The value of his feeling for his mother was determined precisely by the fact that he was standing by her. I may say that I love a certain friend enough to sacrifice such or such a sum of money for him, but I cannot prove that unless I have done it. I may say, "I love my mother enough to remain with her," if actually I have remained with her. I can only estimate the strength of this affection if I have performed an action by which it is defined and ratified. But if I then appeal to this affection to justify my action, I find myself drawn into a vicious circle.

· · ·

In other words, feeling is formed by the deeds that one does; therefore I cannot consult it as a guide to action. And that is to say that I can neither seek within myself for an authentic impulse to action, nor can I expect, from some ethic, formulae that will enable me to act. You may say that the youth did, at least, go to a professor to ask for advice. But if you seek counsel—from a priest, for example—you have selected that priest; and at bottom you already knew, more or less, what he would advise. In other words, to choose an adviser is nevertheless to commit oneself by that choice. If you are a Christian, you will say, Consult a priest; but there are collaborationists, priests who are resisters and priests who wait for the tide to turn: which will you choose? Had this young man chosen a priest of the resistance, or one of the collaboration, he would have decided beforehand the kind of advice he was to receive. Similarly, in coming to me, he knew what advice I should give him, and I had but one reply to make. You are free, therefore choose—that is to say, invent. No rule of general morality can show you what you ought to do.

To say that it does not matter what you choose is not correct. In one sense choice is possible, but what is not possible is not to choose. I can always choose but I must know that if I do not choose, that is still a choice. This although it may appear merely formal, is of great importance as a limit to fantasy and caprice. For, when I confront a real situation—for example, that I am a sexual being, able to have relations with a being of the other sex and able to have children—I am obliged to choose my attitude to it, and in every respect I bear the responsibility of the choice which, in committing myself, also commits the whole of humanity. . . . Man finds himself in an organized situation in which he is himself involved: his choice involves mankind in its entirety, and he cannot avoid choosing. Either he must remain single, or he must marry without having children, or he must marry and have children. In any case, and whichever he may choose, it is impossible for him, in respect of this situation, not to take complete responsibility. Doubtless he chooses without reference to any pre-established values, but it is unjust to tax him with caprice. Rather let us say that the moral choice is comparable to the construction of a work of art.

. . .

No one can tell what the painting of tomorrow will be like; one cannot judge a painting until it is done. What has that to do with morality: We are in the same creative situation. We never speak of a work of art as irresponsible; when we are discussing a canvas by Picasso, we understand very well that the composition became what it is at the time when he was painting it, and that his works are part and parcel of his entire life.

It is the same upon the plane of morality. There is this in common between art and morality, that in both we have to do with creation and invention. We cannot decide a priori what it is that should be done. I think it was made sufficiently clear to you in the case of that student who came to see me, that to whatever ethical system he might appeal, the Kantian or any other, he could find no sort of guidance whatever; he was obliged to invent the law for himself. Certainly we cannot say that this man, in choosing to remain with his mother—that is, in taking sentiment, personal devotion and concrete charity as his moral foundations—would be making an irresponsible choice, nor could we do so if he preferred the sacrifice of going away to England. Man makes himself; he is not found ready-made; he makes himself by the choice of his morality, and he cannot but choose a morality, such is the pressure of circumstances upon him.

Sartre says that "man makes himself." He believes this to be true both individually and collectively. It is through my actions that I commit myself to values, not through principles I accept a priori or rules that are imposed upon me by God or society. If you accept the voice of some authority, you have chosen to accept that authority rather than some other. If you appeal for advice or help, you have chosen to seek that kind of advice rather than some other kind. If you refuse to choose between alternatives, then you are responsible for neglecting both or all the alternatives, for "copping-out." In any case, you must do something, even if what you do is "doing nothing" (that is, not choosing one of the important alternatives before you).

Here is Sartre's reply to his predecessors: We are no longer in the position of Aristotle, in which morality appears to us as a given, as "natural," and without alternatives of the most irresolvable kind. We can no longer trust our "sentiments," as Hume did, for we now find ourselves torn with conflicting sentiments of every kind. We can no longer accept the a priori moralizing of Kant, for we now see that the circumstances in which we must act are never so simple that a simple "categorical" imperative will resolve our quandaries. And even "the greatest good for the greatest number" no longer provides a guide for our actions, for we no longer pretend that we can calculate the consequences of our actions with any such accuracy. Besides, who is to say what "the greatest good" or, for that matter, "the greatest number" is today? Against all this, Sartre argues that there is simply our choice of actions and values, together with their consequences, whatever they are. There is no justification for these choices and no "right" or "wrong." This does not mean that we need not choose or that it is all "arbitrary." To the contrary, the upshot of Sartre's thesis is precisely that we are

"There is this in common between art and morality, that in both we have to do with creation and invention. We cannot decide a priori what it is that should be done."

– JEAN-PAUL SARTRE

always choosing and that morality is nothing other than our commitments, at least for the present, to the values that we choose to follow through our actions.

- Do you see affinities between Nietzsche and Aristotle on ethics?
- What are "master morality" and "slave morality"? What do these two ethical perspectives suggest about the nature of morality?
- Does anything make an act good for Sartre? In what way is Sartre's view still in the Kantian tradition? (Hint: "In choosing for himself he chooses for all men.") How is it very different?
- Do you see any problems with Sartre's ideas that morality amounts to the commitments that we make and that each of us, by making choices, is constructing an individual morality?

J. Pragmatism in Ethics

The existentialist movement was not alone in criticizing the traditional Western approach to morality. The pragmatist movement also saw problems in the approach taken by absolutist views of morality, such as that of Kant. The pragmatists criticized these theories for their failure to acknowledge the situated character of all experience and the need for change in response to new situations. John Dewey, in particular, argued that ethics should be concerned with our actual experience and the problems we actually confront.

Dewey rejects a distinction that moral theorists since Plato have venerated, that between what is instrumentally and what is intrinsically good. The goods that are clearly useful in our everyday lives have traditionally been considered merely "instrumental" goods, less valuable than the intrinsic goods, whose use is less obvious but that are supposed to be fixed and final. The upshot is to devalue practical living, and doing so has pernicious consequences. One of these consequences is obnoxious materialism—the mindless treatment of enjoyments as intrinsic goods without any thought as to whether particular enjoyments are desirable. Another is the tendency of ethical systems to remain overly abstract and ignore problems that occur in the real social world.

Dewey takes issue with Hume's view that we cannot derive values from facts. The facts about our particular situation indicate where problems lie and determine what is valuable under the circumstances. Judgments about what is good are thus factual judgments. The upshot is that moral thought should avail itself of the methods that we make use of to investigate the facts of our situation generally in order to be able to develop sound plans for remedying problems as we encounter them.

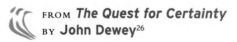 FROM *The Quest for Certainty*
BY **John Dewey**[26]

The scientific revolution came about when material or direct and uncontrolled experience was taken as problematic as supplying material to be transformed by reflective operations into known objects. The contrast between experienced and known objects was found to be a temporal one; namely, one between empirical subject-matters which were had or "given" prior to the acts of experimental variation and redisposition and those which succeeded these acts and issued from them. The

---

[26] John Dewey, *The Quest for Certainty* (New York: G. P. Putnam's Sons, 1929).

notion of an act whether of sense or thought which supplied a valid measure of thought in immediate knowledge was discredited. Consequences of operations became the important thing. The suggestion almost imperatively follows that escape from the defects of transcendental absolutism is not to be had by setting up as values enjoyments that happen anyhow, but in defining value by enjoyments which are the consequences of intelligent action. Without the intervention of thought, enjoyments are not values but problematic goods, becoming values when they re-issue in a changed

John Dewey (1859-1952)

An American pragmatist, social critic, and reformer. The author of a great many influential books on education as well as the central topics of philosophy.

FIG. 7.30 John Dewey
(The New York Public Library / Art Resource, NY)

form from intelligent behavior. The fundamental trouble with the current empirical theory of values is that it merely formulates and justifies the socially prevailing habit of regarding enjoyments as they are actually experienced as values in and of themselves. It completely side-steps the question of regulation of these enjoyments. This issue involves nothing less than the problem of the directed reconstruction of economic, political and religious institutions.

There was seemingly a paradox involved in the notion that if we turned our backs upon the immediately perceived qualities of things, we should be enabled to form valid conceptions of objects, and that these conceptions could be used to bring about a more secure and more significant experience of them. But the method terminated in disclosing the connections or interactions upon which perceived objects, viewed as events, depend. Formal analogy suggests that we regard our direct and original experience of things liked and enjoyed as only *possibilities* of values to be achieved; that enjoyment becomes a value when we discover the relations upon which its presence depends. Such a causal and operational definition gives only a conception of a value, not a value itself. But the utilization of the conception in action results in an object having secure and significant value.

The formal statement may be given concrete content by pointing to the difference between the enjoyed and the enjoyable, the desired and the desirable, the satisfy-ing and the satisfactory. To say that something is enjoyed is to make a statement about a fact, something already in existence; it is not to judge the value of that fact. There is no difference between such a proposition and one which says that something is sweet or sour, red or black. It is just correct or incorrect and that is the end of the matter. But to call an object a value is to assert that it satisfies or fulfills certain conditions. Function and status in meeting conditions is a different matter from bare existence. The fact that something is desired only raises the *question* of its desirability; it does not settle it. Only a child in the degree of his immaturity thinks to settle the question of desirability by reiterated proclamation: "I want it, I want it, I want it." What is objected to in the current empirical theory of values is not connection of them with desire and enjoyment but failure to distinguish between enjoyments of radically different sorts. There are many common expressions in which the difference of the two kinds is clearly recognized. Take for example the difference between the ideas of "satisfying" and "satisfactory." To say that something satisfies is to report something as an isolated finality. To assert that it is satis*factory* is to define it in its connections and interactions. The fact that it pleases or is immediately congenial poses a problem to judgment. How shall the satisfaction be rated? Is it a value or is it not? Is it something to be prized and cherished, *to be* enjoyed? Not stern moralists alone but everyday experience informs us that finding satisfaction in a thing may be a warning, a summons to be on the lookout for consequences. To declare something satis*factory* is to assert that it meets specifiable conditions. It is, in effect, a judgment that the thing "will do." It involves a prediction; it contemplates a future in which the thing will continue to serve; it *will* do. It asserts a consequence the thing will actively institute; it will *do*. That it is satisfying is the content of a proposition of fact; that it is satisfactory is a judgment, an estimate, an appraisal. It denotes an attitude *to be* taken, that of striving to perpetuate and to make secure. . . .

Propositions about what is or has been liked are of instrumental value in reaching judgments of value, in as far as the conditions and consequences of the thing liked are thought about. In themselves they make no claims; they put forth no demand upon subsequent attitudes and acts; they profess no authority to direct. If one likes a thing he likes it; that *is* a point about which there can be no dispute:— although it is not so easy to state just *what* is liked as is frequently assumed. A judgment about what is *to be* desired and enjoyed is, on the other hand, a claim on future action; it possesses *de jure* and not merely *de facto* quality. It is a matter of frequent experience that likings and enjoyments are of all kinds, and that many are such as reflective judgments condemn. By way of self-justification and "rationalization," an enjoyment creates a tendency to assert that the thing enjoyed is a value. This assertion of validity adds authority to the fact. It is a decision that the object has a right to exist and hence a claim upon action to further its existence. . . .

Not even the most devoted adherents of the notion that enjoyment and value are equivalent facts would venture to assert that because we have once liked a thing we should go on liking it; they are compelled to introduce the idea that *some* tastes are to be cultivated. Logically, there is no ground for introducing the idea of cultivation; liking is liking, and one is as good as another. If enjoyments *are* values, the judgment of value cannot regulate the form which liking takes, it cannot regulate its own conditions. Desire and purpose, and hence action, are left without guidance, although the question of regulation of their formation is the supreme problem of practical life. Values (to sum up) may be connected inherently with liking, and yet not with *every* liking but only with those that judgment has approved, after examination of the relation upon which the object liked depends. . . .

Because morality should be concerned with our actual activity, Dewey emphasizes the uniqueness of every situation. Every resolution to some practical problem results in a new situation, with its own limitations. Perceived inadequacies in a particular situation are the problems that ethics should confront, and the focus of moral thinking should be how to resolve these problems in a way that is consistent with satisfying other needs as well. Absolute rules that are supposed to apply to all cases are inappropriate because every case is singular. This is not to say that we can apply our intelligence to our problems without using principles. But moral principles cannot be devised once and for all. They are of value only if they are useful in particular cases. The method for evaluating proposed moral principles is the same as the method used in science. The scientific method formulates hypotheses and then tests them by experimenting on particular cases. In the same way, we formulate moral principles as hypotheses, and we come to know their value only by seeing if they actually work in resolving practical problems.

When theories of values do not afford intellectual assistance in framing ideas and beliefs about values that are adequate to direct action, the gap must be filled

by other means. If intelligent method is lacking, prejudice, the pressure of immediate circumstance, self-interest and class-interest, traditional customs, institutions
of accidental historic origin, are *not* lacking, and they tend to take the place of
intelligence. Thus we are led to our main proposition: *Judgments about values are
judgments about the conditions and the results of experienced objects; judgments about that
which should regulate the formation of our desires, affections and enjoyments.* For whatever
decides their formation will determine the main course of our conduct, personal
and social.

If it sounds strange to hear that we should frame our judgments as to what has
value by considering the connections in existence of what we like and enjoy, the
reply is not far to seek. As long as we do not engage in this inquiry enjoyments
(values if we choose to apply that term) are casual; they are given by "nature," not
constructed by art. Like natural objects in their qualitative existence, they at most
only supply material for elaboration in rational discourse. A *feeling* of good or excellence is as far removed from goodness in fact as a feeling that objects are intellectually thus and so is removed from their being actually so. To recognize that the
truth of natural objects can be reached only by the greatest care in selecting and
arranging directed operations, and then to suppose that values can be truly determined by the mere fact of liking seems to leave us in an incredible position. All the
serious perplexities of life come back to the genuine difficulty of forming a judgment as to the values of the situation; they come back to a conflict of goods. Only
dogmatism can suppose that serious moral conflict is between something clearly
bad and something known to be good, and that uncertainty lies wholly in the will
of the one choosing. Most conflicts of importance are conflicts between things
which are or have been satisfying, not between good and evil. And to suppose that
we can make a hierarchical table of values at large once for all, a kind of catalogue
in which they are arranged in an order of ascending or descending worth, is to indulge in a gloss on our inability to frame intelligent judgments in the concrete. Or
else it is to dignify customary choice and prejudice by a title of honor. . . .

To assume that anything can be known in isolation from its connections with
other things is to identify knowing with merely having some object before perception or in feeling, and is thus to lose the key to the traits that distinguish an object
as known. It is futile, even silly, to suppose that some quality that is directly present
constitutes the whole of the thing presenting the quality. It does not do so when
the quality is that of being hot or fluid or heavy, and it does not when the quality
is that of giving pleasure, or being enjoyed. Such qualities are, once more, effects,
ends in the sense of closing termini of processes involving causal connections. They
are something to be investigated, challenges to inquiry and judgment. The more
connections and interactions we ascertain, the more we *know* the object in question. Thinking is search for these connections. Heat experienced as a consequence
of directed operations has a meaning quite different from the heat that is casually
experienced without knowledge of how it came about. The same is true of enjoyments. Enjoyments that issue from conduct directed by insight into relations have
a meaning and a validity due to the way in which they are experienced. Such
enjoyments are not repented of; they generate no after-taste of bitterness. Even in
the midst of direct enjoyment, there is a sense of validity, of authorization, which
intensifies the enjoyment. There is solicitude for perpetuation of the *object* having
value which is radically different from mere anxiety to perpetuate the *feeling* of
enjoyment. . . .

The time will come when it will be found passing strange that we of this age should take such pains to control by every means at command the formation of ideas of physical things, even those most remote from human concern, and yet are content with haphazard beliefs about the qualities of objects that regulate our deepest interests; that we are scrupulous as to methods of forming ideas of natural objects, and either dogmatic or else driven by immediate conditions in framing those about values. There is, by implication, if not explicitly, a prevalent notion that values are already well known and that all which is lacking is the will to cultivate them in the order of their worth. In fact the most profound lack is not the will to act upon goods already known but the will to know what they are.

It is not a dream that it is possible to exercise some degree of regulation of the occurrence of enjoyments which are of value. Realization of the possibility is exemplified, for example, in the technologies and arts of industrial life—that is, up to a definite limit. Men desired heat, light, and speed of transit and of communication beyond what nature provides of itself. These things have been attained not by lauding the enjoyment of these things and preaching their desirability, but by study of the conditions of their manifestation. Knowledge of relations having been obtained, ability to produce followed, and enjoyment ensued as a matter of course. . . .

Knowledge of conditions and consequences is regarded as wholly indifferent to judging what is of serious value, though it is useful in a prudential way in trying to actualize it. In consequence, the existence of values that are by common consent of a secondary and technical sort are under a fair degree of control, while those denominated supreme and imperative are subject to all the winds of impulse, custom and arbitrary authority.

This distinction between higher and lower types of value is itself something to be looked into. Why should there be a sharp division made between some goods as physical and material and others as ideal and "spiritual"? The question touches the whole dualism of the material and the ideal at its root. To denominate anything "matter" or "material" is not in truth to disparage it. It is, if the designation is correctly applied, a way of indicating that the thing in question is a condition or means of the existence of something else. And disparagement of effective means is practically synonymous with disregard of the things that are termed, in eulogistic fashion, ideal and spiritual. For the latter terms if they have any concrete application at all signify something which is a desirable consummation of conditions, a cherished fulfillment of means. The sharp separation between material and ideal good thus deprives the latter of the underpinning of effective support while it opens the way for treating things which should be employed as means as ends in themselves. For since men cannot after all live without some measure of possession of such matters as health and wealth, the latter things will be viewed as values and ends in isolation unless they are treated as integral constituents of the goods that are deemed supreme and final.

The relations that determine the occurrence of what human beings experience, especially when social connections are taken into account, are indefinitely wider and more complex than those that determine the events termed physical; the latter are the outcome of definite selective operations. This is the reason why we know something about remote objects like the stars better than we know significantly characteristic things about our own bodies and minds. We forget the infinite number of things we do not know about the stars, or rather that what we call a star is itself the product of the elimination, enforced and deliberate, of most of the traits that belong to an actual existence. The amount of knowledge we possess about stars would not seem very great or very important if it were carried over to human beings and exhausted our knowledge of them. It is inevitable that genuine knowledge of man and society should lag far behind physical knowledge.

But this difference is not a ground for making a sharp division between the two, nor does it account for the fact that we make so little use of the experimental method of forming our ideas and beliefs about the concerns of man in his characteristic social relations. For this separation religions and philosophies must admit some responsibility. They have erected a distinction between a narrower scope of relations and a wider and fuller one into a difference of kind, naming one kind material, and the other mental and moral. They have charged themselves gratuitously with the office of diffusing belief in the necessity of the division, and with instilling contempt for the material as something inferior in kind in its intrinsic nature and worth. Formal philosophies undergo evaporation of their technical solid contents; in a thinner and more viable form they find their way into the minds of those who know nothing of their original forms. When these diffuse and, so to say, airy emanations re-crystallize in the popular mind they form a hard deposit of opinion that alters slowly and with great difficulty.

What difference would it actually make in the arts of conduct, personal and social, if the experimental theory were adopted not as a mere theory, but as a part of the working equipment of habitual attitudes on the part of everyone? It would be impossible, even were time given, to answer the question in adequate detail, just as men could not foretell in advance the consequences for knowledge of adopting the experimental method. It is the nature of the method that it has to be tried. But there are generic lines of difference which, within the limits of time at disposal, may be sketched.

Change from forming ideas and judgments of value on the basis of conformity to antecedent objects, to constructing enjoyable objects directed by knowledge of consequences, is a change from looking to the past to looking to the future. I do not for a moment suppose that the experiences of the past, personal and social, are of no importance. For without them we should not be able to frame any ideas whatever of the conditions under which objects are enjoyed nor any estimate of the consequences of esteeming and liking them. But past experiences are significant in giving us intellectual instrumentalities of judging just these points. They are tools, not finalities. Reflection upon what we have liked and have enjoyed is a necessity. But it tells us nothing about the *value* of these things until enjoyments are themselves reflectively controlled, or, until, as they are recalled, we form the best judgment possible about what led us to like this sort of thing and what has issued from the fact that we liked it.

We are not, then, to get away from enjoyments experienced in the past and from recall of them, but from the notion that they are the arbiters of things to be further enjoyed. At present, the arbiter is found in the past, although there are many ways of interpreting what in the past is authoritative. Nominally, the most influential conception doubtless is that of a revelation once had or a perfect life once lived. Reliance upon precedent, upon institutions created in the past, especially in law, upon rules of morals that have come to us through unexamined customs, upon uncriticized tradition, are other forms of dependence. It is not for a moment suggested that we can get away from customs and established institutions. A mere break would doubtless result simply in chaos. But there is no danger of such a break. Mankind is too inertly conservative both by constitution and by education to give the idea of this danger actuality. What there is genuine danger of is that the force of new conditions will produce disruption externally and mechanically: this is an ever present danger. The prospect is increased, not mitigated, by that conservatism which insists upon the adequacy of old standards to meet new conditions. What is needed is intelligent examination of the consequences that are actually effected by inherited institutions and customs, in order that there may be intelligent consideration of the ways in which they are to be intentionally modified in behalf of generation of different consequences.

This is the significant meaning of transfer of experimental method from the technical field of physical experience to the wider field of human life. We trust the method in forming our beliefs about things not directly connected with human life. In effect, we distrust it in moral, political and economic affairs. In the fine arts, there are many signs of a change. In the past, such a change has often been an omen and precursor of changes in other human attitudes. But, generally speaking, the idea of actively adopting experimental method in social affairs, in the matters deemed of most enduring and ultimate worth, strikes most persons as a surrender of all standards and regulative authority. But in principle, experimental method does not signify random and aimless action; it implies direction by ideas and knowledge. The question at issue is a practical one. Are there in existence the ideas and the knowledge that permit experimental method to be effectively used in social interests and affairs?

Where will regulation come from if we surrender familiar and traditionally prized values as our directive standards? Very largely from the findings of the natural sciences. For one of the effects of the separation drawn between knowledge and action is to deprive scientific knowledge of its proper service as a guide of conduct—except once more in those technological fields which have been degraded to an inferior rank. Of course, the complexity of the conditions upon which objects of human and liberal value depend is a great obstacle, and it would be too optimistic to say that we have as yet enough knowledge of the scientific type to enable us to regulate our judgments of value very extensively. But we have more knowledge than we try to put to use, and until we try more systematically we shall not know what are the important gaps in our sciences judged from the point of view of their moral and humane use.

For moralists usually draw a sharp line between the field of the natural sciences and the conduct that is regarded as moral. But a moral that frames its judgments of value on the basis of consequences must depend in a most intimate manner upon the conclusions of science. For the knowledge of the relations between changes which enable us to connect things as antecedents and consequences *is* science. The narrow scope which moralists often give to morals, their isolation of some conduct as virtuous and vicious from other large ranges of conduct, those having to do with health and vigor, business, education, with all the affairs in which desires and affection are implicated, is perpetuated by this habit of exclusion of the subject-matter of natural science from a rôle in formation of moral standards and ideals. The same attitude operates in the other direction to keep natural science a technical specialty, and it works unconsciously to encourage its use exclusively in regions where it can be turned to personal and class advantage, as in war and trade. . . .

We recognize in Dewey's ethical views the same insight as that motivating the pragmatic theory of truth: the view that truth amounts to what is useful in living a good life in this world. The test of a statement's truth, according to this view, is whether it has practical use in our world. It has "cash value," in the words of William James. The value of a moral theory or principle is, similarly, its usefulness in resolving difficulties in our experience. Dewey argues that the theory he proposes, the adoption of experimental method in our moral investigations, would indeed have pragmatic value. It would help people to deal with their changing circumstances and encourage them to view themselves as agents who can improve their world.

Another great difference to be made by carrying the experimental habit into all matter of practice is that it cuts the roots of what is often called subjectivism, but which is better termed egoism. The subjective attitude is much more widespread than would be inferred from the philosophies which have that label attached. It is as rampant in realistic philosophies as in any others, sometimes even more so, although disguised from those who hold these philosophies under the cover of reverence for and enjoyment of ultimate values. For the implication of placing the standard of thought and knowledge in antecedent existence is that our thought makes no difference in what is significantly real. It then affects only our own attitude toward it. . . .

The nature in detail of the revolution that would be wrought by carrying into the region of values the principle now embodied in scientific practice cannot be told; to attempt it would violate the fundamental idea that we know only after we have acted and in consequences of the outcome of action. But it would surely effect a transfer of attention and energy from the subjective to the objective. Men would think of themselves as agents not as ends; ends would be found in experienced enjoyment of the fruits of a transforming activity. In as far as the subjectivity of modern thought represents a discovery of the part played by personal responses, organic and acquired, in the causal production of the qualities and values of objects, it marks the possibility of a decisive gain. It puts us in possession of some of the conditions that control the occurrence of experienced objects, and thereby it supplies us with an instrument of regulation. There is something querulous in the sweeping denial that things as experienced, as perceived and enjoyed, in any way depend upon interaction with human selves. The error of doctrines that have exploited the part played by personal and subjective reactions in determining what is perceived and enjoyed lies either in exaggerating this factor of constitution into the sole condition—as happens in subjective idealism—or else in treating it as a finality instead of, as with all knowledge, an instrument in direction of further action.

A third significant change that would issue from carrying over experimental method from physics to man concerns the import of standards, principles, rules. With the transfer, these, and all tenets and creeds about good and goods, would be recognized to be hypotheses. Instead of being rigidly fixed, they would be treated as intellectual instruments to be tested and confirmed—and altered—through consequences effected by acting upon them. They would lose all pretense of finality—the ulterior source of dogmatism. It is both astonishing and depressing that so much of the energy of mankind has gone into fighting for (with weapons of the flesh as well as of the spirit) the truth of creeds, religious, moral and political, as distinct from what has gone into effort to try creeds by putting them to the test of acting upon them. The change would do away with the intolerance and fanaticism that attend the notion that beliefs and judgments are capable of inherent truth and authority; inherent in the sense of being independent of what they lead to when used as directive principles. The transformation does not imply merely that men are responsible for acting upon what they profess to believe; that is an old doctrine. It goes much further. Any belief as such is tentative, hypothetical; it is not just to be acted upon, but is to be *framed* with reference to its office as a guide to action. Consequently, it should be the last thing in the world to be picked up casually and then clung to rigidly. When it is apprehended as a tool and only a tool, an instrumentality of direction, the same scrupulous attention will go to its formation as now goes into the making of instruments of precision in technical fields. Men, instead of being proud of accepting and asserting beliefs and "principles" on the ground of loyalty, will be as ashamed of that procedure as they would now be to confess their assent to a scientific theory out of reverence for Newton or Helmholz or whomever, without regard to evidence. . . .

The various modifications that would result from adoption in social and humane subjects of the experimental way of thinking are perhaps summed up in saying that it would place *method and means* upon the level of importance that has, in the past, been imputed exclusively to ends. Means have been regarded as menial, and the useful as the servile. Means have been treated as poor relations to be endured, but not inherently welcome. The very meaning of the word "ideals" is significant of the divorce which has obtained between means and ends. "Ideals" are thought to be remote and inaccessible of attainment; they are too high and fine to be sullied by realization. They serve vaguely to arouse "aspiration," but they do not evoke and direct strivings for embodiment in actual existence. They hover in an indefinite way over the actual scene; they are expiring ghosts of a once significant kingdom of divine reality whose rule penetrated to every detail of life.

- Do you agree with Dewey that the purpose of morality is to improve our actual situation in the world?
- Consider a particular moral problem in the contemporary world. How might the scientific method be applied to it?
- Do you see any problems that may result from giving up the ideas of intrinsic goods and ultimate ends?

K. Ethics and Gender

One of the most obvious features of much of the moral philosophy we have been examining is its focus on (or occasionally the denial of) the centrality of abstract principles of reason. Kant, most obviously, celebrates the a priori dictates of practical reason as the core of morality. Mill, although the nature of his utilitarian principles may be quite different, nevertheless emphasizes the importance of a calculative impersonal principle in the determination of right and wrong. More recent decades, however, have seen the appearance of an enormous amount of literature that has challenged this view that morality is something essentially rational, principled, and impersonal. In 1982 Harvard psychologist Carol Gilligan argued at some length that women tend to think about moral issues differently from men, attending more to the impact that particular actions have on relationships than to the conformity of these actions to abstract rules. Ever since, there has been a booming business in trying to elaborate and sort out the relative merits of these diverging perspectives. Theories of feminist ethics often draw upon this work, arguing that traditional moral theory has paid too little attention to relationships. This is not to deny that many of the features that are emphasized in feminist ethics, for instance, a healthy attention to personal feelings as well as (or rather than) impersonal reason, were anticipated by earlier male philosophers, such as Hume and Rousseau. But feminist ethicists have defended the centrality of relational considerations to ethics in an unprecedented way. Some have emphasized the moral relevance of experiences that are distinctively female, such as the experience of motherhood. In the following essay, **Virginia Held**, philosopher and feminist, attempts to spell out some grounds for a feminist critique of traditional ethical theories and suggests new directions for moral thinking on women's experience.

On Feminist Ethics
BY **Virginia Held** [27]

The history of philosophy, including the history of ethics, has been constructed from male points of view, and has been built on assumptions and concepts that are by no means gender-neutral. Feminists characteristically begin with different concerns and give different emphases to the issues we consider than do non-feminist approaches. And, as Lorraine Code expresses it, "starting points and focal points shape the impact of theoretical discussion." Within philosophy, feminists often start with, and focus on, quite different issues than those found in standard philosophy and ethics, however "standard" is understood. Far from providing mere additional insights which can be incorporated into traditional theory, feminist explorations often require radical transformations of existing fields of inquiry and theory. From a feminist point of view, moral theory along with almost all theory will have to be transformed to take adequate account of the experience of women.

. . .

THE HISTORY OF ETHICS

Consider the ideals embodied in the phrase "the man of reason." As Genevieve Lloyd has told the story, what has been taken to characterize the man of reason may have changed from historical period to historical period, but in each, the character ideal of the man of reason has been constructed in conjunction with a rejection of whatever has been taken to be characteristic of the feminine. "Rationality," Lloyd writes, "has been conceived as transcendence of the 'feminine,' and the 'feminine' itself has been partly constituted by its occurrence within this structure."

This has of course fundamentally affected the history of philosophy and of ethics. The split between reason and emotion is one of the most familiar of philosophical conceptions. And the advocacy of reason "controlling" unruly emotion, of rationality guiding responsible human action against the blindness of passion, has a long and highly influential history, almost as familiar to non-philosophers as to philosophers. We should

Virginia Held (1929-)

An American philosopher, specializing in feminist epistemology. She is Professor Emerita at Hunter College of the City University of New York.

[27] Virginia Held, "Feminist Transformations of Moral Theory," in *Philosophy and Phenomenological Research*, Vol. L, Supplement (Fall 1990). Reprinted by permission of Blackwell Publishing Ltd.

certainly now be alert to the ways in which reason has been associated with male endeavor, emotion with female weakness, and the ways in which this is of course not an accidental association. As Lloyd writes, "From the beginnings of philosophical thought, femaleness was symbolically associated with what Reason supposedly left behind—the dark powers of the earth goddesses, immersion in unknown forces associated with mysterious female powers. The early Greeks saw women's capacity to conceive as connecting them with the fertility of Nature. As Plato later expressed the thought, women 'imitate the earth.'"

. . .

The associations, between Reason, form, knowledge, and maleness, have persisted in various guises, and have permeated what has been thought to be moral knowledge as well as what has been thought to be scientific knowledge, and what has been thought to be the practice of morality. The associations between the philosophical concepts and gender cannot be merely dropped, and the concepts retained regardless of gender, because gender has been built into them in such a way that without it, they will have to be different concepts. As feminists repeatedly show, if the concept of "human" were built on what we think about "woman" rather than what we think about "man," it would be a very different concept. Ethics, thus, has not been a search for universal, or truly human guidance, but a gender-biased enterprise.

Other distinctions and associations have supplemented and reinforced the identification of reason with maleness, and of the irrational with the female; on this and other grounds "man" has been associated with the human, "woman" with the natural. Prominent among distinctions reinforcing the latter view has been that between the public and the private, because of the way they have been interpreted. Again, these provide as familiar and entrenched a framework as do reason and emotion, and they have been as influential for non-philosophers as for philosophers. It has been supposed that in the public realm, man transcends his animal nature and creates human history. As *citizen*, he creates government and law; as warrior, he protects society by his willingness to risk death; and as artist or philosopher, he overcomes his human mortality. Here, in the public realm, morality should guide human decision. In the household, in contrast, it has been supposed that women merely "reproduce" life as natural, biological matter. Within the household, the "natural" needs of man for food and shelter are served, and new instances of the biological creature that man is are brought into being. But what is distinctively human, and what transcends any given level of development to create human progress, are thought to occur elsewhere.

This contrast was made highly explicit in Aristotle's conceptions of polis and household; it has continued to affect the basic assumptions of a remarkably broad swath of thought ever since. In ancient Athens, women were confined to the household; the public sphere was literally a male domain. In more recent history, though women have been permitted to venture into public space, the associations of the public, historically male sphere with the distinctively human, and of the household, historically a female sphere, with the merely natural and repetitious, have persisted. These associations have deeply affected moral theory, which has often supposed the transcendent, public domain to be relevant to the foundations of morality in ways that the natural behavior of women in the household could not be. To take some recent and representative examples, David Heyd, in his discussion of supererogation, dismisses a mother's sacrifice for her child as an example of the supererogatory because it belongs, in his view, to "the sphere of natural relationships and instinctive feelings (which lie outside morality)." J. O. Urmson had earlier taken a similar position. In his discussion of supererogation, Urmson said, "Let us be clear that we are not now considering cases of natural affection, such as the sacrifice made by a mother for her child; such cases may be said with some justice not to fall under the concept of morality. . . ." And in a recent article called "Distrusting Economics," Alan Ryan argues persuasively about the questionableness of economics and other branches of the social sciences built on the assumption that human beings are rational, self-interested calculators; he discusses various examples of non self-interested behavior, such as of men in wartime, which show the assumption to be false, but nowhere in the article is there any mention of the activity of mothering, which would seem to be a fertile locus for doubts about the usual picture of rational man. Although Ryan does not provide the kind of explicit reason offered by Heyd and Urmson for omitting the context of mothering from consideration as relevant to his discussion, it is difficult to understand the omission without a comparable assumption being implicit here, as it so often is elsewhere. Without feminist insistence on the relevance for morality of the experience in mothering, this context is largely ignored by moral theorists. And yet, from a gender-neutral point of view, how can this vast and fundamental domain of human experience possibly be imagined to lie "outside morality"?

The result of the public/private distinction, as usually formulated, has been to privilege the points of view of men in the public domains of state and law, and later in the marketplace, and to discount the experience of women. Mothering has been conceptualized as a primarily biological activity, even when performed by humans, and virtually no moral theory in the history of ethics has taken mothering, as experienced by women, seriously as a source of moral insight, until feminists in recent years have begun to. Women have been seen as emotional rather than as rational beings, and thus as incapable of full moral personhood. Women's behavior has been interpreted as either "natural" and driven by instinct, and thus as irrelevant to morality and to the construction of moral principles, or it has been interpreted as, at best, in need of instruction and supervision by males better able to know what morality requires and better able to live up to its demands.

The Hobbesian conception of reason is very different from the Platonic or Aristotelian conceptions before it, and from the conceptions of Rousseau or Kant or Hegel later; all have in common that they ignore and disparage the experience and reality of women. Consider Hobbes' account of man in the state of nature contracting with other men to establish society. These men hypothetically come into existence fully formed and independent of one another, and decide on entering or staying outside of civil society. As Christine Di Stefano writes, "What we find in Hobbes's account of human nature and political order is a vital concern with the survival of a self conceived in masculine terms . . . This masculine dimension of Hobbes's atomistic egoism is powerfully underscored in his state of nature, which is effectively built on the foundation of denied maternity." In Citizen, where Hobbes gave his first systematic exposition of the state of nature, he asks us to "consider men as if but even now sprung out of the earth, and suddenly, like mushrooms, come to full maturity, without all kinds of engagement with each other." As Di Stefano says, it is a most incredible and problematic feature of Hobbes's state of nature that the men in it "are not born of, much less nurtured by, women, or anyone else." To abstract from the complex web of human reality an abstract man for rational perusal, Hobbes has, Di Stefano continues, "expunged human reproduction and early nurturance, two of the most basic and typically female-identified features of distinctively human life, from his account of basic human nature. Such a strategy ensures that he

"Mothering has been conceptualized as a primarily biological activity, even when performed by humans, and virtually no moral theory in the history of ethics has taken mothering, as experienced by women, seriously as a source of moral insight."

– VIRGINIA HELD

can present a thoroughly atomistic subject. . . ." From the point of view of women's experience, such a subject or self is unbelievable and misleading, even as a theoretical construct. The Leviathan, Di Stefano writes, "is effectively comprised of a body politic of orphans who have reared themselves, whose desires are situated within and reflect nothing but independently generated movement. . . . These essential elements are natural human beings conceived along masculine lines."

Rousseau, and Kant, and Hegel, paid homage to the emotional power, the aesthetic sensibility, and the familial concerns, respectively, of women. But since in their views morality must be based on rational principle, and women were incapable of full rationality, or a degree or kind of rationality comparable to that of men, women were deemed, in the view of these moralists, to be inherently wanting in morality. For Rousseau, women must be trained from childhood to submit to the will of men lest their sexual power lead both men and women to disaster. For Kant, women were thought incapable of achieving full moral personhood, and women lose all charm if they try to behave like men by engaging in rational pursuits. For Hegel, women's moral concern for their families could be admirable in its proper place, but is a threat to the more universal aims to which men, as members of the state, should aspire.

These images, of the feminine as what must be overcome if knowledge and morality are to be achieved, of female experience as naturally irrelevant to morality, and of women as inherently deficient moral creatures, are built into the history of ethics. Feminists examine these images, and see that they are not the incidental or merely idiosyncratic suppositions of a few philosophers whose views on many topics depart far from the ordinary anyway. Such views are the nearly uniform reflection in philosophical and ethical theory of patriarchal attitudes pervasive throughout human history. Or they are exaggerations even of ordinary male experience, which exaggerations then reinforce rather than temper other patriarchal conceptions and institutions. They distort the actual experience and aspirations of many men as well as of women. Annette Baier recently speculated about why it is that moral philosophy has so seriously overlooked the trust between human beings that in her view is an utterly central aspect of moral life. She noted that "the great moral theorists in our tradition not only are all men, they are mostly

men who had minimal adult dealings with (and so were then minimally influenced by) women." They were for the most part "clerics, misogynists, and puritan bachelors," and thus it is not surprising that they focus their philosophical attention "so single-mindedly on cool, distanced relations between more or less free and equal adult strangers. . . ."

As feminists, we deplore the patriarchal attitudes that so much of philosophy and moral theory reflect. But we recognize that the problem is more serious even than changing those attitudes. For moral theory as so far developed is incapable of correcting itself without an almost total transformation. It cannot simply absorb the gender that has been "left behind," even if both genders would want it to. To continue to build morality on rational principles opposed to the emotions and to include women among the rational will leave no one to reflect the promptings of the

FIG. 7.31 According to Virginia Held, the moral importance of mothering has been unappreciated by the ethical tradition. *(Image © Calek, 2011. Used under license from Shutterstock.com)*

heart, which promptings can be moral rather than merely instinctive. To simply bring women into the public and male domain of the polis will leave no one to speak for the household. Its values have been hitherto unrecognized, but they are often moral values. Or to continue to seek contractual restraints on the pursuits of self-interest by atomistic individuals, and to have women join men in devotion to these pursuits, will leave no one involved in the nurturance of children and cultivation of social relations, which nurturance and cultivation can be of greatest moral import.

There are very good reasons for women not to want simply to be accorded entry as equals into the enterprise of morality as so far developed. In a recent survey of types of feminist moral theory, Kathryn Morgan notes that "many women who engage in philosophical reflection are acutely aware of the masculine nature of the profession and tradition, and feel their own moral concerns as women silenced or trivialized in virtually all the official settings that define the practice." Women should clearly not agree, as the price of admission to the masculine realm of traditional morality, to abandon our own moral concerns as women.

And so we are groping to shape new moral theory. Understandably, we do not yet have fully worked out feminist moral theories to offer. But we can suggest some directions our project of developing such theories is taking. As Kathryn Morgan points out, there is not likely to be a "star" feminist moral theorist on the order of a Rawls or Nozick: "There will be no individual singled out for two reasons. One reason is that vital moral and theoretical conversations are taking place on a large dialectical scale as the feminist community struggles to develop a feminist ethic. The second reason is that this community of feminist theoreticians is calling into question the very model of the individualized autonomous self presupposed by a star-centered male-dominated tradition. . . . We experience it as a common labour, a common task."

The dialogues that are enabling feminist approaches to moral theory to develop are proceeding. As Alison Jaggar makes clear in her useful overview of them, there is no unitary view of ethics that can be identified as "feminist ethics." Feminist approaches to ethics share a commitment to "rethinking ethics with a view to correcting whatever forms of male bias it may contain." While those who develop these approaches are "united by a shared project, they diverge widely in their views as to how this project is to be accomplished."

Not all feminists, by any means, agree that there are distinctive feminist virtues or values. Some are especially skeptical of the attempt to give positive value to such traditional "feminine virtues" as a willingness to nurture, or an affinity with caring, or reluctance to seek independence. They see this approach as playing into the hands of those who would confine women to traditional roles. Other feminists are skeptical of all claims about women as such, emphasizing that women are divided by class and race and sexual orientation in ways that make any conclusions drawn from "women's experience" dubious.

FIG. 7.32 A modern woman contending with the demands of both the public and private spheres. (© Images.com/Corbis)

Still, it is possible, I think, to discern various important focal points evident in current feminist attempts to transform ethics into a theoretical and practical activity that could be acceptable from a feminist point of view. In the glimpse I have presented of bias in the history of ethics, I focused on what, from a feminist point of view, are three of its most questionable aspects: (1) the split between reason and emotion and the devaluation of emotion; (2) the public/private distinction and the relegation of the private to the natural; and (3) the concept of the self as constructed from a male point of view.

- Do you think that men and women tend to have different approaches to moral reasoning? What might count as evidence for your view?
- What are some major differences between traditional morality and feminist morality? Is Held committed to a form of ethical relativism? Why or why not?
- Can you think of ways in which the role and experience of mothers may offer insights of use to moral theory?

SUMMARY AND CONCLUSION

In this chapter, we have reviewed a variety of theories of morality. (1) Aristotle takes the key to morality to be the concept of "virtue," which he argues to be activity in accordance with rational principles. He bases this argument on a concept of what is "natural" for man, but his discussion is clearly limited to a small class of Greek male citizens, whom he views as the ideal specimens of humanity. (2) Hume and Rousseau both argue that morality must be based on certain kinds of feelings or "sentiments." "Reason is and ought to be the slave of the passions," Hume argues, and Rousseau similarly argues that man is "naturally" good. (3) Kant insists that morality is strictly a matter of rational principle divorced from all personal interests and desires ("inclinations"). His moral theory includes a rejection of the views of Hume and Rousseau, who base morality on feelings (which are inclinations in Kant's sense). It also rejects Aristotle's position. Although both philosophers use the notion of a "rational principle," Kant intends his notion to apply to every human being, and therefore every person has the same duties and obligations. (4) The utilitarians, Bentham and Mill, reject Kant's divorce between morality and personal interest and argue that morality is our guide to the satisfaction of the greatest number of interests of the greatest number of people. (5) Nietzsche rejects both Kant and the utilitarians, preferring a return to the elitism and "virtue" orientation of Aristotle's ethics. He argues that we create our values and live with them according to our personal needs. Following him, the existentialists, particularly Jean-Paul Sartre, argue that all values are chosen by us; there is no "true" morality, only those values to which we have voluntarily committed ourselves. (6) Dewey argues that ethics are concerned with improving human life and confronting problems that arise. He urges the use of the scientific method in our moral inquiry to help us evaluate what courses of action best address our practical problems. (7) Finally, recent feminists have challenged the "male bias" of these traditional theories and have suggested the possibility of a different *kind* of moral view.

CHAPTER REVIEW QUESTIONS

1. Compare Rousseau's notion of conscience to Hume's notion of sentiment. Does one theory seem to be stronger than the other, based on the differences and similarities between the notions of sentiment and conscience?

2. Does Aristotle's model of virtue ethics depend only upon social expectations, or does it also leave room for individual autonomy?

3. Aristotle claims that "actions are called just or temperate when they are the sort that a just or temperate person would do." Does this account seem circular to you? How would Aristotle deny the charge that it is circular?

4. Hobbes (and Xunzi) insist that humankind is naturally evil. Rousseau (and Mencius), on the other hand, believe in the natural goodness of humanity. What do you think? If humankind is naturally good, how does evil enter the picture?

5. Consider how one might reconcile the rule-based system of Kant with the consequence-based system of utilitarianism. Do the two ethical systems complement one another, or are they at odds?

6. Think of a moral dilemma that cannot be satisfactorily solved by either Kant or Mill. Does Nietzsche provide a solution? How would Dewey approach the problem?

7. What are the moral dangers of suggesting, as Nietzsche and Sartre do, that individuals create their own value systems? Could a prison guard in a Nazi concentration camp have described himself as a "good person" on existentialist grounds?

8. How plausible is the idea that men and women make their moral choices using different criteria?

9. Given the choice between saving your own child's life and the lives of someone else's two children, what would you do and why? What do you think Aristotle would say? Kant? Mill?

KEY TERMS

altruism	existentialism	natural law
a priori	Golden Rule	obligation
autonomy	happiness	ought
categorical imperative	happiness calculus	principle of utility
commitment	(or felicity calculus)	psychological egoism
conscience	hedonism	rationality
contemplation (the life of)	hypothetical imperative	relativism
cultural relativism	immoralist	selfishness
deontology	imperative	sentiment
duty	inclination	slave morality
egoism	law	sympathy
ethical absolutism	master morality	utilitarians
ethical egoism	maxim	virtue
ethical relativism	mean (between	will
ethics	the extremes)	will to power
eudaimonia	morality	

BIBLIOGRAPHY AND FURTHER READING

A comprehensive but brief history of ethics is A. MacIntyre, *A Short History of Ethics*, 2nd ed. (New York: Macmillan, 1998).

A general schematic discussion of the problems of ethics is W. Fankena, *Ethics*, 2nd ed. (Englewood Cliffs, NJ: Prentice-Hall, 1973).

A lively summary of ethical issues is S. Blackburn, *Being Good: A Short Introduction to Ethics* (New York: Oxford University Press, 2001).

A much more detailed survey of the problems and history of ethics is R. R. Brandt, *Ethical Theory* (Englewood Cliffs, NJ: Prentice-Hall, 1959).

The classic arguments against egoism are in Joseph Butler, *Fifteen Sermons Preached at the Rolls Chapel* (Gloucestershire, U.K.: Dodo Press, 2009).

A more modern and technical set of arguments is in T. Nagel, *The Possibility of Altruism* (Oxford, U.K.: Clarendon Press, 1970).

Textbooks that include various discussions of ethical options are *Ethics: History, Theory, and Contemporary Issues*, ed. S. Cahn and P. Markie, 4th ed. (New York: Oxford University Press, 2008), and L. M. Hinman. *Ethics: A Pluralistic Approach to Ethical Theory*, 4th ed. (Belmont, CA: Wadsworth, 2007).

Aristotle's *Nicomachean Ethics* was translated by W. D. Ross (Oxford, U.K.: Oxford University Press, 1925). Ross also has a good summary of the arguments in his *Aristotle*, rev. ed. (New York: Barnes & Noble, 1964).

Some excellent articles on Aristotle's ethics are collected in J. J. Walsh and H. L. Shapiro, eds., *Aristotle's Ethics* (Belmont, CA: Wadsworth, 1967), and J. Moravscik, ed., *Aristotle* (New York: Doubleday Anchor, 1967).

David Hume's moral philosophy is most accessible in his *Enquiry Concerning the Principles of Morals* (La Salle, IL: Open Court Press, 1966).

Jean-Jacques Rousseau's moral theories are to be found in his second discourse "On the Origins of Inequality" in *The Social Contract*, trans. E. D. H. Cole (New York: Dutton, 1950) and in *Émile*, trans. B. Foxley (New York: Dutton, 1972).

The best summary of Immanuel Kant's moral philosophy is his own *Foundations of the Metaphysics of Morals*, available in various translations. One recent one is *Groundwork of the Metaphysics of Morals*, trans. M. Gregor (New York: Cambridge University Press, 1998). See also Immanuel Kant, *Lectures on Ethics*, trans. P. Heath (New York: Cambridge University Press, 2001).

John Stuart Mill's utilitarianism is well summarized in his pamphlet *Utilitarianism* (New York: Dutton, 1910).

An account of Friedrich Nietzsche's ethics can be found in W. Kaufmann, *Nietzsche*, 4th ed. (Princeton, NJ: Princeton University Press, 1974).

A good summary of existentialist ethics is M. Warnock, *Existentialist Ethics* (New York: St. Martin's Press, 1967).

For a survey of feminist ethics, see H. Lindemann, *An Invitation to Feminist Ethics* (New York: McGraw-Hill, 2005).

A good collection of essays on feminism and values is M. Pearsall, *Women and Values*, 2nd ed. (Belmont, CA: Wadsworth, 1993).

An excellent historical overview is J. McCracken, *Thinking About Gender: A Historical Anthology* (Fort Worth, TX: Harcourt Brace, 1997).

Two all-purpose collections are P. Singer, ed., *A Companion to Ethics* (Oxford, U.K.: Blackwell, 1991), and P. Singer, ed., *Ethics* (New York: Oxford University Press, 1994).

Also recommended are H. LaFollette, *The Blackwell Guide to Ethical Theory* (Oxford, U.K.: Blackwell, 2000), and J. Rachels, *Ethical Theory*, 2 vols. (New York: Oxford University Press, 1998).

8 | Justice

We hold these truths to be self-evident, that all men are created equal, that they are endowed by their creator with certain unalienable Rights, that among these are Life, Liberty and the Pursuit of Happiness.

THOMAS JEFFERSON ET AL.

"Man is a social animal," wrote Aristotle. Therefore, he is a political animal as well. We live with other people, not just our friends and families, but thousands and millions of others, most of whom we will never meet and many of whom we come across in only the most casual way—passing them as we cross the street or buying a ticket at the movie theater. Yet we have to be concerned about them, and they about us, for there is a sense in which we are all clearly dependent on each other. For example, we depend on them not to attack us without reason or to steal our possessions. Of course, our confidence varies from person to person and from city to city. But it is clear that, in general, we have duties toward people we will never know, such as the duty not to contaminate their water or air supplies or to place their lives in danger. And they have similar duties to us. We also claim certain rights for ourselves, such as the right not to be attacked as we walk down the street, the right to speak our mind about politically controversial issues without being thrown in jail, and the right to believe in this or that religion or no religion at all, without having our jobs, our homes, or our freedom taken from us.

Political and social philosophy is the study of people in societies. It pays particular attention to the abstract claims that people have on each other in the form of "rights," "duties," and "privileges" and their demands for "justice," "equality," and "freedom." (It is important to distinguish this sense of *political* freedom from the causal or metaphysical freedom that we discussed earlier. These types of freedom can be discussed independently of each other.) At least ideally, politics is continuous with morality. Our political duties and obligations, for example, are often the same as our moral duties and obligations. Our claims to certain "moral rights" are often claims to political rights as well. And political rights—particularly those very general and absolute rights that we call human rights (for example, the right not to be tortured or degraded or the right not to be exploited by powerful institutions or persons)—are typically defended on the basis of moral principles. The virtues of **government** are ideally the same as the virtues of individuals: government should be just, temperate,

FIG. 8.1 A blindfolded woman holding scales is a traditional representation of justice. *(© iStockphoto.com/Andrey Burmakin)*

courageous, honest, humane, considerate, and reasonable. Plato and Aristotle portrayed their visions of the ideal **state** in precisely these terms. (Both Plato and Aristotle, unlike most modern philosophers, actually had the opportunity to set up such governments; both failed, but for reasons that were not their fault.)

We do not mean to say that all politics or all politicians are moral. We all know better than that. But it is to say that our politics are constrained and determined by our sense of morality. Morality is more concerned with relations between particular people, while politics is more concerned with large and impersonal groups. But the difference is one of degree. In ancient Greece, Plato and Aristotle lived in relatively small "city-states" (each called a *polis*), with fewer citizens than even most U.S. towns. It was not a stretch for them to treat morality and politics together. But even today, we still speak hopefully of "the human family" and "international brotherhood," which is to reassert our enduring belief that politics—even at the international level—ought to be based on interpersonal moral principles.

The key to a successful **society** is cooperation. If people do not cooperate, the success of society requires that some authority have the power to bring individual interests into line with the public interest. This authority is generally called the state. The state passes laws and enforces them; its purpose is to protect the public interest. But is it only this? We would probably say *no*. Its purpose is also to protect individual rights, for example, against powerful corporations and against strongly mobilized pressure groups that try to interfere with individual lives. In general, we may say that the function of the state is to protect justice. But there has been disagreement ever since ancient times about what protecting justice means and how much the primary emphasis should be placed on the public interest and how much on individual rights and interests.

Our concept of the state and the extent of its power and **authority** depends very much on our conception of human nature and of people's willingness to cooperate without being forced to do so. At one extreme are those who place such strong emphasis on the smooth workings of society that they are willing to sacrifice most individual rights and interests. They are generally called "authoritarians," and their confidence in willing individual cooperation is slight compared to their confidence in a strong authoritarian state. ("He makes the trains run on time" was often said of the fascist Italian dictator Benito Mussolini.) At the other extreme are people with so much confidence in individual cooperation and so little confidence in the state that they argue that the state should be eliminated altogether. They are called **anarchists**. Between these extremes are more moderate positions. For example, many people have some confidence both in individual cooperation and in the possibility of a reasonably just state, but do not have complete confidence in either. Democrats and Republicans, for example, both believe in a government that is at least partially run by the people themselves but with sufficient power to enforce its laws over individual interests when necessary. All these people believe in different solutions to the same central problem: the problem of a balance between the public interest and the need for cooperation, on the one hand, and individual rights and interests, on the other. They are concerned, in other words, with the problem of **justice**.

A. The Problem of Justice

When we think of justice, we tend first to think of criminal cases and of punishment. Justice, in this sense, is catching the criminal and "making him pay for his crime." The oldest sense of the word *justice*, therefore, is what philosophers call **retributive justice**, or simply, "getting even." Retribution for a crime is making the criminal suffer or pay an amount appropriate to the severity of the crime. In ancient traditions, the key phrase was "an eye for an eye, a tooth for a tooth." If a criminal caused a person to be blind, he was, in turn, blinded. We now view this form of justice as brutal and less than civilized. But is it so clear that we have in fact given up this retributive sense of justice? Do we demand retribution from our criminals by punishing them, or do we sincerely attempt to reform them? Or is the purpose of prison simply to keep them off the street? Should we ever punish people for crimes, or should we simply protect ourselves against their doing the same thing again? If a man commits an atrocious murder, is it enough that we guarantee that he will not commit another one? Or does he deserve punishment even if we know that he will not do it again?

Retributive justice and the problems of punishment, however, are really only a small piece of a much larger concern. Justice is not just "getting even" for crimes and offenses. It concerns the running of society as a whole in day-to-day civil matters, as well as in the more dramatic criminal cases. Given the relative scarcity of wealth and goods, how should they be distributed? Should everyone receive exactly the same amount? Should the person who works hard at an unpleasant job receive no more than the person who refuses to work at all and prefers to spend the day watching television and engaging in other amusements? Should the person who uses his or her wealth to the benefit of others receive no more than the person who "throws away" his or her money on gambling, drinking, and debauchery? If a class of people has historically been deprived of its adequate share because of the color of their skins, their religious beliefs, or their sex or age, should that class now be given more than its share in compensation? Or is this, too, an injustice against other people?

Not only wealth and goods are at issue here. Distribution of privileges and power are equally important. Who will be allowed to vote? Will everyone's vote count equally? Should the opinions of an illiterate who does not even know the name of his political leaders have as much say in the government as the political scientist or economist who has studied these matters for years? Should everyone be allowed to drive? Or to drink? Should everyone receive exactly the same treatment before the law? Or are there concerns that would indicate that some people (for example, members of Congress or foreign diplomats) should receive special privileges?

Enjoyment of society's cultural gifts is also at issue. Should everyone receive the same education? What if doing so turns out to be "impractical" (since job training is much more efficient than "liberal arts")? If only some are educated in more than occupational skills, doesn't that mean that some—the workers and career persons who are trained to do a job—are deprived of the education necessary to enjoy great books, music, poetry, philosophy,

FIG. 8.2 Is getting even the essence of justice? (© iStockphoto.com/bruce7)

intellectual debate, or proficiency in foreign languages, all of which give considerable enjoyment to those who have been taught to appreciate them?

There are also questions of status. Should there be social classes? What if it could be proved that such divisions make a society run more smoothly? How minimal should distinctions in status be? This question, in turn, leads to the more general question: Shouldn't all members of society be able to expect equal treatment and respect not only by the law but in every conceivable social situation? All these are the concerns of justice. But what is just? Who decides? And how?

B. Two Ancient Theories of Justice: Plato and Aristotle

Theories of justice, in one sense, are as old as human society. The ancient codes of the Hebrews, the Persians, and the Babylonians were theories of justice in the sense that they were efforts to develop rules to cover fair dealing and distribution of goods, the punishment of criminals, and the settling of disputes. A fully developed theory of justice, however, should go beyond making rules and try to analyze the nature of justice itself. The first great western theories of justice were those of Plato and Aristotle. In *The Republic*, Plato argues that justice in the state is precisely the same as justice in the individual. Justice in both cases is a harmony among the various parts for the good of the whole. In other words, cooperation among all for the sake of a successful society is the key to justice. But this means that the interests of the individual take a clearly secondary role to the interests of society. In ancient Greece, individual interests may have been an occasional concern of the wealthy and powerful, but for the majority of people—especially the slaves—this secondary role was the norm. Because their docile submission was seen as necessary to the overall success of society, their individual interests and rights were extremely minimal. They expected to be rewarded and satisfied only insofar as their efforts benefited their betters, and they expected their betters to reap far more reward from their labor than they themselves. In Plato's universe, everyone has his or her "place," and justice means that they act and are treated accordingly:

 FROM **The *Republic***
BY **Plato**[1]

I think that justice is the very thing, or some form of the thing which, when we were beginning to found our city, we said had to be established throughout. We stated, and often repeated, if you remember, that everyone must pursue one occupation of those in the city, that for which his nature best fitted him.

Yes, we kept saying that.

Further, we have heard many people say, and have often said ourselves, that justice is to perform one's own task, and not to meddle with that of others.

We have said that.

This then, my friend, I said, when it happens, is in some way justice, to do one's own job. And do you know what I take to be a proof of this?

No, tell me.

I think what is left over of those things we have been investigating, after moderation and courage and wisdom have been found, was that which made it possible for those three qualities to appear in the city and to continue as long as it was present. We also said that what remained after we found the other three was justice.

[1] Plato, *The Republic*, Bk. VI, trans. G. M. A. Grube. Copyright © 1974 by Hackett Publishing Company, Inc. Reprinted by permission. All rights reserved.

It had to be.

And surely, I said, if we had to decide which of the four will make the city good by its presence, it would be hard to judge whether it is a common belief among the rulers and the ruled, or the preservation among the soldiers of a law-inspired belief as to the nature of what is, and what is not, to be feared, or the knowledge and guardianship of the rulers, or whether it is, above all, the presence of this fourth in child and woman, slave and free, artisan, ruler and subject, namely that each man, a unity in himself, performed his own task and was not meddling with that of others.

How could this not be hard to judge?

It seems then that the capacity for each in the city to perform his own task rivals wisdom, moderation, and courage as a source of excellence for the city.

It certainly does.

You would then describe justice as a rival to them for excellence in the city?

Most certainly.

Look at it this way and see whether you agree: you will order your rulers to act as judges in the courts of the city?

Surely.

And will their exclusive aim in delivering judgment not be that no citizen should have what belongs to another or be deprived of what is his own?

That would be their aim.

That being just?

Yes.

In some way then possession of one's own and the performance of one's own task could be agreed to be justice.

That is so.

Consider then whether you agree with me in this: if a carpenter attempts to do the work of a cobbler, or a cobbler that of a carpenter, and they exchange their tools and the esteem that goes with the job, or the same man tries to do both, and all the other exchanges are made, do you think that this does any great harm to the city?

No.

But I think that when one who is by nature a worker or some other kind of moneymaker is puffed up by wealth, or by the mob, or by his own strength, or some other such thing, and attempts to enter the warrior class, or one of the soldiers tries to enter the group of counselors or guardians, though he is unworthy of it, and these exchange their tools and the public esteem, or when the same man tries to perform all these jobs together, then I think you will agree that these exchanges and this meddling bring the city to ruin.

They certainly do.

The meddling and exchange between the three established orders does very great harm to the city and would most correctly be called wickedness.

Very definitely.

And you would call the greatest wickedness worked against one's own city injustice?

Of course.

That then is injustice. And let us repeat that the doing of one's own job by the moneymaking, auxiliary, and guardian groups, when each group is performing its own task in the city, is the opposite, it is justice and makes the city just.

I agree with you that this is so.

"[T]he doing of one's own job by the moneymaking, auxiliary, and guardian groups, when each group is performing its own task in the city . . . is justice and makes the city just."

– PLATO'S CHARACTER SOCRATES

Plato's rigid hierarchy of social classes and insistence on the inequality of people offends our sense of universal **equality**. The same is true of Aristotle's theory of justice. But it is important to see that equality (or, more properly, **egalitarianism**, the view that all men and women are equal just by virtue of their being human) is a position that must be argued. It is not a "natural" state of affairs or a belief that has always been accepted by everyone.

In his *Politics*, Aristotle gives an unabashed defense of slavery, not only on the grounds that slaves are efficient and good for society as a whole, but because those who are slaves are "naturally" meant to be slaves. They would be unhappy, he claims, and unable to cope if they were granted freedom and made citizens. (This is not just an ancient argument. You may have heard similar arguments about other groups of people in your own lifetime.) According to Plato and Aristotle, different people have different roles, and to treat unequals equally is as unjust as it is to treat equals unequally. Plato and Aristotle would consider the view that the retarded and children and foreigners deserve the same respect and treatment as citizens to be ridiculous. So, too, would they find the contemporary argument that we should treat men and women as equals.[2]

Despite these opinions, however, Plato and Aristotle laid the foundations for much of our own conception of justice. The idea that equals must be treated as equals is the foundation of our sense of justice just as much as it was theirs—the difference is that we are taught to believe that everybody is an equal. Similarly, the theory of what is called **distributive justice**, the fair distribution of wealth and goods among the members of society, is a current international as well as national concern that owes much to Aristotle's original formulations. The idea that individuals are due certain rewards for their labor is also Aristotle's idea. And despite his aristocratic opinions and his harsh elitism, Aristotle saw quite clearly that the members of society who depended most upon an adequate theory of justice were the poorer and less powerful members. It was for them that the just society was most vital (since the powerful and wealthy had a much better chance of taking care of themselves). It was also Aristotle who made the vital distinction, with which we began this section, between justice in the restricted sense of righting certain wrongs (in crimes, in bad business deals, and in public misfortunes) and justice as the more general concern for a well-balanced and reasonable society.

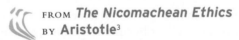 FROM *The Nicomachean Ethics*
BY **Aristotle**[3]

Let us take as a starting-point, then, the various meanings of "an unjust man." Both the lawless man and the greedy and unfair man are thought to be unjust, so that evidently both the law-abiding and the fair man will be just. The just, then, is the lawful and the fair, the unjust the unlawful and the unfair.

Since the lawless man was seen to be unjust and the law-abiding man just, evidently all lawful acts are in a sense just acts; for the acts laid down by the legislative art are lawful, and each of these, we say, is just. Now the laws in their enactments on all subjects aim at the common advantage either of all or of the best of those who hold power, or something of the sort; so that in one sense we call those acts just that tend to produce and preserve happiness and its components for the political society. And the law bids us do both the acts of a brave man (e.g. not to desert our post nor take to flight nor throw away our arms), and those of a temperate man (e.g. not to commit adultery nor to gratify one's lust), and those of a good-tempered man

2 Plato did venture that women as well as men ought to be rulers.

3 Aristotle, *The Nicomachean Ethics*, trans. W. D. Ross (Oxford, U.K. : Oxford University Press, 1925).

(e.g. not to strike another nor to speak evil), and similarly with regard to the other virtues and forms of wickedness, commanding some acts and forbidding others; and the rightly-framed law does this rightly, and the hastily conceived one less well.

This form of justice, then, is complete virtue, but not absolutely, but in relation to our neighbour. And therefore justice is often thought to be the greatest of virtues, and "neither evening nor morning star" is so wonderful; and proverbially "in justice is every virtue comprehended." And it is complete virtue in its fullest sense, because it is the actual exercise of complete virtue. It is complete because he who possesses it can exercise his virtue not only in himself but towards his neighbour also; for many men can exercise virtue in their own affairs, but not in their relations to their neighbour.

. . .

But at all events what we are investigating is the justice which is a *part* of virtue; for there is a justice of this kind, as we maintain. Similarly it is with injustice in the particular sense that we are concerned.

FIG. 8.3 Distributive justice is fairness in the allocation of goods. (© iStockphoto.com/John Kounadeas)

That there is such a thing is indicated by the fact that while the man who exhibits in action the other forms of wickedness acts wrongly indeed, but not graspingly (e.g. the man who throws away his shield through cowardice or speaks harshly through bad temper or fails to help a friend with money through meanness), when a man acts graspingly he often exhibits none of these vices—no, nor all together, but certainly wickedness of some kind (for we blame him) and injustice. There is, then, another kind of injustice which is a part of injustice in the wide sense, and a use of the word "unjust" which answers to a part of what is unjust in the wide sense of "contrary to the law." Again, if one man commits adultery for the sake of gain and makes money by it, while another does so at the bidding of appetite though he loses money and is penalized for it, the latter would be held to be self-indulgent rather than grasping, but the former is unjust, but not self-indulgent; evidently, therefore, he is unjust by reason of his making gain by his act. Again, all other unjust acts are ascribed invariably to some particular kind of wickedness, for example adultery to self-indulgence, the desertion of a comrade in battle to cowardice, physical violence to anger; but if a man makes gain, his action is ascribed to no form of wickedness but injustice. Evidently, therefore, there is apart from injustice in the wide sense another, "particular," injustice which shares the name and nature of the first, because its definition falls within the same genus; for the significance of both consists in a relation to one's neighbour, but the one is concerned with honour or money or safety—or that which includes all these, if we had a single name for it—and its motive is the pleasure that arises from gain; while the other is concerned with all the objects with which the good man is concerned.

It is clear, then, that there is more than one kind of justice, and that there is one which is distinct from virtue entire; we must try to grasp its genus and differentia.

. . .

Of particular justice and that which is just in the corresponding sense, (A) one kind is that which is manifested in distributions of honour or money or the other things that fall to be divided among those who have a share in the constitution (for in these it is possible for one man to have a share either unequal or equal to that of another), and (B) one is that which plays a rectifying part in transactions between man and man. Of this there are two divisions; of transactions (1) some are voluntary, and (2) others involuntary—voluntary such transactions as sale, purchase, loan for consumption, pledging, loan for use, depositing, letting (they are called voluntary because the origin of these transactions is voluntary), while of the involuntary (a) some are clandestine, such as theft, adultery, poisoning, procuring, enticement of slaves, assassination, false witness, and (b) others are violent, such as assault, imprisonment, murder, robbery with violence, mutilation, abuse, insult.

. . .

(A) We have shown that both the unjust man and the unjust act are unfair or unequal; now it is clear that there is also an intermediate between the two unequals involved in either case. And this is the equal; for in any kind of action in which there is a more and a less there is also what is equal. If, then, the unjust is unequal, the just is equal, as all men suppose it to be, even apart from argument. And since the equal is intermediate, the just will be an intermediate. Now equality implies at least two things. The just, then, must be both intermediate and equal and relative (*i.e.* for certain persons). And *qua* intermediate it must be between certain things (which are respectively greater and less); *qua* equal, it involves *two* things; *qua* just, it is for certain people. The just, therefore, involves at least four terms; for the persons for whom it is in fact just are two, and the things in which it is manifested, the objects distributed, are two. And the same equality will exist between the persons and between the things concerned; for as the latter—the things concerned—are related, so are the former; if they are not equal, they will not have what is equal, but this is the origin of quarrels and complaints—when either equals have and are awarded unequal shares, or unequals equal shares. Further, this is plain from the fact that awards should be "according to merit"; for all men agree that what is just in distribution must be according to merit in some sense, though they do not all specify the same sort of merit, but democrats identify it with the status of freeman, supporters of oligarchy with wealth (or with noble birth), and supporters of aristocracy with excellence.

This, then, is what the just is—the proportional; the unjust is what violates the proportion. Hence one term becomes too great, the other too small, as indeed happens in practice, for the man who acts unjustly has too much, and the man who is unjustly treated too little, of what is good. In the case of evil the reverse is true; for the lesser evil is reckoned a good in comparison with the greater, and what is worthy of choice is good, and what is worthier of choice a greater good.

This, then, is one species of the just.

. . .

(B) The remaining one is the rectificatory, which arises in connexion with transactions both voluntary and involuntary. This form of the just has a different specific character from the former. For the justice which distributes common possessions is always in accordance with the kind of proportion mentioned above (for in the case also in which the distribution is made from the common funds of a partnership it will be according to the same ratio which the funds put into the business by the partners bear to one another); and the injustice opposed to this kind of justice is that

FIG. 8.4 Peter Van Lint's painting *The Judgment of Solomon* illustrates some of the grave difficulties in determining what is just. *(Réunion des Musées Nationaux / Art Resource, NY)*

which violates the proportion. But the justice in transactions between man and man is a sort of equality indeed, and the injustice a sort of inequality; not according to that kind of proportion, however, but according to arithmetical proportion. For it makes no difference whether a good man has defrauded a bad man or a bad man a good one, nor whether it is a good or a bad man that has committed adultery; the law looks only to the distinctive character of the injury, and treats the parties as equal, if one is in the wrong and the other is being wronged, and if one inflicted injury and the other has received it. Therefore, this kind of injustice being an inequality, the judge tries to equalize it; for in the case also in which one has received and the other has inflicted a wound, or one has slain and the other has been slain, the suffering and the action have been unequally distributed; but the judge tries to equalize things by means of the penalty, taking away from the gain of the assailant. For the term "gain" is applied generally to such cases, even if it be not a term appropriate to certain cases, for example to the person who inflicts a wound—and "loss" to the sufferer; at all events when the suffering has been estimated, the one is called loss and the other gain. Therefore the equal is intermediate between the greater and less in contrary ways; more of the good and less of the evil are gain, and the contrary is loss; intermediate between them is, as we saw, the equal, which we say is just; therefore corrective justice will be the intermediate between loss and gain. This is why, when people dispute, they take refuge in the judge; and to go to the judge is to go to justice; for the nature of the judge is to be a sort of animate justice; and they seek the judge as an

"[T]o go to the judge is to go to justice; for the nature of the judge is to be a sort of animate justice."

– ARISTOTLE

intermediate; and in some states they call judges mediators, on the assumption that if they get what is intermediate they will get what is just. The just, then, is an intermediate, since the judge is so. The judge restores equality.

- What is retributive justice? What is distributive justice? Provide an example of each. Do you think that one concept (theory) fits them both, or are they very different?
- Why must individuals submit themselves to the authority of the state for the sake of justice?
- Plato's conception of justice is antiegalitarian. In what respects does our society remain antiegalitarian (or inegalitarian) today?
- Aristotle gives one definition of justice that requires that each be given his due according to merit. Is this notion of justice compatible with equality?
- Why should we treat others equally? Can you think of circumstances in which it is unjust to treat people equally?
- What does Aristotle mean when he claims that "the just is the proportional"?

C. Two Modern Theories of Justice: Hume and Mill on Utility and Rights

In contrast to the Greeks, the premise of most modern theories of justice has been the equality of everyone with everyone else. No one is "better" than anyone else, whatever his or her talents, achievements, wealth, family, or intelligence. This view rules out slavery on principle, whatever the benefits to society as a whole and whatever the alleged benefits to the slaves. Slavery is an extreme form of inequality and is thus to be condemned.

But our egalitarian principle has its problems, too. It is obvious that, as a matter of fact, all people are not equally endowed with intelligence or talent, good looks or abilities. Is it therefore to the good of all that everyone should be treated equally? One person is a doctor, capable of saving many lives; another is a chronic profligate and drunkard. If they were to commit exactly the same crime, would it be to the public interest to give them equal jail terms? Obviously not. But would it be just to give them different terms? It doesn't appear so. One problem that recent theorists have tried to answer is connected with cases in which the public interest seems at odds with the demands for equal treatment.

A similar problem, which we mentioned before, gives rise to one of the "paradoxes of democracy." Does it make sense to treat the opinions of an ignorant person whose only knowledge of current events comes from fifteen minutes (at best) of television news a day in the way that we treat the opinions of a skilled political veteran? But the ballots these individuals cast make no such distinction. At the same time, it is obvious that our society, despite its egalitarian principles, treats people who are cleverer at business or power-brokering much better than everyone else. Is this an example of systematic injustice? Or are there cases, even for us, in which inequality can still be defended as compatible with justice?

The theory of justice has been one of the central concerns of British philosophy for several centuries. **Thomas Hobbes** developed a theory that began with the idea that equality is a "natural fact" and justice is that which "assured peace and security to all" when enforced by the government. There is no justice in "the state of nature," Hobbes argued. Justice, like law, comes into existence only with society, through a "social compact" in which everyone agrees to abide by certain rules and to cooperate rather than compete—all for their mutual benefit. Subsequently, John Locke and later David Hume argued a similar theory of justice.

Again, their premises were equality and mutual agreement as the basis of government authority. For both philosophers, the ultimate criterion of justice was utility, the public interest, and therefore the satisfaction of the interests of at least most citizens. This criterion would have been rejected by Plato and Aristotle.

Hume exemplifies the modern view—that justice is to be characterized not just in terms of the structure of the overall society and everyone's "place" in it, but by the interests and well-being of each and every individual. But what about an instance, Hume asks, in which a particular act of justice is clearly contrary to the public interests, such as the case in which an obviously guilty criminal is released for technical reasons or a disgusting pornographer is allowed to publish and sell his or her wares under the protection of "free speech"? Hume replies that there is a need to distinguish between the utility of a single act and the utility of an

FIG. 8.5 Thomas Hobbes *(New York Public Library / Art Resource, NY)*

Thomas Hobbes (1588–1679)

The author of *Leviathan* (1651) and one of England's first great modern philosophers. He is generally credited with the formulation of the theory of the "social contract" for the establishment of governments and society, and he was one of the first philosophers to base his theory of government on a conception of man prior to his "civilization," in what he called "the state of nature." This life was, according to Hobbes, "solitary, poor, nasty, brutish, and short." Therefore, people were motivated to become part of society for their mutual protection. Hobbes also defended a materialist conception of the universe. Even the human mind, he argued, was nothing more than "matter in motion."

overall system; that although a specific act of justice may go against the public interest, the system of justice necessarily will be in the public interest. According to Hume, a single unjust act is to be challenged not as an isolated occurrence, but as an example of a general set of rules and practices.

 On "Justice and Utility"
By David Hume[4]

To make this more evident, consider, that though the rules of justice are established merely by interest, their connection with interest is somewhat singular, and is different from what may be observed on other occasions. A single act of justice is frequently contrary to *public interest;* and were it to stand alone, without being followed by other acts, may, in itself, be very prejudicial to society. When a man of merit, of a beneficent disposition, restores a great fortune to a miser, or a seditious bigot, he has acted justly and laudably, but the public is a real sufferer. Nor is every single act of justice, considered apart, more conducive to private interest, than to public; and it is easily conceived how a man may impoverish himself by a single instance of integrity, and have reason to wish that with regard to that single act, the laws of justice were for a moment suspended in the universe. But however single acts of justice may be contrary, either to public or private interest, it is certain, that the whole plan or scheme is highly conducive, or indeed absolutely requisite, both to the support of society, and the well-being of every individual.

The most explicitly "utilitarian" statement of justice as utility is found in John Stuart Mill's influential pamphlet, *Utilitarianism*.

---

4 David Hume, *Enquiry Concerning the Principles of Morals* (La Salle, IL: Open Court Press, 1912).

FROM *Utilitarianism*
BY **John Stuart Mill**[5]

In the case of this, as of our other moral sentiments, there is no necessary connection between the question of its origin and that of its binding force. That a feeling is bestowed on us by nature does not necessarily legitimate all its promptings. The feeling of justice might be a peculiar instinct, and might yet require, like our other instincts, to be controlled and enlightened by a higher reason. If we have intellectual instincts leading us to judge in a particular way, as well as animal instincts that prompt us to act in a particular way, there is no necessity that the former should be more infallible in their sphere than the latter in theirs: it may as well happen that wrong judgments are occasionally suggested by those, as wrong actions by these.

. . .

In the first place, it is mostly considered unjust to deprive any one of his personal liberty, his property, or any other thing which belongs to him by law. Here, therefore, is one instance of the application of the terms Just and Unjust in a perfectly definite sense; namely, that it is just to respect, unjust to violate, the *legal rights* of any one. But this judgment admits of several exceptions, arising from the other forms in which the notions of justice and injustice present themselves. For example: the person who suffers the deprivation may (as the phrase is) have *forfeited* the rights which he is so deprived of; a case to which we shall return presently.

. . .

Secondly, The legal rights of which he is deprived may be rights which *ought* not to have belonged to him: in other words, the law which confers on him these rights may be a bad law. When it is so, or when (which is the same thing for our purpose) it is supposed to be so, opinions will differ as to the justice or injustice of infringing it. Some maintain that no law, however bad, ought to be disobeyed by an individual citizen; that his opposition to it, if shown at all, should only be shown in endeavoring to get it altered by competent authority. This opinion (which condemns many of the most illustrious benefactors of mankind, and would often protect pernicious institutions against the only weapons, which, in the state of things existing at the time, have any chance of succeeding against them) is defended, by those who hold it, on grounds of expediency; principally on that of the importance, to the common interest of mankind, of maintaining inviolate the sentiment of submission to law. Other persons, again, hold the directly contrary opinion, that any law, judged to be bad, may blamelessly be disobeyed, even though it be not judged to be unjust, but only inexpedient; while others would confine the license of disobedience to the case of unjust laws. But, again, some say that all laws which are inexpedient are unjust, since every law imposes some restriction on the natural liberty of mankind; which restriction is an injustice, unless legitimated by tending to their good. Among these diversities of opinion, it seems to be universally admitted that there may be unjust laws, and that law, consequently, is not the ultimate criterion of justice, but may give to one person a benefit, or impose on another an evil, which justice condemns. When, however, a law is thought to be unjust, it seems always to be regarded as being so in the same way in which a breach of law is unjust—namely, by infringing somebody's right; which, as it cannot in this case be a legal right, receives a different appellation, and is

---

5 John Stuart Mill, *Utilitarianism*, (London: J. M. Dent, 1910).

called a moral right. We may say, therefore, that a second case of injustice consists in taking or withholding from any person that to which he has a *moral right*.

Thirdly, It is universally considered just, that each person should obtain that (whether good or evil) which he *deserves;* and unjust, that he should obtain a good, or be made to undergo an evil, which he does not deserve. This is, perhaps, the clearest and most emphatic form in which the idea of justice is conceived by the general mind. As it involves the notion of desert, the question arises, What constitutes desert? Speaking in a general way, a person is understood to deserve good if he does right; evil, if he does wrong: and, in a more particular sense, to deserve good from those to whom he does or has done good, and evil from those to whom he does or has done evil. The precept of returning good for evil has never been regarded as a case of the fulfilment of justice, but as one in which the claims of justice are waived, in obedience to other considerations.

Fourthly, It is confessedly unjust to *break faith* with any one; to violate an engagement, either express or implied; or disappoint expectations raised by our own conduct, at least if we have raised those expectations knowingly and voluntarily. Like the other obligations of justice already spoken of, this one is not regarded as absolute, but as capable of being overruled by a stronger obligation of justice on the other side, or by such conduct on the part of the person concerned as is deemed to absolve us from our obligation to him, and to constitute a *forfeiture* of the benefit which he has been led to expect.

Fifthly, It is, by universal admission, inconsistent with justice to be *partial;* to show favor or preference to one person over another in matters to which favor and preference do not properly apply. Impartiality, however, does not seem to be regarded as a duty in itself, but rather as instrumental to some other duty; for it is admitted that favor and preference are not always censurable, and indeed the cases in which they are condemned are rather the exception than the rule. A person would be more likely to be blamed than applauded for giving his family or friends no superiority in good offices over strangers, when he could do so without violating any other duty; and no one thinks it unjust to seek one person in preference to another as a friend, connection, or companion. Impartiality, where rights are concerned, is of course obligatory; but this is involved in the more general obligation of giving to every one his right. A tribunal, for example, must be impartial, because it is bound to award, without regard to any other consideration, a disputed object to the one of two parties who has the right to it. There are other cases in which impartiality means, being solely influenced by desert; as with those who, in the capacity of judges, preceptors, or parents, administer reward and punishment as such. There are cases, again, in which it means being solely influenced by consideration for the public interest; as in making a selection among candidates for a government employment. Impartiality, in short, as an obligation of justice, may be said to mean being exclusively influenced by the considerations which it is supposed ought to influence the particular case in hand, and resisting the solicitation of any motives which prompt to conduct different from what those considerations would dictate.

Nearly allied to the idea of impartiality is that of *equality;* which often enters as a component part both into the conception of justice and into the practice of it, and, in the eyes of many persons, constitutes its essence. But, in this still more than in any other case, the notion of justice varies in different persons, and always conforms in its variations to their notion of utility. Each person maintains that equality is the dictate of justice, except where he thinks that expediency requires inequality. The justice of giving equal protection to the rights of all is maintained by those who support the most outrageous inequality in the rights themselves. Even in slave countries, it is theoretically admitted that the rights of the slave, such as they are, ought to be as sacred as those of the master, and that a tribunal which fails to enforce them with equal strictness is wanting in justice; while, at the same time, institutions which leave to the slave scarcely any rights to enforce are not deemed unjust, because they are not deemed inexpedient. Those who think that utility requires distinctions of rank do not consider it unjust that riches and social privileges should be unequally dispensed; but those who think this inequality inexpedient think it unjust also. Whoever thinks that government is necessary sees no injustice in as much inequality as is constituted by giving to the magistrate powers not granted to other people. Even among those who hold levelling doctrines, there are as many questions of justice as there are differences of opinion about expediency. Some Communists consider it unjust that the produce of the labor of the community should be shared on any other principle than that of exact equality; others think it just that those should receive most whose wants are greatest; while others hold that those who work harder, or who produce more, or whose services are more valuable to the community, may justly claim a larger quota in the division of the produce. And the sense of natural justice may be plausibly appealed to in behalf of every one of these opinions.

Mill then goes on to define a **right**:

When we call any thing a person's right, we mean that he has a valid claim on society to protect him in the possession of it, either by the force of law, or by that of education and opinion. If he has what we consider a sufficient claim, on whatever account, to have something guaranteed to him by society, we say that he has a right to it. If we desire to prove that any thing does not belong to him by right, we think this done as soon as it is admitted that society ought not to take measures for securing it to him, but should leave him to chance, or to his own exertions. Thus a person is said to have a right to what he can earn in fair professional competition, because society ought not to allow any other person to hinder him from endeavoring to earn in that manner as much as he can. But he has not a right to three hundred a year, though he may happen to be earning it, because society is not called on to provide that he shall earn that sum. On the contrary, if he owns ten thousand pounds three-per-cent stock, he *has* a right to three hundred a year, because society has come under an obligation to provide him with an income of that amount.

To have a right, then, is, I conceive, to have something which society ought to defend me in the possession of. If the objector goes on to ask why it ought, I can give him no other reason than general utility. If that expression does not seem to convey a sufficient feeling of the strength of the obligation, nor to account for the peculiar energy of the feeling, it is because there goes to the composition of the sentiment, not a rational only, but also an animal element—the thirst for retaliation; and this thirst derives its intensity, as well as its moral justification, from the extraordinarily important and impressive kind of utility which is concerned. The interest involved is that of security; to every one's feelings, the most vital of all interests. All other earthly benefits are needed by one person, not needed by another; and many of them can, if necessary, be cheerfully foregone, or replaced by something else. But security no human being can possibly do without: on it we depend for all our immunity from evil, and for the whole value of all and every good, beyond the passing moment; since nothing but the gratification of the instant could be of any worth to us if we could

"When we call any thing a person's right, we mean that he has a valid claim on society to protect him in the possession of it, either by the force of law, or by that of education and opinion."

– JOHN STUART MILL

be deprived of everything the next instant by whoever was momentarily stronger than ourselves. Now, this most indispensable of all necessaries, after physical nutriment, cannot be had, unless the machinery for providing it is kept unintermittedly in active play. Our notion, therefore, of the claim we have on our fellow-creatures to join in making safe for us the very groundwork of our existence, gathers feelings around it so much more intense than those concerned in any of the more common cases of utility, that the difference in degree (as is often the case in psychology) becomes a real difference in kind. The claim assumes that character of absoluteness, that apparent infinity, and incommensurability with all other considerations, which constitute the distinction between the feeling of right and wrong and that of ordinary expediency and inexpediency. The feelings concerned are so powerful, and we count so positively on finding a responsive feeling in others (all being alike interested), that *ought* and *should* grow into *must*, and recognized indispensability becomes a moral necessity, analogous to physical, and often not inferior to it in binding force.

Mill's utilitarian theory of justice is a logical extension of his ethical theories: What is good and desirable is what is best for the greatest number of people. But although it may at first seem as if the greatest happiness of the greatest number leaves no room for such abstract concerns as justice, Mill argues that, to the contrary, only the principle of utility can give that abstract sense of justice some concrete basis in human life.

The problem with the utilitarian theory of justice is identical to the problem that we saw with the utilitarian theory of morals. Could there not be a case in which the public interest and general utility would be served only at the clearly unjust expense of a single unfortunate individual? Suppose we lived in a society that ran extremely well, such that we had few, if any, complaints about our government and the way it was run, when a single muckraking journalist started turning the peace upside down with his insistence that something was very wrong in the government. We might easily suppose that, at least in the short run, the public confusion and trauma would be much more harmful to the public interest than the slight correction the muckraker might accomplish by publically exposing corrupt politicians. Should the government forcefully silence the journalist? We would say no. He has a right to his inquiries and a right to speak his mind. Or suppose that the most efficient way to solve a series of ongoing crimes was to torture a recently captured suspect and hold him without evidence? Here, again, public interest and justice are at odds. Or more generally, should the government have the authority to throw people in jail just because it has reason (even good reason) to believe that they will create a public disturbance or commit certain crimes? Public interest says yes; justice says no.

This is the problem with utilitarian theories of justice in general: although we may well agree that justice *ought* to serve the public interest and every individual's interests as well, the utilitarian view is always in an awkward position when serving the public interest would come at the intolerable expense of injustice toward a small number of individuals or even

FIG. 8.6 Justice, according to Mill, is of fundamental importance to utilitarians because it deals with our security, one of our most basic needs. (© iStockphoto.com/Stephen Morris)

a single individual. Consider the extreme example of an entire city that would prosper if it would sacrifice the life of one innocent child. Arguably, utilitarianism would seem to defend the sacrifice; justice, however, says that such a sacrifice is inexcusable.

- In what important respect do modern conceptions of justice differ from those of the ancients?
- How are interests and rights important considerations for justice?
- Can justice demand that we break a law? How does Mill argue this point? Can you think of an example in which breaking the law would be the just thing to do? How so?
- How does Mill define a right? Does his definition agree with our general understanding of rights? Is utilitarianism compatible with rights? (Bentham did not think so.) Why might they be incompatible?

D. The Social Contract

The single most influential conception of justice in modern times has been called the "social contract theory." The **social contract** is an agreement among people to share certain interests and make certain compromises for the good of them all. It is a "consent of the governed" theory. In one form or another, it existed even in ancient times. For example, read Socrates' argument in the *Crito*, in which he says that by staying in Athens, he had implicitly agreed to abide by its laws, even when those laws unfairly condemned him to death.

What is most important in understanding the nature of this social contract is that, as Socrates' argument makes clear, there need not have been any actual, physical contract or even oral agreement. We are bound by a social contract, even if we never signed or saw such a contract. Moreover, it may not be the case that there was ever such a contract, even in past history. It happens that Americans are among the few people in the world whose state was actually formed explicitly by such a contract, namely, our Constitution. But the actual existence of such a piece of paper is not necessary for the existence of a social contract. Simply to live in a society, according to these philosophers, is to have accepted, at least implicitly, the terms of such an agreement. (Thus, living in a society, you are expected to obey its laws. "Ignorance is no excuse," and you cannot get out of an arrest by saying "I don't really live here," much less "I don't recognize your right to arrest me.")

Two different pictures of the original social contract are presented by the English philosopher Thomas Hobbes and the French-Swiss philosopher Jean-Jacques Rousseau. Both begin by considering man in "the state of nature," without laws and without society, before men and women came together to accept the social contract. Hobbes bases his conception of the social contract on an extremely unfavorable conception of human nature. He attacks the idealistic political philosophies of Plato and Aristotle for being unrealistic and assuming wrongly that people are naturally capable of virtue and wisdom. Hobbes considers himself a "realist," and like most self-avowed realists, he focuses on the nasty side of things. According to his theory of human nature, natural man is a selfish beast, fighting for his own interests against everyone else. In the natural state human life is a "war of all against all," and a person's life, consequently, is "nasty, brutish and short." Hobbes dismisses the view that people are fundamentally rational, and his sense of human nature emphasizes the passions, particularly the passion for self-preservation. The social contract, accordingly, is mainly an agreement among equally selfish and self-seeking persons not to commit mutual murder.

 FROM *Leviathan*
BY **Thomas Hobbes**[6]

OF THE NATURAL CONDITION OF MANKIND AS CONCERNING THEIR FELICITY, AND MISERY

Men by nature equal. Nature hath made men so equal, in the faculties of the body, and mind; as that though there be found one man sometimes manifestly stronger in body, or of quicker mind than another; yet when all is reckoned together, the difference between man, and man, is not so considerable, as that one man can thereupon claim to himself any benefit, to which another may not pretend, as well as he. For as to the strength of the body, the weakest has strength enough to kill the strongest, either by secret machination or by confederacy with others, that are in the same danger with himself.

· · ·

For such is the nature of men, that howsoever they may acknowledge many others to be more witty, or more eloquent, or more learned; yet they will hardly believe there be many so wise as themselves; for they see their own wit at hand, and other men's at a distance. But this proveth rather that men are in that point equal, than unequal. For there is not ordinarily a greater sign of the equal distribution of any thing, than that every man is contented with his share.

From equality proceeds diffidence. From this equality of ability, ariseth equality of hope in the attaining of our ends. And therefore if any two men desire the same thing, which nevertheless they cannot both enjoy, they become enemies; and in the way to their end, which is principally their own conservation, and sometimes their delectation only, endeavour to destroy, or subdue one another. And from hence it comes to pass, that where an invader hath no more to fear, than another man's single power; if one plant, sow, build, or possess a convenient seat, others may probably be expected to come prepared with forces united, to dispossess, and deprive him, not only of the fruit of his labour, but also of his life, or liberty. And the invader again is in the like danger of another.

From diffidence war. And from this diffidence of one another, there is no way for any man to secure himself, so reasonable, as anticipation; that is, by force, or wiles, to master the persons of all men he can, so long, till he see no other power great enough to endanger him: and this is no more than his own conservation requireth, and is generally allowed. Also because there be some, that taking pleasure in contemplating their own power in the acts of conquest, which they pursue farther than their security requires; if others, that otherwise would be glad to be at ease within modest bounds, should not by invasion increase their power, they would not be able, long time, by standing only on their defence, to subsist. And by consequence, such augmentation of dominion over men being necessary to a man's conservation, it ought to be allowed him.

Again, men have no pleasure, but on the contrary a great deal of grief, in keeping company, where there is no power able to over-awe them all. For every man looketh that his companion should value him, at the same rate he sets upon himself: and upon all signs of contempt, or undervaluing, naturally endeavors, as far as he dares (which amongst them that have no common power to keep them in quiet, is far enough

"If any two men desire the same thing, which nevertheless they cannot both enjoy, they become enemies; and in the way to their end, which is principally their own conservation, and sometimes their delectation only, endeavour to destroy, or subdue one another."

– THOMAS HOBBES

---

6 Thomas Hobbes, *Leviathan* (New York: Hafner, 1926).

FIG. 8.7 Without organized society, says Hobbes, human life would be a war of all against all. *(© iStockphoto.com/TZU-LAN HSIEH)*

to make them destroy each other), to extort a greater value from his contemners, by damage; and from others, by the example.

So that in the nature of man, we find three principal causes of quarrel. First, competition; secondly, diffidence; thirdly, glory.

The first, maketh men invade for gain; the second, for safety; and the third, for reputation. The first use violence, to make themselves masters of other men's persons, wives, children, and cattle; the second, to defend them; the third, for trifles, as a word, a smile, a different opinion, and any other sign of undervalue, either direct in their persons, or by reflection in their kindred, their friends, their nation, their profession, or their name.

Out of civil states, there is always war of every one against every one. Hereby it is manifest, that during the time men live without a common power to keep them all in awe, they are in that condition which is called war; and such a war, as is of every man, against every man. For war, consisteth not in battle only, or the act of fighting, but in a tract of time, wherein the will to contend by battle is sufficiently known.

· · ·

The incommodities of such a war. Whatsoever therefore is consequent to a time of war, where every man is enemy to every man; the same is consequent to the time, wherein men live without other security, than what their own strength, and their own invention shall furnish them withal. In such condition, there is no place for industry; because the fruit thereof is uncertain: and consequently no culture of the earth; no navigation, nor use of the commodities that may be imported by sea; no commodious building; no instruments of moving, and removing, such things as require much force; no knowledge of the face of the earth; no account of time; no arts; no letters; no society; and which is worst of all, continual fear, and danger of violent death; and the life of man, solitary, poor, nasty, brutish, and short.

It may seem strange to some man, that has not well weighed these things; that nature should thus dissociate, and render men apt to invade, and destroy one another: and he may therefore, not trusting to this inference, made from the passions, desire perhaps to have the same confirmed by experience. Let him therefore consider with himself, when taking a journey, he arms himself, and seeks to go well accompanied; when going to sleep, he locks his doors; when even in his house he locks his chests; and this when he knows there be laws, and public officers, armed to revenge all injuries shall be done him; what opinion he has of his fellow-subjects, when he rides armed; of his fellow citizens, when he locks his doors; and of his children, and servants, when he locks his chests. Does he not there as much accuse mankind by his actions, as I do by my words? But neither of us accuse men's nature in it. The desires, and other passions of man, are in themselves no sin. No more are the actions, that proceed from those passions, till they know a law that forbids them: which till laws be made they cannot know: nor can any law be made, till they have agreed upon the person that shall make it.

It may peradventure be thought, there was never such a time, nor condition of war as this; and I believe it was never generally so, over all the world: but there are many places, where they live so now. For the savage people in many places of America, except the government of small families, the concord whereof dependeth on natural lust, have no government at all; and live at this day in that brutish manner, as I said before. Howsoever, it may be perceived what manner of life there would be, where there were no common power to fear, by the manner of life, which men that have formerly lived under a peaceful government, use to degenerate into, in a civil war.

OF THE FIRST AND SECOND NATURAL LAWS, AND OF CONTRACTS

Right of nature what. The right of nature, which writers commonly call *jus naturale*, is the liberty each man hath, to use his own power, as he will himself, for the preservation of his own nature; that is to say, of his own life; and consequently, of doing any thing, which in his own judgment, and reason, he shall conceive to be the aptest means thereunto.

Liberty what. By liberty, is understood, according to the proper signification of the word, the absence of external impediments: which impediments, may oft take away part of a man's power to do what he would; but cannot hinder him from using the power left him, according as his judgment, and reason shall dictate to him.

A law of nature what. A law of nature, *lex naturalis*, is a precept or general rule, found out by reason, by which a man is forbidden to do that, which is destructive of his life, or taketh away the means of preserving the same; and to omit that, by which he thinketh it may be best preserved.

Difference of right and law. For though they that speak of this subject, use to confound *jus*, and *lex*, *right* and *law:* yet they ought to be distinguished; because right, consisteth in liberty to do, or to forbear: whereas law, determineth, and bindeth to one of them: so that law, and right, differ as much, as obligation, and liberty; which in one and the same matter are inconsistent.

Naturally every man has right to every thing. And because the condition of man, as hath been declared in the precedent chapter, is a condition of war of every one against every one; in which case every one is governed by his own reason; and there is nothing he can make use of, that may not be of help unto him, in preserving his life against his enemies; it followeth, that in such a condition, every man has a right to every thing; even to one another's body. And therefore, as long as this natural right of every man to every thing endureth, there can be no security to any man, how strong or wise soever he be, of living out the time, which nature ordinarily alloweth men to live.

The fundamental law of nature. And consequently it is a precept, or general rule of reason, *that every man, ought to endeavour peace, as far as he has hope of obtaining it; and when he cannot obtain it, that he may seek, and use, all helps, and advantages of war.*

· · ·

The second law of nature. From this fundamental law of nature, by which men are commanded to endeavour peace, is derived this second law; *that a man be willing, when others are so too, as far-forth, as for peace, and defence of himself he shall think it necessary, to lay down this right to all things; and be contented with so much liberty against other men, as he would allow other men against himself.* For as long as every man holdeth this right, of doing any thing he liketh; so long are all men in the condition of war. But if other men will not lay down their right, as well as he; then there is no reason for any one, to divest himself of his: for that were to expose himself to prey, which no man is bound to, rather than to dispose himself to peace. This is that law of the Gospel; *whatsoever you require that others should do to you, that do ye to them.*

. . .

What it is to lay down a right. To *lay down* man's *right to* any thing, is to *divest* himself of the *liberty*, of hindering another of the benefit of his own right to the same. For he that renounceth, or passeth away his right, giveth not to any other man a right which he had not before; because there is nothing to which every man had not right by nature: but only standeth out of his way, that he may enjoy his own original right, without hindrance from him; not without hindrance from another. So that the effect which redoundeth to one man, by another man's defect of right, is but so much diminution of impediments to the use of his own right original.

. . .

Not all rights are alienable. Whensoever a man transferreth his right, or renounceth it; it is either in consideration of some right reciprocally transferred to himself; or for some other good he hopeth for thereby. For it is a voluntary act: and of the voluntary acts of every man, the object is some *good to himself.* And therefore there be some rights, which no man can be understood by any words, or other signs, to have abandoned, or transferred. As first a man cannot lay down the right of resisting them, that assault him by force, to take away his life; because he cannot be understood to aim thereby, at any good to himself. The same may be said of wounds, and chains, and imprisonment; both because there is no benefit consequent to such patience; as there is to the patience of suffering another to be wounded, or imprisoned: as also because a man cannot tell, when he seeth men proceed against him by violence, whether they intend his death or not. And lastly the motive, and end for which this renouncing, and transferring of right is introduced, is nothing else but the security of man's person, in his life, and in the means of so preserving life, as not to be weary of it. And therefore if a man by words, or other signs, seem to despoil himself of the end, for which those signs were intended; he is not to be understood as if he meant it, or that it was his will; but that he was ignorant of how such words and actions were to be interpreted.

Contract what. The mutual transferring of right, as that which men call CONTRACT.

. . .

Covenants of mutual trust, when invalid. If a covenant be made, wherein neither of the parties perform presently, but trust one another;

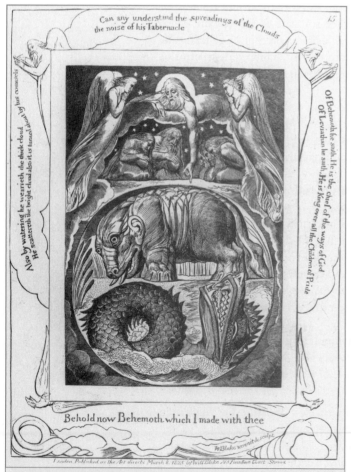

FIG. 8.8 William Blake's engraving of Behemoth and Leviathan. *(Tate, London / Art Resource, NY)*

in the condition of mere nature, which is a condition of war of every man against every man, upon any reasonable suspicion, it is void: but if there be a common power set over them both, with right and force sufficient to compel performance, it is not void. For he that performeth first, has no assurance the other will perform after; because the bonds of words are too weak to bridle men's ambition, avarice, anger, and other passions, without the fear of some coercive power; which in the condition of mere nature, where all men are equal, and judges of the justness of their own fears, cannot possibly be supposed. And therefore he which performeth first, does but betray himself to his enemy; contrary to the right, he can never abandon, of defending his life, and means of living.

But in a civil estate, where there is a power set up to constrain those that would otherwise violate their faith, that fear is no more reasonable; and for that cause, he which by the covenant is to perform first, is obliged so to do.

The cause of fear, which maketh such a covenant invalid, must be always something arising after the covenant made; as some new fact, or other sign of the will not to perform: else it cannot make the covenant void. For that which could not hinder a man from promising, ought not to be admitted as a hindrance of performing.

Right to the end, containeth right to the means. He that transferreth any right, transferreth the means of enjoying it, as far as lieth in his power. As he that selleth land, is understood to transfer the herbage, and whatsoever grows upon it: nor can he that sells a mill turn away the stream that drives it. And they that give to a man the right of government in sovereignty, are understood to give him the right of levying money to maintain soldiers; and of appointing magistrates for the administration of justice.

Hobbes begins his argument with the perhaps surprising observation that people are basically equal in nature. He is not talking here about legal equality or equal rights (for there are no laws and no legal rights), but rather equality in abilities, talents, and power. This observation seems strange because in considering the issue of equality, we usually pay attention to the great differences between people. Instead Hobbes points out our similarities. In particular, he points out that almost everyone is strong and smart enough to kill or inflict grievous injury on others. Even a puny, intellectually challenged individual can, with a knife or a handgun, kill the strongest and smartest person on earth. Accordingly, the basis of the social contract (or "covenant"), according to Hobbes, is our mutual protection. Everyone agrees not to kill other people and in return is guaranteed that he or she will not be killed. Although Hobbes has a cynical view of human nature, his analysis continues to be one of the most powerful arguments for strong governments. (Hobbes himself was a conservative monarchist.)

Rousseau, quite to the contrary, had an extremely optimistic view of human nature, as we showed in the preceding chapter. He believed that people are "naturally good," and it is only the corruptions of society that makes them selfish and destructive. Rousseau does not take the social contract, therefore, to be simply a doctrine of protection between mutually brutish individuals. The function of the political state is rather to allow people to develop the "natural goodness" that they had in the absence of any state at all. This is not to say (although he is often interpreted this way) that Rousseau was nostalgic and wanted to "go back to the state of nature." (It is not even clear that Rousseau believed that there ever was a "state of nature" as such. His example, like Hobbes's, is a way of conveying a picture of "human nature," whether or not it is historically accurate.) We are already in society; that is a given fact. Rousseau's aim is to develop a conception of the state that will allow us to live

"If a covenant be made, wherein neither of the parties perform presently, but trust one another; in the condition of mere nature, which is a condition of war of every man against every man, upon any reasonable suspicion, it is void: but if there be a common power set over them both, with right and force sufficient to compel performance, it is not void."

– THOMAS HOBBES

as morally as possible. This is important, for Rousseau, unlike most social contract theorists, is not a utilitarian. It is not happiness that is most important, but goodness. (Hobbes, by way of contrast, took utility, pleasure and well-being, in addition to self-preservation, to be the purpose of the social contract.)

Rousseau's ambition, therefore, is not to "get us back to nature" but rather to revise our conception of the state. His blueprint for this "revision," however, is one of the most radical documents in modern history and has rightly been cited as one of the causes of both the American and French revolutions. Rousseau's main thesis is inherited from Locke: The state has legitimate power only as long as it serves the people it governs. The revolutionary corollary is that when a state ceases to serve its citizens, the citizens have a right to overthrow that government. This was a radical claim. Even Rousseau was not comfortable with it. (Locke had made his statement to this effect *after* the English Revolution.) Rousseau called revolution "the most horrible alternative," to be avoided wherever possible. But subsequent French history took his theories quite literally. It also demonstrated the "horror" that may follow too radical and abrupt a change in the authority that citizens accept as legitimate.

In earlier works, Rousseau argued his famous thesis that "natural man" is "naturally good" and that contemporary society has corrupted him (and her). He went on to say that competition and the artificiality of our lust for private property are responsible for this corruption. He even included marriage and romantic love as forms of this "lust for private property." In the state of nature, he suggested, people mated when they felt like it, with whomever they felt like, and duels fought between rivals were unheard of. Rousseau does not suggest that we return to prehistoric customs, but he does use his account of them as a wedge to pry open even the most sacred of our modern civil institutions. All these institutions, he argues, must be reexamined, and the tool for that reexamination is the social contract.

The key, as Rousseau argues in his most famous book, appropriately called *The Social Contract*, is that man must regain his freedom within society. This does not mean, however, that a person can do whatever he or she would like to do. Quite the contrary—to be a citizen, according to Rousseau, is to want and do what is good for the society as well. Being free, in fact, means wanting to do what is good for society. In one of the most problematic statements of the social contract, Rousseau says that a person who does not act for the good of the society may have to "be forced to be free." Here we see a strange paradox. On the one hand, Rousseau has properly been regarded as the father of the most liberal and revolutionary political theories of our time. (Marx, for example, claims a great debt to Rousseau.) Rousseau's political philosophy stresses individual freedom and rights above all, even above the state itself. But another side to Rousseau emerges in his paradoxical phrase about forcing freedom. His stress on the subservience of the individual to the state, which is an entity in itself ("the **sovereign**," presumably the king, but essentially

FIG. 8.9 The title page from Thomas Hobbes's *Leviathan* depicted the sovereign as ruling over all. *(HIP / Art Resource, NY)*

any government), has also caused him to be labeled as an authoritarian and the forerunner of totalitarian and fascist governments.

This paradox is not easily resolved, but we can at least explain how it comes about. Rousseau believes that the state is subject to and receives its **legitimacy** from the people it governs. But this does not mean that the individual person necessarily has any real power in determining the form or functions of government. Rousseau is not a democrat. What he says instead is that the state is subject to what he calls the general will, and this is not simply a collection of individuals but something more. We talk about "the spirit of the revolution" or "the discontent of the working class," but these are not simply the sum of every individual person's spirit or discontent. The revolution may have spirit even though some participants do not; indeed, some may even dislike the whole idea.

Here is the source of the paradox: Legitimacy is given to the state by the general will, not by every individual person. The person who does not agree with the general will, therefore, may very well find himself or herself coerced into compliance with the state ("forced to be free"). How much force should be used, however, is a matter about which Rousseau is not very clear; nor have his many followers agreed on that crucial point. On one extreme, Rousseau's authoritarian followers have insisted that all dissent from the general will must be stifled. On the other extreme, Rousseau's most libertarian and anarchist followers have insisted that the individual's rights to be free from government intervention and to live according to his or her own "natural goodness" outweigh any claims that the state may have. What follows are a few selections from *The Social Contract*, beginning with one of Rousseau's best-known slogans.

FROM *The Social Contract* BY **Jean-Jacques Rousseau**[7]

Man is born free; and everywhere he is in chains. One thinks himself the master of others, and still remains a greater slave than they. How did this change come about? I do not know. What can make it legitimate? That question I think I can answer.

If I took into account only force, and the effects derived from it, I should say: "As long as a people is compelled to obey, and obeys, it does well; as soon as it can shake off the yoke, and shakes it off, it does still better; for, regaining its liberty by the same right as took it away, either it is justified in resuming it, or there was no justification for those who took it away." But the social order is a sacred right which is the basis of all other rights. Nevertheless, this right does not come from nature, and must therefore be founded on conventions. Before coming to that, I have to prove what I have just asserted.

THE FIRST SOCIETIES

The most ancient of all societies, and the only one that is natural, is the family: and even so the children remain attached to the father only so long as they need him for their preservation. As soon as this need ceases, the natural bond is dissolved. The children, released from the obedience

FIG. 8.10 (© iStockphoto.com/Royce DeGrie)

[7] Jean-Jacques Rousseau, *The Social Contract and Discourses*, trans. G. D. H. Cole, J. M. Dent, Ltd., 1947. Reprinted by permission of Everyman's Library, an imprint of Alfred A. Knopf.

they owed to the father, and the father, released from the care he owed his children, return equally to independence. If they remain united, they continue so no longer naturally, but voluntarily; and the family itself is then maintained only by convention.

This common liberty results from the nature of man. His first law is to provide for his own preservation, his first cares are those which he owes to himself; and, as soon as he reaches years of discretion, he is the sole judge of the proper means of preserving himself, and consequently becomes his own master.

The family then may be called the first model of political societies; the ruler corresponds to the father, and the people to the children; and all, being born free and equal, alienate their liberty only for their own advantage. The whole difference is that, in the family, the love of the father for his children repays him for the care he takes of them, while, in the State, the pleasure of commanding takes the place of the love which the chief cannot have for the peoples under him.

. . .

THE SOCIAL CONTRACT

I suppose men to have reached the point at which the obstacles in the way of their preservation in the state of nature show their power of resistance to be greater than the resources at the disposal of each individual for his maintenance in that state. That primitive condition can then subsist no longer; and the human race would perish unless it changed its manner of existence.

But, as men cannot engender new forces, but only unite and direct existing ones, they have no other means of preserving themselves than the formation, by aggregation, of a sum of forces great enough to overcome the resistance. These they have to bring into play by means of a single motive power, and cause to act in concert.

This sum of forces can arise only where several persons come together: but, as the force and liberty of each man are the chief instruments of his self-preservation, how can he pledge them without harming his own interests, and neglecting the care he owes to himself? This difficulty, in its bearing on my present subject, may be stated in the following terms:

"The problem is to find a form of association which will defend and protect with the whole common force the person and goods of each associate, and in which each, while uniting himself with all, may still obey himself alone, and remain as free as before." This is the fundamental problem of which the *Social Contract* provides the solution.

The clauses of this contract are so determined by the nature of the act that the slightest modification would make them vain and ineffective; so that, although they have perhaps never been formally set forth, they are everywhere the same and everywhere tacitly admitted and recognized, until, on the violation of the social compact, each regains his original rights and resumes his natural liberty, while losing the conventional liberty in favour of which he renounced it.

These clauses, properly understood, may be reduced to one—the total alienation of each associate, together with all his rights, to the whole community; for,

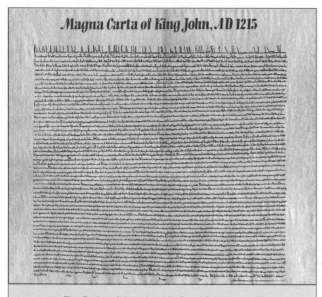

FIG. 8.11 The first social contract in Great Britain was the Magna Carta, which extended rights to citizens and set limits on the rights of the king. (© iStockphoto.com/Roel Smart)

in the first place, as each gives himself absolutely, the conditions are the same for all; and, this being so, no one has any interest in making them burdensome to others.

Moreover, the alienation being without reserve, the union is as perfect as it can be, and no associate has anything more to demand: for, if the individuals retained certain rights, as there would be no common superior to decide between them and the public, each, being on one point his own judge, would ask to be so on all; the state of nature would thus continue, and the association would necessarily become inoperative or tyrannical.

Finally, each man, in giving himself to all, gives himself to nobody; and as there is no associate over which he does not acquire the same right as he yields others over himself, he gains an equivalent for everything he loses, and an increase of force for the preservation of what he has.

If then we discard from the social contract what is not of its essence, we shall find that it reduces itself to the following terms:

"Each of us puts his person and all his power in common under the supreme direction of the general will, and, in our corporate capacity, we receive each member as an indivisible part of the whole."

At once, in place of the individual personality of each contracting party, this act of association creates a moral and collective body, composed of as many members as the assembly contains voters, and receiving from this act its unity, its common identity, its life, and its will. This public person, so formed by the union of all other persons, formerly took the name of *city*, and now takes that of *Republic* or *body* politic; it is called by its members *State* when passive, *Sovereign* when active, and *Power* when compared with others like itself. Those who are associated in it take collectively the name of *people*, and severally are called *citizens*, as sharing in the sovereign power, and *subjects*, as being under the laws of the State. But these terms are often confused and take one for another: it is enough to know how to distinguish them when they are being used with precision.

THE SOVEREIGN

This formula shows us that the act of association comprises a mutual understanding between the public and the individuals, and that each individual, in making a contract, as we may say, with himself, is bound in a double capacity; as a member of the Sovereign he is bound to the individuals, and as a member of the State to the Sovereign. But the maxim of civil right, that no one is bound by undertakings made to himself, does not apply in this case; for there is a great difference between incurring an obligation to yourself and incurring one to a whole of which you form a part.

Attention must further be called to the fact that public deliberation, while competent to bind all the subjects to the Sovereign, because of the two different capacities in which each of them may be regarded, cannot, for the opposite reason, bind that Sovereign to itself; and that it is consequently against the nature of the body politic for the Sovereign to impose on itself a law which it cannot infringe. Being able to regard itself in only one capacity, it is in the position of an individual who makes a contract with himself; and this makes it clear that there neither is nor can be any kind of fundamental law binding on the body of the people—not even the social contract itself. This does not mean that the body politic cannot enter into undertakings with others, provided the contract is not infringed by them; for in relation to what is external to it, it becomes a simple being, an individual.

"[E]ach individual, in making a contract, as we may say, with himself, is bound in a double capacity; as a member of the Sovereign he is bound to the individuals, and as a member of the State to the Sovereign."

— JEAN-JACQUES ROUSSEAU

But the body politic or the Sovereign, drawing its being wholly from the sanctity of the contract, can never bind itself, even to an outsider, to do anything derogatory to the original act, for instance, to alienate any part of itself, or to submit to another Sovereign. Violation of the act by which it exists would be self-annihilation; and that which is itself nothing can create nothing.

As soon as this multitude is so united in one body, it is impossible to offend against one of the members without attacking the body, and still more to offend against the body without the members resenting it. Duty and interest therefore equally oblige the two contracting parties to give each other help; and the same men should seek to combine, in their double capacity, all the advantages dependent upon that capacity.

Again, the Sovereign, being formed wholly of the individuals who compose it, neither has nor can have any interest contrary to theirs; and consequently the sovereign power need give no guarantee to its subjects, because it is impossible for the body to wish to hurt all its members.

. . .

In fact, each individual, as a man, may have a particular will contrary or dissimilar to the general will which he has as a citizen. His particular interest may speak to him quite differently from the common interest: his absolute and naturally independent existence may make him look upon what he owes to the common cause as a gratuitous contribution, the loss of which will do less harm to others than the payment of it is burdensome to himself; and, regarding the moral person which constitutes the State as a *persona ficta*, because not a man, he may wish to enjoy the rights of citizenship without being ready to fulfil the duties of a subject. The continuance of such an injustice could not but prove the undoing of the body politic.

In order then that the social compact may not be an empty formula, it tacitly includes the undertaking, which alone can give force to the rest, that whoever refuses to obey the general will shall be compelled to do so by the whole body. This means nothing less than that he will be forced to be free; for this is the condition which, by giving each citizen to his country, secures him against all personal dependence. In this lies the key to the working of the political machine; this alone legitimizes civil undertakings, which, without it, would be absurd, tyrannical, and liable to the most frightful abuses.

THE CIVIL STATE

The passage from the state of nature to the civil state produces a very remarkable change in man, by substituting justice for instinct in his conduct, and giving his actions the morality they had formerly lacked. Then only, when the voice of duty takes the place of physical impulses and right of appetite, does man, who so far had considered only himself, find that he is forced to act on different principles, and to consult his reason before listening to his inclinations. Although, in this state, he deprives himself of some advantages which he got from nature, he gains in return others so great, his faculties are so stimulated and developed, his ideas so extended, his feelings so ennobled, and his whole soul so uplifted, that, did not the abuses of this new condition often degrade him below that which he left, he would be bound to bless continually the happy moment which took him from it for ever, and, instead of a stupid and unimaginative animal, made him an intelligent being and a man.

Let us draw up the whole account in terms easily commensurable. What man loses by the social contract is his natural liberty and an unlimited right to everything he tries to get and succeeds in getting; what he gains is civil liberty and the proprietorship of all he possesses. If we are to avoid mistake in weighing one against the other, we must clearly distinguish natural liberty, which is bounded only by the strength of the individual, from civil liberty, which is limited by the general will; and possession, which is merely the effect of force or the right of the first occupier, from property, which can be founded only on a positive title.

We might, over and above all this, add, to what man acquires in the civil state, moral liberty, which alone makes him truly master of himself; for the mere impulse of appetite is slavery, while obedience to a law which we prescribe to ourselves is liberty.

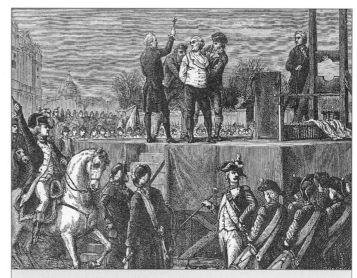

FIG. 8.12 Rousseau's ideas and other social contract theories inspired the French Revolution and the overturning of monarchies throughout Europe. (© iStockphoto.com/HultonArchive)

Although Rousseau shares with Hobbes a belief in the social contract theory, the differences between them could not be more striking. Where Hobbes begins with a brutal view of human nature forced into agreement by fear of mutual violence, Rousseau begins by saying that "man is born free." For Rousseau, the social contract is not an instrument of mutual protection but a means of improving people and bringing out what is best in them. His central theme is not our mutual antagonism, but humanity's "natural goodness." With unmistakable clarity, Rousseau rejects all might-makes-right theories and insists that legitimacy must always be a matter of the consent of the governed. "The general will" is not a general compromise but the creation of a new power, the power of the people, which for Rousseau is the ultimate voice of authority.

The most famous example of social contract theory at work is our own Declaration of Independence. In that document, social contract theory combined with a theory of "natural" ("unalienable") rights to provide an epoch-making announcement of the right of a people to overthrow an established government:

 FROM **The Declaration of Independence** BY **Thomas Jefferson** et al.

We hold these Truths to be self-evident, that all Men are created equal, that they are endowed by their Creator with certain unalienable Rights, that among these are Life, Liberty, and the pursuit of Happiness—That to secure these rights, Governments are instituted among Men, deriving their just Powers from the Consent of the Governed, that whenever any Form of Government becomes destructive of these Ends, it is the Right of the People to alter or to abolish it, and to institute new Government, laying its Foundation on such Principles, and organizing its Powers in such Form, as to them shall seem most likely to effect their Safety and Happiness. Prudence, indeed, will indicate that Governments long established should not be changed for light and transient causes; and accordingly all Experience hath shewn, that Mankind are more disposed to suffer, while Evils are sufferable, than to right themselves by abolishing the Forms to which they are accustomed. But when a long Train of Abuses and Usurpations, pursuing invariably the same Object, evinces a Design to reduce them under absolute Despotism, it is their Right, it is their Duty, to throw off such Government, and to provide new Guards for their future Security.

- What is a social contract? Does it matter whether there is an actual meeting or agreement? To what extent is our own society or government based on a social contract?
- What is meant by the "state of nature"? Given that the state of nature does not describe an actual historical state of affairs, what purpose does referring to the state of nature serve?
- What does Hobbes mean when he claims that equality is a "natural fact"? How are we naturally equal?
- How does Hobbes describe human nature? How does his view differ from Plato's, Aristotle's, and Rousseau's views of human nature?
- Does the social contract function differently in Hobbes's view as compared with Rousseau's?
- What does it mean to be free, according to Rousseau? What is the difference between natural liberty and civil liberty? What kind of freedom does civil liberty involve?

E. Fairness and Entitlement

Because of increased sensitivity to the unacceptability of scenarios in which the good of individuals is sacrificed to the general will, a very different conception of justice has once again begun to dominate. This conception is articulated in a set of views that recognizes the desirability of serving every individual's interests and interprets the primary concern for justice not in terms of utility, but in terms of *rights*. On this account, public interest is important, but respect for every individual's rights is even more important. This view dates back (at least) to Kant, who defended the notions of "duty" and "obligation" as morally basic to any concern for utility. In its modern conception, its most able defense has been Harvard philosopher **John Rawls's** profound work entitled *A Theory of Justice*. For nearly six hundred pages, Rawls essentially defends two principles in order of priority. The first (and more fundamental) principle asserts that we all have basic and equal rights, in particular with reference to our personal freedom. The second principle (which assumes the first) asserts that although we cannot expect everyone in society to enjoy equal wealth, equal health, and equal opportunities, we can and should insist that the way in which inequalities are arranged is to every individual's advantage. For example, it should not be such that society allows that "the rich get richer and the poor get poorer." Rawls's actual statement from *Theory of Justice* is as follows:

> *First: each person is to have an equal right to the most extensive basic liberty compatible with a similar liberty for others.*

> *Second: social and economic inequalities are to be arranged so that they are both (a) reasonably expected to be to everyone's advantage, and (b) attached to positions and offices open to all.*[8]

John Rawls (1921–2002)

The author of *A Theory of Justice* (1971) and professor of philosophy at Harvard University.

Rawls's justification for establishing the rationality and necessity of these "liberal" principles derives from his view that we should consider what we would deem fair if all of us (or our ancestors) were in "the original position"–prior to organized

---

8 John Rawls, *A Theory of Justice* (Cambridge, MA: The Belknap Press of Harvard University Press, 1971), p. 60.

society, like Hobbes's "state of nature," but without any knowledge of our particular traits or interests. In such a situation, what would be rational for us to choose by way of the principles according to which society would be run? Because we do not know, in the essential sense, who we will be in that society, it does us no good to adopt principles that benefit the persons we are now. For example, in a society composed entirely of purple people and green people (remembering that in the original position we do not know which we will be), it would only be rational, Rawls argues, to enact a law that would treat all people equally, whether purple or green. It is much like (but much more complicated and uncertain than) the childhood example involving one of us being asked to cut a pie into sections, giving everyone else first choice. The only rational decision—even if you suspect that the other children are dullards—is to divide the pie equally. Similarly, the aim of Rawls's dual principles is to cut for all of us—if not equal pieces of the social pie, at least pieces that are as equal as possible.

The following selection from one of Rawls's early essays elaborates on his principles of justice:

 ### FROM **"Justice as Fairness"** BY **John Rawls**[9]

Throughout I consider justice only as a virtue of social institutions, or what I shall call practices.[10] The principles of justice are regarded as formulating restrictions as to how practices may define positions and offices, and assign thereto powers and liabilities, rights and duties. Justice as a virtue of particular actions or of persons I do not take up at all. It is important to distinguish these various subjects of justice, since the meaning of the concept varies according to whether it is applied to practices, particular actions, or persons. These meanings are, indeed, connected, but they are not identical. I shall confine my discussion to the sense of justice as applied to practices, since this sense is the basic one. Once it is understood, the other senses should go quite easily.

The conception of justice which I want to develop may be stated in the form of two principles as follows: first, each person participating in a practice, or affected by it, has an equal right to the most extensive liberty compatible with a like liberty for all; and second, inequalities are arbitrary unless it is reasonable to expect that they will work out for everyone's advantage, and provided the positions and offices to which they attach, or from which they may be gained, are open to all. These principles express justice as a complex of three ideas: liberty, equality, and reward for services contributing to the common good.

The term "person" is to be construed variously depending on the circumstances. On some occasions it will mean human individuals, but in others it may refer to nations, provinces, business firms, churches, teams, and so on. The principles of justice apply in all these instances, although there is a certain logical priority to the case of human individuals. As I shall use the term "person," it will be ambiguous in the manner indicated.

> "Inequalities are arbitrary unless it is reasonable to expect that they will work out for everyone's advantage."
>
> – JOHN RAWLS

---

9 John Rawls, "Justice as Fairness," in *The Philosophical Review* 67 (April 1958). Copyright © 1958 by Cornell University. Reprinted by permission of the publisher.

10 We use the word *practice* throughout as a sort of technical term meaning any form of activity specified by a system of rules which defines offices, roles, moves, penalties, defences, and so on, and which gives the activity its structure. As examples one may think of games and rituals, trials and parliaments, markets and systems or property. A partial analysis of the notion of a practice appears in R. C. Solomon's, "Two Concepts of Rules," *Philosophical Review* 64 (1955), pp. 3-32 [Rawls's note].

FIG. 8.13 What social arrangements, asks Rawls, would be acceptable to all parties concerned? *(Image © Nolte Lourens, 2011. Used under license from Shutterstock.com)*

The first principle holds, of course, only if other things are equal: that is, while there must always be a justification for departing from the initial position of equal liberty (which is defined by the pattern of rights and duties, powers and liabilities, established by a practice), and the burden or proof is placed on him who would depart from it, nevertheless, there can be, and often there is, a justification for doing so. Now, that similar particular cases, as defined by a practice, should be treated similarly as they arise, is part of the very concept of a practice; it is involved in the notion of an activity in accordance with rules. The first principle expresses an analogous conception, but as applied to the structure of practices themselves. It holds, for example, that there is a presumption against the distinctions and classifications made by legal systems and other practices to the extent that they infringe on the original and equal liberty of the persons participating in them. The second principle defines how this presumption may be rebutted.

It might be argued at this point that justice requires only an equal liberty. If, however, a greater liberty were possible for all without loss or conflict, then it would be irrational to settle on a lesser liberty. There is no reason for circumscribing rights unless their exercise would be incompatible, or would render the practice defining them less effective. Therefore no serious distortion of the concept of justice is likely to follow from including within it the concept of the greatest equal liberty.

The second principle defines what sorts of inequalities are permissible; it specifies how the presumption laid down by the first principle may be put aside. Now by inequalities it is best to understand not *any* differences between offices and positions, but differences in the benefits and burdens attached to them either directly or indirectly, such as prestige and wealth, or liability to taxation and compulsory services. Players in a game do not protest against there being different positions, such as batter, pitcher, catcher, and the like, nor to there being various privileges and powers as specified by the rules; nor do the citizens of a country object to there being the different offices of government such as president, senator, governor, judge, and so on, each with their special rights and duties. It is not differences in the resulting distribution established by a practice, or made possible by it, of the things men strive to attain or avoid. Thus they may complain about the pattern of honors and rewards set up by a practice (e.g., the privileges and salaries of government officials) or they may object to the distribution of power and wealth which results from the various ways in which men avail themselves of the opportunities allowed by it (e.g., the concentration of wealth which may develop in a free price system allowing large entrepreneurial or speculative gains).

It should be noted that the second principle holds that an inequality is allowed only if there is reason to believe that the practice with the inequality, or resulting from it, will work for the advantage of *every* party engaging in it. Here it is important to stress that *every* party must gain from the inequality. Since the principle applies to practices, it implies that the representative man in every office or position defined by a practice, when he views it as a going concern, must find it reasonable to prefer his condition and prospects with the inequality to what they would be under the practice without it. The principle excludes, therefore, the justification of inequalities on the grounds that the disadvantages of those in one position are outweighed by the greater advantages of those in another position. This rather simple restriction is the main modification I wish to make in the utilitarian principle as usually understood.

Rawls, like Hume in particular, ties the concept of "justice" to the concept of "equality." The main theme of his work is an attempt to develop this connection and to state precisely the kind of "equality" that is most important for justice. Against the conservative suggestion that people should be considered equal in legal rights and "opportunities" alone, without any right to material goods and social services, Rawls argues that a just society will consider the welfare of the worst-off members of society as an obligation. Here he differs with Mill and the utilitarians, who would say that providing such help must be justified as a matter of utility; for Rawls, it is more like a Kantian duty. Moreover, Rawls clearly distinguishes himself from socialists as well, who would argue that all property should be shared. He says only that it is obligatory to help out the worst-off members of society. Nowhere does he suggest that all people ought therefore to have equal wealth and property. Justice, for Rawls, does not equate fair distribution with equal distribution. Equality becomes a far more complex notion than simple egalitarianism often takes it to be.

Is equality the primary concern of justice? Even Rawls admits that a society in which everyone had exactly equal shares of social goods is impossible. But why is it impossible? We can all imagine a situation—and some radical thinkers even propose it—in which all material goods (at least) would be collected and cataloged by the state, then redistributed to every citizen in precisely equal shares. Most of us, including Rawls, find this suggestion intolerable. Yet why, if it realizes the equality that justice demands? Something stops us, and it is not simply the idea that we might lose our own goods, for many of us would in fact benefit from such a redistribution scheme.

What bothers us initially is the very idea of anyone, including (perhaps especially) the government, intruding into our lives and exerting such power. However, we also sense that such a scheme for redistributing the wealth violates something that is very basic to justice—namely, the rights we have to our possessions. Rawls, of course, gives rights top priority in his theory, but the rights he is concerned with have to do with liberty in general, not with having possessions as such. We all feel, with whatever reservations, that we have a right to what we earn and that we have a right to keep what we already possess. Many of us resent that the government takes from us a substantial percentage of our earnings to use in ways that are not directly (or perhaps even indirectly) under our control. And we believe we have the right, for instance, to the modest sum that grandfather left us in his will (presumably the residue of earlier taxation), even though we did not earn it in any sense. In response to such considerations, many philosophers have become increasingly aware of another kind of right that is not treated adequately by such liberal theories of Rawls's—in fact, a right that goes against the modest scheme of redistribution (for example, through taxation) encouraged by his principles. This other kind of right, known as **entitlement**, gives rise to a very different theory of justice.

The popular name for this alternative theory is libertarianism, and it has recently become a powerful force in American politics. Libertarianism is an "entitlement theory" that puts the right to private property first and foremost and couples this idea with a deep skepticism as to the wisdom or fairness of government. The original entitlement theory was developed by John Locke. Locke argued that the right to private property was so basic that it preceded any social conventions or laws, and existed quite independent of any government or state. What gave a person the right to a piece of property, Locke argued, was that he had "mixed his labor with it," in other words, the person worked with it and improved it and so had the right to it. By "property," Locke was thinking mainly of land. In today's society—where what is at stake consists mainly of salaries and what we can buy with them—we would say that a person has the basic right to keep what he or she earns. In the 1970s, Locke's theory was updated considerably and argued forcefully by John Rawls's younger Harvard colleague, **Robert Nozick**. In *Anarchy, State, and Utopia*, Nozick argues for the entitlement theory and against any attempt to set "patterns" of fair distribution. The enforcement of any such pattern, he contends, must result in the violation of people's rights.

FROM *Anarchy, State, and Utopia* BY **Robert Nozick**[11]

> "A minimal state, limited to the narrow functions of protection against force, theft, fraud, enforcement of contracts, and so on, is justified."
>
> – ROBERT NOZICK

Individuals have rights, and there are things no person or group may do to them (without violating their rights). So strong and far-reaching are these rights that they raise the question of what, if anything, the state and its officials may do. How much room do individual rights leave for the state? . . . Our main conclusions about the state are that a minimal state, limited to the narrow functions of protection against force, theft, fraud, enforcement of contracts, and so on, is justified; that any more extensive state will violate persons' rights to not be forced to do certain things, and is unjustified; and that the minimal state is inspiring as well as right. Two noteworthy implications are that the state may not use its coercive apparatus for the purpose of getting some citizens to aid others, or in order to prohibit activities to people for their *own* good or protection.

· · ·

THE ENTITLEMENT THEORY

The subject of justice in holdings consists of three major topics. The first is the *original acquisition of holdings*, the appropriation of unheld things. This includes the issues of how unheld things may come to be held, the process, or processes, by which unheld things may come to be held, the things that may come to be held by these processes, the extent of what comes to be held by a particular process, and so on. We shall refer to the complicated truth about this topic, which we shall not formulate here, as the principle of justice in acquisition. The second topic concerns the *transfer of holdings* from one person to another. By what processes may a person transfer holdings to another? How may a person acquire a holding from another who holds it? Under this topic come general descriptions of voluntary exchange, and gift and (on the other hand) fraud, as well as reference to particular conventional details fixed upon in a given society. The complicated truth about this subject (with placeholders for conventional details) we shall call the principle of justice in transfer. (And we shall suppose it also includes principles governing how a person may divest himself of a holding, passing it into an unheld state.)

If the world were wholly just, the following inductive definition would exhaustively cover the subject of justice in holdings.

1. A person who acquires a holding in accordance with the principle of justice in acquisition is entitled to that holding.

2. A person who acquires a holding in accordance with the principle of justice in transfer, from someone else entitled to the holding, is entitled to the holding.

3. No one is entitled to a holding except by (repeated) applications of 1 and 2.

The complete principle of distributive justice would say simply that a distribution is just if everyone is entitled to the holdings they possess under the distribution.

A distribution is just if it arises from another just distribution by legitimate means. The legitimate means of moving from one distribution to another are specified by the principle of justice in transfer. The legitimate first "moves" are specified by the principle of justice in acquisition. Whatever arises from a just situation by just steps is itself just.

· · ·

Not all actual situations are generated in accordance with the two principles of justice in holdings: the principle of justice in acquisition and the principle of justice in transfer. Some people steal from others, or defraud them, or enslave them, seizing their product and preventing them from living as they choose, or forcibly exclude others from com-

FIG. 8.14 An illustration of Thomas More's island of "Utopia" *(Bildarchiv Preussischer Kulturbesitz / Art Resource, NY)*

peting in exchanges. None of these are permissible modes of transition from one situation to another. And some persons acquire holdings by means not sanctioned by the principle of justice in acquisition. The existence of past injustice (previous violations of the first two principles of justice in holdings) raises the third major topic under justice in holdings: the rectification of injustice in holdings. If past injustice has shaped present holdings in various ways, some identifiable and some not, what now, if anything, ought to be done to rectify these injustices? What obligations do the performers of injustice have toward those whose position is worse than it would have been had the injustice not been done? Or, than it would have had compensation been paid promptly? How, if at all, do things change if the beneficiaries and those made worse off are not the direct parties in the act of injustice, but, for example, their descendants? Is an injustice done to someone whose holding was itself based upon an unrectified injustice? How far back must one go in wiping clean the historical slate of injustices? What may victims of injustice permissibly do in order to rectify the injustices being done to them, including the many injustices done by persons acting through their government? I do not know of a thorough or theoretically sophisticated treatment of such issues. Idealizing greatly, let us suppose theoretical investigations will produce a principle of rectification. This principle uses historical information about previous situations and injustices done in them (as defined by the first two principles of justice and rights against interference), and information about the actual course of events that flowed from these injustices, until the present, and it yields a description (or descriptions) of holdings in the society.

. . .

HISTORICAL PRINCIPLES AND END-RESULT PRINCIPLES

The general outlines of the entitlement theory illuminate the nature and defects of other conceptions of distributive justice. The entitlement theory of justice in distribution is *historical;* whether a distribution is just depends upon how it came about. In contrast, *current time-slice principles* of justice hold that the justice of a distribution is determined by how things are distributed (who has what) as judged by some *structural* principle(s) of just distribution. A utilitarian who judges between any two distributions by seeing which has the greater sum of utility and, if the sums tie, applies some fixed equality criterion to choose the more equal distribution, would hold a current time-slice principle of justice. As would someone who had a fixed schedule of trade-offs between the sum of happiness and equality. According to a current time-slice principle, all that needs to be looked at, in judging the justice of a distribution, is who ends up with what; in comparing any two distributions one need look only at the matrix presenting the distributions. No further information need be fed into a principle of justice. It is a consequence of such principles of justice that any two structurally identical distributions are equally just. (Two distributions are structurally identical if they present the same profile, but perhaps have different persons occupying the particular slots. My having ten and your having five, and my having five and your having ten are structurally identical distributions.) Welfare economics is the theory of current time-slice principles of justice. The subject is conceived as operating on matrices representing only current information about distribution. This, as well as some of the usual conditions (for example, the choice of distribution is invariant under relabeling of columns), guarantees that welfare economics will be a current time-slice theory, with all of its inadequacies.

Most persons do not accept current time-slice principles as constituting the whole story about distributive shares. They think it relevant in assessing the justice of a situation to consider not only the distribution it embodies, but also how that distribution came about. If some persons are in prison for murder or war crimes, we do not say that to assess the justice of the distribution in the society we must look only at what this person has, and that person has, and that person has, . . . at the current time. We think it relevant to ask whether someone did something so that he *deserved* to be punished, deserved to have a lower share. Most will agree to the relevance of further information with regard to punishments and penalties. Consider also desired things. One traditional socialist view is that workers are entitled to the product and full fruits of their labor; thay have earned it; a distribution is unjust if it does not give the workers what they are entitled to. Such entitlements are based upon some past history. No socialist holding this view would find it comforting to be told that because the actual distribution *A* happens to coincide structurally with the one he desires *D*, therefore is no less just than *D*; . . . This socialist rightly, in my view, holds onto the notions of earning, producing, entitlement, desert, and so forth, and he rejects current time-slice principles that look only to the structure of the resulting set of holdings. . . . His mistake lies in his view of what entitlements arise out of what sorts of productive processes.

- What does Rawls mean by "justice as fairness"? When are inequalities tolerable?
- Do you think that envisioning what people in "the original position" would find acceptable if they were designing the ground rules of society is an effective means for determining what is fair? Why or why not?
- How does the entitlement theory differ from Rawls's conception of justice as fairness? Which view is more similar to Aristotle's conception of justice?

F. Justice or Care: A Feminist Perspective

The debate about justice has gone on for almost 2,500 years. But it may be noted that most of the voices in the debate have been male voices. This fact raises the question of whether there is some male bias to the perspective in which justice has been debated or, indeed, some male bias in the very notion of justice itself. **Cheshire Calhoun** has argued that this is the case. Here is an excerpt from her argument.

FROM **"Justice, Care, Gender Bias"**
BY **Cheshire Calhoun**[12]

Carol Gilligan poses two separable, though in her work not separate, challenges to moral theory. The first is a challenge to the adequacy of current moral theory that is dominated by the ethics of justice. The ethics of justice, on her view, excludes some dimensions of moral experience, such as contextual decision making, special obligations, the moral motives of compassion and sympathy, and the relevance of considering one's own integrity in making moral decisions. The second is a challenge to moral theory's presumed gender neutrality. The ethics of justice is not gender neutral, she argues, because it advocates ideals of agency, moral motivation, and correct moral reasoning which women are less likely than men to achieve; and because the moral dimensions excluded from the ethics of justice are just the ones figuring more prominently in women's than men's moral experience.

The adequacy and gender bias charges are, for Gilligan, linked. She claims that the ethics of justice and the ethics of care are two different moral orientations. Whereas individuals may use both orientations, the shift from one to the other requires a Gestalt shift, since "the terms of one perspective do not contain the terms of the other." The exclusion of the care perspective from the ethics of justice simultaneously undermines the adequacy of the ethics of justice (it cannot give a complete account of moral life) and renders it gender-biased.

Some critics have responded by arguing that there is no logical incompatibility between the two moral orientations. Because the ethics of justice does not in

"The exclusion of the care perspective from the ethics of justice simultaneously undermines the adequacy of the ethics of justice . . . and renders it gender-biased."

– CHESHIRE CALHOUN

[12] Cheshire Calhoun, "Justice, Care, Gender Bias," in *Journal of Philosophy* 85 (1988). Reprinted by permission.

Cheshire Calhoun (1954–)

A professor of philosophy at Arizona State University, Tempe.

FIG. 8.15 Feminist philosopher Cheshire Calhoun *(Used by permission of Cheshire Calhoun)*

principle exclude the ethics of care (even if theorists within the justice tradition have had little to say about care issues), it is neither inadequate nor gender-biased. Correctly applying moral rules and principles, for instance, requires, rather than excludes, knowledge of contextual details. Both orientations are crucial to correct moral reasoning and an adequate understanding of moral life. Thus, the ethics of justice and the ethics of care are not in fact rivaling, alternative moral theories. The so-called ethics of care merely makes focal issues that are already implicitly contained in the ethics of justice.

Suppose the two are logically compatible. Would the charge of gender bias evaporate? Yes, so long as gender neutrality only requires that the ethics of justice could, consistently, make room for the central moral concerns of the ethics of care. But perhaps gender neutrality requires more than this. Since the spectre of gender bias in theoretical knowledge is itself a moral issue, we would be well advised to consider the question of gender bias more carefully before concluding that our moral theory speaks in an androgynous voice. Although we can and should test the ethics of justice by asking whether it could consistently include the central moral issues in the ethics of care, we might also ask what ideologies of the moral life are likely to result from the repeated inclusion or exclusion of particular topics in moral theorizing.

Theorizing that crystallizes into a tradition has nonlogical as well as logical implications. In order to explain why a tradition has the contours it does, one may need to suppose general acceptance of particular beliefs that are not logically entailed by any particular theory and might be denied by individual theorists were those beliefs articulated. When behavioral researchers, for example, focus almost exclusively on aggression and its role in human life, neglecting other behavioral motives, their doing so has the nonlogical implication that aggression is, indeed, the most important behavioral motive. This is because only a belief like this would explain the rationality of this pattern of research. Such nonlogical implications become ideologies when politically loaded (as the importance of aggression is when coupled with observations about women's lower level of aggression).

When understood as directed at moral theory's nonlogical implications, the gender-bias charge takes a different form. Even if the ethics of justice could consistently accommodate the ethics of care, the critical point is that theorists in the justice tradition have not said much, except in passing, about the ethics of care, and are unlikely to say much in the future without a radical shift in theoretical priorities; and concentrating almost exclusively on rights of noninterference, impartiality, rationality, autonomy, and principles creates an ideology of the moral domain which has undesirable political implications for women. This formulation shifts the justice-care debate from one about logical compatibility to a debate about which theoretical priorities would improve the lot of women.

- In what sense are notions of justice "masculine"? What contribution or revisions can a feminist perspective offer?
- Do you think an ethics of justice and an ethics of care are compatible? If so, how? If it is necessary to choose between considerations of justice and considerations of care, should justice necessarily prevail? If this is the case, what understanding of "justice" would be most caring?

G. Individual Rights and Freedom

If our concern were only the smooth workings of society, almost any government would do—the stronger the better, the more authoritarian, the more efficient. But efficiency is only one of several concerns and probably not the most important. You may argue that the public interest could be served by an efficient, authoritarian government, but it is clear that justice and individual rights could not. The most important feature of social contract theory (and consent-of-the-governed theories in general) is the clear emphasis on justice and rights. However, the social contract theory by itself is not entirely clear about the status of individual rights, as Nozick makes clear in his criticism of Rawls. Those rights concerning freedom are of particular concern here. How much personal freedom does the social contract guarantee us?

Any discussion of justice and the state must include some special concern for the status of basic freedoms and **unalienable rights** (that is, rights that no one and no government may take away). Among these are the freedom to speak one's political opinions without harassment, freedom to worship (or not worship) without being penalized or punished, freedom to defend oneself against attack ("the right to bear arms" is a controversial case), and the freedom to pursue one's own interests (when these interests do not interfere with the rights of others). In addition, we can add the right not to be imprisoned without reason, accused without a fair trial, or punished unduly for a crime committed. Our best-known list of such freedoms and rights is the American Bill of Rights, appended to the main body of the U.S. Constitution as a kind of contractual guarantee of personal rights.

But even if the importance of such rights is indisputable, the precise formulation and extent of those rights are highly debatable. We speak of "unalienable rights," but should such rights be left unrestricted, for example, even in wartime? It is clear, to mention the most common example, that freedom of speech does not extend so far as the right to falsely yell "fire" in a crowded theater. Freedom of speech, therefore, like other rights, is limited by considerations of public welfare and utility. But how limited? Is mere annoyance to the government sufficient reason to limit it, or the populace becoming sick of some message? Similarly, we can go back to the difficult examples we raised in earlier sections. Is the right not to be subjected to harsh punishment always legitimate, even against overwhelming public interest? For example, is it valid in the case of a person who has committed violent crimes repeatedly? Or, to take a difficult example, is "free enterprise" an "unalienable" right in our society? Or is free enterprise rather a theory (and a debatable one) that suggests that public interest and justice will best be served by open competition and a free market? That theory evolved before modern monopolies developed and before it was obvious that "free" markets could be

FIG. 8.16 *(Image © Sylvana Rega, 2011. Used under license from Shutterstock.com)*

manipulated so as not to be either free or in the public interest at all. Is that "freedom" still a right? Or should it also be tempered by other concerns?

One of the most important basic rights is the presumed right to own private property. John Locke, writing just after the English ("Glorious") Revolution of 1688, listed three basic rights that would become the main ingredients of both the American Declaration of Independence and a still-prominent political philosophy called liberalism. Foremost among them were "life, liberty, and the right to own private property." (The original draft of the American Declaration included just these three, but Jefferson replaced the last with the less committal "pursuit of happiness.") For Locke, private property is the bulwark of freedom and the basis of other human rights. One's own body is private property in the most basic sense; no one else has the authority to violate or use it without permission. Most contemporary societies recognize this right to one's own body as fundamental. But then Locke adds that the right to own property that one has helped cultivate with his or her body (that one "hath mixed his labour with") is also basic to freedom and human dignity. The Protestant work ethic is powerfully evident in this view, in which work and rights are treated together, the first being our way of earning the second:

 FROM *The Second Treatise on Government*
BY **John Locke**[13]

Though the earth and all inferior creatures be common to all men, yet every man has a *property* in his own *person*. This nobody has any right to but himself. The *labour* of his body and the *work* of his hands, we may say, are properly his. Whatsoever, then, he removes out of the state that nature hath provided and left it in, he hath mixed his labour with it, and joined to it something that is his own, and thereby makes it his property. It being by him removed from the common state nature placed it in, it hath by this labour something annexed to it that excludes the common right of other men. For his labour being the unquestionable property of the labourer, no man but he can have a right to what that is once joined to, at least where there is enough, and as good left in common for others.

He that is nourished by the acorns he picked up under an oak, or the apples he gathered from the trees in the wood, has certainly appropriated them to himself. Nobody can deny but the nourishment is his. I ask, then, when did they begin to be his? when he digested? or when he ate? or when he boiled? or when he brought them home? or when he picked them up? And 'tis plain, if the first gathering made them not his, nothing else could. That labour put a distinction between them and common. That added something to them more than Nature, the common mother of all, had done, and so they became his private right. And will any one say he had not right to those acorns or apples he thus appropriated because he had not the consent of all mankind to make them his? Was it a robbery thus to assume to himself what belonged to all in common? If such a consent as that was necessary, man had starved, notwithstanding the plenty God had given him. We see in commons, which remain so by compact, that 'tis the taking any part of what is common, and removing it out of the state Nature leaves it in, which begins the property, without which the common is of no use. And the taking of this or that part does not depend on the express consent of all the commoners. Thus, the grass my horse has bit, the turfs my servant has cut, and the ore I have digged in any place, where I have a right to them in com-

"For his labour being the unquestionable property of the labourer, no man but he can have a right to what that is once joined to, at least where there is enough, and as good left in common for others."

–JOHN LOCKE

13 John Locke, *The Second Treatise on Government*, (Oxford, U.K.: Clarendon, 1690), pp. 26–27, 51.

mon with others, become my property without the assignation or consent of any body. The labour that was mine, removing them out of that common state they were in, hath fixed my property in them.

. . .

And thus, I think, it is very easy to conceive, without any difficulty, how labour could at first begin a title of property in the common things of nature, and how the spending it upon our uses bounded it; so that there could then be no reason of quarrelling about title, nor any doubt about the largeness of possession it gave. Right and conveniency went together. For as a man had a right to all he could employ his labour upon, so he had no temptation to labour for more than he could make use of. This left no room for controversy about the title, nor for encroachment on the right of others. What portion a man carved to himself was easily seen; and it was useless as well as dishonest to carve himself too much, or take more than he needed.

A right is a kind of demand, the demand that one is owed something by society and the state, usually a certain sort of consideration or treatment. But most of the rights we have been discussing are in fact rights to freedom or to liberty, that is, the right to be left alone and not interfered with. A belief in individual freedom forms the basis of the liberal political philosophy, which is defined most of all by a commitment to the right of each individual to be free to do whatever he or she wishes as long as it does not interfere with similar rights of others. The classic statement of this position is another pamphlet by John Stuart Mill, *On Liberty* (1859). In it, Mill defends the rights of individuals and minorities against the tyranny of democratic majorities, for he sees that liberty can be as endangered in a **democracy** as it can in an authoritarian state. Mill goes on to offer a "very simple principle," that individual liberty is to be considered inviolable except when other people are threatened with harm.

 FROM *On Liberty*
BY **John Stuart Mill**[14]

The object of this Essay is to assert one very simple principle, as entitled to govern absolutely the dealings of society with the individual in the way of compulsion and control, whether the means used be physical force in the form of legal penalties, or the moral coercion of public opinion. That principle is, that the sole end for which mankind are warranted, individually or collectively, in interfering with the liberty of action of any of their number, is self-protection. That the only purpose for which power can be rightfully exercised over any member of a civilized community, against his will, is to prevent harm to others. His own good, either physical or moral, is not a sufficient warrant. He cannot rightfully be compelled to do or forbear because it will be better for him to do so, because it will make him happier, because, in the opinions of others, to do so would be wise, or even right. These are good reasons for remonstrating with him, or reasoning with him, or persuading him, or entreating him, but not for compelling him, or visiting with any evil in case he do otherwise. To justify that, the conduct from which it is desired to deter him must be calculated to produce evil to some one else. The only part of the conduct of any one, for which he is amenable to society, is that which concerns others. In the part which merely concerns

---

[14] John Stuart Mill, *On Liberty*, (London: Longmans, 1859).

himself, his independence is, of right, absolute. Over himself, over his own body and mind, the individual is sovereign.

It is, perhaps, hardly necessary to say that this doctrine is meant to apply only to human beings in the maturity of their faculties. We are not speaking of children, or of young persons below the age which the law may fix as that of manhood or womanhood. Those who are still in a state to require being taken care of by others, must be protected against their own actions as well as against external injury. For the same reason, we may leave out of consideration those backward states of society in which the race itself may be considered as in its nonage. The early difficulties in the way of spontaneous progress are so great, that there is seldom any choice of means for overcoming them; and a ruler full of the spirit of improvement is warranted in the use of any expedients that will attain an end, perhaps otherwise unattainable. Despotism is a legitimate mode of government in dealing with barbarians, provided the end be their improvement,[15] and the means justified by actually affecting that end. Liberty, as a principle, has no application to any state of things anterior to the time when mankind have become capable of being improved by free and equal discussion.

It is proper to state that I forego any advantage which could be derived to my argument from the idea of abstract right, as a thing independent of utility. I regard utility as the ultimate appeal on all ethical questions; but it must be utility in the largest sense, grounded on the permanent interests of a man as a progressive being. Those interests, I contend, authorise the subjection of individual spontaneity to external control, only in respect to those actions of each, which concern the interest of other people. If any one does an act hurtful to others, there is a prima facie case for punishing him, by law, or, where legal penalties are not safely applicable, by general disapprobation. There are also many positive acts for the benefit of others, which he may rightfully be compelled to perform; such as to give evidence in a court of justice; to bear his fair share in the common defence, or in any other joint work necessary to the interest of the society of which he enjoys the protection; and to perform certain acts of individual beneficence, such as saving a fellow creature's life, or interposing to protect the defenceless against ill-usage, things which whenever it is obviously a man's duty to do, he may rightfully be made responsible to society for not doing. A person may cause evil to others not only by his actions but by his inaction, and in either case is justly accountable to them for the injury. The latter case, it is true, requires a much more cautious exercise of compulsion than the former. To make any one answerable for doing evil to others is the rule; to make him answerable for not preventing evil is, comparatively speaking, the exception. Yet there are many cases clear enough and grave enough to justify that exception. In all things which regard the external relations of the individual, he is de jure amenable to those whose interests are concerned, and, if need be, to society as their protector. There are often good reasons for not holding him to the responsibility; but these reasons must arise from the special expediencies of the case: either because it is a kind of case in which he is on the whole likely to act better, when left to his own discretion, than when controlled in any way in which society have it in their power to control him; or because the attempt to exercise control would produce other evils, greater than those which it would prevent. When such reasons as these preclude the enforcement of

---

[15] Notice the political implications for this qualification, however, in "underdeveloped" countries and colonies. The principle of *paternalism*—that one ought to take care of those who cannot take care of themselves—is easily abused and therefore dangerous.

responsibility, the conscience of the agent himself should step into the vacant judgment seat, and protect those interests of others which have no external protection; judging himself all the more rigidly, because the case does not admit of his being made accountable to the judgment of his fellow creatures.

But there is a sphere of action in which society, as distinguished from the individual, has, if any, only an indirect interest; comprehending all that portion of a person's life and conduct which affects only himself, or if it also affects others, only with their free, voluntary, and undeceived consent and participation. When I say only himself, I mean directly, and in the first instance; for whatever affects himself, may affect others through himself; and the objection which may be grounded on this contingency, will receive consideration in the sequel. This, then, is the appropriate region of human liberty. It comprises, first, the inward domain of consciousness; demanding liberty of conscience in the most comprehensive sense; liberty of thought and feeling; absolute freedom of opinion and sentiment on all subjects, practical or speculative, scientific, moral, or theological. The liberty of expressing and publishing opinions may seem to fall under a different principle, since it belongs to that part of the conduct of an individual which concerns other people; but, being almost of as much importance as the liberty of thought itself, and resting in great part on the same reasons, is practically inseparable from it. Secondly, the principle requires liberty of tastes and pursuits; of framing the plan of our life to suit our own character; of doing as we like, subject to such consequences as may follow: without impediment from our fellow creatures, so long as what we do does not harm them, even though they should think our conduct foolish, perverse, or wrong. Thirdly, from this liberty of each individual, follows the liberty, within the same limits, of combination among individuals; freedom to unite, for any purpose not involving harm to others: the persons combining being supposed to be of full age, and not forced or deceived.

No society in which these liberties are not, on the whole, respected, is free, whatever may be its form of government and unqualified. The only freedom which deserves the name, is that of pursuing our own good in our own way, so long as we do not attempt to deprive others of theirs, or impede their efforts to obtain it. Each is the proper guardian of his own health, whether bodily, *or* mental and spiritual. Mankind are greater gainers by suffering each other to live as seems good to themselves, than by compelling each to live as seems good to the rest.

FIG. 8.17 John Stuart Mill thought that censorship is rarely justified. *(© iStockphoto.com/Srdjan Srdjanov)*

Mill's main concern in his essay is the extent to which the government and public interest have authority over individuals and individual actions. If an action harms other people or presents a public menace, then the government does have the authority to prevent it or punish a person for doing it. But if an action is not harmful to others, the government has no such authority. In the question of freedom of speech, for example, this means that governments have no authority to censor some comment or publication unless it clearly harms

> "The only freedom which deserves the name, is that of pursuing our own good in our own way, so long as we do not attempt to deprive others of theirs, or impede their efforts to obtain it."
>
> – JOHN STUART MILL

other people, not merely annoys or personally offends them. Mill is particularly concerned with protecting individuals against "the tyranny of the majority." The public interest is authoritative to "a limit," but it does not justify interference with personal affairs or opinions.

We have been discussing the right to behave as one likes, so long as one does not harm others. But it is important to point out that discussions of rights should never be set apart from discussions of political duties and obligations. As the several versions of the social contract make clear, these are always part of one and the same agreement—certain rights in return for certain obligations. To discuss freedom of speech, for example, without also discussing the obligation to be well informed and logically coherent, is to provide a dangerously one-sided view of the problem. The theme that all rights and "freedoms from" must be coupled with duties and obligations and the freedom to perform them has recurred since the ancient Greeks. Recall Rousseau's idea, for example, that the citizen's obligations to the state are just as important as the state's obligations to its citizens.

One way of developing this idea of an exchange of rights and obligations has been to distinguish two different senses of "freedom": a *negative* freedom from interference and a *positive* freedom to realize one's own potential and find one's place in society. Freedom from interference may be necessary for a person to enjoy life and contribute to the welfare of those around him or her, but a person also needs positive goods—health and education, for example. Thus freedom takes on a double meaning, freedom *from* interference but freedom *to* participate in society, too. Since positive freedom also includes a person's being able to take on responsibilities, some philosophers have pointed out the paradox that one can be "free to perform obligations."

The idea that one is "free to perform obligations" may sound odd to us because we are so used to talking exclusively about freedom from constraints and the demands made by authority. But many philosophers are concerned that simple freedom from constraint leaves people without moral direction and can easily degenerate into chaos and anarchy. Thus these philosophers stress the necessity of certain supports and guidelines as an essential part of freedom. They call it "positive" freedom, since it necessarily includes "positive" goods (health and education) as well as a set of roles, duties, obligations, and constraints. This notion can be abused easily, for "positive freedom" can be made compatible with the most authoritarian state. (The Soviet Union, for example, often used the term *freedom* in this "positive" sense.) But despite possible abuses, it is important to see that there is more to freedom than simple freedom from interference. Whenever someone demands freedom, it is important to ask not only "from what?" but "for what?"

It is also worth distinguishing several different kinds of rights. We can distinguish between "negative" and "positive" rights as well as freedoms; one has a right not to be interfered with, and one has rights *to* certain goods that society can provide. We have mostly been discussing negative rights (the right to be left alone, the right not to be arrested without good reason). But there are positive rights that are equally important for a good human life, although they are often controversial in this society. They include, for example, the right to a minimal income regardless of the type of work one performs and the right to adequate health care regardless of one's ability to pay for it. Many rights are clearly localized within a particular state or community, as, for example, the right of university regents to free tickets to football games and lunches at taxpayers' expense. These rights exist by convention only and cannot be generalized from one community to another.

More generally, however, there are **civil rights**, rights that are guaranteed in a particular state or nation. One example is the right to equal treatment despite differences in skin color, sex, or religion, as required by various state and federal laws. These civil rights are obviously much more important than conventional rights, and they have a clearly moral basis. For this reason, even though they are defined by reference to a particular state and society, they are often generalized to apply to other societies as well. Rights that are justifiably generalized in this way should be recognized as *moral* rights or **human rights**, extendable to all people, in any society, regardless of the laws and customs of the society in which they live. Some apparent human rights have been hotly debated: for example, whether the U.S. government has the moral authority to interfere with the harsh abuses of human rights in, say, China or Castro's Cuba. If the right in question is harsh punishment for a seemingly minor crime, it could be argued that their system of punishment is simply more severe than ours, and we should not apply our values. If the right in question is the ability of citizens to speak out against the government without threat of imprisonment or worse, strong arguments have been made that the U.S. government does indeed have the moral authority to interfere. (Whether or not it wishes to risk the consequences is another matter.) If the right in question is one of the basic human rights—such as the right not to be tortured or debased or pointlessly murdered—then it can be argued that everyone has a moral obligation to defend such rights. Human rights are those that transcend all social and national boundaries. They demand that people deserve certain treatment just because they are human, regardless of all else.

Human rights, according to Malcolm X, were at stake in the civil rights movement of the 1960s. Malcolm X was one of the leaders of the "Black Nationalist" movement of that era, and he pursued not just justice, but an independent and separate state for black people of all nations. In the following passage, he argues that the rights being denied to African Americans were fundamental human rights, and they should be recognized as such at the international level.

FIG. 8.18 Why is freedom of expression a "negative right"? (© iStockphoto.com/Claudelle Girard)

On Civil and Human Rights
BY Malcolm X[16]

Civil rights actually keeps the struggle within the domestic confines of America. It keeps it under the jurisdiction of the American government, which means that as long as our struggle for what we're seeking is labeled civil rights, we can only go to Washington, D.C., and then we rely upon either the Supreme Court, the President or the Congress or the senators. These senators—many of them are racists. Many of the congressmen are racists. Many of the judges are racists and oftentimes the president himself is a very shrewdly camouflaged racist. And so we really can't get meaningful redress for our grievances when we are depending upon these grievances being redressed just within the jurisdiction of the United States government.

On the other hand, human rights go beyond the jurisdiction of this government. Human rights are international. Human rights are something that a man has by dint of his having been born. The labeling of our struggle in this country under the title civil rights of the past 12 years has actually made it impossible for us to get

---

16 From *Two Speeches by Malcolm X*. Copyright © 1990 by Betty Shabazz and Pathfinder Press. Reprinted by permission.

FIG. 8.19 Civil rights leader Malcolm X *(AP Photo)*

outside help. Many foreign nations, many of our brothers and sisters on the African continent who have gotten their independence, have restrained themselves, have refrained from becoming vocally or actively involved in our struggle for fear that they would be violating U.S. protocol, that they would be accused of getting involved in America's domestic affairs.

On the other hand, when we label it human rights, it internationalizes the problem and puts it at a level that makes it possible for any nation or any people anywhere on this earth to speak out in behalf of our human rights struggle.

So we feel that by calling it civil rights for the past 12 years, we've actually been barking up the wrong tree, that ours is a problem of *human* rights.

Plus, if we have our human rights, our civil rights are automatic. If we're respected as a human being, we'll be respected as a citizen; and in this country the black man not only is not respected as a citizen, he is not even respected as a human being.

And the proof is that you find in many instances people can come to this country from other countries—they can come to this country from behind the Iron Curtain—and despite the fact that they come here from these other places, they don't have to have civil-rights legislation passed in order for their rights to be safeguarded.

No new legislation is necessary for foreigners who come here to have their rights safeguarded. The Constitution is sufficient, but when it comes to the black men who were born here—whenever we are asking for our rights, they tell us that new legislation is necessary.

Well, we don't believe that. The Organization of Afro-American Unity feels that as long as our people in this country confine their struggle within the limitations and under the jurisdiction of the United States government, we remain within the confines of the vicious system that has done nothing but exploit and oppress us ever since we've been here. So we feel that our only real hope is to make known that our problem is not a Negro problem or an American problem but rather, it has become a human problem, a world problem, and it has to be attacked at the world level, at a level at which all segments of humanity can intervene in our behalf.

In the heated discussion of rights that has defined a great deal of the debate about justice in the advanced industrialized countries—whether there should be limitations on freedom of speech and whether or not a government has the right to tax the income of its citizens—what is often neglected is the crisis that threatens so much of the developing world (and to a shocking extent the developed world as well). Many people lack the most essential necessities of human life: clean air to breathe, clean water to drink, and enough food to eat. The lack of food is not so much a problem of supply—there is plenty of food in the world—but a problem of justice. Some political thinkers have begun to address this issue of justice in terms of rights, claiming that people have fundamental human rights to the basic necessities for living. All too often, they argue, the rights to property are defended even when the consequence is that thousands or millions of people will starve. Here, Nobel Prize-winning economist Amartya

Sen defends the idea that hunger deserves much more dedicated attention than it has been getting from economists and philosophers.

FROM "Property and Hunger" BY Amartya Sen[17]

Moral claims based on intrinsically valuable rights are often used in political and social arguments. Rights related to ownership have been invoked for ages. But there are also other types of rights which have been seen as "inherent and inalienable," and the American Declaration of Independence refers to "certain unalienable rights," among which are "life, liberty and the pursuit of happiness." The Indian constitution talks even of "the right to an adequate means of livelihood." The "right not to be hungry" has often been invoked in recent discussions on the obligation to help the famished.

PROPERTY AND DEPRIVATION

The right to hold, use and bequeath property that one has legitimately acquired is often taken to be inherently valuable. In fact, however, many of its defenses seem to be actually of the instrumental type, e.g., arguing that property rights make people more free to choose one kind of a life rather than another. Even the traditional attempt at founding "natural property rights" on the principles of "natural liberty" (with or without John Locke's proviso) has some instrumental features. But even if we do accept that property rights may have some intrinsic value, this does not in any way amount to an overall justification of property rights, since property rights may have consequences which themselves will require assessment. Indeed, the causation of hunger as well as its prevention may materially depend on how property rights are structured. If a set of property rights leads, say, to starvation, as it well might, then the moral approval of these rights would certainly be compromised severely. In general, the need for consequential analysis of property rights is inescapable whether or not such rights are seen as having any intrinsic value. . . .

If starvation and hunger are seen in terms of failures of entitlements, then it becomes immediately clear that the total availability of food in a country is only one of several variables that are relevant. Many famines occur without any decline in the availability of food. For example, in the Great Bengal famine of 1943, the total food availability in Bengal was not particularly bad (considerably higher than two years earlier when there was no famine), and yet three million people died, in a famine mainly affecting the rural areas, through rather violent shifts in the relative purchasing powers of different groups, hitting the rural laborers the hardest. The Ethiopian famine of 1973 took place in a year of average per capita food availability, but the cultivators and other occupation groups in the province of Wollo had lost their means of subsistence

FIG. 8.20 Nobel laureate, economist, and philosopher Amartya Sen *(AP Photo/Pavel Rahman)*

Amartya Sen (on left) (1933–)

An Indian economist and philosopher. He won the Nobel Prize for economics in 1998. He teaches at Harvard University.

[17] Sen, Amartya, "Property and Hunger," from *Economics and Philosophy*, vol. 4 (1988) pp. 57-68. Copyright © Cambridge University Press. Reprinted by permission of Cambridge University Press and the author.

(through loss of crops and a decline of economic activity, related to a local drought) and had no means of commanding food from elsewhere in the country. Indeed, some food moved *out* of Wollo to more prosperous people in other parts of Ethiopia, repeating a pattern of contrary movement of food that was widely observed during the Irish famine of the 1840s (with food moving out of famine-stricken Ireland to prosperous England which had greater power in the battle of entitlements). The Bangladesh famine of 1974 took place in a year of *peak* food availability, but several occupation groups had lost their entitlement to food through loss of employment and other economic changes (including inflationary pressures causing prices to outrun wages). Other examples of famines without significant (or any) decline in food availability can be found, and there is nothing particularly surprising about this fact once it is recognized that the availability of food is only one influence among many on the entitlement of each occupation group. Even when a famine is associated with a decline of food availability, the entitlement changes have to be studied to understand the particular nature of the famine, e.g., why one occupation group is hit but not another. The causation of starvation can be sensibly sought in failures of entitlements of the respective groups.

The causal analysis of famines in terms of entitlements also points to possible public policies of prevention. The main economic strategy would have to take the form of increasing the entitlements of the deprived groups, and in general, of guaranteeing minimum entitlements for everyone, paying particular attention to the vulnerable groups. This can, in the long run, be done in many different ways, involving both economic growth (including growth of food output) and distributional adjustments. Some of these policies may, however, require that the property rights and the corresponding entitlements of the more prosperous groups be violated.

There is, however, no great moral dilemma in this if property rights are treated as purely *instrumental*. If the goals of relief of hunger and poverty are sufficiently powerful, then it would be just right to violate whatever property rights come in the way, since—in this view—property rights have no intrinsic status. On the other hand, if property rights are taken to be morally inviolable irrespective of their consequences, then it will follow that these policies cannot be morally acceptable even though they might save thousands, or even millions, from dying. The inflexible moral "constraint" of respecting people's legitimately acquired entitlements would rule out such policies.

The issue here is not the valuing of property rights, but their alleged inviolability. There is no dilemma here either for the purely instrumental view of property rights or for treating the fulfillment of property rights as one goal among many, but specifically for consequence-independent assertions of property rights and for the corresponding constraint-based approaches to moral entitlement of ownership.

That property and hunger are closely related cannot possibly come as a great surprise. Hunger is primarily associated with not owning enough food and thus property rights over food are immediately and directly involved. Fights over that property right can be a major part of the reality of a poor country, and any system of moral assessment has to take note of that phenomenon. The tendency to see hunger in purely technocratic terms of food output and availability may help to hide the crucial role of entitlements in the genesis of hunger, but a fuller economic analysis cannot overlook that crucial role. Since property rights over food are derived from property rights over other goods and resources (through production and trade), the entire system of rights of acquisition and transfer is implicated in the emergence and survival of hunger and starvation.

THE RIGHT NOT TO BE HUNGRY

Property rights have been championed for a long time. In contrast, the assertion of "the right not to be hungry" is a comparatively recent phenomenon. While this right is much invoked in political debates, there is a good deal of skepticism about treating this as truly a right in any substantial way. It is often asserted that this concept of "right not to be hungry" stands essentially for nothing at all ("simple nonsense," as Bentham called "natural rights" in general). That piece of sophisticated cynicism reveals not so much a penetrating insight into the practical affairs of the world, but a refusal to investigate what people mean when they assert the existence of rights that for the bulk of humanity, are not in fact guaranteed by the existing institutional arrangements.

The right not to be hungry is not asserted as a recognition of an institutional right that already exists, as the right to property typically is. The assertion is primarily a moral claim as to what should be valued, and what institutional structure we should aim for, and try to guarantee if feasible. It can also be seen in terms of Ronald Dworkin's category of "background rights"—rights that provide a justification for political decisions by society in abstract. This interpretation serves as the basis for a reason to change the existing institutional structure and state policy.

- What is a right? What does it mean to say that rights are unalienable? Are rights ever actually absolute or unalienable?
- What is the only justification for the exercise of power, according to Mill? Is despotism ever a legitimate form of government?
- How is liberty related to a notion of rights? Which of the rights guaranteed under the U.S. Constitution can you identify in Mill's article?
- What is the relationship between rights and obligations? Provide an example. Do the concepts of negative freedom and positive freedom help to clarify the distinction between rights and obligations? How are these two notions of freedom related to positive and negative rights?
- What is the difference between a civil right and a human right? Does Hobbes think that there are any human rights?
- How might our political institutions respond if the right not to be hungry was taken seriously?

H. Fighting for Rights and Justice: Civil Disobedience

If one accepts Mill's argument for limited government, one may also be tempted to favor a still more radical step–to no government at all. The idea that people can get along and work together without a government requires a robust confidence in the capacity and willingness of both the average person and the most powerful members of society to cooperate without the need of force from above, the opposite of Thomas Hobbes's view of men as selfish and requiring a sovereign in order to get along. Another extreme alternative would be to question the need for living in society at all. **Henry David Thoreau** is well known for his grand experiment of living in the Massachusetts woods at Walden pond, minimizing his needs and, for the most part, living virtually alone. Of course one may object that he was able to do so only with the support of other people (not the least because the land itself was owned by his friend, Ralph Waldo Emerson). But the point, repeated by many defenders of "the simple life" over

Henry David Thoreau (1817-1862)

An American essayist, naturalist, and philosopher; a champion of individualism. His most famous work was *Walden*.

FIG. 8.21 Henry David Thoreau *(© iStockphoto .com/Steven Wynn)*

the centuries, is that we can all get along with much less than we who live in a "civilized" society typically think we can. This point is being widely promoted in the United States and other "advanced" societies today, in the name of the environment and the ultimate viability of life on earth. Thoreau's experiment spoke to something quite different, however, and that was the independence and self-reliance of the individual.

Despite his experiment with isolation, Thoreau lived in society like the rest of us and could thus be argued to be beholden to its laws. But should one obey the laws of the land? Socrates (in the *Crito*) certainly thought so, even in the case when those laws were unfairly turned against him. But not everyone agrees. One of the founding principles of the United States, expressed so clearly in the Declaration of Independence, is that a people has the right to rebel against unjust laws and an oppressive government. This principle is directly entailed by the very idea of a social contract. But what about individuals? What are their obligations?

Thoreau turned his ferocious sense of independence to defend the individual's right to disobey unjust laws in his essay "Resistance to Civil Government" (later published as "Civil Disobedience"), in which he defends his decision not to pay his taxes. Indeed, he claims that for a person to obey the laws of a government that behaves unjustly would be the same as his behaving unjustly himself. While "lesser men"—degraded, immoral, and unthinking pawns of government—may go along year after year, obeying the laws, no man of moral character would do so, Thoreau claimed. But being a man of moral character himself, he absolved himself of any obligations to his country other than to "do what he believed right."

FROM "Resistance to Civil Government" ("Civil Disobedience") BY Henry David Thoreau[18]

I heartily accept the motto,—"That government is best which governs least;" and I should like to see it acted up to more rapidly and systematically. Carried out, it finally amounts to this, which also I believe,—"That government is best which governs not at all;" and when men are prepared for it, that will be the kind of government which they will have. Government is at best but an expedient; but most governments are usually, and all governments are sometimes, inexpedient. The objections which have been brought against a standing army, and they are many and weighty, and deserve to prevail, may also at least be brought against a standing government. The standing army is only an arm of the standing government. The government itself, which is only the mode which the people have chosen to execute their will, is equally liable to be abused and perverted before the people can act through it. Witness the present Mexican war, the work of comparatively a few individuals using the standing government as their tool; for, in the outset, the people would not have consented to this measure.

This American government,—what is it but a tradition, though a recent one, endeavoring to transmit itself unimpaired to posterity, but each instant losing some

---

[18] Henry David Thoreau, "Resistance to Civil Government," 1849.

of its integrity? It has not the vitality and force of a single living man; for a single man can bend it to his will. It is a sort of wooden gun to the people themselves; and, if ever they should use it in earnest as a real one against each other, it will surely split. But it is not the less necessary for this; for the people must have some complicated machinery or other, and hear its din, to satisfy that idea of government which they have. Governments show thus how successfully men can be imposed on, even impose on themselves, for their own advantage. It is excellent, we must allow; yet this government never of itself furthered any enterprise, but by the alacrity with which it got out of its way. *It* does not keep the country free. *It* does not settle the West. *It* does not educate. The character inherent in the American people has done all that has been accomplished; and it would have done somewhat more, if the government had not sometimes got in its way. For government is an expedient by which men would fain succeed in letting one another alone; and, as has been said, when it is most expedient, the governed are most let alone by it. Trade and commerce, if they were not made of India rubber, would never manage to bound over the obstacles which legislators are continually putting in their way; and, if one were to judge these men wholly by the effects of their actions, and not partly by their intentions, they would deserve to be classed and punished with those mischievous persons who put obstructions on the railroads.

But, to speak practically and as a citizen, unlike those who call themselves no-government men, I ask for, not *at once* no government, but at once a better government. Let every man make known what kind of government would command his respect, and that will be one step toward obtaining it.

After all, the practical reason why, when the power is once in the hands of the people, a majority are permitted, and for a long period continue, to rule, is not because they are most likely to be in the right, nor because this seems fairest to the minority, but because they are physically the strongest. But a government in which the majority rule in all cases cannot be based on justice, even as far as men understand it. Can there not be a government in which majorities do not virtually decide right and wrong, but conscience?—in which majorities decide only those questions to which the rule of expediency is applicable? Must the citizen ever for a moment, or in the least degree, resign his conscience to the legislator? Why has every man a conscience, then? I think that we should be men first, and subjects afterward. It is not desirable to cultivate a respect for the law, so much as for the right. The only obligation which I have a right to assume, is to do at any time what I think right. It is truly enough said, that a corporation has no conscience; but a corporation of conscientious men is a corporation *with* a conscience. Law never made men a whit more just; and, by means of their respect for it, even the well-disposed are daily made the agents of injustice. A common and natural result of an undue respect for law is, that you may see a file of soldiers, colonel, captain, corporal, privates, powder-monkeys and all, marching in admirable order over hill and dale to the wars, against their wills, aye, against their common sense and consciences, which makes it very steep marching indeed, and produces a palpitation of the heart. They have no doubt that it is a damnable business in which they are concerned; they are all peaceably inclined. Now, what are they? Men at all? or small moveable forts and magazines, at the service of some unscrupulous man in power?

. . .

Under a government which imprisons any unjustly, the true place for a just man is also a prison. The proper place to-day, the only place which Massachusetts has

"Must the citizen ever for a moment, or in the least degree, resign his conscience to the legislator? Why has every man a conscience, then?"

– HENRY DAVID THOREAU

provided for her freer and less desponding spirits, is in her prisons, to be put out and locked out of the State by her own act, as they have already put themselves out by their principles. It is there that the fugitive slave, and the Mexican prisoner on parole, and the Indian come to plead the wrongs of his race, should find them; on that separate, but more free and honorable ground, where the State places those who are not *with* her but *against* her,—the only house in a slave-state in which a free man can abide with honor. If any think that their influence would be lost there, and their voices no longer afflict the ear of the State, that they would not be as an enemy within its walls, they do not know by how much truth is stronger than error, nor how much more eloquently and effectively he can combat injustice who has experienced a little in his own person. Cast your whole vote, not a strip of paper merely, but your whole influence. A minority is powerless while it conforms to the majority; it is not even a minority then; but it is irresistible when it clogs by its whole weight. If the alternative is to keep all just men in prison, or give up war and slavery, the State will not hesitate which to choose. If a thousand men were not to pay their tax-bills this year, that would not be a violent and bloody measure, as it would be to pay them, and enable the State to commit violence and shed innocent blood. This is, in fact, the definition of a peaceable revolution, if any such is possible. If the tax-gatherer, or any other public officer, asks me, as one has done, "But what shall I do?" my answer is, "If you really wish to do any thing, resign your office." When the subject has refused allegiance, and the officer has resigned his office, then the revolution is accomplished. But even suppose blood should flow. Is there not a sort of blood shed when the conscience is wounded? Through this wound a man's real manhood and immortality flow out, and he bleeds to an everlasting death. I see this blood flowing now.

· · ·

Thus the State never intentionally confronts a man's sense, intellectual or moral, but only his body, his senses. It is not armed with superior wit or honesty, but with superior physical strength. I was not born to be forced. I will breathe after my own fashion. Let us see who is the strongest. What force has a multitude? They only can force me who obey a higher law than I. They force me to become like themselves. I do not hear of *men* being *forced* to live this way or that by masses of men. What sort of life were that to live? When I meet a government which says to me, "Your money or your life," why should I be in haste to give it my money? It may be in a great strait, and not know what to do: I cannot help that. It must help itself; do as I do. It is not worth the while to snivel about it. I am not responsible for the successful working of the machinery of society. I am not the son of the engineer. I perceive that, when an acorn and a chestnut fall side by side, the one does not remain inert to make way for the other, but both obey their own laws, and spring and grow and flourish as best they can, till one, perchance, overshadows and destroys the other. If a plant cannot live according to its nature, it dies; and so a man.

Thoreau did not reject the idea of living in society, despite his insistence on independence and self-reliance, nor did he reject the idea of government as such. He rather insisted on a just government and just laws as the precondition of his cooperation. A little more than a hundred years later, in 1963, **Martin Luther King, Jr.**, used similar reasoning in his decision to participate in the civil rights protests in Birmingham, Alabama. King was famous for his advocacy of nonviolent protest; nonetheless, King did believe in protest. In fact, he claims that disobeying the law was his moral—and Christian—obligation. We close this chapter with his famous "Letter from Birmingham Jail," in which he makes this argument.

 FROM **"Letter from Birmingham Jail"**
BY **Martin Luther King, Jr.**[19]

I think I should indicate why I am here in Birmingham, since you have been influenced by the view which argues against "outsiders coming in." I have the honor of serving as president of the Southern Christian Leadership Conference, an organization operating in every southern state, with headquarters in Atlanta, Georgia. We have some eighty-five affiliated organizations across the South, and one of them is the Alabama Christian Movement for Human Rights. Frequently we share staff, educational and financial resources with our affiliates. Several months ago the affiliate here in Birmingham asked us to be on call to engage in a nonviolent direct-action program if such were deemed necessary. We readily consented, and when the hour came we lived up to our promise. So I, along with several members of my staff, am here because I was invited here. I am here because I have organizational ties here.

But more basically, I am in Birmingham because injustice is here. Just as the prophets of the eighth century B.C. left their villages and carried their "thus saith the Lord" far beyond the boundaries of their home towns, and just as the Apostle Paul left his village of Tarsus and carried the gospel of Jesus Christ to the far corners of the Greco-Roman world, so am I compelled to carry the gospel of freedom beyond my own home town. Like Paul, I must constantly respond to the Macedonian call for aid.

Moreover, I am cognizant of the interrelatedness of all communities and states. I cannot sit idly by in Atlanta and not be concerned about what happens in Birmingham. Injustice anywhere is a threat to justice everywhere. We are caught in an inescapable network of mutuality, tied in a single garment of destiny. Whatever affects one directly, affects all indirectly. Never again can we afford to live with the narrow, provincial "outside agitator" idea. Anyone who lives inside the United States can never be considered an outsider anywhere within its bounds.

You deplore the demonstrations taking place in Birmingham. But your statement, I am sorry to say, fails to express a similar concern for the conditions that brought about the demonstration. I am sure that none of you would want to rest content with the superficial kind of social analysis that deals merely

"Injustice anywhere is a threat to justice everywhere. We are caught in an inescapable network of mutuality, tied in a single garment of destiny. Whatever affects one directly, affects all indirectly."

— MARTIN LUTHER KING, JR.

Martin Luther King, Jr. (1929-1968)

An American Baptist minister, civil rights leader, and Nobel Prize Laureate. He was assassinated in 1968.

FIG. 8.22 A 1968 photograph of Dr. Martin Luther King, Jr., in Memphis, Tennessee. *(AP Photo/Charles Kelly)*

with effects and does not grapple with underlying causes. It is unfortunate that demonstrations are taking place in Birmingham, but it is even more unfortunate that the city's white power structure left the Negro community with no alternative.

In any nonviolent campaign there are four basic steps: collection of the facts to determine whether injustices exist; negotiation; self-purification; and direct action. We have gone through all these steps in Birmingham. There can be no gainsaying the fact that racial injustice engulfs this community. Birmingham is probably the most thoroughly segregated city in the United States. Its ugly record of brutality is widely known. Negroes have experienced grossly unjust treatment in the courts. There have been more unsolved bombings of Negro homes and churches in Birmingham than in any other city in the nation. These are the hard, brutal facts of the case. On the basis of these conditions, Negro leaders sought to negotiate with the city fathers. But the latter consistently refused to engage in good-faith negotiation.

Then, last September, came the opportunity to talk with leaders of Birmingham's economic community. In the course of the negotiations, certain promises were made by the merchants—for example, to remove the stores' humiliating racial signs. On the basis of these promises, the Reverend Fred Shuttlesworth and the leaders of the Alabama Christian Movement for Human Rights agreed to a moratorium on all demonstrations. As the weeks and months went by, we realized that we were the victims of a broken promise. A few signs, briefly removed, returned; the others remained.

As in so many past experiences, our hopes had been blasted, and the shadow of deep disappointment settled upon us. We had no alternative except to prepare for direct action, whereby we would present our very bodies as a means of laying our case before the conscience of the local and the national community. Mindful of the difficulties involved, we decided to undertake a process of self-purification. We began a series of workshops on nonviolence, and we repeatedly asked ourselves: "Are you able to accept blows without retaliating?" "Are you able to endure the ordeal of jail?" We decided to schedule our direct-action program for the Easter season, realizing that except for Christmas, this is the main shopping period of the year. Knowing that a strong economic-withdrawal program would be the by-product of direct action, we felt that this would be the best time to bring pressure to bear on the merchants for the needed change.

Then it occurred to us that Birmingham's mayoralty election was coming up in March, and we speedily decided to postpone action until after election day. When we discovered that the Commissioner of Public Safety, Eugene "Bull" Connor, had piled up enough votes to be in the run-off, we decided again to postpone action until the day after the run-off so that the demonstrations could not be used to cloud the issues. Like many others, we waited to see Mr. Connor defeated, and to this end we endured postponement after postponement. Having aided in this community need, we felt that our direct-action program could be delayed no longer.

You may well ask: "Why direct action? Why sit-ins, marches and so forth? Isn't negotiation a better path?" You are quite right in calling for negotiation. Indeed, this is the very purpose of direct action. Nonviolent direct action seeks to create such a crisis and foster such a tension that a community which has constantly refused to negotiate is forced to confront the issue. It seeks so to dramatize the issue that it can no longer be ignored. My citing the creation of tension as part of the work of the nonviolent-resister may sound rather shocking. But I must confess that I am not afraid of the word "tension." I have earnestly opposed violent tension, but there is a type of constructive, nonviolent tension which is necessary for growth. Just as Socrates felt that it was necessary to create a tension in the mind so that individuals could rise from the bondage of myths and half-truths to the unfettered realm of creative analysis and objective appraisal, so must we see the need for nonviolent gadflies to create the kind of tension in society that will help men rise from the dark depths of prejudice and racism to the majestic heights of understanding and brotherhood.

The purpose of our direct-action program is to create a situation so crisis-packed that it will inevitably open the door to negotiation. I therefore concur with you in your call for negotiation. Too long has our beloved Southland been bogged down in a tragic effort to live in monologue rather than dialogue.

. . .

We know through painful experience that freedom is never voluntarily given by the oppressor; it must be demanded by the oppressed. Frankly, I have yet to engage in a direct-action campaign that was "well timed" in the view of those who have not suffered unduly from the disease of segregation. For years now I have heard the word "Wait!" It rings in the ear of every Negro with piercing familiarity. This "Wait" has almost always meant "Never." We must come to see, with one of our distinguished jurists, that "justice too long delayed is justice denied."

You express a great deal of anxiety over our willingness to break laws. This is certainly a legitimate concern. Since we so diligently urge people to obey the Supreme Court's decision of 1954 outlawing segregation in the public schools, at first glance it may seem rather paradoxical for us consciously to break laws. One may well ask: "How can you advocate breaking some laws and obeying others?" The answer lies in the fact that there are two types of laws: just and unjust. I would be the first to advocate obeying just laws. One has not only a legal but a moral responsibility to obey just laws. Conversely, one has a moral responsibility to disobey unjust laws. I would agree with St. Augustine that "an unjust law is no law at all."

Now, what is the difference between the two? How does one determine whether a law is just or unjust? A just law is a man-made code that squares with the moral law or the law of God. An unjust law is a code that is out of harmony with the moral law. To put it in the terms of St. Thomas Aquinas: An unjust law is a human law that is not rooted in eternal law and natural law. Any law that uplifts human personality is just. Any law that degrades human personality is unjust. All segregation statutes are unjust because segregation distorts the soul and damages the personality. It gives the segregator a false sense of superiority and the segregated a false sense of inferiority. Segregation, to use the terminology of the Jewish philosopher Martin Buber, substitutes an "I-it" relationship for an "I-thou" relationship and ends up relegating persons to the status of things. Hence segregation is not only politically, economically and sociologically unsound, it is morally wrong and sinful. Paul Tillich has said that sin is separation. Is not segregation an existential expression of man's tragic separation, his awful estrangement, his terrible sinfulness? Thus it is that I can urge men to obey the 1954 decision of the Supreme Court, for it is morally right; and I can urge them to disobey segregation ordinances, for they are morally wrong.

Let us consider a more concrete example of just and unjust laws. An unjust law is a code that a numerical or power majority group compels a minority group to obey but does not make binding on itself. This is *difference* made legal. By the same token, a just law is a code that a majority compels a minority to follow and that it is willing to follow itself. This is *sameness* made legal.

Let me give another explanation. A law is unjust if it is inflicted on a minority that, as a result of being denied the right to vote, had no part in enacting or devising the law. Who can say that the legislature of Alabama which set up that state's segregation laws was democratically elected? Throughout Alabama all sorts of devious methods are used to prevent Negroes from becoming registered voters, and there are some counties in which, even though Negroes constitute a majority of the population, not a single Negro is registered. Can any law enacted under such circumstances be considered democratically structured?

Sometimes a law is just on its face and unjust in its application. For instance, I have been arrested on a charge of parading without a permit. Now, there is nothing wrong in having an ordinance which requires a permit for a parade. But such an ordinance becomes unjust when it is used to maintain segregation and to deny citizens the First-Amendment privilege of peaceful assembly and protest.

. . .

Oppressed people cannot remain oppressed forever. The yearning for freedom eventually manifests itself, and that is what has happened to the American Negro. Something within has reminded him of his birthright of freedom, and something without has reminded him that it can be gained. Consciously or unconsciously, he has been caught up by the *Zeitgeist*, and with his black brothers of Africa and his brown and yellow brothers of Asia, South America and the Caribbean, the United States Negro is moving with a sense of great urgency toward the promised land of racial justice. If one recognizes this vital urge that has engulfed the Negro community, one should readily understand why public demonstrations are taking place. The Negro has many pent-up resentments and latent frustrations, and he must release them. So let him march; let him make prayer pilgrimages to the city hall; let him go on freedom rides—and try to understand why he must do so. If his repressed emotions are not released in nonviolent ways, they will seek expression through violence; this is not a threat but a fact of history. So I have not said to my people: "Get rid of your discontent." Rather, I have tried to say that this normal and healthy discontent can be channeled into the creative outlet of nonviolent direct action. And now this approach is being termed extremist.

But though I was initially disappointed at being categorized as an extremist, as I continued to think about the matter I gradually gained a measure of satisfaction from the label. Was not Jesus an extremist for love: "Love your enemies, bless them that curse you, do good to them that hate you, and pray for them which despitefully use you, and persecute you." Was not Amos an extremist for justice: "Let justice roll down like waters and righteousness like an ever-flowing stream." Was not Paul an extremist for the Christian gospel: "I bear in my body the marks of the Lord Jesus." Was not Martin Luther an extremist: "Here I stand; I cannot do otherwise, so help me God." And John Bunyan: "I will stay in jail to the end of my days before I make a butchery of my conscience." And Abraham Lincoln: "This nation cannot survive half slave and half free." And Thomas Jefferson: "We hold these truths to be self-evident, that all men are created equal. . . ." So the question is not whether we will be extremists, but what kind of extremists we will be. Will we be extremists for hate or for love? Will we be extremists for the preservation of injustice or for the extension of justice? In that dramatic scene on Calvary's hill three men were crucified. We must never forget that all three were crucified for the same crime—the crime of extremism. Two were extremists for immorality, and thus fell below their environment. The other, Jesus Christ, was an extremist for love, truth, and goodness, and therefore rose above his environment. Perhaps the South, the nation and the world are in dire need of creative extremists.

- On what basis is civil disobedience justified, according to Thoreau? In what respects is Thoreau's view similar to Rousseau's or Locke's?
- Can you think of a current law that you believe to be unjust? Do you think that you are acting unjustly in obeying such laws? How would you respond to Thoreau?
- Are pacifists justified in not paying their federal income tax because they believe war (and by extension, military expenditures) to be immoral?
- Is disobedience by violent means ever justified? How might one draw a moral distinction between the Fathers of the American Revolution and political terrorist groups?

SUMMARY AND CONCLUSION

In some areas of philosophy, the question arises, What does this have to do with everyday life? In political philosophy, as in moral philosophy, the connection between philosophy and "everyday life" is obvious. It is no coincidence that the major revolutions of the eighteenth and nineteenth centuries came soon after a flurry of philosophical radicalism. And we know that much of the world is divided and ruled according to rival political philosophies at the present time.

What is always at issue is the concept of justice. The ideas that people are equal and should be treated equally, that people have natural or human rights that no one and no government can take away from them, that people should equally share the material goods of society—these have all been the subject of constant debate, and sometimes wars and revolutions, for most of modern times. The nature of the state itself has been part of that debate as well, with the state serving as the stage on which the debate has been carried out. How much should the state serve the people, and how much should the people serve the state? What constitutes a good state? And when, if ever, do people have the right to overthrow the state, or a particular regime, or a particular law? We cannot even begin to give adequate answers to these complex questions in the context of a general introduction to philosophy. But neither can we avoid asking them in the world as it is today.

CHAPTER REVIEW QUESTIONS

1. Does a utilitarian description of the state necessarily compromise the rights of the individual? Mill doesn't think so. How can rights be used to protect the individual from the "tyranny of the majority"? How could a utilitarian defend a robust conception of individual rights?

2. Recall John Rawls's two principles of justice. Give a short argument detailing how those two principles can be derived from his "original position." Rawls insists that for this derivation to work, individuals must be self-interested and rational. Explain why this is so. Are individuals self-interested and rational in your view?

3. Can you envision situations in which "positive" and "negative" rights may conflict? If so, how should such conflicts be resolved?

4. What rights would you include in a list of unalienable human rights? What kind of coercive measures may be justified in order to satisfy these rights?

5. We have seen a number of different conceptions of justice: as an orderly society in which members perform their well-defined social function, as giving each his due, as defending some notion of equality, as fairness, and as entitlement. Can you think of how these different definitions could be unified under a single concept of justice?

KEY TERMS

alienation	equality	retributive justice
anarchists	fascism	rights
authority	freedom	social contract
civil rights	government	society
democracy	human rights	sovereign
distributive justice	justice	state
egalitarianism	legitimacy	unalienable rights
entitlement	liberty (political freedom)	

BIBLIOGRAPHY AND FURTHER READING

Plato, *The Republic*, trans. F. M. Cornford (Oxford, U.K.: Oxford University Press, 1941), is still standard reading for the basics and some thought-provoking alternatives in political philosophy.

See also Aristotle, *Politics*, in *The Basic Works of Aristotle*, ed. R. McKeon (New York: Random House, 1941).

Our own national documents, the Declaration of Independence and the Constitution, are always important reading.

John Stuart Mill, *On Liberty*, ed. E. Rapaport (Indianapolis: Hackett, 1978), has long been the classic defense of liberalism.

M. Oakeshott, *Rationalism in Politics and Other Essays* (New York: Basic Books, 1962), is an important challenge to liberal philosophy. So is M. Sandel, *Liberalism and the Limits of Justice*, 2nd ed. (New York: Cambridge University Press, 1998). See also Robert Nisbet, *Conservatism: Dream and Reality* (Minneapolis: University of Minnesota Press, 1986).

Karl Marx's *Communist Manifesto*, trans. S. Moore (Chicago: Regnery, 1969), and his *Early Writings*, trans. T. Bottomore (New York: McGraw-Hill, 1963), are essential reading for beginning students in political philosophy.

Niccolò Machiavelli, *The Prince*, trans. D. Wootton (Indianapolis: Hackett, 1995), and Jean-Jacques Rousseau, *The Social Contract*, trans. E. D. H. Cole (New York: Dutton, 1950), are both important and rewarding reading.

For more general discussions of the philosophy of politics, see *A Companion to Contemporary Political Philosophy*, ed. R. E. Goodin, P. Pettit, and T. Pogge (New York: Wiley-Blackwell, 1995), and R. E. Goodin and P. Pettit, eds., *Contemporary Political Philosophy: An Anthology*, 2nd ed. (New York: Wiley-Blackwell, 2006).

More of Amartya Sen's ideas about justice and the limitations of traditional theories of rights can be found in his book *The Idea of Justice* (Cambridge, MA: Harvard University Press, 2009).

For a discussion of justice issues in relation to women, see M. C. Nussbaum, *Sex and Social Justice* (New York: Oxford University Press, 1999).

For further consideration of the feminist discussion of justice in relation to an ethics of care, see Annette Baier, "The Need for More than Justice," in her book *Moral Prejudices: Essays on Ethics* (Cambridge, MA: Harvard University Press, 1995), pp. 18–32.

For further discussions of justice in relation to civil rights and the civil rights movement of the 1960s see *The Autobiography of Malcolm X*, coauthored with Alex Haley (New York: Ballantine, 1992), and Martin Luther King, Jr., *A Testament of Hope*, ed. J. M. Washington (San Francisco: HarperCollins, 1991).

Two good collections are R. Simon, *Blackwell Guide to Social and Political Philosophy* (Oxford, U.K.: Wiley-Blackwell, 2002), and R. Solomon and M. Murphy, *What Is Justice?* 2nd ed. (New York: Oxford University Press, 2003).

Glossary

Abrahamic religions The Western monotheisms: Judaism, Christianity, and Islam (which all trace their roots from the prophet Abraham).

absolute space and absolute time The view that space and time exist independently of objects and events "in" them, a view defended by Newton. In general, absolute, as used in philosophy, means independent and nonrelative, unqualified and all-inclusive.

absolutism The thesis that there is but one correct view of reality. Opposed to relativism.

abstract Overly general, not concrete, independent of particular concerns or objects. For example, a philosopher may attempt to ascertain the nature of justice without particular reference to any concrete practical case.

action-at-a-distance The idea that one object can have a causal effect on another from a distance, as in Newton's laws of gravitational attraction. Leibniz's rejection of this idea as "absurd" led him to develop a noncausal interpretation of the same phenomena.

ad hominem argument An argument against the person instead of the position; for example, attacking a philosopher's living habits instead of asking whether or not his theories are true.

agnosticism The refusal to believe either that God exists or that He does not exist, usually on the grounds that there can be no sufficient evidence for either belief.

Ahura Mazda The supreme God of Zoroastrianism.

alienation In Marx, the unnatural separation of a person from the products he or she makes, from other people, or from oneself.

altruism The thesis that one ought to act for the sake of the interests of others.

Analects, The One of the major works of Confucianism.

analytic (of a sentence or truth) Demonstrably true (and necessarily true) by virtue of the logical form or the meanings of the component words. The concept was introduced by Kant, who defined it in terms of a sentence (he called it a "judgment") in which the "predicate was contained in the subject" and "added nothing to it." For example, in "a horse is an animal," he would say that the concept of "horse" already includes the concept of being an animal; we would say that "horse" means "an animal that . . ." and thus "is an animal" adds nothing to what we already know just from "horse." Kant also says that the criterion or test for analytic sentences is the principle of contradiction; an analytic sentence is one for which denial yields a self-contradiction.

analytic philosophy The movement in twentieth-century philosophy, particularly in the United States and Britain, that focuses its primary attention on language and linguistic analysis.

anarchism The view that no government has the legitimate authority to coerce people and that the public interest and individual rights can be served only without a state of any kind.

Angra Mainyush The evil spirit in Zoroastrianism.

animism The view that things (or, at the extreme, all things) are alive. It may also be the view that the universe as a whole is one gigantic organism.

antecedent conditions Those circumstances, states of affairs, or events that regularly precede and can be said to cause an event. The antecedent conditions of boiling water, for example, are the application of heat to water under normal atmospheric pressure, and so on. A determinist would say that the antecedent conditions of a human action would be the state of the agent's nervous system, a developed character (with personality traits), certain desires and beliefs, and the circumstances (or "stimulus") in which the action takes place.

anthropomorphic Humanlike. An anthropomorphic conception of God ascribes human attributes to Him.

apeiron In Anaximander, "the unlimited," the basic stuff of the universe.

aphorism A short, striking general observation, usually just a sentence or two.

a posteriori (knowledge) "After experience" or empirical. (See *empirical*.)

appearance The way something seems to us through our senses. Usually philosophers worry about something's being a mere appearance, such that it bears no faithful resemblance to the reality of which it is the appearance.

a priori (knowledge) "Before experience" or, more accurately, independent of all experience. A priori knowledge is always necessary, for there can be no imaginable instances that would refute it and no intelligible doubting of it. One may come to know something a priori through experience (for example, you may find out that no parallel lines ever touch each other by drawing tens of thousands of parallel lines), but what is essential to a priori knowledge is that no such experience is needed. Knowledge is a priori if it can be proved independently of experience. The most obvious examples of a priori knowledge are analytic sentences, such as "a horse is an animal" and "if all men are mammals and Socrates is a man, then Socrates is a mammal."

argument The process of reasoning from one claim to another. An argument may, but need not, be directed against an explicit alternative. A philosophical argument does not require an opponent or a disagreement.

argument from design See *teleological argument*.

asceticism A life of self-denial and material simplicity, often to further philosophical or religious goals.

Asha Immortal spirit or "righteousness" in Zoroastrianism.

assertion A statement or declaration, taking a position. Mere assertion, when presented as an argument, is a fallacy; arguments consist not only of assertions but of reasons for them as well.

association of ideas A central idea of empiricist philosophy, according to which all knowledge is composed of separate ideas that are connected by their resemblance to one another (e.g., "this one looks exactly like that one"), by their contiguity in space and time (e.g., "every time I see this, I see that as well"), and by their causality (e.g., "every time a thing of that sort happens, it is followed by something of this sort"). (The three different "associations" here are Hume's.)

assumption A principle taken for granted without argument or proof.

atheism The belief that there is no God. A person who believes that there is no God is an *atheist*.

attribute In Spinoza, an essential property of God; for example, having a physical nature, having thoughts. In general, an attribute is a property (as in Aristotle).

authority That which controls; usually, that which has the right to control. (For example, the government has the authority to tax your income.)

autonomy Intellectual independence and freedom from authority. Moral autonomy is the ability of every rational person to reach his or her own moral conclusions about what is right and what is wrong. (This does not mean that they will therefore come to different conclusions.)

axiom A principle that is generally accepted from the beginning and so may be used without further debate as a starting point of an argument.

bad faith Sartre's characterization of a person's refusal to acknowledge the degree to which he or she is free and responsible for his or her choices. This sometimes means not accepting the facts that are true about you. More often it means accepting the facts about you as conclusive about your identity, as in the statement "Oh, I couldn't do that, I'm too shy."

Becoming (in Plato) The "world of Becoming" is the changing world of our daily experience, in which things and people come into being and pass away.

begging the question Merely restating as the conclusion of an argument one of its premises. For example, "Why do oysters give me indigestion? Because they upset my stomach."

behaviorism In psychology, the radical methodological thesis that insists that only what is publicly observable can be used as subject matter or as evidence in scientific research regarding human beings. In particular, all talk of "minds" and "mental events," "desires," "purposes," "ideas," "perceptions," and "experiences" is to be given up in favor of terms that refer only to the experimental situation or the behavior of the creature (or person) in question (for example, "stimulus," "response," "reinforcements"). In philosophy and metaphysics, behaviorism is the logical thesis that there are no "covert" or "private" mental events, only patterns of behavior and psychological ways of talking about behavior as "intelligent," "deceitful," "calculating," or "inattentive." All these patterns of behavior must be understood not in terms of some process ("intelligence," "deceitful thinking," "calculating," or "lack of attending") going on "in the mind" but, rather, as ways of interpreting, predicting, and otherwise describing and evaluating behavior.

Being (in Plato) The "world of Being" is the realm of eternal Forms, in which nothing ever changes. It is, for Plato, reality, and, in general, Being is used by philosophers to refer to whatever they consider ultimately real (substance, God).

best of all possible worlds This world, according to Leibniz's view that God demands a perfect universe and makes it "the best possible," all things considered.

Bhagavadgītā ("Gītā") The "Song of God" of ancient Hinduism; a segment of the epic poem the *Mahabhavata* in which the character Krishna reveals himself to be God incarnate.

Brahman The Hindu idea of the One, the unity underlying all things.

Buddha "The awakened one"; the historical founder of Buddhism.

Cartesian Concerning Descartes. In particular, concerning his philosophical method. (Descartes's followers are generally called "Cartesians" and their method "Cartesianism.") The Cartesian method is essentially a deductive method, as in geometry, starting with self-evident axioms and deducing the rest.

categorical imperative In Kant's philosophy, a moral law, a command that is unqualified and not dependent on any conditions or qualifications. In particular, that rule that tells us to act in such a way that we would rationally will that everyone else act the same way.

categories Kant's word (borrowed from Aristotle) for those most basic and a priori concepts of human knowledge, for example, causality and substance.

causal interactionism The theory that mind and body causally interact, that mental events (for example, an "act of will") can cause a bodily consequence (for instance, raising one's arm), and that a bodily change (such as a puncture of the skin) can cause a mental consequence (for example, a pain).

causal theory of perception The view that our experience (our sensations and ideas) are the effects of physical objects acting upon our sense organs.

causation *or* causality The relation of cause and effect, one event bringing about another according to natural law. In Hume, (1) one event following another necessarily (or so it seems to us) or (2) one type of event regularly following another (See *association of ideas*).

cause That which brings something about. On the hard determinist interpretation, a cause is an antecedent condition that, together with other antecedent conditions, is sufficient to make the occurrence of some event necessary, according to the laws of nature. On a weaker interpretation, a cause may simply be an event (or condition) that regularly precedes another event and thus can be used to predict when the latter will occur. (For example, if we say "a cause of forest fires is lightning," we mean "whenever lightning strikes a sufficiently dry forest, fire will occur.") In Aristotle, "cause" means something like "reason," and he distinguishes four different kinds of "causes" of a change: (1) the *formal* cause, the principle or essential idea according to which a change comes about (think of a blueprint for a building or the plans for a project); (2) the *material* cause, the matter that undergoes the change (think of the raw materials for building a house—lumber, bricks, cement); (3) the *efficient* cause, that which initiates the change (the construction workers and their tools); and (4) the *final* cause, or the purpose of the change (to build a place where Socrates and his family can live, for example).

cause-of-itself (*causa sui*) That which brings about its own existence or whose essence involves existence, often said of God.

certainty Beyond doubt. But it is important to insist that certainty in the philosophical sense is more than the common psychological use of *certain* ("feeling certain"). One can feel certain and yet be wrong or foolish. One can be certain, in this philosophical sense, only if one can prove that the matter is beyond doubt, that no reasons for doubt could be raised.

civil rights Those rights that are determined by a particular state and its laws; constitutional rights, for example, are civil rights in this sense, guaranteed by the law of the land.

cogito, ergo sum Or "I think, therefore I am" is Descartes's only principle that he finds "beyond doubt" and "perfectly certain." (*Think* here refers to any kind of idea or experience in the mind, not just what we would call *thinking*.) It is the premise of his entire philosophy.

coherence Logical connection. A statement by a witness in a courtroom coheres with other testimony and evidence when it fits in and is consistent with that other testimony and evidence. To say that a philosophy must be coherent is to say that its various principles must fit together in an orderly and logically agreeable fashion.

coherence theory of truth A statement or a belief is true if and only if it "coheres" with a system of statements or beliefs. A truth of mathematics is "true" because it forms part of the nexus in the complex of mathematical truths. A geometrical theorem is "true" because it can be proved from other theorems (axioms, definitions) of the geometrical system. A "factual" statement is "true" insofar as other "factual" statements, including general statements about experience that are logically relevant to the original statement, support it. Since we can never get "outside" our experience, the only sense in saying that a belief is true (according to this theory) is that it "coheres" with the rest of our experience.

commitment To form a binding obligation voluntarily. In Sartre's moral philosophy, a commitment is the freely chosen adoption of a moral principle or project that one thereby vows to defend and practice, even in the absence of any other reasons for doing so. Since, according to Sartre, there are never conclusive reasons for adopting any particular moral position, one must always defend his or her position through commitment and nothing else.

compatibilism The thesis that both determinism (on some interpretations) and free action can be true. According to compatibilists, determinism does not rule out free action and the possibility of free action does not require that determinism be false. They are compatible positions.

compulsion "Being forced to do something." One acts from compulsion (or is compelled to act) when he or she could not have done otherwise. Some philosophers distinguish between *external* compulsions (for example, being pushed) and *internal* compulsions (for instance, a neurotic obsession).

conceptual truth A statement that is true and that we can see to be true by virtue of the meanings of the words (or we should say, the "concepts") that compose it. For example, "a horse is an animal" is a conceptual truth because anyone who speaks English and knows the meaning of the words *horse* and *animal* knows that such a statement must be true; part of the definition of the word *horse* is "an animal." In Plato, a conceptual truth is a truth about Forms. In Aristotle, a conceptual truth is a matter of describing the essence of a thing. (See *essence, Form.*)

conscience A sense or feeling about what is right and wrong, usually without argument. (It is like intuition in matters of knowledge.) In Christian moral theory, it is a moral sense instilled in us by God. In Freudian psychology, it is the internalization of the moral lessons taught us as children by our parents and teachers.

consistent Fitting together in an orderly logical way. Two principles are consistent if they do not contradict each other. A philosophy is consistent if none of its principles contradict each other.

constitute To put together, "set up," or synthesize experience through categories or concepts. First used by Kant, later by Husserl.

contemplation (the life of) According to Aristotle (and other philosophers), the happiest life, the life of thought and philosophy.

contingent (truth) Dependent on the facts; neither logically necessary nor logically impossible. A contingent state of affairs could have been otherwise. One test to see if a state of affairs is contingent is to see if it is conceivable that it could be other than it is. It is contingent, for example, that heavy objects fall toward the earth, since it is easily imaginable what it would be like if they did not. This is so even though, in another sense, we say that it is (physically) necessary that heavy objects fall. The philosophical terms *contingent* and *necessary* refer to logical possibility, not to the factual question of whether a statement is true or not.

continuity (spatiotemporal continuity) The uninterrupted identifiability of an object over time in the same location or in a sequence of tangent locations.

contradiction The logical relation of two principles in which the truth of one requires the falsity of the other. A witness's statement in court contradicts other testimony if both statements cannot be true.

correspondence theory of truth A statement or belief is true if and only if it "corresponds" to "the facts." Even when restricting our attention to statements of fact, however, this common-sense "theory" gets into trouble as soon as it tries to pick out what corresponds to what. How can we identify a "fact," for example, apart from the language we use to identify it? And what does it mean to say that a statement "corresponds" to a fact?

cosmogony The study of the origins of the universe in its entirety.

cosmological argument An argument (or set of arguments) that undertakes to "prove" that God exists on the basis of the idea that there must have been a first cause or an ultimate reason for the existence of the universe (the cosmos).

cosmology The study of the universe in its entirety (from the Greek word for "universe"–*cosmos*).

counterexample An example that contradicts a generalization, such as "all elephants have tusks." A counterexample would be an elephant without tusks.

criterion The test or standard according to which a judgment or an evaluation can be made. For example, a test for a substance being an acid is whether or not it turns litmus paper red. Or a sure mark or standard. In ancient skepticism, a sufficient guarantee of truth.

critical Thinking so as to be mindful of mistakes in reasoning; to be critical is not necessarily to be unpleasant.

cultural relativism The descriptive anthropological thesis that different societies have different moralities. It is important to stress that these moralities must be fundamentally different, not only different in details. Some societies consider an act as stealing while others do not, but a society that does not have a conception of private property may be fundamentally different from one that does.

Dao The "Way"; in Confucianism, the "way" to be a gentleman, for example, following the rituals; in Daoism, the underlying and ineffable "way" of nature or reality.

datum Latin, literally, "what is given." (plural, *data*)

declarative sentence A sentence in which one takes a position, states a fact, asserts a proposition.

deconstruction Initiated by Jacques Derrida, a school of philosophical thought that encourages critical reading "against the grain," exposing and resisting the text's binary assumptions (the text's hierarchy of what is valuable and what is not) and displacing the analytical structure that is based on them.

deduction (deductive argument) A process of reasoning from one principle to another by means of accepted rules of inference. In a deductive argument, a conclusion follows necessarily from the premises, so if you are certain of the premises, you can be certain of the conclusion, too.

deism A variation of the Judeo-Christian religion that was extremely popular in the science-minded eighteenth century. Deism holds that God must have existed to create the universe with all its laws (and thereby usually accepts some form of the cosmological argument) but also holds that there is no justification for our belief that God has any special concern for man, any concern for justice, or any of those anthropomorphic attributes assumed when we worship Him, pray to Him, and believe in biblical stories about Him.

democracy That form of government in which policies or, at least, the makers of policy are chosen by popular mandate.

deontology Ethics based on duty (Gk: *dein*). Kant's ethic is deontological in that it stresses obedience to principle, rather than attention to consequences (including happiness).

determinism The view that every event in the universe is dependent upon other events, which are its causes. On this view, all human actions and decisions, even those that we would normally describe as "free" and "undetermined," are totally dependent on prior events that cause them.

dharma In Hinduism, righteousness, the way of the good; one's duties and obligations, based on the role one occupies.

dialectic Argument through dialogue, disagreement, and successive revisions, out of which comes agreement. Alternately, a "logic" developed by Hegel in which different forms or philosophies are arranged according to increasing sophistication and scope. The "logic" is a development from one form, whose inadequacies are demonstrated, to another, which corrects these inadequacies, and so on. Marx borrows this "dialectic" and gives it a social interpretation. (The "logic" need not be anything like the form "thesis-antithesis-synthesis.")

distributive justice The ideal of everyone receiving his or her fair share. For example, concerns over ownership of land, just wages, and fair prices are all matters of distributive justice.

divine preordination God's knowledge of and power over all that will happen, including our own future actions.

doubt Lack of certainty; lack of reasons to believe and perhaps having reasons not to believe. It is important to distinguish doubt in this philosophical sense from doubt in the ordinary psychological sense. Mere personal uncertainty or distrust is not sufficient; there must be a demonstrable reason for doubt, that is, a reason for not accepting the belief in question.

dual aspect theory The theory (for example, in Spinoza) that mind and body are simply different aspects (or "attributes") of one and the same substance, thus avoiding the problem of interaction between substances.

dualism In general, the distinction between mind and body as separate substances, or very different kinds of states and events with radically different properties.

duty What one is morally bound to do.

egalitarianism The view that all people are equal in rights and equally deserving of respect.

egoism The thesis that people act for their own interests. *Psychological egoism* is merely the thesis that people act in their own interests; *ethical egoism* is the thesis that people ought to act in their own interests.

eliminative materialism The thesis that increasing knowledge of neurology eventually will allow us to give up our "folk psychological" terminology of mental states.

empirical (knowledge) Derived from and to be defended by appeal to experience. Empirical knowledge can only be so derived and so defended (as opposed to a priori knowledge, which need not be).

empirical ego All the characteristics of a person that can be discovered through experience and that distinguish each of us from other persons qualitatively; that which makes each of us a particular man or woman and gives us a particular "character." Compare *transcendental ego*.

empiricism The philosophy that demands that all knowledge, except for certain logical truths and principles of mathematics, comes from experience. British empiricism is often used to refer specifically to the three philosophers Locke, Berkeley, and Hume. Empiricism is still very much alive, however, and includes Bertrand Russell and a great many philosophers of the first half of the twentieth century who called themselves "logical empiricists" (better known as logical positivists).

emptiness In Buddhism, in Nāgārjuna, being without substance: the proper understanding of being as without substance.

Enlightenment A cultural and philosophical movement in the eighteenth century in Europe defined by a new confidence in human reason and individual autonomy. Some of the major figures of this movement were Descartes, the metaphysician d'Holbach, the political philosopher Rousseau, and the political reformer-writer Voltaire in France. In Great Britain, Enlightenment philosophers were Locke and Hume; in Germany, Kant.

entitlement A right; for instance, a right to own property.

epiphenomenalism The thesis that mental events are epiphenomena, that is, side effects of various physical processes in the brain and nervous system but of little importance themselves. The model is a one-way causal model: body states cause changes in the mind, but mental states have no effect in themselves on the body.

epistemology The study of human knowledge, its nature, its sources, and its justification.

equality In political philosophy, the nondiscriminatory treatment of every person, regardless of sex, race, religion, physical or mental abilities, wealth, social status, and so forth.

essence (or an essential property) The necessary or defining characteristics or properties of a thing. The essence of a person is that without which we would not say one is *that* particular person (Fred rather than Mary, for example). In Husserl's writings, "essence" or "essential intuition" refers to those ideal objects and laws that constitute necessary truths. The term *essence* is borrowed from Aristotle (and the medieval philosophers) and used in much the same way, except that Husserl's notion of essence is always tied to "intuition" and consciousness.

ethical absolutism The thesis that there is one and only one correct morality.

ethical egoism The thesis that people ought to act in their own interests.

ethical relativism The thesis that different moralities should be considered equally correct even if they directly contradict each other. A morality is "correct," according to this thesis, merely if it is correct according to the particular society that accepts it.

ethics A system of general moral principles and a conception of morality and its foundation. Or, the study of moral principles.

eudaimonia Aristotle's word for "happiness," or, more literally, "living well."

existentialism A modern movement in philosophy that puts great emphasis on individual choice and the voluntary acceptance (or creation) of one's values. In Sartre's terms, existentialism is the philosophy that teaches that "man's existence precedes his essence." That is, people have no given self-identity; they have to choose their identities and work for them through their actions. (Neglect and omission, however, are also actions. One can be a certain type of person just by not bothering to perform particular actions.)

explanation An account—usually a causal account—of something; it is opposed to *justification*, which also defends. One can, for example, explain one's action (say, by claiming that one was drunk) without thereby justifying it, that is, showing it to be right. Hume ultimately explains our knowledge but does not justify it.

extended Having spatial dimensions. Philosophers (for example, Descartes, Leibniz, and Spinoza) often define bodies as "extended" and minds and ideas as "unextended."

extended (substance) Physical matter in space and time, material objects.

facticity Sartre's term (borrowed from Heidegger) for the totality of facts that are true of a person at any given time.

faith In the popular sense, believing in something for which you have inadequate evidence or little good reason. In theology, faith usually refers to the trust that a believer should have in God's ultimate grace and fairness. Sometimes, faith is defended as a rational belief in God (for example, in Kant). More often, faith is defended against rationality (as in Kierkegaard).

fallacy An apparently persuasive argument that is really an error in reasoning; an unsound or invalid argument.

fascism The view that the best government is the strongest and that the government has the right—and perhaps the duty—to control the lives of every citizen for the sake of the most efficient society.

fatalism The thesis that certain events (or perhaps all events) are going to happen inevitably, regardless of what efforts we take to prevent them.

first principles Those axioms and assumptions from which a philosophy begins. They must be solid and indisputable principles; they need not be those principles that one happens to believe first.

Form (in Plato) An independently existing entity in the world of Being, which determines the nature of the particular things of this world that "participate" in it. In Aristotle, forms have no independent existence.

formal logic A branch of logic that is concerned with the principles of reasoning as such, in which the relationships between symbols are studied, not their interpretation.

Four Noble Truths Among the most important teachings of the Buddha: "All is suffering (and transitory)," the need to eliminate desire, the way to eliminate desire, and the right path to the good.

freedom The idea that a human decision or action is a person's own responsibility and that praise and blame may be appropriately ascribed. The most extreme interpretation of *freedom* is the absence of any causes or determinations. Thus an indeterminist would say that an event was free if it had no causes; a libertarian would say that a human act was free if it was only self-caused, but not determined by anything else (including a person's character). Certain determinists, however ("soft determinists"), would say that an act is free if only it is "in character" and based upon a person's desire and personality. Most generally, we say that a person's act was free if we would say that he or she could have done otherwise, whether or not it was the result of a conscious decision and whether or not certain causes may have been involved. (See also *liberty*.)

freedom of the will The condition in which actions are undetermined by external causes, including the power of God (although how God can leave us this "indeterminacy" in spite of God's power and knowledge over us is and must be incomprehensible to us).

free will Among philosophers, a somewhat antiquated expression (as in "he did it of his own free will"), which means that a person is capable of making decisions that are not determined by antecedent conditions. Of course, there may be antecedent considerations, such as what a person wants or what a person believes, but free will means that such considerations never determine a person's decision. At most they "enter into the decision."

functionalism The view that the mind is the product of a pattern in the brain, as in a computer, rather than a product of the matter of the brain as such.

generalization Usually, a proposition about all of a group or set of things on the basis of a limited acquaintance with some of its members. In logic, however, a generalization may be universal ("all x's are y's") or existential ("there are some x's that are y's").

generalization from experience (or inductive generalization) Inference from observation, experience, and experiment to a generalization about all members of a certain class. For example, in a laboratory, a researcher finds that certain experiments on tobacco plants always have the same result. He or she generalizes, through induction, from experimental observations to a claim (or *hypothesis*) about all tobacco plants. But notice that this generalization is never certain (like the generalization in geometry from a proof of a theorem about this triangle to a theorem about all triangles). It may always turn out that there was a fluke in the experiment or that the experimenter chose a peculiar sample of plants.

God In traditional Judeo-Christian theology, the being who created the universe and exists independently of it, who is all-powerful, all-knowing, everywhere at once, and concerned with justice and the ultimate welfare of humankind. When spelled with a small "g," the word refers to any supernatural being worthy of worship or, at least, extraordinary respect.

Golden Rule "Do unto others as you would have them do unto you."

government The instrument of authority; the body that rules, passes and enforces laws, and so forth.

happiness The achievement of the good life. In Aristotle, the name we all agree to give to the good life, whatever it is. Happiness, in this sense, must not be confused with pleasure, which is but one (among many) concerns and conceptions of the good life.

happiness calculus (also *felicity calculus*) Bentham's technique for quantifying and adding up pleasures and pains as a way of deciding what to do.

hedonism The conception of the good life that takes pleasure to be the ultimate good. Hedonism is the premise of most forms of utilitarianism. It is often the premise—although sometimes a consequence—of ethical egoism. (These two are not the same: hedonism refers to the *end*; egoism refers to *whose* ends.)

Heisenberg uncertainty principle An important principle of recent physics that demonstrates that we cannot know both the position and the momentum of certain subatomic particles, for in our attempts to know one, we make it impossible to know the other. This principle has been used to attack the very idea of "determinism" in its classical formulations, for determinism requires the "certainty" of possible prediction that the Heisenberg uncertainty principle rejects.

hermeneutics The discipline of interpretation of texts. Broadly conceived (as by Heidegger and Gadamer), it is the "uncovering" of meanings in everyday life, the attempt to understand the signs and symbols of one's culture and tradition in juxtaposition with other cultures and traditions.

historicism A philosophy that localizes truth and different views of reality to particular times, places, and peoples in history. It is generally linked to a very strong relativist thesis as well, that there is no truth apart from these various historical commitments.

human rights Those rights that are considered to be universal, "unalienable," and common to every person regardless of where or when he or she lives. For example, freedom from torture and degradation would be a human right.

Hume's fork Hume's insistence that every belief be justified either as a "relation between ideas" or as a "matter of fact."

hypothesis A provisional conclusion, accepted as most probable in the light of the known facts or tentatively adopted as a basis for analysis.

hypothetical imperative In Kant, a command that is conditional, depending upon particular aims or inclinations. For example, "if you want to be a doctor, then go to medical school." According to Kant, all other philosophers (Aristotle, Hume, Rousseau) took morality to be a hypothetical imperative. He does not.

idea In epistemology, almost any mental phenomenon (not typically, as in Plato, with existence independent of individual minds). The terminology varies slightly; Locke uses *idea* to refer to virtually any "mental content"; Hume reserves *idea* for those mental atoms that are derived by the mind from impressions. In Plato, a Form.

idealism The metaphysical view that only minds and their ideas exist.

Identity of Indiscernibles A principle of Leibniz's philosophy according to which no two things can possibly have all the same properties or be absolutely identical in all respects.

identity theory The thesis that the mind and brain are ontologically one and the same or, more accurately, that mental states and events are in fact certain brain and nervous system processes. The theory is usually presented as a form of materialism, but it is important to emphasize that unlike many materialistic theories, it does not deny the existence of mental events. It denies only that they have independent existence. Mental events are nothing other than certain bodily events.

illusion A false belief motivated by intense wishes. According to Marx, religion is an illusion that is intended to compensate for an intolerable social situation. According to Freud, religion is an illusion that attempts to hold onto our childhood desires for fatherly protection and security.

immaterialism The metaphysical view that accepts the existence of nonspatial, nonsensory entities, such as numbers, minds, and ideas. The weak version asserts merely that there are such entities. The strong version asserts that there are *only* such entities (that is, there are no physical objects).

immediate For certain and without need for argument.

immoralist A person who rejects the ultimate claims of morality. An immoralist need not actually break the rules of morality; he or she does not consider them absolute rules and claims that other considerations (even personal considerations) may override them.

immortality The idea that the soul survives death (and, in some belief systems, precedes birth).

imperative A command.

implication One statement logically follows from another. Statements imply one another: We infer one from the other.

impression Hume's word for sensations or sense-data, that which is given to the mind through the senses.

inclination Kant's term for all personal considerations: desires, feelings, emotions, attitudes, moods, and so on.

incoherent Not fitting together in an orderly or logically agreeable fashion. Using fancy jargon that has no precise meaning may be a source of incoherence. So is a mere list of random beliefs, without any order or logic to hold them together. (They may even contradict each other.) An incoherent philosophy may be insightful and true in parts, but because it never coheres into a single system, it may well appear to be nonsense or simply a jumble of words and phrases. In other cases, an incoherent philosophy may be one that makes no sense, whose terms are utter gibberish or whose principles are mere ramblings without intelligible connection or interpretation. (Opposite of coherent.)

inconsistent Not compatible; contradictory. One may also say that a person's actions are inconsistent with his or her principles. People as well as other principles can be inconsistent with a principle.

incorrigibility Impossible to correct; cannot be mistaken. It has long been argued that our claims about our own mental states are incorrigible—we cannot be mistaken about them.

indeterminism The thesis that at least some events in the universe are not determined, are not caused by antecedent conditions, and may not be predictable.

induction; inductive reasoning; inductive generalization Induction is the process of inferring general conclusions (for example, "all swans are white") from a sufficiently large sample of particular observations ("this swan is white, that swan is white, and that one, and that one, and that one. . . . "). It is usually contrasted with *deduction,* in that, while deductive reasoning guarantees that the conclusion shall be as certain as the premises, induction never gives us a conclusion as certain as the premises. Its conclusions are, at most, merely probable. ("There may always be some black swan somewhere," and there are, in Western Australia.) (See A Brief Introduction to Logic, pp. 23-39.)

inductive argument A process of reasoning in which the characteristics of an entire class or set of things is inferred on the basis of an acquaintance with some of its members. In an inductive argument, although the conclusion is supported by the premises, it does not follow necessarily from the premises, and its truth is not guaranteed by them.

ineffable Indescribable.

inference Reasoning from one set of principles to another, as in an argument. Deductive inference is but a single kind of inference.

inference-ticket Ryle's term for referring to the proper function of a mental state: talk, as a description of a pattern of behavior and, therefore, as an "inference-ticket" that allows us to infer what a person will do in the future. (To say "George wants an olive" is to give us an inference-ticket regarding his future behavior around olives.)

infinite regress A sequence going back endlessly. For example, "A is caused by B, and B by C, and C by D . . . and so on to infinity." Aristotle believed such a regress to be an intellectual absurdity.

innate ideas Literally, ideas that are "born into the mind"; knowledge that is "programmed" into us from birth and need not be learned. Experience may be necessary to "trigger off" such ideas, but they are already "in" all of us. In Plato, the theory of innate ideas is part of a general theory of the immortality of the soul. Locke's famous attack on such ideas took them to be literally ideas that all men share from birth. The rationalist philosophers he was supposedly attacking, however, held a much more sophisticated notion; they did not believe that ideas are literally "born into us," but they did believe that we are born with certain "innate" capacities and dispositions, which will develop with proper education (and mental health). And, most important, these ideas can be defended or justified without appeal to any particular experiences or experiments. This is the claim that Locke ultimately rejected.

intentionality The "aboutness" of mental states (and other intentional states). A belief is always *about* something. A desire is always *for* something. An emotion is *directed* at someone or some situation. The importance of this concept in phenomenology is that it undercuts the metaphor of mental "contents" (as in a theater, an image explicitly used by Hume, for example). The concept was used by Husserl's teacher, Franz Brentano, who borrowed it from some medieval philosophers before Husserl used it and made it famous. McGinn, on the other hand, treats intentionality as the content of consciousness.

intuition Immediate knowledge of the truth without the aid of any reasoning and without appeal to experience. Intuition, as rational intuition (there are other kinds), is a central concern of the rationalist philosophers, who consider intuition one of the main functions of reason. But because of its very nature, intuition cannot be argued for, nor can it be defended by experience. Accordingly, many philosophers, especially empiricists, reject the notion of intuition and accept it only when absolutely unavoidable. In the twentieth century, Edmund Husserl defended the appeal to intuition in his phenomenology.

invalid Not correctly following agreed-upon rules of inference in an argument. Always applied to arguments, not to statements. (Opposite of valid.)

justice In the general sense, the virtues of an ideal society. In the more particular sense, the balance of public interest and individual rights, the fair sharing of the available goods of society, the proper punishment of criminals, and the fair restitution to victims of crime and misfortune within society.

justification An attempt to defend a position or an act, to show that it is correct (or at least reasonable). (Compare with *explanation*.)

karma In Hinduism, the tendency of any course of action to be repeated; the limitation of one's free will by one's own habits and dispositions (even into the next life).

Krishna In Hinduism, an avatar, God incarnate.

law An objective rule that is binding on individuals whether they personally accept it or not. Contrasted with *maxim*.

law of contradiction That basic rule of logic that demands that a sentence and its denial cannot both be true. "Not (P and not P)." This law is used by many philosophers (Kant, Leibniz, and Hume, for example) as a criterion for analyticity or analytic truth.

law of the excluded middle That rule of logic that says that either a sentence or its denial must be true: "Either P or not P." In formal logic, this law, together with the law of contradiction, forms the basis of a great many arguments (for example, that form of argument called *reductio ad absurdum*, in which the consequences of one premise are shown to be absurd, and therefore its denial is accepted). Many logicians are now reconsidering this law, for it is becoming evident that not all sentences are either true or false. For example, consider Russell's famous example, "the King of France is bald" (when there is no king of France); is that true or false? It surely is not true, but neither can it be false, for there is no king of France who is not bald. Or what of, "green ideas sleep furiously"? Many philosophers would say that these are neither true nor false, thus rejecting the law of the excluded middle.

legitimacy The right to have authority; sanctioned power (for example, through the grace of God, by means of legal succession, by appeal to justice, or to the general consent of the people governed).

liberty (political freedom) The ability to act without restraint or threat of punishment. For example, the ability to travel between states without a passport, the ability to speak one's opinions without prosecution, or the ability to work for or choose one's profession or career. This ability, however, is not mere physical or mental ability; one may have the liberty to travel or to try to become a doctor without having the means to do so. It is also important to distinguish this political sense of liberty or freedom from the metaphysical or causal sense discussed previously. Whether our acts are really free in that sense must be distinguished from the question of whether we are constrained or free to act in this political sense. The first refers to the causes of human behavior; the second refers only to the existence of legislation and political forces constraining our behavior.

logic The study of the rules of valid inference and "rational argument." In general, a sense of order.

logical truth A sentence that can be shown to be true by virtue of its logical form alone (by virtue of the connectives, "and," "or," and so forth).

masculinist From the point of view of men's interests and advantage, as opposed to those of women.

master morality In Nietzsche, a morality that takes personal self-realization as primary, so-called because it was the morality of the "masters" in the slave states of the ancient world (including Greece).

materialism The metaphysical view that only physical matter and its properties exist. Such intangible entities as numbers, minds, and ideas are really properties of physical bodies. To talk about energy, for example, is, in a way, to talk about physical potential; to talk about minds is, as a kind of shorthand, to talk about behavior; to talk about ideas is, in a misleading way, to talk about the various structures and interrelationships between objects. Numbers have no existence of their own but only represent sets of sets of objects (the set of all sets of eight things is the number eight, for example). Materialism has always been a powerful worldview in modern scientific culture. It is also the most common view among the pre-Socratic philosophers.

matter of fact (in Hume) An empirical claim, to be confirmed or falsified through experience.

maxim In Kant, a personal rule or intention. Contrasted with *law*.

mean (between the extremes) In Aristotle, the middle course, not too much, not too little. Courage, for example, is a mean because a person with courage is neither too timid to fight nor so lacking in fear that he or she is rash or reckless in the face of danger.

metaphysics Most simply, the study of the most basic (or "first") principles. Traditionally, the study of ultimate reality, or "Being as such." Popularly, any kind of very abstract or obscure thinking. Most philosophers today would define metaphysics as the study of the most general concepts of science and human life, for example, reality, existence, freedom, God, soul, action, mind. In general, we can divide metaphysics among ontology, cosmology, and an ill-defined set of problems concerning God and the immortality of the human soul. (See *ontology, cosmology*.)

method (sometimes, methodology) An approach and strategy for resolving philosophical problems. For example, the appeal to experience, the appeal to divine revelation, the insistence upon mathematical logic, confidence in reason, or trust in authority—all these are aspects of philosophical methodology.

method of doubt (or methodological doubt) Descartes' technique for discovering those principles of which we can be "perfectly certain," namely, doubt everything, until you discover those principles that cannot be doubted.

modes (in Spinoza) Inessential properties or modifications of attributes.

monad (in Leibniz) The simple immaterial substances that are the ultimate constituents of all reality. God, the one uncreated monad, created all the others as self-enclosed ("windowless"), predetermined entities.

monism The metaphysical view that there is ultimately only one substance, that all reality is one. Less strictly, it may be applied to philosophers who believe in only one kind of substance.

monotheism Belief in one God.

morality In general, the rules for right action and prohibitions against wrong acts. Sometimes morality is the single set of absolute rules and prohibitions that are valid for all men at all times and all societies. More loosely, a morality can be any set of ultimate principles, and there may be any number of moralities in different societies.

mysticism The belief that one can come to grasp certain fundamental religious truths (the existence of God, the oneness of the universe) through direct experience, but of a very special kind, different from ordinary understanding and often at odds with reason.

natural law The moral law as it is revealed through the way that nature (particularly our human nature) has been constructed. St. Thomas Aquinas, among others, defends this idea, arguing that God has prescribed rules for our conduct in the very way he designed us.

naturalism The belief that ultimate reality is a natural property.

necessary (truth) Cannot be otherwise and cannot be imagined to be otherwise. In philosophy, it is not enough that something be "necessary" according to physical laws (for example, the law of gravity) or "necessary" according to custom or habit (for example, the "necessity" of laws against rape or the felt necessity of having a cigarette after dinner). Necessary allows for not even imaginary counterexamples; hence it is a necessary truth that two plus two equals four. Not only do we believe thus with certainty and find ourselves incapable of intelligibly doubting it, but we cannot even suggest what it would be for it to be false, no matter how wild our imaginations.

necessary and sufficient conditions A is necessary and sufficient for B when A is both logically required and enough to guarantee B ("A if and only if B").

necessity In accordance with a necessary truth.

nihility "The Nothing," "nothingness."

obligation Bound by duty. For example, "you have an obligation to keep your promises."

omnipotent All powerful, usually said of God.

omnipresent Everywhere at once, usually said of God.

omniscient All knowing, usually said of God.

ontological argument An argument (or set of arguments) that tries to "prove" the existence of God from the very concept of "God." For example, "God," by definition, is that being with all possible perfection; existence is a perfection; therefore, God exists.

ontology The study of being. That is, that part of metaphysics that asks such questions as, What is there? What is it for something to exist? What is an individual thing? How do things interact? Traditionally, these questions were formulated as questions about substance. Today, much of ontology is part of logic and linguistics and is the study of the concepts we use to discuss such matters. Sometimes ontology is used as a synonym for metaphysics, but usually the latter is the broader discipline.

ought The term most often used to express moral duty or obligation. Sometimes *should* is used, but this word is ambiguously between *ought* and merely *preferable*. Sometimes *must* or *have to* is used, but this word is ambiguously between *ought to* and *forced to*. In Hume's ethics (and in many others as well), *ought* is contrasted with *is* as the hallmark of value (especially moral) judgment.

pantheism The belief that God is identical to the universe as a whole, everything is divine, or that God is in everything. Spinoza, for example, was a pantheist. Hinduism is a form of pantheism in that it includes a conception of the divine in all things, rather than as a separate Creator.

paradox A self-contradictory conclusion drawn from seemingly acceptable premises. For example, suppose you try to help all and only those people who do not help themselves. That sounds reasonable enough. But then, do you help yourself? If you do help everyone, then you would also help yourself. But if you do not help yourself, then you are not helping all who do not help themselves. This is a paradox.

parallelism The thesis that mental events and bodily events parallel each other and occur in perfect coordination but do not interact.

participation Plato's obscure and unexplained relationship between the things of this world and the Forms of which they are manifestations. He tells us that individual things "participate" in their Forms.

perception A kind of knowledge, sense experience.

phenomenology A contemporary European philosophy, founded by the German-Czech philosopher Edmund Husserl, that begins with a "pure description of consciousness." Originally developed as an answer to certain questions of necessary truth in the foundations of arithmetic, it was later expanded to answer more general philosophical questions and, in the hands of its later practitioners, it became a "philosophy of man" as well as a theory of knowledge.

pluralism The metaphysical view that there are many distinct substances in the universe and, perhaps, many different kinds of substances as well.

polytheism Belief in many gods.

pragmatic theory of truth A statement or belief that is true if and only if it "works," that is, if it allows us to predict certain results and function effectively in everyday life, and if it encourages further inquiry and helps us lead better lives.

pragmatism A distinctly American philosophical movement founded by Charles Sanders Peirce at the turn of the twentieth century and popularized by William James and John Dewey. Its central thesis is obvious in its name, that truth and value are always to be determined by reference to practical (pragmatic) considerations. Only those metaphysical distinctions that make some difference in practice are worth considering, and the only ultimate defense of any belief is that "it works."

predestination The thesis (usually in a theological context) that every event is destined to happen (as in fatalism) whatever efforts we make to prevent it. The usual version is that God knows and perhaps causes all things to happen, and therefore everything must happen precisely as He knows (and possibly causes) it to happen.

predicate That which is asserted or denied of a thing, which refers to a property of things. Some familiar predicates would be "is red," "is an animal."

prediction To say that some event will happen before it happens. Determinism normally includes the thesis that if we know enough about the antecedent conditions of an event, we can always predict that it will occur. But prediction does not require determinism. One may predict the outcome of some state of affairs on the basis of statistical probabilities without knowing any antecedent conditions and perhaps even without assuming that there are any such conditions (in quantum physics, for example). It is also possible that a person may predict the future on the basis of lucky guesses or ESP, again without necessarily accepting determinism.

preestablished harmony The belief that the order of the universe is prearranged by God. In Leibniz, this view allows him an alternative to Newton's theory of causal relationships, namely, that the coordination between our ideas and the physical events of the world and our bodies was set up by God in perfect order.

premise The principle or one of the principles upon which an argument is based. The starting point of an argument.

presupposition A principle that is assumed as a precondition for whatever else one believes, which itself may remain unexamined and uncriticized throughout the argument. For example, a lawyer presupposes that the court aims at justice and has some idea what is just. It is the philosopher, not the lawyer, who challenges such claims.

primary qualities In Locke, those properties ("qualities") that inhere in the object.

prime mover (in Aristotle) The "cause-of-itself," the first cause, which (Who) initiates all changes but is not itself (Himself) affected by anything prior. Aristotle believes there must be a prime mover if we are to avoid an infinite regress, which he considers an absurdity. Aristotle also refers to the prime mover as "God," and medieval philosophers (for example, St. Thomas Aquinas) developed these views into Christian theology.

principle of induction The belief that the laws of nature will continue to hold in the future as they have in the past. (Crudely, "the future will be like the past.")

Principle of Sufficient Reason (in Leibniz) The insistence that all events must have a justification and that ultimately all events must be justified by God's reasons. The principle is sometimes invoked to assert that everything must have some explanation, whether or not God is involved. (For example, scientists use such a principle in their work, as was shown in Chapter 3.)

principle of universal causation The belief that every event has its cause (or causes). In scientific circles, it is usually added, "its sufficient natural cause," in order to eliminate the possibility of miracles and divine intervention (which are allowed in Leibniz's similar but broader Principle of Sufficient Reason).

principle of utility In Bentham, the principle that one ought to do what gives the greatest pleasure to the greatest number of people.

privacy The seeming inaccessibility of mental states and events to anyone other than the person who "has" them.

private language argument Wittgenstein's argument that even if there were such "private objects" as mental states and events, it would be impossible for us to talk about them and impossible for us to identify them, even in our own case.

privileged access The technical term used by philosophers to refer to the curious fact that a person usually (if not always) can immediately know, simply by paying attention, what is going on in his own mind, while other people can find out what is going on—if they can at all—only by watching the person's behavior, listening to what he or she says, or asking (and hoping they get a truthful answer). It is important to distinguish privileged access from incorrigibility. The first means that a person knows directly what is "in his mind" without having to observe his behavior; the second means that he knows for certain and beyond the possibility of error.

probable Likely or supported by the evidence (but not conclusively). The empiricist's middle step between the extremities of certainty and doubt. (Probability is the measure of how probable something is.)

problem of evil The dilemma that emerges from trying to reconcile the belief that God is omnipotent, omniscient, and just with the suffering and evil in the world.

proof In a deductive argument, a proof is a sequence of steps, each according to an acceptable rule of inference, to the conclusion to be proved.

property Properties are generally distinguished from the substances in which they "inhere" by pointing to the fact that a property cannot exist without being a property of something; for example, there can be any number of red things but no redness that exists independently. (Many philosophers have challenged this idea, but this problem, which is called the "problem of universals," is not discussed in this introductory volume.)

proposition An assertion that is either true or false.

psychological egoism The thesis that people always act for their own self-interest, even when it seems as if they are acting for other people's benefit (for example, in giving to charity, the egoist would say, a person is simply making himself or herself feel self-righteous).

purposiveness without a purpose (Kant) The idea that the elements of a beautiful object seem to cohere as if toward a purpose, but we can find no definite purpose. For example, a sunset seems to us a unified aesthetic phenomenon, but there obviously is no "purpose" to a sunset.

quality In Locke (and other authors), a property.

rational In accordance with the rules of effective thought: coherence, consistency, practicability, simplicity, comprehensiveness, looking at the evidence and weighing it carefully, not jumping to conclusions, and so forth. Rationality may not guarantee truth; all the evidence and everything we believe may point to one conclusion, while later generations, who know things that we do not, may see that our conclusion was incorrect. Yet it would still be, for us, the rational conclusion. Rationality points to the manner of thinking, rather than its ultimate conclusions. Philosophically, the stress on rationality takes the emphasis off reality and places it on our manner of philosophizing.

rationalism The philosophy that is characterized by its confidence in reason, and intuition in particular, to know reality independently of experience. (See *reason* and *intuition*.) *Continental rationalism* is usually reserved for three European philosophers: Descartes, Spinoza, and Leibniz.

rationality Acting in the best possible way; according to reason. Sometimes, rationality means simply doing what is best under the circumstances, without insisting that there is only one rational way of acting. In other words, rationality is considered relative to particular interests and circumstances. In Kant's philosophy, however, rationality refers to the faculty that allows us to act in the correct way, without reference to particular interests and circumstances.

realism The thesis that reality exists in itself and is independent of our consciousness of it.

reason The ability to think abstractly, to form arguments and make inferences. Sometimes referred to as a "faculty" of the human mind (a leftover from eighteenth-century philosophy). In rationalism, the term describes the faculty that allows us to know reality, through intuition. In empiricism, simply the ability to recognize certain principles that are "relations of ideas," for example, trivial truths ("a cat is an animal") and, more complicated, principles of arithmetic and geometry. Empiricists deny that reason allows us special insight into reality, however; it tells us only relationships between ideas. In metaphysics, however, reason often has a more controversial meaning, namely, the human ability to go beyond experience to determine, through thought alone, what reality is really like.

reasons Explanations, justifications, evidence, or some other basis for accepting a proposition.

reductio ad absurdum A form of argument in which one refutes a statement by showing that it leads to self-contradiction or an otherwise intolerable conclusion.

reflection To think about something, to "put it in perspective." We often do so with our beliefs and emotions. For example, "This morning I was furious at you, but after reflecting on it at lunch, I decided that it was nothing to be angry about." One may say that philosophy is reflection about life and knowledge in general.

relations of ideas In empiricism, knowledge that is restricted to the logical and conceptual connections between ideas, not to the correspondence of those ideas to experience or to reality. Such knowledge can therefore be demonstrated without appeal to experience. Arithmetic and geometry were taken to be paradigmatic examples of relations of ideas.

relativism The thesis that there is no single correct view of reality, no single truth. Relativists often talk about the possibility of "different conceptual frameworks," "alternative lifestyles," and various "forms of consciousness." They are opposed, often violently, to realists and absolutists. Also, the thesis that morals are relative to particular societies, particular interests, particular circumstances, or particular individuals. (See *cultural relativism, ethical relativism*.)

resemblance Having the same features. All people resemble each other (or, at least, most do) in having one and only one head; you resemble yourself five years ago in (perhaps) having the same hair texture, the same color eyes, the same fear of spiders, and the same skill at chess.

responsibility Answerability or accountability for some act or event presumed to be within a person's control.

retributive justice "Getting even" or "an eye for an eye."

retrodiction To say, on the basis of certain present evidence, what must have happened in the past. For example, the astronomer who looks at the present course of a comet can retrodict certain facts about its history. For the determinist, retrodiction is as important to his or her thesis as prediction.

rhetoric The persuasive use of language to convince other people to accept your beliefs.

rights Demands that a member of society is entitled to make upon his or her society. Everyone, for example, has a right to police protection. Some people, by virtue of their position, have special rights; for example, members of Congress have the right to send mail to their constituents without paying postage.

rule of inference A generally accepted principle according to which one may infer one statement from another; those rules of logic according to which validity is defined. All such rules are analytic, but there is considerable disagreement about whether all are so by virtue of their own logical form or whether some are so because they are derived from other, more basic rules. There is also the following question: Given that these rules define correct logical form, how is it possible to say that they have correct logical form?

secondary qualities In Locke, those properties ("qualities") that are caused in us by objects, but do not inhere in the objects themselves (for example, color).

self-consciousness Being aware of oneself, whether "as others see you" (looking in a mirror or "watching yourself play a role" at a party) or just "looking into yourself " (as when you reflect on your goals in life or wonder, in a moment of philosophical perversity, whether you really exist or not.) Self-consciousness requires having some concept of your "self." Accordingly, it is logically tied to questions of self-identity.

self-contradictory A contradiction within one and the same statement or set of statements. What I say may contradict what you say; but what I say may also contradict something else that I said, in which case I am being self-contradictory. Moreover, in a few strange cases, my own statement may be self-contradictory; for example, "I do not exist."

self-evident Obvious without proof or argument; for Descartes, a "clear and distinct idea," about which there could be no doubt, and it is obvious that there could be no doubt.

self-identity The way you characterize yourself, either in general (as a human being, as a man or as a woman, as a creature before God, or as one among many animals) or in particular (as the person who can run the fastest mile, as an all-"C" student, or as the worst-dressed slob in your class). Self-identity, on this characterization, requires self-consciousness. The self-identity of a person, in other words, is not merely the same as the identity of a "thing," for example, the identity of a human body.

selfishness Acting in one's own interest to the exclusion of others' interests. The word has a nasty connotation and so should be separated from the more neutral claims of the psychological egoist. To say that a person is acting selfishly is to condemn him or her and say that the action is blameworthy. It is possible to act for one's own interests, however, and not be selfish, for one may also act for the benefit of others. A selfish act is to the exclusion of other people's interests; an act may be both in one's own interests and in the interests of others, however.

semantics The meanings of a sentence and its various components. Also, the study of those meanings. (So, we can talk about the semantics of a sentence, and we can talk about doing semantics.) "Merely semantic" is a nasty way of referring to conceptual truths, analytic sentences that are true just by virtue of meanings.

semantic theory of truth A formal theory, best known from the work of Alfred Tarski, that defines "true" in terms of a technical notion of *satisfaction*. According to the theory, every sentence in the language is either satisfied or not by a distinct class of individuals. This theory is adequate, however, only for artificially constructed languages. Generalizing the theory to natural language (for example, American English), we can say that the theory suggests that we (but not each of us personally) set up the rules according to which our sentences do or do not "correspond with the facts" of the world.

sensation The experimental result of the stimulation of a sense organ, for example, *seeing* red, *hearing* a ringing noise, *smelling* something burning. The simplest of mental phenomena.

sense-data That which is given to the senses, prior to any reasoning or organization on our part.

sentiment Feeling, emotion, particularly moral feelings (as in Hume, Rousseau).

skepticism A philosophical belief that knowledge is not possible, that doubt will not be overcome by any valid arguments. A philosopher who holds this belief is called a skeptic. Again, skepticism is not mere personal doubt; it requires systematic doubt with reasons for that doubt.

slave morality In Nietzsche's moral philosophy, a morality that takes duties and obligations as primary, so called because it was the morality of the slaves who were not allowed to aspire any higher than mere efficiency and personal comfort.

social contract An agreement, tacit or explicit, that all members of society shall abide by the laws of the state in order to maximize the public interest and ensure cooperation among themselves. Such a contract need never have actually been signed in history; what is important is that every member of a society, by choosing to remain in that society, implicitly makes such an agreement.

society A group of people with common historical and cultural ties, usually but not always, members of the same state and ruled by the same government.

soft determinism A thesis that accepts determinism but claims that certain kinds of causes, namely, a person's character, still allow us to call his or her actions "free." Soft determinists are therefore compatibilists, for they believe in both freedom and determinism.

sophists Ancient Greek philosophers and teachers who believed that no reality exists except for what we take to be reality.

sound Refers to an argument whose premises are true and that is valid.

sovereign Independent. A sovereign state is one that is subject to the laws of no other state. A sovereign is a person (for example, a king) who is not subject or answerable to the commands of anyone else. A people are sovereign when their wishes are ultimate in the same way and not subject to commands by anyone else or any government. (To say that a people is sovereign is not to say that the will of any individual or group is sovereign within it.)

Spenta Mainyush The good spirit of Zoroastrianism.

state The center of authority in a society, for example, the largest political unit in a society. Usually a state is a nation, for example, the United States or Germany. Usually, but not always, coextensive with a society and usually, but not always, distinguished by a single form of government and a single government (for example, the U.S. federal government).

subjective idealism The view that only ideas and mind exist and that there are no substances, matter, or material objects. In particular, the philosophy of Bishop Berkeley.

subjective truth In Kierkegaard, the "truth" of strong feelings and commitment.

substance A "unit" of existence, a being; something that "stands by itself"; the essential reality of a thing or things that underlies the various properties and changes of properties. Its most common definitions: "that which is independent and can exist by itself" and "the essence of a thing which does not and cannot change." In traditional metaphysics, substance is the same as "ultimate reality," and the study of substance is that branch of metaphysics that studies reality, namely, ontology. In Descartes, a thing that so exists that it needs no other thing in order to exist (God). Created substances need only the occurrence of God to exist. (See *essence, ontology*.)

sufficient cause Capable of bringing something about by itself (for example, four healthy people are sufficient to push a Volkswagen up a hill).

Sufism Islamic mysticism.

syllogism A three-line deductive argument; the best-known examples are those arguments of this form:

> All P's are Q's. (Major premise)
> S is a P. (Minor premise)
> Therefore S is a Q. (Conclusion)

The major premise asserts something about the predicate of the conclusion (in this case, Q). The minor premise asserts something about the subject of the conclusion (in this case, S).

sympathy Fellow feeling; a felt concern for other people's welfare. In the ethics of Hume and Rousseau, the necessary and universal sentiment without which morals—and society—would be impossible.

synonym "Meaning the same." Two words are synonymous if they are interchangeable in a sentence without losing the meaning of the sentence. For example, the words *criminal* and *felon* are synonyms in most contexts. The test of a supposedly conceptual truth is to replace certain words with synonyms and then see if its denial yields a self-contradiction. In other words, substituting synonyms turns a conceptual truth into an analytic truth. For example, "ferns are plants"; substituting for *fern* its synonym (or, in this case, also its definition) "a primitive plant that bears spores, etc." we have "a plant is a plant," whose denial is a contradiction ("a plant is not a plant") and thus is analytic.

synthetic (statement) A noncontradictory proposition in which the predicate is not entailed by the subject, for example, "horses are generally obstinate." (*Synthetic* is opposed, in this sense, to *analytic*.) A synthetic sentence cannot be shown to be true by appeal to the logical form or the meanings of the component words. Kant defined a synthetic sentence as one that "adds an idea to the subject which is not already contained in it." For example, "a horse is the source of a large income for some people" is a strictly synthetic sentence. No appeal to the meaning of *horse* will help you find out whether it is true or not, and its denial surely does not result in self-contradiction. But, according to Kant, it must not be concluded that all synthetic sentences can be shown to be true solely by appeal to experience. Some, he claimed, are known a priori.

synthetic a priori knowledge Knowledge that is necessary and known independently of experience (and thus a priori), but that does not derive its truth from the logic or meaning of sentences (thus synthetic). This is the focal concept of Kant's philosophy.

system An orderly formulation of principles (together with reasons, implications, evidence, methods, and presuppositions) that is comprehensive, consistent, and coherent and in which the various principles are interconnected as tightly as possible by logical implications.

tabula rasa In Locke's philosophy, the "blank tablet" metaphor of the mind, in opposition to the doctrine that there are innate ideas. In other words, the mind is a "blank" at birth, and everything we know must be "stamped in" through experience.

tautology A trivial truth that is true by virtue of logical form alone and tells us nothing about the world. (Popularly, a bit of repetitive nonsense, for example, "a rose is a rose is a rose." Technically (in logic), a sentence that can be shown to be true no matter what the truth or falsity of its component parts.)

teleological argument An argument that attempts to "prove" that God exists because of the intricacy and "design" of nature. It is sometimes called the "argument from design," since the basis of the argument is that since the universe is evidently designed, it must have a designer. The analogy most often used is our inference from finding a complex mechanism on the beach (for example, a watch) that some intelligent being must have created it.

teleology (teleological) The belief that every phenomenon has a purpose, end, or goal (from the Greek *telos*, meaning "purpose"). Aristotle's metaphysics is a teleology, which means that he believes that the universe itself—and consequently everything in it—operates for purposes and can be explained according to goals.

theism Belief in God.

transcendence Sartre's term for a person's plan, ambitions, intentions, and hopes for the future. (Do not confuse this use of the word with those introduced in Chapters 1 and 4.)

transcendent Independent of. In the philosophy of religion, a *transcendent God* is one who is distinct and separate from the universe he created. This is contrasted with the concept of an immanent God, for example, in pantheism, where God is identical with his creation or, to take a different example, in certain forms of humanism, in which God is identical with humankind. (Hegel argued such a thesis.)

transcendental Referring to the basic rules of human knowledge, usually with an absolutist suggestion that there can be but a single set of such basic rules. Thus Kant's "transcendental deduction" attempted to deduce the one possible set of basic rules for human understanding, and Husserl's transcendental phenomenology attempted to lay bare the one set of basic ("essential") laws of human consciousness. Contemporary philosophers sometimes talk about "the transcendental turn" in philosophy, in other words, the attempt to move beyond claims that may apply only to ourselves and our way of viewing things to the way that things must be viewed.

transcendental deduction Kant's elaborate attempt to prove that there is but one set of categories (basic rules or a priori concepts) that all rational creatures must use in constituting their experience.

transcendental ego The bare, logical fact of one's own self-consciousness: Descartes' "I think"; the self "behind" all our experiences; the mental activity that unifies our various thoughts and sensations. (The term comes from Kant's *Critique of Pure Reason*.)

trivial Obvious and not worth saying.

truth of reason In traditional rationalism, a belief that can be justified solely by appeal to intuition or deduction from premises based upon intuition. Arithmetic and geometry were, for the rationalists as for the empiricists, paradigmatic cases of such truths. The rationalists and empiricists disagreed mainly on the scope of such truths and the restrictions to be placed on the problematic appeal to intuition.

unalienable rights The rights that no one and no government can take away, for example, the right of a person to protect his or her own life. In other words, *human rights*.

unconscious Freud's famous way of referring to the fact that there are ideas, desires, memories, and experiences in our minds to which we do not have privileged access, that we may be wrong about (and, therefore, about which our claims are not incorrigible), and that may be more evident to other people than to us. Freud also distinguishes a *preconscious* ("the antechamber of consciousness"). Preconscious ideas can be made conscious simply by being attended to. (For example, you do know what the capital of California is, but you were not conscious of it before I mentioned it; it was preconscious.) Truly unconscious ideas, however, cannot be made conscious, even when one tries to do so.

unextended Not having spatial dimensions. Philosophers (for example, Descartes, Leibniz, and Spinoza) often define mind and ideas as unextended.

unsound Refers to an argument whose premises are false or that is invalid.

Upanishads The text containing the "secret doctrines" that form the basis of Hinduism and Buddhism.

utilitarianism The moral philosophy that says we should act in such ways as to make the greatest number of people as happy as possible.

valid Refers to an argument that correctly follows agreed-upon rules of inference. Always applies to arguments, not statements.

vicious circle The use of two propositions or arguments to support one another with no other support. For example, "He must be guilty because he's got such a guilty look on his face. . . . Well, I can tell it's a guilty look because he's the one who is guilty."

virtue Moral excellence. In Aristotle's philosophy, a state of character according to which we enjoy doing what is right. In Kant, willing what is right (whether or not we enjoy it, in fact, especially if we don't enjoy it).

void Empty space.

will The power of mind that allows us to choose our own actions or, at least, what we shall try to do. In Kant, a good will is the only thing that is good "without qualification," in other words, acting for the right reasons and good intentions.

will to power In Nietzsche's philosophy, the thesis that every act is ultimately aimed at greater capability or control, sometimes over other people, but, more important, superiority according to one's own standards. In other words, it is what Aristotle meant by excellence. (Nietzsche has often been interpreted, however, to mean political power.)

Zend-Avesta The scripture of Zoroastrianism.

Zoroastrianism The religion founded by Zarathustra ("Zoroaster") in ancient Persia.

Index